For

Not to be taken
from the room.

reference

AMERICAN TIME USE

Who Spends How Long at What

2nd EDITION

BY THE EDITORS OF NEW STRATEGIST PUBLICATIONS

New Strategist Publications, Inc.
Ithaca, New York

New Strategist Publications, Inc.
P.O. Box 242, Ithaca, New York 14851
800/848-0842; 607/273-0913
www.newstrategist.com

ISBN 978-1-935114-84-0 (hardcover)
ISBN 978-1-935114-85-7 (paper)

Printed in the United States of America

Table of Contents

The average person spends more time sleeping than doing any other activity. After sleep, work is the most time-consuming activity, with television coming in third.

The priorities of teenagers are starkly different from those of their elders. Most teens still live with their parents, attend school, and prize nothing more than time with their friends.

Many young adults have shouldered the responsibilities of a home, a job, and a family, while others are still in school and not yet living on their own. Their time use reflects this diversity.

With young children in the home and the mortgage payment due, both men and women of this age are busy earning a paycheck and managing a family. Leisure time is in short supply.

Work is second only to sleep among activities that the average 35-to-44-year-old spends the most time doing. Caring for and helping household children are ahead of grooming and socializing.

The average 45-to-54-year-old spends more time grooming and socializing than caring for children and has more time to indulge in personal interests.

People aged 55 to 64 are a diverse group. Some are already retired and enjoying more leisure time. Others are still in the workforce.

Most people aged 65 to 74 have put work behind them and made leisure pursuits their top priorities. After sleep, watching television is their most important activity.

The oldest Americans are the ones with the greatest amount of leisure time. Alas, they also suffer the most from sleeplessness.

Tables

Chapter 3. Time Use by People Aged 20 to 24

Chapter 4. Time Use by People Aged 25 to 34

Chapter 5. Time Use by People Aged 35 to 44

Chapter 6. Time Use by People Aged 45 to 54

Chapter 7. Time Use by People Aged 55 to 64

Chapter 8. Time Use by People Aged 65 to 74

Chapter 9. Time Use by People Aged 75 or Older

Introduction

Every day each of us gets 24 hours to accomplish what we need to do and enjoy what we want to do. The activities we choose to do during those 24 hours and the amount of time we allot to each activity determines the quality of our family life, the unique features of our culture, and the driving forces of our economy.

Several years ago, the federal government initiated a survey to collect data on how Americans spend their time during an average day. Called the American Time Use Survey (ATUS), this ongoing collection of data allows economists, policy makers, and sociologists to better understand our economy and lifestyle and how policy decisions affect our lives. Through telephone interviews with a nationally representative sample of Americans aged 15 or older, ATUS collects information in minute detail about what survey respondents did during the previous 24 hours—or "diary day" (For more about ATUS methodology, see Appendix A).

American Time Use: Who Spends How Long at What is your window into the vast collection of American Time Use Survey data. Presented here are detailed tables and analysis of results from the 2008 survey.

If you have ever wondered while watching TV why advertisers are so intent on selling snacks or sleep aids or cleaning products—or even why they spend so much money on television advertising itself—time use data has the answer. On an average day, eating ranks fourth in our priorities, behind only sleep, work, and watching television (which is why advertisers spend so much money on television spots). Cleaning the house ranks eighth among our most time-consuming activities. And on an average night, millions of Americans are sleepless, time-use statistics reveal.

American Time Use presents detailed time use data for the single most important demographic characteristic for determining how people spend their time—their age. A person's age determines his or her lifecycle stage, and lifecycle stage determines whether he or she is in school, in the work force, married, or a parent. Lifecycle stage sets our priorities, determining how we spend our 24-hour allotment of time. *How Americans Spend Their Time* puts you in the know, showing you what others are doing—from teens (15-to-19-year-olds) to young adults (20-to-24-year-olds), from parents (25-to-34- and 35-to-44-year-olds) to empty-nesters (45-to-54- and 55-to-64-year-olds) and from the go-go elderly to the slow-go elderly (65-to-74-year-olds and those aged 75 or older).

The detailed time use data presented in *American Time Use* are not available on any government web site. They were obtained by special request from the Bureau of Labor Statistics. The comparisons of time use by lifecycle stage contained in this book are also not available from the federal government. New Strategist's statisticians analyzed the raw time use data—number of people, average time, and participant time—to produce the percentages of people participating in activities, the indexes, and the rankings—each of which reveals significant differences in time use by lifecycle stage. Government web sites are useful for obtaining either general information (summary data) or for tapping into enormous databases that require analysis by statistical programs. New Strategist has done the work for you, providing analysis and comparisons, placing the important American Time Use Survey at your fingertips.

How to analyze time use data

To analyze time use data, you need to understand three simple concepts: primary activity, average time, and participant time. An examination of the amount of time people spend sleepless will help explain these three concepts.

• **Primary activity** ATUS collects data on the amount of time people spend engaged in "primary" activities on an average day, meaning the main activity a respondent is doing at a given moment. For example, if a respondent is watching television and eating, one of those activities will be recorded as the primary activity, and the fact that the respondent is also doing the other activity at the same time will not appear in the data. This is an important concept to keep in mind because the amount of time people spend doing some activities might appear to be low because the activity is rarely a primary activity—such as listening to the radio. Sleeplessness is a primary activity if a respondent reports trying to go to sleep but is instead tossing and turning, lying awake, counting sheep, or otherwise experiencing insomnia.

• **Average time** Data collected by the 2008 American Time Use Survey found that people aged 15 or older spent an average of 0.06 hours—or about 4 minutes—sleepless on diary day. (To convert decimal hours to minutes, multiply 60 by the decimal. In this case, multiply 60 by .06 and the result is 3.6—or nearly 4 minutes) This doesn't sound like much time spent sleepless, but that is because the percentage of people who experience sleeplessness is small, and the average time spent sleepless includes both those who tossed and turned on diary day (or night) and those who slept like a log. Average time is an artificial measure based on two factors—the percentage of people who engaged in an activity and the amount of time participants spent doing the activity. Because average time calculations include both those engaging in an activity and those who did not, average time figures will be less than the actual time participants spent doing an activity—particularly for activities in which few people participate or which take little time. But the average is a most valuable number, because it allows researchers to compare time use by demographic characteristic, revealing differences in priorities.

• **Participant time** During an average day in 2008, a substantial 5.2 percent of people aged 15 or older experienced sleeplessness. Among those who were sleepless, the average amount of time they spent counting sheep was a significant 0.85 hours—or 51 minutes. This is participant time, which tells you how much time people who engaged in an activity on diary day spent doing the activity. Participant time provides an important reality check, revealing how much time people devote to activities. But because participant time includes only those engaging in an activity, it does not allow for the comparison of time use across demographic segments.

This analysis of the time people spend sleepless shows sleeplessness to be a big problem for some—which may explain why television advertisers spend so much money on marketing sleep aids. The problem gets worse with advancing age. The percentage of people experiencing sleeplessness rises above average in the 45-to-54 age group and peaks at 8.1 percent among people aged 75 or older. The amount of time spent sleepless by "participants" also increases with age, to more than 1.5 hours for those aged 65 or older. These two factors—the percentage of people experiencing sleeplessness and the amount of time spent sleepless by those experiencing it—are statistically combined and result in average time spent sleepless. By indexing average time, you can see at a glance how sleeplessness varies by age in this chart:

Sleeplessness

(indexed average time spent per day in sleeplessness as a primary activity, by age, 2008; 100 equals the time spent by the average person doing the activity)

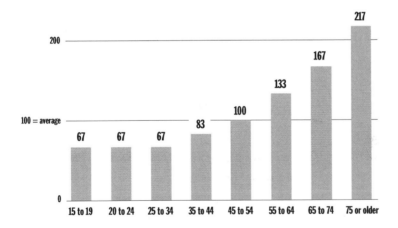

How time use differs by lifecycle stage

Teenagers go to school, the middle-aged go to work, and the elderly have the most leisure time. These characteristics of time use by lifecycle stage are well known. But going beyond the generalities reveals the surprising priorities of Americans at every stage of life. In some cases, time use data confirm stereotypes. In other cases, they disprove common knowledge. In every case, however, a more thorough understanding of how Americans spend their time can be the key to better business and policy decisions.

Let's start with teenagers. Anyone who has ever lived with teens knows they spend a lot of time in the bathroom. The time use statistics confirm this stereotype. People aged 15 to 19 spend more time grooming as a primary activity than any other age group, an average of

0.78 hours per day (or about 47 minutes). When those figures are indexed to the average, grooming patterns by age look like this:

Grooming

(indexed average time spent per day grooming as a primary activity, by age, 2008; 100 equals the time spent by the average person doing the activity)

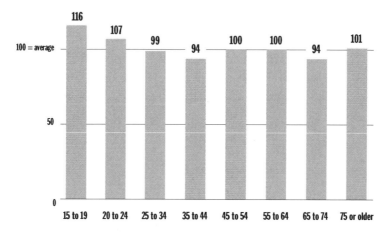

Teens are also known for being on the phone too much. Again, time use statistics uphold the stereotype. People aged 15 to 19 spend more time on the phone with friends as a primary activity than any other age group.

Telephone calls to or from friends

(indexed average time spent per day on the telephone with friends, neighbors, or acquaintances as a primary activity, by age, 2008; 100 equals the time spent by the average person doing the activity)

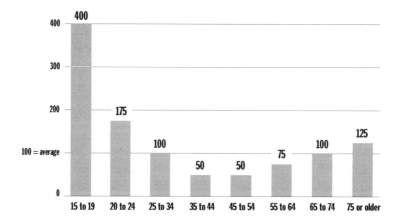

But teens are not the ones most likely to talk to family members on the telephone. Older Americans spend more time than younger ones talking to family members on the phone.

Telephone calls to or from family members

(indexed average time spent per day on the telephone with family members as a primary activity, by age, 2008; 100 equals the time spent by the average person doing the activity)

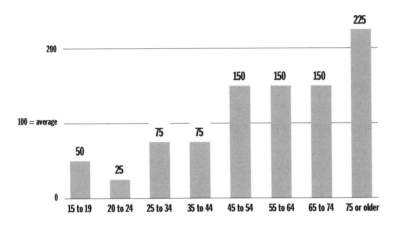

Older Americans spend more time than younger ones at a variety of activities because they have more free time. Interestingly, they spend much more time than younger adults watching television as a primary activity. In fact, people aged 75 or older spend more than one-quarter of their waking hours watching television as a primary activity.

Watching television

(indexed average time spent per day watching television as a primary activity, by age, 2008; 100 equals the time spent by the average person doing the activity)

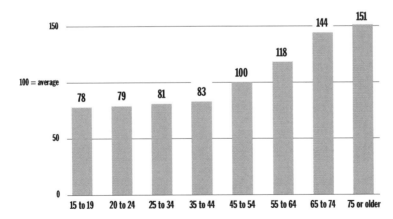

Older Americans spend much more time than younger adults reading. In fact, among people aged 55 or older, reading for personal interest ranks among the ten most time-consuming daily activities. Among those aged 75 or older it ranks fourth, behind only sleeping, watching television, and eating.

Reading

(indexed average time spent per day reading for personal interest as a primary activity, by age, 2008; 100 equals the time spent by the average person doing the activity)

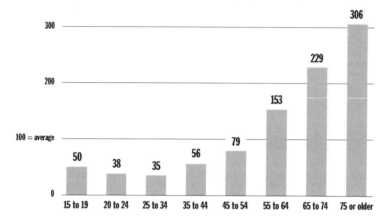

Playing games is an interesting category in the ATUS survey because it includes computer games as well as board games and card games such as poker or bridge. Because the category spans such a variety of activities, time spent playing games as a primary activity peaks in two age groups—among teens and young adults, and among people aged 65 or older. The younger group is mostly playing computer games. The older group is more likely playing board games or bridge.

Playing games

(indexed average time spent per day playing games as a primary activity, by age, 2008; 100 equals the time spent by the average person doing the activity)

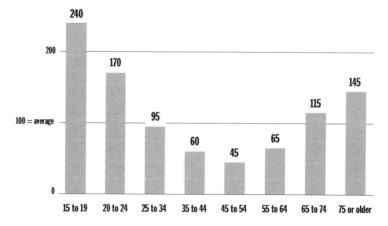

The middle-aged, and specifically people aged 45 to 54, spend the most time working. In fact, men aged 45 to 54 who worked on diary day spent as much time at their main job as they did sleeping. Surprisingly, however, the middle-aged do not spend the most time on household chores—despite the fact that they have the largest households. Older Americans spend the most time doing chores, People aged 65 or older spend more time than any other age group cleaning house and preparing meals.

Housecleaning

(indexed average time spent per day cleaning the interior of the house as a primary activity, by age, 2008; 100 equals the time spent by the average person doing the activity)

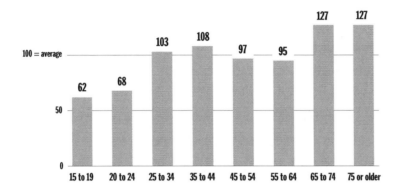

People aged 65 to 74 spend the most time grocery shopping. People aged 55 or older spend the most time on lawn care. The observation that work expands to fill the time available helps to explain these facts. Older Americans have much more free time than younger adults (even more than teenagers). They spend much of their free time puttering around cleaning, fixing, and improving.

Lawn, garden, and houseplant care

(indexed average time spent per day in lawn, garden, or houseplant care as a primary activity, by age, 2008; 100 equals the time spent by the average person doing the activity)

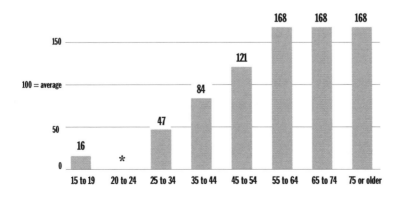

* Data for 20-to-24-year-olds are unavailable.

Not surprisingly, the time spent caring for household children peaks among people with young children at home—in the 25 to 44 age groups. Time spent caring for children in other households (i.e. grandchildren) peaks in the 55-to-74 age groups. The average time spent caring for pets is greatest among people aged 55 or older.

Pet care

(indexed average time spent per day caring for animals or pets as a primary activity, by age, 2008; 100 equals the time spent by the average person doing the activity)

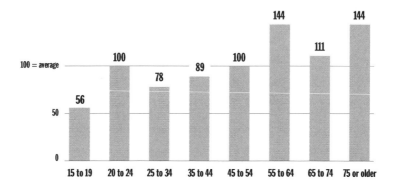

Time use statistics reveal the defining elements of our culture, and no element defines us more than the automobile. The time use survey data show "traveling" to be one of our most time consuming daily activities. On an average day, people aged 15 or older spend 1.20 hours (or 1 hour, 12 minutes) traveling. The category "traveling" is defined as going from one destination to another. While any mode of transportation is included in the category, the automobile by far is the dominant mode of transportation in the United States. The average amount of time spent traveling does not vary much by lifecycle stage, except for a decline in the oldest age group.

Traveling

(indexed average time spent per day traveling as a primary activity, by age, 2008; 100 equals the time spent by the average person doing the activity)

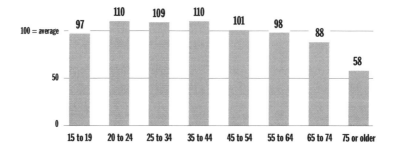

The time use data also show the most important reasons for daily travel at each lifecycle stage. Overall, travel related to work (i.e. commuting) is the most time-consuming travel subcategory. But among teenagers, travel related to education is number one, followed by travel related to socializing. Among people aged 65 or older, travel related to shopping is the most time-consuming travel subcategory.

Regardless of lifecycle stage, however, we all spend a good portion of our day in automobiles. This explains why advertisements for cars are so common on television and in newspapers. Cars are one of our top priorities. To learn more about our other priorities, dive into *American Time Use: Who Spends How Long at What.*

A step-by-step guide to using the tables

Each chapter of *American Time Use* includes 20 tables (except for the Total Population chapter, which has only 14 tables because it does not include tables indexing time use and participation to the average). Each table reveals how an age group spends its time in the following ways.

• **Tables 1 to 3: Average Time Use** The first three tables in each chapter present the entire range of time use information for the age group. Table 1 presents data for total people in the age group, Table 2 for men in the age group, and Table 3 for women in the age group. Tables 1 through 3 present data in four columns:

1. Column one shows the estimated number of people in the age group participating in the primary activity on an average day. Among men aged 45 to 54, for example, 13.3 million worked at their main job on diary day.

2. Column two shows the percentage of people in the age group who participate in the primary activity on diary day. (Note: Activities in which fewer than 2 percent of people in an age group participate are not shown because of small sample sizes.) Those 13.3 million men who worked at their main job on diary day represented 61.7 percent of men in the age group.

3. Column three shows the number of hours per day the average person in the age group spent doing the primary activity. The amount of time spent by the average person on many activities will appear low because it includes everyone—both those participating in the activity on that day and those not participating in the activity. The average man aged 45 to 54 spent 5.03 hours working at his main job on diary day, for example. This is well below the usual eight-hour workday because it includes both men who worked on diary day and men who did not work on diary day.

4. Column four shows the hours spent by participants doing the primary activity on diary day. Among men aged 45 to 54, those who worked on diary day spent 8.16 hours at their main job, significantly more than the 5.03 average.

• **Tables 4 to 6: Indexed Time Use** The next set of three tables compares the average amount of time people in an age group spend doing a primary activity with the average for the total population aged 15 or older. Table 4 presents data for total people in the age group, Table 5 for men in the age group, and Table 6 for women in the age group. Tables 4 through 6 present data in three columns.

1. Column one shows the number of hours per day the average person in the age group spends doing a primary activity. (This information also appears in column 3 of Tables 1 through 3.)

2. Column two shows the number of hours per day spent by the average person aged 15 or older doing the primary activity.

3. Column three compares time use in the age group with time use by the total population aged 15 or older. The comparison is accomplished by creating an index—dividing the number of hours people in the age group spend doing an activity by the number of hours total people aged 15 or older spend doing the activity and multiplying by 100. The average man aged 45 to 54, for example, spent 5.03 hours on diary day working at his main job. The average man aged 15 or older spent 3.96 hours on diary day working at his main job. The index is calculated by dividing 5.03 by 3.96 and multiplying the resulting figure by 100. If you subtract 100 from the index figure, the result is the percentage difference between the age group and the average. In this case, the index is 127. The difference between the index figure of 127 and 100 is 27. This means men aged 45 to 54 spend 27 percent more time working at their main job on an average day than all men aged 15 or older.

• **Table 7: Indexed Time Use by Sex** Table 7 compares the time use of men and women in an age group. The table presents data in three columns.

1. Column one shows the average hours per day men in the age group spend doing primary activities.

2. Column two shows the average hours per day women in the age group spend doing primary activities.

3. Column three indexes women's time use to men's. The average man aged 45 to 54 spent 5.03 hours working at his main job on diary day. The average woman aged 45 to 54 spent 3.75 hours working at her main job on diary day. The index of women's time to men's (3.75/5.03 * 100) is 75. When you subtract 100 from the index figure of 75, the result is –25, which means women aged 45 to 54 spend 25 percent less time working at their main job on an average day than their male counterparts. In another example, the average woman aged 45 to 54 spent 0.33 hours on diary day doing the laundry. The average man in the age group spent 0.08 hours on diary day doing laundry. The index is 413 (0.33/0.08*100=413), meaning women aged 45 to 54 spend far more time doing the laundry on an average day than their male counterparts.

• **Tables 8 to 10: Indexed Participation in Activities** The next three tables, 8 through 10, offer another perspective on time use, comparing the percentage of people in an age group participating in a primary activity on an average day with the percentage of total people aged 15 or older participating in the primary activity. Table 8 presents data for total people in the age group, Table 9 for men in the age group, and Table 10 for women in the age group. Tables 8 through 10 present data in three columns.

1. Column one shows the percentage of people in the age group doing a primary activity on an average day. (This information also appears in column 2 of Tables 1 through 3.)

2. Column two shows the percentage of total people aged 15 or older doing the primary activity on an average day.

3. Column three compares the percentage of people in the age group who participate in the activity with the percentage of total people aged 15 or older who do. Among men aged 45 to 54, for example, 14.6 percent participated in lawn, garden, and houseplant care as a primary activity on diary day. Among all men aged 15 or older, a smaller 11.0 percent participated in this activity on diary day. Dividing 14.6 by 11.0 and multiplying by 100 results in an index of 133. Subtracting 100 from 133 shows that men aged 45 to 54 are 33 percent more likely than all men aged 15 or older to participate in lawn, garden, and houseplant care on an average day.

• **Table 11: Indexed Participation by Sex** Table 7 compares the percentage of men and women in an age group participating in an activity. Table 7 presents data in three columns.

1. Column one shows the percentage of men in the age group doing the primary activity on an average day.

2. Column two shows the percentage of women in the age group doing the primary activity on an average day.

3. Column three indexes women's participation to men's. For example, 32.5 percent of women aged 45 to 54 did the laundry as a primary activity on diary day. Among men in the age group, only 7.7 percent did the laundry on diary day. The index of women's participation to men's is 425 (32.5/7.7*100) and means women aged 45 to 54 are more than four times more likely than their male counterparts to do laundry on an average day. In another example, 79.8 percent of women aged 45 to 54 watch television as a primary activity on an average day. Among men aged 45 to 54, the figure is a larger 84.3 percent. The index of 95 (79.8/84.3*100) means women aged 45 to 54 are 5 percent less likely (95 minus 100 = -5) than men aged 45 to 54 to watch television on an average day.

• **Tables 12 to 14: Ranking, Average Time** Tables 12 through 14 rank the number of hours per day people in an age group spend doing a primary activity on an average day. Table 12 ranks average time use for everyone in the age group, Table 13 for men in the age group, and Table 14 for women in the age group.

- **Tables 15 to 17: Ranking, Percent Participating** Tables 15 through 17 rank the percentage of people in an age group doing a primary activity on an average day. Table 15 ranks the percentage of total people in the age group doing the primary activity on an average day, Table 16 ranks the percentage of men doing the activity, and Table 14 ranks the percentage of women doing the activity.

- **Tables 18 to 20: Ranking, Participant Time** Tables 18 through 20 rank the number of hours participants spend doing a primary activity on an average day. Table 18 ranks the time all participants in an age group spend doing an activity on an average day. Table 19 ranks the time male participants spend doing the activity, and Table 20 ranks the time female participants spend doing the activity.

For more information

For more information about the history and methodology of the American Time Use Survey, see Appendix A at the back of this book. For more information about the time use categories themselves and what activities they include, see Appendix B: Time Use Category Examples. A brief perusal of the examples will assure you that just about any possible activity has been considered and categorized by Bureau of Labor Statistics researchers. Caring for an orphaned animal, shoveling snow, going to a wedding, taking vitamins, singing karaoke--it is all included in the American Time Use Survey. Also at the back of the book is the Glossary, which defines the survey's commonly used terms. The index there will help you see at a glance which time use categories are available for each age group and the pages on which the information is located.

American Time Use: Who Spends How Long at What is certain to make you stop and think about how you spend your day and arrange your priorities. It will have you comparing yourself to friends and neighbors. Most important, it will reveal how your clients, customers, and constituents value their time and allow you to better meet their needs.

1

Time Use, 2008: Total People

The average person spends more time sleeping than doing any other activity, an average of 8.60 hours a day. After sleep, work is the number-one most time-consuming activity, with the average person spending 3.28 hours per day working at a main job. (This figure appears low because it includes weekdays and weekends, working-age people and retirees.) Not surprisingly, the percentage of people who work and the amount of time spent on the job peaks in middle age. Men aged 45 to 54 who work spend as much time working as they do sleeping on an average day.

Television is the third most time-consuming activity for the average American, who spends 2.77 hours per day watching television as a primary activity. The amount of time people devote to television rises with age, starting at just 2.16 hours per day among 15-to-19-year-olds and rising to 4.19 hours a day among people aged 75 or older.

Three household chores appear in the top ten list of time-consuming activities—cooking, house-cleaning, and caring for children. Interestingly, the amount of time people spend cooking and cleaning peaks in the oldest age group—among people aged 75 or older—rather than in the crowded-nest ages of 25 to 54. Caring for household children ranks eighth on the list of time consuming activities (excluding sleep), and rises as high as fourth place among 25-to-44-year-olds. It falls off the top-ten list entirely in the 45-to-54 age group as children grow up and leave home.

Work and television are the top priorities of Americans

(average hours per day spent by people aged 15 or older doing primary activities, for the 10 activities on which the average person spends the most time, excluding sleep, 2008)

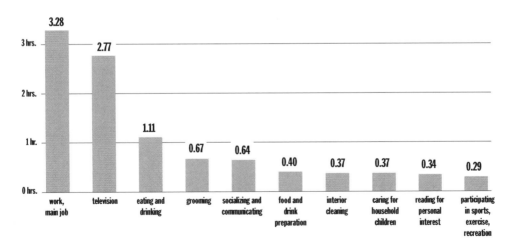

Although computers and the Internet are changing the way people communicate, computer use does not even begin to crack the top-ten list of time-consuming activities. Leisure computer use ranks 20th in time use (excluding sleep). The average American devotes much more time to reading for personal interest, putting reading in ninth place on the time-use list. Reading becomes an increasingly important priority with advancing age. Whether this continues to be true as younger, computer-oriented generations age remains to be seen.

Men's and women's time use differs considerably in every age group in stereotypical ways. Women spend much more time than men caring for children, doing the laundry, cooking, cleaning, and grocery shopping. Men spend more time than women tending the lawn, doing home maintenance, and caring for vehicles. Women spend more time reading than men. Men spend more time involved in leisure computer use than women. Women are much more likely than men to talk to family members on the phone during an average day.

Table 1.1 Time Use by Total People Aged 15 or Older, 2008

(number and percent of total people aged 15 or older participating in primary activities on an average day, hours spent doing activity by the average person aged 15 or older and by those aged 15 or older who participated in the activity, 2008; numbers of participants in thousands)

	total people aged 15 or older participating		time spent doing activity (hours)	
	number	percent	average person aged 15 or older	participants aged 15 or older
TOTAL, ALL ACTIVITIES	238,007	100.0%	24.00	24.00
Personal care	237,922	100.0	9.38	9.38
Sleeping	237,789	99.9	8.60	8.61
Sleeplessness	12,390	5.2	0.06	0.85
Grooming	188,788	79.3	0.67	0.85
Health-related self-care	15,121	6.4	0.09	1.38
Household activities	179,767	75.5	1.77	2.34
Housework	84,381	35.5	0.58	1.64
Interior cleaning	58,281	24.5	0.37	1.50
Laundry	38,467	16.2	0.17	1.06
Storing interior household items, including food	11,877	5.0	0.02	0.35
Food and drink preparation, presentation, and clean-up	124,475	52.3	0.52	1.00
Food and drink preparation	117,317	49.3	0.40	0.82
Kitchen and food clean-up	49,622	20.8	0.12	0.56
Interior maintenance, repair, and decoration	7,200	3.0	0.07	2.22
Interior arrangement, decoration, and repairs	4,685	2.0	0.05	2.76
Exterior maintenance, repair, and decoration	6,535	2.7	0.06	2.04
Lawn, garden, and houseplants	22,346	9.4	0.19	2.00
Animals and pets (not veterinary care)	34,523	14.5	0.09	0.63
Walking, exercising, and playing with pets	13,726	5.8	0.04	0.76
Vehicles	6,408	2.7	0.04	1.48
Household management	69,041	29.0	0.21	0.72
Financial management	9,637	4.0	0.03	0.83
Household and personal organization and planning	33,452	14.1	0.09	0.65
Household and personal mail and messages (except email)	16,310	6.9	0.02	0.32
Household and personal email	22,456	9.4	0.06	0.63
Caring for and helping household members	62,109	26.1	0.45	1.73
Caring for and helping household children	52,120	21.9	0.37	1.69
Physical care for household children	37,309	15.7	0.17	1.07
Reading to or with household children	6,231	2.6	0.01	0.48
Playing with household children (except sports)	12,915	5.4	0.09	1.61
Talking with, listening to household children	7,230	3.0	0.02	0.57
Looking after household children as a primary activity	5,405	2.3	0.03	1.12
Picking up or dropping off household children	21,947	9.2	0.02	0.20
Activities related to household children's education	9,092	3.8	0.04	0.93
Helping household children with homework	8,194	3.4	0.03	0.83
Helping household adults	8,625	3.6	0.01	0.34
Caring for and helping people in other households	31,600	13.3	0.16	1.23
Caring for and helping children in other households	13,236	5.6	0.09	1.54

	total people aged 15 or older participating		time spent doing activity (hours)	
	number	percent	average person aged 15 or older	participants aged 15 or older
Helping adults in other households	19,082	8.0%	0.06	0.78
Picking up or dropping off adults in other households	11,801	5.0	0.01	0.16
Work and work-related activities	**110,959**	**46.6**	**3.45**	**7.41**
Work, main job	104,476	43.9	3.28	7.46
Work, other job(s)	5,655	2.4	0.09	3.99
Education	**18,822**	**7.9**	**0.44**	**5.55**
Taking class	12,323	5.2	0.27	5.22
Taking class for degree, certification, or licensure	11,328	4.8	0.26	5.44
Research, homework	13,916	5.8	0.16	2.72
Consumer purchases (store, telephone, Internet)	**96,755**	**40.7**	**0.38**	**0.94**
Grocery shopping	30,743	12.9	0.10	0.76
Purchasing gas	9,448	4.0	0.01	0.17
Purchasing food (except groceries)	28,677	12.0	0.02	0.17
Shopping, except groceries, food, and gas	55,919	23.5	0.25	1.08
Professional and personal care services	**21,158**	**8.9**	**0.08**	**0.92**
Financial services and banking	7,693	3.2	0.01	0.24
Banking	7,200	3.0	0.01	0.18
Medical and care services	8,638	3.6	0.05	1.34
Using health and care services outside the home	8,172	3.4	0.04	1.13
Household services	**4,970**	**2.1**	**0.01**	**0.65**
Eating and drinking	**228,537**	**96.0**	**1.11**	**1.15**
Socializing, relaxing, and leisure	**227,105**	**95.4**	**4.62**	**4.85**
Socializing and communicating	89,468	37.6	0.64	1.69
Attending or hosting social events	5,535	2.3	0.07	3.17
Relaxing and leisure	217,332	91.3	3.83	4.19
Relaxing, thinking	47,425	19.9	0.27	1.34
Television	192,536	80.9	2.77	3.42
Listening to the radio	4,787	2.0	0.03	1.30
Listening to or playing music (not radio)	6,204	2.6	0.03	1.07
Playing games (including computer)	21,402	9.0	0.20	2.22
Computer use for leisure (except games)	22,627	9.5	0.14	1.49
Reading for personal interest	56,846	23.9	0.34	1.44
Arts and entertainment (except sports)	7,689	3.2	0.09	2.63
Sports, exercise, and recreation	**44,944**	**18.9**	**0.33**	**1.76**
Participating in sports, exercise, or recreation	42,688	17.9	0.29	1.64
Using cardiovascular equipment	5,202	2.2	0.02	0.72
Walking	11,448	4.8	0.04	0.85
Working out, unspecified	7,598	3.2	0.03	0.94
Religious and spiritual activities	**21,950**	**9.2**	**0.14**	**1.55**
Attending religious services	11,599	4.9	0.09	1.80
Participation in religious practices	10,882	4.6	0.04	0.88

	total people aged 15 or older participating		time spent doing activity (hours)	
	number	percent	average person aged 15 or older	participants aged 15 or older
Volunteer activities	**15,965**	**6.7%**	**0.15**	**2.19**
Administrative and support activities	6,026	2.5	0.04	1.46
Telephone calls	**36,576**	**15.4**	**0.13**	**0.83**
Telephone calls to or from family members	17,493	7.3	0.04	0.60
Telephone calls to or from friends, neighbors, or acquaintances	13,292	5.6	0.04	0.78
Traveling	**206,854**	**86.9**	**1.20**	**1.38**
Travel related to personal care	6,006	2.5	0.01	0.52
Travel related to household activities	22,337	9.4	0.04	0.41
Travel related to household management	14,539	6.1	0.02	0.41
Travel related to caring for and helping household members	32,374	13.6	0.08	0.60
Travel related to caring for and helping household children	26,071	11.0	0.06	0.55
Travel related to helping household adults	6,086	2.6	0.02	0.64
Travel related to caring for and helping people in other households	24,954	10.5	0.06	0.60
Travel related to caring for and helping children in other households	8,381	3.5	0.02	0.49
Travel related to helping adults in other households	16,908	7.1	0.04	0.59
Travel related to work	90,803	38.2	0.28	0.73
Travel related to education	11,958	5.0	0.03	0.64
Travel related to taking class	10,474	4.4	0.03	0.59
Travel related to consumer purchases	94,287	39.6	0.24	0.60
Travel related to grocery shopping	30,682	12.9	0.05	0.40
Travel related to purchasing gas	9,347	3.9	0.02	0.58
Travel related to purchasing food (except groceries)	26,746	11.2	0.04	0.36
Travel related to shopping (except groceries, food, and gas)	54,081	22.7	0.12	0.55
Travel related to using professional and personal care services	19,326	8.1	0.04	0.46
Travel related to using financial services and banking	7,225	3.0	0.01	0.26
Travel related to using medical services	7,889	3.3	0.02	0.59
Travel related to eating and drinking	59,488	25.0	0.12	0.47
Travel related to socializing, relaxing, and leisure	68,139	28.6	0.18	0.63
Travel related to socializing and communicating	44,153	18.6	0.09	0.50
Travel related to attending or hosting social events	4,755	2.0	0.01	0.66
Travel related to relaxing and leisure	21,232	8.9	0.04	0.40
Travel related to arts and entertainment	6,165	2.6	0.02	0.68
Travel related to sports, exercise, and recreation	22,747	9.6	0.04	0.46
Travel related to participating in sports, exercise, recreation	20,369	8.6	0.04	0.42
Travel related to religious and spiritual activities	12,212	5.1	0.02	0.41
Travel related to volunteer activities	10,185	4.3	0.02	0.42

Note: Primary activities are those respondents identified as their main activity. Other activities done simultaneously, such as eating while watching TV, are not included. Numbers may not add to total because not all subcategories are shown. If fewer than 2.0 percent of the total population participated in a primary activity, then the primary activity is not shown.
Source: Bureau of Labor Statistics, unpublished tables from the 2008 American Time Use Survey, Internet site http://www.bls .gov/tus/home.htm; calculations by New Strategist

Table 1.2 Time Use by Men Aged 15 or Older, 2008

(number and percent of men aged 15 or older participating in primary activities on an average day, hours spent doing activity by the average man aged 15 or older and by men aged 15 or older who participated in the activity, 2008; numbers of participants in thousands)

	men aged 15 or older participating		time spent doing activity (hours)	
	number	percent	average man aged 15 or older	male participants aged 15 or older
TOTAL, ALL ACTIVITIES	**115,339**	**100.0%**	**24.00**	**24.00**
Personal care	**115,303**	**100.0**	**9.21**	**9.21**
Sleeping	115,220	99.9	8.56	8.57
Sleeplessness	5,215	4.5	0.05	0.73
Grooming	88,389	76.6	0.56	0.73
Health-related self-care	5,550	4.8	0.07	1.39
Household activities	**76,760**	**66.6**	**1.32**	**1.99**
Housework	22,688	19.7	0.24	1.23
Interior cleaning	15,525	13.5	0.17	1.26
Laundry	7,237	6.3	0.06	0.97
Storing interior household items, including food	3,314	2.9	0.01	0.40
Food and drink preparation, presentation, and clean-up	44,316	38.4	0.30	0.78
Food and drink preparation	41,542	36.0	0.25	0.68
Kitchen and food clean-up	10,940	9.5	0.05	0.53
Interior maintenance, repair, and decoration	4,508	3.9	0.10	2.50
Interior arrangement, decoration, and repairs	2,823	2.4	0.08	3.18
Exterior maintenance, repair, and decoration	4,370	3.8	0.08	2.22
Lawn, garden, and houseplants	12,658	11.0	0.26	2.35
Animals and pets (not veterinary care)	14,006	12.1	0.08	0.69
Walking, exercising, and playing with pets	6,027	5.2	0.04	0.86
Vehicles	5,199	4.5	0.07	1.65
Household management	27,633	24.0	0.16	0.67
Financial management	3,675	3.2	0.03	0.87
Household and personal organization and planning	12,805	11.1	0.07	0.62
Household and personal mail and messages (except email)	6,307	5.5	0.02	0.30
Household and personal email	8,571	7.4	0.05	0.62
Caring for and helping household members	**23,883**	**20.7**	**0.30**	**1.45**
Caring for and helping household children	19,365	16.8	0.25	1.49
Physical care for household children	11,995	10.4	0.09	0.89
Reading to or with household children	1,979	1.7	0.01	0.51
Playing with household children (except sports)	5,445	4.7	0.08	1.76
Talking with, listening to household children	2,011	1.7	0.01	0.58
Looking after household children as a primary activity	1,680	1.5	0.02	1.31
Picking up or dropping off household children	7,139	6.2	0.01	0.17
Activities related to household children's education	2,506	2.2	0.02	0.97
Helping household children with homework	2,341	2.0	0.02	0.97
Helping household adults	4,035	3.5	0.01	0.40
Caring for and helping people in other households	**12,645**	**11.0**	**0.13**	**1.14**
Caring for and helping children in other households	4,197	3.6	0.05	1.26

	men aged 15 or older participating		time spent doing activity (hours)	
	number	percent	average man aged 15 or older	male participants aged 15 or older
Helping adults in other households	8,615	7.5%	0.07	0.95
Picking up or dropping off adults in other households	5,129	4.4	0.01	0.17
Work and work-related activities	**61,541**	**53.4**	**4.16**	**7.79**
Work, main job	57,839	50.1	3.96	7.89
Work, other job(s)	2,674	2.3	0.10	4.23
Education	**7,905**	**6.9**	**0.39**	**5.75**
Taking class	5,785	5.0	0.27	5.37
Taking class for degree, certification, or licensure	5,550	4.8	0.27	5.52
Research, homework	5,341	4.6	0.12	2.49
Consumer purchases (store, telephone, Internet)	**41,032**	**35.6**	**0.28**	**0.79**
Grocery shopping	11,031	9.6	0.06	0.67
Purchasing gas	4,926	4.3	0.01	0.17
Purchasing food (except groceries)	13,616	11.8	0.02	0.16
Shopping, except groceries, food, and gas	22,595	19.6	0.19	0.96
Professional and personal care services	**7,687**	**6.7**	**0.06**	**0.84**
Financial services and banking	3,613	3.1	0.01	0.25
Banking	3,208	2.8	0.00	0.16
Medical and care services	2,809	2.4	0.04	1.52
Using health and care services outside the home	2,646	2.3	0.03	1.29
Household services	**2,419**	**2.1**	**0.01**	**0.66**
Eating and drinking	**111,287**	**96.5**	**1.15**	**1.19**
Socializing, relaxing, and leisure	**110,020**	**95.4**	**4.83**	**5.07**
Socializing and communicating	40,248	34.9	0.59	1.70
Attending or hosting social events	2,268	2.0	0.06	3.27
Relaxing and leisure	106,209	92.1	4.09	4.44
Relaxing, thinking	23,479	20.4	0.27	1.34
Television	94,958	82.3	3.01	3.66
Listening to the radio	2,919	2.5	0.03	1.18
Listening to or playing music (not radio)	3,773	3.3	0.04	1.18
Playing games (including computer)	11,042	9.6	0.25	2.58
Computer use for leisure (except games)	10,975	9.5	0.15	1.55
Reading for personal interest	24,307	21.1	0.29	1.36
Arts and entertainment (except sports)	3,824	3.3	0.09	2.70
Sports, exercise, and recreation	**25,422**	**22.0**	**0.44**	**2.02**
Participating in sports, exercise, or recreation	24,266	21.0	0.40	1.90
Using cardiovascular equipment	2,130	1.8	0.01	0.76
Walking	5,686	4.9	0.04	0.79
Working out, unspecified	4,065	3.5	0.04	1.04
Religious and spiritual activities	**8,885**	**7.7**	**0.12**	**1.54**
Attending religious services	4,629	4.0	0.07	1.83
Participation in religious practices	4,258	3.7	0.03	0.92

	men aged 15 or older participating		time spent doing activity (hours)	
	number	percent	average man aged 15 or older	male participants aged 15 or older
Volunteer activities	**6,614**	**5.7%**	**0.14**	**2.41**
Administrative and support activities	2,248	1.9	0.03	1.49
Telephone calls	**11,514**	**10.0**	**0.07**	**0.72**
Telephone calls to or from family members	4,393	3.8	0.02	0.49
Telephone calls to or from friends, neighbors, or acquaintances	4,264	3.7	0.02	0.68
Traveling	**102,032**	**88.5**	**1.23**	**1.39**
Travel related to personal care	3,542	3.1	0.01	0.49
Travel related to household activities	9,756	8.5	0.04	0.46
Travel related to household management	6,320	5.5	0.03	0.48
Travel related to caring for and helping household members	11,424	9.9	0.06	0.57
Travel related to caring for and helping household children	8,482	7.4	0.04	0.52
Travel related to helping household adults	2,750	2.4	0.02	0.67
Travel related to caring for and helping people in other households	10,670	9.3	0.06	0.61
Travel related to caring for and helping children in other households	2,852	2.5	0.01	0.49
Travel related to helping adults in other households	7,779	6.7	0.04	0.63
Travel related to work	51,252	44.4	0.36	0.81
Travel related to education	5,349	4.6	0.03	0.59
Travel related to taking class	4,776	4.1	0.02	0.55
Travel related to consumer purchases	39,831	34.5	0.21	0.60
Travel related to grocery shopping	10,998	9.5	0.04	0.45
Travel related to purchasing gas	4,843	4.2	0.02	0.56
Travel related to purchasing food (except groceries)	12,683	11.0	0.04	0.34
Travel related to shopping (except groceries, food, and gas)	21,764	18.9	0.11	0.56
Travel related to using professional and personal care services	7,315	6.3	0.03	0.44
Travel related to using financial services and banking	3,479	3.0	0.01	0.28
Travel related to using medical services	2,661	2.3	0.01	0.60
Travel related to eating and drinking	31,492	27.3	0.13	0.47
Travel related to socializing, relaxing, and leisure	32,289	28.0	0.18	0.66
Travel related to socializing and communicating	20,213	17.5	0.09	0.50
Travel related to attending or hosting social events	1,957	1.7	0.01	0.71
Travel related to relaxing and leisure	10,820	9.4	0.04	0.42
Travel related to arts and entertainment	3,205	2.8	0.02	0.71
Travel related to sports, exercise, and recreation	13,261	11.5	0.06	0.48
Travel related to participating in sports, exercise, recreation	12,042	10.4	0.05	0.44
Travel related to religious and spiritual activities	5,065	4.4	0.02	0.43
Travel related to volunteer activities	4,401	3.8	0.02	0.43

Note: Primary activities are those respondents identified as their main activity. Other activities done simultaneously, such as eating while watching TV, are not included. Numbers may not add to total because not all subcategories are shown. If fewer than 2.0 percent of the total population participated in a primary activity, then the primary activity is not shown.
Source: Bureau of Labor Statistics, unpublished tables from the 2008 American Time Use Survey, Internet site http://www.bls .gov/tus/home.htm; calculations by New Strategist

Table 1.3 Time Use by Women Aged 15 or Older, 2008

(number and percent of women aged 15 or older participating in primary activities on an average day, hours spent doing activity by the average woman aged 15 or older and by women aged 15 or older who participated in the activity, 2008; numbers of participants in thousands)

	women aged 15 or older participating		time spent doing activity (hours)	
	number	percent	average woman aged 15 or older	female participants aged 15 or older
TOTAL, ALL ACTIVITIES	**122,668**	**100.0%**	**24.00**	**24.00**
Personal care	**122,618**	**100.0**	**9.54**	**9.54**
Sleeping	122,569	99.9	8.64	8.64
Sleeplessness	7,175	5.8	0.07	0.95
Grooming	100,399	81.8	0.78	0.95
Health-related self-care	9,572	7.8	0.11	1.38
Household activities	**103,006**	**84.0**	**2.19**	**2.61**
Housework	61,694	50.3	0.90	1.79
Interior cleaning	42,756	34.9	0.55	1.58
Laundry	31,231	25.5	0.28	1.08
Storing interior household items, including food	8,562	7.0	0.02	0.33
Food and drink preparation, presentation, and clean-up	80,160	65.3	0.73	1.12
Food and drink preparation	75,775	61.8	0.55	0.89
Kitchen and food clean-up	38,682	31.5	0.18	0.57
Interior maintenance, repair, and decoration	2,692	2.2	0.04	1.73
Interior arrangement, decoration, and repairs	1,862	1.5	0.03	2.12
Exterior maintenance, repair, and decoration	2,164	1.8	0.03	1.68
Lawn, garden, and houseplants	9,687	7.9	0.12	1.56
Animals and pets (not veterinary care)	20,517	16.7	0.10	0.59
Walking, exercising, and playing with pets	7,699	6.3	0.04	0.69
Vehicles	1,209	1.0	0.01	0.73
Household management	41,407	33.8	0.25	0.75
Financial management	5,962	4.9	0.04	0.80
Household and personal organization and planning	20,647	16.8	0.11	0.67
Household and personal mail and messages (except email)	10,003	8.2	0.03	0.34
Household and personal email	13,885	11.3	0.07	0.64
Caring for and helping household members	**38,226**	**31.2**	**0.59**	**1.90**
Caring for and helping household children	32,755	26.7	0.48	1.80
Physical care for household children	25,314	20.6	0.24	1.15
Reading to or with household children	4,252	3.5	0.02	0.46
Playing with household children (except sports)	7,471	6.1	0.09	1.50
Talking with, listening to household children	5,219	4.3	0.02	0.57
Looking after household children as a primary activity	3,725	3.0	0.03	1.04
Picking up or dropping off household children	14,808	12.1	0.03	0.22
Activities related to household children's education	6,585	5.4	0.05	0.91
Helping household children with homework	5,853	4.8	0.04	0.78
Helping household adults	4,590	3.7	0.01	0.29
Caring for and helping people in other households	**18,955**	**15.5**	**0.20**	**1.28**
Caring for and helping children in other households	9,039	7.4	0.12	1.67

	women aged 15 or older participating		time spent doing activity (hours)	
	number	percent	average woman aged 15 or older	female participants aged 15 or older
Helping adults in other households	10,467	8.5%	0.05	0.64
Picking up or dropping off adults in other households	6,672	5.4	0.01	0.14
Work and work-related activities	**49,418**	**40.3**	**2.79**	**6.93**
Work, main job	46,637	38.0	2.63	6.93
Work, other job(s)	2,981	2.4	0.09	3.78
Education	**10,917**	**8.9**	**0.48**	**5.41**
Taking class	6,538	5.3	0.27	5.09
Taking class for degree, certification, or licensure	5,778	4.7	0.25	5.37
Research, homework	8,575	7.0	0.20	2.87
Consumer purchases (store, telephone, Internet)	**55,723**	**45.4**	**0.48**	**1.05**
Grocery shopping	19,712	16.1	0.13	0.81
Purchasing gas	4,522	3.7	0.01	0.17
Purchasing food (except groceries)	15,061	12.3	0.02	0.17
Shopping, except groceries, food, and gas	33,324	27.2	0.31	1.16
Professional and personal care services	**13,471**	**11.0**	**0.11**	**0.97**
Financial services and banking	4,081	3.3	0.01	0.23
Banking	3,992	3.3	0.01	0.19
Medical and care services	5,830	4.8	0.06	1.26
Using health and care services outside the home	5,526	4.5	0.05	1.05
Household services	**2,551**	**2.1**	**0.01**	**0.65**
Eating and drinking	**117,250**	**95.6**	**1.07**	**1.12**
Socializing, relaxing, and leisure	**117,085**	**95.4**	**4.42**	**4.63**
Socializing and communicating	49,220	40.1	0.68	1.69
Attending or hosting social events	3,267	2.7	0.08	3.10
Relaxing and leisure	111,123	90.6	3.58	3.95
Relaxing, thinking	23,946	19.5	0.26	1.34
Television	97,578	79.5	2.54	3.20
Listening to the radio	1,868	1.5	0.02	1.49
Listening to or playing music (not radio)	2,430	2.0	0.02	0.91
Playing games (including computer)	10,360	8.4	0.15	1.83
Computer use for leisure (except games)	11,652	9.5	0.14	1.44
Reading for personal interest	32,540	26.5	0.40	1.50
Arts and entertainment (except sports)	3,865	3.2	0.08	2.57
Sports, exercise, and recreation	**19,522**	**15.9**	**0.23**	**1.42**
Participating in sports, exercise, or recreation	18,422	15.0	0.20	1.30
Using cardiovascular equipment	3,072	2.5	0.02	0.70
Walking	5,761	4.7	0.04	0.90
Working out, unspecified	3,533	2.9	0.02	0.81
Religious and spiritual activities	**13,065**	**10.7**	**0.17**	**1.55**
Attending religious services	6,969	5.7	0.10	1.78
Participation in religious practices	6,624	5.4	0.05	0.86

	women aged 15 or older participating		time spent doing activity (hours)	
	number	percent	average woman aged 15 or older	female participants aged 15 or older
Volunteer activities	**9,351**	**7.6%**	**0.16**	**2.04**
Administrative and support activities	3,778	3.1	0.04	1.44
Telephone calls	**25,061**	**20.4**	**0.18**	**0.89**
Telephone calls to or from family members	13,100	10.7	0.07	0.64
Telephone calls to or from friends, neighbors, or acquaintances	9,028	7.4	0.06	0.83
Traveling	**104,822**	**85.5**	**1.17**	**1.36**
Travel related to personal care	2,464	2.0	0.01	0.57
Travel related to household activities	12,581	10.3	0.04	0.37
Travel related to household management	8,220	6.7	0.02	0.35
Travel related to caring for and helping household members	20,950	17.1	0.11	0.62
Travel related to caring for and helping household children	17,589	14.3	0.08	0.57
Travel related to helping household adults	3,336	2.7	0.02	0.61
Travel related to caring for and helping people in other households	14,285	11.6	0.07	0.59
Travel related to caring for and helping children in other households	5,530	4.5	0.02	0.49
Travel related to helping adults in other households	9,129	7.4	0.04	0.56
Travel related to work	39,552	32.2	0.20	0.62
Travel related to education	6,609	5.4	0.04	0.68
Travel related to taking class	5,698	4.6	0.03	0.63
Travel related to consumer purchases	54,455	44.4	0.27	0.61
Travel related to grocery shopping	19,684	16.0	0.06	0.36
Travel related to purchasing gas	4,504	3.7	0.02	0.61
Travel related to purchasing food (except groceries)	14,063	11.5	0.04	0.39
Travel related to shopping (except groceries, food, and gas)	32,318	26.3	0.14	0.54
Travel related to using professional and personal care services	12,011	9.8	0.05	0.48
Travel related to using financial services and banking	3,746	3.1	0.01	0.25
Travel related to using medical services	5,229	4.3	0.02	0.58
Travel related to eating and drinking	27,996	22.8	0.11	0.48
Travel related to socializing, relaxing, and leisure	35,850	29.2	0.17	0.59
Travel related to socializing and communicating	23,940	19.5	0.10	0.50
Travel related to attending or hosting social events	2,798	2.3	0.01	0.62
Travel related to relaxing and leisure	10,412	8.5	0.03	0.38
Travel related to arts and entertainment	2,960	2.4	0.02	0.65
Travel related to sports, exercise, and recreation	9,486	7.7	0.03	0.43
Travel related to participating in sports, exercise, recreation	8,328	6.8	0.03	0.38
Travel related to religious and spiritual activities	7,146	5.8	0.02	0.40
Travel related to volunteer activities	5,784	4.7	0.02	0.41

Note: Primary activities are those respondents identified as their main activity. Other activities done simultaneously, such as eating while watching TV, are not included. Numbers may not add to total because not all subcategories are shown. If fewer than 2.0 percent of the total population participated in a primary activity, then the primary activity is not shown.
Source: Bureau of Labor Statistics, unpublished tables from the 2008 American Time Use Survey, Internet site http://www.bls .gov/tus/home.htm; calculations by New Strategist

Table 1.4 Indexed Time Use on of People Aged 15 or Older by Sex, 2008

(average hours spent by people aged 15 or older doing primary activities on an average day by sex, and index of women's time to men's, 2008)

	average hours, 15 or older		index of women to men
	men	women	
TOTAL, ALL ACTIVITIES	**24.00**	**24.00**	**100**
Personal care	**9.21**	**9.54**	**104**
Sleeping	8.56	8.64	101
Sleeplessness	0.05	0.07	140
Grooming	0.56	0.78	139
Health-related self-care	0.07	0.11	157
Household activities	**1.32**	**2.19**	**166**
Housework	0.24	0.90	375
Interior cleaning	0.17	0.55	324
Laundry	0.06	0.28	467
Storing interior household items, including food	0.01	0.02	200
Food and drink preparation, presentation, and clean-up	0.30	0.73	243
Food and drink preparation	0.25	0.55	220
Kitchen and food clean-up	0.05	0.18	360
Interior maintenance, repair, and decoration	0.10	0.04	40
Interior arrangement, decoration, and repairs	0.08	0.03	38
Exterior maintenance, repair, and decoration	0.08	0.03	38
Lawn, garden, and houseplants	0.26	0.12	46
Animals and pets (not veterinary care)	0.08	0.10	125
Walking, exercising, and playing with pets	0.04	0.04	100
Vehicles	0.07	0.01	14
Household management	0.16	0.25	156
Financial management	0.03	0.04	133
Household and personal organization and planning	0.07	0.11	157
Household and personal mail and messages (except email)	0.02	0.03	150
Household and personal email	0.05	0.07	140
Caring for and helping household members	**0.30**	**0.59**	**197**
Caring for and helping household children	0.25	0.48	192
Physical care for household children	0.09	0.24	267
Reading to or with household children	0.01	0.02	200
Playing with household children (except sports)	0.08	0.09	113
Talking with, listening to household children	0.01	0.02	200
Looking after household children as a primary activity	0.02	0.03	150
Picking up or dropping off household children	0.01	0.03	300
Activities related to household children's education	0.02	0.05	250
Helping household children with homework	0.02	0.04	200
Helping household adults	0.01	0.01	100
Caring for and helping people in other households	**0.13**	**0.20**	**154**
Caring for and helping children in other households	0.05	0.12	240

	average hours, 15 or older		index of women to men
	men	women	
Helping adults in other households	0.07	0.05	71
Picking up or dropping off adults in other households	0.01	0.01	100
Work and work-related activities	**4.16**	**2.79**	**67**
Work, main job	3.96	2.63	66
Work, other job(s)	0.10	0.09	90
Education	**0.39**	**0.48**	**123**
Taking class	0.27	0.27	100
Taking class for degree, certification, or licensure	0.27	0.25	93
Research, homework	0.12	0.20	167
Consumer purchases (store, telephone, Internet)	**0.28**	**0.48**	**171**
Grocery shopping	0.06	0.13	217
Purchasing gas	0.01	0.01	100
Purchasing food (except groceries)	0.02	0.02	100
Shopping, except groceries, food, and gas	0.19	0.31	163
Professional and personal care services	**0.06**	**0.11**	**183**
Financial services and banking	0.01	0.01	100
Banking	0.00	0.01	—
Medical and care services	0.04	0.06	150
Using health and care services outside the home	0.03	0.05	167
Household services	**0.01**	**0.01**	**100**
Eating and drinking	**1.15**	**1.07**	**93**
Socializing, relaxing, and leisure	**4.83**	**4.42**	**92**
Socializing and communicating	0.59	0.68	115
Attending or hosting social events	0.06	0.08	133
Relaxing and leisure	4.09	3.58	88
Relaxing, thinking	0.27	0.26	96
Television	3.01	2.54	84
Listening to the radio	0.03	0.02	67
Listening to or playing music (not radio)	0.04	0.02	50
Playing games (including computer)	0.25	0.15	60
Computer use for leisure (except games)	0.15	0.14	93
Reading for personal interest	0.29	0.40	138
Arts and entertainment (except sports)	0.09	0.08	89
Sports, exercise, and recreation	**0.44**	**0.23**	**52**
Participating in sports, exercise, or recreation	0.40	0.20	50
Using cardiovascular equipment	0.01	0.02	200
Walking	0.04	0.04	100
Working out, unspecified	0.04	0.02	50
Religious and spiritual activities	**0.12**	**0.17**	**142**
Attending religious services	0.07	0.10	143
Participation in religious practices	0.03	0.05	167

	average hours, 15 or older		index of women to men
	men	women	
Volunteer activities	**0.14**	**0.16**	**114**
Administrative and support activities	0.03	0.04	133
Telephone calls	**0.07**	**0.18**	**257**
Telephone calls to or from family members	0.02	0.07	350
Telephone calls to or from friends, neighbors, or acquaintances	0.02	0.06	300
Traveling	**1.23**	**1.17**	**95**
Travel related to personal care	0.01	0.01	100
Travel related to household activities	0.04	0.04	100
Travel related to household management	0.03	0.02	67
Travel related to caring for and helping household members	0.06	0.11	183
Travel related to caring for and helping household children	0.04	0.08	200
Travel related to helping household adults	0.02	0.02	100
Travel related to caring for and helping people in other households	0.06	0.07	117
Travel related to caring for and helping children in other households	0.01	0.02	200
Travel related to helping adults in other households	0.04	0.04	100
Travel related to work	0.36	0.20	56
Travel related to education	0.03	0.04	133
Travel related to taking class	0.02	0.03	150
Travel related to consumer purchases	0.21	0.27	129
Travel related to grocery shopping	0.04	0.06	150
Travel related to purchasing gas	0.02	0.02	100
Travel related to purchasing food (except groceries)	0.04	0.04	100
Travel related to shopping (except groceries, food, and gas)	0.11	0.14	127
Travel related to using professional and personal care services	0.03	0.05	167
Travel related to using financial services and banking	0.01	0.01	100
Travel related to using medical services	0.01	0.02	200
Travel related to eating and drinking	0.13	0.11	85
Travel related to socializing, relaxing, and leisure	0.18	0.17	94
Travel related to socializing and communicating	0.09	0.10	111
Travel related to attending or hosting social events	0.01	0.01	100
Travel related to relaxing and leisure	0.04	0.03	75
Travel related to arts and entertainment	0.02	0.02	100
Travel related to sports, exercise, and recreation	0.06	0.03	50
Travel related to participating in sports, exercise, and recreation	0.05	0.03	60
Travel related to religious and spiritual activities	0.02	0.02	100
Travel related to volunteer activities	0.02	0.02	100

Note: The index is calculated by dividing women's time by men's and multiplying by 100. Primary activities are those respondents identified as their main activity. Other activities done simultaneously, such as eating while watching TV, are not included. If fewer than 2.0 percent of the total population participated in a primary activity, then the primary activity is not shown. "–" means denominator is zero.
Source: Bureau of Labor Statistics, unpublished tables from the 2008 American Time Use Survey, Internet site http://www.bls.gov/tus/home.htm; calculations by New Strategist

Table 1.5 Indexed Participation in Primary Activities of People Aged 15 or Older by Sex, 2008

(percent of people aged 15 or older participating in primary activities on an average day by sex, and index of women's participation to men's, 2008)

	aged 15 or older, percent participating		index of women to men
	men	women	
TOTAL, ALL ACTIVITIES	**100.0%**	**100.0%**	**100**
Personal care	**100.0**	**100.0**	**100**
Sleeping	99.9	99.9	100
Sleeplessness	4.5	5.8	129
Grooming	76.6	81.8	107
Health-related self-care	4.8	7.8	162
Household activities	**66.6**	**84.0**	**126**
Housework	19.7	50.3	256
Interior cleaning	13.5	34.9	259
Laundry	6.3	25.5	406
Storing interior household items, including food	2.9	7.0	243
Food and drink preparation, presentation, and clean-up	38.4	65.3	170
Food and drink preparation	36.0	61.8	172
Kitchen and food clean-up	9.5	31.5	332
Interior maintenance, repair, and decoration	3.9	2.2	56
Interior arrangement, decoration, and repairs	2.4	1.5	62
Exterior maintenance, repair, and decoration	3.8	1.8	47
Lawn, garden, and houseplants	11.0	7.9	72
Animals and pets (not veterinary care)	12.1	16.7	138
Walking, exercising, and playing with pets	5.2	6.3	120
Vehicles	4.5	1.0	22
Household management	24.0	33.8	141
Financial management	3.2	4.9	153
Household and personal organization and planning	11.1	16.8	152
Household and personal mail and messages (except email)	5.5	8.2	149
Household and personal email	7.4	11.3	152
Caring for and helping household members	**20.7**	**31.2**	**150**
Caring for and helping household children	16.8	26.7	159
Physical care for household children	10.4	20.6	198
Reading to or with household children	1.7	3.5	202
Playing with household children (except sports)	4.7	6.1	129
Talking with, listening to household children	1.7	4.3	244
Looking after household children as a primary activity	1.5	3.0	208
Picking up or dropping off household children	6.2	12.1	195
Activities related to household children's education	2.2	5.4	247
Helping household children with homework	2.0	4.8	235
Helping household adults	3.5	3.7	107
Caring for and helping people in other households	**11.0**	**15.5**	**141**
Caring for and helping children in other households	3.6	7.4	203

	aged 15 or older, percent participating		index of women to men
	men	women	
Helping adults in other households	7.5%	8.5%	114
Picking up or dropping off adults in other households	4.4	5.4	122
Work and work-related activities	**53.4**	**40.3**	**76**
Work, main job	50.1	38.0	76
Work, other job(s)	2.3	2.4	105
Education	**6.9**	**8.9**	**130**
Taking class	5.0	5.3	106
Taking class for degree, certification, or licensure	4.8	4.7	98
Research, homework	4.6	7.0	151
Consumer purchases (store, telephone, Internet)	**35.6**	**45.4**	**128**
Grocery shopping	9.6	16.1	168
Purchasing gas	4.3	3.7	86
Purchasing food (except groceries)	11.8	12.3	104
Shopping, except groceries, food, and gas	19.6	27.2	139
Professional and personal care services	**6.7**	**11.0**	**165**
Financial services and banking	3.1	3.3	106
Banking	2.8	3.3	117
Medical and care services	2.4	4.8	195
Using health and care services outside the home	2.3	4.5	196
Household services	**2.1**	**2.1**	**99**
Eating and drinking	**96.5**	**95.6**	**99**
Socializing, relaxing, and leisure	**95.4**	**95.4**	**100**
Socializing and communicating	34.9	40.1	115
Attending or hosting social events	2.0	2.7	135
Relaxing and leisure	92.1	90.6	98
Relaxing, thinking	20.4	19.5	96
Television	82.3	79.5	97
Listening to the radio	2.5	1.5	60
Listening to or playing music (not radio)	3.3	2.0	61
Playing games (including computer)	9.6	8.4	88
Computer use for leisure (except games)	9.5	9.5	100
Reading for personal interest	21.1	26.5	126
Arts and entertainment (except sports)	3.3	3.2	95
Sports, exercise, and recreation	**22.0**	**15.9**	**72**
Participating in sports, exercise, or recreation	21.0	15.0	71
Using cardiovascular equipment	1.8	2.5	136
Walking	4.9	4.7	95
Working out, unspecified	3.5	2.9	82
Religious and spiritual activities	**7.7**	**10.7**	**138**
Attending religious services	4.0	5.7	142
Participation in religious practices	3.7	5.4	146

	aged 15 or older, percent participating		index of women to men
	men	women	
Volunteer activities	**5.7%**	**7.6%**	**133**
Administrative and support activities	1.9	3.1	158
Telephone calls	**10.0**	**20.4**	**205**
Telephone calls to or from family members	3.8	10.7	280
Telephone calls to or from friends, neighbors, or acquaintances	3.7	7.4	199
Traveling	**88.5**	**85.5**	**97**
Travel related to personal care	3.1	2.0	65
Travel related to household activities	8.5	10.3	121
Travel related to household management	5.5	6.7	122
Travel related to caring for and helping household members	9.9	17.1	172
Travel related to caring for and helping household children	7.4	14.3	195
Travel related to helping household adults	2.4	2.7	114
Travel related to caring for and helping people in other households	9.3	11.6	126
Travel related to caring for and helping children in other households	2.5	4.5	182
Travel related to helping adults in other households	6.7	7.4	110
Travel related to work	44.4	32.2	73
Travel related to education	4.6	5.4	116
Travel related to taking class	4.1	4.6	112
Travel related to consumer purchases	34.5	44.4	129
Travel related to grocery shopping	9.5	16.0	168
Travel related to purchasing gas	4.2	3.7	87
Travel related to purchasing food (except groceries)	11.0	11.5	104
Travel related to shopping (except groceries, food, and gas)	18.9	26.3	140
Travel related to using professional and personal care services	6.3	9.8	154
Travel related to using financial services and banking	3.0	3.1	101
Travel related to using medical services	2.3	4.3	185
Travel related to eating and drinking	27.3	22.8	84
Travel related to socializing, relaxing, and leisure	28.0	29.2	104
Travel related to socializing and communicating	17.5	19.5	111
Travel related to attending or hosting social events	1.7	2.3	134
Travel related to relaxing and leisure	9.4	8.5	90
Travel related to arts and entertainment	2.8	2.4	87
Travel related to sports, exercise, and recreation	11.5	7.7	67
Travel related to participating in sports, exercise, recreation	10.4	6.8	65
Travel related to religious and spiritual activities	4.4	5.8	133
Travel related to volunteer activities	3.8	4.7	124

Note: The index is calculated by dividing percent of women participating in primary activity by percent of men participating in primary activity and multiplying by 100. Primary activities are those respondents identified as their main activity. Other activities done simultaneously, such as eating while watching TV, are not included. If fewer than 2.0 percent of the total population participated in a primary activity, then the primary activity is not shown.
Source: Bureau of Labor Statistics, unpublished tables from the 2008 American Time Use Survey, Internet site http://www.bls .gov/tus/home.htm; calculations by New Strategist

Table 1.6 Ranking: Average Hours per Day Spent Doing Primary Activities by Total People Aged 15 or Older, 2008

(average hours per day spent by people aged 15 or older doing primary activities, ranked by time spent doing activity, 2008)

		average hours per day spent by people aged 15 or older
	Total, all activities	**24.00**
1.	Sleeping	8.60
2.	Work, main job	3.28
3.	Television	2.77
4.	Eating and drinking	1.11
5.	Grooming	0.67
6.	Socializing and communicating	0.64
7.	Food and drink preparation	0.40
8.	Interior cleaning	0.37
9.	Caring for and helping household children	0.37
10.	Reading for personal interest	0.34
11.	Participating in sports, exercise, or recreation	0.29
12.	Travel related to work	0.28
13.	Taking class	0.27
14.	Relaxing, thinking	0.27
15.	Shopping, except groceries, food, and gas	0.25
16.	Playing games (including computer)	0.20
17.	Lawn, garden, and houseplants	0.19
18.	Laundry	0.17
19.	Research, homework	0.16
20.	Volunteer activities	0.15
21.	Computer use for leisure (except games)	0.14
22.	Telephone calls	0.13
23.	Kitchen and food clean-up	0.12
24.	Travel related to shopping (except groceries, food, and gas)	0.12
25.	Travel related to eating and drinking	0.12
26.	Grocery shopping	0.10
27.	Health-related self-care	0.09
28.	Animals and pets (not veterinary care)	0.09
29.	Household and personal organization and planning	0.09
30.	Caring for and helping children in other households	0.09
31.	Work, other job(s)	0.09
32.	Arts and entertainment (except sports)	0.09
33.	Attending religious services	0.09
34.	Travel related to socializing and communicating	0.09
35.	Interior maintenance, repair, and decoration	0.07
36.	Attending or hosting social events	0.07
37.	Exterior maintenance, repair, and decoration	0.06
38.	Household and personal email	0.06
39.	Helping adults in other households	0.06

	average hours per day spent by people aged 15 or older
40. Travel related to caring for and helping household children	0.06
41. Medical and care services	0.05
42. Travel related to grocery shopping	0.05
43. Vehicles	0.04
44. Activities related to household children's education	0.04
45. Participation in religious practices	0.04
46. Travel related to household activities	0.04
47. Travel related to helping adults in other households	0.04
48. Travel related to purchasing food (except groceries)	0.04
49. Travel related to relaxing and leisure	0.04
50. Travel related to sports, exercise, and recreation	0.04
51. Financial management	0.03
52. Listening to the radio	0.03
53. Listening to or playing music (not radio)	0.03
54. Travel related to education	0.03
55. Storing interior household items, including food	0.02
56. Household and personal mail and messages (except email)	0.02
57. Purchasing food (except groceries)	0.02
58. Travel related to helping household adults	0.02
59. Travel related to caring for and helping children in other households	0.02
60. Travel related to purchasing gas	0.02
61. Travel related to using medical services	0.02
62. Travel related to arts and entertainment	0.02
63. Travel related to religious and spiritual activities	0.02
64. Travel related to volunteer activities	0.02
65. Helping household adults	0.01
66. Purchasing gas	0.01
67. Financial services and banking	0.01
68. Household services	0.01
69. Travel related to personal care	0.01
70. Travel related to using financial services and banking	0.01
71. Travel related to attending or hosting social events	0.01

Note: Primary activities are those respondents identified as their main activity. Other activities done simultaneously, such as eating while watching TV, are not included. If fewer than 2.0 percent of the total population participated in a primary activity, then the primary activity is not shown.
Source: Bureau of Labor Statistics, unpublished tables from the 2008 American Time Use Survey, Internet site http://www.bls .gov/tus/home.htm; calculations by New Strategist

Table 1.7 Ranking: Average Hours per Day Spent Doing Primary Activities by Men Aged 15 or Older, 2008

(average hours per day spent by men aged 15 or older doing primary activities, ranked by time spent doing activity, 2008)

		average hours per day spent by men aged 15 or older
	Total, all activities	**24.00**
1.	Sleeping	8.56
2.	Work, main job	3.96
3.	Television	3.01
4.	Eating and drinking	1.15
5.	Socializing and communicating	0.59
6.	Grooming	0.56
7.	Participating in sports, exercise, or recreation	0.40
8.	Travel related to work	0.36
9.	Reading for personal interest	0.29
10.	Taking class	0.27
11.	Relaxing, thinking	0.27
12.	Lawn, garden, and houseplants	0.26
13.	Food and drink preparation	0.25
14.	Caring for and helping household children	0.25
15.	Playing games (including computer)	0.25
16.	Shopping, except groceries, food, and gas	0.19
17.	Interior cleaning	0.17
18.	Computer use for leisure (except games)	0.15
19.	Volunteer activities	0.14
20.	Travel related to eating and drinking	0.13
21.	Research, homework	0.12
22.	Travel related to shopping (except groceries, food, and gas)	0.11
23.	Interior maintenance, repair, and decoration	0.10
24.	Work, other job(s)	0.10
25.	Arts and entertainment (except sports)	0.09
26.	Travel related to socializing and communicating	0.09
27.	Exterior maintenance, repair, and decoration	0.08
28.	Animals and pets (not veterinary care)	0.08
29.	Health-related self-care	0.07
30.	Vehicles	0.07
31.	Household and personal organization and planning	0.07
32.	Helping adults in other households	0.07
33.	Attending religious services	0.07
34.	Telephone calls	0.07
35.	Laundry	0.06
36.	Grocery shopping	0.06
37.	Attending or hosting social events	0.06
38.	Travel related to sports, exercise, and recreation	0.06
39.	Kitchen and food clean-up	0.05

	average hours per day spent by men aged 15 or older
40. Household and personal email	0.05
41. Caring for and helping children in other households	0.05
42. Medical and care services	0.04
43. Listening to or playing music (not radio)	0.04
44. Travel related to household activities	0.04
45. Travel related to caring for and helping household children	0.04
46. Travel related to helping adults in other households	0.04
47. Travel related to grocery shopping	0.04
48. Travel related to purchasing food (except groceries)	0.04
49. Travel related to relaxing and leisure	0.04
50. Financial management	0.03
51. Listening to the radio	0.03
52. Participation in religious practices	0.03
53. Travel related to education	0.03
54. Household and personal mail and messages (except email)	0.02
55. Activities related to household children's education	0.02
56. Purchasing food (except groceries)	0.02
57. Travel related to helping household adults	0.02
58. Travel related to purchasing gas	0.02
59. Travel related to arts and entertainment	0.02
60. Travel related to religious and spiritual activities	0.02
61. Travel related to volunteer activities	0.02
62. Storing interior household items, including food	0.01
63. Helping household adults	0.01
64. Purchasing gas	0.01
65. Financial services and banking	0.01
66. Household services	0.01
67. Travel related to personal care	0.01
68. Travel related to caring for and helping children in other households	0.01
69. Travel related to using financial services and banking	0.01
70. Travel related to using medical services	0.01
71. Travel related to attending or hosting social events	0.01

Note: Primary activities are those respondents identified as their main activity. Other activities done simultaneously, such as eating while watching TV, are not included. If fewer than 2.0 percent of the total population participated in a primary activity, then the primary activity is not shown.

Source: Bureau of Labor Statistics, unpublished tables from the 2005 American Time Use Survey, Internet site http://www.bls .gov/tus/home.htm; calculations by New Strategist

Table 1.8 Ranking: Average Hours per Day Spent Doing Primary Activities by Women Aged 15 or Older, 2008

(average hours per day spent by women aged 15 or older doing primary activities, ranked by time spent doing activity, 2008)

		average hours per day spent by women aged 15 or older
	Total, all activities	**24.00**
1.	Sleeping	8.64
2.	Work, main job	2.63
3.	Television	2.54
4.	Eating and drinking	1.07
5.	Grooming	0.78
6.	Socializing and communicating	0.68
7.	Interior cleaning	0.55
8.	Food and drink preparation	0.55
9.	Caring for and helping household children	0.48
10.	Reading for personal interest	0.40
11.	Shopping, except groceries, food, and gas	0.31
12.	Laundry	0.28
13.	Taking class	0.27
14.	Relaxing, thinking	0.26
15.	Research, homework	0.20
16.	Participating in sports, exercise, or recreation	0.20
17.	Travel related to work	0.20
18.	Kitchen and food clean-up	0.18
19.	Telephone calls	0.18
20.	Volunteer activities	0.16
21.	Playing games (including computer)	0.15
22.	Computer use for leisure (except games)	0.14
23.	Travel related to shopping (except groceries, food, and gas)	0.14
24.	Grocery shopping	0.13
25.	Lawn, garden, and houseplants	0.12
26.	Caring for and helping children in other households	0.12
27.	Health-related self-care	0.11
28.	Household and personal organization and planning	0.11
29.	Travel related to eating and drinking	0.11
30.	Animals and pets (not veterinary care)	0.10
31.	Attending religious services	0.10
32.	Travel related to socializing and communicating	0.10
33.	Work, other job(s)	0.09
34.	Attending or hosting social events	0.08
35.	Arts and entertainment (except sports)	0.08
36.	Travel related to caring for and helping household children	0.08
37.	Household and personal email	0.07
38.	Medical and care services	0.06
39.	Travel related to grocery shopping	0.06

	average hours per day spent by women aged 15 or older
40. Activities related to household children's education	0.05
41. Helping adults in other households	0.05
42. Participation in religious practices	0.05
43. Interior maintenance, repair, and decoration	0.04
44. Financial management	0.04
45. Travel related to household activities	0.04
46. Travel related to helping adults in other households	0.04
47. Travel related to education	0.04
48. Travel related to purchasing food (except groceries)	0.04
49. Exterior maintenance, repair, and decoration	0.03
50. Household and personal mail and messages (except email)	0.03
51. Travel related to relaxing and leisure	0.03
52. Travel related to sports, exercise, and recreation	0.03
53. Storing interior household items, including food	0.02
54. Purchasing food (except groceries)	0.02
55. Listening to the radio	0.02
56. Listening to or playing music (not radio)	0.02
57. Travel related to helping household adults	0.02
58. Travel related to caring for and helping children in other households	0.02
59. Travel related to purchasing gas	0.02
60. Travel related to using medical services	0.02
61. Travel related to arts and entertainment	0.02
62. Travel related to religious and spiritual activities	0.02
63. Travel related to volunteer activities	0.02
64. Vehicles	0.01
65. Helping household adults	0.01
66. Purchasing gas	0.01
67. Financial services and banking	0.01
68. Household services	0.01
69. Travel related to personal care	0.01
70. Travel related to using financial services and banking	0.01
71. Travel related to attending or hosting social events	0.01

Note: Primary activities are those respondents identified as their main activity. Other activities done simultaneously, such as eating while watching TV, are not included. If fewer than 2.0 percent of the total population participated in a primary activity, then the primary activity is not shown.
Source: Bureau of Labor Statistics, unpublished tables from the 2008 American Time Use Survey, Internet site http://www.bls .gov/tus/home.htm; calculations by New Strategist

Table 1.9   Ranking: Percent of Total People Aged 15 or Older Participating in Primary Activities on an Average Day, 2008

(percent of people aged 15 or older participating in primary activities on an average day, ranked by percent participating, 2008)

		percent of people aged 15 or older participating in activity
	Total, all activities	**100.0%**
1.	Sleeping	99.9
2.	Eating and drinking	96.0
3.	Television	80.9
4.	Grooming	79.3
5.	Food and drink preparation	49.3
6.	Work, main job	43.9
7.	Travel related to work	38.2
8.	Socializing and communicating	37.6
9.	Travel related to eating and drinking	25.0
10.	Interior cleaning	24.5
11.	Reading for personal interest	23.9
12.	Shopping, except groceries, food, and gas	23.5
13.	Travel related to shopping (except groceries, food, and gas)	22.7
14.	Caring for and helping household children	21.9
15.	Kitchen and food clean-up	20.8
16.	Relaxing, thinking	19.9
17.	Sports, exercise, and recreation	18.9
18.	Travel related to socializing and communicating	18.6
19.	Laundry	16.2
20.	Telephone calls	15.4
21.	Animals and pets (not veterinary care)	14.5
22.	Household and personal organization and planning	14.1
23.	Grocery shopping	12.9
24.	Travel related to grocery shopping	12.9
25.	Purchasing food (except groceries)	12.0
26.	Travel related to purchasing food (except groceries)	11.2
27.	Travel related to caring for and helping household children	11.0
28.	Travel related to sports, exercise, and recreation	9.6
29.	Computer use for leisure (except games)	9.5
30.	Household and personal email	9.4
31.	Lawn, garden, and houseplants	9.4
32.	Travel related to household activities	9.4
33.	Playing games (including computer)	9.0
34.	Travel related to relaxing and leisure	8.9
35.	Helping adults in other households	8.0
36.	Travel related to helping adults in other households	7.1
37.	Household and personal mail and messages (except email)	6.9
38.	Volunteer activities	6.7
39.	Health-related self-care	6.4

	percent of people aged 15 or older participating in activity
40. Research, homework	5.8%
41. Caring for and helping children in other households	5.6
42. Taking class	5.2
43. Travel related to religious and spiritual activities	5.1
44. Travel related to education	5.0
45. Storing interior household items, including food	5.0
46. Attending religious services	4.9
47. Participation in religious practices	4.6
48. Travel related to volunteer activities	4.3
49. Financial management	4.0
50. Purchasing gas	4.0
51. Travel related to purchasing gas	3.9
52. Activities related to household children's education	3.8
53. Medical and care services	3.6
54. Helping household adults	3.6
55. Travel related to caring for and helping children in other households	3.5
56. Travel related to using medical services	3.3
57. Financial services and banking	3.2
58. Arts and entertainment (except sports)	3.2
59. Travel related to using financial services and banking	3.0
60. Interior maintenance, repair, and decoration	3.0
61. Exterior maintenance, repair, and decoration	2.7
62. Vehicles	2.7
63. Listening to or playing music (not radio)	2.6
64. Travel related to arts and entertainment	2.6
65. Travel related to helping household adults	2.6
66. Travel related to personal care	2.5
67. Work, other job(s)	2.4
68. Attending or hosting social events	2.3
69. Household services	2.1
70. Listening to the radio	2.0
71. Travel related to attending or hosting social events	2.0

Note: Primary activities are those respondents identified as their main activity. Other activities done simultaneously, such as eating while watching TV, are not included. If fewer than 2.0 percent of the total population participated in a primary activity, then the primary activity is not shown.
Source: Bureau of Labor Statistics, unpublished tables from the 2008 American Time Use Survey, Internet site http://www.bls .gov/tus/home.htm; calculations by New Strategist

Table 1.10 Ranking: Percent of Men Aged 15 or Older Participating in Primary Activities on an Average Day, 2008

(percent of men aged 15 or older participating in primary activities on an average day, ranked by percent participating, 2008)

		percent of men aged 15 or older participating in activity
	Total, all activities	**100.0%**
1.	Sleeping	99.9
2.	Eating and drinking	96.5
3.	Television	82.3
4.	Grooming	76.6
5.	Work, main job	50.1
6.	Travel related to work	44.4
7.	Food and drink preparation	36.0
8.	Socializing and communicating	34.9
9.	Travel related to eating and drinking	27.3
10.	Sports, exercise, and recreation	22.0
11.	Reading for personal interest	21.1
12.	Relaxing, thinking	20.4
13.	Shopping, except groceries, food, and gas	19.6
14.	Travel related to shopping (except groceries, food, and gas)	18.9
15.	Travel related to socializing and communicating	17.5
16.	Caring for and helping household children	16.8
17.	Interior cleaning	13.5
18.	Animals and pets (not veterinary care)	12.1
19.	Purchasing food (except groceries)	11.8
20.	Travel related to sports, exercise, and recreation	11.5
21.	Household and personal organization and planning	11.1
22.	Travel related to purchasing food (except groceries)	11.0
23.	Lawn, garden, and houseplants	11.0
24.	Telephone calls	10.0
25.	Playing games (including computer)	9.6
26.	Grocery shopping	9.6
27.	Travel related to grocery shopping	9.5
28.	Computer use for leisure (except games)	9.5
29.	Kitchen and food clean-up	9.5
30.	Travel related to relaxing and leisure	9.4
31.	Travel related to household activities	8.5
32.	Helping adults in other households	7.5
33.	Household and personal email	7.4
34.	Travel related to caring for and helping household children	7.4
35.	Travel related to helping adults in other households	6.7
36.	Laundry	6.3
37.	Volunteer activities	5.7
38.	Household and personal mail and messages (except email)	5.5
39.	Taking class	5.0

	percent of men aged 15 or older participating in activity
40. Health-related self-care	4.8%
41. Travel related to education	4.6
42. Research, homework	4.6
43. Vehicles	4.5
44. Travel related to religious and spiritual activities	4.4
45. Purchasing gas	4.3
46. Travel related to purchasing gas	4.2
47. Attending religious services	4.0
48. Interior maintenance, repair, and decoration	3.9
49. Travel related to volunteer activities	3.8
50. Exterior maintenance, repair, and decoration	3.8
51. Participation in religious practices	3.7
52. Caring for and helping children in other households	3.6
53. Helping household adults	3.5
54. Arts and entertainment (except sports)	3.3
55. Listening to or playing music (not radio)	3.3
56. Financial management	3.2
57. Financial services and banking	3.1
58. Travel related to personal care	3.1
59. Travel related to using financial services and banking	3.0
60. Storing interior household items, including food	2.9
61. Travel related to arts and entertainment	2.8
62. Listening to the radio	2.5
63. Travel related to caring for and helping children in other households	2.5
64. Medical and care services	2.4
65. Travel related to helping household adults	2.4
66. Work, other job(s)	2.3
67. Travel related to using medical services	2.3
68. Activities related to household children's education	2.2
69. Household services	2.1
70. Attending or hosting social events	2.0
71. Travel related to attending or hosting social events	1.7

Note: Primary activities are those respondents identified as their main activity. Other activities done simultaneously, such as eating while watching TV, are not included. If fewer than 2.0 percent of the total population participated in a primary activity, then the primary activity is not shown.
Source: Bureau of Labor Statistics, unpublished tables from the 2008 American Time Use Survey, Internet site http://www.bls.gov/tus/home.htm; calculations by New Strategist

Table 1.11 Ranking: Percent of Women Aged 15 or Older Participating in Primary Activities on an Average Day, 2008

(percent of women aged 15 or older participating in primary activities on an average day, ranked by percent participating, 2008)

		percent of women aged 15 or older participating in activity
	Total, all activities	**100.0%**
1.	Sleeping	99.9
2.	Eating and drinking	95.6
3.	Grooming	81.8
4.	Television	79.5
5.	Food and drink preparation	61.8
6.	Socializing and communicating	40.1
7.	Work, main job	38.0
8.	Interior cleaning	34.9
9.	Travel related to work	32.2
10.	Kitchen and food clean-up	31.5
11.	Shopping, except groceries, food, and gas	27.2
12.	Caring for and helping household children	26.7
13.	Reading for personal interest	26.5
14.	Travel related to shopping (except groceries, food, and gas)	26.3
15.	Laundry	25.5
16.	Travel related to eating and drinking	22.8
17.	Telephone calls	20.4
18.	Relaxing, thinking	19.5
19.	Travel related to socializing and communicating	19.5
20.	Household and personal organization and planning	16.8
21.	Animals and pets (not veterinary care)	16.7
22.	Grocery shopping	16.1
23.	Travel related to grocery shopping	16.0
24.	Sports, exercise, and recreation	15.9
25.	Travel related to caring for and helping household children	14.3
26.	Purchasing food (except groceries)	12.3
27.	Travel related to purchasing food (except groceries)	11.5
28.	Household and personal email	11.3
29.	Travel related to household activities	10.3
30.	Computer use for leisure (except games)	9.5
31.	Helping adults in other households	8.5
32.	Travel related to relaxing and leisure	8.5
33.	Playing games (including computer)	8.4
34.	Household and personal mail and messages (except email)	8.2
35.	Lawn, garden, and houseplants	7.9
36.	Health-related self-care	7.8
37.	Travel related to sports, exercise, and recreation	7.7
38.	Volunteer activities	7.6

	percent of women aged 15 or older participating in activity
39. Travel related to helping adults in other households	7.4%
40. Caring for and helping children in other households	7.4
41. Research, homework	7.0
42. Storing interior household items, including food	7.0
43. Travel related to religious and spiritual activities	5.8
44. Attending religious services	5.7
45. Participation in religious practices	5.4
46. Travel related to education	5.4
47. Activities related to household children's education	5.4
48. Taking class	5.3
49. Financial management	4.9
50. Medical and care services	4.8
51. Travel related to volunteer activities	4.7
52. Travel related to caring for and helping children in other households	4.5
53. Travel related to using medical services	4.3
54. Helping household adults	3.7
55. Purchasing gas	3.7
56. Travel related to purchasing gas	3.7
57. Financial services and banking	3.3
58. Arts and entertainment (except sports)	3.2
59. Travel related to using financial services and banking	3.1
60. Travel related to helping household adults	2.7
61. Attending or hosting social events	2.7
62. Work, other job(s)	2.4
63. Travel related to arts and entertainment	2.4
64. Travel related to attending or hosting social events	2.3
65. Interior maintenance, repair, and decoration	2.2
66. Household services	2.1
67. Travel related to personal care	2.0
68. Listening to or playing music (not radio)	2.0
69. Exterior maintenance, repair, and decoration	1.8
70. Listening to the radio	1.5
71. Vehicles	1.0

Note: Primary activities are those respondents identified as their main activity. Other activities done simultaneously, such as eating while watching TV, are not included. If fewer than 2.0 percent of the total population participated in a primary activity, then the primary activity is not shown.
Source: Bureau of Labor Statistics, unpublished tables from the 2008 American Time Use Survey, Internet site http://www.bls .gov/tus/home.htm; calculations by New Strategist

Table 1.12 Ranking: Average Hours per Day Spent Doing Primary Activities by Total Participants Aged 15 or Older, 2008

(hours per day spent by participants aged 15 or older doing primary activities, ranked by time spent doing activity, 2008)

		average hours per day spent by participants aged 15 or older
	Total, all activities	**24.00**
1.	Sleeping	8.61
2.	Work, main job	7.46
3.	Taking class	5.22
4.	Work, other job(s)	3.99
5.	Television	3.42
6.	Attending or hosting social events	3.17
7.	Research, homework	2.72
8.	Arts and entertainment (except sports)	2.63
9.	Interior maintenance, repair, and decoration	2.22
10.	Playing games (including computer)	2.22
11.	Volunteer activities	2.19
12.	Exterior maintenance, repair, and decoration	2.04
13.	Lawn, garden, and houseplants	2.00
14.	Attending religious services	1.80
15.	Sports, exercise, and recreation	1.76
16.	Caring for and helping household children	1.69
17.	Socializing and communicating	1.69
18.	Caring for and helping children in other households	1.54
19.	Interior cleaning	1.50
20.	Computer use for leisure (except games)	1.49
21.	Vehicles	1.48
22.	Reading for personal interest	1.44
23.	Health-related self-care	1.38
24.	Medical and care services	1.34
25.	Relaxing, thinking	1.34
26.	Listening to the radio	1.30
27.	Eating and drinking	1.15
28.	Shopping, except groceries, food, and gas	1.08
29.	Listening to or playing music (not radio)	1.07
30.	Laundry	1.06
31.	Activities related to household children's education	0.93
32.	Participation in religious practices	0.88
33.	Grooming	0.85
34.	Financial management	0.83
35.	Telephone calls	0.83
36.	Food and drink preparation	0.82
37.	Helping adults in other households	0.78
38.	Grocery shopping	0.76
39.	Travel related to work	0.73

	average hours per day spent by participants aged 15 or older
40. Travel related to arts and entertainment	0.68
41. Travel related to attending or hosting social events	0.66
42. Household and personal organization and planning	0.65
43. Household services	0.65
44. Travel related to helping household adults	0.64
45. Travel related to education	0.64
46. Animals and pets (not veterinary care)	0.63
47. Household and personal email	0.63
48. Travel related to helping adults in other households	0.59
49. Travel related to using medical services	0.59
50. Travel related to purchasing gas	0.58
51. Kitchen and food clean-up	0.56
52. Travel related to caring for and helping household children	0.55
53. Travel related to shopping (except groceries, food, and gas)	0.55
54. Travel related to personal care	0.52
55. Travel related to socializing and communicating	0.50
56. Travel related to caring for and helping children in other households	0.49
57. Travel related to eating and drinking	0.47
58. Travel related to sports, exercise, and recreation	0.46
59. Travel related to volunteer activities	0.42
60. Travel related to household activities	0.41
61. Travel related to religious and spiritual activities	0.41
62. Travel related to grocery shopping	0.40
63. Travel related to relaxing and leisure	0.40
64. Travel related to purchasing food (except groceries)	0.36
65. Storing interior household items, including food	0.35
66. Helping household adults	0.34
67. Household and personal mail and messages (except email)	0.32
68. Travel related to using financial services and banking	0.26
69. Financial services and banking	0.24
70. Purchasing gas	0.17
71. Purchasing food (except groceries)	0.17

Note: Primary activities are those respondents identified as their main activity. Other activities done simultaneously, such as eating while watching TV, are not included. If fewer than 2.0 percent of the total population participated in a primary activity, then the primary activity is not shown.
Source: Bureau of Labor Statistics, unpublished tables from the 2008 American Time Use Survey, Internet site http://www.bls .gov/tus/home.htm; calculations by New Strategist

Table 1.13 Ranking: Average Hours per Day Spent Doing Primary Activities by Male Participants Aged 15 or Older, 2008

(hours per day spent by male participants aged 15 or older doing primary activities, ranked by time spent doing activity, 2008)

		average hours per day spent by male participants aged 15 or older
	Total, all activities	**24.00**
1.	Sleeping	8.57
2.	Work, main job	7.89
3.	Taking class	5.37
4.	Work, other job(s)	4.23
5.	Television	3.66
6.	Attending or hosting social events	3.27
7.	Arts and entertainment (except sports)	2.70
8.	Playing games (including computer)	2.58
9.	Interior maintenance, repair, and decoration	2.50
10.	Research, homework	2.49
11.	Volunteer activities	2.41
12.	Lawn, garden, and houseplants	2.35
13.	Exterior maintenance, repair, and decoration	2.22
14.	Sports, exercise, and recreation	2.02
15.	Attending religious services	1.83
16.	Socializing and communicating	1.70
17.	Vehicles	1.65
18.	Computer use for leisure (except games)	1.55
19.	Medical and care services	1.52
20.	Caring for and helping household children	1.49
21.	Health-related self-care	1.39
22.	Reading for personal interest	1.36
23.	Relaxing, thinking	1.34
24.	Interior cleaning	1.26
25.	Caring for and helping children in other households	1.26
26.	Eating and drinking	1.19
27.	Listening to the radio	1.18
28.	Listening to or playing music (not radio)	1.18
29.	Laundry	0.97
30.	Activities related to household children's education	0.97
31.	Shopping, except groceries, food, and gas	0.96
32.	Helping adults in other households	0.95
33.	Participation in religious practices	0.92
34.	Financial management	0.87
35.	Travel related to work	0.81
36.	Grooming	0.73
37.	Telephone calls	0.72
38.	Travel related to attending or hosting social events	0.71
39.	Travel related to arts and entertainment	0.71

	average hours per day spent by male participants aged 15 or older
40. Animals and pets (not veterinary care)	0.69
41. Food and drink preparation	0.68
42. Grocery shopping	0.67
43. Travel related to helping household adults	0.67
44. Household services	0.66
45. Travel related to helping adults in other households	0.63
46. Household and personal organization and planning	0.62
47. Household and personal email	0.62
48. Travel related to using medical services	0.60
49. Travel related to education	0.59
50. Travel related to purchasing gas	0.56
51. Travel related to shopping (except groceries, food, and gas)	0.56
52. Kitchen and food clean-up	0.53
53. Travel related to caring for and helping household children	0.52
54. Travel related to socializing and communicating	0.50
55. Travel related to personal care	0.49
56. Travel related to caring for and helping children in other households	0.49
57. Travel related to sports, exercise, and recreation	0.48
58. Travel related to eating and drinking	0.47
59. Travel related to household activities	0.46
60. Travel related to grocery shopping	0.45
61. Travel related to religious and spiritual activities	0.43
62. Travel related to volunteer activities	0.43
63. Travel related to relaxing and leisure	0.42
64. Storing interior household items, including food	0.40
65. Helping household adults	0.40
66. Travel related to purchasing food (except groceries)	0.34
67. Household and personal mail and messages (except email)	0.30
68. Travel related to using financial services and banking	0.28
69. Financial services and banking	0.25
70. Purchasing gas	0.17
71. Purchasing food (except groceries)	0.16

Note: Primary activities are those respondents identified as their main activity. Other activities done simultaneously, such as eating while watching TV, are not included. If fewer than 2.0 percent of the total population participated in a primary activity, then the primary activity is not shown.
Source: Bureau of Labor Statistics, unpublished tables from the 2008 American Time Use Survey, Internet site http://www.bls.gov/tus/home.htm; calculations by New Strategist

Table 1.14 Ranking: Average Hours per Day Spent Doing Primary Activities by Female Participants Aged 15 or Older, 2008

(hours per day spent by female participants aged 15 or older doing primary activities, ranked by time spent doing activity, 2008)

		average hours per day spent by female participants aged 15 or older
	Total, all activities	**24.00**
1.	Sleeping	8.64
2.	Work, main job	6.93
3.	Taking class	5.09
4.	Work, other job(s)	3.78
5.	Television	3.20
6.	Attending or hosting social events	3.10
7.	Research, homework	2.87
8.	Arts and entertainment (except sports)	2.57
9.	Volunteer activities	2.04
10.	Playing games (including computer)	1.83
11.	Caring for and helping household children	1.80
12.	Attending religious services	1.78
13.	Interior maintenance, repair, and decoration	1.73
14.	Socializing and communicating	1.69
15.	Exterior maintenance, repair, and decoration	1.68
16.	Caring for and helping children in other households	1.67
17.	Interior cleaning	1.58
18.	Lawn, garden, and houseplants	1.56
19.	Reading for personal interest	1.50
20.	Listening to the radio	1.49
21.	Computer use for leisure (except games)	1.44
22.	Sports, exercise, and recreation	1.42
23.	Health-related self-care	1.38
24.	Relaxing, thinking	1.34
25.	Medical and care services	1.26
26.	Shopping, except groceries, food, and gas	1.16
27.	Eating and drinking	1.12
28.	Laundry	1.08
29.	Grooming	0.95
30.	Activities related to household children's education	0.91
31.	Listening to or playing music (not radio)	0.91
32.	Food and drink preparation	0.89
33.	Telephone calls	0.89
34.	Participation in religious practices	0.86
35.	Grocery shopping	0.81
36.	Financial management	0.80
37.	Vehicles	0.73
38.	Travel related to education	0.68
39.	Household and personal organization and planning	0.67

	average hours per day spent by female participants aged 15 or older
40. Household services	0.65
41. Travel related to arts and entertainment	0.65
42. Household and personal email	0.64
43. Helping adults in other households	0.64
44. Travel related to work	0.62
45. Travel related to attending or hosting social events	0.62
46. Travel related to helping household adults	0.61
47. Travel related to purchasing gas	0.61
48. Animals and pets (not veterinary care)	0.59
49. Travel related to using medical services	0.58
50. Kitchen and food clean-up	0.57
51. Travel related to personal care	0.57
52. Travel related to caring for and helping household children	0.57
53. Travel related to helping adults in other households	0.56
54. Travel related to shopping (except groceries, food, and gas)	0.54
55. Travel related to socializing and communicating	0.50
56. Travel related to caring for and helping children in other households	0.49
57. Travel related to eating and drinking	0.48
58. Travel related to sports, exercise, and recreation	0.43
59. Travel related to volunteer activities	0.41
60. Travel related to religious and spiritual activities	0.40
61. Travel related to purchasing food (except groceries)	0.39
62. Travel related to relaxing and leisure	0.38
63. Travel related to household activities	0.37
64. Travel related to grocery shopping	0.36
65. Household and personal mail and messages (except email)	0.34
66. Storing interior household items, including food	0.33
67. Helping household adults	0.29
68. Travel related to using financial services and banking	0.25
69. Financial services and banking	0.23
70. Purchasing gas	0.17
71. Purchasing food (except groceries)	0.17

Note: Primary activities are those respondents identified as their main activity. Other activities done simultaneously, such as eating while watching TV, are not included. If fewer than 2.0 percent of the total population participated in a primary activity, then the primary activity is not shown.
Source: Bureau of Labor Statistics, unpublished tables from the 2008 American Time Use Survey, Internet site http://www.bls .gov/tus/home.htm; calculations by New Strategist

Time Use, 2008: People Aged 15 to 19

The priorities of teenagers are different from those of their elders. Most teens still live with their parents, attend school, and prize nothing more than time with their friends. These factors explain much of teen time use. Nearly half of teens socialize on an average day, despite the demands of school and parents. Teens, more than any other age group, are likely to devote time to looking good, and 83 percent spend time grooming as a primary activity. Not only are they most likely to spend time grooming, but those who do spend more time grooming than any other age group—nearly one hour a day. Thirty-seven percent of 15-to-19-year-olds are in class on an average day (these averages include weekends as well as weekdays), and 32 percent can be found doing homework. A substantial 20 percent spend time at work on an average day.

Teens' well-documented attachment to computers can be seen in the time use data as well. Teens are more likely than their elders to spend time on the computer as a leisure pursuit—a category that does not include playing computer games. Twenty-two percent of 15-to-19-year-olds spend leisure time on the computer as a primary activity on an average day. Nearly the same proportion (21 percent) play games as a primary activity on an average day—again, a larger percentage than in any other age group. The Bureau of Labor Statistics includes board games as well computer games in this category, but it is a safe assumption that among 15-to-19-year-olds the category is all about computer games.

Playing games and using computers are top priorities among teens

(average hours per day spent by people aged 15 to 19 doing primary activities, for the 10 activities on which the average 15-to-19-year-old spends the most time, excluding sleep, 2008)

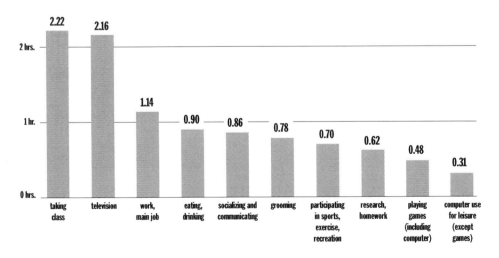

The proof lies in the fact that the percentage of teens who play games rises to 29 percent among teen boys, ranking 7th among activities on which the average teen boy spends the most time (excluding sleep)—even ahead of grooming.

Teenagers are more likely than other age groups to spend time talking with friends on the telephone as a primary activity. Thirteen percent of 15-to-19-year-olds talk on the phone with friends on an average day, a figure that seems low but does not include the time teens spend on the phone while doing other activities such as homework.

How does time use differ between teen boys and girls? The time use statistics uphold the stereotypes. Girls spend more time grooming, doing household chores, babysitting, and shopping. Boys spend more time playing games (mostly computer games) and sports.

Table 2.1 **Time Use by Total People Aged 15 to 19, 2008**

(number and percent of people aged 15 to 19 participating in primary activities on an average day, hours spent doing an activity by the average 15-to-19-year-old and by 15-to-19-year-olds who participated in the activity, 2008; numbers of participants in thousands)

	participants aged 15 to 19		time spent doing activity (hours)	
	number	percent	average person aged 15 to 19	participants aged 15 to 19
TOTAL, ALL ACTIVITIES	**21,292**	**100.0%**	**24.00**	**24.00**
Personal care	**21,292**	**100.0**	**10.35**	**10.35**
Sleeping	21,292	100.0	9.55	9.55
Sleeplessness	969	4.6	0.04	–
Grooming	17,592	82.6	0.78	0.95
Health-related self-care	412	1.9	0.01	–
Household activities	**11,410**	**53.6**	**0.74**	**1.39**
Housework	4,217	19.8	0.28	1.41
Interior cleaning	3,539	16.6	0.23	1.40
Laundry	1,101	5.2	0.04	–
Storing interior household items, including food	229	1.1	0.00	–
Food and drink preparation, presentation, and clean-up	4,496	21.1	0.13	0.63
Food and drink preparation	3,762	17.7	0.10	0.58
Kitchen and food clean-up	1,358	6.4	0.03	–
Interior maintenance, repair, and decoration	285	1.3	0.01	–
Interior arrangement, decoration, and repairs	152	0.7	0.01	–
Exterior maintenance, repair, and decoration	325	1.5	0.02	–
Lawn, garden, and houseplants	485	2.3	0.03	–
Animals and pets (not veterinary care)	1,907	9.0	0.05	0.60
Walking, exercising, and playing with pets	763	3.6	0.02	–
Vehicles	537	2.5	0.05	–
Household management	5,756	27.0	0.17	0.62
Financial management	119	0.6	0.00	–
Household and personal organization and planning	3,583	16.8	0.06	0.38
Household and personal mail and messages (except email)	207	1.0	0.00	–
Household and personal email	2,360	11.1	0.10	0.91
Caring for and helping household members	**2,883**	**13.5**	**0.09**	**0.67**
Caring for and helping household children	2,160	10.1	0.07	0.69
Physical care for household children	493	2.3	0.02	–
Reading to or with household children				
Playing with household children (except sports)	366	1.7	0.02	–
Talking with, listening to household children	217	1.0	0.01	–
Looking after household children as a primary activity	186	0.9	0.01	–
Picking up or dropping off household children	1,038	4.9	0.01	–
Activities related to household children's education	132	0.6	0.00	–
Helping household children with homework	112	0.5	0.00	–
Helping household adults	537	2.5	0.01	–
Caring for and helping people in other households	**3,942**	**18.5**	**0.15**	**0.81**
Caring for and helping children in other households	2,147	10.1	0.08	0.81

	participants aged 15 to 19		time spent doing activity (hours)	
	number	percent	average person aged 15 to 19	participants aged 15 to 19
Helping adults in other households	1,975	9.3%	0.07	0.72
Picking up or dropping off adults in other households	1,203	5.7	0.01	–
Work and work-related activities	**5,095**	**23.9**	**1.28**	**5.36**
Work, main job	4,266	20.0	1.14	5.71
Work, other job(s)	58	0.3	0.02	–
Education	**9,999**	**47.0**	**2.92**	**6.21**
Taking class	7,845	36.8	2.22	6.03
Taking class for degree, certification, or licensure	7,728	36.3	2.20	6.06
Research, homework	6,821	32.0	0.62	1.94
Consumer purchases (store, telephone, Internet)	**7,520**	**35.3**	**0.30**	**0.84**
Grocery shopping	1,295	6.1	0.04	–
Purchasing gas	622	2.9	0.00	–
Purchasing food (except groceries)	3,278	15.4	0.02	0.16
Shopping, except groceries, food, and gas	4,314	20.3	0.22	1.09
Professional and personal care services	**1,035**	**4.9**	**0.05**	**–**
Financial services and banking	393	1.8	0.00	–
Banking	373	1.8	0.00	–
Medical and care services	419	2.0	0.02	–
Using health and care services outside the home	419	2.0	0.01	–
Household services	**296**	**1.4**	**0.00**	**–**
Eating and drinking	**20,347**	**95.6**	**0.90**	**0.94**
Socializing, relaxing, and leisure	**20,417**	**95.9**	**4.53**	**4.73**
Socializing and communicating	10,501	49.3	0.86	1.75
Attending or hosting social events	530	2.5	0.07	–
Relaxing and leisure	19,273	90.5	3.44	3.79
Relaxing, thinking	3,053	14.3	0.14	0.97
Television	15,837	74.4	2.16	2.90
Listening to the radio	611	2.9	0.03	–
Listening to or playing music (not radio)	2,342	11.0	0.10	0.92
Playing games (including computer)	4,450	20.9	0.48	2.29
Computer use for leisure (except games)	4,614	21.7	0.31	1.41
Reading for personal interest	2,485	11.7	0.17	1.43
Arts and entertainment (except sports)	1,295	6.1	0.16	2.67
Sports, exercise, and recreation	**6,828**	**32.1**	**0.80**	**2.49**
Participating in sports, exercise, or recreation	6,304	29.6	0.70	–
Using cardiovascular equipment	122	0.6	0.01	–
Walking	402	1.9	0.02	–
Working out, unspecified	523	2.5	0.02	–
Religious and spiritual activities	**1,318**	**6.2**	**0.10**	**1.54**
Attending religious services	705	3.3	0.06	–
Participation in religious practices	556	2.6	0.02	–

	participants aged 15 to 19		time spent doing activity (hours)	
	number	percent	average person aged 15 to 19	participants aged 15 to 19
Volunteer activities	**1,436**	**6.7%**	**0.14**	–
Administrative and support activities	232	1.1	0.01	–
Telephone calls	**4,548**	**21.4**	**0.27**	**1.29**
Telephone calls to or from family members	890	4.2	0.02	–
Telephone calls to or from friends, neighbors, or acquaintances	2,711	12.7	0.16	1.26
Traveling	**20,077**	**94.3**	**1.16**	**1.23**
Travel related to personal care	922	4.3	0.02	–
Travel related to household activities	1,792	8.4	0.03	0.38
Travel related to household management	1,163	5.5	0.02	–
Travel related to caring for and helping household members	1,370	6.4	0.03	–
Travel related to caring for and helping household children	1,005	4.7	0.02	–
Travel related to helping household adults	355	1.7	0.01	–
Travel related to caring for and helping people in other households	3,325	15.6	0.07	0.44
Travel related to caring for and helping children in other households	1,693	8.0	0.03	0.38
Travel related to helping adults in other households	1,793	8.4	0.04	0.42
Travel related to work	4,203	19.7	0.09	0.44
Travel related to education	7,212	33.9	0.17	0.51
Travel related to taking class	6,474	30.4	0.14	0.47
Travel related to consumer purchases	7,230	34.0	0.19	0.55
Travel related to grocery shopping	1,319	6.2	0.02	–
Travel related to purchasing gas	613	2.9	0.03	–
Travel related to purchasing food (except groceries)	3,127	14.7	0.04	0.29
Travel related to shopping (except groceries, food, and gas)	4,102	19.3	0.09	0.47
Travel related to using professional and personal care services	1,035	4.9	0.02	–
Travel related to using financial services and banking	393	1.8	0.00	–
Travel related to using medical services	419	2.0	0.01	–
Travel related to eating and drinking	5,550	26.1	0.11	0.43
Travel related to socializing, relaxing, and leisure	9,701	45.6	0.27	0.58
Travel related to socializing and communicating	6,158	28.9	0.12	0.42
Travel related to attending or hosting social events	454	2.1	0.01	–
Travel related to relaxing and leisure	4,104	19.3	0.06	0.32
Travel related to arts and entertainment	1,055	5.0	0.04	–
Travel related to sports, exercise, and recreation	4,496	21.1	0.09	0.44
Travel related to participating in sports, exercise, and recreation	3,839	18.0	0.07	0.39
Travel related to religious and spiritual activities	962	4.5	0.02	–
Travel related to volunteer activities	1,056	5.0	0.02	–

Note: Primary activities are those respondents identified as their main activity. Other activities done simultaneously, such as eating while watching TV, are not included. Numbers may not add to total because not all subcategories are shown. If fewer than 2.0 percent of the total population participated in a primary activity, then the primary activity is not shown. "–" means sample is too small to make a reliable estimate.
Source: Bureau of Labor Statistics, unpublished tables from the 2008 American Time Use Survey, Internet site http://www.bls .gov/tus/home.htm; calculations by New Strategist

Table 2.2 Time Use by Men Aged 15 to 19, 2008

(number and percent of men aged 15 to 19 participating in primary activities on an average day, hours spent doing activity by the average 15-to-19-year-old man and by 15-to-19-year-old men who participated in the activity, 2008; numbers of participants in thousands)

	men aged 15 to 19 participating		time spent doing activity (hours)	
	number	percent	average man aged 15 to 19	male participants aged 15 to 19
TOTAL, ALL ACTIVITIES	**10,800**	**100.0%**	**24.00**	**24.00**
Personal care	**10,800**	**100.0**	**10.28**	**10.28**
Sleeping	10,800	100.0	9.64	9.64
Sleeplessness	439	4.1	0.03	–
Grooming	8,878	82.2	0.62	0.75
Health-related self-care	244	2.3	0.01	–
Household activities	**5,464**	**50.6**	**0.60**	**1.19**
Housework	1,704	15.8	0.17	1.09
Interior cleaning	1,371	12.7	0.14	–
Laundry	433	4.0	0.03	–
Storing interior household items, including food	60	0.6	0.00	–
Food and drink preparation, presentation, and clean-up	2,095	19.4	0.10	0.50
Food and drink preparation	1,776	16.4	0.07	0.44
Kitchen and food clean-up	571	5.3	0.02	–
Interior maintenance, repair, and decoration	186	1.7	0.01	–
Interior arrangement, decoration, and repairs	53	0.5	0.01	–
Exterior maintenance, repair, and decoration	163	1.5	0.01	–
Lawn, garden, and houseplants	359	3.3	0.05	–
Animals and pets (not veterinary care)	920	8.5	0.05	–
Walking, exercising, and playing with pets	382	3.5	0.02	–
Vehicles	485	4.5	0.09	–
Household management	2,571	23.8	0.12	0.48
Financial management	56	0.5	0.00	–
Household and personal organization and planning	1,874	17.4	0.06	0.36
Household and personal mail and messages (except email)	46	0.4	0.00	–
Household and personal email	715	6.6	0.05	–
Caring for and helping household members	**1,098**	**10.2**	**0.05**	**–**
Caring for and helping household children	746	6.9	0.03	–
Physical care for household children	56	0.5	0.00	–
Reading to or with household children	–	–	–	–
Playing with household children (except sports)	151	1.4	0.01	–
Talking with, listening to household children	89	0.8	0.01	–
Looking after household children as a primary activity	97	0.9	0.00	–
Picking up or dropping off household children	373	3.5	0.00	–
Activities related to household children's education	63	0.6	0.00	–
Helping household children with homework	63	0.6	0.00	–
Helping household adults	267	2.5	0.01	–
Caring for and helping people in other households	**1,460**	**13.5**	**0.09**	**0.64**
Caring for and helping children in other households	761	7.0	0.05	–

	men aged 15 to 19 participating		time spent doing activity (hours)	
	number	percent	average man aged 15 to 19	male participants aged 15 to 19
Helping adults in other households	777	7.2%	0.04	–
Picking up or dropping off adults in other households	479	4.4	0.01	–
Work and work-related activities	**2,274**	**21.1**	**1.16**	**5.51**
Work, main job	1,862	17.2	1.05	6.11
Work, other job(s)	30	0.3	0.01	–
Education	**5,040**	**46.7**	**2.96**	**6.35**
Taking class	4,280	39.6	2.39	6.03
Taking class for degree, certification, or licensure	4,216	39.0	2.37	6.08
Research, homework	3,020	28.0	0.48	1.73
Consumer purchases (store, telephone, Internet)	**3,182**	**29.5**	**0.19**	**0.63**
Grocery shopping	608	5.6	0.03	
Purchasing gas	350	3.2	0.01	–
Purchasing food (except groceries)	1,536	14.2	0.02	0.13
Shopping, except groceries, food, and gas	1,675	15.5	0.13	0.84
Professional and personal care services	**302**	**2.8**	**0.02**	–
Financial services and banking	106	1.0	0.00	–
Banking	85	0.8	0.00	–
Medical and care services	152	1.4	0.02	–
Using health and care services outside the home	152	1.4	0.01	–
Household services	**177**	**1.6**	**0.01**	–
Eating and drinking	**10,334**	**95.7**	**0.94**	**0.98**
Socializing, relaxing, and leisure	**10,414**	**96.4**	**4.83**	**5.01**
Socializing and communicating	5,555	51.4	0.87	1.70
Attending or hosting social events	306	2.8	0.08	–
Relaxing and leisure	9,879	91.5	3.72	4.06
Relaxing, thinking	1,487	13.8	0.12	–
Television	8,086	74.9	2.23	2.98
Listening to the radio	253	2.3	0.03	–
Listening to or playing music (not radio)	1,427	13.2	0.13	–
Playing games (including computer)	3,168	29.3	0.76	2.57
Computer use for leisure (except games)	2,276	21.1	0.27	1.26
Reading for personal interest	1,236	11.4	0.16	–
Arts and entertainment (except sports)	710	6.6	0.16	–
Sports, exercise, and recreation	**4,565**	**42.3**	**1.09**	**2.59**
Participating in sports, exercise, or recreation	4,306	39.9	1.00	–
Using cardiovascular equipment	33	0.3	0.00	–
Walking	193	1.8	0.01	–
Working out, unspecified	295	2.7	0.02	–
Religious and spiritual activities	**481**	**4.5**	**0.08**	–
Attending religious services	177	1.6	0.04	–
Participation in religious practices	225	2.1	0.04	–

	men aged 15 to 19 participating		time spent doing activity (hours)	
	number	percent	average man aged 15 to 19	male participants aged 15 to 19
Volunteer activities	**825**	**7.6%**	**0.15**	–
Administrative and support activities	136	1.3	0.01	–
Telephone calls	**1,938**	**17.9**	**0.18**	**0.99**
Telephone calls to or from family members	325	3.0	0.00	–
Telephone calls to or from friends, neighbors, or acquaintances	1,207	11.2	0.10	–
Traveling	**10,179**	**94.3**	**1.19**	**1.26**
Travel related to personal care	505	4.7	0.01	–
Travel related to household activities	1,000	9.3	0.04	–
Travel related to household management	757	7.0	0.03	–
Travel related to caring for and helping household members	493	4.6	0.03	–
Travel related to caring for and helping household children	336	3.1	0.02	–
Travel related to helping household adults	167	1.5	0.01	–
Travel related to caring for and helping people in other households	1,271	11.8	0.05	0.44
Travel related to caring for and helping children in other households	637	5.9	0.03	–
Travel related to helping adults in other households	688	6.4	0.03	–
Travel related to work	1,741	16.1	0.07	0.44
Travel related to education	3,747	34.7	0.17	0.50
Travel related to taking class	3,382	31.3	0.15	0.47
Travel related to consumer purchases	3,060	28.3	0.17	0.61
Travel related to grocery shopping	618	5.7	0.02	–
Travel related to purchasing gas	342	3.2	0.05	–
Travel related to purchasing food (except groceries)	1,464	13.6	0.03	–
Travel related to shopping (except groceries, food, and gas)	1,572	14.6	0.08	0.52
Travel related to using professional and personal care services	302	2.8	0.01	–
Travel related to using financial services and banking	106	1.0	0.00	–
Travel related to using medical services	152	1.4	0.01	–
Travel related to eating and drinking	3,088	28.6	0.14	0.47
Travel related to socializing, relaxing, and leisure	4,993	46.2	0.28	0.60
Travel related to socializing and communicating	3,359	31.1	0.11	0.36
Travel related to attending or hosting social events	277	2.6	0.01	–
Travel related to relaxing and leisure	1,947	18.0	0.06	0.36
Travel related to arts and entertainment	573	5.3	0.05	–
Travel related to sports, exercise, and recreation	2,928	27.1	0.12	0.43
Travel related to participating in sports, exercise, recreation	2,624	24.3	0.09	0.39
Travel related to religious and spiritual activities	379	3.5	0.02	–
Travel related to volunteer activities	623	5.8	0.02	–

Note: Primary activities are those respondents identified as their main activity. Other activities done simultaneously, such as eating while watching TV, are not included. Numbers may not add to total because not all subcategories are shown. If fewer than 2.0 percent of the total population participated in a primary activity, then the primary activity is not shown. "–" means sample is too small to make a reliable estimate.
Source: Bureau of Labor Statistics, unpublished tables from the 2008 American Time Use Survey, Internet site http://www.bls .gov/tus/home.htm; calculations by New Strategist

Table 2.3 Time Use by Women Aged 15 to 19, 2008

(number and percent of women aged 15 to 19 participating in primary activities on an average day, hours spent doing activity by the average 15-to-19-year-old woman and by 15-to-19-year-old women who participated in the activity, 2008; numbers of participants in thousands)

	women aged 15 to 19 participating		time spent doing activity (hours)	
	number	percent	average woman aged 15 to 19	female participants aged 15 to 19
TOTAL, ALL ACTIVITIES	**10,491**	**100.0%**	**24.00**	**24.00**
Personal care	**10,491**	**100.0**	**10.43**	**10.43**
Sleeping	10,491	100.0	9.46	9.46
Sleeplessness	530	5.1	0.04	–
Grooming	8,714	83.1	0.95	1.15
Health-related self-care	168	1.6	0.01	–
Household activities	**5,947**	**56.7**	**0.89**	**1.57**
Housework	2,513	24.0	0.39	1.63
Interior cleaning	2,167	20.7	0.33	1.58
Laundry	668	6.4	0.06	–
Storing interior household items, including food	169	1.6	0.00	–
Food and drink preparation, presentation, and clean-up	2,402	22.9	0.17	0.73
Food and drink preparation	1,987	18.9	0.13	0.70
Kitchen and food clean-up	787	7.5	0.03	–
Interior maintenance, repair, and decoration	99	0.9	0.01	–
Interior arrangement, decoration, and repairs	99	0.9	0.01	–
Exterior maintenance, repair, and decoration	162	1.5	0.02	–
Lawn, garden, and houseplants	126	1.2	0.02	–
Animals and pets (not veterinary care)	987	9.4	0.05	–
Walking, exercising, and playing with pets	381	3.6	0.03	–
Vehicles	52	0.5	0.00	–
Household management	3,185	30.4	0.22	0.73
Financial management	63	0.6	0.00	–
Household and personal organization and planning	1,708	16.3	0.06	0.40
Household and personal mail and messages (except email)	162	1.5	0.00	–
Household and personal email	1,645	15.7	0.15	0.97
Caring for and helping household members	**1,785**	**17.0**	**0.14**	**0.80**
Caring for and helping household children	1,414	13.5	0.11	–
Physical care for household children	437	4.2	0.04	–
Reading to or with household children	–	–		
Playing with household children (except sports)	214	2.0	0.03	–
Talking with, listening to household children	128	1.2	0.01	–
Looking after household children as a primary activity	89	0.8	0.01	–
Picking up or dropping off household children	665	6.3	0.01	–
Activities related to household children's education	69	0.7	0.01	–
Helping household children with homework	49	0.5	0.00	–
Helping household adults	269	2.6	0.01	–
Caring for and helping people in other households	**2,482**	**23.7**	**0.22**	**0.91**
Caring for and helping children in other households	1,386	13.2	0.12	–

| | women aged 15 to 19 participating | | time spent doing activity (hours) | |
---	number	percent	average woman aged 15 to 19	female participants aged 15 to 19
Helping adults in other households	1,198	11.4%	0.10	–
Picking up or dropping off adults in other households	724	6.9	0.01	–
Work and work-related activities	**2,822**	**26.9**	**1.41**	**5.25**
Work, main job	2,404	22.9	1.24	5.40
Work, other job(s)	28	0.3	0.02	–
Education	**4,959**	**47.3**	**2.87**	**6.07**
Taking class	3,565	34.0	2.05	6.02
Taking class for degree, certification, or licensure	3,512	33.5	2.02	6.03
Research, homework	3,801	36.2	0.76	2.10
Consumer purchases (store, telephone, Internet)	**4,338**	**41.3**	**0.41**	**1.00**
Grocery shopping	687	6.5	0.05	–
Purchasing gas	272	2.6	0.00	–
Purchasing food (except groceries)	1,741	16.6	0.03	0.19
Shopping, except groceries, food, and gas	2,639	25.2	0.31	1.25
Professional and personal care services	**733**	**7.0**	**0.07**	**–**
Financial services and banking	288	2.7	0.00	–
Banking	288	2.7	0.00	–
Medical and care services	267	2.5	0.03	–
Using health and care services outside the home	267	2.5	0.02	–
Household services	**119**	**1.1**	**0.00**	**–**
Eating and drinking	**10,013**	**95.4**	**0.85**	**0.90**
Socializing, relaxing, and leisure	**10,003**	**95.3**	**4.23**	**4.43**
Socializing and communicating	4,946	47.1	0.85	1.81
Attending or hosting social events	224	2.1	0.06	–
Relaxing and leisure	9,393	89.5	3.15	3.51
Relaxing, thinking	1,566	14.9	0.15	–
Television	7,751	73.9	2.08	2.82
Listening to the radio	358	3.4	0.04	–
Listening to or playing music (not radio)	914	8.7	0.07	–
Playing games (including computer)	1,283	12.2	0.19	–
Computer use for leisure (except games)	2,338	22.3	0.35	1.56
Reading for personal interest	1,249	11.9	0.18	–
Arts and entertainment (except sports)	585	5.6	0.16	–
Sports, exercise, and recreation	**2,263**	**21.6**	**0.50**	**2.31**
Participating in sports, exercise, or recreation	1,998	19.0	0.39	–
Using cardiovascular equipment	89	0.8	0.01	–
Walking	209	2.0	0.03	–
Working out, unspecified	228	2.2	0.02	–
Religious and spiritual activities	**836**	**8.0**	**0.11**	**–**
Attending religious services	528	5.0	0.08	–
Participation in religious practices	330	3.1	0.01	–

	women aged 15 to 19 participating		time spent doing activity (hours)	
	number	percent	average woman aged 15 to 19	female participants aged 15 to 19
Volunteer activities	**612**	**5.8%**	**0.12**	–
Administrative and support activities	97	0.9	0.01	–
Telephone calls	**2,610**	**24.9**	**0.38**	**1.51**
Telephone calls to or from family members	565	5.4	0.03	–
Telephone calls to or from friends, neighbors, or acquaintances	1,505	14.3	0.22	1.57
Traveling	**9,898**	**94.3**	**1.14**	**1.20**
Travel related to personal care	418	4.0	0.03	–
Travel related to household activities	792	7.5	0.02	–
Travel related to household management	407	3.9	0.02	–
Travel related to caring for and helping household members	877	8.4	0.04	–
Travel related to caring for and helping household children	670	6.4	0.02	–
Travel related to helping household adults	187	1.8	0.02	–
Travel related to caring for and helping people in other households	2,054	19.6	0.09	0.44
Travel related to caring for and helping children in other households	1,056	10.1	0.04	–
Travel related to helping adults in other households	1,106	10.5	0.05	–
Travel related to work	2,462	23.5	0.10	0.45
Travel related to education	3,465	33.0	0.17	0.52
Travel related to taking class	3,092	29.5	0.14	0.47
Travel related to consumer purchases	4,170	39.7	0.20	0.50
Travel related to grocery shopping	701	6.7	0.03	–
Travel related to purchasing gas	272	2.6	0.02	–
Travel related to purchasing food (except groceries)	1,663	15.9	0.05	0.32
Travel related to shopping (except groceries, food, and gas)	2,529	24.1	0.10	0.43
Travel related to using professional and personal care services	733	7.0	0.02	–
Travel related to using financial services and banking	288	2.7	0.01	–
Travel related to using medical services	267	2.5	0.01	–
Travel related to eating and drinking	2,462	23.5	0.09	0.37
Travel related to socializing, relaxing, and leisure	4,708	44.9	0.25	0.56
Travel related to socializing and communicating	2,799	26.7	0.13	0.48
Travel related to attending or hosting social events	177	1.7	0.01	–
Travel related to relaxing and leisure	2,157	20.6	0.06	0.29
Travel related to arts and entertainment	482	4.6	0.04	–
Travel related to sports, exercise, and recreation	1,568	14.9	0.07	–
Travel related to participating in sports, exercise, recreation	1,215	11.6	0.05	–
Travel related to religious and spiritual activities	583	5.6	0.02	–
Travel related to volunteer activities	433	4.1	0.01	–

Note: Primary activities are those respondents identified as their main activity. Other activities done simultaneously, such as eating while watching TV, are not included. Numbers may not add to total because not all subcategories are shown. If fewer than 2.0 percent of the total population participated in a primary activity, then the primary activity is not shown. "–" means sample is too small to make a reliable estimate.
Source: Bureau of Labor Statistics, unpublished tables from the 2008 American Time Use Survey, Internet site http://www.bls.gov/tus/home.htm; calculations by New Strategist

Table 2.4 Indexed Time Use of Total People Aged 15 to 19, 2008

(hours spent doing primary activities on an average day by people aged 15 to 19 and by total people aged 15 or older, and index of time spent by 15-to-19-year-olds to total people, 2008)

	average hours		index, people aged 15 to 19 to total people
	people aged 15 to 19	total people	
TOTAL, ALL ACTIVITIES	**24.00**	**24.00**	**100**
Personal care	**10.35**	**9.38**	**110**
Sleeping	9.55	8.60	111
Sleeplessness	0.04	0.06	67
Grooming	0.78	0.67	116
Health-related self-care	0.01	0.09	11
Household activities	**0.74**	**1.77**	**42**
Housework	0.28	0.58	48
Interior cleaning	0.23	0.37	62
Laundry	0.04	0.17	24
Storing interior household items, including food	0.00	0.02	0
Food and drink preparation, presentation, and clean-up	0.13	0.52	25
Food and drink preparation	0.10	0.40	25
Kitchen and food clean-up	0.03	0.12	25
Interior maintenance, repair, and decoration	0.01	0.07	14
Interior arrangement, decoration, and repairs	0.01	0.05	20
Exterior maintenance, repair, and decoration	0.02	0.06	33
Lawn, garden, and houseplants	0.03	0.19	16
Animals and pets (not veterinary care)	0.05	0.09	56
Walking, exercising, and playing with pets	0.02	0.04	50
Vehicles	0.05	0.04	125
Household management	0.17	0.21	81
Financial management	0.00	0.03	0
Household and personal organization and planning	0.06	0.09	67
Household and personal mail and messages (except email)	0.00	0.02	0
Household and personal email	0.10	0.06	167
Caring for and helping household members	**0.09**	**0.45**	**20**
Caring for and helping household children	0.07	0.37	19
Physical care for household children	0.02	0.17	12
Reading to or with household children	0.00	0.01	0
Playing with household children (except sports)	0.02	0.09	22
Talking with, listening to household children	0.01	0.02	50
Looking after household children as a primary activity	0.01	0.03	33
Picking up or dropping off household children	0.01	0.02	50
Activities related to household children's education	0.00	0.04	0
Helping household children with homework	0.00	0.03	0
Helping household adults	0.01	0.01	100
Caring for and helping people in other households	**0.15**	**0.16**	**94**
Caring for and helping children in other households	0.08	0.09	89

	average hours		index, people aged 15 to 19
	people aged 15 to 19	total people	to total people
Helping adults in other households	0.07	0.06	117
Picking up or dropping off adults in other households	0.01	0.01	100
Work and work-related activities	**1.28**	**3.45**	**37**
Work, main job	1.14	3.28	35
Work, other job(s)	0.02	0.09	22
Education	**2.92**	**0.44**	**664**
Taking class	2.22	0.27	822
Taking class for degree, certification, or licensure	2.20	0.26	846
Research, homework	0.62	0.16	388
Consumer purchases (store, telephone, Internet)	**0.30**	**0.38**	**79**
Grocery shopping	0.04	0.10	40
Purchasing gas	0.00	0.01	0
Purchasing food (except groceries)	0.02	0.02	100
Shopping, except groceries, food, and gas	0.22	0.25	88
Professional and personal care services	**0.05**	**0.08**	**63**
Financial services and banking	0.00	0.01	0
Banking	0.00	0.01	0
Medical and care services	0.02	0.05	40
Using health and care services outside the home	0.01	0.04	25
Household services	**0.00**	**0.01**	**0**
Eating and drinking	**0.90**	**1.11**	**81**
Socializing, relaxing, and leisure	**4.53**	**4.62**	**98**
Socializing and communicating	0.86	0.64	134
Attending or hosting social events	0.07	0.07	100
Relaxing and leisure	3.44	3.83	90
Relaxing, thinking	0.14	0.27	52
Television	2.16	2.77	78
Listening to the radio	0.03	0.03	100
Listening to or playing music (not radio)	0.10	0.03	333
Playing games (including computer)	0.48	0.20	240
Computer use for leisure (except games)	0.31	0.14	221
Reading for personal interest	0.17	0.34	50
Arts and entertainment (except sports)	0.16	0.09	178
Sports, exercise, and recreation	**0.80**	**0.33**	**242**
Participating in sports, exercise, or recreation	0.70	0.29	241
Using cardiovascular equipment	0.01	0.02	50
Walking	0.02	0.04	50
Working out, unspecified	0.02	0.03	67
Religious and spiritual activities	**0.10**	**0.14**	**71**
Attending religious services	0.06	0.09	67
Participation in religious practices	0.02	0.04	50

	average hours		index, people aged 15 to 19 to total people
	people aged 15 to 19	total people	
Volunteer activities	**0.14**	**0.15**	**93**
Administrative and support activities	0.01	0.04	25
Telephone calls	**0.27**	**0.13**	**208**
Telephone calls to or from family members	0.02	0.04	50
Telephone calls to or from friends, neighbors, or acquaintances	0.16	0.04	400
Traveling	**1.16**	**1.20**	**97**
Travel related to personal care	0.02	0.01	200
Travel related to household activities	0.03	0.04	75
Travel related to household management	0.02	0.02	100
Travel related to caring for and helping household members	0.03	0.08	38
Travel related to caring for and helping household children	0.02	0.06	33
Travel related to helping household adults	0.01	0.02	50
Travel related to caring for and helping people in other households	0.07	0.06	117
Travel related to caring for and helping children in other households	0.03	0.02	150
Travel related to helping adults in other households	0.04	0.04	100
Travel related to work	0.09	0.28	32
Travel related to education	0.17	0.03	567
Travel related to taking class	0.14	0.03	467
Travel related to consumer purchases	0.19	0.24	79
Travel related to grocery shopping	0.02	0.05	40
Travel related to purchasing gas	0.03	0.02	150
Travel related to purchasing food (except groceries)	0.04	0.04	100
Travel related to shopping (except groceries, food, and gas)	0.09	0.12	75
Travel related to using professional and personal care services	0.02	0.04	50
Travel related to using financial services and banking	0.00	0.01	0
Travel related to using medical services	0.01	0.02	50
Travel related to eating and drinking	0.11	0.12	92
Travel related to socializing, relaxing, and leisure	0.27	0.18	150
Travel related to socializing and communicating	0.12	0.09	133
Travel related to attending or hosting social events	0.01	0.01	100
Travel related to relaxing and leisure	0.06	0.04	150
Travel related to arts and entertainment	0.04	0.02	200
Travel related to sports, exercise, and recreation	0.09	0.04	225
Travel related to participating in sports, exercise, recreation	0.07	0.04	175
Travel related to religious and spiritual activities	0.02	0.02	100
Travel related to volunteer activities	0.02	0.02	100

Note: The index is calculated by dividing average time spent by people in the age group doing primary activity by average time spent by total people doing primary activity and multiplying by 100. Primary activities are those respondents identified as their main activity. Other activities done simultaneously, such as eating while watching TV, are not included. Numbers may not add to total because not all subcategories are shown. If fewer than 2.0 percent of the total population participated in a primary activity, then the primary activity is not shown.
Source: Bureau of Labor Statistics, unpublished tables from the 2008 American Time Use Survey, Internet site http://www.bls .gov/tus/home.htm; calculations by New Strategist

Table 2.5 Indexed Time Use of Men Aged 15 to 19, 2008

(hours spent doing primary activities on an average day by men aged 15 to 19 and by total men aged 15 or older, and index of time spent by 15-to-19-year-old men to total men, 2008)

	average hours		index, men aged 15 to 19
	men aged 15 to 19	total men	to total men
TOTAL, ALL ACTIVITIES	**24.00**	**24.00**	**100**
Personal care	**10.28**	**9.21**	**112**
Sleeping	9.64	8.56	113
Sleeplessness	0.03	0.05	60
Grooming	0.62	0.56	111
Health-related self-care	0.01	0.07	14
Household activities	**0.60**	**1.32**	**45**
Housework	0.17	0.24	71
Interior cleaning	0.14	0.17	82
Laundry	0.03	0.06	50
Storing interior household items, including food	0.00	0.01	0
Food and drink preparation, presentation, and clean-up	0.10	0.30	33
Food and drink preparation	0.07	0.25	28
Kitchen and food clean-up	0.02	0.05	40
Interior maintenance, repair, and decoration	0.01	0.10	10
Interior arrangement, decoration, and repairs	0.01	0.08	13
Exterior maintenance, repair, and decoration	0.01	0.08	13
Lawn, garden, and houseplants	0.05	0.26	19
Animals and pets (not veterinary care)	0.05	0.08	63
Walking, exercising, and playing with pets	0.02	0.04	50
Vehicles	0.09	0.07	129
Household management	0.12	0.16	75
Financial management	0.00	0.03	0
Household and personal organization and planning	0.06	0.07	86
Household and personal mail and messages (except email)	0.00	0.02	0
Household and personal email	0.05	0.05	100
Caring for and helping household members	**0.05**	**0.30**	**17**
Caring for and helping household children	0.03	0.25	12
Physical care for household children	0.00	0.09	0
Reading to or with household children	0.00	0.01	0
Playing with household children (except sports)	0.01	0.08	13
Talking with, listening to household children	0.01	0.01	100
Looking after household children as a primary activity	0.00	0.02	0
Picking up or dropping off household children	0.00	0.01	0
Activities related to household children's education	0.00	0.02	0
Helping household children with homework	0.00	0.02	0
Helping household adults	0.01	0.01	100
Caring for and helping people in other households	**0.09**	**0.13**	**69**
Caring for and helping children in other households	0.05	0.05	100

	average hours		index, men aged 15 to 19 to total men
	men aged 15 to 19	total men	
Helping adults in other households	0.04	0.07	57
Picking up or dropping off adults in other households	0.01	0.01	100
Work and work-related activities	**1.16**	**4.16**	**28**
Work, main job	1.05	3.96	27
Work, other job(s)	0.01	0.10	10
Education	**2.96**	**0.39**	**759**
Taking class	2.39	0.27	885
Taking class for degree, certification, or licensure	2.37	0.27	878
Research, homework	0.48	0.12	400
Consumer purchases (store, telephone, Internet)	**0.19**	**0.28**	**68**
Grocery shopping	0.03	0.06	50
Purchasing gas	0.01	0.01	100
Purchasing food (except groceries)	0.02	0.02	100
Shopping, except groceries, food, and gas	0.13	0.19	68
Professional and personal care services	**0.02**	**0.06**	**33**
Financial services and banking	0.00	0.01	0
Banking	0.00	0.00	0
Medical and care services	0.02	0.04	50
Using health and care services outside the home	0.01	0.03	33
Household services	**0.01**	**0.01**	**100**
Eating and drinking	**0.94**	**1.15**	**82**
Socializing, relaxing, and leisure	**4.83**	**4.83**	**100**
Socializing and communicating	0.87	0.59	147
Attending or hosting social events	0.08	0.06	133
Relaxing and leisure	3.72	4.09	91
Relaxing, thinking	0.12	0.27	44
Television	2.23	3.01	74
Listening to the radio	0.03	0.03	100
Listening to or playing music (not radio)	0.13	0.04	325
Playing games (including computer)	0.76	0.25	304
Computer use for leisure (except games)	0.27	0.15	180
Reading for personal interest	0.16	0.29	55
Arts and entertainment (except sports)	0.16	0.09	178
Sports, exercise, and recreation	**1.09**	**0.44**	**248**
Participating in sports, exercise, or recreation	1.00	0.40	250
Using cardiovascular equipment	0.00	0.01	0
Walking	0.01	0.04	25
Working out, unspecified	0.02	0.04	50
Religious and spiritual activities	**0.08**	**0.12**	**67**
Attending religious services	0.04	0.07	57
Participation in religious practices	0.04	0.03	133

	average hours		index, men aged 15 to 19 to total men
	men aged 15 to 19	total men	
Volunteer activities	**0.15**	**0.14**	**107**
Administrative and support activities	0.01	0.03	33
Telephone calls	**0.18**	**0.07**	**257**
Telephone calls to or from family members	0.00	0.02	0
Telephone calls to or from friends, neighbors, or acquaintances	0.10	0.02	500
Traveling	**1.19**	**1.23**	**97**
Travel related to personal care	0.01	0.01	100
Travel related to household activities	0.04	0.04	100
Travel related to household management	0.03	0.03	100
Travel related to caring for and helping household members	0.03	0.06	50
Travel related to caring for and helping household children	0.02	0.04	50
Travel related to helping household adults	0.01	0.02	50
Travel related to caring for and helping people in other households	0.05	0.06	83
Travel related to caring for and helping children in other households	0.03	0.01	300
Travel related to helping adults in other households	0.03	0.04	75
Travel related to work	0.07	0.36	19
Travel related to education	0.17	0.03	567
Travel related to taking class	0.15	0.02	750
Travel related to consumer purchases	0.17	0.21	81
Travel related to grocery shopping	0.02	0.04	50
Travel related to purchasing gas	0.05	0.02	250
Travel related to purchasing food (except groceries)	0.03	0.04	75
Travel related to shopping (except groceries, food, and gas)	0.08	0.11	73
Travel related to using professional and personal care services	0.01	0.03	33
Travel related to using financial services and banking	0.00	0.01	0
Travel related to using medical services	0.01	0.01	100
Travel related to eating and drinking	0.14	0.13	108
Travel related to socializing, relaxing, and leisure	0.28	0.18	156
Travel related to socializing and communicating	0.11	0.09	122
Travel related to attending or hosting social events	0.01	0.01	100
Travel related to relaxing and leisure	0.06	0.04	150
Travel related to arts and entertainment	0.05	0.02	250
Travel related to sports, exercise, and recreation	0.12	0.06	200
Travel related to participating in sports, exercise, recreation	0.09	0.05	180
Travel related to religious and spiritual activities	0.02	0.02	100
Travel related to volunteer activities	0.02	0.02	100

Note: The index is calculated by dividing average time spent by men in the age group doing primary activity by average time spent by total men doing primary activity and multiplying by 100. Primary activities are those respondents identified as their main activity. Other activities done simultaneously, such as eating while watching TV, are not included. Numbers may not add to total because not all subcategories are shown. If fewer than 2.0 percent of the total population participated in a primary activity, then the primary activity is not shown.
Source: Bureau of Labor Statistics, unpublished tables from the 2008 American Time Use Survey, Internet site http://www.bls.gov/tus/home.htm; calculations by New Strategist

Table 2.6 Indexed Time Use of Women Aged 15 to 19, 2008

(hours spent doing primary activities on an average day by women aged 15 to 19 and by total women aged 15 or older, and index of time spent by 15-to-19-year-old women to total women, 2008)

	average hours		index, women aged 15 to 19 to total women
	women aged 15 to 19	total women	
TOTAL, ALL ACTIVITIES	**24.00**	**24.00**	**100**
Personal care	**10.43**	**9.54**	**109**
Sleeping	9.46	8.64	109
Sleeplessness	0.04	0.07	57
Grooming	0.95	0.78	122
Health-related self-care	0.01	0.11	9
Household activities	**0.89**	**2.19**	**41**
Housework	0.39	0.90	43
Interior cleaning	0.33	0.55	60
Laundry	0.06	0.28	21
Storing interior household items, including food	0.00	0.02	0
Food and drink preparation, presentation, and clean-up	0.17	0.73	23
Food and drink preparation	0.13	0.55	24
Kitchen and food clean-up	0.03	0.18	17
Interior maintenance, repair, and decoration	0.01	0.04	25
Interior arrangement, decoration, and repairs	0.01	0.03	33
Exterior maintenance, repair, and decoration	0.02	0.03	67
Lawn, garden, and houseplants	0.02	0.12	17
Animals and pets (not veterinary care)	0.05	0.10	50
Walking, exercising, and playing with pets	0.03	0.04	75
Vehicles	0.00	0.01	0
Household management	0.22	0.25	88
Financial management	0.00	0.04	0
Household and personal organization and planning	0.06	0.11	55
Household and personal mail and messages (except email)	0.00	0.03	0
Household and personal email	0.15	0.07	214
Caring for and helping household members	**0.14**	**0.59**	**24**
Caring for and helping household children	0.11	0.48	23
Physical care for household children	0.04	0.24	17
Reading to or with household children	0.00	0.02	0
Playing with household children (except sports)	0.03	0.09	33
Talking with, listening to household children	0.01	0.02	50
Looking after household children as a primary activity	0.01	0.03	33
Picking up or dropping off household children	0.01	0.03	33
Activities related to household children's education	0.01	0.05	20
Helping household children with homework	0.00	0.04	0
Helping household adults	0.01	0.01	100
Caring for and helping people in other households	**0.22**	**0.20**	**110**
Caring for and helping children in other households	0.12	0.12	100

	average hours		index, women aged 15 to 19 to total women
	women aged 15 to 19	total women	
Helping adults in other households	0.10	0.05	200
Picking up or dropping off adults in other households	0.01	0.01	100
Work and work-related activities	**1.41**	**2.79**	**51**
Work, main job	1.24	2.63	47
Work, other job(s)	0.02	0.09	22
Education	**2.87**	**0.48**	**598**
Taking class	2.05	0.27	759
Taking class for degree, certification, or licensure	2.02	0.25	808
Research, homework	0.76	0.20	380
Consumer purchases (store, telephone, Internet)	**0.41**	**0.48**	**85**
Grocery shopping	0.05	0.13	38
Purchasing gas	0.00	0.01	0
Purchasing food (except groceries)	0.03	0.02	150
Shopping, except groceries, food, and gas	0.31	0.31	100
Professional and personal care services	**0.07**	**0.11**	**64**
Financial services and banking	0.00	0.01	0
Banking	0.00	0.01	0
Medical and care services	0.03	0.06	50
Using health and care services outside the home	0.02	0.05	40
Household services	**0.00**	**0.01**	**0**
Eating and drinking	**0.85**	**1.07**	**79**
Socializing, relaxing, and leisure	**4.23**	**4.42**	**96**
Socializing and communicating	0.85	0.68	125
Attending or hosting social events	0.06	0.08	75
Relaxing and leisure	3.15	3.58	88
Relaxing, thinking	0.15	0.26	58
Television	2.08	2.54	82
Listening to the radio	0.04	0.02	200
Listening to or playing music (not radio)	0.07	0.02	350
Playing games (including computer)	0.19	0.15	127
Computer use for leisure (except games)	0.35	0.14	250
Reading for personal interest	0.18	0.40	45
Arts and entertainment (except sports)	0.16	0.08	200
Sports, exercise, and recreation	**0.50**	**0.23**	**217**
Participating in sports, exercise, or recreation	0.39	0.20	195
Using cardiovascular equipment	0.01	0.02	50
Walking	0.03	0.04	75
Working out, unspecified	0.02	0.02	100
Religious and spiritual activities	**0.11**	**0.17**	**65**
Attending religious services	0.08	0.10	80
Participation in religious practices	0.01	0.05	20

	average hours		index, women aged 15 to 19
	women aged 15 to 19	total women	to total women
Volunteer activities	**0.12**	**0.16**	**75**
Administrative and support activities	0.01	0.04	25
Telephone calls	**0.38**	**0.18**	**211**
Telephone calls to or from family members	0.03	0.07	43
Telephone calls to or from friends, neighbors, or acquaintances	0.22	0.06	367
Traveling	**1.14**	**1.17**	**97**
Travel related to personal care	0.03	0.01	300
Travel related to household activities	0.02	0.04	50
Travel related to household management	0.02	0.02	100
Travel related to caring for and helping household members	0.04	0.11	36
Travel related to caring for and helping household children	0.02	0.08	25
Travel related to helping household adults	0.02	0.02	100
Travel related to caring for and helping people in other households	0.09	0.07	129
Travel related to caring for and helping children in other households	0.04	0.02	200
Travel related to helping adults in other households	0.05	0.04	125
Travel related to work	0.10	0.20	50
Travel related to education	0.17	0.04	425
Travel related to taking class	0.14	0.03	467
Travel related to consumer purchases	0.20	0.27	74
Travel related to grocery shopping	0.03	0.06	50
Travel related to purchasing gas	0.02	0.02	100
Travel related to purchasing food (except groceries)	0.05	0.04	125
Travel related to shopping (except groceries, food, and gas)	0.10	0.14	71
Travel related to using professional and personal care services	0.02	0.05	40
Travel related to using financial services and banking	0.01	0.01	100
Travel related to using medical services	0.01	0.02	50
Travel related to eating and drinking	0.09	0.11	82
Travel related to socializing, relaxing, and leisure	0.25	0.17	147
Travel related to socializing and communicating	0.13	0.10	130
Travel related to attending or hosting social events	0.01	0.01	100
Travel related to relaxing and leisure	0.06	0.03	200
Travel related to arts and entertainment	0.04	0.02	200
Travel related to sports, exercise, and recreation	0.07	0.03	233
Travel related to participating in sports, exercise, recreation	0.05	0.03	167
Travel related to religious and spiritual activities	0.02	0.02	100
Travel related to volunteer activities	0.01	0.02	50

Note: The index is calculated by dividing average time spent by women in the age group doing primary activity by average time spent by total women doing primary activity and multiplying by 100. Primary activities are those respondents identified as their main activity. Other activities done simultaneously, such as eating while watching TV, are not included. Numbers may not add to total because not all subcategories are shown. If fewer than 2.0 percent of the total population participated in a primary activity, then the primary activity is not shown.
Source: Bureau of Labor Statistics, unpublished tables from the 2008 American Time Use Survey, Internet site http://www.bls .gov/tus/home.htm; calculations by New Strategist

Table 2.7 Indexed Time Use of People Aged 15 to 19 by Sex, 2008

(average hours spent by people aged 15 to 19 doing primary activities on an average day by sex, and index of women's time to men's, 2008)

	average hours, aged 15 to 19		index of women to men
	men	women	
TOTAL, ALL ACTIVITIES	**24.00**	**24.00**	**100**
Personal care	**10.28**	**10.43**	**101**
Sleeping	9.64	9.46	98
Sleeplessness	0.03	0.04	133
Grooming	0.62	0.95	153
Health-related self-care	0.01	0.01	100
Household activities	**0.60**	**0.89**	**148**
Housework	0.17	0.39	229
Interior cleaning	0.14	0.33	236
Laundry	0.03	0.06	200
Storing interior household items, including food	0.00	0.00	–
Food and drink preparation, presentation, and clean-up	0.10	0.17	170
Food and drink preparation	0.07	0.13	186
Kitchen and food clean-up	0.02	0.03	150
Interior maintenance, repair, and decoration	0.01	0.01	100
Interior arrangement, decoration, and repairs	0.01	0.01	100
Exterior maintenance, repair, and decoration	0.01	0.02	200
Lawn, garden, and houseplants	0.05	0.02	40
Animals and pets (not veterinary care)	0.05	0.05	100
Walking, exercising, and playing with pets	0.02	0.03	150
Vehicles	0.09	0.00	0
Household management	0.12	0.22	183
Financial management	0.00	0.00	–
Household and personal organization and planning	0.06	0.06	100
Household and personal mail and messages (except email)	0.00	0.00	–
Household and personal email	0.05	0.15	300
Caring for and helping household members	**0.05**	**0.14**	**280**
Caring for and helping household children	0.03	0.11	367
Physical care for household children	0.00	0.04	–
Reading to or with household children	0.00	0.00	–
Playing with household children (except sports)	0.01	0.03	300
Talking with, listening to household children	0.01	0.01	100
Looking after household children as a primary activity	0.00	0.01	–
Picking up or dropping off household children	0.00	0.01	–
Activities related to household children's education	0.00	0.01	–
Helping household children with homework	0.00	0.00	–
Helping household adults	0.01	0.01	100
Caring for and helping people in other households	**0.09**	**0.22**	**244**
Caring for and helping children in other households	0.05	0.12	240

	average hours, aged 15 to 19		index of women to men
	men	women	
Helping adults in other households	0.04	0.10	250
Picking up or dropping off adults in other households	0.01	0.01	100
Work and work-related activities	**1.16**	**1.41**	**122**
Work, main job	1.05	1.24	118
Work, other job(s)	0.01	0.02	200
Education	**2.96**	**2.87**	**97**
Taking class	2.39	2.05	86
Taking class for degree, certification, or licensure	2.37	2.02	85
Research, homework	0.48	0.76	158
Consumer purchases (store, telephone, Internet)	**0.19**	**0.41**	**216**
Grocery shopping	0.03	0.05	167
Purchasing gas	0.01	0.00	0
Purchasing food (except groceries)	0.02	0.03	150
Shopping, except groceries, food, and gas	0.13	0.31	238
Professional and personal care services	**0.02**	**0.07**	**350**
Financial services and banking	0.00	0.00	–
Banking	0.00	0.00	–
Medical and care services	0.02	0.03	150
Using health and care services outside the home	0.01	0.02	200
Household services	**0.01**	**0.00**	**0**
Eating and drinking	**0.94**	**0.85**	**90**
Socializing, relaxing, and leisure	**4.83**	**4.23**	**88**
Socializing and communicating	0.87	0.85	98
Attending or hosting social events	0.08	0.06	75
Relaxing and leisure	3.72	3.15	85
Relaxing, thinking	0.12	0.15	125
Television	2.23	2.08	93
Listening to the radio	0.03	0.04	133
Listening to or playing music (not radio)	0.13	0.07	54
Playing games (including computer)	0.76	0.19	25
Computer use for leisure (except games)	0.27	0.35	130
Reading for personal interest	0.16	0.18	113
Arts and entertainment (except sports)	0.16	0.16	100
Sports, exercise, and recreation	**1.09**	**0.50**	**46**
Participating in sports, exercise, or recreation	1.00	0.39	39
Using cardiovascular equipment	0.00	0.01	–
Walking	0.01	0.03	300
Working out, unspecified	0.02	0.02	100
Religious and spiritual activities	**0.08**	**0.11**	**138**
Attending religious services	0.04	0.08	200
Participation in religious practices	0.04	0.01	25

	average hours, aged 15 to 19		index of women to men
	men	women	
Volunteer activities	**0.15**	**0.12**	**80**
Administrative and support activities	0.01	0.01	100
Telephone calls	**0.18**	**0.38**	**211**
Telephone calls to or from family members	0.00	0.03	–
Telephone calls to or from friends, neighbors, or acquaintances	0.10	0.22	220
Traveling	**1.19**	**1.14**	**96**
Travel related to personal care	0.01	0.03	300
Travel related to household activities	0.04	0.02	50
Travel related to household management	0.03	0.02	67
Travel related to caring for and helping household members	0.03	0.04	133
Travel related to caring for and helping household children	0.02	0.02	100
Travel related to helping household adults	0.01	0.02	200
Travel related to caring for and helping people in other households	0.05	0.09	180
Travel related to caring for and helping children in other households	0.03	0.04	133
Travel related to helping adults in other households	0.03	0.05	167
Travel related to work	0.07	0.10	143
Travel related to education	0.17	0.17	100
Travel related to taking class	0.15	0.14	93
Travel related to consumer purchases	0.17	0.20	118
Travel related to grocery shopping	0.02	0.03	150
Travel related to purchasing gas	0.05	0.02	40
Travel related to purchasing food (except groceries)	0.03	0.05	167
Travel related to shopping (except groceries, food, and gas)	0.08	0.10	125
Travel related to using professional and personal care services	0.01	0.02	200
Travel related to using financial services and banking	0.00	0.01	–
Travel related to using medical services	0.01	0.01	100
Travel related to eating and drinking	0.14	0.09	64
Travel related to socializing, relaxing, and leisure	0.28	0.25	89
Travel related to socializing and communicating	0.11	0.13	118
Travel related to attending or hosting social events	0.01	0.01	100
Travel related to relaxing and leisure	0.06	0.06	100
Travel related to arts and entertainment	0.05	0.04	80
Travel related to sports, exercise, and recreation	0.12	0.07	58
Travel related to participating in sports, exercise, recreation	0.09	0.05	56
Travel related to religious and spiritual activities	0.02	0.02	100
Travel related to volunteer activities	0.02	0.01	50

Note: The index is calculated by dividing women's time by men's time and multiplying by 100. Primary activities are those respondents identified as their main activity. Other activities done simultaneously, such as eating while watching TV, are not included. Numbers may not add to total because not all subcategories are shown. If fewer than 2.0 percent of the total population participated in a primary activity, then the primary activity is not shown. "–" means denominator is zero.
Source: Bureau of Labor Statistics, unpublished tables from the 2008 American Time Use Survey, Internet site http://www.bls.gov/tus/home.htm; calculations by New Strategist

Table 2.8 Indexed Participation in Primary Activities by Total People Aged 15 to 19, 2008

(percent of people aged 15 to 19 and total people aged 15 or older participating in primary activities on an average day, and index of participation by 15-to-19-year-olds to total people, 2008)

	percent participating		index, people aged 15 to 19 to total
	people aged 15 to 19	total people	
TOTAL, ALL ACTIVITIES	**100.0%**	**100.0%**	**100**
Personal care	**100.0**	**100.0**	**100**
Sleeping	100.0	99.9	100
Sleeplessness	4.6	5.2	87
Grooming	82.6	79.3	104
Health-related self-care	1.9	6.4	30
Household activities	**53.6**	**75.5**	**71**
Housework	19.8	35.5	56
Interior cleaning	16.6	24.5	68
Laundry	5.2	16.2	32
Storing interior household items, including food	1.1	5.0	22
Food and drink preparation, presentation, and clean-up	21.1	52.3	40
Food and drink preparation	17.7	49.3	36
Kitchen and food clean-up	6.4	20.8	31
Interior maintenance, repair, and decoration	1.3	3.0	44
Interior arrangement, decoration, and repairs	0.7	2.0	36
Exterior maintenance, repair, and decoration	1.5	2.7	56
Lawn, garden, and houseplants	2.3	9.4	24
Animals and pets (not veterinary care)	9.0	14.5	62
Walking, exercising, and playing with pets	3.6	5.8	62
Vehicles	2.5	2.7	94
Household management	27.0	29.0	93
Financial management	0.6	4.0	14
Household and personal organization and planning	16.8	14.1	120
Household and personal mail and messages (except email)	1.0	6.9	14
Household and personal email	11.1	9.4	117
Caring for and helping household members	**13.5**	**26.1**	**52**
Caring for and helping household children	10.1	21.9	46
Physical care for household children	2.3	15.7	15
Reading to or with household children	0.0	2.6	0
Playing with household children (except sports)	1.7	5.4	32
Talking with, listening to household children	1.0	3.0	34
Looking after household children as a primary activity	0.9	2.3	38
Picking up or dropping off household children	4.9	9.2	53
Activities related to household children's education	0.6	3.8	16
Helping household children with homework	0.5	3.4	15
Helping household adults	2.5	3.6	70
Caring for and helping people in other households	**18.5**	**13.3**	**139**
Caring for and helping children in other households	10.1	5.6	181

	percent participating		index, people aged 15 to 19
	people aged 15 to 19	total people	to total
Helping adults in other households	9.3%	8.0%	116
Picking up or dropping off adults in other households	5.7	5.0	114
Work and work-related activities	**23.9**	**46.6**	**51**
Work, main job	20.0	43.9	46
Work, other job(s)	0.3	2.4	11
Education	**47.0**	**7.9**	**594**
Taking class	36.8	5.2	712
Taking class for degree, certification, or licensure	36.3	4.8	763
Research, homework	32.0	5.8	548
Consumer purchases (store, telephone, Internet)	**35.3**	**40.7**	**87**
Grocery shopping	6.1	12.9	47
Purchasing gas	2.9	4.0	74
Purchasing food (except groceries)	15.4	12.0	128
Shopping, except groceries, food, and gas	20.3	23.5	86
Professional and personal care services	**4.9**	**8.9**	**55**
Financial services and banking	1.8	3.2	57
Banking	1.8	3.0	58
Medical and care services	2.0	3.6	54
Using health and care services outside the home	2.0	3.4	57
Household services	**1.4**	**2.1**	**67**
Eating and drinking	**95.6**	**96.0**	**100**
Socializing, relaxing, and leisure	**95.9**	**95.4**	**100**
Socializing and communicating	49.3	37.6	131
Attending or hosting social events	2.5	2.3	107
Relaxing and leisure	90.5	91.3	99
Relaxing, thinking	14.3	19.9	72
Television	74.4	80.9	92
Listening to the radio	2.9	2.0	143
Listening to or playing music (not radio)	11.0	2.6	422
Playing games (including computer)	20.9	9.0	232
Computer use for leisure (except games)	21.7	9.5	228
Reading for personal interest	11.7	23.9	49
Arts and entertainment (except sports)	6.1	3.2	188
Sports, exercise, and recreation	**32.1**	**18.9**	**170**
Participating in sports, exercise, or recreation	29.6	17.9	165
Using cardiovascular equipment	0.6	2.2	26
Walking	1.9	4.8	39
Working out, unspecified	2.5	3.2	77
Religious and spiritual activities	**6.2**	**9.2**	**67**
Attending religious services	3.3	4.9	68
Participation in religious practices	2.6	4.6	57

	percent participating		index, people aged 15 to 19
	people aged 15 to 19	total people	to total
Volunteer activities	**6.7%**	**6.7%**	**101**
Administrative and support activities	1.1	2.5	43
Telephone calls	**21.4**	**15.4**	**139**
Telephone calls to or from family members	4.2	7.3	57
Telephone calls to or from friends, neighbors, or acquaintances	12.7	5.6	228
Traveling	**94.3**	**86.9**	**108**
Travel related to personal care	4.3	2.5	172
Travel related to household activities	8.4	9.4	90
Travel related to household management	5.5	6.1	89
Travel related to caring for and helping household members	6.4	13.6	47
Travel related to caring for and helping household children	4.7	11.0	43
Travel related to helping household adults	1.7	2.6	65
Travel related to caring for and helping people in other households	15.6	10.5	149
Travel related to caring for and helping children in other households	8.0	3.5	226
Travel related to helping adults in other households	8.4	7.1	119
Travel related to work	19.7	38.2	52
Travel related to education	33.9	5.0	674
Travel related to taking class	30.4	4.4	691
Travel related to consumer purchases	34.0	39.6	86
Travel related to grocery shopping	6.2	12.9	48
Travel related to purchasing gas	2.9	3.9	73
Travel related to purchasing food (except groceries)	14.7	11.2	131
Travel related to shopping (except groceries, food, and gas)	19.3	22.7	85
Travel related to using professional and personal care services	4.9	8.1	60
Travel related to using financial services and banking	1.8	3.0	61
Travel related to using medical services	2.0	3.3	59
Travel related to eating and drinking	26.1	25.0	104
Travel related to socializing, relaxing, and leisure	45.6	28.6	159
Travel related to socializing and communicating	28.9	18.6	156
Travel related to attending or hosting social events	2.1	2.0	107
Travel related to relaxing and leisure	19.3	8.9	216
Travel related to arts and entertainment	5.0	2.6	191
Travel related to sports, exercise, and recreation	21.1	9.6	221
Travel related to participating in sports, exercise, and recreation	18.0	8.6	211
Travel related to religious and spiritual activities	4.5	5.1	88
Travel related to volunteer activities	5.0	4.3	116

Note: The index is calculated by dividing percent of people in the age group doing primary activity by percent of total people doing primary activity and multiplying by 100. Primary activities are those respondents identified as their main activity. Other activities done simultaneously, such as eating while watching TV, are not included. If fewer than 2.0 percent of the total population participated in a primary activity, then the primary activity is not shown.
Source: Bureau of Labor Statistics, unpublished tables from the 2008 American Time Use Survey, Internet site http://www.bls .gov/tus/home.htm; calculations by New Strategist

Table 2.9 Indexed Participation in Primary Activities by Men Aged 15 to 19, 2008

(percent of men aged 15 to 19 and total men aged 15 or older participating in primary activities on an average day, and index of participation by 15-to-19-year-old men to total men, 2008)

	percent participating		index, men aged 15 to 19 to total men
	men aged 15 to 19	total men	
TOTAL, ALL ACTIVITIES	**100.0%**	**100.0%**	**100**
Personal care	**100.0**	**100.0**	**100**
Sleeping	100.0	99.9	100
Sleeplessness	4.1	4.5	90
Grooming	82.2	76.6	107
Health-related self-care	2.3	4.8	47
Household activities	**50.6**	**66.6**	**76**
Housework	15.8	19.7	80
Interior cleaning	12.7	13.5	94
Laundry	4.0	6.3	64
Storing interior household items, including food	0.6	2.9	19
Food and drink preparation, presentation, and clean-up	19.4	38.4	50
Food and drink preparation	16.4	36.0	46
Kitchen and food clean-up	5.3	9.5	56
Interior maintenance, repair, and decoration	1.7	3.9	44
Interior arrangement, decoration, and repairs	0.5	2.4	20
Exterior maintenance, repair, and decoration	1.5	3.8	40
Lawn, garden, and houseplants	3.3	11.0	30
Animals and pets (not veterinary care)	8.5	12.1	70
Walking, exercising, and playing with pets	3.5	5.2	68
Vehicles	4.5	4.5	100
Household management	23.8	24.0	99
Financial management	0.5	3.2	16
Household and personal organization and planning	17.4	11.1	156
Household and personal mail and messages (except email)	0.4	5.5	8
Household and personal email	6.6	7.4	89
Caring for and helping household members	**10.2**	**20.7**	**49**
Caring for and helping household children	6.9	16.8	41
Physical care for household children	0.5	10.4	5
Reading to or with household children	0.0	1.7	0
Playing with household children (except sports)	1.4	4.7	30
Talking with, listening to household children	0.8	1.7	47
Looking after household children as a primary activity	0.9	1.5	62
Picking up or dropping off household children	3.5	6.2	56
Activities related to household children's education	0.6	2.2	27
Helping household children with homework	0.6	2.0	29
Helping household adults	2.5	3.5	71
Caring for and helping people in other households	**13.5**	**11.0**	**123**
Caring for and helping children in other households	7.0	3.6	194

	percent participating		index, men aged 15 to 19 to total men
	men aged 15 to 19	total men	
Helping adults in other households	7.2%	7.5%	96
Picking up or dropping off adults in other households	4.4	4.4	100
Work and work-related activities	**21.1**	**53.4**	**39**
Work, main job	17.2	50.1	34
Work, other job(s)	0.3	2.3	12
Education	**46.7**	**6.9**	**681**
Taking class	39.6	5.0	790
Taking class for degree, certification, or licensure	39.0	4.8	811
Research, homework	28.0	4.6	604
Consumer purchases (store, telephone, Internet)	**29.5**	**35.6**	**83**
Grocery shopping	5.6	9.6	59
Purchasing gas	3.2	4.3	76
Purchasing food (except groceries)	14.2	11.8	120
Shopping, except groceries, food, and gas	15.5	19.6	79
Professional and personal care services	**2.8**	**6.7**	**42**
Financial services and banking	1.0	3.1	31
Banking	0.8	2.8	28
Medical and care services	1.4	2.4	58
Using health and care services outside the home	1.4	2.3	61
Household services	**1.6**	**2.1**	**78**
Eating and drinking	**95.7**	**96.5**	**99**
Socializing, relaxing, and leisure	**96.4**	**95.4**	**101**
Socializing and communicating	51.4	34.9	147
Attending or hosting social events	2.8	2.0	144
Relaxing and leisure	91.5	92.1	99
Relaxing, thinking	13.8	20.4	68
Television	74.9	82.3	91
Listening to the radio	2.3	2.5	93
Listening to or playing music (not radio)	13.2	3.3	404
Playing games (including computer)	29.3	9.6	306
Computer use for leisure (except games)	21.1	9.5	221
Reading for personal interest	11.4	21.1	54
Arts and entertainment (except sports)	6.6	3.3	198
Sports, exercise, and recreation	**42.3**	**22.0**	**192**
Participating in sports, exercise, or recreation	39.9	21.0	190
Using cardiovascular equipment	0.3	1.8	17
Walking	1.8	4.9	36
Working out, unspecified	2.7	3.5	78
Religious and spiritual activities	**4.5**	**7.7**	**58**
Attending religious services	1.6	4.0	41
Participation in religious practices	2.1	3.7	56

	percent participating		index, men aged 15 to 19 to total men
	men aged 15 to 19	total men	
Volunteer activities	**7.6%**	**5.7%**	**133**
Administrative and support activities	1.3	1.9	65
Telephone calls	**17.9**	**10.0**	**180**
Telephone calls to or from family members	3.0	3.8	79
Telephone calls to or from friends, neighbors, or acquaintances	11.2	3.7	302
Traveling	**94.3**	**88.5**	**107**
Travel related to personal care	4.7	3.1	152
Travel related to household activities	9.3	8.5	109
Travel related to household management	7.0	5.5	128
Travel related to caring for and helping household members	4.6	9.9	46
Travel related to caring for and helping household children	3.1	7.4	42
Travel related to helping household adults	1.5	2.4	65
Travel related to caring for and helping people in other households	11.8	9.3	127
Travel related to caring for and helping children in other households	5.9	2.5	239
Travel related to helping adults in other households	6.4	6.7	94
Travel related to work	16.1	44.4	36
Travel related to education	34.7	4.6	748
Travel related to taking class	31.3	4.1	756
Travel related to consumer purchases	28.3	34.5	82
Travel related to grocery shopping	5.7	9.5	60
Travel related to purchasing gas	3.2	4.2	75
Travel related to purchasing food (except groceries)	13.6	11.0	123
Travel related to shopping (except groceries, food, and gas)	14.6	18.9	77
Travel related to using professional and personal care services	2.8	6.3	44
Travel related to using financial services and banking	1.0	3.0	33
Travel related to using medical services	1.4	2.3	61
Travel related to eating and drinking	28.6	27.3	105
Travel related to socializing, relaxing, and leisure	46.2	28.0	165
Travel related to socializing and communicating	31.1	17.5	177
Travel related to attending or hosting social events	2.6	1.7	151
Travel related to relaxing and leisure	18.0	9.4	192
Travel related to arts and entertainment	5.3	2.8	191
Travel related to sports, exercise, and recreation	27.1	11.5	236
Travel related to participating in sports, exercise, recreation	24.3	10.4	233
Travel related to religious and spiritual activities	3.5	4.4	80
Travel related to volunteer activities	5.8	3.8	151

Note: The index is calculated by dividing percent of men in the age group doing primary activity by percent of total men doing primary activity and multiplying by 100. Primary activities are those respondents identified as their main activity. Other activities done simultaneously, such as eating while watching TV, are not included. If fewer than 2.0 percent of the total population participated in a primary activity, then the primary activity is not shown.
Source: Bureau of Labor Statistics, unpublished tables from the 2008 American Time Use Survey, Internet site http://www.bls.gov/tus/home.htm; calculations by New Strategist

Table 2.10 Indexed Participation in Primary Activities by Women Aged 15 to 19, 2008

(percent of women aged 15 to 19 and total women aged 15 or older participating in primary activities on an average day, and index of participation by 15-to-19-year-old women to total women, 2008)

	percent participating		index, women aged 15 to 19
	women aged 15 to 19	total women	to total women
TOTAL, ALL ACTIVITIES	**100.0%**	**100.0%**	**100**
Personal care	**100.0**	**100.0**	**100**
Sleeping	100.0	99.9	100
Sleeplessness	5.1	5.8	86
Grooming	83.1	81.8	101
Health-related self-care	1.6	7.8	21
Household activities	**56.7**	**84.0**	**68**
Housework	24.0	50.3	48
Interior cleaning	20.7	34.9	59
Laundry	6.4	25.5	25
Storing interior household items, including food	1.6	7.0	23
Food and drink preparation, presentation, and clean-up	22.9	65.3	35
Food and drink preparation	18.9	61.8	31
Kitchen and food clean-up	7.5	31.5	24
Interior maintenance, repair, and decoration	0.9	2.2	43
Interior arrangement, decoration, and repairs	0.9	1.5	62
Exterior maintenance, repair, and decoration	1.5	1.8	88
Lawn, garden, and houseplants	1.2	7.9	15
Animals and pets (not veterinary care)	9.4	16.7	56
Walking, exercising, and playing with pets	3.6	6.3	58
Vehicles	0.5	1.0	50
Household management	30.4	33.8	90
Financial management	0.6	4.9	12
Household and personal organization and planning	16.3	16.8	97
Household and personal mail and messages (except email)	1.5	8.2	19
Household and personal email	15.7	11.3	139
Caring for and helping household members	**17.0**	**31.2**	**55**
Caring for and helping household children	13.5	26.7	50
Physical care for household children	4.2	20.6	20
Reading to or with household children	0.0	3.5	0
Playing with household children (except sports)	2.0	6.1	33
Talking with, listening to household children	1.2	4.3	29
Looking after household children as a primary activity	0.8	3.0	28
Picking up or dropping off household children	6.3	12.1	53
Activities related to household children's education	0.7	5.4	12
Helping household children with homework	0.5	4.8	10
Helping household adults	2.6	3.7	69
Caring for and helping people in other households	**23.7**	**15.5**	**153**
Caring for and helping children in other households	13.2	7.4	179

	percent participating		index, women aged 15 to 19
	women aged 15 to 19	total women	to total women
Helping adults in other households	11.4%	8.5%	134
Picking up or dropping off adults in other households	6.9	5.4	127
Work and work-related activities	**26.9**	**40.3**	**67**
Work, main job	22.9	38.0	60
Work, other job(s)	0.3	2.4	11
Education	**47.3**	**8.9**	**531**
Taking class	34.0	5.3	638
Taking class for degree, certification, or licensure	33.5	4.7	711
Research, homework	36.2	7.0	518
Consumer purchases (store, telephone, Internet)	**41.3**	**45.4**	**91**
Grocery shopping	6.5	16.1	41
Purchasing gas	2.6	3.7	70
Purchasing food (except groceries)	16.6	12.3	135
Shopping, except groceries, food, and gas	25.2	27.2	93
Professional and personal care services	**7.0**	**11.0**	**64**
Financial services and banking	2.7	3.3	83
Banking	2.7	3.3	84
Medical and care services	2.5	4.8	54
Using health and care services outside the home	2.5	4.5	56
Household services	**1.1**	**2.1**	**55**
Eating and drinking	**95.4**	**95.6**	**100**
Socializing, relaxing, and leisure	**95.3**	**95.4**	**100**
Socializing and communicating	47.1	40.1	117
Attending or hosting social events	2.1	2.7	80
Relaxing and leisure	89.5	90.6	99
Relaxing, thinking	14.9	19.5	76
Television	73.9	79.5	93
Listening to the radio	3.4	1.5	224
Listening to or playing music (not radio)	8.7	2.0	440
Playing games (including computer)	12.2	8.4	145
Computer use for leisure (except games)	22.3	9.5	235
Reading for personal interest	11.9	26.5	45
Arts and entertainment (except sports)	5.6	3.2	177
Sports, exercise, and recreation	**21.6**	**15.9**	**136**
Participating in sports, exercise, or recreation	19.0	15.0	127
Using cardiovascular equipment	0.8	2.5	34
Walking	2.0	4.7	42
Working out, unspecified	2.2	2.9	75
Religious and spiritual activities	**8.0**	**10.7**	**75**
Attending religious services	5.0	5.7	89
Participation in religious practices	3.1	5.4	58

	percent participating		index, women aged 15 to 19 to total women
	women aged 15 to 19	total women	
Volunteer activities	**5.8%**	**7.6%**	77
Administrative and support activities	0.9	3.1	30
Telephone calls	**24.9**	**20.4**	122
Telephone calls to or from family members	5.4	10.7	50
Telephone calls to or from friends, neighbors, or acquaintances	14.3	7.4	195
Traveling	**94.3**	**85.5**	110
Travel related to personal care	4.0	2.0	198
Travel related to household activities	7.5	10.3	74
Travel related to household management	3.9	6.7	58
Travel related to caring for and helping household members	8.4	17.1	49
Travel related to caring for and helping household children	6.4	14.3	45
Travel related to helping household adults	1.8	2.7	66
Travel related to caring for and helping people in other households	19.6	11.6	168
Travel related to caring for and helping children in other households	10.1	4.5	223
Travel related to helping adults in other households	10.5	7.4	142
Travel related to work	23.5	32.2	73
Travel related to education	33.0	5.4	613
Travel related to taking class	29.5	4.6	634
Travel related to consumer purchases	39.7	44.4	90
Travel related to grocery shopping	6.7	16.0	42
Travel related to purchasing gas	2.6	3.7	71
Travel related to purchasing food (except groceries)	15.9	11.5	138
Travel related to shopping (except groceries, food, and gas)	24.1	26.3	91
Travel related to using professional and personal care services	7.0	9.8	71
Travel related to using financial services and banking	2.7	3.1	90
Travel related to using medical services	2.5	4.3	60
Travel related to eating and drinking	23.5	22.8	103
Travel related to socializing, relaxing, and leisure	44.9	29.2	154
Travel related to socializing and communicating	26.7	19.5	137
Travel related to attending or hosting social events	1.7	2.3	74
Travel related to relaxing and leisure	20.6	8.5	242
Travel related to arts and entertainment	4.6	2.4	190
Travel related to sports, exercise, and recreation	14.9	7.7	193
Travel related to participating in sports, exercise, recreation	11.6	6.8	171
Travel related to religious and spiritual activities	5.6	5.8	95
Travel related to volunteer activities	4.1	4.7	88

Note: The index is calculated by dividing percent of women in the age group doing primary activity by percent of total women doing primary activity and multiplying by 100. Primary activities are those respondents identified as their main activity. Other activities done simultaneously, such as eating while watching TV, are not included. If fewer than 2.0 percent of the total population participated in a primary activity, then the primary activity is not shown.
Source: Bureau of Labor Statistics, unpublished tables from the 2008 American Time Use Survey, Internet site http://www.bls .gov/tus/home.htm; calculations by New Strategist

Table 2.11 Indexed Participation in Primary Activities of People Aged 15 to 19 by Sex, 2008

(percent of people aged 15 to 19 participating in primary activities on an average day by sex, and index of women's participation to men's, 2008)

	aged 15 to 19, percent participating		index of women to men
	men	women	
TOTAL, ALL ACTIVITIES	**100.0%**	**100.0%**	**100**
Personal care	**100.0**	**100.0**	**100**
Sleeping	100.0	100.0	100
Sleeplessness	4.1	5.1	124
Grooming	82.2	83.1	101
Health-related self-care	2.3	1.6	71
Household activities	**50.6**	**56.7**	**112**
Housework	15.8	24.0	152
Interior cleaning	12.7	20.7	163
Laundry	4.0	6.4	159
Storing interior household items, including food	0.6	1.6	290
Food and drink preparation, presentation, and clean-up	19.4	22.9	118
Food and drink preparation	16.4	18.9	115
Kitchen and food clean-up	5.3	7.5	142
Interior maintenance, repair, and decoration	1.7	0.9	55
Interior arrangement, decoration, and repairs	0.5	0.9	192
Exterior maintenance, repair, and decoration	1.5	1.5	102
Lawn, garden, and houseplants	3.3	1.2	36
Animals and pets (not veterinary care)	8.5	9.4	110
Walking, exercising, and playing with pets	3.5	3.6	103
Vehicles	4.5	0.5	11
Household management	23.8	30.4	128
Financial management	0.5	0.6	116
Household and personal organization and planning	17.4	16.3	94
Household and personal mail and messages (except email)	0.4	1.5	363
Household and personal email	6.6	15.7	237
Caring for and helping household members	**10.2**	**17.0**	**167**
Caring for and helping household children	6.9	13.5	195
Physical care for household children	0.5	4.2	803
Reading to or with household children	0.0	0.0	–
Playing with household children (except sports)	1.4	2.0	146
Talking with, listening to household children	0.8	1.2	148
Looking after household children as a primary activity	0.9	0.8	94
Picking up or dropping off household children	3.5	6.3	184
Activities related to household children's education	0.6	0.7	113
Helping household children with homework	0.6	0.5	80
Helping household adults	2.5	2.6	104
Caring for and helping people in other households	**13.5**	**23.7**	**175**
Caring for and helping children in other households	7.0	13.2	187

	aged 15 to 19, percent participating		index of women to men
	men	women	
Helping adults in other households	7.2%	11.4%	159
Picking up or dropping off adults in other households	4.4	6.9	156
Work and work-related activities	**21.1**	**26.9**	**128**
Work, main job	17.2	22.9	133
Work, other job(s)	0.3	0.3	96
Education	**46.7**	**47.3**	**101**
Taking class	39.6	34.0	86
Taking class for degree, certification, or licensure	39.0	33.5	86
Research, homework	28.0	36.2	130
Consumer purchases (store, telephone, Internet)	**29.5**	**41.3**	**140**
Grocery shopping	5.6	6.5	116
Purchasing gas	3.2	2.6	80
Purchasing food (except groceries)	14.2	16.6	117
Shopping, except groceries, food, and gas	15.5	25.2	162
Professional and personal care services	**2.8**	**7.0**	**250**
Financial services and banking	1.0	2.7	280
Banking	0.8	2.7	349
Medical and care services	1.4	2.5	181
Using health and care services outside the home	1.4	2.5	181
Household services	**1.6**	**1.1**	**69**
Eating and drinking	**95.7**	**95.4**	**100**
Socializing, relaxing, and leisure	**96.4**	**95.3**	**99**
Socializing and communicating	51.4	47.1	92
Attending or hosting social events	2.8	2.1	75
Relaxing and leisure	91.5	89.5	98
Relaxing, thinking	13.8	14.9	108
Television	74.9	73.9	99
Listening to the radio	2.3	3.4	146
Listening to or playing music (not radio)	13.2	8.7	66
Playing games (including computer)	29.3	12.2	42
Computer use for leisure (except games)	21.1	22.3	106
Reading for personal interest	11.4	11.9	104
Arts and entertainment (except sports)	6.6	5.6	85
Sports, exercise, and recreation	**42.3**	**21.6**	**51**
Participating in sports, exercise, or recreation	39.9	19.0	48
Using cardiovascular equipment	0.3	0.8	278
Walking	1.8	2.0	111
Working out, unspecified	2.7	2.2	80
Religious and spiritual activities	**4.5**	**8.0**	**179**
Attending religious services	1.6	5.0	307
Participation in religious practices	2.1	3.1	151

	aged 15 to 19, percent participating		index of women to men
	men	women	
Volunteer activities	**7.6%**	**5.8%**	**76**
Administrative and support activities	1.3	0.9	73
Telephone calls	**17.9**	**24.9**	**139**
Telephone calls to or from family members	3.0	5.4	179
Telephone calls to or from friends, neighbors, or acquaintances	11.2	14.3	128
Traveling	**94.3**	**94.3**	**100**
Travel related to personal care	4.7	4.0	85
Travel related to household activities	9.3	7.5	82
Travel related to household management	7.0	3.9	55
Travel related to caring for and helping household members	4.6	8.4	183
Travel related to caring for and helping household children	3.1	6.4	205
Travel related to helping household adults	1.5	1.8	115
Travel related to caring for and helping people in other households	11.8	19.6	166
Travel related to caring for and helping children in other households	5.9	10.1	171
Travel related to helping adults in other households	6.4	10.5	165
Travel related to work	16.1	23.5	146
Travel related to education	34.7	33.0	95
Travel related to taking class	31.3	29.5	94
Travel related to consumer purchases	28.3	39.7	140
Travel related to grocery shopping	5.7	6.7	117
Travel related to purchasing gas	3.2	2.6	82
Travel related to purchasing food (except groceries)	13.6	15.9	117
Travel related to shopping (except groceries, food, and gas)	14.6	24.1	166
Travel related to using professional and personal care services	2.8	7.0	250
Travel related to using financial services and banking	1.0	2.7	280
Travel related to using medical services	1.4	2.5	181
Travel related to eating and drinking	28.6	23.5	82
Travel related to socializing, relaxing, and leisure	46.2	44.9	97
Travel related to socializing and communicating	31.1	26.7	86
Travel related to attending or hosting social events	2.6	1.7	66
Travel related to relaxing and leisure	18.0	20.6	114
Travel related to arts and entertainment	5.3	4.6	87
Travel related to sports, exercise, and recreation	27.1	14.9	55
Travel related to participating in sports, exercise, recreation	24.3	11.6	48
Travel related to religious and spiritual activities	3.5	5.6	158
Travel related to volunteer activities	5.8	4.1	72

Note: The index is calculated by dividing percent of women participating in primary activity by percent of men participating in primary activity and multiplying by 100. Primary activities are those respondents identified as their main activity. Other activities done simultaneously, such as eating while watching TV, are not included. If fewer than 2.0 percent of the total population participated in a primary activity, then the primary activity is not shown. "−" means denominator is zero.
Source: Bureau of Labor Statistics, unpublished tables from the 2008 American Time Use Survey, Internet site http://www.bls
.gov/tus/home.htm; calculations by New Strategist

Table 2.12 Ranking: Average Hours per Day Spent Doing Primary Activities by Total People Aged 15 to 19, 2008

(average hours per day spent by people aged 15 to 19 doing primary activities, ranked by time spent doing activity, 2008)

		average hours per day spent by people aged 15 to 19
	Total, all activities	**24.00**
1.	Sleeping	9.55
2.	Taking class	2.22
3.	Television	2.16
4.	Work, main job	1.14
5.	Eating and drinking	0.90
6.	Socializing and communicating	0.86
7.	Grooming	0.78
8.	Participating in sports, exercise, or recreation	0.70
9.	Research, homework	0.62
10.	Playing games (including computer)	0.48
11.	Computer use for leisure (except games)	0.31
12.	Telephone calls	0.27
13.	Interior cleaning	0.23
14.	Shopping, except groceries, food, and gas	0.22
15.	Reading for personal interest	0.17
16.	Travel related to education	0.17
17.	Arts and entertainment (except sports)	0.16
18.	Relaxing, thinking	0.14
19.	Volunteer activities	0.14
20.	Travel related to socializing and communicating	0.12
21.	Travel related to eating and drinking	0.11
22.	Food and drink preparation	0.10
23.	Household and personal email	0.10
24.	Listening to or playing music (not radio)	0.10
25.	Travel related to work	0.09
26.	Travel related to shopping (except groceries, food, and gas)	0.09
27.	Travel related to sports, exercise, and recreation	0.09
28.	Caring for and helping children in other households	0.08
29.	Caring for and helping household children	0.07
30.	Helping adults in other households	0.07
31.	Attending or hosting social events	0.07
32.	Household and personal organization and planning	0.06
33.	Attending religious services	0.06
34.	Travel related to relaxing and leisure	0.06
35.	Animals and pets (not veterinary care)	0.05
36.	Vehicles	0.05
37.	Laundry	0.04
38.	Grocery shopping	0.04
39.	Travel related to helping adults in other households	0.04

		average hours per day spent by people aged 15 to 19
40.	Travel related to purchasing food (except groceries)	0.04
41.	Travel related to arts and entertainment	0.04
42.	Kitchen and food clean-up	0.03
43.	Lawn, garden, and houseplants	0.03
44.	Listening to the radio	0.03
45.	Travel related to household activities	0.03
46.	Travel related to caring for and helping children in other households	0.03
47.	Travel related to purchasing gas	0.03
48.	Exterior maintenance, repair, and decoration	0.02
49.	Work, other job(s)	0.02
50.	Purchasing food (except groceries)	0.02
51.	Medical and care services	0.02
52.	Participation in religious practices	0.02
53.	Travel related to personal care	0.02
54.	Travel related to caring for and helping household children	0.02
55.	Travel related to grocery shopping	0.02
56.	Travel related to religious and spiritual activities	0.02
57.	Travel related to volunteer activities	0.02
58.	Health-related self-care	0.01
59.	Interior maintenance, repair, and decoration	0.01
60.	Helping household adults	0.01
61.	Travel related to helping household adults	0.01
62.	Travel related to using medical services	0.01
63.	Travel related to attending or hosting social events	0.01
64.	Storing interior household items, including food	0.00
65.	Financial management	0.00
66.	Household and personal mail and messages (except email)	0.00
67.	Activities related to household children's education	0.00
68.	Purchasing gas	0.00
69.	Financial services and banking	0.00
70.	Household services	0.00
71.	Travel related to using financial services and banking	0.00

Note: Primary activities are those respondents identified as their main activity. Other activities done simultaneously, such as eating while watching TV, are not included. If fewer than 2.0 percent of the total population participated in a primary activity, then the primary activity is not shown.
Source: Bureau of Labor Statistics, unpublished tables from the 2008 American Time Use Survey, Internet site http://www.bls .gov/tus/home.htm; calculations by New Strategist

Table 2.13 Ranking: Average Hours per Day Spent Doing Primary Activities by Men Aged 15 to 19, 2008

(average hours per day spent by men aged 15 to 19 doing primary activities, ranked by time spent doing activity, 2008)

		average hours per day spent by men aged 15 to 19
	Total, all activities	**24.00**
1.	Sleeping	9.64
2.	Taking class	2.39
3.	Television	2.23
4.	Work, main job	1.05
5.	Participating in sports, exercise, or recreation	1.00
6.	Eating and drinking	0.94
7.	Socializing and communicating	0.87
8.	Playing games (including computer)	0.76
9.	Grooming	0.62
10.	Research, homework	0.48
11.	Computer use for leisure (except games)	0.27
12.	Telephone calls	0.18
13.	Travel related to education	0.17
14.	Reading for personal interest	0.16
15.	Arts and entertainment (except sports)	0.16
16.	Volunteer activities	0.15
17.	Interior cleaning	0.14
18.	Travel related to eating and drinking	0.14
19.	Shopping, except groceries, food, and gas	0.13
20.	Listening to or playing music (not radio)	0.13
21.	Relaxing, thinking	0.12
22.	Travel related to sports, exercise, and recreation	0.12
23.	Travel related to socializing and communicating	0.11
24.	Vehicles	0.09
25.	Attending or hosting social events	0.08
26.	Travel related to shopping (except groceries, food, and gas)	0.08
27.	Food and drink preparation	0.07
28.	Travel related to work	0.07
29.	Household and personal organization and planning	0.06
30.	Travel related to relaxing and leisure	0.06
31.	Lawn, garden, and houseplants	0.05
32.	Animals and pets (not veterinary care)	0.05
33.	Household and personal email	0.05
34.	Caring for and helping children in other households	0.05
35.	Travel related to purchasing gas	0.05
36.	Travel related to arts and entertainment	0.05
37.	Helping adults in other households	0.04
38.	Attending religious services	0.04
39.	Participation in religious practices	0.04

	average hours per day spent by men aged 15 to 19
40. Travel related to household activities	0.04
41. Laundry	0.03
42. Caring for and helping household children	0.03
43. Grocery shopping	0.03
44. Listening to the radio	0.03
45. Travel related to caring for and helping children in other households	0.03
46. Travel related to helping adults in other households	0.03
47. Travel related to purchasing food (except groceries)	0.03
48. Kitchen and food clean-up	0.02
49. Purchasing food (except groceries)	0.02
50. Medical and care services	0.02
51. Travel related to caring for and helping household children	0.02
52. Travel related to grocery shopping	0.02
53. Travel related to religious and spiritual activities	0.02
54. Travel related to volunteer activities	0.02
55. Health-related self-care	0.01
56. Interior maintenance, repair, and decoration	0.01
57. Exterior maintenance, repair, and decoration	0.01
58. Helping household adults	0.01
59. Work, other job(s)	0.01
60. Purchasing gas	0.01
61. Household services	0.01
62. Travel related to personal care	0.01
63. Travel related to helping household adults	0.01
64. Travel related to using medical services	0.01
65. Travel related to attending or hosting social events	0.01
66. Storing interior household items, including food	0.00
67. Financial management	0.00
68. Household and personal mail and messages (except email)	0.00
69. Activities related to household children's education	0.00
70. Financial services and banking	0.00
71. Travel related to using financial services and banking	0.00

Note: Primary activities are those respondents identified as their main activity. Other activities done simultaneously, such as eating while watching TV, are not included. If fewer than 2.0 percent of the total population participated in a primary activity, then the primary activity is not shown.
Source: Bureau of Labor Statistics, unpublished tables from the 2005 American Time Use Survey, Internet site http://www.bls .gov/tus/home.htm; calculations by New Strategist

Table 2.14 Ranking: Average Hours per Day Spent Doing Primary Activities by Women Aged 15 to 19, 2008

(average hours per day spent by women aged 15 to 19 doing primary activities, ranked by time spent doing activity, 2008)

		average hours per day spent by women aged 15 to 19
	Total, all activities	24.00
1.	Sleeping	9.46
2.	Television	2.08
3.	Taking class	2.05
4.	Work, main job	1.24
5.	Grooming	0.95
6.	Eating and drinking	0.85
7.	Socializing and communicating	0.85
8.	Research, homework	0.76
9.	Participating in sports, exercise, or recreation	0.39
10.	Telephone calls	0.38
11.	Computer use for leisure (except games)	0.35
12.	Interior cleaning	0.33
13.	Shopping, except groceries, food, and gas	0.31
14.	Playing games (including computer)	0.19
15.	Reading for personal interest	0.18
16.	Travel related to education	0.17
17.	Arts and entertainment (except sports)	0.16
18.	Household and personal email	0.15
19.	Relaxing, thinking	0.15
20.	Food and drink preparation	0.13
21.	Travel related to socializing and communicating	0.13
22.	Caring for and helping children in other households	0.12
23.	Volunteer activities	0.12
24.	Caring for and helping household children	0.11
25.	Helping adults in other households	0.10
26.	Travel related to work	0.10
27.	Travel related to shopping (except groceries, food, and gas)	0.10
28.	Travel related to eating and drinking	0.09
29.	Attending religious services	0.08
30.	Listening to or playing music (not radio)	0.07
31.	Travel related to sports, exercise, and recreation	0.07
32.	Laundry	0.06
33.	Household and personal organization and planning	0.06
34.	Attending or hosting social events	0.06
35.	Travel related to relaxing and leisure	0.06
36.	Animals and pets (not veterinary care)	0.05
37.	Grocery shopping	0.05
38.	Travel related to helping adults in other households	0.05
39.	Travel related to purchasing food (except groceries)	0.05

	average hours per day spent by women aged 15 to 19
40. Listening to the radio	0.04
41. Travel related to caring for and helping children in other households	0.04
42. Travel related to arts and entertainment	0.04
43. Kitchen and food clean-up	0.03
44. Purchasing food (except groceries)	0.03
45. Medical and care services	0.03
46. Travel related to personal care	0.03
47. Travel related to grocery shopping	0.03
48. Exterior maintenance, repair, and decoration	0.02
49. Lawn, garden, and houseplants	0.02
50. Work, other job(s)	0.02
51. Travel related to household activities	0.02
52. Travel related to caring for and helping household children	0.02
53. Travel related to helping household adults	0.02
54. Travel related to purchasing gas	0.02
55. Travel related to religious and spiritual activities	0.02
56. Health-related self-care	0.01
57. Interior maintenance, repair, and decoration	0.01
58. Activities related to household children's education	0.01
59. Helping household adults	0.01
60. Participation in religious practices	0.01
61. Travel related to using financial services and banking	0.01
62. Travel related to using medical services	0.01
63. Travel related to attending or hosting social events	0.01
64. Travel related to volunteer activities	0.01
65. Storing interior household items, including food	0.00
66. Vehicles	0.00
67. Financial management	0.00
68. Household and personal mail and messages (except email)	0.00
69. Purchasing gas	0.00
70. Financial services and banking	0.00
71. Household services	0.00

Note: Primary activities are those respondents identified as their main activity. Other activities done simultaneously, such as eating while watching TV, are not included. If fewer than 2.0 percent of the total population participated in a primary activity, then the primary activity is not shown.
Source: Bureau of Labor Statistics, unpublished tables from the 2008 American Time Use Survey, Internet site http://www.bls .gov/tus/home.htm; calculations by New Strategist

Table 2.15 Ranking: Percent of Total People Aged 15 to 19 Participating in Primary Activities on an Average Day, 2008

(percent of people aged 15 to 19 participating in primary activities on an average day, ranked by percent participating, 2008)

		percent of people aged 15 to 19 participating in activity
	Total, all activities	**100.0%**
1.	Sleeping	100.0
2.	Eating and drinking	95.6
3.	Grooming	82.6
4.	Television	74.4
5.	Socializing and communicating	49.3
6.	Taking class	36.8
7.	Travel related to education	33.9
8.	Research, homework	32.0
9.	Participating in sports, exercise, or recreation	29.6
10.	Travel related to socializing and communicating	28.9
11.	Travel related to eating and drinking	26.1
12.	Computer use for leisure (except games)	21.7
13.	Telephone calls	21.4
14.	Travel related to sports, exercise, and recreation	21.1
15.	Playing games (including computer)	20.9
16.	Shopping, except groceries, food, and gas	20.3
17.	Work, main job	20.0
18.	Travel related to work	19.7
19.	Travel related to relaxing and leisure	19.3
20.	Travel related to shopping (except groceries, food, and gas)	19.3
21.	Food and drink preparation	17.7
22.	Household and personal organization and planning	16.8
23.	Interior cleaning	16.6
24.	Purchasing food (except groceries)	15.4
25.	Travel related to purchasing food (except groceries)	14.7
26.	Relaxing, thinking	14.3
27.	Reading for personal interest	11.7
28.	Household and personal email	11.1
29.	Listening to or playing music (not radio)	11.0
30.	Caring for and helping household children	10.1
31.	Caring for and helping children in other households	10.1
32.	Helping adults in other households	9.3
33.	Animals and pets (not veterinary care)	9.0
34.	Travel related to helping adults in other households	8.4
35.	Travel related to household activities	8.4
36.	Travel related to caring for and helping children in other households	8.0
37.	Volunteer activities	6.7
38.	Kitchen and food clean-up	6.4
39.	Travel related to grocery shopping	6.2

	percent of people aged 15 to 19 participating in activity
40. Arts and entertainment (except sports)	6.1%
41. Grocery shopping	6.1
42. Laundry	5.2
43. Travel related to volunteer activities	5.0
44. Travel related to arts and entertainment	5.0
45. Travel related to caring for and helping household children	4.7
46. Travel related to religious and spiritual activities	4.5
47. Travel related to personal care	4.3
48. Attending religious services	3.3
49. Purchasing gas	2.9
50. Travel related to purchasing gas	2.9
51. Listening to the radio	2.9
52. Participation in religious practices	2.6
53. Vehicles	2.5
54. Helping household adults	2.5
55. Attending or hosting social events	2.5
56. Lawn, garden, and houseplants	2.3
57. Travel related to attending or hosting social events	2.1
58. Medical and care services	2.0
59. Travel related to using medical services	2.0
60. Health-related self-care	1.9
61. Financial services and banking	1.8
62. Travel related to using financial services and banking	1.8
63. Travel related to helping household adults	1.7
64. Exterior maintenance, repair, and decoration	1.5
65. Household services	1.4
66. Interior maintenance, repair, and decoration	1.3
67. Storing interior household items, including food	1.1
68. Household and personal mail and messages (except email)	1.0
69. Activities related to household children's education	0.6
70. Financial management	0.6
71. Work, other job(s)	0.3

Note: Primary activities are those respondents identified as their main activity. Other activities done simultaneously, such as eating while watching TV, are not included. If fewer than 2.0 percent of the total population participated in a primary activity, then the primary activity is not shown.
Source: Bureau of Labor Statistics, unpublished tables from the 2008 American Time Use Survey, Internet site http://www.bls .gov/tus/home.htm; calculations by New Strategist

Table 2.16 Ranking: Percent of Men Aged 15 to 19 Participating in Primary Activities on an Average Day, 2008

(percent of men aged 15 to 19 participating in primary activities on an average day, ranked by percent participating, 2008)

		percent of men aged 15 to 19 participating in activity
	Total, all activities	**100.0%**
1.	Sleeping	100.0
2.	Eating and drinking	95.7
3.	Grooming	82.2
4.	Television	74.9
5.	Socializing and communicating	51.4
6.	Participating in sports, exercise, or recreation	39.9
7.	Taking class	39.6
8.	Travel related to education	34.7
9.	Travel related to socializing and communicating	31.1
10.	Playing games (including computer)	29.3
11.	Travel related to eating and drinking	28.6
12.	Research, homework	28.0
13.	Travel related to sports, exercise, and recreation	27.1
14.	Computer use for leisure (except games)	21.1
15.	Travel related to relaxing and leisure	18.0
16.	Telephone calls	17.9
17.	Household and personal organization and planning	17.4
18.	Work, main job	17.2
19.	Food and drink preparation	16.4
20.	Travel related to work	16.1
21.	Shopping, except groceries, food, and gas	15.5
22.	Travel related to shopping (except groceries, food, and gas)	14.6
23.	Purchasing food (except groceries)	14.2
24.	Relaxing, thinking	13.8
25.	Travel related to purchasing food (except groceries)	13.6
26.	Listening to or playing music (not radio)	13.2
27.	Interior cleaning	12.7
28.	Reading for personal interest	11.4
29.	Travel related to household activities	9.3
30.	Animals and pets (not veterinary care)	8.5
31.	Volunteer activities	7.6
32.	Helping adults in other households	7.2
33.	Caring for and helping children in other households	7.0
34.	Caring for and helping household children	6.9
35.	Household and personal email	6.6
36.	Arts and entertainment (except sports)	6.6
37.	Travel related to helping adults in other households	6.4
38.	Travel related to caring for and helping children in other households	5.9
39.	Travel related to volunteer activities	5.8

	percent of men aged 15 to 19 participating in activity
40. Travel related to grocery shopping	5.7%
41. Grocery shopping	5.6
42. Travel related to arts and entertainment	5.3
43. Kitchen and food clean-up	5.3
44. Travel related to personal care	4.7
45. Vehicles	4.5
46. Laundry	4.0
47. Travel related to religious and spiritual activities	3.5
48. Lawn, garden, and houseplants	3.3
49. Purchasing gas	3.2
50. Travel related to purchasing gas	3.2
51. Travel related to caring for and helping household children	3.1
52. Attending or hosting social events	2.8
53. Travel related to attending or hosting social events	2.6
54. Helping household adults	2.5
55. Listening to the radio	2.3
56. Health-related self-care	2.3
57. Participation in religious practices	2.1
58. Interior maintenance, repair, and decoration	1.7
59. Attending religious services	1.6
60. Household services	1.6
61. Travel related to helping household adults	1.5
62. Exterior maintenance, repair, and decoration	1.5
63. Medical and care services	1.4
64. Travel related to using medical services	1.4
65. Financial services and banking	1.0
66. Travel related to using financial services and banking	1.0
67. Activities related to household children's education	0.6
68. Storing interior household items, including food	0.6
69. Financial management	0.5
70. Household and personal mail and messages (except email)	0.4
71. Work, other job(s)	0.3

Note: Primary activities are those respondents identified as their main activity. Other activities done simultaneously, such as eating while watching TV, are not included. If fewer than 2.0 percent of the total population participated in a primary activity, then the primary activity is not shown.
Source: Bureau of Labor Statistics, unpublished tables from the 2008 American Time Use Survey, Internet site http://www.bls .gov/tus/home.htm; calculations by New Strategist

Table 2.17 Ranking: Percent of Women Aged 15 to 19 Participating in Primary Activities on an Average Day, 2008

(percent of women aged 15 to 19 participating in primary activities on an average day, ranked by percent participating, 2008)

		percent of women aged 15 to 19 participating in activity
	Total, all activities	**100.0%**
1.	Sleeping	100.0
2.	Eating and drinking	95.4
3.	Grooming	83.1
4.	Television	73.9
5.	Socializing and communicating	47.1
6.	Research, homework	36.2
7.	Taking class	34.0
8.	Travel related to education	33.0
9.	Travel related to socializing and communicating	26.7
10.	Shopping, except groceries, food, and gas	25.2
11.	Telephone calls	24.9
12.	Travel related to shopping (except groceries, food, and gas)	24.1
13.	Travel related to work	23.5
14.	Travel related to eating and drinking	23.5
15.	Work, main job	22.9
16.	Computer use for leisure (except games)	22.3
17.	Interior cleaning	20.7
18.	Travel related to relaxing and leisure	20.6
19.	Participating in sports, exercise, or recreation	19.0
20.	Food and drink preparation	18.9
21.	Purchasing food (except groceries)	16.6
22.	Household and personal organization and planning	16.3
23.	Travel related to purchasing food (except groceries)	15.9
24.	Household and personal email	15.7
25.	Travel related to sports, exercise, and recreation	14.9
26.	Relaxing, thinking	14.9
27.	Caring for and helping household children	13.5
28.	Caring for and helping children in other households	13.2
29.	Playing games (including computer)	12.2
30.	Reading for personal interest	11.9
31.	Helping adults in other households	11.4
32.	Travel related to helping adults in other households	10.5
33.	Travel related to caring for and helping children in other households	10.1
34.	Animals and pets (not veterinary care)	9.4
35.	Listening to or playing music (not radio)	8.7
36.	Travel related to household activities	7.5
37.	Kitchen and food clean-up	7.5
38.	Travel related to grocery shopping	6.7
39.	Grocery shopping	6.5

	percent of women aged 15 to 19 participating in activity
40. Travel related to caring for and helping household children	6.4%
41. Laundry	6.4
42. Volunteer activities	5.8
43. Arts and entertainment (except sports)	5.6
44. Travel related to religious and spiritual activities	5.6
45. Attending religious services	5.0
46. Travel related to arts and entertainment	4.6
47. Travel related to volunteer activities	4.1
48. Travel related to personal care	4.0
49. Listening to the radio	3.4
50. Participation in religious practices	3.1
51. Travel related to using financial services and banking	2.7
52. Financial services and banking	2.7
53. Travel related to purchasing gas	2.6
54. Purchasing gas	2.6
55. Helping household adults	2.6
56. Medical and care services	2.5
57. Travel related to using medical services	2.5
58. Attending or hosting social events	2.1
59. Travel related to helping household adults	1.8
60. Travel related to attending or hosting social events	1.7
61. Storing interior household items, including food	1.6
62. Health-related self-care	1.6
63. Exterior maintenance, repair, and decoration	1.5
64. Household and personal mail and messages (except email)	1.5
65. Lawn, garden, and houseplants	1.2
66. Household services	1.1
67. Interior maintenance, repair, and decoration	0.9
68. Activities related to household children's education	0.7
69. Financial management	0.6
70. Vehicles	0.5
71. Work, other job(s)	0.3

Note: Primary activities are those respondents identified as their main activity. Other activities done simultaneously, such as eating while watching TV, are not included. If fewer than 2.0 percent of the total population participated in a primary activity, then the primary activity is not shown.
Source: Bureau of Labor Statistics, unpublished tables from the 2008 American Time Use Survey, Internet site http://www.bls .gov/tus/home.htm; calculations by New Strategist

Table 2.18 Ranking: Average Hours per Day Spent Doing Primary Activities by Total Participants Aged 15 to 19, 2008

(hours per day spent by participants aged 15 to 19 doing primary activities, ranked by time spent doing activity, 2008)

		average hours per day spent by participants aged 15 to 19
	Total, all activities	**24.00**
1.	Sleeping	9.55
2.	Taking class	6.03
3.	Work, main job	5.71
4.	Television	2.90
5.	Arts and entertainment (except sports)	2.67
6.	Playing games (including computer)	2.29
7.	Research, homework	1.94
8.	Socializing and communicating	1.75
9.	Reading for personal interest	1.43
10.	Computer use for leisure (except games)	1.41
11.	Interior cleaning	1.40
12.	Telephone calls	1.29
13.	Shopping, except groceries, food, and gas	1.09
14.	Relaxing, thinking	0.97
15.	Grooming	0.95
16.	Eating and drinking	0.94
17.	Listening to or playing music (not radio)	0.92
18.	Household and personal email	0.91
19.	Caring for and helping children in other households	0.81
20.	Helping adults in other households	0.72
21.	Caring for and helping household children	0.69
22.	Animals and pets (not veterinary care)	0.60
23.	Food and drink preparation	0.58
24.	Travel related to education	0.51
25.	Travel related to shopping (except groceries, food, and gas)	0.47
26.	Travel related to sports, exercise, and recreation	0.44
27.	Travel related to work	0.44
28.	Travel related to eating and drinking	0.43
29.	Travel related to socializing and communicating	0.42
30.	Travel related to helping adults in other households	0.42
31.	Household and personal organization and planning	0.38
32.	Travel related to household activities	0.38
33.	Travel related to caring for and helping children in other households	0.38
34.	Travel related to relaxing and leisure	0.32
35.	Travel related to purchasing food (except groceries)	0.29
36.	Purchasing food (except groceries)	0.16

Note: Primary activities are those respondents identified as their main activity. Other activities done simultaneously, such as eating while watching TV, are not included. The primary activities shown are those for which data by age are available.
Source: Bureau of Labor Statistics, unpublished tables from the 2008 American Time Use Survey, Internet site http://www.bls .gov/tus/home.htm; calculations by New Strategist

Table 2.19 Ranking: Average Hours per Day Spent Doing Primary Activities by Male Participants Aged 15 to 19, 2008

(hours per day spent by male participants aged 15 to 19 doing primary activities, ranked by time spent doing activity, 2008)

		average hours per day spent by male participants aged 15 to 19
	Total, all activities	**24.00**
1.	Sleeping	9.64
2.	Work, main job	6.11
3.	Taking class	6.03
4.	Television	2.98
5.	Playing games (including computer)	2.57
6.	Research, homework	1.73
7.	Socializing and communicating	1.70
8.	Computer use for leisure (except games)	1.26
9.	Telephone calls	0.99
10.	Eating and drinking	0.98
11.	Shopping, except groceries, food, and gas	0.84
12.	Grooming	0.75
13.	Travel related to shopping (except groceries, food, and gas)	0.52
14.	Travel related to education	0.50
15.	Travel related to eating and drinking	0.47
16.	Food and drink preparation	0.44
17.	Travel related to work	0.44
18.	Travel related to sports, exercise, and recreation	0.43
19.	Travel related to socializing and communicating	0.36
20.	Travel related to relaxing and leisure	0.36
21.	Household and personal organization and planning	0.36
22.	Purchasing food (except groceries)	0.13

Note: Primary activities are those respondents identified as their main activity. Other activities done simultaneously, such as eating while watching TV, are not included. The primary activities shown are those for which data by age are available.
Source: Bureau of Labor Statistics, unpublished tables from the 2008 American Time Use Survey, Internet site http://www.bls .gov/tus/home.htm; calculations by New Strategist

Table 2.20 Ranking: Average Hours per Day Spent Doing Primary Activities by Female Participants Aged 15 to 19, 2008

(hours per day spent by female participants aged 15 to 19 doing primary activities, ranked by time spent doing activity, 2008)

		average hours per day spent by female participants aged 15 to 19
	Total, all activities	24.00
1.	Sleeping	9.46
2.	Taking class	6.02
3.	Work, main job	5.40
4.	Television	2.82
5.	Research, homework	2.10
6.	Socializing and communicating	1.81
7.	Interior cleaning	1.58
8.	Computer use for leisure (except games)	1.56
9.	Telephone calls	1.51
10.	Shopping, except groceries, food, and gas	1.25
11.	Grooming	1.15
12.	Household and personal email	0.97
13.	Eating and drinking	0.90
14.	Food and drink preparation	0.70
15.	Travel related to education	0.52
16.	Travel related to socializing and communicating	0.48
17.	Travel related to work	0.45
18.	Travel related to shopping (except groceries, food, and gas)	0.43
19.	Household and personal organization and planning	0.40
20.	Travel related to eating and drinking	0.37
21.	Travel related to purchasing food (except groceries)	0.32
22.	Travel related to relaxing and leisure	0.29
23.	Purchasing food (except groceries)	0.19

Note: Primary activities are those respondents identified as their main activity. Other activities done simultaneously, such as eating while watching TV, are not included. The primary activities shown are those for which data by age are available.
Source: Bureau of Labor Statistics, unpublished tables from the 2008 American Time Use Survey, Internet site http://www.bls .gov/tus/home.htm; calculations by New Strategist

Time Use, 2008: People Aged 20 to 24

The lifestyles of young adults are diverse. Many have shouldered the responsibilities of a home, a job, and a family, while others are still in school and not yet living on their own. This split in priorities distinguishes the time use of people aged 20 to 24 from that of younger and older people.

For the average 20-to-24-year-old, work is a top priority. Among all 20-to-24-year-olds, work at a main job ranks first in time use on an average day (excluding sleep). Caring for and helping household children has entered the top-ten list, ranking eighth. But taking class and doing homework appear in the top ten list because many in the age group are still in school. And, not surprisingly, socializing and communicating are among the top ten activities of young adults.

Fifty-one percent of 20-to-24-year-olds work at a main job on an average day (these data include both weekdays and weekends). Twenty percent care for household children. Eleven percent go to class and 18 percent do homework. This age group is least likely to talk on the phone with family members as a primary activity. Only 2 percent do so on an average day. They are simply too busy juggling all the other aspects of their lives to spend much time talking to mom and dad.

People aged 20 to 24 are computer-savvy, but cannot spend as much time on the computer as 15-to-19-year-olds. Nine percent of 20-to-24-year-olds use a computer for leisure as a primary activity on an average day (not including playing games), far below the 22 percent among 15-to-19-

Work is a top priority for 20-to-24-year-olds

(average hours per day spent by people aged 20 to 24 doing primary activities, for the 10 activities on which the average 20-to-24-year-old spends the most time, excluding sleep, 2008)

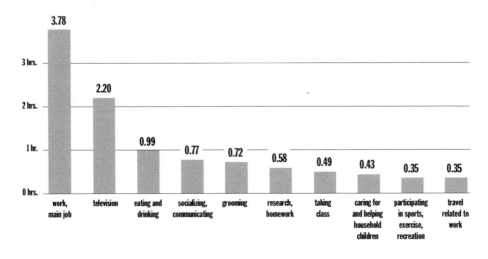

year-olds. Thirteen percent of 20-to-24-year-olds play games (mostly computer games) as a primary activity on an average day, less than the 21 percent among 15-to-19-year-olds. Playing games ranks 11th in average time use among 20-to-24-year-olds (excluding sleep), lower than its ninth place ranking among 15-to-19-year-olds. Among men in the age group, however, playing games ranks sixth in average time use.

There are sharp differences in time use between men and women in the 20-to-24 age group. Women spend much more time than men doing household chores such as cooking, cleaning, and laundry. Women spend much more time than men caring for household children. Women also spend more time shopping. Men spend more time working than women, and they spend more time participating in sports, watching television, and working on vehicles.

Table 3.1 Time Use by Total People Aged 20 to 24, 2008

(number and percent of people aged 20 to 24 participating in primary activities on an average day, hours spent doing an activity by the average 20-to-24-year-old and by 20-to-24-year-olds who participated in the activity, 2008; numbers of participants in thousands)

	participants aged 20 to 24		time spent doing activity (hours)	
	number	percent	average person aged 20 to 24	participants aged 20 to 24
TOTAL, ALL ACTIVITIES	**20,409**	**100.0%**	**24.00**	**24.00**
Personal care	**20,402**	**100.0**	**9.61**	**9.62**
Sleeping	20,402	100.0	8.84	8.84
Sleeplessness	887	4.3	0.04	–
Grooming	16,386	80.3	0.72	0.89
Health-related self-care	491	2.4	0.02	–
Household activities	**12,445**	**61.0**	**1.05**	**1.73**
Housework	4,702	23.0	0.36	1.58
Interior cleaning	3,228	15.8	0.25	1.61
Laundry	1,867	9.1	0.11	–
Storing interior household items, including food	427	2.1	0.00	–
Food and drink preparation, presentation, and clean-up	7,133	35.0	0.29	0.83
Food and drink preparation	6,771	33.2	0.25	0.76
Kitchen and food clean-up	1,373	6.7	0.03	–
Interior maintenance, repair, and decoration	398	2.0	0.05	–
Interior arrangement, decoration, and repairs	314	1.5	0.05	–
Exterior maintenance, repair, and decoration	64	0.3	0.00	–
Lawn, garden, and houseplants	591	2.9	0.07	–
Animals and pets (not veterinary care)	2,530	12.4	0.09	–
Walking, exercising, and playing with pets	1,149	5.6	0.06	–
Vehicles	593	2.9	0.04	–
Household management	4,882	23.9	0.14	0.59
Financial management	863	4.2	0.01	–
Household and personal organization and planning	2,179	10.7	0.08	–
Household and personal mail and messages (except email)	243	1.2	0.00	–
Household and personal email	1,941	9.5	0.05	–
Caring for and helping household members	**4,719**	**23.1**	**0.48**	**2.07**
Caring for and helping household children	4,096	20.1	0.43	2.13
Physical care for household children	3,520	17.2	0.24	1.37
Reading to or with household children	257	1.3	0.01	–
Playing with household children (except sports)	1,448	7.1	0.11	–
Talking with, listening to household children	5	0.0	0.00	–
Looking after household children as a primary activity	512	2.5	0.05	–
Picking up or dropping off household children	870	4.3	0.01	–
Activities related to household children's education	228	1.1	0.01	–
Helping household children with homework	228	1.1	0.01	–
Helping household adults	812	4.0	0.01	–
Caring for and helping people in other households	**3,358**	**16.5**	**0.17**	**1.02**
Caring for and helping children in other households	983	4.8	0.05	–

	participants aged 20 to 24		time spent doing activity (hours)	
	number	percent	average person aged 20 to 24	participants aged 20 to 24
Helping adults in other households	2,511	12.3%	0.09	0.77
Picking up or dropping off adults in other households	1,728	8.5	0.01	—
Work and work-related activities	**11,226**	**55.0**	**4.01**	**7.29**
Work, main job	10,390	50.9	3.78	7.43
Work, other job(s)	612	3.0	0.14	—
Education	**4,028**	**19.7**	**1.11**	**5.60**
Taking class	2,238	11.0	0.49	—
Taking class for degree, certification, or licensure	2,238	11.0	0.48	—
Research, homework	3,611	17.7	0.58	3.30
Consumer purchases (store, telephone, Internet)	**8,170**	**40.0**	**0.40**	**0.99**
Grocery shopping	1,884	9.2	0.07	—
Purchasing gas	714	3.5	0.01	—
Purchasing food (except groceries)	3,208	15.7	0.02	0.16
Shopping, except groceries, food, and gas	4,984	24.4	0.30	1.21
Professional and personal care services	**1,483**	**7.3**	**0.04**	**—**
Financial services and banking	885	4.3	0.01	—
Banking	822	4.0	0.01	—
Medical and care services	273	1.3	0.01	—
Using health and care services outside the home	243	1.2	0.01	—
Household services	**374**	**1.8**	**0.01**	**—**
Eating and drinking	**19,242**	**94.3**	**0.99**	**1.05**
Socializing, relaxing, and leisure	**19,154**	**93.9**	**4.03**	**4.29**
Socializing and communicating	7,453	36.5	0.77	2.12
Attending or hosting social events	494	2.4	0.10	—
Relaxing and leisure	17,873	87.6	3.04	3.47
Relaxing, thinking	3,669	18.0	0.18	1.02
Television	15,625	76.6	2.20	2.87
Listening to the radio	432	2.1	0.01	—
Listening to or playing music (not radio)	844	4.1	0.06	—
Playing games (including computer)	2,644	13.0	0.34	—
Computer use for leisure (except games)	1,789	8.8	0.10	—
Reading for personal interest	2,551	12.5	0.13	—
Arts and entertainment (except sports)	794	3.9	0.11	—
Sports, exercise, and recreation	**4,038**	**19.8**	**0.40**	**2.02**
Participating in sports, exercise, or recreation	3,744	18.3	0.35	1.90
Using cardiovascular equipment	264	1.3	0.01	—
Walking	489	2.4	0.03	—
Working out, unspecified	890	4.4	0.05	—
Religious and spiritual activities	**643**	**3.2**	**0.06**	**—**
Attending religious services	347	1.7	0.03	—
Participation in religious practices	319	1.6	0.02	—

	participants aged 20 to 24		time spent doing activity (hours)	
	number	percent	average person aged 20 to 24	participants aged 20 to 24
Volunteer activities	**547**	**2.7%**	**0.04**	–
Administrative and support activities	229	1.1	0.01	–
Telephone calls	**3,071**	**15.0**	**0.17**	**1.16**
Telephone calls to or from family members	456	2.2	0.01	–
Telephone calls to or from friends, neighbors, or acquaintances	1,745	8.6	0.07	–
Traveling	**19,249**	**94.3**	**1.32**	**1.40**
Travel related to personal care	980	4.8	0.02	–
Travel related to household activities	2,391	11.7	0.05	0.42
Travel related to household management	1,454	7.1	0.02	–
Travel related to caring for and helping household members	2,038	10.0	0.05	0.53
Travel related to caring for and helping household children	1,389	6.8	0.04	–
Travel related to helping household adults	687	3.4	0.01	–
Travel related to caring for and helping people in other households	2,774	13.6	0.08	0.55
Travel related to caring for and helping children in other households	713	3.5	0.01	–
Travel related to helping adults in other households	2,212	10.8	0.05	–
Travel related to work	10,244	50.2	0.35	0.70
Travel related to education	2,592	12.7	0.11	–
Travel related to taking class	2,175	10.7	0.09	–
Travel related to consumer purchases	7,982	39.1	0.23	0.59
Travel related to grocery shopping	1,867	9.1	0.04	–
Travel related to purchasing gas	714	3.5	0.01	–
Travel related to purchasing food (except groceries)	2,857	14.0	0.06	0.43
Travel related to shopping (except groceries, food, and gas)	4,834	23.7	0.11	0.48
Travel related to using professional and personal care services	1,304	6.4	0.02	–
Travel related to using financial services and banking	885	4.3	0.01	–
Travel related to using medical services	200	1.0	0.01	–
Travel related to eating and drinking	5,800	28.4	0.11	0.39
Travel related to socializing, relaxing, and leisure	7,346	36.0	0.21	0.59
Travel related to socializing and communicating	4,125	20.2	0.11	0.55
Travel related to attending or hosting social events	506	2.5	0.01	–
Travel related to relaxing and leisure	3,477	17.0	0.07	0.43
Travel related to arts and entertainment	658	3.2	0.02	–
Travel related to sports, exercise, and recreation	2,920	14.3	0.06	0.43
Travel related to participating in sports, exercise, recreation	2,637	12.9	0.05	–
Travel related to religious and spiritual activities	461	2.3	0.01	–
Travel related to volunteer activities	373	1.8	0.00	–

Note: Primary activities are those respondents identified as their main activity. Other activities done simultaneously, such as eating while watching TV, are not included. Numbers may not add to total because not all subcategories are shown. If fewer than 2.0 percent of the total population participated in a primary activity, then the primary activity is not shown. "–" means sample is too small to make a reliable estimate.
Source: Bureau of Labor Statistics, unpublished tables from the 2008 American Time Use Survey, Internet site http://www.bls.gov/tus/home.htm; calculations by New Strategist

Table 3.2 Time Use by Men Aged 20 to 24, 2008

(number and percent of men aged 20 to 24 participating in primary activities on an average day, hours spent doing activity by the average 20-to-24-year-old man and by 20-to-24-year-old men who participated in the activity, 2008; numbers of participants in thousands)

	men aged 20 to 24 participating		time spent doing activity (hours)	
	number	percent	average man aged 20 to 24	male participants aged 20 to 24
TOTAL, ALL ACTIVITIES	**10,290**	**100.0%**	**24.00**	**24.00**
Personal care	**10,290**	**100.0**	**9.57**	**9.57**
Sleeping	10,290	100.0	8.89	8.89
Sleeplessness	666	6.5	0.05	–
Grooming	8,334	81.0	0.59	0.73
Health-related self-care	221	2.1	0.01	–
Household activities	**5,196**	**50.5**	**0.86**	**1.71**
Housework	1,342	13.0	0.20	–
Interior cleaning	715	6.9	0.14	–
Laundry	729	7.1	0.06	–
Storing interior household items, including food	189	1.8	0.01	–
Food and drink preparation, presentation, and clean-up	2,788	27.1	0.19	0.70
Food and drink preparation	2,726	26.5	0.18	0.66
Kitchen and food clean-up	297	2.9	0.01	–
Interior maintenance, repair, and decoration	204	2.0	0.08	–
Interior arrangement, decoration, and repairs	183	1.8	0.07	–
Exterior maintenance, repair, and decoration	46	0.4	0.00	–
Lawn, garden, and houseplants	414	4.0	0.13	–
Animals and pets (not veterinary care)	1,515	14.7	0.13	–
Walking, exercising, and playing with pets	787	7.6	0.10	–
Vehicles	466	4.5	0.06	–
Household management	1,848	18.0	0.07	–
Financial management	420	4.1	0.01	–
Household and personal organization and planning	710	6.9	0.02	–
Household and personal mail and messages (except email)	153	1.5	0.00	–
Household and personal email	641	6.2	0.03	–
Caring for and helping household members	**1,193**	**11.6**	**0.17**	**–**
Caring for and helping household children	858	8.3	0.14	–
Physical care for household children	619	6.0	0.07	–
Reading to or with household children	76	0.7	0.00	–
Playing with household children (except sports)	443	4.3	0.05	–
Talking with, listening to household children	0	0.0	0.00	–
Looking after household children as a primary activity	33	0.3	0.01	–
Picking up or dropping off household children	234	2.3	0.01	–
Activities related to household children's education	0	0.0	0.00	–
Helping household children with homework	0	0.0	0.00	–
Helping household adults	287	2.8	0.01	–
Caring for and helping people in other households	**1,397**	**13.6**	**0.12**	**–**
Caring for and helping children in other households	264	2.6	0.03	–

	men aged 20 to 24 participating		time spent doing activity (hours)	
	number	percent	average man aged 20 to 24	male participants aged 20 to 24
Helping adults in other households	1,077	10.5%	0.06	–
Picking up or dropping off adults in other households	815	7.9	0.01	–
Work and work-related activities	**6,553**	**63.7**	**4.86**	**7.63**
Work, main job	6,106	59.3	4.69	7.90
Work, other job(s)	221	2.1	0.11	–
Education	**1,174**	**11.4**	**0.56**	–
Taking class	785	7.6	0.26	–
Taking class for degree, certification, or licensure	785	7.6	0.26	–
Research, homework	937	9.1	0.28	–
Consumer purchases (store, telephone, Internet)	**2,977**	**28.9**	**0.22**	**0.77**
Grocery shopping	848	8.2	0.06	–
Purchasing gas	264	2.6	0.00	–
Purchasing food (except groceries)	1,513	14.7	0.02	–
Shopping, except groceries, food, and gas	1,257	12.2	0.13	–
Professional and personal care services	**695**	**6.8**	**0.03**	–
Financial services and banking	568	5.5	0.02	–
Banking	505	4.9	0.01	–
Medical and care services	30	0.3	0.00	–
Using health and care services outside the home	0	0.0	0.00	–
Household services	**155**	**1.5**	**0.02**	–
Eating and drinking	**9,735**	**94.6**	**0.94**	**1.02**
Socializing, relaxing, and leisure	**9,752**	**94.8**	**4.54**	**4.79**
Socializing and communicating	3,690	35.9	0.82	2.29
Attending or hosting social events	241	2.3	0.13	–
Relaxing and leisure	9,364	91.0	3.47	3.82
Relaxing, thinking	1,920	18.7	0.14	–
Television	8,112	78.8	2.41	3.05
Listening to the radio	432	4.2	0.02	–
Listening to or playing music (not radio)	634	6.2	0.10	–
Playing games (including computer)	1,875	18.2	0.57	–
Computer use for leisure (except games)	883	8.6	0.11	–
Reading for personal interest	1,467	14.3	0.10	–
Arts and entertainment (except sports)	370	3.6	0.12	–
Sports, exercise, and recreation	**2,362**	**23.0**	**0.50**	–
Participating in sports, exercise, or recreation	2,244	21.8	0.44	–
Using cardiovascular equipment	69	0.7	0.00	–
Walking	206	2.0	0.02	–
Working out, unspecified	660	6.4	0.08	–
Religious and spiritual activities	**397**	**3.9**	**0.05**	–
Attending religious services	132	1.3	0.02	–
Participation in religious practices	239	2.3	0.02	–

	men aged 20 to 24 participating		time spent doing activity (hours)	
	number	percent	average man aged 20 to 24	male participants aged 20 to 24
Volunteer activities	**261**	**2.5%**	**0.03**	–
Administrative and support activities	34	0.3	0.00	–
Telephone calls	**1,376**	**13.4**	**0.12**	–
Telephone calls to or from family members	141	1.4	0.01	–
Telephone calls to or from friends, neighbors, or acquaintances	848	8.2	0.05	–
Traveling	**9,679**	**94.1**	**1.27**	**1.35**
Travel related to personal care	483	4.7	0.01	–
Travel related to household activities	839	8.2	0.03	–
Travel related to household management	577	5.6	0.02	–
Travel related to caring for and helping household members	494	4.8	0.02	–
Travel related to caring for and helping household children	253	2.5	0.02	–
Travel related to helping household adults	196	1.9	0.00	–
Travel related to caring for and helping people in other households	1,347	13.1	0.07	–
Travel related to caring for and helping children in other households	264	2.6	0.01	–
Travel related to helping adults in other households	1,043	10.1	0.05	–
Travel related to work	6,185	60.1	0.45	0.75
Travel related to education	920	8.9	0.08	–
Travel related to taking class	803	7.8	0.06	–
Travel related to consumer purchases	2,876	27.9	0.17	0.62
Travel related to grocery shopping	831	8.1	0.05	–
Travel related to purchasing gas	264	2.6	0.01	–
Travel related to purchasing food (except groceries)	1,431	13.9	0.06	–
Travel related to shopping (except groceries, food, and gas)	1,237	12.0	0.06	–
Travel related to using professional and personal care services	663	6.4	0.01	–
Travel related to using financial services and banking	568	5.5	0.01	–
Travel related to using medical services	19	0.2	0.00	–
Travel related to eating and drinking	2,972	28.9	0.12	0.40
Travel related to socializing, relaxing, and leisure	3,550	34.5	0.19	0.53
Travel related to socializing and communicating	1,739	16.9	0.09	–
Travel related to attending or hosting social events	253	2.5	0.01	–
Travel related to relaxing and leisure	1,964	19.1	0.07	–
Travel related to arts and entertainment	309	3.0	0.02	–
Travel related to sports, exercise, and recreation	1,789	17.4	0.06	–
Travel related to participating in sports, exercise, recreation	1,671	16.2	0.05	–
Travel related to religious and spiritual activities	296	2.9	0.01	–
Travel related to volunteer activities	150	1.5	0.00	–

Note: Primary activities are those respondents identified as their main activity. Other activities done simultaneously, such as eating while watching TV, are not included. Numbers may not add to total because not all subcategories are shown. If fewer than 2.0 percent of the total population participated in a primary activity, then the primary activity is not shown. "–" means sample is too small to make a reliable estimate.
Source: Bureau of Labor Statistics, unpublished tables from the 2008 American Time Use Survey, Internet site http://www.bls .gov/tus/home.htm; calculations by New Strategist

Table 3.3 Time Use by Women Aged 20 to 24, 2008

(number and percent of women aged 20 to 24 participating in primary activities on an average day, hours spent doing activity by the average 20-to-24-year-old woman and by 20-to-24-year-old women who participated in the activity, 2008; numbers of participants in thousands)

	women aged 20 to 24 participating		time spent doing activity (hours)	
	number	percent	average woman aged 20 to 24	female participants aged 20 to 24
TOTAL, ALL ACTIVITIES	**10,119**	**100.0%**	**24.00**	**24.00**
Personal care	**10,113**	**99.9**	**9.65**	**9.66**
Sleeping	10,113	99.9	8.78	8.79
Sleeplessness	221	2.2	0.03	–
Grooming	8,052	79.6	0.85	1.07
Health-related self-care	270	2.7	0.02	–
Household activities	**7,249**	**71.6**	**1.25**	**1.74**
Housework	3,359	33.2	0.53	1.59
Interior cleaning	2,513	24.8	0.39	1.48
Laundry	1,138	11.2	0.15	–
Storing interior household items, including food	238	2.4	0.00	–
Food and drink preparation, presentation, and clean-up	4,345	42.9	0.39	0.91
Food and drink preparation	4,045	40.0	0.33	0.83
Kitchen and food clean-up	1,076	10.6	0.06	–
Interior maintenance, repair, and decoration	194	1.9	0.02	–
Interior arrangement, decoration, and repairs	132	1.3	0.02	–
Exterior maintenance, repair, and decoration	18	0.2	0.00	–
Lawn, garden, and houseplants	177	1.7	0.00	–
Animals and pets (not veterinary care)	1,015	10.0	0.05	–
Walking, exercising, and playing with pets	363	3.6	0.02	–
Vehicles	126	1.2	0.01	–
Household management	3,034	30.0	0.22	0.73
Financial management	443	4.4	0.01	–
Household and personal organization and planning	1,469	14.5	0.14	–
Household and personal mail and messages (except email)	89	0.9	0.00	–
Household and personal email	1,300	12.8	0.07	–
Caring for and helping household members	**3,526**	**34.8**	**0.80**	**2.29**
Caring for and helping household children	3,238	32.0	0.72	2.24
Physical care for household children	2,901	28.7	0.41	1.43
Reading to or with household children	181	1.8	0.01	–
Playing with household children (except sports)	1,005	9.9	0.17	–
Talking with, listening to household children	5	0.0	0.00	–
Looking after household children as a primary activity	478	4.7	0.08	–
Picking up or dropping off household children	637	6.3	0.02	–
Activities related to household children's education	228	2.3	0.01	–
Helping household children with homework	228	2.3	0.01	–
Helping household adults	524	5.2	0.01	–
Caring for and helping people in other households	**1,961**	**19.4**	**0.22**	**–**
Caring for and helping children in other households	719	7.1	0.07	–

	women aged 20 to 24 participating		time spent doing activity (hours)	
	number	percent	average woman aged 20 to 24	female participants aged 20 to 24
Helping adults in other households	1,434	14.2%	0.13	–
Picking up or dropping off adults in other households	913	9.0	0.01	–
Work and work-related activities	**4,673**	**46.2**	**3.14**	**6.81**
Work, main job	4,284	42.3	2.86	6.75
Work, other job(s)	391	3.9	0.16	–
Education	**2,854**	**28.2**	**1.66**	**–**
Taking class	1,453	14.4	0.71	–
Taking class for degree, certification, or licensure	1,453	14.4	0.71	–
Research, homework	2,675	26.4	0.89	–
Consumer purchases (store, telephone, Internet)	**5,193**	**51.3**	**0.58**	**1.13**
Grocery shopping	1,036	10.2	0.08	–
Purchasing gas	449	4.4	0.01	–
Purchasing food (except groceries)	1,695	16.8	0.03	–
Shopping, except groceries, food, and gas	3,727	36.8	0.46	1.26
Professional and personal care services	**788**	**7.8**	**0.04**	**–**
Financial services and banking	317	3.1	0.00	–
Banking	317	3.1	0.00	–
Medical and care services	243	2.4	0.02	–
Using health and care services outside the home	243	2.4	0.01	–
Household services	**219**	**2.2**	**0.01**	**–**
Eating and drinking	**9,508**	**94.0**	**1.02**	**1.09**
Socializing, relaxing, and leisure	**9,403**	**92.9**	**3.51**	**3.77**
Socializing and communicating	3,763	37.2	0.73	1.96
Attending or hosting social events	253	2.5	0.08	–
Relaxing and leisure	8,509	84.1	2.60	3.09
Relaxing, thinking	1,748	17.3	0.22	–
Television	7,513	74.2	1.99	2.68
Listening to the radio	0	0.0	0.00	–
Listening to or playing music (not radio)	209	2.1	0.01	–
Playing games (including computer)	769	7.6	0.12	–
Computer use for leisure (except games)	907	9.0	0.08	–
Reading for personal interest	1,084	10.7	0.15	–
Arts and entertainment (except sports)	424	4.2	0.10	–
Sports, exercise, and recreation	**1,676**	**16.6**	**0.29**	**–**
Participating in sports, exercise, or recreation	1,500	14.8	0.26	–
Using cardiovascular equipment	195	1.9	0.01	–
Walking	283	2.8	0.04	–
Working out, unspecified	230	2.3	0.03	–
Religious and spiritual activities	**246**	**2.4**	**0.06**	**–**
Attending religious services	215	2.1	0.04	–
Participation in religious practices	80	0.8	0.02	–

	women aged 20 to 24 participating		time spent doing activity (hours)	
	number	percent	average woman aged 20 to 24	female participants aged 20 to 24
Volunteer activities	**286**	**2.8%**	**0.04**	–
Administrative and support activities	195	1.9	0.01	–
Telephone calls	**1,694**	**16.7**	**0.23**	–
Telephone calls to or from family members	315	3.1	0.01	–
Telephone calls to or from friends, neighbors, or acquaintances	897	8.9	0.08	–
Traveling	**9,570**	**94.6**	**1.38**	**1.46**
Travel related to personal care	496	4.9	0.02	–
Travel related to household activities	1,552	15.3	0.07	–
Travel related to household management	876	8.7	0.02	–
Travel related to caring for and helping household members	1,544	15.3	0.08	–
Travel related to caring for and helping household children	1,136	11.2	0.06	–
Travel related to helping household adults	491	4.9	0.02	–
Travel related to caring for and helping people in other households	1,427	14.1	0.08	–
Travel related to caring for and helping children in other households	450	4.4	0.02	–
Travel related to helping adults in other households	1,170	11.6	0.06	–
Travel related to work	4,059	40.1	0.25	0.62
Travel related to education	1,672	16.5	0.13	–
Travel related to taking class	1,373	13.6	0.11	–
Travel related to consumer purchases	5,106	50.5	0.29	0.57
Travel related to grocery shopping	1,036	10.2	0.04	–
Travel related to purchasing gas	449	4.4	0.02	–
Travel related to purchasing food (except groceries)	1,426	14.1	0.07	–
Travel related to shopping (except groceries, food, and gas)	3,597	35.5	0.16	0.46
Travel related to using professional and personal care services	641	6.3	0.03	–
Travel related to using financial services and banking	317	3.1	0.01	–
Travel related to using medical services	181	1.8	0.01	–
Travel related to eating and drinking	2,827	27.9	0.11	0.38
Travel related to socializing, relaxing, and leisure	3,796	37.5	0.23	0.63
Travel related to socializing and communicating	2,386	23.6	0.13	0.55
Travel related to attending or hosting social events	253	2.5	0.01	–
Travel related to relaxing and leisure	1,513	15.0	0.08	–
Travel related to arts and entertainment	349	3.4	0.02	–
Travel related to sports, exercise, and recreation	1,131	11.2	0.06	–
Travel related to participating in sports, exercise, recreation	966	9.5	0.05	–
Travel related to religious and spiritual activities	165	1.6	0.01	–
Travel related to volunteer activities	223	2.2	0.00	–

Note: Primary activities are those respondents identified as their main activity. Other activities done simultaneously, such as eating while watching TV, are not included. Numbers may not add to total because not all subcategories are shown. If fewer than 2.0 percent of the total population participated in a primary activity, then the primary activity is not shown. "–" means sample is too small to make a reliable estimate.
Source: Bureau of Labor Statistics, unpublished tables from the 2008 American Time Use Survey, Internet site http://www.bls .gov/tus/home.htm; calculations by New Strategist

Table 3.4 Indexed Time Use of Total People Aged 20 to 24, 2008

(hours spent doing primary activities on an average day by people aged 20 to 24 and by total people aged 15 or older, and index of time spent by 20-to-24-year-olds to total people, 2008)

	average hours		index, people aged 20 to 24 to total people
	people aged 20 to 24	total people	
TOTAL, ALL ACTIVITIES	**24.00**	**24.00**	**100**
Personal care	**10.35**	**9.38**	**110**
Sleeping	9.55	8.60	111
Sleeplessness	0.04	0.06	67
Grooming	0.78	0.67	116
Health-related self-care	0.01	0.09	11
Household activities	**0.74**	**1.77**	**42**
Housework	0.28	0.58	48
Interior cleaning	0.23	0.37	62
Laundry	0.04	0.17	24
Storing interior household items, including food	0.00	0.02	0
Food and drink preparation, presentation, and clean-up	0.13	0.52	25
Food and drink preparation	0.10	0.40	25
Kitchen and food clean-up	0.03	0.12	25
Interior maintenance, repair, and decoration	0.01	0.07	14
Interior arrangement, decoration, and repairs	0.01	0.05	20
Exterior maintenance, repair, and decoration	0.02	0.06	33
Lawn, garden, and houseplants	0.03	0.19	16
Animals and pets (not veterinary care)	0.05	0.09	56
Walking, exercising, and playing with pets	0.02	0.04	50
Vehicles	0.05	0.04	125
Household management	0.17	0.21	81
Financial management	0.00	0.03	0
Household and personal organization and planning	0.06	0.09	67
Household and personal mail and messages (except email)	0.00	0.02	0
Household and personal email	0.10	0.06	167
Caring for and helping household members	**0.09**	**0.45**	**20**
Caring for and helping household children	0.07	0.37	19
Physical care for household children	0.02	0.17	12
Reading to or with household children	0.00	0.01	0
Playing with household children (except sports)	0.02	0.09	22
Talking with, listening to household children	0.01	0.02	50
Looking after household children as a primary activity	0.01	0.03	33
Picking up or dropping off household children	0.01	0.02	50
Activities related to household children's education	0.00	0.04	0
Helping household children with homework	0.00	0.03	0
Helping household adults	0.01	0.01	100
Caring for and helping people in other households	**0.15**	**0.16**	**94**
Caring for and helping children in other households	0.08	0.09	89

	average hours		index, people aged 20 to 24 to total people
	people aged 20 to 24	total people	
Helping adults in other households	0.07	0.06	117
Picking up or dropping off adults in other households	0.01	0.01	100
Work and work-related activities	**1.28**	**3.45**	**37**
Work, main job	1.14	3.28	35
Work, other job(s)	0.02	0.09	22
Education	**2.92**	**0.44**	**664**
Taking class	2.22	0.27	822
Taking class for degree, certification, or licensure	2.20	0.26	846
Research, homework	0.62	0.16	388
Consumer purchases (store, telephone, Internet)	**0.30**	**0.38**	**79**
Grocery shopping	0.04	0.10	40
Purchasing gas	0.00	0.01	0
Purchasing food (except groceries)	0.02	0.02	100
Shopping, except groceries, food, and gas	0.22	0.25	88
Professional and personal care services	**0.05**	**0.08**	**63**
Financial services and banking	0.00	0.01	0
Banking	0.00	0.01	0
Medical and care services	0.02	0.05	40
Using health and care services outside the home	0.01	0.04	25
Household services	**0.00**	**0.01**	**0**
Eating and drinking	**0.90**	**1.11**	**81**
Socializing, relaxing, and leisure	**4.53**	**4.62**	**98**
Socializing and communicating	0.86	0.64	134
Attending or hosting social events	0.07	0.07	100
Relaxing and leisure	3.44	3.83	90
Relaxing, thinking	0.14	0.27	52
Television	2.16	2.77	78
Listening to the radio	0.03	0.03	100
Listening to or playing music (not radio)	0.10	0.03	333
Playing games (including computer)	0.48	0.20	240
Computer use for leisure (except games)	0.31	0.14	221
Reading for personal interest	0.17	0.34	50
Arts and entertainment (except sports)	0.16	0.09	178
Sports, exercise, and recreation	**0.80**	**0.33**	**242**
Participating in sports, exercise, or recreation	0.70	0.29	241
Using cardiovascular equipment	0.01	0.02	50
Walking	0.02	0.04	50
Working out, unspecified	0.02	0.03	67
Religious and spiritual activities	**0.10**	**0.14**	**71**
Attending religious services	0.06	0.09	67
Participation in religious practices	0.02	0.04	50

	average hours		index, people aged 20 to 24
	people aged 20 to 24	total people	to total people
Volunteer activities	**0.14**	**0.15**	**93**
Administrative and support activities	0.01	0.04	25
Telephone calls	**0.27**	**0.13**	**208**
Telephone calls to or from family members	0.02	0.04	50
Telephone calls to or from friends, neighbors, or acquaintances	0.16	0.04	400
Traveling	**1.16**	**1.20**	**97**
Travel related to personal care	0.02	0.01	200
Travel related to household activities	0.03	0.04	75
Travel related to household management	0.02	0.02	100
Travel related to caring for and helping household members	0.03	0.08	38
Travel related to caring for and helping household children	0.02	0.06	33
Travel related to helping household adults	0.01	0.02	50
Travel related to caring for and helping people in other households	0.07	0.06	117
Travel related to caring for and helping children in other households	0.03	0.02	150
Travel related to helping adults in other households	0.04	0.04	100
Travel related to work	0.09	0.28	32
Travel related to education	0.17	0.03	567
Travel related to taking class	0.14	0.03	467
Travel related to consumer purchases	0.19	0.24	79
Travel related to grocery shopping	0.02	0.05	40
Travel related to purchasing gas	0.03	0.02	150
Travel related to purchasing food (except groceries)	0.04	0.04	100
Travel related to shopping (except groceries, food, and gas)	0.09	0.12	75
Travel related to using professional and personal care services	0.02	0.04	50
Travel related to using financial services and banking	0.00	0.01	0
Travel related to using medical services	0.01	0.02	50
Travel related to eating and drinking	0.11	0.12	92
Travel related to socializing, relaxing, and leisure	0.27	0.18	150
Travel related to socializing and communicating	0.12	0.09	133
Travel related to attending or hosting social events	0.01	0.01	100
Travel related to relaxing and leisure	0.06	0.04	150
Travel related to arts and entertainment	0.04	0.02	200
Travel related to sports, exercise, and recreation	0.09	0.04	225
Travel related to participating in sports, exercise, recreation	0.07	0.04	175
Travel related to religious and spiritual activities	0.02	0.02	100
Travel related to volunteer activities	0.02	0.02	100

Note: The index is calculated by dividing average time spent by people in the age group doing primary activity by average time spent by total people doing primary activity and multiplying by 100. Primary activities are those respondents identified as their main activity. Other activities done simultaneously, such as eating while watching TV, are not included. Numbers may not add to total because not all subcategories are shown. If fewer than 2.0 percent of the total population participated in a primary activity, then the primary activity is not shown.
Source: Bureau of Labor Statistics, unpublished tables from the 2008 American Time Use Survey, Internet site http://www.bls .gov/tus/home.htm; calculations by New Strategist

Table 3.5 Indexed Time Use of Men Aged 20 to 24, 2008

(hours spent doing primary activities on an average day by men aged 20 to 24 and by total men aged 15 or older, and index of time spent by 20-to-24-year-old men to total men, 2008)

	average hours		index, men aged 20 to 24 to total men
	men aged 20 to 24	total men	
TOTAL, ALL ACTIVITIES	**24.00**	**24.00**	**100**
Personal care	**9.57**	**9.21**	**104**
Sleeping	8.89	8.56	104
Sleeplessness	0.05	0.05	100
Grooming	0.59	0.56	105
Health-related self-care	0.01	0.07	14
Household activities	**0.86**	**1.32**	**65**
Housework	0.20	0.24	83
Interior cleaning	0.14	0.17	82
Laundry	0.06	0.06	100
Storing interior household items, including food	0.01	0.01	100
Food and drink preparation, presentation, and clean-up	0.19	0.30	63
Food and drink preparation	0.18	0.25	72
Kitchen and food clean-up	0.01	0.05	20
Interior maintenance, repair, and decoration	0.08	0.10	80
Interior arrangement, decoration, and repairs	0.07	0.08	88
Exterior maintenance, repair, and decoration	0.00	0.08	0
Lawn, garden, and houseplants	0.13	0.26	50
Animals and pets (not veterinary care)	0.13	0.08	163
Walking, exercising, and playing with pets	0.10	0.04	250
Vehicles	0.06	0.07	86
Household management	0.07	0.16	44
Financial management	0.01	0.03	33
Household and personal organization and planning	0.02	0.07	29
Household and personal mail and messages (except email)	0.00	0.02	0
Household and personal email	0.03	0.05	60
Caring for and helping household members	**0.17**	**0.30**	**57**
Caring for and helping household children	0.14	0.25	56
Physical care for household children	0.07	0.09	78
Reading to or with household children	0.00	0.01	0
Playing with household children (except sports)	0.05	0.08	63
Talking with, listening to household children	0.00	0.01	0
Looking after household children as a primary activity	0.01	0.02	50
Picking up or dropping off household children	0.01	0.01	100
Activities related to household children's education	0.00	0.02	0
Helping household children with homework	0.00	0.02	0
Helping household adults	0.01	0.01	100
Caring for and helping people in other households	**0.12**	**0.13**	**92**
Caring for and helping children in other households	0.03	0.05	60

	average hours		index, men aged 20 to 24
	men aged 20 to 24	total men	to total men
Helping adults in other households	0.06	0.07	86
Picking up or dropping off adults in other households	0.01	0.01	100
Work and work-related activities	**4.86**	**4.16**	**117**
Work, main job	4.69	3.96	118
Work, other job(s)	0.11	0.10	110
Education	**0.56**	**0.39**	**144**
Taking class	0.26	0.27	96
Taking class for degree, certification, or licensure	0.26	0.27	96
Research, homework	0.28	0.12	233
Consumer purchases (store, telephone, Internet)	**0.22**	**0.28**	**79**
Grocery shopping	0.06	0.06	100
Purchasing gas	0.00	0.01	0
Purchasing food (except groceries)	0.02	0.02	100
Shopping, except groceries, food, and gas	0.13	0.19	68
Professional and personal care services	**0.03**	**0.06**	**50**
Financial services and banking	0.02	0.01	200
Banking	0.01	0.00	–
Medical and care services	0.00	0.04	0
Using health and care services outside the home	0.00	0.03	0
Household services	**0.02**	**0.01**	**200**
Eating and drinking	**0.94**	**1.15**	**82**
Socializing, relaxing, and leisure	**4.54**	**4.83**	**94**
Socializing and communicating	0.82	0.59	139
Attending or hosting social events	0.13	0.06	217
Relaxing and leisure	3.47	4.09	85
Relaxing, thinking	0.14	0.27	52
Television	2.41	3.01	80
Listening to the radio	0.02	0.03	67
Listening to or playing music (not radio)	0.10	0.04	250
Playing games (including computer)	0.57	0.25	228
Computer use for leisure (except games)	0.11	0.15	73
Reading for personal interest	0.10	0.29	34
Arts and entertainment (except sports)	0.12	0.09	133
Sports, exercise, and recreation	**0.50**	**0.44**	**114**
Participating in sports, exercise, or recreation	0.44	0.40	110
Using cardiovascular equipment	0.00	0.01	
Walking	0.02	0.04	50
Working out, unspecified	0.08	0.04	200
Religious and spiritual activities	**0.05**	**0.12**	**42**
Attending religious services	0.02	0.07	29
Participation in religious practices	0.02	0.03	67

	average hours		index, men aged 20 to 24 to total men
	men aged 20 to 24	total men	
Volunteer activities	**0.03**	**0.14**	**21**
Administrative and support activities	0.00	0.03	0
Telephone calls	**0.12**	**0.07**	**171**
Telephone calls to or from family members	0.01	0.02	50
Telephone calls to or from friends, neighbors, or acquaintances	0.05	0.02	250
Traveling	**1.27**	**1.23**	**103**
Travel related to personal care	0.01	0.01	100
Travel related to household activities	0.03	0.04	75
Travel related to household management	0.02	0.03	67
Travel related to caring for and helping household members	0.02	0.06	33
Travel related to caring for and helping household children	0.02	0.04	50
Travel related to helping household adults	0.00	0.02	0
Travel related to caring for and helping people in other households	0.07	0.06	117
Travel related to caring for and helping children in other households	0.01	0.01	100
Travel related to helping adults in other households	0.05	0.04	125
Travel related to work	0.45	0.36	125
Travel related to education	0.08	0.03	267
Travel related to taking class	0.06	0.02	300
Travel related to consumer purchases	0.17	0.21	81
Travel related to grocery shopping	0.05	0.04	125
Travel related to purchasing gas	0.01	0.02	50
Travel related to purchasing food (except groceries)	0.06	0.04	150
Travel related to shopping (except groceries, food, and gas)	0.06	0.11	55
Travel related to using professional and personal care services	0.01	0.03	33
Travel related to using financial services and banking	0.01	0.01	100
Travel related to using medical services	0.00	0.01	0
Travel related to eating and drinking	0.12	0.13	92
Travel related to socializing, relaxing, and leisure	0.19	0.18	106
Travel related to socializing and communicating	0.09	0.09	100
Travel related to attending or hosting social events	0.01	0.01	100
Travel related to relaxing and leisure	0.07	0.04	175
Travel related to arts and entertainment	0.02	0.02	100
Travel related to sports, exercise, and recreation	0.06	0.06	100
Travel related to participating in sports, exercise, recreation	0.05	0.05	100
Travel related to religious and spiritual activities	0.01	0.02	50
Travel related to volunteer activities	0.00	0.02	0

Note: The index is calculated by dividing average time spent by men in the age group doing primary activity by average time spent by total men doing primary activity and multiplying by 100. Primary activities are those respondents identified as their main activity. Other activities done simultaneously, such as eating while watching TV, are not included. Numbers may not add to total because not all subcategories are shown. If fewer than 2.0 percent of the total population participated in a primary activity, then the primary activity is not shown. "–" means denominator is zero.
Source: Bureau of Labor Statistics, unpublished tables from the 2008 American Time Use Survey, Internet site http://www.bls .gov/tus/home.htm; calculations by New Strategist

Table 3.6 Indexed Time Use of Women Aged 20 to 24, 2008

(hours spent doing primary activities on an average day by women aged 20 to 24 and by total women aged 15 or older, and index of time spent by 20-to-24-year-old women to total women, 2008)

	average hours		index, women aged 20 to 24 to total women
	women aged 20 to 24	total women	
TOTAL, ALL ACTIVITIES	**24.00**	**24.00**	**100**
Personal care	**9.65**	**9.54**	**101**
Sleeping	8.78	8.64	102
Sleeplessness	0.03	0.07	43
Grooming	0.85	0.78	109
Health-related self-care	0.02	0.11	18
Household activities	**1.25**	**2.19**	**57**
Housework	0.53	0.90	59
Interior cleaning	0.39	0.55	71
Laundry	0.15	0.28	54
Storing interior household items, including food	0.00	0.02	0
Food and drink preparation, presentation, and clean-up	0.39	0.73	53
Food and drink preparation	0.33	0.55	60
Kitchen and food clean-up	0.06	0.18	33
Interior maintenance, repair, and decoration	0.02	0.04	50
Interior arrangement, decoration, and repairs	0.02	0.03	67
Exterior maintenance, repair, and decoration	0.00	0.03	0
Lawn, garden, and houseplants	0.00	0.12	0
Animals and pets (not veterinary care)	0.05	0.10	50
Walking, exercising, and playing with pets	0.02	0.04	50
Vehicles	0.01	0.01	100
Household management	0.22	0.25	88
Financial management	0.01	0.04	25
Household and personal organization and planning	0.14	0.11	127
Household and personal mail and messages (except email)	0.00	0.03	0
Household and personal email	0.07	0.07	100
Caring for and helping household members	**0.80**	**0.59**	**136**
Caring for and helping household children	0.72	0.48	150
Physical care for household children	0.41	0.24	171
Reading to or with household children	0.01	0.02	50
Playing with household children (except sports)	0.17	0.09	189
Talking with, listening to household children	0.00	0.02	0
Looking after household children as a primary activity	0.08	0.03	267
Picking up or dropping off household children	0.02	0.03	67
Activities related to household children's education	0.01	0.05	20
Helping household children with homework	0.01	0.04	25
Helping household adults	0.01	0.01	100
Caring for and helping people in other households	**0.22**	**0.20**	**110**
Caring for and helping children in other households	0.07	0.12	58

	average hours		index, women aged 20 to 24 to total women
	women aged 20 to 24	total women	
Helping adults in other households	0.13	0.05	260
Picking up or dropping off adults in other households	0.01	0.01	100
Work and work-related activities	**3.14**	**2.79**	**113**
Work, main job	2.86	2.63	109
Work, other job(s)	0.16	0.09	178
Education	**1.66**	**0.48**	**346**
Taking class	0.71	0.27	263
Taking class for degree, certification, or licensure	0.71	0.25	284
Research, homework	0.89	0.20	445
Consumer purchases (store, telephone, Internet)	**0.58**	**0.48**	**121**
Grocery shopping	0.08	0.13	62
Purchasing gas	0.01	0.01	100
Purchasing food (except groceries)	0.03	0.02	150
Shopping, except groceries, food, and gas	0.46	0.31	148
Professional and personal care services	**0.04**	**0.11**	**36**
Financial services and banking	0.00	0.01	0
Banking	0.00	0.01	0
Medical and care services	0.02	0.06	33
Using health and care services outside the home	0.01	0.05	20
Household services	**0.01**	**0.01**	**100**
Eating and drinking	**1.02**	**1.07**	**95**
Socializing, relaxing, and leisure	**3.51**	**4.42**	**79**
Socializing and communicating	0.73	0.68	107
Attending or hosting social events	0.08	0.08	100
Relaxing and leisure	2.60	3.58	73
Relaxing, thinking	0.22	0.26	85
Television	1.99	2.54	78
Listening to the radio	0.00	0.02	0
Listening to or playing music (not radio)	0.01	0.02	50
Playing games (including computer)	0.12	0.15	80
Computer use for leisure (except games)	0.08	0.14	57
Reading for personal interest	0.15	0.40	38
Arts and entertainment (except sports)	0.10	0.08	125
Sports, exercise, and recreation	**0.29**	**0.23**	**126**
Participating in sports, exercise, or recreation	0.26	0.20	130
Using cardiovascular equipment	0.01	0.02	50
Walking	0.04	0.04	100
Working out, unspecified	0.03	0.02	150
Religious and spiritual activities	**0.06**	**0.17**	**35**
Attending religious services	0.04	0.10	40
Participation in religious practices	0.02	0.05	40

	average hours		index, women aged 20 to 24
	women aged 20 to 24	total women	to total women
Volunteer activities	**0.04**	**0.16**	**25**
Administrative and support activities	0.01	0.04	25
Telephone calls	**0.23**	**0.18**	**128**
Telephone calls to or from family members	0.01	0.07	14
Telephone calls to or from friends, neighbors, or acquaintances	0.08	0.06	133
Traveling	**1.38**	**1.17**	**118**
Travel related to personal care	0.02	0.01	200
Travel related to household activities	0.07	0.04	175
Travel related to household management	0.02	0.02	100
Travel related to caring for and helping household members	0.08	0.11	73
Travel related to caring for and helping household children	0.06	0.08	75
Travel related to helping household adults	0.02	0.02	100
Travel related to caring for and helping people in other households	0.08	0.07	114
Travel related to caring for and helping children in other households	0.02	0.02	100
Travel related to helping adults in other households	0.06	0.04	150
Travel related to work	0.25	0.20	125
Travel related to education	0.13	0.04	325
Travel related to taking class	0.11	0.03	367
Travel related to consumer purchases	0.29	0.27	107
Travel related to grocery shopping	0.04	0.06	67
Travel related to purchasing gas	0.02	0.02	100
Travel related to purchasing food (except groceries)	0.07	0.04	175
Travel related to shopping (except groceries, food, and gas)	0.16	0.14	114
Travel related to using professional and personal care services	0.03	0.05	60
Travel related to using financial services and banking	0.01	0.01	100
Travel related to using medical services	0.01	0.02	50
Travel related to eating and drinking	0.11	0.11	100
Travel related to socializing, relaxing, and leisure	0.23	0.17	135
Travel related to socializing and communicating	0.13	0.10	130
Travel related to attending or hosting social events	0.01	0.01	100
Travel related to relaxing and leisure	0.08	0.03	267
Travel related to arts and entertainment	0.02	0.02	100
Travel related to sports, exercise, and recreation	0.06	0.03	200
Travel related to participating in sports, exercise, recreation	0.05	0.03	167
Travel related to religious and spiritual activities	0.01	0.02	50
Travel related to volunteer activities	0.00	0.02	0

Note: The index is calculated by dividing average time spent by women in the age group doing primary activity by average time spent by total women doing primary activity and multiplying by 100. Primary activities are those respondents identified as their main activity. Other activities done simultaneously, such as eating while watching TV, are not included. Numbers may not add to total because not all subcategories are shown. If fewer than 2.0 percent of the total population participated in a primary activity, then the primary activity is not shown.
Source: Bureau of Labor Statistics, unpublished tables from the 2008 American Time Use Survey, Internet site http://www.bls .gov/tus/home.htm; calculations by New Strategist

Table 3.7 Indexed Time Use of People Aged 20 to 24 by Sex, 2008

(average hours spent by people aged 20 to 24 doing primary activities on an average day by sex, and index of women's time to men's, 2008)

	average hours, aged 20 to 24		index of women to men
	men	women	
TOTAL, ALL ACTIVITIES	**24.00**	**24.00**	**100**
Personal care	**9.57**	**9.65**	**101**
Sleeping	8.89	8.78	99
Sleeplessness	0.05	0.03	60
Grooming	0.59	0.85	144
Health-related self-care	0.01	0.02	200
Household activities	**0.86**	**1.25**	**145**
Housework	0.20	0.53	265
Interior cleaning	0.14	0.39	279
Laundry	0.06	0.15	250
Storing interior household items, including food	0.01	0.00	0
Food and drink preparation, presentation, and clean-up	0.19	0.39	205
Food and drink preparation	0.18	0.33	183
Kitchen and food clean-up	0.01	0.06	600
Interior maintenance, repair, and decoration	0.08	0.02	25
Interior arrangement, decoration, and repairs	0.07	0.02	29
Exterior maintenance, repair, and decoration	0.00	0.00	–
Lawn, garden, and houseplants	0.13	0.00	0
Animals and pets (not veterinary care)	0.13	0.05	38
Walking, exercising, and playing with pets	0.10	0.02	20
Vehicles	0.06	0.01	17
Household management	0.07	0.22	314
Financial management	0.01	0.01	100
Household and personal organization and planning	0.02	0.14	700
Household and personal mail and messages (except email)	0.00	0.00	–
Household and personal email	0.03	0.07	233
Caring for and helping household members	**0.17**	**0.80**	**471**
Caring for and helping household children	0.14	0.72	514
Physical care for household children	0.07	0.41	586
Reading to or with household children	0.00	0.01	–
Playing with household children (except sports)	0.05	0.17	340
Talking with, listening to household children	0.00	0.00	–
Looking after household children as a primary activity	0.01	0.08	800
Picking up or dropping off household children	0.01	0.02	200
Activities related to household children's education	0.00	0.01	–
Helping household children with homework	0.00	0.01	–
Helping household adults	0.01	0.01	100
Caring for and helping people in other households	**0.12**	**0.22**	**183**
Caring for and helping children in other households	0.03	0.07	233

	average hours, aged 20 to 24		index of women to men
	men	women	
Helping adults in other households	0.06	0.13	217
Picking up or dropping off adults in other households	0.01	0.01	100
Work and work-related activities	**4.86**	**3.14**	**65**
Work, main job	4.69	2.86	61
Work, other job(s)	0.11	0.16	145
Education	**0.56**	**1.66**	**296**
Taking class	0.26	0.71	273
Taking class for degree, certification, or licensure	0.26	0.71	273
Research, homework	0.28	0.89	318
Consumer purchases (store, telephone, Internet)	**0.22**	**0.58**	**264**
Grocery shopping	0.06	0.08	133
Purchasing gas	0.00	0.01	–
Purchasing food (except groceries)	0.02	0.03	150
Shopping, except groceries, food, and gas	0.13	0.46	354
Professional and personal care services	**0.03**	**0.04**	**133**
Financial services and banking	0.02	0.00	0
Banking	0.01	0.00	0
Medical and care services	0.00	0.02	–
Using health and care services outside the home	0.00	0.01	–
Household services	**0.02**	**0.01**	**50**
Eating and drinking	**0.94**	**1.02**	**109**
Socializing, relaxing, and leisure	**4.54**	**3.51**	**77**
Socializing and communicating	0.82	0.73	89
Attending or hosting social events	0.13	0.08	62
Relaxing and leisure	3.47	2.60	75
Relaxing, thinking	0.14	0.22	157
Television	2.41	1.99	83
Listening to the radio	0.02	0.00	0
Listening to or playing music (not radio)	0.10	0.01	10
Playing games (including computer)	0.57	0.12	21
Computer use for leisure (except games)	0.11	0.08	73
Reading for personal interest	0.10	0.15	150
Arts and entertainment (except sports)	0.12	0.10	83
Sports, exercise, and recreation	**0.50**	**0.29**	**58**
Participating in sports, exercise, or recreation	0.44	0.26	59
Using cardiovascular equipment	0.00	0.01	–
Walking	0.02	0.04	200
Working out, unspecified	0.08	0.03	38
Religious and spiritual activities	**0.05**	**0.06**	**120**
Attending religious services	0.02	0.04	200
Participation in religious practices	0.02	0.02	100

	average hours, aged 20 to 24		index of women to men
	men	women	
Volunteer activities	**0.03**	**0.04**	**133**
Administrative and support activities	0.00	0.01	–
Telephone calls	**0.12**	**0.23**	**192**
Telephone calls to or from family members	0.01	0.01	100
Telephone calls to or from friends, neighbors, or acquaintances	0.05	0.08	160
Traveling	**1.27**	**1.38**	**109**
Travel related to personal care	0.01	0.02	200
Travel related to household activities	0.03	0.07	233
Travel related to household management	0.02	0.02	100
Travel related to caring for and helping household members	0.02	0.08	400
Travel related to caring for and helping household children	0.02	0.06	300
Travel related to helping household adults	0.00	0.02	–
Travel related to caring for and helping people in other households	0.07	0.08	114
Travel related to caring for and helping children in other households	0.01	0.02	200
Travel related to helping adults in other households	0.05	0.06	120
Travel related to work	0.45	0.25	56
Travel related to education	0.08	0.13	163
Travel related to taking class	0.06	0.11	183
Travel related to consumer purchases	0.17	0.29	171
Travel related to grocery shopping	0.05	0.04	80
Travel related to purchasing gas	0.01	0.02	200
Travel related to purchasing food (except groceries)	0.06	0.07	117
Travel related to shopping (except groceries, food, and gas)	0.06	0.16	267
Travel related to using professional and personal care services	0.01	0.03	300
Travel related to using financial services and banking	0.01	0.01	100
Travel related to using medical services	0.00	0.01	–
Travel related to eating and drinking	0.12	0.11	92
Travel related to socializing, relaxing, and leisure	0.19	0.23	121
Travel related to socializing and communicating	0.09	0.13	144
Travel related to attending or hosting social events	0.01	0.01	100
Travel related to relaxing and leisure	0.07	0.08	114
Travel related to arts and entertainment	0.02	0.02	100
Travel related to sports, exercise, and recreation	0.06	0.06	100
Travel related to participating in sports, exercise, recreation	0.05	0.05	100
Travel related to religious and spiritual activities	0.01	0.01	100
Travel related to volunteer activities	0.00	0.00	–

Note: The index is calculated by dividing women's time by men's time and multiplying by 100. Primary activities are those respondents identified as their main activity. Other activities done simultaneously, such as eating while watching TV, are not in-cluded. Numbers may not add to total because not all subcategories are shown. If fewer than 2.0 percent of the total population participated in a primary activity, then the primary activity is not shown. "–" means denominator is zero.
Source: Bureau of Labor Statistics, unpublished tables from the 2008 American Time Use Survey, Internet site http://www.bls .gov/tus/home.htm; calculations by New Strategist

Table 3.8 Indexed Participation in Primary Activities by Total People Aged 20 to 24, 2008

(percent of people aged 20 to 24 and total people aged 15 or older participating in primary activities on an average day, and index of participation by 20-to-24-year-olds to total people, 2008)

	percent participating		index, people aged 20 to 24
	people aged 20 to 24	total people	to total
TOTAL, ALL ACTIVITIES	**100.0%**	**100.0%**	**100**
Personal care	**100.0**	**100.0**	**100**
Sleeping	100.0	99.9	100
Sleeplessness	4.3	5.2	83
Grooming	80.3	79.3	101
Health-related self-care	2.4	6.4	38
Household activities	**61.0**	**75.5**	**81**
Housework	23.0	35.5	65
Interior cleaning	15.8	24.5	65
Laundry	9.1	16.2	57
Storing interior household items, including food	2.1	5.0	42
Food and drink preparation, presentation, and clean-up	35.0	52.3	67
Food and drink preparation	33.2	49.3	67
Kitchen and food clean-up	6.7	20.8	32
Interior maintenance, repair, and decoration	2.0	3.0	64
Interior arrangement, decoration, and repairs	1.5	2.0	78
Exterior maintenance, repair, and decoration	0.3	2.7	11
Lawn, garden, and houseplants	2.9	9.4	31
Animals and pets (not veterinary care)	12.4	14.5	85
Walking, exercising, and playing with pets	5.6	5.8	98
Vehicles	2.9	2.7	108
Household management	23.9	29.0	82
Financial management	4.2	4.0	104
Household and personal organization and planning	10.7	14.1	76
Household and personal mail and messages (except email)	1.2	6.9	17
Household and personal email	9.5	9.4	101
Caring for and helping household members	**23.1**	**26.1**	**89**
Caring for and helping household children	20.1	21.9	92
Physical care for household children	17.2	15.7	110
Reading to or with household children	1.3	2.6	48
Playing with household children (except sports)	7.1	5.4	131
Talking with, listening to household children	0.0	3.0	0
Looking after household children as a primary activity	2.5	2.3	110
Picking up or dropping off household children	4.3	9.2	46
Activities related to household children's education	1.1	3.8	29
Helping household children with homework	1.1	3.4	32
Helping household adults	4.0	3.6	110
Caring for and helping people in other households	**16.5**	**13.3**	**124**
Caring for and helping children in other households	4.8	5.6	87

	percent participating		index, people aged 20 to 24 to total
	people aged 20 to 24	total people	
Helping adults in other households	12.3%	8.0%	153
Picking up or dropping off adults in other households	8.5	5.0	171
Work and work-related activities	**55.0**	**46.6**	**118**
Work, main job	50.9	43.9	116
Work, other job(s)	3.0	2.4	126
Education	**19.7**	**7.9**	**250**
Taking class	11.0	5.2	212
Taking class for degree, certification, or licensure	11.0	4.8	230
Research, homework	17.7	5.8	303
Consumer purchases (store, telephone, Internet)	**40.0**	**40.7**	**98**
Grocery shopping	9.2	12.9	71
Purchasing gas	3.5	4.0	88
Purchasing food (except groceries)	15.7	12.0	130
Shopping, except groceries, food, and gas	24.4	23.5	104
Professional and personal care services	**7.3**	**8.9**	**82**
Financial services and banking	4.3	3.2	134
Banking	4.0	3.0	133
Medical and care services	1.3	3.6	37
Using health and care services outside the home	1.2	3.4	35
Household services	**1.8**	**2.1**	**88**
Eating and drinking	**94.3**	**96.0**	**98**
Socializing, relaxing, and leisure	**93.9**	**95.4**	**98**
Socializing and communicating	36.5	37.6	97
Attending or hosting social events	2.4	2.3	104
Relaxing and leisure	87.6	91.3	96
Relaxing, thinking	18.0	19.9	90
Television	76.6	80.9	95
Listening to the radio	2.1	2.0	105
Listening to or playing music (not radio)	4.1	2.6	159
Playing games (including computer)	13.0	9.0	144
Computer use for leisure (except games)	8.8	9.5	92
Reading for personal interest	12.5	23.9	52
Arts and entertainment (except sports)	3.9	3.2	120
Sports, exercise, and recreation	**19.8**	**18.9**	**105**
Participating in sports, exercise, or recreation	18.3	17.9	102
Using cardiovascular equipment	1.3	2.2	59
Walking	2.4	4.8	50
Working out, unspecified	4.4	3.2	137
Religious and spiritual activities	**3.2**	**9.2**	**34**
Attending religious services	1.7	4.9	35
Participation in religious practices	1.6	4.6	34

	percent participating		index, people aged 20 to 24 to total
	people aged 20 to 24	total people	
Volunteer activities	**2.7%**	**6.7%**	**40**
Administrative and support activities	1.1	2.5	44
Telephone calls	**15.0**	**15.4**	**98**
Telephone calls to or from family members	2.2	7.3	30
Telephone calls to or from friends, neighbors, or acquaintances	8.6	5.6	153
Traveling	**94.3**	**86.9**	**109**
Travel related to personal care	4.8	2.5	190
Travel related to household activities	11.7	9.4	125
Travel related to household management	7.1	6.1	117
Travel related to caring for and helping household members	10.0	13.6	73
Travel related to caring for and helping household children	6.8	11.0	62
Travel related to helping household adults	3.4	2.6	132
Travel related to caring for and helping people in other households	13.6	10.5	130
Travel related to caring for and helping children in other households	3.5	3.5	99
Travel related to helping adults in other households	10.8	7.1	153
Travel related to work	50.2	38.2	132
Travel related to education	12.7	5.0	253
Travel related to taking class	10.7	4.4	242
Travel related to consumer purchases	39.1	39.6	99
Travel related to grocery shopping	9.1	12.9	71
Travel related to purchasing gas	3.5	3.9	89
Travel related to purchasing food (except groceries)	14.0	11.2	125
Travel related to shopping (except groceries, food, and gas)	23.7	22.7	104
Travel related to using professional and personal care services	6.4	8.1	79
Travel related to using financial services and banking	4.3	3.0	143
Travel related to using medical services	1.0	3.3	30
Travel related to eating and drinking	28.4	25.0	114
Travel related to socializing, relaxing, and leisure	36.0	28.6	126
Travel related to socializing and communicating	20.2	18.6	109
Travel related to attending or hosting social events	2.5	2.0	124
Travel related to relaxing and leisure	17.0	8.9	191
Travel related to arts and entertainment	3.2	2.6	124
Travel related to sports, exercise, and recreation	14.3	9.6	150
Travel related to participating in sports, exercise, recreation	12.9	8.6	151
Travel related to religious and spiritual activities	2.3	5.1	44
Travel related to volunteer activities	1.8	4.3	43

Note: The index is calculated by dividing percent of people in the age group doing primary activity by percent of total people doing primary activity and multiplying by 100. Primary activities are those respondents identified as their main activity. Other activities done simultaneously, such as eating while watching TV, are not included. If fewer than 2.0 percent of the total population participated in a primary activity, then the primary activity is not shown.
Source: Bureau of Labor Statistics, unpublished tables from the 2008 American Time Use Survey, Internet site http://www.bls .gov/tus/home.htm; calculations by New Strategist

Table 3.9 Indexed Participation in Primary Activities by Men Aged 20 to 24, 2008

(percent of men aged 20 to 24 and total men aged 15 or older participating in primary activities on an average day, and index of participation by 20-to-24-year-old men to total men, 2008)

	percent participating		index, men aged 20 to 24
	men aged 20 to 24	total men	to total men
TOTAL, ALL ACTIVITIES	**100.0%**	**100.0%**	**100**
Personal care	**100.0**	**100.0**	**100**
Sleeping	100.0	99.9	100
Sleeplessness	6.5	4.5	143
Grooming	81.0	76.6	106
Health-related self-care	2.1	4.8	45
Household activities	**50.5**	**66.6**	**76**
Housework	13.0	19.7	66
Interior cleaning	6.9	13.5	52
Laundry	7.1	6.3	113
Storing interior household items, including food	1.8	2.9	64
Food and drink preparation, presentation, and clean-up	27.1	38.4	71
Food and drink preparation	26.5	36.0	74
Kitchen and food clean-up	2.9	9.5	30
Interior maintenance, repair, and decoration	2.0	3.9	51
Interior arrangement, decoration, and repairs	1.8	2.4	73
Exterior maintenance, repair, and decoration	0.4	3.8	12
Lawn, garden, and houseplants	4.0	11.0	37
Animals and pets (not veterinary care)	14.7	12.1	121
Walking, exercising, and playing with pets	7.6	5.2	146
Vehicles	4.5	4.5	100
Household management	18.0	24.0	75
Financial management	4.1	3.2	128
Household and personal organization and planning	6.9	11.1	62
Household and personal mail and messages (except email)	1.5	5.5	27
Household and personal email	6.2	7.4	84
Caring for and helping household members	**11.6**	**20.7**	**56**
Caring for and helping household children	8.3	16.8	50
Physical care for household children	6.0	10.4	58
Reading to or with household children	0.7	1.7	43
Playing with household children (except sports)	4.3	4.7	91
Talking with, listening to household children	0.0	1.7	0
Looking after household children as a primary activity	0.3	1.5	22
Picking up or dropping off household children	2.3	6.2	37
Activities related to household children's education	0.0	2.2	0
Helping household children with homework	0.0	2.0	0
Helping household adults	2.8	3.5	80
Caring for and helping people in other households	**13.6**	**11.0**	**124**
Caring for and helping children in other households	2.6	3.6	71

	percent participating		index, men aged 20 to 24 to total men
	men aged 20 to 24	total men	
Helping adults in other households	10.5%	7.5%	140
Picking up or dropping off adults in other households	7.9	4.4	178
Work and work-related activities	**63.7**	**53.4**	**119**
Work, main job	59.3	50.1	118
Work, other job(s)	2.1	2.3	93
Education	**11.4**	**6.9**	**166**
Taking class	7.6	5.0	152
Taking class for degree, certification, or licensure	7.6	4.8	159
Research, homework	9.1	4.6	197
Consumer purchases (store, telephone, Internet)	**28.9**	**35.6**	**81**
Grocery shopping	8.2	9.6	86
Purchasing gas	2.6	4.3	60
Purchasing food (except groceries)	14.7	11.8	125
Shopping, except groceries, food, and gas	12.2	19.6	62
Professional and personal care services	**6.8**	**6.7**	**101**
Financial services and banking	5.5	3.1	176
Banking	4.9	2.8	176
Medical and care services	0.3	2.4	12
Using health and care services outside the home	0.0	2.3	0
Household services	**1.5**	**2.1**	**72**
Eating and drinking	**94.6**	**96.5**	**98**
Socializing, relaxing, and leisure	**94.8**	**95.4**	**99**
Socializing and communicating	35.9	34.9	103
Attending or hosting social events	2.3	2.0	119
Relaxing and leisure	91.0	92.1	99
Relaxing, thinking	18.7	20.4	92
Television	78.8	82.3	96
Listening to the radio	4.2	2.5	166
Listening to or playing music (not radio)	6.2	3.3	188
Playing games (including computer)	18.2	9.6	190
Computer use for leisure (except games)	8.6	9.5	90
Reading for personal interest	14.3	21.1	68
Arts and entertainment (except sports)	3.6	3.3	108
Sports, exercise, and recreation	**23.0**	**22.0**	**104**
Participating in sports, exercise, or recreation	21.8	21.0	104
Using cardiovascular equipment	0.7	1.8	36
Walking	2.0	4.9	41
Working out, unspecified	6.4	3.5	182
Religious and spiritual activities	**3.9**	**7.7**	**50**
Attending religious services	1.3	4.0	32
Participation in religious practices	2.3	3.7	63

	percent participating		index, men aged 20 to 24 to total men
	men aged 20 to 24	total men	
Volunteer activities	**2.5%**	**5.7%**	**44**
Administrative and support activities	0.3	1.9	17
Telephone calls	**13.4**	**10.0**	**134**
Telephone calls to or from family members	1.4	3.8	36
Telephone calls to or from friends, neighbors, or acquaintances	8.2	3.7	223
Traveling	**94.1**	**88.5**	**106**
Travel related to personal care	4.7	3.1	153
Travel related to household activities	8.2	8.5	96
Travel related to household management	5.6	5.5	102
Travel related to caring for and helping household members	4.8	9.9	48
Travel related to caring for and helping household children	2.5	7.4	33
Travel related to helping household adults	1.9	2.4	80
Travel related to caring for and helping people in other households	13.1	9.3	142
Travel related to caring for and helping children in other households	2.6	2.5	104
Travel related to helping adults in other households	10.1	6.7	150
Travel related to work	60.1	44.4	135
Travel related to education	8.9	4.6	193
Travel related to taking class	7.8	4.1	188
Travel related to consumer purchases	27.9	34.5	81
Travel related to grocery shopping	8.1	9.5	85
Travel related to purchasing gas	2.6	4.2	61
Travel related to purchasing food (except groceries)	13.9	11.0	126
Travel related to shopping (except groceries, food, and gas)	12.0	18.9	64
Travel related to using professional and personal care services	6.4	6.3	102
Travel related to using financial services and banking	5.5	3.0	183
Travel related to using medical services	0.2	2.3	8
Travel related to eating and drinking	28.9	27.3	106
Travel related to socializing, relaxing, and leisure	34.5	28.0	123
Travel related to socializing and communicating	16.9	17.5	96
Travel related to attending or hosting social events	2.5	1.7	145
Travel related to relaxing and leisure	19.1	9.4	203
Travel related to arts and entertainment	3.0	2.8	108
Travel related to sports, exercise, and recreation	17.4	11.5	151
Travel related to participating in sports, exercise, recreation	16.2	10.4	156
Travel related to religious and spiritual activities	2.9	4.4	66
Travel related to volunteer activities	1.5	3.8	38

Note: The index is calculated by dividing percent of men in the age group doing primary activity by percent of total men doing primary activity and multiplying by 100. Primary activities are those respondents identified as their main activity. Other activities done simultaneously, such as eating while watching TV, are not included. If fewer than 2.0 percent of the total population participated in a primary activity, then the primary activity is not shown.
Source: Bureau of Labor Statistics, unpublished tables from the 2008 American Time Use Survey, Internet site http://www.bls .gov/tus/home.htm; calculations by New Strategist

Table 3.10 Indexed Participation in Primary Activities by Women Aged 20 to 24, 2008

(percent of women aged 20 to 24 and total women aged 15 or older participating in primary activities on an average day, and index of participation by 20-to-24-year-old women to total women, 2008)

	percent participating		index, women aged 20 to 24 to total women
	women aged 20 to 24	total women	
TOTAL, ALL ACTIVITIES	**100.0%**	**100.0%**	**100**
Personal care	**99.9**	**100.0**	**100**
Sleeping	99.9	99.9	100
Sleeplessness	2.2	5.8	37
Grooming	79.6	81.8	97
Health-related self-care	2.7	7.8	34
Household activities	**71.6**	**84.0**	**85**
Housework	33.2	50.3	66
Interior cleaning	24.8	34.9	71
Laundry	11.2	25.5	44
Storing interior household items, including food	2.4	7.0	34
Food and drink preparation, presentation, and clean-up	42.9	65.3	66
Food and drink preparation	40.0	61.8	65
Kitchen and food clean-up	10.6	31.5	34
Interior maintenance, repair, and decoration	1.9	2.2	87
Interior arrangement, decoration, and repairs	1.3	1.5	86
Exterior maintenance, repair, and decoration	0.2	1.8	10
Lawn, garden, and houseplants	1.7	7.9	22
Animals and pets (not veterinary care)	10.0	16.7	60
Walking, exercising, and playing with pets	3.6	6.3	57
Vehicles	1.2	1.0	126
Household management	30.0	33.8	89
Financial management	4.4	4.9	90
Household and personal organization and planning	14.5	16.8	86
Household and personal mail and messages (except email)	0.9	8.2	11
Household and personal email	12.8	11.3	113
Caring for and helping household members	**34.8**	**31.2**	**112**
Caring for and helping household children	32.0	26.7	120
Physical care for household children	28.7	20.6	139
Reading to or with household children	1.8	3.5	52
Playing with household children (except sports)	9.9	6.1	163
Talking with, listening to household children	0.0	4.3	0
Looking after household children as a primary activity	4.7	3.0	156
Picking up or dropping off household children	6.3	12.1	52
Activities related to household children's education	2.3	5.4	42
Helping household children with homework	2.3	4.8	47
Helping household adults	5.2	3.7	138
Caring for and helping people in other households	**19.4**	**15.5**	**125**
Caring for and helping children in other households	7.1	7.4	96

	percent participating		index, women aged 20 to 24
	women aged 20 to 24	total women	to total women
Helping adults in other households	14.2%	8.5%	166
Picking up or dropping off adults in other households	9.0	5.4	166
Work and work-related activities	**46.2**	**40.3**	**115**
Work, main job	42.3	38.0	111
Work, other job(s)	3.9	2.4	159
Education	**28.2**	**8.9**	**317**
Taking class	14.4	5.3	269
Taking class for degree, certification, or licensure	14.4	4.7	305
Research, homework	26.4	7.0	378
Consumer purchases (store, telephone, Internet)	**51.3**	**45.4**	**113**
Grocery shopping	10.2	16.1	64
Purchasing gas	4.4	3.7	120
Purchasing food (except groceries)	16.8	12.3	136
Shopping, except groceries, food, and gas	36.8	27.2	136
Professional and personal care services	**7.8**	**11.0**	**71**
Financial services and banking	3.1	3.3	94
Banking	3.1	3.3	96
Medical and care services	2.4	4.8	51
Using health and care services outside the home	2.4	4.5	53
Household services	**2.2**	**2.1**	**104**
Eating and drinking	**94.0**	**95.6**	**98**
Socializing, relaxing, and leisure	**92.9**	**95.4**	**97**
Socializing and communicating	37.2	40.1	93
Attending or hosting social events	2.5	2.7	94
Relaxing and leisure	84.1	90.6	93
Relaxing, thinking	17.3	19.5	88
Television	74.2	79.5	93
Listening to the radio	0.0	1.5	0
Listening to or playing music (not radio)	2.1	2.0	104
Playing games (including computer)	7.6	8.4	90
Computer use for leisure (except games)	9.0	9.5	94
Reading for personal interest	10.7	26.5	40
Arts and entertainment (except sports)	4.2	3.2	133
Sports, exercise, and recreation	**16.6**	**15.9**	**104**
Participating in sports, exercise, or recreation	14.8	15.0	99
Using cardiovascular equipment	1.9	2.5	77
Walking	2.8	4.7	60
Working out, unspecified	2.3	2.9	79
Religious and spiritual activities	**2.4**	**10.7**	**23**
Attending religious services	2.1	5.7	37
Participation in religious practices	0.8	5.4	15

	percent participating		index, women aged 20 to 24 to total women
	women aged 20 to 24	total women	
Volunteer activities	**2.8%**	**7.6%**	**37**
Administrative and support activities	1.9	3.1	63
Telephone calls	**16.7**	**20.4**	**82**
Telephone calls to or from family members	3.1	10.7	29
Telephone calls to or from friends, neighbors, or acquaintances	8.9	7.4	120
Traveling	**94.6**	**85.5**	**111**
Travel related to personal care	4.9	2.0	244
Travel related to household activities	15.3	10.3	150
Travel related to household management	8.7	6.7	129
Travel related to caring for and helping household members	15.3	17.1	89
Travel related to caring for and helping household children	11.2	14.3	78
Travel related to helping household adults	4.9	2.7	178
Travel related to caring for and helping people in other households	14.1	11.6	121
Travel related to caring for and helping children in other households	4.4	4.5	97
Travel related to helping adults in other households	11.6	7.4	155
Travel related to work	40.1	32.2	124
Travel related to education	16.5	5.4	307
Travel related to taking class	13.6	4.6	292
Travel related to consumer purchases	50.5	44.4	114
Travel related to grocery shopping	10.2	16.0	64
Travel related to purchasing gas	4.4	3.7	121
Travel related to purchasing food (except groceries)	14.1	11.5	123
Travel related to shopping (except groceries, food, and gas)	35.5	26.3	135
Travel related to using professional and personal care services	6.3	9.8	65
Travel related to using financial services and banking	3.1	3.1	103
Travel related to using medical services	1.8	4.3	42
Travel related to eating and drinking	27.9	22.8	122
Travel related to socializing, relaxing, and leisure	37.5	29.2	128
Travel related to socializing and communicating	23.6	19.5	121
Travel related to attending or hosting social events	2.5	2.3	110
Travel related to relaxing and leisure	15.0	8.5	176
Travel related to arts and entertainment	3.4	2.4	143
Travel related to sports, exercise, and recreation	11.2	7.7	145
Travel related to participating in sports, exercise, recreation	9.5	6.8	141
Travel related to religious and spiritual activities	1.6	5.8	28
Travel related to volunteer activities	2.2	4.7	47

Note: The index is calculated by dividing percent of women in the age group doing primary activity by percent of total women doing primary activity and multiplying by 100. Primary activities are those respondents identified as their main activity. Other activities done simultaneously, such as eating while watching TV, are not included. If fewer than 2.0 percent of the total population participated in a primary activity, then the primary activity is not shown.
Source: Bureau of Labor Statistics, unpublished tables from the 2008 American Time Use Survey, Internet site http://www.bls .gov/tus/home.htm; calculations by New Strategist

Table 3.11 Indexed Participation in Primary Activities of People Aged 20 to 24 by Sex, 2008

(percent of people aged 20 to 24 participating in primary activities on an average day by sex, and index of women's participation to men's, 2008)

	aged 20 to 24, percent participating		index of women to men
	men	women	
TOTAL, ALL ACTIVITIES	**100.0%**	**100.0%**	**100**
Personal care	**100.0**	**99.9**	**100**
Sleeping	100.0	99.9	100
Sleeplessness	6.5	2.2	34
Grooming	81.0	79.6	98
Health-related self-care	2.1	2.7	124
Household activities	**50.5**	**71.6**	**142**
Housework	13.0	33.2	255
Interior cleaning	6.9	24.8	357
Laundry	7.1	11.2	159
Storing interior household items, including food	1.8	2.4	128
Food and drink preparation, presentation, and clean-up	27.1	42.9	158
Food and drink preparation	26.5	40.0	151
Kitchen and food clean-up	2.9	10.6	368
Interior maintenance, repair, and decoration	2.0	1.9	97
Interior arrangement, decoration, and repairs	1.8	1.3	73
Exterior maintenance, repair, and decoration	0.4	0.2	40
Lawn, garden, and houseplants	4.0	1.7	43
Animals and pets (not veterinary care)	14.7	10.0	68
Walking, exercising, and playing with pets	7.6	3.6	47
Vehicles	4.5	1.2	27
Household management	18.0	30.0	167
Financial management	4.1	4.4	107
Household and personal organization and planning	6.9	14.5	210
Household and personal mail and messages (except email)	1.5	0.9	59
Household and personal email	6.2	12.8	206
Caring for and helping household members	**11.6**	**34.8**	**301**
Caring for and helping household children	8.3	32.0	384
Physical care for household children	6.0	28.7	477
Reading to or with household children	0.7	1.8	242
Playing with household children (except sports)	4.3	9.9	231
Talking with, listening to household children	0.0	0.0	–
Looking after household children as a primary activity	0.3	4.7	1,473
Picking up or dropping off household children	2.3	6.3	277
Activities related to household children's education	0.0	2.3	–
Helping household children with homework	0.0	2.3	–
Helping household adults	2.8	5.2	186
Caring for and helping people in other households	**13.6**	**19.4**	**143**
Caring for and helping children in other households	2.6	7.1	277

	aged 20 to 24, percent participating		index of women to men
	men	women	
Helping adults in other households	10.5%	14.2%	135
Picking up or dropping off adults in other households	7.9	9.0	114
Work and work-related activities	**63.7**	**46.2**	**73**
Work, main job	59.3	42.3	71
Work, other job(s)	2.1	3.9	180
Education	**11.4**	**28.2**	**247**
Taking class	7.6	14.4	188
Taking class for degree, certification, or licensure	7.6	14.4	188
Research, homework	9.1	26.4	290
Consumer purchases (store, telephone, Internet)	**28.9**	**51.3**	**177**
Grocery shopping	8.2	10.2	124
Purchasing gas	2.6	4.4	173
Purchasing food (except groceries)	14.7	16.8	114
Shopping, except groceries, food, and gas	12.2	36.8	302
Professional and personal care services	**6.8**	**7.8**	**115**
Financial services and banking	5.5	3.1	57
Banking	4.9	3.1	64
Medical and care services	0.3	2.4	824
Using health and care services outside the home	0.0	2.4	–
Household services	**1.5**	**2.2**	**144**
Eating and drinking	**94.6**	**94.0**	**99**
Socializing, relaxing, and leisure	**94.8**	**92.9**	**98**
Socializing and communicating	35.9	37.2	104
Attending or hosting social events	2.3	2.5	107
Relaxing and leisure	91.0	84.1	92
Relaxing, thinking	18.7	17.3	93
Television	78.8	74.2	94
Listening to the radio	4.2	0.0	0
Listening to or playing music (not radio)	6.2	2.1	34
Playing games (including computer)	18.2	7.6	42
Computer use for leisure (except games)	8.6	9.0	104
Reading for personal interest	14.3	10.7	75
Arts and entertainment (except sports)	3.6	4.2	117
Sports, exercise, and recreation	**23.0**	**16.6**	**72**
Participating in sports, exercise, or recreation	21.8	14.8	68
Using cardiovascular equipment	0.7	1.9	287
Walking	2.0	2.8	140
Working out, unspecified	6.4	2.3	35
Religious and spiritual activities	**3.9**	**2.4**	**63**
Attending religious services	1.3	2.1	166
Participation in religious practices	2.3	0.8	34

	aged 20 to 24, percent participating		index of women to men
	men	women	
Volunteer activities	**2.5%**	**2.8%**	**111**
Administrative and support activities	0.3	1.9	583
Telephone calls	**13.4**	**16.7**	**125**
Telephone calls to or from family members	1.4	3.1	227
Telephone calls to or from friends, neighbors, or acquaintances	8.2	8.9	108
Traveling	**94.1**	**94.6**	**101**
Travel related to personal care	4.7	4.9	104
Travel related to household activities	8.2	15.3	188
Travel related to household management	5.6	8.7	154
Travel related to caring for and helping household members	4.8	15.3	318
Travel related to caring for and helping household children	2.5	11.2	457
Travel related to helping household adults	1.9	4.9	255
Travel related to caring for and helping people in other households	13.1	14.1	108
Travel related to caring for and helping children in other households	2.6	4.4	173
Travel related to helping adults in other households	10.1	11.6	114
Travel related to work	60.1	40.1	67
Travel related to education	8.9	16.5	185
Travel related to taking class	7.8	13.6	174
Travel related to consumer purchases	27.9	50.5	181
Travel related to grocery shopping	8.1	10.2	127
Travel related to purchasing gas	2.6	4.4	173
Travel related to purchasing food (except groceries)	13.9	14.1	101
Travel related to shopping (except groceries, food, and gas)	12.0	35.5	296
Travel related to using professional and personal care services	6.4	6.3	98
Travel related to using financial services and banking	5.5	3.1	57
Travel related to using medical services	0.2	1.8	969
Travel related to eating and drinking	28.9	27.9	97
Travel related to socializing, relaxing, and leisure	34.5	37.5	109
Travel related to socializing and communicating	16.9	23.6	140
Travel related to attending or hosting social events	2.5	2.5	102
Travel related to relaxing and leisure	19.1	15.0	78
Travel related to arts and entertainment	3.0	3.4	115
Travel related to sports, exercise, and recreation	17.4	11.2	64
Travel related to participating in sports, exercise, recreation	16.2	9.5	59
Travel related to religious and spiritual activities	2.9	1.6	57
Travel related to volunteer activities	1.5	2.2	151

Note: The index is calculated by dividing percent of women participating in primary activity by percent of men participating in primary activity and multiplying by 100. Primary activities are those respondents identified as their main activity. Other activities done simultaneously, such as eating while watching TV, are not included. If fewer than 2.0 percent of the total population participated in a primary activity, then the primary activity is not shown. "–" means denominator is zero.
Source: Bureau of Labor Statistics, unpublished tables from the 2008 American Time Use Survey, Internet site http://www.bls.gov/tus/home.htm; calculations by New Strategist

Table 3.12   Ranking: Average Hours per Day Spent Doing Primary Activities by Total People Aged 20 to 24, 2008

(average hours per day spent by people aged 20 to 24 doing primary activities, ranked by time spent doing activity, 2008)

		average hours per day spent by people aged 20 to 24
	Total, all activities	**24.00**
1.	Sleeping	8.84
2.	Work, main job	3.78
3.	Television	2.20
4.	Eating and drinking	0.99
5.	Socializing and communicating	0.77
6.	Grooming	0.72
7.	Research, homework	0.58
8.	Taking class	0.49
9.	Caring for and helping household children	0.43
10.	Participating in sports, exercise, or recreation	0.35
11.	Travel related to work	0.35
12.	Playing games (including computer)	0.34
13.	Shopping, except groceries, food, and gas	0.30
14.	Interior cleaning	0.25
15.	Food and drink preparation	0.25
16.	Relaxing, thinking	0.18
17.	Telephone calls	0.17
18.	Work, other job(s)	0.14
19.	Reading for personal interest	0.13
20.	Laundry	0.11
21.	Arts and entertainment (except sports)	0.11
22.	Travel related to education	0.11
23.	Travel related to shopping (except groceries, food, and gas)	0.11
24.	Travel related to eating and drinking	0.11
25.	Travel related to socializing and communicating	0.11
26.	Attending or hosting social events	0.10
27.	Computer use for leisure (except games)	0.10
28.	Animals and pets (not veterinary care)	0.09
29.	Helping adults in other households	0.09
30.	Household and personal organization and planning	0.08
31.	Lawn, garden, and houseplants	0.07
32.	Grocery shopping	0.07
33.	Travel related to relaxing and leisure	0.07
34.	Listening to or playing music (not radio)	0.06
35.	Travel related to purchasing food (except groceries)	0.06
36.	Travel related to sports, exercise, and recreation	0.06
37.	Interior maintenance, repair, and decoration	0.05
38.	Household and personal email	0.05
39.	Caring for and helping children in other households	0.05

	average hours per day spent by people aged 20 to 24
40. Travel related to household activities	0.05
41. Travel related to helping adults in other households	0.05
42. Vehicles	0.04
43. Volunteer activities	0.04
44. Travel related to caring for and helping household children	0.04
45. Travel related to grocery shopping	0.04
46. Kitchen and food clean-up	0.03
47. Attending religious services	0.03
48. Health-related self-care	0.02
49. Purchasing food (except groceries)	0.02
50. Participation in religious practices	0.02
51. Travel related to personal care	0.02
52. Travel related to arts and entertainment	0.02
53. Financial management	0.01
54. Activities related to household children's education	0.01
55. Helping household adults	0.01
56. Purchasing gas	0.01
57. Financial services and banking	0.01
58. Medical and care services	0.01
59. Household services	0.01
60. Listening to the radio	0.01
61. Travel related to helping household adults	0.01
62. Travel related to caring for and helping children in other households	0.01
63. Travel related to purchasing gas	0.01
64. Travel related to using financial services and banking	0.01
65. Travel related to using medical services	0.01
66. Travel related to attending or hosting social events	0.01
67. Travel related to religious and spiritual activities	0.01
68. Storing interior household items, including food	0.00
69. Exterior maintenance, repair, and decoration	0.00
70. Household and personal mail and messages (except email)	0.00
71. Travel related to volunteer activities	0.00

Note: Primary activities are those respondents identified as their main activity. Other activities done simultaneously, such as eating while watching TV, are not included. If fewer than 2.0 percent of the total population participated in a primary activity, then the primary activity is not shown.
Source: Bureau of Labor Statistics, unpublished tables from the 2008 American Time Use Survey, Internet site http://www.bls .gov/tus/home.htm; calculations by New Strategist

Table 3.13 Ranking: Average Hours per Day Spent Doing Primary Activities by Men Aged 20 to 24, 2008

(average hours per day spent by men aged 20 to 24 doing primary activities, ranked by time spent doing activity, 2008)

		average hours per day spent by men aged 20 to 24
	Total, all activities	**24.00**
1.	Sleeping	8.89
2.	Work, main job	4.69
3.	Television	2.41
4.	Eating and drinking	0.94
5.	Socializing and communicating	0.82
6.	Grooming	0.59
7.	Playing games (including computer)	0.57
8.	Travel related to work	0.45
9.	Participating in sports, exercise, or recreation	0.44
10.	Research, homework	0.28
11.	Taking class	0.26
12.	Food and drink preparation	0.18
13.	Interior cleaning	0.14
14.	Caring for and helping household children	0.14
15.	Relaxing, thinking	0.14
16.	Lawn, garden, and houseplants	0.13
17.	Animals and pets (not veterinary care)	0.13
18.	Shopping, except groceries, food, and gas	0.13
19.	Attending or hosting social events	0.13
20.	Arts and entertainment (except sports)	0.12
21.	Telephone calls	0.12
22.	Travel related to eating and drinking	0.12
23.	Work, other job(s)	0.11
24.	Computer use for leisure (except games)	0.11
25.	Listening to or playing music (not radio)	0.10
26.	Reading for personal interest	0.10
27.	Travel related to socializing and communicating	0.09
28.	Interior maintenance, repair, and decoration	0.08
29.	Travel related to education	0.08
30.	Travel related to relaxing and leisure	0.07
31.	Laundry	0.06
32.	Vehicles	0.06
33.	Helping adults in other households	0.06
34.	Grocery shopping	0.06
35.	Travel related to purchasing food (except groceries)	0.06
36.	Travel related to shopping (except groceries, food, and gas)	0.06
37.	Travel related to sports, exercise, and recreation	0.06
38.	Travel related to helping adults in other households	0.05
39.	Travel related to grocery shopping	0.05

	average hours per day spent by men aged 20 to 24
40. Household and personal email	0.03
41. Caring for and helping children in other households	0.03
42. Volunteer activities	0.03
43. Travel related to household activities	0.03
44. Household and personal organization and planning	0.02
45. Purchasing food (except groceries)	0.02
46. Financial services and banking	0.02
47. Household services	0.02
48. Listening to the radio	0.02
49. Attending religious services	0.02
50. Participation in religious practices	0.02
51. Travel related to caring for and helping household children	0.02
52. Travel related to arts and entertainment	0.02
53. Health-related self-care	0.01
54. Storing interior household items, including food	0.01
55. Kitchen and food clean-up	0.01
56. Financial management	0.01
57. Helping household adults	0.01
58. Travel related to personal care	0.01
59. Travel related to caring for and helping children in other households	0.01
60. Travel related to purchasing gas	0.01
61. Travel related to using financial services and banking	0.01
62. Travel related to attending or hosting social events	0.01
63. Travel related to religious and spiritual activities	0.01
64. Exterior maintenance, repair, and decoration	0.00
65. Household and personal mail and messages (except email)	0.00
66. Activities related to household children's education	0.00
67. Purchasing gas	0.00
68. Medical and care services	0.00
69. Travel related to helping household adults	0.00
70. Travel related to using medical services	0.00
71. Travel related to volunteer activities	0.00

Note: Primary activities are those respondents identified as their main activity. Other activities done simultaneously, such as eating while watching TV, are not included. If fewer than 2.0 percent of the total population participated in a primary activity, then the primary activity is not shown.
Source: Bureau of Labor Statistics, unpublished tables from the 2005 American Time Use Survey, Internet site http://www.bls .gov/tus/home.htm; calculations by New Strategist

Table 3.14 Ranking: Average Hours per Day Spent Doing Primary Activities by Women Aged 20 to 24, 2008

(average hours per day spent by women aged 20 to 24 doing primary activities, ranked by time spent doing activity, 2008)

		average hours per day spent by women aged 20 to 24
	Total, all activities	**24.00**
1.	Sleeping	8.78
2.	Work, main job	2.86
3.	Television	1.99
4.	Eating and drinking	1.02
5.	Research, homework	0.89
6.	Grooming	0.85
7.	Socializing and communicating	0.73
8.	Caring for and helping household children	0.72
9.	Taking class	0.71
10.	Shopping, except groceries, food, and gas	0.46
11.	Interior cleaning	0.39
12.	Food and drink preparation	0.33
13.	Participating in sports, exercise, or recreation	0.26
14.	Travel related to work	0.25
15.	Telephone calls	0.23
16.	Relaxing, thinking	0.22
17.	Work, other job(s)	0.16
18.	Travel related to shopping (except groceries, food, and gas)	0.16
19.	Laundry	0.15
20.	Reading for personal interest	0.15
21.	Household and personal organization and planning	0.14
22.	Helping adults in other households	0.13
23.	Travel related to education	0.13
24.	Travel related to socializing and communicating	0.13
25.	Playing games (including computer)	0.12
26.	Travel related to eating and drinking	0.11
27.	Arts and entertainment (except sports)	0.10
28.	Grocery shopping	0.08
29.	Attending or hosting social events	0.08
30.	Computer use for leisure (except games)	0.08
31.	Travel related to relaxing and leisure	0.08
32.	Household and personal email	0.07
33.	Caring for and helping children in other households	0.07
34.	Travel related to household activities	0.07
35.	Travel related to purchasing food (except groceries)	0.07
36.	Kitchen and food clean-up	0.06
37.	Travel related to caring for and helping household children	0.06
38.	Travel related to helping adults in other households	0.06
39.	Travel related to sports, exercise, and recreation	0.06

	average hours per day spent by women aged 20 to 24
40. Animals and pets (not veterinary care)	0.05
41. Attending religious services	0.04
42. Volunteer activities	0.04
43. Travel related to grocery shopping	0.04
44. Purchasing food (except groceries)	0.03
45. Health-related self-care	0.02
46. Interior maintenance, repair, and decoration	0.02
47. Medical and care services	0.02
48. Participation in religious practices	0.02
49. Travel related to personal care	0.02
50. Travel related to helping household adults	0.02
51. Travel related to caring for and helping children in other households	0.02
52. Travel related to purchasing gas	0.02
53. Travel related to arts and entertainment	0.02
54. Vehicles	0.01
55. Financial management	0.01
56. Activities related to household children's education	0.01
57. Helping household adults	0.01
58. Purchasing gas	0.01
59. Household services	0.01
60. Listening to or playing music (not radio)	0.01
61. Travel related to using financial services and banking	0.01
62. Travel related to using medical services	0.01
63. Travel related to attending or hosting social events	0.01
64. Travel related to religious and spiritual activities	0.01
65. Storing interior household items, including food	0.00
66. Exterior maintenance, repair, and decoration	0.00
67. Lawn, garden, and houseplants	0.00
68. Household and personal mail and messages (except email)	0.00
69. Financial services and banking	0.00
70. Listening to the radio	0.00
71. Travel related to volunteer activities	0.00

Note: Primary activities are those respondents identified as their main activity. Other activities done simultaneously, such as eating while watching TV, are not included. If fewer than 2.0 percent of the total population participated in a primary activity, then the primary activity is not shown.
Source: Bureau of Labor Statistics, unpublished tables from the 2008 American Time Use Survey, Internet site http://www.bls .gov/tus/home.htm; calculations by New Strategist

Table 3.15 Ranking: Percent of Total People Aged 20 to 24 Participating in Primary Activities on an Average Day, 2008

(percent of people aged 20 to 24 participating in primary activities on an average day, ranked by percent participating, 2008)

		percent of people aged 20 to 24 participating in activity
	Total, all activities	**100.0%**
1.	Sleeping	100.0
2.	Eating and drinking	94.3
3.	Grooming	80.3
4.	Television	76.6
5.	Work, main job	50.9
6.	Travel related to work	50.2
7.	Socializing and communicating	36.5
8.	Food and drink preparation	33.2
9.	Travel related to eating and drinking	28.4
10.	Shopping, except groceries, food, and gas	24.4
11.	Travel related to shopping (except groceries, food, and gas)	23.7
12.	Travel related to socializing and communicating	20.2
13.	Caring for and helping household children	20.1
14.	Participating in sports, exercise, or recreation	18.3
15.	Relaxing, thinking	18.0
16.	Research, homework	17.7
17.	Travel related to relaxing and leisure	17.0
18.	Interior cleaning	15.8
19.	Purchasing food (except groceries)	15.7
20.	Telephone calls	15.0
21.	Travel related to sports, exercise, and recreation	14.3
22.	Travel related to purchasing food (except groceries)	14.0
23.	Playing games (including computer)	13.0
24.	Travel related to education	12.7
25.	Reading for personal interest	12.5
26.	Animals and pets (not veterinary care)	12.4
27.	Helping adults in other households	12.3
28.	Travel related to household activities	11.7
29.	Taking class	11.0
30.	Travel related to helping adults in other households	10.8
31.	Household and personal organization and planning	10.7
32.	Household and personal email	9.5
33.	Grocery shopping	9.2
34.	Laundry	9.1
35.	Travel related to grocery shopping	9.1
36.	Computer use for leisure (except games)	8.8
37.	Travel related to caring for and helping household children	6.8
38.	Kitchen and food clean-up	6.7
39.	Caring for and helping children in other households	4.8

		percent of people aged 20 to 24 participating in activity
40.	Travel related to personal care	4.8%
41.	Financial services and banking	4.3
42.	Travel related to using financial services and banking	4.3
43.	Financial management	4.2
44.	Listening to or playing music (not radio)	4.1
45.	Helping household adults	4.0
46.	Arts and entertainment (except sports)	3.9
47.	Purchasing gas	3.5
48.	Travel related to purchasing gas	3.5
49.	Travel related to caring for and helping children in other households	3.5
50.	Travel related to helping household adults	3.4
51.	Travel related to arts and entertainment	3.2
52.	Work, other job(s)	3.0
53.	Vehicles	2.9
54.	Lawn, garden, and houseplants	2.9
55.	Volunteer activities	2.7
56.	Travel related to attending or hosting social events	2.5
57.	Attending or hosting social events	2.4
58.	Health-related self-care	2.4
59.	Travel related to religious and spiritual activities	2.3
60.	Listening to the radio	2.1
61.	Storing interior household items, including food	2.1
62.	Interior maintenance, repair, and decoration	2.0
63.	Household services	1.8
64.	Travel related to volunteer activities	1.8
65.	Attending religious services	1.7
66.	Participation in religious practices	1.6
67.	Medical and care services	1.3
68.	Household and personal mail and messages (except email)	1.2
69.	Activities related to household children's education	1.1
70.	Travel related to using medical services	1.0
71.	Exterior maintenance, repair, and decoration	0.3

Note: Primary activities are those respondents identified as their main activity. Other activities done simultaneously, such as eating while watching TV, are not included. If fewer than 2.0 percent of the total population participated in a primary activity, then the primary activity is not shown.
Source: Bureau of Labor Statistics, unpublished tables from the 2008 American Time Use Survey, Internet site http://www.bls.gov/tus/home.htm; calculations by New Strategist

Table 3.16 Ranking: Percent of Men Aged 20 to 24 Participating in Primary Activities on an Average Day, 2008

(percent of men aged 20 to 24 participating in primary activities on an average day, ranked by percent participating, 2008)

		percent of men aged 20 to 24 participating in activity
	Total, all activities	**100.0%**
1.	Sleeping	100.0
2.	Eating and drinking	94.6
3.	Grooming	81.0
4.	Television	78.8
5.	Travel related to work	60.1
6.	Work, main job	59.3
7.	Socializing and communicating	35.9
8.	Travel related to eating and drinking	28.9
9.	Food and drink preparation	26.5
10.	Participating in sports, exercise, or recreation	21.8
11.	Travel related to relaxing and leisure	19.1
12.	Relaxing, thinking	18.7
13.	Playing games (including computer)	18.2
14.	Travel related to sports, exercise, and recreation	17.4
15.	Travel related to socializing and communicating	16.9
16.	Animals and pets (not veterinary care)	14.7
17.	Purchasing food (except groceries)	14.7
18.	Reading for personal interest	14.3
19.	Travel related to purchasing food (except groceries)	13.9
20.	Telephone calls	13.4
21.	Shopping, except groceries, food, and gas	12.2
22.	Travel related to shopping (except groceries, food, and gas)	12.0
23.	Helping adults in other households	10.5
24.	Travel related to helping adults in other households	10.1
25.	Research, homework	9.1
26.	Travel related to education	8.9
27.	Computer use for leisure (except games)	8.6
28.	Caring for and helping household children	8.3
29.	Grocery shopping	8.2
30.	Travel related to household activities	8.2
31.	Travel related to grocery shopping	8.1
32.	Taking class	7.6
33.	Laundry	7.1
34.	Interior cleaning	6.9
35.	Household and personal organization and planning	6.9
36.	Household and personal email	6.2
37.	Listening to or playing music (not radio)	6.2
38.	Financial services and banking	5.5
39.	Travel related to using financial services and banking	5.5

	percent of men aged 20 to 24 participating in activity
40. Travel related to personal care	4.7%
41. Vehicles	4.5
42. Listening to the radio	4.2
43. Financial management	4.1
44. Lawn, garden, and houseplants	4.0
45. Arts and entertainment (except sports)	3.6
46. Travel related to arts and entertainment	3.0
47. Kitchen and food clean-up	2.9
48. Travel related to religious and spiritual activities	2.9
49. Helping household adults	2.8
50. Caring for and helping children in other households	2.6
51. Travel related to caring for and helping children in other households	2.6
52. Travel related to purchasing gas	2.6
53. Purchasing gas	2.6
54. Volunteer activities	2.5
55. Travel related to caring for and helping household children	2.5
56. Travel related to attending or hosting social events	2.5
57. Attending or hosting social events	2.3
58. Participation in religious practices	2.3
59. Work, other job(s)	2.1
60. Health-related self-care	2.1
61. Interior maintenance, repair, and decoration	2.0
62. Travel related to helping household adults	1.9
63. Storing interior household items, including food	1.8
64. Household services	1.5
65. Household and personal mail and messages (except email)	1.5
66. Travel related to volunteer activities	1.5
67. Attending religious services	1.3
68. Exterior maintenance, repair, and decoration	0.4
69. Medical and care services	0.3
70. Travel related to using medical services	0.2
71. Activities related to household children's education	0.0

Note: Primary activities are those respondents identified as their main activity. Other activities done simultaneously, such as eating while watching TV, are not included. If fewer than 2.0 percent of the total population participated in a primary activity, then the primary activity is not shown.
Source: Bureau of Labor Statistics, unpublished tables from the 2008 American Time Use Survey, Internet site http://www.bls .gov/tus/home.htm; calculations by New Strategist

Table 3.17 Ranking: Percent of Women Aged 20 to 24 Participating in Primary Activities on an Average Day, 2008

(percent of women aged 20 to 24 participating in primary activities on an average day, ranked by percent participating, 2008)

		percent of women aged 20 to 24 participating in activity
	Total, all activities	**100.0%**
1.	Sleeping	99.9
2.	Eating and drinking	94.0
3.	Grooming	79.6
4.	Television	74.2
5.	Work, main job	42.3
6.	Travel related to work	40.1
7.	Food and drink preparation	40.0
8.	Socializing and communicating	37.2
9.	Shopping, except groceries, food, and gas	36.8
10.	Travel related to shopping (except groceries, food, and gas)	35.5
11.	Caring for and helping household children	32.0
12.	Travel related to eating and drinking	27.9
13.	Research, homework	26.4
14.	Interior cleaning	24.8
15.	Travel related to socializing and communicating	23.6
16.	Relaxing, thinking	17.3
17.	Purchasing food (except groceries)	16.8
18.	Telephone calls	16.7
19.	Travel related to education	16.5
20.	Travel related to household activities	15.3
21.	Travel related to relaxing and leisure	15.0
22.	Participating in sports, exercise, or recreation	14.8
23.	Household and personal organization and planning	14.5
24.	Taking class	14.4
25.	Helping adults in other households	14.2
26.	Travel related to purchasing food (except groceries)	14.1
27.	Household and personal email	12.8
28.	Travel related to helping adults in other households	11.6
29.	Laundry	11.2
30.	Travel related to caring for and helping household children	11.2
31.	Travel related to sports, exercise, and recreation	11.2
32.	Reading for personal interest	10.7
33.	Kitchen and food clean-up	10.6
34.	Grocery shopping	10.2
35.	Travel related to grocery shopping	10.2
36.	Animals and pets (not veterinary care)	10.0
37.	Computer use for leisure (except games)	9.0
38.	Playing games (including computer)	7.6
39.	Caring for and helping children in other households	7.1

	percent of women aged 20 to 24 participating in activity
40. Helping household adults	5.2%
41. Travel related to personal care	4.9
42. Travel related to helping household adults	4.9
43. Travel related to caring for and helping children in other households	4.4
44. Travel related to purchasing gas	4.4
45. Purchasing gas	4.4
46. Financial management	4.4
47. Arts and entertainment (except sports)	4.2
48. Work, other job(s)	3.9
49. Travel related to arts and entertainment	3.4
50. Travel related to using financial services and banking	3.1
51. Financial services and banking	3.1
52. Volunteer activities	2.8
53. Health-related self-care	2.7
54. Attending or hosting social events	2.5
55. Travel related to attending or hosting social events	2.5
56. Medical and care services	2.4
57. Storing interior household items, including food	2.4
58. Activities related to household children's education	2.3
59. Travel related to volunteer activities	2.2
60. Household services	2.2
61. Attending religious services	2.1
62. Listening to or playing music (not radio)	2.1
63. Interior maintenance, repair, and decoration	1.9
64. Travel related to using medical services	1.8
65. Lawn, garden, and houseplants	1.7
66. Travel related to religious and spiritual activities	1.6
67. Vehicles	1.2
68. Household and personal mail and messages (except email)	0.9
69. Participation in religious practices	0.8
70. Exterior maintenance, repair, and decoration	0.2
71. Listening to the radio	0.0

Note: Primary activities are those respondents identified as their main activity. Other activities done simultaneously, such as eating while watching TV, are not included. If fewer than 2.0 percent of the total population participated in a primary activity, then the primary activity is not shown.
Source: Bureau of Labor Statistics, unpublished tables from the 2008 American Time Use Survey, Internet site http://www.bls .gov/tus/home.htm; calculations by New Strategist

Table 3.18 Ranking: Average Hours per Day Spent Doing Primary Activities by Total Participants Aged 20 to 24, 2008

(hours per day spent by participants aged 20 to 24 doing primary activities, ranked by time spent doing activity, 2008)

		average hours per day spent by participants aged 20 to 24
	Total, all activities	**24.00**
1.	Sleeping	8.84
2.	Work, main job	7.43
3.	Research, homework	3.30
4.	Television	2.87
5.	Caring for and helping household children	2.13
6.	Socializing and communicating	2.12
7.	Participating in sports, exercise, or recreation	1.90
8.	Interior cleaning	1.61
9.	Shopping, except groceries, food, and gas	1.21
10.	Telephone calls	1.16
11.	Eating and drinking	1.05
12.	Relaxing, thinking	1.02
13.	Grooming	0.89
14.	Helping adults in other households	0.77
15.	Food and drink preparation	0.76
16.	Travel related to work	0.70
17.	Travel related to socializing and communicating	0.55
18.	Travel related to shopping (except groceries, food, and gas)	0.48
19.	Travel related to relaxing and leisure	0.43
20.	Travel related to sports, exercise, and recreation	0.43
21.	Travel related to purchasing food (except groceries)	0.43
22.	Travel related to household activities	0.42
23.	Travel related to eating and drinking	0.39
24.	Purchasing food (except groceries)	0.16

Note: Primary activities are those respondents identified as their main activity. Other activities done simultaneously, such as eating while watching TV, are not included. The primary activities shown are those for which data by age are available.
Source: Bureau of Labor Statistics, unpublished tables from the 2008 American Time Use Survey, Internet site http://www.bls .gov/tus/home.htm; calculations by New Strategist

Table 3.19 Ranking: Average Hours per Day Spent Doing Primary Activities by Male Participants Aged 20 to 24, 2008

(hours per day spent by male participants aged 20 to 24 doing primary activities, ranked by time spent doing activity, 2008)

		average hours per day spent by male participants aged 20 to 24
	Total, all activities	**24.00**
1.	Sleeping	8.89
2.	Work, main job	7.90
3.	Television	3.05
4.	Socializing and communicating	2.29
5.	Eating and drinking	1.02
6.	Travel related to work	0.75
7.	Grooming	0.73
8.	Food and drink preparation	0.66
9.	Travel related to eating and drinking	0.40

Note: Primary activities are those respondents identified as their main activity. Other activities done simultaneously, such as eating while watching TV, are not included. The primary activities shown are those for which data by age are available.
Source: Bureau of Labor Statistics, unpublished tables from the 2008 American Time Use Survey, Internet site http://www.bls .gov/tus/home.htm; calculations by New Strategist

Table 3.20 Ranking: Average Hours per Day Spent Doing Primary Activities by Female Participants Aged 20 to 24, 2008

(hours per day spent by female participants aged 20 to 24 doing primary activities, ranked by time spent doing activity, 2008)

		average hours per day spent by female participants aged 20 to 24
	Total, all activities	**24.00**
1.	Sleeping	8.79
2.	Work, main job	6.75
3.	Television	2.68
4.	Caring for and helping household children	2.24
5.	Socializing and communicating	1.96
6.	Interior cleaning	1.48
7.	Shopping, except groceries, food, and gas	1.26
8.	Eating and drinking	1.09
9.	Grooming	1.07
10.	Food and drink preparation	0.83
11.	Travel related to work	0.62
12.	Travel related to socializing and communicating	0.55
13.	Travel related to shopping (except groceries, food, and gas)	0.46
14.	Travel related to eating and drinking	0.38

Note: Primary activities are those respondents identified as their main activity. Other activities done simultaneously, such as eating while watching TV, are not included. The primary activities shown are those for which data by age are available.
Source: Bureau of Labor Statistics, unpublished tables from the 2008 American Time Use Survey, Internet site http://www.bls .gov/tus/home.htm; calculations by New Strategist

Time Use, 2008: People Aged 25 to 34

Life begins in earnest in the 25-to-34 age group. At this lifestage, most people start a career, marry, have children, and buy a home. Work and family are the dominant priorities. Leisure time is in short supply. With young children in the home and the mortgage payment due, both men and women are busy earning a paycheck and managing a family.

Children are a top priority at this lifestage. Caring for household children as a primary activity ranks fourth in time use among 25-to-34-year-olds (excluding sleep), ahead of grooming or socializing (but, interestingly, not ahead of time spent watching television or eating). Forty-one percent of 25-to-34-year-olds care for household children as a primary activity on an average day. Among women in the age group, the figure is a higher 54 percent. Among men, 29 percent spend time caring for household children as a primary activity on an average day.

Household chores also take up a lot of time. Cleaning house and cooking meals are two of the top ten items on which the average 25-to-34-year-olds spends the most time (excluding sleep). Work is also increasingly important, with 56 percent of the age group working at their main job on an average day (including both weekdays and weekends). Commuting to work makes the top ten list of time-consuming activities as well, with the average person in the age group devoting 0.37 hours going to and from work. Among commuters, the time spent on the road is a much greater 0.74 hours (or 44 minutes).

For 25-to-34-year-olds, children take up a lot of time

(average hours per day spent by people aged 25 to 34 doing primary activities, for the 10 activities on which the average 25-to-34-year-old spends the most time, excluding sleep, 2008)

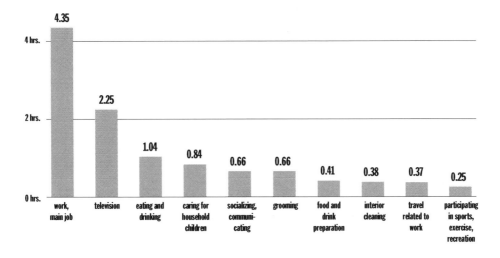

This lifestage is not all work and no play. Watching television as a primary activity ranks second in time use among 25-to-34-year-olds (not including sleep), and socializing ranks fifth. Nine percent of men in the age group play games on an average day (mostly computer games). Nineteen percent participate in sports, exercise, or recreation. Among women, 25 percent shop on an average day for items other than food or gas. Fifteen percent read for personal interest.

The time use of men and women diverges in the 25-to-34 age group, with women spending much more time than men in the laundry room, as well as cleaning house, cooking meals, and washing dishes. Twenty-four percent of women aged 25 to 34 do the laundry on an average day, compared with only 7 percent of men. Men spend more time than women on lawn care and working on vehicles. Not surprisingly, women spend more than twice as much time as men caring for children. Men spend more time at work.

Table 4.1 Time Use by Total People Aged 25 to 34, 2008

(number and percent of total people aged 25 to 34 participating in primary activities on an average day, hours spent doing activity by the average person aged 25 to 34 and by those aged 25 to 34 who participated in the activity, 2008; numbers of participants in thousands)

	participants aged 25 to 34		time spent doing activity (hours)	
	number	percent	average person aged 25 to 34	participants aged 25 to 34
TOTAL, ALL ACTIVITIES	**39,994**	**100.0%**	**24.00**	**24.00**
Personal care	**39,994**	**100.0**	**9.28**	**9.28**
Sleeping	39,985	100.0	8.54	8.54
Sleeplessness	1,619	4.0	0.04	0.93
Grooming	32,594	81.5	0.66	0.81
Health-related self-care	951	2.4	0.07	–
Household activities	**29,530**	**73.8**	**1.50**	**2.03**
Housework	13,978	35.0	0.56	1.60
Interior cleaning	9,836	24.6	0.38	1.56
Laundry	6,168	15.4	0.16	1.03
Storing interior household items, including food	1,455	3.6	0.01	0.34
Food and drink preparation, presentation, and clean-up	21,226	53.1	0.53	1.00
Food and drink preparation	20,303	50.8	0.41	0.80
Kitchen and food clean-up	7,890	19.7	0.12	0.60
Interior maintenance, repair, and decoration	691	1.7	0.03	–
Interior arrangement, decoration, and repairs	537	1.3	0.03	–
Exterior maintenance, repair, and decoration	596	1.5	0.02	–
Lawn, garden, and houseplants	1,927	4.8	0.09	1.80
Animals and pets (not veterinary care)	4,456	11.1	0.07	0.43
Walking, exercising, and playing with pets	2,153	5.4	0.04	0.75
Vehicles	950	2.4	0.03	–
Household management	9,803	24.5	0.15	0.59
Financial management	1,070	2.7	0.02	–
Household and personal organization and planning	4,825	12.1	0.07	0.56
Household and personal mail and messages (except email)	1,499	3.7	0.01	–
Household and personal email	3,731	9.3	0.05	0.59
Caring for and helping household members	**17,541**	**43.9**	**0.93**	**2.13**
Caring for and helping household children	16,515	41.3	0.84	2.05
Physical care for household children	13,970	34.9	0.41	1.17
Reading to or with household children	2,442	6.1	0.03	0.48
Playing with household children (except sports)	5,680	14.2	0.25	1.79
Talking with, listening to household children	1,571	3.9	0.02	0.51
Looking after household children as a primary activity	1,593	4.0	0.05	1.25
Picking up or dropping off household children	6,548	16.4	0.04	0.23
Activities related to household children's education	2,483	6.2	0.05	0.85
Helping household children with homework	2,191	5.5	0.04	0.80
Helping household adults	1,553	3.9	0.01	0.31
Caring for and helping people in other households	**4,232**	**10.6**	**0.09**	**0.84**
Caring for and helping children in other households	1,252	3.1	0.03	–

	participants aged 25 to 34		time spent doing activity (hours)	
	number	percent	average person aged 25 to 34	participants aged 25 to 34
Helping adults in other households	3,006	7.5%	0.04	0.52
Picking up or dropping off adults in other households	2,137	5.3	0.01	0.14
Work and work-related activities	**23,756**	**59.4**	**4.57**	**7.69**
Work, main job	22,456	56.1	4.35	7.74
Work, other job(s)	1,002	2.5	0.11	–
Education	**2,356**	**5.9**	**0.29**	**4.88**
Taking class	1,146	2.9	0.10	–
Taking class for degree, certification, or licensure	900	2.3	0.09	–
Research, homework	1,847	4.6	0.19	4.05
Consumer purchases (store, telephone, Internet)	**16,699**	**41.8**	**0.37**	**0.88**
Grocery shopping	5,068	12.7	0.09	0.74
Purchasing gas	1,803	4.5	0.01	0.17
Purchasing food (except groceries)	5,887	14.7	0.02	0.16
Shopping, except groceries, food, and gas	8,997	22.5	0.24	1.06
Professional and personal care services	**3,067**	**7.7**	**0.06**	**0.82**
Financial services and banking	941	2.4	0.01	–
Banking	796	2.0	0.00	–
Medical and care services	887	2.2	0.03	–
Using health and care services outside the home	856	2.1	0.02	–
Household services	**839**	**2.1**	**0.01**	–
Eating and drinking	**38,223**	**95.6**	**1.04**	**1.08**
Socializing, relaxing, and leisure	**37,510**	**93.8**	**3.82**	**4.08**
Socializing and communicating	14,302	35.8	0.66	1.84
Attending or hosting social events	1,079	2.7	0.11	3.98
Relaxing and leisure	35,145	87.9	2.97	3.38
Relaxing, thinking	7,044	17.6	0.19	1.08
Television	31,101	77.8	2.25	2.90
Listening to the radio	444	1.1	0.01	–
Listening to or playing music (not radio)	692	1.7	0.02	–
Playing games (including computer)	2,651	6.6	0.19	2.87
Computer use for leisure (except games)	3,970	9.9	0.18	1.80
Reading for personal interest	4,932	12.3	0.12	0.94
Arts and entertainment (except sports)	1,373	3.4	0.09	2.55
Sports, exercise, and recreation	**6,812**	**17.0**	**0.28**	**1.63**
Participating in sports, exercise, or recreation	6,545	16.4	0.25	1.51
Using cardiovascular equipment	1,050	2.6	0.02	–
Walking	1,258	3.1	0.03	–
Working out, unspecified	1,142	2.9	0.03	–
Religious and spiritual activities	**2,515**	**6.3**	**0.10**	**1.61**
Attending religious services	1,501	3.8	0.07	1.90
Participation in religious practices	843	2.1	0.02	–

	participants aged 25 to 34		time spent doing activity (hours)	
	number	percent	average person aged 25 to 34	participants aged 25 to 34
Volunteer activities	**1,762**	**4.4%**	**0.08**	**1.86**
Administrative and support activities	618	1.5	0.02	–
Telephone calls	**4,784**	**12.0**	**0.09**	**0.76**
Telephone calls to or from family members	2,151	5.4	0.03	0.61
Telephone calls to or from friends, neighbors, or acquaintances	1,670	4.2	0.04	0.85
Traveling	**36,456**	**91.2**	**1.31**	**1.44**
Travel related to personal care	1,073	2.7	0.01	–
Travel related to household activities	3,601	9.0	0.04	0.43
Travel related to household management	2,201	5.5	0.03	0.48
Travel related to caring for and helping household members	8,683	21.7	0.13	0.62
Travel related to caring for and helping household children	7,725	19.3	0.11	0.56
Travel related to helping household adults	1,021	2.6	0.02	–
Travel related to caring for and helping people in other households	3,640	9.1	0.05	0.56
Travel related to caring for and helping children in other households	914	2.3	0.01	–
Travel related to helping adults in other households	2,755	6.9	0.04	–
Travel related to work	19,758	49.4	0.37	0.74
Travel related to education	1,148	2.9	0.02	–
Travel related to taking class	990	2.5	0.02	–
Travel related to consumer purchases	16,121	40.3	0.24	0.60
Travel related to grocery shopping	5,089	12.7	0.05	0.38
Travel related to purchasing gas	1,750	4.4	0.04	1.01
Travel related to purchasing food (except groceries)	5,317	13.3	0.04	0.33
Travel related to shopping (except groceries, food, and gas)	8,546	21.4	0.10	0.48
Travel related to using professional and personal care services	2,812	7.0	0.03	0.37
Travel related to using financial services and banking	887	2.2	0.00	–
Travel related to using medical services	850	2.1	0.01	–
Travel related to eating and drinking	10,245	25.6	0.13	0.51
Travel related to socializing, relaxing, and leisure	10,775	26.9	0.20	0.74
Travel related to socializing and communicating	7,550	18.9	0.10	0.52
Travel related to attending or hosting social events	967	2.4	0.01	0.60
Travel related to relaxing and leisure	2,957	7.4	0.03	0.46
Travel related to arts and entertainment	1,019	2.5	0.02	0.74
Travel related to sports, exercise, and recreation	3,672	9.2	0.04	0.45
Travel related to participating in sports, exercise, recreation	3,393	8.5	0.03	0.41
Travel related to religious and spiritual activities	1,685	4.2	0.02	0.36
Travel related to volunteer activities	1,081	2.7	0.01	0.36

Note: Primary activities are those respondents identified as their main activity. Other activities done simultaneously, such as eating while watching TV, are not included. Numbers may not add to total because not all subcategories are shown. If fewer than 2.0 percent of the total population participated in a primary activity, then the primary activity is not shown. "–" means sample is too small to make a reliable estimate.
Source: Bureau of Labor Statistics, unpublished tables from the 2008 American Time Use Survey, Internet site http://www.bls.gov/tus/home.htm; calculations by New Strategist

Table 4.2 Time Use by Men Aged 25 to 34, 2008

(number and percent of men aged 25 to 34 participating in primary activities on an average day, hours spent doing activity by the average man aged 25 to 34 and by men aged 25 to 34 who participated in the activity, 2008; numbers of participants in thousands)

	men aged 25 to 34 participating		time spent doing activity (hours)	
	number	percent	average man aged 25 to 34	male participants aged 25 to 34
TOTAL, ALL ACTIVITIES	**20,008**	**100.0%**	**24.00**	**24.00**
Personal care	**20,008**	**100.0**	**9.14**	**9.14**
Sleeping	19,999	100.0	8.48	8.48
Sleeplessness	882	4.4	0.04	–
Grooming	15,919	79.6	0.56	0.70
Health-related self-care	397	2.0	0.09	–
Household activities	**12,613**	**63.0**	**1.06**	**1.68**
Housework	4,424	22.1	0.28	1.28
Interior cleaning	3,046	15.2	0.21	1.38
Laundry	1,363	6.8	0.07	0.98
Storing interior household items, including food	521	2.6	0.04	–
Food and drink preparation, presentation, and clean-up	7,599	38.0	0.32	0.85
Food and drink preparation	7,243	36.2	0.26	0.71
Kitchen and food clean-up	1,985	9.9	0.06	0.64
Interior maintenance, repair, and decoration	445	2.2	0.04	–
Interior arrangement, decoration, and repairs	352	1.8	0.03	–
Exterior maintenance, repair, and decoration	333	1.7	0.03	–
Lawn, garden, and houseplants	1,116	5.6	0.12	2.12
Animals and pets (not veterinary care)	1,403	7.0	0.05	–
Walking, exercising, and playing with pets	806	4.0	0.03	–
Vehicles	744	3.7	0.06	–
Household management	4,136	20.7	0.13	0.62
Financial management	436	2.2	0.01	–
Household and personal organization and planning	1,982	9.9	0.06	0.63
Household and personal mail and messages (except email)	748	3.7	0.01	–
Household and personal email	1,635	8.2	0.04	–
Caring for and helping household members	**6,367**	**31.8**	**0.56**	**1.76**
Caring for and helping household children	5,820	29.1	0.52	1.78
Physical care for household children	4,418	22.1	0.19	0.86
Reading to or with household children	746	3.7	0.02	–
Playing with household children (except sports)	2,332	11.7	0.23	2.01
Talking with, listening to household children	354	1.8	0.01	–
Looking after household children as a primary activity	414	2.1	0.04	–
Picking up or dropping off household children	1,636	8.2	0.01	0.16
Activities related to household children's education	429	2.1	0.02	–
Helping household children with homework	392	2.0	0.02	–
Helping household adults	763	3.8	0.02	–
Caring for and helping people in other households	**2,041**	**10.2**	**0.07**	**0.68**
Caring for and helping children in other households	433	2.2	0.02	–

	men aged 25 to 34 participating		time spent doing activity (hours)	
	number	percent	average man aged 25 to 34	male participants aged 25 to 34
Helping adults in other households	1,581	7.9%	0.04	0.56
Picking up or dropping off adults in other households	1,191	6.0	0.01	–
Work and work-related activities	**13,539**	**67.7**	**5.47**	**8.09**
Work, main job	12,804	64.0	5.23	8.17
Work, other job(s)	519	2.6	0.09	–
Education	**1,054**	**5.3**	**0.30**	–
Taking class	510	2.5	0.10	–
Taking class for degree, certification, or licensure	466	2.3	0.09	–
Research, homework	957	4.8	0.20	–
Consumer purchases (store, telephone, Internet)	**7,588**	**37.9**	**0.30**	**0.78**
Grocery shopping	1,864	9.3	0.07	0.74
Purchasing gas	1,028	5.1	0.01	–
Purchasing food (except groceries)	2,936	14.7	0.02	0.14
Shopping, except groceries, food, and gas	3,969	19.8	0.19	0.98
Professional and personal care services	**1,060**	**5.3**	**0.03**	–
Financial services and banking	475	2.4	0.01	–
Banking	362	1.8	0.00	–
Medical and care services	142	0.7	0.01	–
Using health and care services outside the home	125	0.6	0.01	–
Household services	**301**	**1.5**	**0.01**	–
Eating and drinking	**19,261**	**96.3**	**1.06**	**1.10**
Socializing, relaxing, and leisure	**18,628**	**93.1**	**3.93**	**4.22**
Socializing and communicating	6,864	34.3	0.61	1.78
Attending or hosting social events	326	1.6	0.07	–
Relaxing and leisure	17,548	87.7	3.13	3.57
Relaxing, thinking	4,100	20.5	0.22	1.05
Television	15,669	78.3	2.34	2.99
Listening to the radio	350	1.7	0.01	–
Listening to or playing music (not radio)	412	2.1	0.02	–
Playing games (including computer)	1,814	9.1	0.28	3.09
Computer use for leisure (except games)	1,781	8.9	0.18	2.01
Reading for personal interest	1,859	9.3	0.07	0.73
Arts and entertainment (except sports)	780	3.9	0.11	–
Sports, exercise, and recreation	**3,842**	**19.2**	**0.35**	**1.84**
Participating in sports, exercise, or recreation	3,714	18.6	0.32	1.70
Using cardiovascular equipment	266	1.3	0.01	–
Walking	792	4.0	0.03	–
Working out, unspecified	474	2.4	0.03	–
Religious and spiritual activities	**1,206**	**6.0**	**0.08**	**1.34**
Attending religious services	635	3.2	0.05	–
Participation in religious practices	582	2.9	0.02	–

	men aged 25 to 34 participating		time spent doing activity (hours)	
	number	percent	average man aged 25 to 34	male participants aged 25 to 34
Volunteer activities	**709**	**3.5%**	**0.06**	–
Administrative and support activities	266	1.3	0.01	–
Telephone calls	**1,931**	**9.7**	**0.06**	**0.64**
Telephone calls to or from family members	762	3.8	0.02	–
Telephone calls to or from friends, neighbors, or acquaintances	600	3.0	0.02	–
Traveling	**18,420**	**92.1**	**1.38**	**1.50**
Travel related to personal care	743	3.7	0.01	–
Travel related to household activities	1,899	9.5	0.05	0.52
Travel related to household management	1,139	5.7	0.03	–
Travel related to caring for and helping household members	2,296	11.5	0.06	0.53
Travel related to caring for and helping household children	1,907	9.5	0.05	0.52
Travel related to helping household adults	434	2.2	0.01	–
Travel related to caring for and helping people in other households	1,828	9.1	0.05	0.54
Travel related to caring for and helping children in other households	326	1.6	0.01	–
Travel related to helping adults in other households	1,469	7.3	0.04	–
Travel related to work	11,432	57.1	0.49	0.86
Travel related to education	498	2.5	0.02	–
Travel related to taking class	425	2.1	0.01	–
Travel related to consumer purchases	7,240	36.2	0.22	0.60
Travel related to grocery shopping	1,864	9.3	0.05	0.48
Travel related to purchasing gas	978	4.9	0.03	–
Travel related to purchasing food (except groceries)	2,552	12.8	0.04	0.34
Travel related to shopping (except groceries, food, and gas)	3,766	18.8	0.09	0.50
Travel related to using professional and personal care services	1,034	5.2	0.01	–
Travel related to using financial services and banking	475	2.4	0.01	–
Travel related to using medical services	142	0.7	0.00	–
Travel related to eating and drinking	5,541	27.7	0.16	0.58
Travel related to socializing, relaxing, and leisure	5,185	25.9	0.22	0.84
Travel related to socializing and communicating	3,551	17.7	0.09	0.49
Travel related to attending or hosting social events	298	1.5	0.01	–
Travel related to relaxing and leisure	1,642	8.2	0.04	0.45
Travel related to arts and entertainment	524	2.6	0.02	–
Travel related to sports, exercise, and recreation	2,108	10.5	0.05	0.51
Travel related to participating in sports, exercise, recreation	1,959	9.8	0.05	0.46
Travel related to religious and spiritual activities	678	3.4	0.01	–
Travel related to volunteer activities	420	2.1	0.01	–

Note: Primary activities are those respondents identified as their main activity. Other activities done simultaneously, such as eating while watching TV, are not included. Numbers may not add to total because not all subcategories are shown. If fewer than 2.0 percent of the total population participated in a primary activity, then the primary activity is not shown. "–" means sample is too small to make a reliable estimate.
Source: Bureau of Labor Statistics, unpublished tables from the 2008 American Time Use Survey, Internet site http://www.bls.gov/tus/home.htm; calculations by New Strategist

Table 4.3 **Time Use by Women Aged 25 to 34, 2008**

(number and percent of women aged 25 to 34 participating in primary activities on an average day, hours spent doing activity by the average woman aged 25 to 34 and by women aged 25 to 34 who participated in the activity, 2008; numbers of participants in thousands)

	women aged 25 to 34 participating		time spent doing activity (hours)	
	number	percent	average woman aged 25 to 34	female participants aged 25 to 34
TOTAL, ALL ACTIVITIES	**19,986**	**100.0%**	**24.00**	**24.00**
Personal care	**19,986**	**100.0**	**9.43**	**9.43**
Sleeping	19,986	100.0	8.57	8.60
Sleeplessness	737	3.7	0.03	–
Grooming	16,676	83.4	0.76	0.91
Health-related self-care	554	2.8	0.04	–
Household activities	**16,917**	**84.6**	**1.93**	**2.29**
Housework	9,554	47.8	0.83	1.74
Interior cleaning	6,789	34.0	0.56	1.64
Laundry	4,805	24.0	0.25	1.05
Storing interior household items, including food	935	4.7	0.02	0.39
Food and drink preparation, presentation, and clean-up	13,627	68.2	0.74	1.08
Food and drink preparation	13,060	65.3	0.56	0.85
Kitchen and food clean-up	5,906	29.6	0.17	0.59
Interior maintenance, repair, and decoration	246	1.2	0.02	–
Interior arrangement, decoration, and repairs	185	0.9	0.02	–
Exterior maintenance, repair, and decoration	263	1.3	0.02	–
Lawn, garden, and houseplants	810	4.1	0.05	–
Animals and pets (not veterinary care)	3,503	17.5	0.09	0.40
Walking, exercising, and playing with pets	1,347	6.7	0.05	–
Vehicles	205	1.0	0.01	–
Household management	5,667	28.4	0.16	0.57
Financial management	635	3.2	0.02	–
Household and personal organization and planning	2,843	14.2	0.07	0.51
Household and personal mail and messages (except email)	751	3.8	0.01	–
Household and personal email	2,096	10.5	0.07	0.63
Caring for and helping household members	**11,173**	**55.9**	**1.31**	**2.35**
Caring for and helping household children	10,695	53.5	1.17	2.19
Physical care for household children	9,551	47.8	0.63	1.31
Reading to or with household children	1,696	8.5	0.04	0.47
Playing with household children (except sports)	3,348	16.8	0.27	1.64
Talking with, listening to household children	1,216	6.1	0.03	0.51
Looking after household children as a primary activity	1,179	5.9	0.06	1.08
Picking up or dropping off household children	4,912	24.6	0.06	0.25
Activities related to household children's education	2,054	10.3	0.09	0.87
Helping household children with homework	1,800	9.0	0.07	0.80
Helping household adults	790	4.0	0.01	–
Caring for and helping people in other households	**2,191**	**11.0**	**0.11**	**0.98**
Caring for and helping children in other households	819	4.1	0.05	

	women aged 25 to 34 participating		time spent doing activity (hours)	
	number	percent	average woman aged 25 to 34	female participants aged 25 to 34
Helping adults in other households	1,425	7.1%	0.03	0.49
Picking up or dropping off adults in other households	946	4.7	0.01	0.15
Work and work-related activities	**10,218**	**51.1**	**3.66**	**7.15**
Work, main job	9,652	48.3	3.47	7.18
Work, other job(s)	484	2.4	0.12	–
Education	**1,320**	**6.6**	**0.27**	**4.18**
Taking class	636	3.2	0.10	–
Taking class for degree, certification, or licensure	433	2.2	0.08	–
Research, homework	889	4.4	0.17	–
Consumer purchases (store, telephone, Internet)	**9,110**	**45.6**	**0.44**	**0.96**
Grocery shopping	3,205	16.0	0.12	0.75
Purchasing gas	775	3.9	0.01	–
Purchasing food (except groceries)	2,951	14.8	0.03	0.18
Shopping, except groceries, food, and gas	5,028	25.2	0.28	1.12
Professional and personal care services	**2,007**	**10.0**	**0.09**	**0.91**
Financial services and banking	465	2.3	0.01	–
Banking	434	2.2	0.00	–
Medical and care services	745	3.7	0.05	–
Using health and care services outside the home	732	3.7	0.04	–
Household services	**538**	**2.7**	**0.02**	**–**
Eating and drinking	**18,962**	**94.9**	**1.01**	**1.06**
Socializing, relaxing, and leisure	**18,882**	**94.5**	**3.72**	**3.94**
Socializing and communicating	7,438	37.2	0.70	1.89
Attending or hosting social events	753	3.8	0.14	–
Relaxing and leisure	17,597	88.0	2.81	3.19
Relaxing, thinking	2,945	14.7	0.16	1.10
Television	15,432	77.2	2.16	2.80
Listening to the radio	95	0.5	0.00	–
Listening to or playing music (not radio)	280	1.4	0.02	–
Playing games (including computer)	837	4.2	0.10	–
Computer use for leisure (except games)	2,189	11.0	0.18	1.63
Reading for personal interest	3,072	15.4	0.16	1.06
Arts and entertainment (except sports)	593	3.0	0.06	–
Sports, exercise, and recreation	**2,970**	**14.9**	**0.20**	**1.37**
Participating in sports, exercise, or recreation	2,831	14.2	0.18	1.25
Using cardiovascular equipment	784	3.9	0.03	–
Walking	466	2.3	0.02	–
Working out, unspecified	668	3.3	0.03	–
Religious and spiritual activities	**1,309**	**6.5**	**0.12**	**1.86**
Attending religious services	866	4.3	0.09	2.07
Participation in religious practices	261	1.3	0.01	–

	women aged 25 to 34 participating		time spent doing activity (hours)	
	number	percent	average woman aged 25 to 34	female participants aged 25 to 34
Volunteer activities	**1,053**	**5.3%**	**0.11**	**2.04**
Administrative and support activities	353	1.8	0.02	–
Telephone calls	**2,853**	**14.3**	**0.12**	**0.83**
Telephone calls to or from family members	1,388	6.9	0.04	0.59
Telephone calls to or from friends, neighbors, or acquaintances	1,070	5.4	0.05	–
Traveling	**18,036**	**90.2**	**1.24**	**1.38**
Travel related to personal care	330	1.7	0.01	–
Travel related to household activities	1,702	8.5	0.03	0.33
Travel related to household management	1,063	5.3	0.02	0.35
Travel related to caring for and helping household members	6,387	32.0	0.21	0.65
Travel related to caring for and helping household children	5,818	29.1	0.17	0.57
Travel related to helping household adults	587	2.9	0.03	–
Travel related to caring for and helping people in other households	1,812	9.1	0.05	0.58
Travel related to caring for and helping children in other households	588	2.9	0.01	–
Travel related to helping adults in other households	1,287	6.4	0.04	–
Travel related to work	8,326	41.7	0.24	0.58
Travel related to education	650	3.3	0.03	–
Travel related to taking class	564	2.8	0.02	–
Travel related to consumer purchases	8,881	44.4	0.26	0.60
Travel related to grocery shopping	3,226	16.1	0.05	0.32
Travel related to purchasing gas	772	3.9	0.06	–
Travel related to purchasing food (except groceries)	2,765	13.8	0.04	0.32
Travel related to shopping (except groceries, food, and gas)	4,780	23.9	0.11	0.47
Travel related to using professional and personal care services	1,778	8.9	0.04	0.42
Travel related to using financial services and banking	412	2.1	0.00	–
Travel related to using medical services	708	3.5	0.02	–
Travel related to eating and drinking	4,704	23.5	0.10	0.44
Travel related to socializing, relaxing, and leisure	5,590	28.0	0.18	0.64
Travel related to socializing and communicating	3,998	20.0	0.11	0.55
Travel related to attending or hosting social events	669	3.3	0.02	–
Travel related to relaxing and leisure	1,315	6.6	0.03	0.46
Travel related to arts and entertainment	496	2.5	0.01	–
Travel related to sports, exercise, and recreation	1,564	7.8	0.03	0.37
Travel related to participating in sports, exercise, recreation	1,434	7.2	0.02	0.33
Travel related to religious and spiritual activities	1,008	5.0	0.02	0.39
Travel related to volunteer activities	661	3.3	0.01	–

Note: Primary activities are those respondents identified as their main activity. Other activities done simultaneously, such as eating while watching TV, are not included. Numbers may not add to total because not all subcategories are shown. If fewer than 2.0 percent of the total population participated in a primary activity, then the primary activity is not shown. "–" means sample is too small to make a reliable estimate.
Source: Bureau of Labor Statistics, unpublished tables from the 2008 American Time Use Survey, Internet site http://www.bls .gov/tus/home.htm; calculations by New Strategist

Table 4.4 Indexed Time Use of Total People Aged 25 to 34, 2008

(hours spent doing primary activities on an average day by people aged 25 to 34 and by total people aged 15 or older, and index of time spent by people aged 25 to 34 to total people, 2008)

	average hours		index, people aged 25 to 34 to total people
	people aged 25 to 34	total people	
TOTAL, ALL ACTIVITIES	**24.00**	**24.00**	**100**
Personal care	**9.28**	**9.38**	**99**
Sleeping	8.54	8.60	99
Sleeplessness	0.04	0.06	67
Grooming	0.66	0.67	99
Health-related self-care	0.07	0.09	78
Household activities	**1.50**	**1.77**	**85**
Housework	0.56	0.58	97
Interior cleaning	0.38	0.37	103
Laundry	0.16	0.17	94
Storing interior household items, including food	0.01	0.02	50
Food and drink preparation, presentation, and clean-up	0.53	0.52	102
Food and drink preparation	0.41	0.40	103
Kitchen and food clean-up	0.12	0.12	100
Interior maintenance, repair, and decoration	0.03	0.07	43
Interior arrangement, decoration, and repairs	0.03	0.05	60
Exterior maintenance, repair, and decoration	0.02	0.06	33
Lawn, garden, and houseplants	0.09	0.19	47
Animals and pets (not veterinary care)	0.07	0.09	78
Walking, exercising, and playing with pets	0.04	0.04	100
Vehicles	0.03	0.04	75
Household management	0.15	0.21	71
Financial management	0.02	0.03	67
Household and personal organization and planning	0.07	0.09	78
Household and personal mail and messages (except email)	0.01	0.02	50
Household and personal email	0.05	0.06	83
Caring for and helping household members	**0.93**	**0.45**	**207**
Caring for and helping household children	0.84	0.37	227
Physical care for household children	0.41	0.17	241
Reading to or with household children	0.03	0.01	300
Playing with household children (except sports)	0.25	0.09	278
Talking with, listening to household children	0.02	0.02	100
Looking after household children as a primary activity	0.05	0.03	167
Picking up or dropping off household children	0.04	0.02	200
Activities related to household children's education	0.05	0.04	125
Helping household children with homework	0.04	0.03	133
Helping household adults	0.01	0.01	100
Caring for and helping people in other households	**0.09**	**0.16**	**56**
Caring for and helping children in other households	0.03	0.09	33

	average hours		index, people aged 25 to 34
	people aged 25 to 34	total people	to total people
Helping adults in other households	0.04	0.06	67
Picking up or dropping off adults in other households	0.01	0.01	100
Work and work-related activities	**4.57**	**3.45**	**132**
Work, main job	4.35	3.28	133
Work, other job(s)	0.11	0.09	122
Education	**0.29**	**0.44**	**66**
Taking class	0.10	0.27	37
Taking class for degree, certification, or licensure	0.09	0.26	35
Research, homework	0.19	0.16	119
Consumer purchases (store, telephone, Internet)	**0.37**	**0.38**	**97**
Grocery shopping	0.09	0.10	90
Purchasing gas	0.01	0.01	100
Purchasing food (except groceries)	0.02	0.02	100
Shopping, except groceries, food, and gas	0.24	0.25	96
Professional and personal care services	**0.06**	**0.08**	**75**
Financial services and banking	0.01	0.01	100
Banking	0.00	0.01	0
Medical and care services	0.03	0.05	60
Using health and care services outside the home	0.02	0.04	50
Household services	**0.01**	**0.01**	**100**
Eating and drinking	**1.04**	**1.11**	**94**
Socializing, relaxing, and leisure	**3.82**	**4.62**	**83**
Socializing and communicating	0.66	0.64	103
Attending or hosting social events	0.11	0.07	157
Relaxing and leisure	2.97	3.83	78
Relaxing, thinking	0.19	0.27	70
Television	2.25	2.77	81
Listening to the radio	0.01	0.03	33
Listening to or playing music (not radio)	0.02	0.03	67
Playing games (including computer)	0.19	0.20	95
Computer use for leisure (except games)	0.18	0.14	129
Reading for personal interest	0.12	0.34	35
Arts and entertainment (except sports)	0.09	0.09	100
Sports, exercise, and recreation	**0.28**	**0.33**	**85**
Participating in sports, exercise, or recreation	0.25	0.29	86
Using cardiovascular equipment	0.02	0.02	100
Walking	0.03	0.04	75
Working out, unspecified	0.03	0.03	100
Religious and spiritual activities	**0.10**	**0.14**	**71**
Attending religious services	0.07	0.09	78
Participation in religious practices	0.02	0.04	50

	average hours		index, people aged 25 to 34 to total people
	people aged 25 to 34	total people	
Volunteer activities	**0.08**	**0.15**	**53**
Administrative and support activities	0.02	0.04	50
Telephone calls	**0.09**	**0.13**	**69**
Telephone calls to or from family members	0.03	0.04	75
Telephone calls to or from friends, neighbors, or acquaintances	0.04	0.04	100
Traveling	**1.31**	**1.20**	**109**
Travel related to personal care	0.01	0.01	100
Travel related to household activities	0.04	0.04	100
Travel related to household management	0.03	0.02	150
Travel related to caring for and helping household members	0.13	0.08	163
Travel related to caring for and helping household children	0.11	0.06	183
Travel related to helping household adults	0.02	0.02	100
Travel related to caring for and helping people in other households	0.05	0.06	83
Travel related to caring for and helping children in other households	0.01	0.02	50
Travel related to helping adults in other households	0.04	0.04	100
Travel related to work	0.37	0.28	132
Travel related to education	0.02	0.03	67
Travel related to taking class	0.02	0.03	67
Travel related to consumer purchases	0.24	0.24	100
Travel related to grocery shopping	0.05	0.05	100
Travel related to purchasing gas	0.04	0.02	200
Travel related to purchasing food (except groceries)	0.04	0.04	100
Travel related to shopping (except groceries, food, and gas)	0.10	0.12	83
Travel related to using professional and personal care services	0.03	0.04	75
Travel related to using financial services and banking	0.00	0.01	0
Travel related to using medical services	0.01	0.02	50
Travel related to eating and drinking	0.13	0.12	108
Travel related to socializing, relaxing, and leisure	0.20	0.18	111
Travel related to socializing and communicating	0.10	0.09	111
Travel related to attending or hosting social events	0.01	0.01	100
Travel related to relaxing and leisure	0.03	0.04	75
Travel related to arts and entertainment	0.02	0.02	100
Travel related to sports, exercise, and recreation	0.04	0.04	100
Travel related to participating in sports, exercise, recreation	0.03	0.04	75
Travel related to religious and spiritual activities	0.02	0.02	100
Travel related to volunteer activities	0.01	0.02	50

Note: The index is calculated by dividing average time spent by people in the age group doing primary activity by average time spent by total people doing primary activity and multiplying by 100. Primary activities are those respondents identified as their main activity. Other activities done simultaneously, such as eating while watching TV, are not included. Numbers may not add to total because not all subcategories are shown. If fewer than 2.0 percent of the total population participated in a primary activity, then the primary activity is not shown.
Source: Bureau of Labor Statistics, unpublished tables from the 2008 American Time Use Survey, Internet site http://www.bls .gov/tus/home.htm; calculations by New Strategist

Table 4.5 Indexed Time Use of Men Aged 25 to 34, 2008

(hours spent doing primary activities on an average day by men aged 25 to 34 and by total men aged 15 or older, and index of time spent by men aged 25 to 34 to total men, 2008)

	average hours		index, men aged 25 to 34 to total men
	men aged 25 to 34	total men	
TOTAL, ALL ACTIVITIES	**24.00**	**24.00**	**100**
Personal care	**9.14**	**9.21**	**99**
Sleeping	8.48	8.56	99
Sleeplessness	0.04	0.05	80
Grooming	0.56	0.56	100
Health-related self-care	0.09	0.07	129
Household activities	**1.06**	**1.32**	**80**
Housework	0.28	0.24	117
Interior cleaning	0.21	0.17	124
Laundry	0.07	0.06	117
Storing interior household items, including food	0.04	0.01	400
Food and drink preparation, presentation, and clean-up	0.32	0.30	107
Food and drink preparation	0.26	0.25	104
Kitchen and food clean-up	0.06	0.05	120
Interior maintenance, repair, and decoration	0.04	0.10	40
Interior arrangement, decoration, and repairs	0.03	0.08	38
Exterior maintenance, repair, and decoration	0.03	0.08	38
Lawn, garden, and houseplants	0.12	0.26	46
Animals and pets (not veterinary care)	0.05	0.08	63
Walking, exercising, and playing with pets	0.03	0.04	75
Vehicles	0.06	0.07	86
Household management	0.13	0.16	81
Financial management	0.01	0.03	33
Household and personal organization and planning	0.06	0.07	86
Household and personal mail and messages (except email)	0.01	0.02	50
Household and personal email	0.04	0.05	80
Caring for and helping household members	**0.56**	**0.30**	**187**
Caring for and helping household children	0.52	0.25	208
Physical care for household children	0.19	0.09	211
Reading to or with household children	0.02	0.01	200
Playing with household children (except sports)	0.23	0.08	288
Talking with, listening to household children	0.01	0.01	100
Looking after household children as a primary activity	0.04	0.02	200
Picking up or dropping off household children	0.01	0.01	100
Activities related to household children's education	0.02	0.02	100
Helping household children with homework	0.02	0.02	100
Helping household adults	0.02	0.01	200
Caring for and helping people in other households	**0.07**	**0.13**	**54**
Caring for and helping children in other households	0.02	0.05	40

	average hours		index, men aged 25 to 34
	men aged 25 to 34	total men	to total men
Helping adults in other households	0.04	0.07	57
Picking up or dropping off adults in other households	0.01	0.01	100
Work and work-related activities	**5.47**	**4.16**	**131**
Work, main job	5.23	3.96	132
Work, other job(s)	0.09	0.10	90
Education	**0.30**	**0.39**	**77**
Taking class	0.10	0.27	37
Taking class for degree, certification, or licensure	0.09	0.27	33
Research, homework	0.20	0.12	167
Consumer purchases (store, telephone, Internet)	**0.30**	**0.28**	**107**
Grocery shopping	0.07	0.06	117
Purchasing gas	0.01	0.01	100
Purchasing food (except groceries)	0.02	0.02	100
Shopping, except groceries, food, and gas	0.19	0.19	100
Professional and personal care services	**0.03**	**0.06**	**50**
Financial services and banking	0.01	0.01	100
Banking	0.00	0.00	–
Medical and care services	0.01	0.04	25
Using health and care services outside the home	0.01	0.03	33
Household services	**0.01**	**0.01**	**100**
Eating and drinking	**1.06**	**1.15**	**92**
Socializing, relaxing, and leisure	**3.93**	**4.83**	**81**
Socializing and communicating	0.61	0.59	103
Attending or hosting social events	0.07	0.06	117
Relaxing and leisure	3.13	4.09	77
Relaxing, thinking	0.22	0.27	81
Television	2.34	3.01	78
Listening to the radio	0.01	0.03	33
Listening to or playing music (not radio)	0.02	0.04	50
Playing games (including computer)	0.28	0.25	112
Computer use for leisure (except games)	0.18	0.15	120
Reading for personal interest	0.07	0.29	24
Arts and entertainment (except sports)	0.11	0.09	122
Sports, exercise, and recreation	**0.35**	**0.44**	**80**
Participating in sports, exercise, or recreation	0.32	0.40	80
Using cardiovascular equipment	0.01	0.01	100
Walking	0.03	0.04	75
Working out, unspecified	0.03	0.04	75
Religious and spiritual activities	**0.08**	**0.12**	**67**
Attending religious services	0.05	0.07	71
Participation in religious practices	0.02	0.03	67

	average hours		index, men aged 25 to 34 to total men
	men aged 25 to 34	total men	
Volunteer activities	**0.06**	**0.14**	**43**
Administrative and support activities	0.01	0.03	33
Telephone calls	**0.06**	**0.07**	**86**
Telephone calls to or from family members	0.02	0.02	100
Telephone calls to or from friends, neighbors, or acquaintances	0.02	0.02	100
Traveling	**1.38**	**1.23**	**112**
Travel related to personal care	0.01	0.01	100
Travel related to household activities	0.05	0.04	125
Travel related to household management	0.03	0.03	100
Travel related to caring for and helping household members	0.06	0.06	100
Travel related to caring for and helping household children	0.05	0.04	125
Travel related to helping household adults	0.01	0.02	50
Travel related to caring for and helping people in other households	0.05	0.06	83
Travel related to caring for and helping children in other households	0.01	0.01	100
Travel related to helping adults in other households	0.04	0.04	100
Travel related to work	0.49	0.36	136
Travel related to education	0.02	0.03	67
Travel related to taking class	0.01	0.02	50
Travel related to consumer purchases	0.22	0.21	105
Travel related to grocery shopping	0.05	0.04	125
Travel related to purchasing gas	0.03	0.02	150
Travel related to purchasing food (except groceries)	0.04	0.04	100
Travel related to shopping (except groceries, food, and gas)	0.09	0.11	82
Travel related to using professional and personal care services	0.01	0.03	33
Travel related to using financial services and banking	0.01	0.01	100
Travel related to using medical services	0.00	0.01	0
Travel related to eating and drinking	0.16	0.13	123
Travel related to socializing, relaxing, and leisure	0.22	0.18	122
Travel related to socializing and communicating	0.09	0.09	100
Travel related to attending or hosting social events	0.01	0.01	100
Travel related to relaxing and leisure	0.04	0.04	100
Travel related to arts and entertainment	0.02	0.02	100
Travel related to sports, exercise, and recreation	0.05	0.06	83
Travel related to participating in sports, exercise, recreation	0.05	0.05	100
Travel related to religious and spiritual activities	0.01	0.02	50
Travel related to volunteer activities	0.01	0.02	50

Note: The index is calculated by dividing average time spent by men in the age group doing primary activity by average time spent by total men doing primary activity and multiplying by 100. Primary activities are those respondents identified as their main activity. Other activities done simultaneously, such as eating while watching TV, are not included. Numbers may not add to total because not all subcategories are shown. If fewer than 2.0 percent of the total population participated in a primary activity, then the primary activity is not shown. "–" means denominator is zero.
Source: Bureau of Labor Statistics, unpublished tables from the 2008 American Time Use Survey, Internet site http://www.bls.gov/tus/home.htm; calculations by New Strategist

Table 4.6 Indexed Time Use of Women Aged 25 to 34, 2008

(hours spent doing primary activities on an average day by women aged 25 to 34 and by total women aged 15 or older, and index of time spent by women aged 25 to 34 to total women, 2008)

	average hours		index, women aged 25 to 34 to total women
	women aged 25 to 34	total women	
TOTAL, ALL ACTIVITIES	**24.00**	**24.00**	**100**
Personal care	**9.43**	**9.54**	**99**
Sleeping	8.57	8.64	99
Sleeplessness	0.03	0.07	43
Grooming	0.76	0.78	97
Health-related self-care	0.04	0.11	36
Household activities	**1.93**	**2.19**	**88**
Housework	0.83	0.90	92
Interior cleaning	0.56	0.55	102
Laundry	0.25	0.28	89
Storing interior household items, including food	0.02	0.02	100
Food and drink preparation, presentation, and clean-up	0.74	0.73	101
Food and drink preparation	0.56	0.55	102
Kitchen and food clean-up	0.17	0.18	94
Interior maintenance, repair, and decoration	0.02	0.04	50
Interior arrangement, decoration, and repairs	0.02	0.03	67
Exterior maintenance, repair, and decoration	0.02	0.03	67
Lawn, garden, and houseplants	0.05	0.12	42
Animals and pets (not veterinary care)	0.09	0.10	90
Walking, exercising, and playing with pets	0.05	0.04	125
Vehicles	0.01	0.01	100
Household management	0.16	0.25	64
Financial management	0.02	0.04	50
Household and personal organization and planning	0.07	0.11	64
Household and personal mail and messages (except email)	0.01	0.03	33
Household and personal email	0.07	0.07	100
Caring for and helping household members	**1.31**	**0.59**	**222**
Caring for and helping household children	1.17	0.48	244
Physical care for household children	0.63	0.24	263
Reading to or with household children	0.04	0.02	200
Playing with household children (except sports)	0.27	0.09	300
Talking with, listening to household children	0.03	0.02	150
Looking after household children as a primary activity	0.06	0.03	200
Picking up or dropping off household children	0.06	0.03	200
Activities related to household children's education	0.09	0.05	180
Helping household children with homework	0.07	0.04	175
Helping household adults	0.01	0.01	100
Caring for and helping people in other households	**0.11**	**0.20**	**55**
Caring for and helping children in other households	0.05	0.12	42

	average hours		index, women aged 25 to 34 to total women
	women aged 25 to 34	total women	
Helping adults in other households	0.03	0.05	60
Picking up or dropping off adults in other households	0.01	0.01	100
Work and work-related activities	**3.66**	**2.79**	**131**
Work, main job	3.47	2.63	132
Work, other job(s)	0.12	0.09	133
Education	**0.27**	**0.48**	**56**
Taking class	0.10	0.27	37
Taking class for degree, certification, or licensure	0.08	0.25	32
Research, homework	0.17	0.20	85
Consumer purchases (store, telephone, Internet)	**0.44**	**0.48**	**92**
Grocery shopping	0.12	0.13	92
Purchasing gas	0.01	0.01	100
Purchasing food (except groceries)	0.03	0.02	150
Shopping, except groceries, food, and gas	0.28	0.31	90
Professional and personal care services	**0.09**	**0.11**	**82**
Financial services and banking	0.01	0.01	100
Banking	0.00	0.01	0
Medical and care services	0.05	0.06	83
Using health and care services outside the home	0.04	0.05	80
Household services	**0.02**	**0.01**	**200**
Eating and drinking	**1.01**	**1.07**	**94**
Socializing, relaxing, and leisure	**3.72**	**4.42**	**84**
Socializing and communicating	0.70	0.68	103
Attending or hosting social events	0.14	0.08	175
Relaxing and leisure	2.81	3.58	78
Relaxing, thinking	0.16	0.26	62
Television	2.16	2.54	85
Listening to the radio	0.00	0.02	0
Listening to or playing music (not radio)	0.02	0.02	100
Playing games (including computer)	0.10	0.15	67
Computer use for leisure (except games)	0.18	0.14	129
Reading for personal interest	0.16	0.40	40
Arts and entertainment (except sports)	0.06	0.08	75
Sports, exercise, and recreation	**0.20**	**0.23**	**87**
Participating in sports, exercise, or recreation	0.18	0.20	90
Using cardiovascular equipment	0.03	0.02	150
Walking	0.02	0.04	50
Working out, unspecified	0.03	0.02	150
Religious and spiritual activities	**0.12**	**0.17**	**71**
Attending religious services	0.09	0.10	90
Participation in religious practices	0.01	0.05	20

	average hours		index, women aged 25 to 34 to total women
	women aged 25 to 34	total women	
Volunteer activities	**0.11**	**0.16**	**69**
Administrative and support activities	0.02	0.04	50
Telephone calls	**0.12**	**0.18**	**67**
Telephone calls to or from family members	0.04	0.07	57
Telephone calls to or from friends, neighbors, or acquaintances	0.05	0.06	83
Traveling	**1.24**	**1.17**	**106**
Travel related to personal care	0.01	0.01	100
Travel related to household activities	0.03	0.04	75
Travel related to household management	0.02	0.02	100
Travel related to caring for and helping household members	0.21	0.11	191
Travel related to caring for and helping household children	0.17	0.08	213
Travel related to helping household adults	0.03	0.02	150
Travel related to caring for and helping people in other households	0.05	0.07	71
Travel related to caring for and helping children in other households	0.01	0.02	50
Travel related to helping adults in other households	0.04	0.04	100
Travel related to work	0.24	0.20	120
Travel related to education	0.03	0.04	75
Travel related to taking class	0.02	0.03	67
Travel related to consumer purchases	0.26	0.27	96
Travel related to grocery shopping	0.05	0.06	83
Travel related to purchasing gas	0.06	0.02	300
Travel related to purchasing food (except groceries)	0.04	0.04	100
Travel related to shopping (except groceries, food, and gas)	0.11	0.14	79
Travel related to using professional and personal care services	0.04	0.05	80
Travel related to using financial services and banking	0.00	0.01	0
Travel related to using medical services	0.02	0.02	100
Travel related to eating and drinking	0.10	0.11	91
Travel related to socializing, relaxing, and leisure	0.18	0.17	106
Travel related to socializing and communicating	0.11	0.10	110
Travel related to attending or hosting social events	0.02	0.01	200
Travel related to relaxing and leisure	0.03	0.03	100
Travel related to arts and entertainment	0.01	0.02	50
Travel related to sports, exercise, and recreation	0.03	0.03	100
Travel related to participating in sports, exercise, recreation	0.02	0.03	67
Travel related to religious and spiritual activities	0.02	0.02	100
Travel related to volunteer activities	0.01	0.02	50

Note: The index is calculated by dividing average time spent by women in the age group doing primary activity by average time spent by total women doing primary activity and multiplying by 100. Primary activities are those respondents identified as their main activity. Other activities done simultaneously, such as eating while watching TV, are not included. Numbers may not add to total because not all subcategories are shown. If fewer than 2.0 percent of the total population participated in a primary activity, then the primary activity is not shown.
Source: Bureau of Labor Statistics, unpublished tables from the 2008 American Time Use Survey, Internet site http://www.bls .gov/tus/home.htm; calculations by New Strategist

Table 4.7 Indexed Time Use of People Aged 25 to 34 by Sex, 2008

(average hours spent by people aged 25 to 34 doing primary activities on an average day by sex, and index of women's time to men's, 2008)

	average hours, aged 25 to 34		index of women to men
	men	women	
TOTAL, ALL ACTIVITIES	**24.00**	**24.00**	**100**
Personal care	**9.14**	**9.43**	**103**
Sleeping	8.48	8.57	101
Sleeplessness	0.04	0.03	75
Grooming	0.56	0.76	136
Health-related self-care	0.09	0.04	44
Household activities	**1.06**	**1.93**	**182**
Housework	0.28	0.83	296
Interior cleaning	0.21	0.56	267
Laundry	0.07	0.25	357
Storing interior household items, including food	0.04	0.02	50
Food and drink preparation, presentation, and clean-up	0.32	0.74	231
Food and drink preparation	0.26	0.56	215
Kitchen and food clean-up	0.06	0.17	283
Interior maintenance, repair, and decoration	0.04	0.02	50
Interior arrangement, decoration, and repairs	0.03	0.02	67
Exterior maintenance, repair, and decoration	0.03	0.02	67
Lawn, garden, and houseplants	0.12	0.05	42
Animals and pets (not veterinary care)	0.05	0.09	180
Walking, exercising, and playing with pets	0.03	0.05	167
Vehicles	0.06	0.01	17
Household management	0.13	0.16	123
Financial management	0.01	0.02	200
Household and personal organization and planning	0.06	0.07	117
Household and personal mail and messages (except email)	0.01	0.01	100
Household and personal email	0.04	0.07	175
Caring for and helping household members	**0.56**	**1.31**	**234**
Caring for and helping household children	0.52	1.17	225
Physical care for household children	0.19	0.63	332
Reading to or with household children	0.02	0.04	200
Playing with household children (except sports)	0.23	0.27	117
Talking with, listening to household children	0.01	0.03	300
Looking after household children as a primary activity	0.04	0.06	150
Picking up or dropping off household children	0.01	0.06	600
Activities related to household children's education	0.02	0.09	450
Helping household children with homework	0.02	0.07	350
Helping household adults	0.02	0.01	50
Caring for and helping people in other households	**0.07**	**0.11**	**157**
Caring for and helping children in other households	0.02	0.05	250

	average hours, aged 25 to 34		index of women to men
	men	women	
Helping adults in other households	0.04	0.03	75
Picking up or dropping off adults in other households	0.01	0.01	100
Work and work-related activities	**5.47**	**3.66**	**67**
Work, main job	5.23	3.47	66
Work, other job(s)	0.09	0.12	133
Education	**0.30**	**0.27**	**90**
Taking class	0.10	0.10	100
Taking class for degree, certification, or licensure	0.09	0.08	89
Research, homework	0.20	0.17	85
Consumer purchases (store, telephone, Internet)	**0.30**	**0.44**	**147**
Grocery shopping	0.07	0.12	171
Purchasing gas	0.01	0.01	100
Purchasing food (except groceries)	0.02	0.03	150
Shopping, except groceries, food, and gas	0.19	0.28	147
Professional and personal care services	**0.03**	**0.09**	**300**
Financial services and banking	0.01	0.01	100
Banking	0.00	0.00	–
Medical and care services	0.01	0.05	500
Using health and care services outside the home	0.01	0.04	400
Household services	**0.01**	**0.02**	**200**
Eating and drinking	**1.06**	**1.01**	**95**
Socializing, relaxing, and leisure	**3.93**	**3.72**	**95**
Socializing and communicating	0.61	0.70	115
Attending or hosting social events	0.07	0.14	200
Relaxing and leisure	3.13	2.81	90
Relaxing, thinking	0.22	0.16	73
Television	2.34	2.16	92
Listening to the radio	0.01	0.00	0
Listening to or playing music (not radio)	0.02	0.02	100
Playing games (including computer)	0.28	0.10	36
Computer use for leisure (except games)	0.18	0.18	100
Reading for personal interest	0.07	0.16	229
Arts and entertainment (except sports)	0.11	0.06	55
Sports, exercise, and recreation	**0.35**	**0.20**	**57**
Participating in sports, exercise, or recreation	0.32	0.18	56
Using cardiovascular equipment	0.01	0.03	300
Walking	0.03	0.02	67
Working out, unspecified	0.03	0.03	100
Religious and spiritual activities	**0.08**	**0.12**	**150**
Attending religious services	0.05	0.09	180
Participation in religious practices	0.02	0.01	50

	average hours, aged 25 to 34		index of women to men
	men	women	
Volunteer activities	**0.06**	**0.11**	**183**
Administrative and support activities	0.01	0.02	200
Telephone calls	**0.06**	**0.12**	**200**
Telephone calls to or from family members	0.02	0.04	200
Telephone calls to or from friends, neighbors, or acquaintances	0.02	0.05	250
Traveling	**1.38**	**1.24**	**90**
Travel related to personal care	0.01	0.01	100
Travel related to household activities	0.05	0.03	60
Travel related to household management	0.03	0.02	67
Travel related to caring for and helping household members	0.06	0.21	350
Travel related to caring for and helping household children	0.05	0.17	340
Travel related to helping household adults	0.01	0.03	300
Travel related to caring for and helping people in other households	0.05	0.05	100
Travel related to caring for and helping children in other households	0.01	0.01	100
Travel related to helping adults in other households	0.04	0.04	100
Travel related to work	0.49	0.24	49
Travel related to education	0.02	0.03	150
Travel related to taking class	0.01	0.02	200
Travel related to consumer purchases	0.22	0.26	118
Travel related to grocery shopping	0.05	0.05	100
Travel related to purchasing gas	0.03	0.06	200
Travel related to purchasing food (except groceries)	0.04	0.04	100
Travel related to shopping (except groceries, food, and gas)	0.09	0.11	122
Travel related to using professional and personal care services	0.01	0.04	400
Travel related to using financial services and banking	0.01	0.00	0
Travel related to using medical services	0.00	0.02	–
Travel related to eating and drinking	0.16	0.10	63
Travel related to socializing, relaxing, and leisure	0.22	0.18	82
Travel related to socializing and communicating	0.09	0.11	122
Travel related to attending or hosting social events	0.01	0.02	200
Travel related to relaxing and leisure	0.04	0.03	75
Travel related to arts and entertainment	0.02	0.01	50
Travel related to sports, exercise, and recreation	0.05	0.03	60
Travel related to participating in sports, exercise, recreation	0.05	0.02	40
Travel related to religious and spiritual activities	0.01	0.02	200
Travel related to volunteer activities	0.01	0.01	100

Note: The index is calculated by dividing women's time by men's time and multiplying by 100. Primary activities are those respondents identified as their main activity. Other activities done simultaneously, such as eating while watching TV, are not included. Numbers may not add to total because not all subcategories are shown. If fewer than 2.0 percent of the total population participated in a primary activity, then the primary activity is not shown. "–" means denominator is zero.
Source: Bureau of Labor Statistics, unpublished tables from the 2008 American Time Use Survey, Internet site http://www.bls.gov/tus/home.htm; calculations by New Strategist

Table 4.8 Indexed Participation in Primary Activities by Total People Aged 25 to 34, 2008

(percent of people aged 25 to 34 and total people aged 15 or older participating in primary activities on an average day, and index of participation by people aged 25 to 34 to total people, 2008)

	percent participating		index, people aged 25 to 34 to total
	people aged 25 to 34	total people	
TOTAL, ALL ACTIVITIES	**100.0%**	**100.0%**	**100**
Personal care	**100.0**	**100.0**	**100**
Sleeping	100.0	99.9	100
Sleeplessness	4.0	5.2	78
Grooming	81.5	79.3	103
Health-related self-care	2.4	6.4	37
Household activities	**73.8**	**75.5**	**98**
Housework	35.0	35.5	99
Interior cleaning	24.6	24.5	100
Laundry	15.4	16.2	95
Storing interior household items, including food	3.6	5.0	73
Food and drink preparation, presentation, and clean-up	53.1	52.3	101
Food and drink preparation	50.8	49.3	103
Kitchen and food clean-up	19.7	20.8	95
Interior maintenance, repair, and decoration	1.7	3.0	57
Interior arrangement, decoration, and repairs	1.3	2.0	68
Exterior maintenance, repair, and decoration	1.5	2.7	54
Lawn, garden, and houseplants	4.8	9.4	51
Animals and pets (not veterinary care)	11.1	14.5	77
Walking, exercising, and playing with pets	5.4	5.8	93
Vehicles	2.4	2.7	88
Household management	24.5	29.0	84
Financial management	2.7	4.0	66
Household and personal organization and planning	12.1	14.1	86
Household and personal mail and messages (except email)	3.7	6.9	55
Household and personal email	9.3	9.4	99
Caring for and helping household members	**43.9**	**26.1**	**168**
Caring for and helping household children	41.3	21.9	189
Physical care for household children	34.9	15.7	223
Reading to or with household children	6.1	2.6	233
Playing with household children (except sports)	14.2	5.4	262
Talking with, listening to household children	3.9	3.0	129
Looking after household children as a primary activity	4.0	2.3	175
Picking up or dropping off household children	16.4	9.2	178
Activities related to household children's education	6.2	3.8	163
Helping household children with homework	5.5	3.4	159
Helping household adults	3.9	3.6	107
Caring for and helping people in other households	**10.6**	**13.3**	**80**
Caring for and helping children in other households	3.1	5.6	56

	percent participating		index, people aged 25 to 34 to total
	people aged 25 to 34	total people	
Helping adults in other households	7.5%	8.0%	94
Picking up or dropping off adults in other households	5.3	5.0	108
Work and work-related activities	**59.4**	**46.6**	**127**
Work, main job	56.1	43.9	128
Work, other job(s)	2.5	2.4	105
Education	**5.9**	**7.9**	**74**
Taking class	2.9	5.2	55
Taking class for degree, certification, or licensure	2.3	4.8	47
Research, homework	4.6	5.8	79
Consumer purchases (store, telephone, Internet)	**41.8**	**40.7**	**103**
Grocery shopping	12.7	12.9	98
Purchasing gas	4.5	4.0	114
Purchasing food (except groceries)	14.7	12.0	122
Shopping, except groceries, food, and gas	22.5	23.5	96
Professional and personal care services	**7.7**	**8.9**	**86**
Financial services and banking	2.4	3.2	73
Banking	2.0	3.0	66
Medical and care services	2.2	3.6	61
Using health and care services outside the home	2.1	3.4	62
Household services	**2.1**	**2.1**	**100**
Eating and drinking	**95.6**	**96.0**	**100**
Socializing, relaxing, and leisure	**93.8**	**95.4**	**98**
Socializing and communicating	35.8	37.6	95
Attending or hosting social events	2.7	2.3	116
Relaxing and leisure	87.9	91.3	96
Relaxing, thinking	17.6	19.9	88
Television	77.8	80.9	96
Listening to the radio	1.1	2.0	55
Listening to or playing music (not radio)	1.7	2.6	66
Playing games (including computer)	6.6	9.0	74
Computer use for leisure (except games)	9.9	9.5	104
Reading for personal interest	12.3	23.9	52
Arts and entertainment (except sports)	3.4	3.2	106
Sports, exercise, and recreation	**17.0**	**18.9**	**90**
Participating in sports, exercise, or recreation	16.4	17.9	91
Using cardiovascular equipment	2.6	2.2	120
Walking	3.1	4.8	65
Working out, unspecified	2.9	3.2	89
Religious and spiritual activities	**6.3**	**9.2**	**68**
Attending religious services	3.8	4.9	77
Participation in religious practices	2.1	4.6	46

	percent participating		index, people aged 25 to 34
	people aged 25 to 34	total people	to total
Volunteer activities	**4.4%**	**6.7%**	**66**
Administrative and support activities	1.5	2.5	61
Telephone calls	**12.0**	**15.4**	**78**
Telephone calls to or from family members	5.4	7.3	73
Telephone calls to or from friends, neighbors, or acquaintances	4.2	5.6	75
Traveling	**91.2**	**86.9**	**105**
Travel related to personal care	2.7	2.5	106
Travel related to household activities	9.0	9.4	96
Travel related to household management	5.5	6.1	90
Travel related to caring for and helping household members	21.7	13.6	160
Travel related to caring for and helping household children	19.3	11.0	176
Travel related to helping household adults	2.6	2.6	100
Travel related to caring for and helping people in other households	9.1	10.5	87
Travel related to caring for and helping children in other households	2.3	3.5	65
Travel related to helping adults in other households	6.9	7.1	97
Travel related to work	49.4	38.2	129
Travel related to education	2.9	5.0	57
Travel related to taking class	2.5	4.4	56
Travel related to consumer purchases	40.3	39.6	102
Travel related to grocery shopping	12.7	12.9	99
Travel related to purchasing gas	4.4	3.9	111
Travel related to purchasing food (except groceries)	13.3	11.2	118
Travel related to shopping (except groceries, food, and gas)	21.4	22.7	94
Travel related to using professional and personal care services	7.0	8.1	87
Travel related to using financial services and banking	2.2	3.0	73
Travel related to using medical services	2.1	3.3	64
Travel related to eating and drinking	25.6	25.0	102
Travel related to socializing, relaxing, and leisure	26.9	28.6	94
Travel related to socializing and communicating	18.9	18.6	102
Travel related to attending or hosting social events	2.4	2.0	121
Travel related to relaxing and leisure	7.4	8.9	83
Travel related to arts and entertainment	2.5	2.6	98
Travel related to sports, exercise, and recreation	9.2	9.6	96
Travel related to participating in sports, exercise, recreation	8.5	8.6	99
Travel related to religious and spiritual activities	4.2	5.1	82
Travel related to volunteer activities	2.7	4.3	63

Note: The index is calculated by dividing percent of people in the age group doing primary activity by percent of total people doing primary activity and multiplying by 100. Primary activities are those respondents identified as their main activity. Other activities done simultaneously, such as eating while watching TV, are not included. If fewer than 2.0 percent of the total population participated in a primary activity, then the primary activity is not shown.
Source: Bureau of Labor Statistics, unpublished tables from the 2008 American Time Use Survey, Internet site http://www.bls.gov/tus/home.htm; calculations by New Strategist

Table 4.9 Indexed Participation in Primary Activities by Men Aged 25 to 34, 2008

(percent of men aged 25 to 34 and total men aged 15 or older participating in primary activities on an average day, and index of participation by men aged 25 to 34 to total men, 2008)

	percent participating		index, men aged 25 to 34 to total men
	men aged 25 to 34	total men	
TOTAL, ALL ACTIVITIES	**100.0%**	**100.0%**	**100**
Personal care	**100.0**	**100.0**	**100**
Sleeping	100.0	99.9	100
Sleeplessness	4.4	4.5	97
Grooming	79.6	76.6	104
Health-related self-care	2.0	4.8	41
Household activities	**63.0**	**66.6**	**95**
Housework	22.1	19.7	112
Interior cleaning	15.2	13.5	113
Laundry	6.8	6.3	109
Storing interior household items, including food	2.6	2.9	91
Food and drink preparation, presentation, and clean-up	38.0	38.4	99
Food and drink preparation	36.2	36.0	101
Kitchen and food clean-up	9.9	9.5	105
Interior maintenance, repair, and decoration	2.2	3.9	57
Interior arrangement, decoration, and repairs	1.8	2.4	72
Exterior maintenance, repair, and decoration	1.7	3.8	44
Lawn, garden, and houseplants	5.6	11.0	51
Animals and pets (not veterinary care)	7.0	12.1	58
Walking, exercising, and playing with pets	4.0	5.2	77
Vehicles	3.7	4.5	82
Household management	20.7	24.0	86
Financial management	2.2	3.2	68
Household and personal organization and planning	9.9	11.1	89
Household and personal mail and messages (except email)	3.7	5.5	68
Household and personal email	8.2	7.4	110
Caring for and helping household members	**31.8**	**20.7**	**154**
Caring for and helping household children	29.1	16.8	173
Physical care for household children	22.1	10.4	212
Reading to or with household children	3.7	1.7	217
Playing with household children (except sports)	11.7	4.7	247
Talking with, listening to household children	1.8	1.7	101
Looking after household children as a primary activity	2.1	1.5	142
Picking up or dropping off household children	8.2	6.2	132
Activities related to household children's education	2.1	2.2	99
Helping household children with homework	2.0	2.0	97
Helping household adults	3.8	3.5	109
Caring for and helping people in other households	**10.2**	**11.0**	**93**
Caring for and helping children in other households	2.2	3.6	59

	percent participating		index, men aged 25 to 34 to total men
	men aged 25 to 34	total men	
Helping adults in other households	7.9%	7.5%	106
Picking up or dropping off adults in other households	6.0	4.4	134
Work and work-related activities	**67.7**	**53.4**	**127**
Work, main job	64.0	50.1	128
Work, other job(s)	2.6	2.3	112
Education	**5.3**	**6.9**	**77**
Taking class	2.5	5.0	51
Taking class for degree, certification, or licensure	2.3	4.8	48
Research, homework	4.8	4.6	103
Consumer purchases (store, telephone, Internet)	**37.9**	**35.6**	**107**
Grocery shopping	9.3	9.6	97
Purchasing gas	5.1	4.3	120
Purchasing food (except groceries)	14.7	11.8	124
Shopping, except groceries, food, and gas	19.8	19.6	101
Professional and personal care services	**5.3**	**6.7**	**79**
Financial services and banking	2.4	3.1	76
Banking	1.8	2.8	65
Medical and care services	0.7	2.4	29
Using health and care services outside the home	0.6	2.3	27
Eating and drinking	**96.3**	**96.5**	**100**
Socializing, relaxing, and leisure	**93.1**	**95.4**	**98**
Socializing and communicating	**34.3**	**34.9**	**98**
Attending or hosting social events	1.6	2.0	83
Relaxing and leisure	87.7	92.1	95
Relaxing, thinking	20.5	20.4	101
Television	78.3	82.3	95
Listening to the radio	1.7	2.5	69
Listening to or playing music (not radio)	2.1	3.3	63
Playing games (including computer)	9.1	9.6	95
Computer use for leisure (except games)	8.9	9.5	94
Reading for personal interest	9.3	21.1	44
Arts and entertainment (except sports)	3.9	3.3	118
Sports, exercise, and recreation	**19.2**	**22.0**	**87**
Participating in sports, exercise, or recreation	18.6	21.0	88
Using cardiovascular equipment	1.3	1.8	72
Walking	4.0	4.9	80
Working out, unspecified	2.4	3.5	67
Religious and spiritual activities	**6.0**	**7.7**	**78**
Attending religious services	3.2	4.0	79
Participation in religious practices	2.9	3.7	79

	percent participating		index, men aged 25 to 34 to total men
	men aged 25 to 34	total men	
Volunteer activities	**3.5%**	**5.7%**	**62**
Administrative and support activities	1.3	1.9	68
Telephone calls	**9.7**	**10.0**	**97**
Telephone calls to or from family members	3.8	3.8	100
Telephone calls to or from friends, neighbors, or acquaintances	3.0	3.7	81
Traveling	**92.1**	**88.5**	**104**
Travel related to personal care	3.7	3.1	121
Travel related to household activities	9.5	8.5	112
Travel related to household management	5.7	5.5	104
Travel related to caring for and helping household members	11.5	9.9	116
Travel related to caring for and helping household children	9.5	7.4	130
Travel related to helping household adults	2.2	2.4	91
Travel related to caring for and helping people in other households	9.1	9.3	99
Travel related to caring for and helping children in other households	1.6	2.5	66
Travel related to helping adults in other households	7.3	6.7	109
Travel related to work	57.1	44.4	129
Travel related to education	2.5	4.6	54
Travel related to taking class	2.1	4.1	51
Travel related to consumer purchases	36.2	34.5	105
Travel related to grocery shopping	9.3	9.5	98
Travel related to purchasing gas	4.9	4.2	116
Travel related to purchasing food (except groceries)	12.8	11.0	116
Travel related to shopping (except groceries, food, and gas)	18.8	18.9	100
Travel related to using professional and personal care services	5.2	6.3	81
Travel related to using financial services and banking	2.4	3.0	79
Travel related to using medical services	0.7	2.3	31
Travel related to eating and drinking	27.7	27.3	101
Travel related to socializing, relaxing, and leisure	25.9	28.0	93
Travel related to socializing and communicating	17.7	17.5	101
Travel related to attending or hosting social events	1.5	1.7	88
Travel related to relaxing and leisure	8.2	9.4	87
Travel related to arts and entertainment	2.6	2.8	94
Travel related to sports, exercise, and recreation	10.5	11.5	92
Travel related to participating in sports, exercise, recreation	9.8	10.4	94
Travel related to religious and spiritual activities	3.4	4.4	77
Travel related to volunteer activities	2.1	3.8	55

Note: The index is calculated by dividing percent of men in the age group doing primary activity by percent of total men doing primary activity and multiplying by 100. Primary activities are those respondents identified as their main activity. Other activities done simultaneously, such as eating while watching TV, are not included. If fewer than 2.0 percent of the total population participated in a primary activity, then the primary activity is not shown.
Source: Bureau of Labor Statistics, unpublished tables from the 2008 American Time Use Survey, Internet site http://www.bls.gov/tus/home.htm; calculations by New Strategist

Table 4.10 Indexed Participation in Primary Activities by Women Aged 25 to 34, 2008

(percent of women aged 25 to 34 and total women aged 15 or older participating in primary activities on an average day, and index of participation by women aged 25 to 34 to total women, 2008)

	percent participating		index, women aged 25 to 34
	women aged 25 to 34	total women	to total women
TOTAL, ALL ACTIVITIES	**100.0%**	**100.0%**	**100**
Personal care	**100.0**	**100.0**	**100**
Sleeping	100.0	99.9	100
Sleeplessness	3.7	5.8	63
Grooming	83.4	81.8	102
Health-related self-care	2.8	7.8	36
Household activities	**84.6**	**84.0**	**101**
Housework	47.8	50.3	95
Interior cleaning	34.0	34.9	97
Laundry	24.0	25.5	94
Storing interior household items, including food	4.7	7.0	67
Food and drink preparation, presentation, and clean-up	68.2	65.3	104
Food and drink preparation	65.3	61.8	106
Kitchen and food clean-up	29.6	31.5	94
Interior maintenance, repair, and decoration	1.2	2.2	56
Interior arrangement, decoration, and repairs	0.9	1.5	61
Exterior maintenance, repair, and decoration	1.3	1.8	75
Lawn, garden, and houseplants	4.1	7.9	51
Animals and pets (not veterinary care)	17.5	16.7	105
Walking, exercising, and playing with pets	6.7	6.3	107
Vehicles	1.0	1.0	104
Household management	28.4	33.8	84
Financial management	3.2	4.9	65
Household and personal organization and planning	14.2	16.8	85
Household and personal mail and messages (except email)	3.8	8.2	46
Household and personal email	10.5	11.3	93
Caring for and helping household members	**55.9**	**31.2**	**179**
Caring for and helping household children	53.5	26.7	200
Physical care for household children	47.8	20.6	232
Reading to or with household children	8.5	3.5	245
Playing with household children (except sports)	16.8	6.1	275
Talking with, listening to household children	6.1	4.3	143
Looking after household children as a primary activity	5.9	3.0	194
Picking up or dropping off household children	24.6	12.1	204
Activities related to household children's education	10.3	5.4	191
Helping household children with homework	9.0	4.8	189
Helping household adults	4.0	3.7	106
Caring for and helping people in other households	**11.0**	**15.5**	**71**
Caring for and helping children in other households	4.1	7.4	56

	percent participating		index, women aged 25 to 34 to total women
	women aged 25 to 34	total women	
Helping adults in other households	7.1%	8.5%	84
Picking up or dropping off adults in other households	4.7	5.4	87
Work and work-related activities	**51.1**	**40.3**	**127**
Work, main job	48.3	38.0	127
Work, other job(s)	2.4	2.4	100
Education	**6.6**	**8.9**	**74**
Taking class	3.2	5.3	60
Taking class for degree, certification, or licensure	2.2	4.7	46
Research, homework	4.4	7.0	64
Consumer purchases (store, telephone, Internet)	**45.6**	**45.4**	**100**
Grocery shopping	16.0	16.1	100
Purchasing gas	3.9	3.7	105
Purchasing food (except groceries)	14.8	12.3	120
Shopping, except groceries, food, and gas	25.2	27.2	93
Professional and personal care services	**10.0**	**11.0**	**91**
Financial services and banking	2.3	3.3	70
Banking	2.2	3.3	67
Medical and care services	3.7	4.8	78
Using health and care services outside the home	3.7	4.5	81
Household services	**2.7**	**2.1**	**129**
Eating and drinking	**94.9**	**95.6**	**99**
Socializing, relaxing, and leisure	**94.5**	**95.4**	**99**
Socializing and communicating	37.2	40.1	93
Attending or hosting social events	3.8	2.7	141
Relaxing and leisure	88.0	90.6	97
Relaxing, thinking	14.7	19.5	75
Television	77.2	79.5	97
Listening to the radio	0.5	1.5	31
Listening to or playing music (not radio)	1.4	2.0	71
Playing games (including computer)	4.2	8.4	50
Computer use for leisure (except games)	11.0	9.5	115
Reading for personal interest	15.4	26.5	58
Arts and entertainment (except sports)	3.0	3.2	94
Sports, exercise, and recreation	**14.9**	**15.9**	**93**
Participating in sports, exercise, or recreation	14.2	15.0	94
Using cardiovascular equipment	3.9	2.5	157
Walking	2.3	4.7	50
Working out, unspecified	3.3	2.9	116
Religious and spiritual activities	**6.5**	**10.7**	**61**
Attending religious services	4.3	5.7	76
Participation in religious practices	1.3	5.4	24

	percent participating		index, women aged 25 to 34
	women aged 25 to 34	total women	to total women
Volunteer activities	**5.3%**	**7.6%**	**69**
Administrative and support activities	1.8	3.1	57
Telephone calls	**14.3**	**20.4**	**70**
Telephone calls to or from family members	6.9	10.7	65
Telephone calls to or from friends, neighbors, or acquaintances	5.4	7.4	73
Traveling	**90.2**	**85.5**	**106**
Travel related to personal care	1.7	2.0	82
Travel related to household activities	8.5	10.3	83
Travel related to household management	5.3	6.7	79
Travel related to caring for and helping household members	32.0	17.1	187
Travel related to caring for and helping household children	29.1	14.3	203
Travel related to helping household adults	2.9	2.7	108
Travel related to caring for and helping people in other households	9.1	11.6	78
Travel related to caring for and helping children in other households	2.9	4.5	65
Travel related to helping adults in other households	6.4	7.4	87
Travel related to work	41.7	32.2	129
Travel related to education	3.3	5.4	60
Travel related to taking class	2.8	4.6	61
Travel related to consumer purchases	44.4	44.4	100
Travel related to grocery shopping	16.1	16.0	101
Travel related to purchasing gas	3.9	3.7	105
Travel related to purchasing food (except groceries)	13.8	11.5	121
Travel related to shopping (except groceries, food, and gas)	23.9	26.3	91
Travel related to using professional and personal care services	8.9	9.8	91
Travel related to using financial services and banking	2.1	3.1	68
Travel related to using medical services	3.5	4.3	83
Travel related to eating and drinking	23.5	22.8	103
Travel related to socializing, relaxing, and leisure	28.0	29.2	96
Travel related to socializing and communicating	20.0	19.5	103
Travel related to attending or hosting social events	3.3	2.3	147
Travel related to relaxing and leisure	6.6	8.5	78
Travel related to arts and entertainment	2.5	2.4	103
Travel related to sports, exercise, and recreation	7.8	7.7	101
Travel related to participating in sports, exercise, recreation	7.2	6.8	106
Travel related to religious and spiritual activities	5.0	5.8	87
Travel related to volunteer activities	3.3	4.7	70

Note: The index is calculated by dividing percent of women in the age group doing primary activity by percent of total women doing primary activity and multiplying by 100. Primary activities are those respondents identified as their main activity. Other activities done simultaneously, such as eating while watching TV, are not included. If fewer than 2.0 percent of the total population participated in a primary activity, then the primary activity is not shown.
Source: Bureau of Labor Statistics, unpublished tables from the 2008 American Time Use Survey, Internet site http://www.bls .gov/tus/home.htm; calculations by New Strategist

Table 4.11 Indexed Participation in Primary Activities of People Aged 25 to 34 by Sex, 2008

(percent of people aged 25 to 34 participating in primary activities on an average day by sex, and index of women's participation to men's, 2008)

	aged 25 to 34, percent participating		index of women to men
	men	women	
TOTAL, ALL ACTIVITIES	**100.0%**	**100.0%**	**100**
Personal care	**100.0**	**100.0**	**100**
Sleeping	100.0	100.0	100
Sleeplessness	4.4	3.7	84
Grooming	79.6	83.4	105
Health-related self-care	2.0	2.8	140
Household activities	**63.0**	**84.6**	**134**
Housework	22.1	47.8	216
Interior cleaning	15.2	34.0	223
Laundry	6.8	24.0	353
Storing interior household items, including food	2.6	4.7	180
Food and drink preparation, presentation, and clean-up	38.0	68.2	180
Food and drink preparation	36.2	65.3	181
Kitchen and food clean-up	9.9	29.6	298
Interior maintenance, repair, and decoration	2.2	1.2	55
Interior arrangement, decoration, and repairs	1.8	0.9	53
Exterior maintenance, repair, and decoration	1.7	1.3	79
Lawn, garden, and houseplants	5.6	4.1	73
Animals and pets (not veterinary care)	7.0	17.5	250
Walking, exercising, and playing with pets	4.0	6.7	167
Vehicles	3.7	1.0	28
Household management	20.7	28.4	137
Financial management	2.2	3.2	146
Household and personal organization and planning	9.9	14.2	144
Household and personal mail and messages (except email)	3.7	3.8	101
Household and personal email	8.2	10.5	128
Caring for and helping household members	**31.8**	**55.9**	**176**
Caring for and helping household children	29.1	53.5	184
Physical care for household children	22.1	47.8	216
Reading to or with household children	3.7	8.5	228
Playing with household children (except sports)	11.7	16.8	144
Talking with, listening to household children	1.8	6.1	344
Looking after household children as a primary activity	2.1	5.9	285
Picking up or dropping off household children	8.2	24.6	301
Activities related to household children's education	2.1	10.3	479
Helping household children with homework	2.0	9.0	460
Helping household adults	3.8	4.0	104
Caring for and helping people in other households	**10.2**	**11.0**	**107**
Caring for and helping children in other households	2.2	4.1	189

	aged 25 to 34, percent participating		index of women to men
	men	women	
Helping adults in other households	7.9%	7.1%	90
Picking up or dropping off adults in other households	6.0	4.7	80
Work and work-related activities	**67.7**	**51.1**	**76**
Work, main job	64.0	48.3	75
Work, other job(s)	2.6	2.4	93
Education	**5.3**	**6.6**	**125**
Taking class	2.5	3.2	125
Taking class for degree, certification, or licensure	2.3	2.2	93
Research, homework	4.8	4.4	93
Consumer purchases (store, telephone, Internet)	**37.9**	**45.6**	**120**
Grocery shopping	9.3	16.0	172
Purchasing gas	5.1	3.9	75
Purchasing food (except groceries)	14.7	14.8	101
Shopping, except groceries, food, and gas	19.8	25.2	127
Professional and personal care services	**5.3**	**10.0**	**190**
Financial services and banking	2.4	2.3	98
Banking	1.8	2.2	120
Medical and care services	0.7	3.7	525
Using health and care services outside the home	0.6	3.7	586
Household services	**1.5**	**2.7**	**179**
Eating and drinking	**96.3**	**94.9**	**99**
Socializing, relaxing, and leisure	**93.1**	**94.5**	**101**
Socializing and communicating	34.3	37.2	108
Attending or hosting social events	1.6	3.8	231
Relaxing and leisure	87.7	88.0	100
Relaxing, thinking	20.5	14.7	72
Television	78.3	77.2	99
Listening to the radio	1.7	0.5	27
Listening to or playing music (not radio)	2.1	1.4	68
Playing games (including computer)	9.1	4.2	46
Computer use for leisure (except games)	8.9	11.0	123
Reading for personal interest	9.3	15.4	165
Arts and entertainment (except sports)	3.9	3.0	76
Sports, exercise, and recreation	**19.2**	**14.9**	**77**
Participating in sports, exercise, or recreation	18.6	14.2	76
Using cardiovascular equipment	1.3	3.9	295
Walking	4.0	2.3	59
Working out, unspecified	2.4	3.3	141
Religious and spiritual activities	**6.0**	**6.5**	**109**
Attending religious services	3.2	4.3	137
Participation in religious practices	2.9	1.3	45

	aged 25 to 34, percent participating		index of women to men
	men	women	
Volunteer activities	**3.5%**	**5.3%**	**149**
Administrative and support activities	1.3	1.8	133
Telephone calls	**9.7**	**14.3**	**148**
Telephone calls to or from family members	3.8	6.9	182
Telephone calls to or from friends, neighbors, or acquaintances	3.0	5.4	179
Traveling	**92.1**	**90.2**	**98**
Travel related to personal care	3.7	1.7	44
Travel related to household activities	9.5	8.5	90
Travel related to household management	5.7	5.3	93
Travel related to caring for and helping household members	11.5	32.0	278
Travel related to caring for and helping household children	9.5	29.1	305
Travel related to helping household adults	2.2	2.9	135
Travel related to caring for and helping people in other households	9.1	9.1	100
Travel related to caring for and helping children in other households	1.6	2.9	181
Travel related to helping adults in other households	7.3	6.4	88
Travel related to work	57.1	41.7	73
Travel related to education	2.5	3.3	131
Travel related to taking class	2.1	2.8	133
Travel related to consumer purchases	36.2	44.4	123
Travel related to grocery shopping	9.3	16.1	173
Travel related to purchasing gas	4.9	3.9	79
Travel related to purchasing food (except groceries)	12.8	13.8	108
Travel related to shopping (except groceries, food, and gas)	18.8	23.9	127
Travel related to using professional and personal care services	5.2	8.9	172
Travel related to using financial services and banking	2.4	2.1	87
Travel related to using medical services	0.7	3.5	499
Travel related to eating and drinking	27.7	23.5	85
Travel related to socializing, relaxing, and leisure	25.9	28.0	108
Travel related to socializing and communicating	17.7	20.0	113
Travel related to attending or hosting social events	1.5	3.3	225
Travel related to relaxing and leisure	8.2	6.6	80
Travel related to arts and entertainment	2.6	2.5	95
Travel related to sports, exercise, and recreation	10.5	7.8	74
Travel related to participating in sports, exercise, recreation	9.8	7.2	73
Travel related to religious and spiritual activities	3.4	5.0	149
Travel related to volunteer activities	2.1	3.3	158

Note: The index is calculated by dividing percent of women participating in primary activity by percent of men participating in primary activity and multiplying by 100. Primary activities are those respondents identified as their main activity. Other activities done simultaneously, such as eating while watching TV, are not included. If fewer than 2.0 percent of the total population participated in a primary activity, then the primary activity is not shown.
Source: Bureau of Labor Statistics, unpublished tables from the 2008 American Time Use Survey, Internet site http://www.bls .gov/tus/home.htm; calculations by New Strategist

Table 4.12 Ranking: Average Hours per Day Spent Doing Primary Activities by Total People Aged 25 to 34, 2008

(average hours per day spent by people aged 25 to 34 doing primary activities, ranked by time spent doing activity, 2008)

		average hours per day spent by people aged 25 to 34
	Total, all activities	**24.00**
1.	Sleeping	8.54
2.	Work, main job	4.35
3.	Television	2.25
4.	Eating and drinking	1.04
5.	Caring for and helping household children	0.84
6.	Socializing and communicating	0.66
7.	Grooming	0.66
8.	Food and drink preparation	0.41
9.	Interior cleaning	0.38
10.	Travel related to work	0.37
11.	Participating in sports, exercise, or recreation	0.25
12.	Shopping, except groceries, food, and gas	0.24
13.	Travel related to socializing, relaxing, and leisure	0.20
14.	Research, homework	0.19
15.	Relaxing, thinking	0.19
16.	Playing games (including computer)	0.19
17.	Computer use for leisure (except games)	0.18
18.	Laundry	0.16
19.	Travel related to eating and drinking	0.13
20.	Reading for personal interest	0.12
21.	Kitchen and food clean-up	0.12
22.	Work, other job(s)	0.11
23.	Travel related to caring for and helping household children	0.11
24.	Attending or hosting social events	0.11
25.	Travel related to socializing and communicating	0.10
26.	Travel related to shopping (except groceries, food, and gas)	0.10
27.	Taking class	0.10
28.	Religious and spiritual activities	0.10
29.	Telephone calls	0.09
30.	Lawn, garden, and houseplants	0.09
31.	Grocery shopping	0.09
32.	Arts and entertainment (except sports)	0.09
33.	Volunteer activities	0.08
34.	Household and personal organization and planning	0.07
35.	Health-related self-care	0.07
36.	Animals and pets (not veterinary care)	0.07
37.	Travel related to grocery shopping	0.05
38.	Household and personal email	0.05
39.	Activities related to household children's education	0.05

	average hours per day spent by people aged 25 to 34
40. Travel related to sports, exercise, and recreation	0.04
41. Travel related to purchasing gas	0.04
42. Travel related to purchasing food (except groceries)	0.04
43. Travel related to household activities	0.04
44. Travel related to helping adults in other households	0.04
45. Helping adults in other households	0.04
46. Vehicles	0.03
47. Travel related to relaxing and leisure	0.03
48. Medical and care services	0.03
49. Interior maintenance, repair, and decoration	0.03
50. Caring for and helping children in other households	0.03
51. Travel related to religious and spiritual activities	0.02
52. Travel related to helping household adults	0.02
53. Travel related to education	0.02
54. Travel related to arts and entertainment	0.02
55. Purchasing food (except groceries)	0.02
56. Listening to or playing music (not radio)	0.02
57. Financial management	0.02
58. Exterior maintenance, repair, and decoration	0.02
59. Travel related to volunteer activities	0.01
60. Travel related to using medical services	0.01
61. Travel related to personal care	0.01
62. Travel related to caring for and helping children in other households	0.01
63. Travel related to attending or hosting social events	0.01
64. Storing interior household items, including food	0.01
65. Purchasing gas	0.01
66. Listening to the radio	0.01
67. Household services	0.01
68. Household and personal mail and messages (except email)	0.01
69. Helping household adults	0.01
70. Financial services and banking	0.01
71. Travel related to using financial services and banking	0.00

Note: Primary activities are those respondents identified as their main activity. Other activities done simultaneously, such as eating while watching TV, are not included. If fewer than 2.0 percent of the total population participated in a primary activity, then the primary activity is not shown.
Source: Bureau of Labor Statistics, unpublished tables from the 2008 American Time Use Survey, Internet site http://www.bls.gov/tus/home.htm; calculations by New Strategist

Table 4.13 Ranking: Average Hours per Day Spent Doing Primary Activities by Men Aged 25 to 34, 2008

(average hours per day spent by men aged 25 to 34 doing primary activities, ranked by time spent doing activity, 2008)

		average hours per day spent by men aged 25 to 34
	Total, all activities	**24.00**
1.	Sleeping	8.48
2.	Work, main job	5.23
3.	Television	2.34
4.	Eating and drinking	1.06
5.	Socializing and communicating	0.61
6.	Grooming	0.56
7.	Caring for and helping household children	0.52
8.	Travel related to work	0.49
9.	Participating in sports, exercise, or recreation	0.32
10.	Playing games (including computer)	0.28
11.	Food and drink preparation	0.26
12.	Relaxing, thinking	0.22
13.	Interior cleaning	0.21
14.	Research, homework	0.20
15.	Shopping, except groceries, food, and gas	0.19
16.	Computer use for leisure (except games)	0.18
17.	Travel related to eating and drinking	0.16
18.	Lawn, garden, and houseplants	0.12
19.	Arts and entertainment (except sports)	0.11
20.	Taking class	0.10
21.	Travel related to shopping (except groceries, food, and gas)	0.09
22.	Travel related to socializing and communicating	0.09
23.	Work, other job(s)	0.09
24.	Health-related self-care	0.09
25.	Grocery shopping	0.07
26.	Reading for personal interest	0.07
27.	Laundry	0.07
28.	Attending or hosting social events	0.07
29.	Kitchen and food clean-up	0.06
30.	Household and personal organization and planning	0.06
31.	Telephone calls	0.06
32.	Vehicles	0.06
33.	Volunteer activities	0.06
34.	Travel related to sports, exercise, and recreation	0.05
35.	Travel related to caring for and helping household children	0.05
36.	Travel related to household activities	0.05
37.	Travel related to grocery shopping	0.05
38.	Animals and pets (not veterinary care)	0.05
39.	Attending religious services	0.05

	average hours per day spent by men aged 25 to 34
40. Travel related to purchasing food (except groceries)	0.04
41. Travel related to relaxing and leisure	0.04
42. Household and personal email	0.04
43. Helping adults in other households	0.04
44. Travel related to helping adults in other households	0.04
45. Storing interior household items, including food	0.04
46. Interior maintenance, repair, and decoration	0.04
47. Travel related to purchasing gas	0.03
48. Exterior maintenance, repair, and decoration	0.03
49. Purchasing food (except groceries)	0.02
50. Helping household adults	0.02
51. Participation in religious practices	0.02
52. Travel related to arts and entertainment	0.02
53. Travel related to education	0.02
54. Caring for and helping children in other households	0.02
55. Activities related to household children's education	0.02
56. Listening to or playing music (not radio)	0.02
57. Purchasing gas	0.01
58. Household and personal mail and messages (except email)	0.01
59. Travel related to personal care	0.01
60. Travel related to religious and spiritual activities	0.01
61. Financial services and banking	0.01
62. Travel related to using financial services and banking	0.01
63. Financial management	0.01
64. Travel related to helping household adults	0.01
65. Travel related to volunteer activities	0.01
66. Listening to the radio	0.01
67. Travel related to caring for and helping children in other households	0.01
68. Household services	0.01
69. Travel related to attending or hosting social events	0.01
70. Medical and care services	0.01
71. Travel related to using medical services	0.00

Note: Primary activities are those respondents identified as their main activity. Other activities done simultaneously, such as eating while watching TV, are not included. If fewer than 2.0 percent of the total population participated in a primary activity, then the primary activity is not shown.
Source: Bureau of Labor Statistics, unpublished tables from the 2008 American Time Use Survey, Internet site http://www.bls.gov/tus/home.htm; calculations by New Strategist

Table 4.14 Ranking: Average Hours per Day Spent Doing Primary Activities by Women Aged 25 to 34, 2008

(average hours per day spent by women aged 25 to 34 doing primary activities, ranked by time spent doing activity, 2008)

		average hours per day spent by women aged 25 to 34
	Total, all activities	**24.00**
1.	Sleeping	8.57
2.	Work, main job	3.47
3.	Television	2.16
4.	Caring for and helping household children	1.17
5.	Eating and drinking	1.01
6.	Grooming	0.76
7.	Socializing and communicating	0.70
8.	Interior cleaning	0.56
9.	Food and drink preparation	0.56
10.	Shopping, except groceries, food, and gas	0.28
11.	Laundry	0.25
12.	Travel related to work	0.24
13.	Computer use for leisure (except games)	0.18
14.	Participating in sports, exercise, or recreation	0.18
15.	Kitchen and food clean-up	0.17
16.	Research, homework	0.17
17.	Travel related to caring for and helping household children	0.17
18.	Relaxing, thinking	0.16
19.	Reading for personal interest	0.16
20.	Attending or hosting social events	0.14
21.	Work, other job(s)	0.12
22.	Grocery shopping	0.12
23.	Telephone calls	0.12
24.	Volunteer activities	0.11
25.	Travel related to shopping (except groceries, food, and gas)	0.11
26.	Travel related to socializing and communicating	0.11
27.	Taking class	0.10
28.	Playing games (including computer)	0.10
29.	Travel related to eating and drinking	0.10
30.	Animals and pets (not veterinary care)	0.09
31.	Activities related to household children's education	0.09
32.	Attending religious services	0.09
33.	Household and personal organization and planning	0.07
34.	Household and personal email	0.07
35.	Arts and entertainment (except sports)	0.06
36.	Travel related to purchasing gas	0.06
37.	Lawn, garden, and houseplants	0.05
38.	Caring for and helping children in other households	0.05
39.	Medical and care services	0.05

	average hours per day spent by women aged 25 to 34
40. Travel related to grocery shopping	0.05
41. Health-related self-care	0.04
42. Travel related to helping adults in other households	0.04
43. Travel related to purchasing food (except groceries)	0.04
44. Helping adults in other households	0.03
45. Purchasing food (except groceries)	0.03
46. Travel related to household activities	0.03
47. Travel related to helping household adults	0.03
48. Travel related to education	0.03
49. Travel related to relaxing and leisure	0.03
50. Travel related to sports, exercise, and recreation	0.03
51. Storing interior household items, including food	0.02
52. Interior maintenance, repair, and decoration	0.02
53. Exterior maintenance, repair, and decoration	0.02
54. Financial management	0.02
55. Household services	0.02
56. Listening to or playing music (not radio)	0.02
57. Travel related to using medical services	0.02
58. Travel related to attending or hosting social events	0.02
59. Travel related to religious and spiritual activities	0.02
60. Vehicles	0.01
61. Household and personal mail and messages (except email)	0.01
62. Helping household adults	0.01
63. Purchasing gas	0.01
64. Financial services and banking	0.01
65. Participation in religious practices	0.01
66. Travel related to personal care	0.01
67. Travel related to caring for and helping children in other households	0.01
68. Travel related to arts and entertainment	0.01
69. Travel related to volunteer activities	0.01
70. Listening to the radio	0.00
71. Travel related to using financial services and banking	0.00

Note: Primary activities are those respondents identified as their main activity. Other activities done simultaneously, such as eating while watching TV, are not included. If fewer than 2.0 percent of the total population participated in a primary activity, then the primary activity is not shown.
Source: Bureau of Labor Statistics, unpublished tables from the 2008 American Time Use Survey, Internet site http://www.bls .gov/tus/home.htm; calculations by New Strategist

Table 4.15   Ranking: Percent of Total People Aged 25 to 34 Participating in Primary Activities on an Average Day, 2008

(percent of people aged 25 to 34 participating in primary activities on an average day, ranked by percent participating, 2008)

		percent of people aged 25 to 34 participating in activity
	Total, all activities	**100.0%**
1.	Sleeping	100.0
2.	Eating and drinking	95.6
3.	Grooming	81.5
4.	Television	77.8
5.	Work, main job	56.1
6.	Food and drink preparation	50.8
7.	Travel related to work	49.4
8.	Caring for and helping household children	41.3
9.	Socializing and communicating	35.8
10.	Travel related to socializing, relaxing, and leisure	26.9
11.	Travel related to eating and drinking	25.6
12.	Interior cleaning	24.6
13.	Shopping, except groceries, food, and gas	22.5
14.	Travel related to shopping (except groceries, food, and gas)	21.4
15.	Kitchen and food clean-up	19.7
16.	Travel related to caring for and helping household children	19.3
17.	Travel related to socializing and communicating	18.9
18.	Relaxing, thinking	17.6
19.	Participating in sports, exercise, or recreation	16.4
20.	Laundry	15.4
21.	Purchasing food (except groceries)	14.7
22.	Travel related to purchasing food (except groceries)	13.3
23.	Travel related to grocery shopping	12.7
24.	Grocery shopping	12.7
25.	Reading for personal interest	12.3
26.	Household and personal organization and planning	12.1
27.	Telephone calls	12.0
28.	Animals and pets (not veterinary care)	11.1
29.	Computer use for leisure (except games)	9.9
30.	Household and personal email	9.3
31.	Travel related to sports, exercise, and recreation	9.2
32.	Travel related to household activities	9.0
33.	Helping adults in other households	7.5
34.	Travel related to relaxing and leisure	7.4
35.	Travel related to helping adults in other households	6.9
36.	Playing games (including computer)	6.6
37.	Religious and spiritual activities	6.3
38.	Activities related to household children's education	6.2
39.	Lawn, garden, and houseplants	4.8

		percent of people aged 25 to 34 participating in activity
40.	Research, homework	4.6%
41.	Purchasing gas	4.5
42.	Volunteer activities	4.4
43.	Travel related to purchasing gas	4.4
44.	Travel related to religious and spiritual activities	4.2
45.	Helping household adults	3.9
46.	Household and personal mail and messages (except email)	3.7
47.	Storing interior household items, including food	3.6
48.	Arts and entertainment (except sports)	3.4
49.	Caring for and helping children in other households	3.1
50.	Travel related to education	2.9
51.	Taking class	2.9
52.	Travel related to volunteer activities	2.7
53.	Attending or hosting social events	2.7
54.	Travel related to personal care	2.7
55.	Financial management	2.7
56.	Travel related to helping household adults	2.6
57.	Travel related to arts and entertainment	2.5
58.	Work, other job(s)	2.5
59.	Travel related to attending or hosting social events	2.4
60.	Health-related self-care	2.4
61.	Vehicles	2.4
62.	Financial services and banking	2.4
63.	Travel related to caring for and helping children in other households	2.3
64.	Medical and care services	2.2
65.	Travel related to using financial services and banking	2.2
66.	Travel related to using medical services	2.1
67.	Household services	2.1
68.	Listening to or playing music (not radio)	1.7
69.	Interior maintenance, repair, and decoration	1.7
70.	Exterior maintenance, repair, and decoration	1.5
71.	Listening to the radio	1.1

Note: Primary activities are those respondents identified as their main activity. Other activities done simultaneously, such as eating while watching TV, are not included. If fewer than 2.0 percent of the total population participated in a primary activity, then the primary activity is not shown.
Source: Bureau of Labor Statistics, unpublished tables from the 2008 American Time Use Survey, Internet site http://www.bls .gov/tus/home.htm; calculations by New Strategist

Table 4.16 Ranking: Percent of Men Aged 25 to 34 Participating in Primary Activities on an Average Day, 2008

(percent of men aged 25 to 34 participating in primary activities on an average day, ranked by percent participating, 2008)

		percent of men aged 25 to 34 participating in activity
	Total, all activities	**100.0%**
1.	Sleeping	100.0
2.	Eating and drinking	96.3
3.	Grooming	79.6
4.	Television	78.3
5.	Work, main job	64.0
6.	Travel related to work	57.1
7.	Food and drink preparation	36.2
8.	Socializing and communicating	34.3
9.	Caring for and helping household children	29.1
10.	Travel related to eating and drinking	27.7
11.	Relaxing, thinking	20.5
12.	Shopping, except groceries, food, and gas	19.8
13.	Travel related to shopping (except groceries, food, and gas)	18.8
14.	Participating in sports, exercise, or recreation	18.6
15.	Travel related to socializing and communicating	17.7
16.	Interior cleaning	15.2
17.	Purchasing food (except groceries)	14.7
18.	Travel related to purchasing food (except groceries)	12.8
19.	Travel related to sports, exercise, and recreation	10.5
20.	Kitchen and food clean-up	9.9
21.	Household and personal organization and planning	9.9
22.	Telephone calls	9.7
23.	Travel related to caring for and helping household children	9.5
24.	Travel related to household activities	9.5
25.	Grocery shopping	9.3
26.	Travel related to grocery shopping	9.3
27.	Reading for personal interest	9.3
28.	Playing games (including computer)	9.1
29.	Computer use for leisure (except games)	8.9
30.	Travel related to relaxing and leisure	8.2
31.	Household and personal email	8.2
32.	Helping adults in other households	7.9
33.	Travel related to helping adults in other households	7.3
34.	Animals and pets (not veterinary care)	7.0
35.	Laundry	6.8
36.	Lawn, garden, and houseplants	5.6
37.	Purchasing gas	5.1
38.	Travel related to purchasing gas	4.9
39.	Research, homework	4.8

	percent of men aged 25 to 34 participating in activity
40. Arts and entertainment (except sports)	3.9%
41. Helping household adults	3.8
42. Household and personal mail and messages (except email)	3.7
43. Vehicles	3.7
44. Travel related to personal care	3.7
45. Volunteer activities	3.5
46. Travel related to religious and spiritual activities	3.4
47. Attending religious services	3.2
48. Participation in religious practices	2.9
49. Travel related to arts and entertainment	2.6
50. Storing interior household items, including food	2.6
51. Work, other job(s)	2.6
52. Taking class	2.5
53. Travel related to education	2.5
54. Financial services and banking	2.4
55. Travel related to using financial services and banking	2.4
56. Interior maintenance, repair, and decoration	2.2
57. Financial management	2.2
58. Travel related to helping household adults	2.2
59. Caring for and helping children in other households	2.2
60. Activities related to household children's education	2.1
61. Travel related to volunteer activities	2.1
62. Listening to or playing music (not radio)	2.1
63. Health-related self-care	2.0
64. Listening to the radio	1.7
65. Exterior maintenance, repair, and decoration	1.7
66. Attending or hosting social events	1.6
67. Travel related to caring for and helping children in other households	1.6
68. Household services	1.5
69. Travel related to attending or hosting social events	1.5
70. Medical and care services	0.7
71. Travel related to using medical services	0.7

Note: Primary activities are those respondents identified as their main activity. Other activities done simultaneously, such as eating while watching TV, are not included. If fewer than 2.0 percent of the total population participated in a primary activity, then the primary activity is not shown.
Source: Bureau of Labor Statistics, unpublished tables from the 2008 American Time Use Survey, Internet site http://www.bls .gov/tus/home.htm; calculations by New Strategist

Table 4.17 Ranking: Percent of Women Aged 25 to 34 Participating in Primary Activities on an Average Day, 2008

(percent of women aged 25 to 34 participating in primary activities on an average day, ranked by percent participating, 2008)

		percent of women aged 25 to 34 participating in activity
	Total, all activities	100.0%
1.	Sleeping	100.0
2.	Eating and drinking	94.9
3.	Grooming	83.4
4.	Television	77.2
5.	Food and drink preparation	65.3
6.	Caring for and helping household children	53.5
7.	Work, main job	48.3
8.	Travel related to work	41.7
9.	Socializing and communicating	37.2
10.	Interior cleaning	34.0
11.	Kitchen and food clean-up	29.6
12.	Travel related to caring for and helping household children	29.1
13.	Shopping, except groceries, food, and gas	25.2
14.	Laundry	24.0
15.	Travel related to shopping (except groceries, food, and gas)	23.9
16.	Travel related to eating and drinking	23.5
17.	Travel related to socializing and communicating	20.0
18.	Animals and pets (not veterinary care)	17.5
19.	Travel related to grocery shopping	16.1
20.	Grocery shopping	16.0
21.	Reading for personal interest	15.4
22.	Purchasing food (except groceries)	14.8
23.	Relaxing, thinking	14.7
24.	Telephone calls	14.3
25.	Household and personal organization and planning	14.2
26.	Participating in sports, exercise, or recreation	14.2
27.	Travel related to purchasing food (except groceries)	13.8
28.	Computer use for leisure (except games)	11.0
29.	Household and personal email	10.5
30.	Activities related to household children's education	10.3
31.	Travel related to household activities	8.5
32.	Travel related to sports, exercise, and recreation	7.8
33.	Helping adults in other households	7.1
34.	Travel related to relaxing and leisure	6.6
35.	Travel related to helping adults in other households	6.4
36.	Volunteer activities	5.3
37.	Travel related to religious and spiritual activities	5.0
38.	Storing interior household items, including food	4.7
39.	Research, homework	4.4

		percent of women aged 25 to 34 participating in activity
40.	Attending religious services	4.3%
41.	Playing games (including computer)	4.2
42.	Caring for and helping children in other households	4.1
43.	Lawn, garden, and houseplants	4.1
44.	Helping household adults	4.0
45.	Purchasing gas	3.9
46.	Travel related to purchasing gas	3.9
47.	Attending or hosting social events	3.8
48.	Household and personal mail and messages (except email)	3.8
49.	Medical and care services	3.7
50.	Travel related to using medical services	3.5
51.	Travel related to attending or hosting social events	3.3
52.	Travel related to volunteer activities	3.3
53.	Travel related to education	3.3
54.	Taking class	3.2
55.	Financial management	3.2
56.	Arts and entertainment (except sports)	3.0
57.	Travel related to caring for and helping children in other households	2.9
58.	Travel related to helping household adults	2.9
59.	Health-related self-care	2.8
60.	Household services	2.7
61.	Travel related to arts and entertainment	2.5
62.	Work, other job(s)	2.4
63.	Financial services and banking	2.3
64.	Travel related to using financial services and banking	2.1
65.	Travel related to personal care	1.7
66.	Listening to or playing music (not radio)	1.4
67.	Exterior maintenance, repair, and decoration	1.3
68.	Participation in religious practices	1.3
69.	Interior maintenance, repair, and decoration	1.2
70.	Vehicles	1.0
71.	Listening to the radio	0.5

Note: Primary activities are those respondents identified as their main activity. Other activities done simultaneously, such as eating while watching TV, are not included. If fewer than 2.0 percent of the total population participated in a primary activity, then the primary activity is not shown.
Source: Bureau of Labor Statistics, unpublished tables from the 2008 American Time Use Survey, Internet site http://www.bls .gov/tus/home.htm; calculations by New Strategist

Table 4.18 **Ranking: Average Hours per Day Spent Doing Primary Activities by Total Participants Aged 25 to 34, 2008**

(hours per day spent by participants aged 25 to 34 doing primary activities, ranked by time spent doing activity, 2008)

		average hours per day spent by participants aged 25 to 34
	Total, all activities	**24.00**
1.	Sleeping	8.54
2.	Work, main job	7.74
3.	Research, homework	4.05
4.	Attending or hosting social events	3.98
5.	Television	2.90
6.	Playing games (including computer)	2.87
7.	Arts and entertainment (except sports)	2.55
8.	Caring for and helping household children	2.05
9.	Volunteer activities	1.86
10.	Socializing and communicating	1.84
11.	Computer use for leisure (except games)	1.80
12.	Lawn, garden, and houseplants	1.80
13.	Religious and spiritual activities	1.61
14.	Interior cleaning	1.56
15.	Participating in sports, exercise, or recreation	1.51
16.	Eating and drinking	1.08
17.	Relaxing, thinking	1.08
18.	Shopping, except groceries, food, and gas	1.06
19.	Laundry	1.03
20.	Travel related to purchasing gas	1.01
21.	Reading for personal interest	0.94
22.	Activities related to household children's education	0.85
23.	Grooming	0.81
24.	Food and drink preparation	0.80
25.	Telephone calls	0.76
26.	Travel related to work	0.74
27.	Travel related to socializing, relaxing, and leisure	0.74
28.	Grocery shopping	0.74
29.	Travel related to arts and entertainment	0.74
30.	Kitchen and food clean-up	0.60
31.	Travel related to attending or hosting social events	0.60
32.	Household and personal email	0.59
33.	Travel related to caring for and helping household children	0.56
34.	Household and personal organization and planning	0.56
35.	Travel related to socializing and communicating	0.52
36.	Helping adults in other households	0.52
37.	Travel related to eating and drinking	0.51
38.	Travel related to shopping (except groceries, food, and gas)	0.48
39.	Travel related to relaxing and leisure	0.46

	average hours per day spent by participants aged 25 to 34
40. Travel related to sports, exercise, and recreation	0.45
41. Animals and pets (not veterinary care)	0.43
42. Travel related to household activities	0.43
43. Travel related to grocery shopping	0.38
44. Travel related to religious and spiritual activities	0.36
45. Travel related to volunteer activities	0.36
46. Storing interior household items, including food	0.34
47. Travel related to purchasing food (except groceries)	0.33
48. Helping household adults	0.31
49. Purchasing gas	0.17
50. Purchasing food (except groceries)	0.16

Note: Primary activities are those respondents identified as their main activity. Other activities done simultaneously, such as eating while watching TV, are not included. The primary activities shown are those for which data by age are available. Source: Bureau of Labor Statistics, unpublished tables from the 2008 American Time Use Survey, Internet site http://www.bls .gov/tus/home.htm; calculations by New Strategist

Table 4.19 Ranking: Average Hours per Day Spent Doing Primary Activities by Male Participants Aged 25 to 34, 2008

(hours per day spent by male participants aged 25 to 34 doing primary activities, ranked by time spent doing activity, 2008)

		average hours per day spent by male participants aged 25 to 34
	Total, all activities	**24.00**
1.	Sleeping	8.48
2.	Work, main job	8.17
3.	Playing games (including computer)	3.09
4.	Television	2.99
5.	Lawn, garden, and houseplants	2.12
6.	Computer use for leisure (except games)	2.01
7.	Socializing and communicating	1.78
8.	Caring for and helping household children	1.78
9.	Participating in sports, exercise, or recreation	1.70
10.	Interior cleaning	1.38
11.	Eating and drinking	1.10
12.	Relaxing, thinking	1.05
13.	Shopping, except groceries, food, and gas	0.98
14.	Laundry	0.98
15.	Travel related to work	0.86
16.	Grocery shopping	0.74
17.	Reading for personal interest	0.73
18.	Food and drink preparation	0.71
19.	Grooming	0.70
20.	Kitchen and food clean-up	0.64
21.	Telephone calls	0.64
22.	Household and personal organization and planning	0.63
23.	Travel related to eating and drinking	0.58
24.	Helping adults in other households	0.56
25.	Travel related to caring for and helping household children	0.52
26.	Travel related to household activities	0.52
27.	Travel related to sports, exercise, and recreation	0.51
28.	Travel related to shopping (except groceries, food, and gas)	0.50
29.	Travel related to socializing and communicating	0.49
30.	Travel related to grocery shopping	0.48
31.	Travel related to relaxing and leisure	0.45
32.	Travel related to purchasing food (except groceries)	0.34
33.	Purchasing food (except groceries)	0.14

Note: Primary activities are those respondents identified as their main activity. Other activities done simultaneously, such as eating while watching TV, are not included. The primary activities shown are those for which data by age are available.
Source: Bureau of Labor Statistics, unpublished tables from the 2008 American Time Use Survey, Internet site http://www.bls.gov/tus/home.htm; calculations by New Strategist

Table 4.20 Ranking: Average Hours per Day Spent Doing Primary Activities by Female Participants Aged 25 to 34, 2008

(hours per day spent by female participants aged 25 to 34 doing primary activities, ranked by time spent doing activity, 2008)

		average hours per day spent by female participants aged 25 to 34
	Total, all activities	**24.00**
1.	Sleeping	8.60
2.	Work, main job	7.18
3.	Television	2.80
4.	Caring for and helping household children	2.19
5.	Attending religious services	2.07
6.	Volunteer activities	2.04
7.	Socializing and communicating	1.89
8.	Interior cleaning	1.64
9.	Computer use for leisure (except games)	1.63
10.	Participating in sports, exercise, or recreation	1.25
11.	Shopping, except groceries, food, and gas	1.12
12.	Relaxing, thinking	1.10
13.	Eating and drinking	1.06
14.	Reading for personal interest	1.06
15.	Laundry	1.05
16.	Grooming	0.91
17.	Activities related to household children's education	0.87
18.	Food and drink preparation	0.85
19.	Telephone calls	0.83
20.	Grocery shopping	0.75
21.	Household and personal email	0.63
22.	Kitchen and food clean-up	0.59
23.	Travel related to work	0.58
24.	Travel related to caring for and helping household children	0.57
25.	Travel related to socializing and communicating	0.55
26.	Household and personal organization and planning	0.51
27.	Helping adults in other households	0.49
28.	Travel related to shopping (except groceries, food, and gas)	0.47
29.	Travel related to relaxing and leisure	0.46
30.	Travel related to eating and drinking	0.44
31.	Animals and pets (not veterinary care)	0.40
32.	Travel related to religious and spiritual activities	0.39
33.	Storing interior household items, including food	0.39
34.	Travel related to sports, exercise, and recreation	0.37
35.	Travel related to household activities	0.33
36.	Travel related to grocery shopping	0.32
37.	Travel related to purchasing food (except groceries)	0.32
38.	Purchasing food (except groceries)	0.18

Note: Primary activities are those respondents identified as their main activity. Other activities done simultaneously, such as eating while watching TV, are not included. The primary activities shown are those for which data by age are available.
Source: Bureau of Labor Statistics, unpublished tables from the 2008 American Time Use Survey, Internet site http://www.bls .gov/tus/home.htm; calculations by New Strategist

Time Use, 2008: People Aged 35 to 44

In the 35-to-44 age group, the demands of work and family are equally compelling. Work is second only to sleep among activities on which the average 35-to-44-year-old spends the most time. Most 35-to-44-year-olds have children at home, which is why caring for and helping household children is the fourth most time consuming primary activity for the age group (excluding sleep)—ahead of grooming or socializing.

Forty-six percent of 35-to-44-year-olds care for household children as a primary activity on an average day. Among women in the age group, the figure is a higher 54 percent. Men in the age group are slightly more likely than those in the younger 25-to-34 age group to spend time caring for household children as a primary activity (37 percent versus 29 percent). One factor behind the greater participation of 35-to-44-year-old men in caring for children is the older age of their children, who require more picking up and dropping off. On an average day, 14 percent of men aged 35 to 44 spend time picking up and dropping off household children as a primary activity. Not surprisingly, women in the age group are even more likely to chauffeur household children, 27 percent doing so on an average day.

Work demands the biggest time commitment from both men and women (after sleep). On an average day, 67 percent of men work at their main job (this figure is low because it includes both

Work and children are the top priorities of 35-to-44-year-olds

(average hours per day spent by people aged 35 to 44 doing primary activities, for the 10 activities on which the average 35-to-44-year-old spends the most time, excluding sleep, 2008)

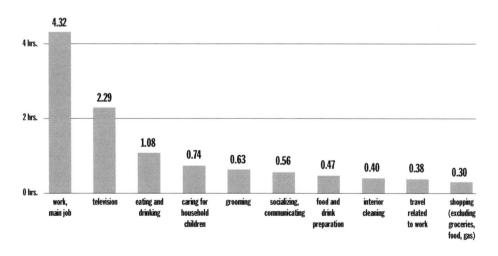

weekdays and weekends). Among women in the age group, 48 percent work on an average day. Commuting to work makes the top ten list of time-consuming activities for this age group.

Housework is at a maximum for 35-to-44-year-olds, many with teens at home. This age group is most likely to do a load of laundry on an average day (21 percent) and is one of the age groups most likely to be found in the grocery store (14 percent go grocery shopping on an average day). Because leisure time is in short supply, they are least likely among the age groups to spend time involved in sports, exercise, or recreation as a primary activity (only 15 percent do so on an average day).

Women aged 35 to 44 spend twice as much time as their male counterparts caring for household children. Women are also more likely than men to be involved in caring for animals on an average day (15 versus 11 percent). Thirty-three percent of women aged 35 to 44 do the laundry on an average day compared with 7 percent of men. But men are more likely than women to care for the lawn, with lawn care ranking tenth in time use for the average man in the age group (excluding sleep).

Table 5.1 Time Use by Total People Aged 35 to 44, 2008

(number and percent of total people aged 35 to 44 participating in primary activities on an average day, hours spent doing activity by the average person aged 35 to 44 and by those aged 35 to 44 who participated in the activity, 2008; numbers of participants in thousands)

	participants aged 35 to 44		time spent doing activity (hours)	
	number	percent	average person aged 35 to 44	participants aged 35 to 44
TOTAL, ALL ACTIVITIES	**41,698**	**100.0%**	**24.00**	**24.00**
Personal care	**41,676**	**99.9**	**9.11**	**9.12**
Sleeping	41,650	99.9	8.38	8.39
Sleeplessness	1,768	4.2	0.05	1.21
Grooming	33,873	81.2	0.63	0.78
Health-related self-care	1,639	3.9	0.08	2.13
Household activities	**33,167**	**79.5**	**1.89**	**2.38**
Housework	15,978	38.3	0.64	1.67
Interior cleaning	10,398	24.9	0.40	1.60
Laundry	8,588	20.6	0.21	1.03
Storing interior household items, including food	1,949	4.7	0.02	0.34
Food and drink preparation, presentation, and clean-up	24,631	59.1	0.61	1.03
Food and drink preparation	23,478	56.3	0.47	0.83
Kitchen and food clean-up	10,450	25.1	0.13	0.53
Interior maintenance, repair, and decoration	1,288	3.1	0.08	2.60
Interior arrangement, decoration, and repairs	729	1.7	0.05	3.14
Exterior maintenance, repair, and decoration	1,181	2.8	0.07	2.33
Lawn, garden, and houseplants	3,374	8.1	0.16	1.97
Animals and pets (not veterinary care)	5,291	12.7	0.08	0.62
Walking, exercising, and playing with pets	2,455	5.9	0.05	0.78
Vehicles	1,164	2.8	0.04	1.61
Household management	12,693	30.4	0.20	0.67
Financial management	1,758	4.2	0.04	1.01
Household and personal organization and planning	6,857	16.4	0.09	0.57
Household and personal mail and messages (except email)	2,208	5.3	0.01	0.20
Household and personal email	4,379	10.5	0.06	0.53
Caring for and helping household members	**20,399**	**48.9**	**0.87**	**1.78**
Caring for and helping household children	19,133	45.9	0.74	1.62
Physical care for household children	13,719	32.9	0.33	1.00
Reading to or with household children	3,095	7.4	0.03	0.47
Playing with household children (except sports)	4,243	10.2	0.14	1.40
Talking with, listening to household children	3,187	7.6	0.04	0.57
Looking after household children as a primary activity	1,901	4.6	0.04	0.98
Picking up or dropping off household children	8,667	20.8	0.04	0.21
Activities related to household children's education	4,072	9.8	0.08	0.85
Helping household children with homework	3,739	9.0	0.07	0.79
Helping household adults	1,446	3.5	0.01	0.26
Caring for and helping people in other households	**4,436**	**10.6**	**0.10**	**0.95**
Caring for and helping children in other households	1,667	4.0	0.04	0.96

	participants aged 35 to 44		time spent doing activity (hours)	
	number	percent	average person aged 35 to 44	participants aged 35 to 44
Helping adults in other households	2,879	6.9%	0.06	0.84
Picking up or dropping off adults in other households	1,727	4.1	0.01	0.14
Work and work-related activities	**25,188**	**60.4**	**4.56**	**7.54**
Work, main job	23,890	57.3	4.32	7.53
Work, other job(s)	1,400	3.4	0.14	4.30
Education	**1,007**	**2.4**	**0.08**	**3.34**
Taking class	454	1.1	0.03	–
Taking class for degree, certification, or licensure	238	0.6	0.02	–
Research, homework	770	1.8	0.05	–
Consumer purchases (store, telephone, Internet)	**18,703**	**44.9**	**0.43**	**0.97**
Grocery shopping	5,851	14.0	0.10	0.74
Purchasing gas	1,737	4.2	0.01	0.16
Purchasing food (except groceries)	6,057	14.5	0.02	0.17
Shopping, except groceries, food, and gas	10,798	25.9	0.30	1.14
Professional and personal care services	**2,764**	**6.6**	**0.06**	**0.86**
Financial services and banking	938	2.2	0.00	0.22
Banking	906	2.2	0.00	0.19
Medical and care services	1,016	2.4	0.03	–
Using health and care services outside the home	1,016	2.4	0.03	–
Household services	**712**	**1.7**	**0.01**	–
Eating and drinking	**39,761**	**95.4**	**1.08**	**1.13**
Socializing, relaxing, and leisure	**39,064**	**93.7**	**3.68**	**3.92**
Socializing and communicating	15,083	36.2	0.56	1.53
Attending or hosting social events	880	2.1	0.07	3.37
Relaxing and leisure	37,032	88.8	2.96	3.33
Relaxing, thinking	6,941	16.6	0.15	0.93
Television	32,774	78.6	2.29	2.92
Listening to the radio	534	1.3	0.01	–
Listening to or playing music (not radio)	548	1.3	0.01	–
Playing games (including computer)	2,495	6.0	0.12	1.94
Computer use for leisure (except games)	4,006	9.6	0.15	1.54
Reading for personal interest	7,212	17.3	0.19	1.11
Arts and entertainment (except sports)	1,371	3.3	0.09	2.60
Sports, exercise, and recreation	**6,902**	**16.6**	**0.30**	**1.80**
Participating in sports, exercise, or recreation	6,277	15.1	0.25	1.67
Using cardiovascular equipment	936	2.2	0.01	–
Walking	1,130	2.7	0.02	0.88
Working out, unspecified	1,394	3.3	0.03	0.76
Religious and spiritual activities	**3,317**	**8.0**	**0.12**	**1.51**
Attending religious services	1,750	4.2	0.08	1.89
Participation in religious practices	1,703	4.1	0.03	0.79

	participants aged 35 to 44		time spent doing activity (hours)	
	number	percent	average person aged 35 to 44	participants aged 35 to 44
Volunteer activities	**2,886**	**6.9%**	**0.14**	**2.03**
Administrative and support activities	1,166	2.8	0.04	1.44
Telephone calls	**4,822**	**11.6**	**0.07**	**0.64**
Telephone calls to or from family members	2,228	5.3	0.03	0.58
Telephone calls to or from friends, neighbors, or acquaintances	1,707	4.1	0.02	0.55
Traveling	**37,764**	**90.6**	**1.32**	**1.46**
Travel related to personal care	751	1.8	0.01	–
Travel related to household activities	3,519	8.4	0.03	0.39
Travel related to household management	2,445	5.9	0.02	0.38
Travel related to caring for and helping household members	11,299	27.1	0.16	0.60
Travel related to caring for and helping household children	10,195	24.4	0.14	0.57
Travel related to helping household adults	1,102	2.6	0.01	–
Travel related to caring for and helping people in other households	3,878	9.3	0.06	0.69
Travel related to caring for and helping children in other households	1,315	3.2	0.02	0.50
Travel related to helping adults in other households	2,571	6.2	0.05	0.74
Travel related to work	20,389	48.9	0.38	0.77
Travel related to education	405	1.0	0.01	–
Travel related to taking class	365	0.9	0.01	–
Travel related to consumer purchases	18,023	43.2	0.26	0.59
Travel related to grocery shopping	5,835	14.0	0.05	0.39
Travel related to purchasing gas	1,732	4.2	0.02	0.37
Travel related to purchasing food (except groceries)	5,646	13.5	0.04	0.31
Travel related to shopping (except groceries, food, and gas)	10,399	24.9	0.15	0.58
Travel related to using professional and personal care services	2,462	5.9	0.03	0.51
Travel related to using financial services and banking	817	2.0	0.00	–
Travel related to using medical services	1,001	2.4	0.01	–
Travel related to eating and drinking	10,396	24.9	0.11	0.44
Travel related to socializing, relaxing, and leisure	10,285	24.7	0.14	0.56
Travel related to socializing and communicating	6,422	15.4	0.08	0.51
Travel related to attending or hosting social events	734	1.8	0.01	0.74
Travel related to relaxing and leisure	2,831	6.8	0.03	0.38
Travel related to arts and entertainment	1,054	2.5	0.01	0.47
Travel related to sports, exercise, and recreation	3,809	9.1	0.05	0.55
Travel related to participating in sports, exercise, recreation	3,204	7.7	0.04	0.48
Travel related to religious and spiritual activities	1,747	4.2	0.02	0.48
Travel related to volunteer activities	2,021	4.8	0.02	0.44

Note: Primary activities are those respondents identified as their main activity. Other activities done simultaneously, such as eating while watching TV, are not included. Numbers may not add to total because not all subcategories are shown. If fewer than 2.0 percent of the total population participated in a primary activity, then the primary activity is not shown. "–" means sample is too small to make a reliable estimate.
Source: Bureau of Labor Statistics, unpublished tables from the 2008 American Time Use Survey, Internet site http://www.bls.gov/tus/home.htm; calculations by New Strategist

Table 5.2 Time Use by Men Aged 35 to 44, 2008

(number and percent of men aged 35 to 44 participating in primary activities on an average day, hours spent doing activity by the average man aged 35 to 44 and by men aged 35 to 44 who participated in the activity, 2008; numbers of participants in thousands)

	men aged 35 to 44 participating		time spent doing activity (hours)	
	number	percent	average man aged 35 to 44	male participants aged 35 to 44
TOTAL, ALL ACTIVITIES	**20,574**	**100.0%**	**24.00**	**24.00**
Personal care	**20,552**	**99.9**	**8.90**	**8.91**
Sleeping	20,526	99.8	8.31	8.33
Sleeplessness	608	3.0	0.04	–
Grooming	16,271	79.1	0.54	0.68
Health-related self-care	567	2.8	0.04	–
Household activities	**14,231**	**69.2**	**1.35**	**1.95**
Housework	4,077	19.8	0.26	1.29
Interior cleaning	2,540	12.3	0.17	1.41
Laundry	1,542	7.5	0.07	0.98
Storing interior household items, including food	494	2.4	0.01	–
Food and drink preparation, presentation, and clean-up	8,509	41.4	0.33	0.79
Food and drink preparation	7,921	38.5	0.28	0.72
Kitchen and food clean-up	2,218	10.8	0.05	0.45
Interior maintenance, repair, and decoration	837	4.1	0.12	–
Interior arrangement, decoration, and repairs	528	2.6	0.09	–
Exterior maintenance, repair, and decoration	879	4.3	0.10	–
Lawn, garden, and houseplants	1,973	9.6	0.23	2.38
Animals and pets (not veterinary care)	2,199	10.7	0.07	0.63
Walking, exercising, and playing with pets	882	4.3	0.04	–
Vehicles	1,010	4.9	0.09	–
Household management	4,921	23.9	0.14	0.59
Financial management	644	3.1	0.02	–
Household and personal organization and planning	2,445	11.9	0.07	0.56
Household and personal mail and messages (except email)	817	4.0	0.01	–
Household and personal email	1,656	8.0	0.04	0.56
Caring for and helping household members	**8,230**	**40.0**	**0.62**	**1.55**
Caring for and helping household children	7,710	37.5	0.52	1.39
Physical care for household children	4,995	24.3	0.21	0.88
Reading to or with household children	1,051	5.1	0.02	0.49
Playing with household children (except sports)	1,832	8.9	0.14	1.58
Talking with, listening to household children	783	3.8	0.02	–
Looking after household children as a primary activity	610	3.0	0.03	–
Picking up or dropping off household children	2,955	14.4	0.03	0.18
Activities related to household children's education	1,152	5.6	0.05	–
Helping household children with homework	1,103	5.4	0.05	–
Helping household adults	525	2.6	0.01	–
Caring for and helping people in other households	**1,947**	**9.5**	**0.11**	**1.15**
Caring for and helping children in other households	525	2.6	0.03	–

	men aged 35 to 44 participating		time spent doing activity (hours)	
	number	percent	average man aged 35 to 44	male participants aged 35 to 44
Helping adults in other households	1,462	7.1%	0.07	1.05
Picking up or dropping off adults in other households	846	4.1	0.01	–
Work and work-related activities	**14,573**	**70.8**	**5.64**	**7.96**
Work, main job	13,799	67.1	5.36	7.99
Work, other job(s)	667	3.2	0.14	–
Education	**353**	**1.7**	**0.04**	**–**
Taking class	106	0.5	0.01	–
Taking class for degree, certification, or licensure	54	0.3	0.01	–
Research, homework	246	1.2	0.03	–
Consumer purchases (store, telephone, Internet)	**7,880**	**38.3**	**0.32**	**0.84**
Grocery shopping	1,910	9.3	0.06	0.68
Purchasing gas	733	3.6	0.01	–
Purchasing food (except groceries)	2,962	14.4	0.02	0.17
Shopping, except groceries, food, and gas	4,286	20.8	0.23	1.09
Professional and personal care services	**883**	**4.3**	**0.02**	**–**
Financial services and banking	464	2.3	0.00	–
Banking	437	2.1	0.00	–
Medical and care services	203	1.0	0.01	–
Using health and care services outside the home	203	1.0	0.01	–
Household services	**412**	**2.0**	**0.01**	**–**
Eating and drinking	**19,716**	**95.8**	**1.14**	**1.19**
Socializing, relaxing, and leisure	**19,339**	**94.0**	**3.73**	**3.97**
Socializing and communicating	6,573	31.9	0.52	1.62
Attending or hosting social events	437	2.1	0.06	–
Relaxing and leisure	18,434	89.6	3.07	3.43
Relaxing, thinking	3,378	16.4	0.15	0.93
Television	16,555	80.5	2.42	3.01
Listening to the radio	263	1.3	0.01	–
Listening to or playing music (not radio)	277	1.3	0.02	–
Playing games (including computer)	1,250	6.1	0.13	2.21
Computer use for leisure (except games)	2,138	10.4	0.16	1.52
Reading for personal interest	2,793	13.6	0.14	1.06
Arts and entertainment (except sports)	646	3.1	0.08	–
Sports, exercise, and recreation	**3,499**	**17.0**	**0.37**	**2.19**
Participating in sports, exercise, or recreation	3,208	15.6	0.33	2.11
Using cardiovascular equipment	255	1.2	0.01	–
Walking	385	1.9	0.02	–
Working out, unspecified	646	3.1	0.03	–
Religious and spiritual activities	**1,426**	**6.9**	**0.10**	**1.46**
Attending religious services	735	3.6	0.07	1.97
Participation in religious practices	671	3.3	0.02	–

	men aged 35 to 44 participating		time spent doing activity (hours)	
	number	percent	average man aged 35 to 44	male participants aged 35 to 44
Volunteer activities	**1,020**	**5.0%**	**0.10**	**2.07**
Administrative and support activities	322	1.6	0.02	–
Telephone calls	**1,357**	**6.6**	**0.05**	**0.69**
Telephone calls to or from family members	509	2.5	0.02	–
Telephone calls to or from friends, neighbors, or acquaintances	500	2.4	0.01	–
Traveling	**18,700**	**90.9**	**1.37**	**1.51**
Travel related to personal care	353	1.7	0.01	–
Travel related to household activities	1,669	8.1	0.04	0.45
Travel related to household management	1,063	5.2	0.02	0.44
Travel related to caring for and helping household members	4,018	19.5	0.10	0.52
Travel related to caring for and helping household children	3,554	17.3	0.09	0.50
Travel related to helping household adults	407	2.0	0.01	–
Travel related to caring for and helping people in other households	1,746	8.5	0.07	0.80
Travel related to caring for and helping children in other households	424	2.1	0.01	–
Travel related to helping adults in other households	1,345	6.5	0.06	0.89
Travel related to work	12,206	59.3	0.50	0.84
Travel related to education	73	0.4	0.00	–
Travel related to taking class	66	0.3	0.00	–
Travel related to consumer purchases	7,537	36.6	0.20	0.55
Travel related to grocery shopping	1,910	9.3	0.04	0.44
Travel related to purchasing gas	727	3.5	0.01	–
Travel related to purchasing food (except groceries)	2,782	13.5	0.04	0.31
Travel related to shopping (except groceries, food, and gas)	4,042	19.6	0.11	0.53
Travel related to using professional and personal care services	881	4.3	0.02	–
Travel related to using financial services and banking	455	2.2	0.01	–
Travel related to using medical services	203	1.0	0.01	–
Travel related to eating and drinking	5,772	28.1	0.12	0.44
Travel related to socializing, relaxing, and leisure	4,756	23.1	0.16	0.69
Travel related to socializing and communicating	2,915	14.2	0.09	0.65
Travel related to attending or hosting social events	386	1.9	0.01	–
Travel related to relaxing and leisure	1,402	6.8	0.03	0.44
Travel related to arts and entertainment	579	2.8	0.01	–
Travel related to sports, exercise, and recreation	1,947	9.5	0.06	0.58
Travel related to participating in sports, exercise, recreation	1,675	8.1	0.05	0.57
Travel related to religious and spiritual activities	861	4.2	0.02	0.44
Travel related to volunteer activities	700	3.4	0.02	–

Note: Primary activities are those respondents identified as their main activity. Other activities done simultaneously, such as eating while watching TV, are not included. Numbers may not add to total because not all subcategories are shown. If fewer than 2.0 percent of the total population participated in a primary activity, then the primary activity is not shown. "–" means sample is too small to make a reliable estimate.
Source: Bureau of Labor Statistics, unpublished tables from the 2008 American Time Use Survey, Internet site http://www.bls .gov/tus/home.htm; calculations by New Strategist

Table 5.3 Time Use by Women Aged 35 to 44, 2008

(number and percent of women aged 35 to 44 participating in primary activities on an average day, hours spent doing activity by the average woman aged 35 to 44 and by women aged 35 to 44 who participated in the activity, 2008; numbers of participants in thousands)

	women aged 35 to 44 participating		time spent doing activity (hours)	
	number	percent	average woman aged 35 to 44	female participants aged 35 to 44
TOTAL, ALL ACTIVITIES	**21,124**	**100.0%**	**24.00**	**24.00**
Personal care	**21,124**	**100.0**	**9.32**	**9.32**
Sleeping	21,124	100.0	8.44	8.44
Sleeplessness	1,160	5.5	0.07	1.21
Grooming	17,602	83.3	0.72	0.87
Health-related self-care	1,071	5.1	0.13	–
Household activities	**18,936**	**89.6**	**2.42**	**2.70**
Housework	11,900	56.3	1.01	1.80
Interior cleaning	7,859	37.2	0.62	1.67
Laundry	7,047	33.4	0.35	1.05
Storing interior household items, including food	1,455	6.9	0.02	0.35
Food and drink preparation, presentation, and clean-up	16,123	76.3	0.88	1.15
Food and drink preparation	15,557	73.6	0.65	0.89
Kitchen and food clean-up	8,232	39.0	0.22	0.55
Interior maintenance, repair, and decoration	450	2.1	0.04	–
Interior arrangement, decoration, and repairs	201	1.0	0.03	–
Exterior maintenance, repair, and decoration	302	1.4	0.03	–
Lawn, garden, and houseplants	1,401	6.6	0.09	1.40
Animals and pets (not veterinary care)	3,091	14.6	0.09	0.62
Walking, exercising, and playing with pets	1,573	7.4	0.05	0.71
Vehicles	154	0.7	0.01	–
Household management	7,772	36.8	0.26	0.72
Financial management	1,114	5.3	0.06	–
Household and personal organization and planning	4,412	20.9	0.12	0.57
Household and personal mail and messages (except email)	1,391	6.6	0.01	0.21
Household and personal email	2,723	12.9	0.07	0.51
Caring for and helping household members	**12,170**	**57.6**	**1.12**	**1.94**
Caring for and helping household children	11,423	54.1	0.96	1.77
Physical care for household children	8,725	41.3	0.44	1.07
Reading to or with household children	2,044	9.7	0.04	0.46
Playing with household children (except sports)	2,411	11.4	0.14	1.27
Talking with, listening to household children	2,404	11.4	0.07	0.61
Looking after household children as a primary activity	1,291	6.1	0.06	0.93
Picking up or dropping off household children	5,712	27.0	0.06	0.22
Activities related to household children's education	2,920	13.8	0.11	0.81
Helping household children with homework	2,636	12.5	0.09	0.71
Helping household adults	921	4.4	0.01	–
Caring for and helping people in other households	**2,489**	**11.8**	**0.09**	**0.80**
Caring for and helping children in other households	1,142	5.4	0.04	0.83t

	women aged 35 to 44 participating		time spent doing activity (hours)	
	number	percent	average woman aged 35 to 44	female participants aged 35 to 44
Helping adults in other households	1,416	6.7%	0.04	0.63
Picking up or dropping off adults in other households	880	4.2	0.01	–
Work and work-related activities	**10,615**	**50.3**	**3.50**	**6.97**
Work, main job	10,091	47.8	3.30	6.90
Work, other job(s)	733	3.5	0.15	–
Education	**654**	**3.1**	**0.12**	**–**
Taking class	348	1.6	0.04	–
Taking class for degree, certification, or licensure	184	0.9	0.02	–
Research, homework	524	2.5	0.08	–
Consumer purchases (store, telephone, Internet)	**10,822**	**51.2**	**0.54**	**1.06**
Grocery shopping	3,941	18.7	0.14	0.77
Purchasing gas	1,004	4.8	0.01	0.15
Purchasing food (except groceries)	3,095	14.7	0.03	0.17
Shopping, except groceries, food, and gas	6,512	30.8	0.36	1.18
Professional and personal care services	**1,881**	**8.9**	**0.09**	**1.02**
Financial services and banking	474	2.2	0.00	–
Banking	469	2.2	0.00	–
Medical and care services	814	3.9	0.05	–
Using health and care services outside the home	814	3.9	0.05	–
Household services	**300**	**1.4**	**0.02**	**–**
Eating and drinking	**20,045**	**94.9**	**1.02**	**1.07**
Socializing, relaxing, and leisure	**19,725**	**93.4**	**3.62**	**3.88**
Socializing and communicating	8,510	40.3	0.59	1.47
Attending or hosting social events	443	2.1	0.08	–
Relaxing and leisure	18,598	88.0	2.86	3.24
Relaxing, thinking	3,563	16.9	0.15	0.92
Television	16,219	76.8	2.17	2.83
Listening to the radio	270	1.3	0.01	–
Listening to or playing music (not radio)	271	1.3	0.01	–
Playing games (including computer)	1,245	5.9	0.10	1.66
Computer use for leisure (except games)	1,868	8.8	0.14	1.57
Reading for personal interest	4,419	20.9	0.24	1.14
Arts and entertainment (except sports)	725	3.4	0.09	–
Sports, exercise, and recreation	**3,403**	**16.1**	**0.23**	**1.40**
Participating in sports, exercise, or recreation	3,068	14.5	0.18	1.22
Using cardiovascular equipment	681	3.2	0.02	–
Walking	746	3.5	0.03	–
Working out, unspecified	748	3.5	0.02	–
Religious and spiritual activities	**1,891**	**9.0**	**0.14**	**1.55**
Attending religious services	1,015	4.8	0.09	1.84
Participation in religious practices	1,032	4.9	0.04	0.82

	women aged 35 to 44 participating		time spent doing activity (hours)	
	number	percent	average woman aged 35 to 44	female participants aged 35 to 44
Volunteer activities	**1,866**	**8.8%**	**0.18**	**2.00**
Administrative and support activities	844	4.0	0.06	–
Telephone calls	**3,465**	**16.4**	**0.10**	**0.61**
Telephone calls to or from family members	1,719	8.1	0.05	0.57
Telephone calls to or from friends, neighbors, or acquaintances	1,207	5.7	0.03	0.59
Traveling	**19,064**	**90.2**	**1.28**	**1.42**
Travel related to personal care	398	1.9	0.02	–
Travel related to household activities	1,850	8.8	0.03	0.34
Travel related to household management	1,382	6.5	0.02	0.34
Travel related to caring for and helping household members	7,281	34.5	0.22	0.65
Travel related to caring for and helping household children	6,641	31.4	0.19	0.61
Travel related to helping household adults	695	3.3	0.02	–
Travel related to caring for and helping people in other households	2,131	10.1	0.06	0.60
Travel related to caring for and helping children in other households	891	4.2	0.02	–
Travel related to helping adults in other households	1,226	5.8	0.03	0.57
Travel related to work	8,183	38.7	0.26	0.67
Travel related to education	333	1.6	0.02	–
Travel related to taking class	299	1.4	0.01	–
Travel related to consumer purchases	10,485	49.6	0.31	0.62
Travel related to grocery shopping	3,925	18.6	0.07	0.36
Travel related to purchasing gas	1,004	4.8	0.02	0.35
Travel related to purchasing food (except groceries)	2,864	13.6	0.04	0.31
Travel related to shopping (except groceries, food, and gas)	6,357	30.1	0.18	0.61
Travel related to using professional and personal care services	1,580	7.5	0.04	0.54
Travel related to using financial services and banking	362	1.7	0.00	–
Travel related to using medical services	798	3.8	0.02	–
Travel related to eating and drinking	4,623	21.9	0.10	0.44
Travel related to socializing, relaxing, and leisure	5,529	26.2	0.11	0.44
Travel related to socializing and communicating	3,507	16.6	0.06	0.39
Travel related to attending or hosting social events	348	1.6	0.01	–
Travel related to relaxing and leisure	1,428	6.8	0.02	0.32
Travel related to arts and entertainment	475	2.2	0.01	–
Travel related to sports, exercise, and recreation	1,862	8.8	0.04	0.51
Travel related to participating in sports, exercise, recreation	1,529	7.2	0.03	0.38
Travel related to religious and spiritual activities	886	4.2	0.02	0.52
Travel related to volunteer activities	1,320	6.2	0.03	0.42

Note: Primary activities are those respondents identified as their main activity. Other activities done simultaneously, such as eating while watching TV, are not included. Numbers may not add to total because not all subcategories are shown. If fewer than 2.0 percent of the total population participated in a primary activity, then the primary activity is not shown. "–" means sample is too small to make a reliable estimate.
Source: Bureau of Labor Statistics, unpublished tables from the 2008 American Time Use Survey, Internet site http://www.bls .gov/tus/home.htm; calculations by New Strategist

Table 5.4 Indexed Time Use of Total People Aged 35 to 44, 2008

(hours spent doing primary activities on an average day by people aged 35 to 44 and by total people aged 15 or older, and index of time spent by people aged 35 to 44 to total people, 2008)

	average hours		index, people aged 35 to 44
	people aged 35 to 44	total people	to total people
TOTAL, ALL ACTIVITIES	**24.00**	**24.00**	**100**
Personal care	**9.11**	**9.38**	**97**
Sleeping	8.38	8.60	97
Sleeplessness	0.05	0.06	83
Grooming	0.63	0.67	94
Health-related self-care	0.08	0.09	89
Household activities	**1.89**	**1.77**	**107**
Housework	0.64	0.58	110
Interior cleaning	0.40	0.37	108
Laundry	0.21	0.17	124
Storing interior household items, including food	0.02	0.02	100
Food and drink preparation, presentation, and clean-up	0.61	0.52	117
Food and drink preparation	0.47	0.40	118
Kitchen and food clean-up	0.13	0.12	108
Interior maintenance, repair, and decoration	0.08	0.07	114
Interior arrangement, decoration, and repairs	0.05	0.05	100
Exterior maintenance, repair, and decoration	0.07	0.06	117
Lawn, garden, and houseplants	0.16	0.19	84
Animals and pets (not veterinary care)	0.08	0.09	89
Walking, exercising, and playing with pets	0.05	0.04	125
Vehicles	0.04	0.04	100
Household management	0.20	0.21	95
Financial management	0.04	0.03	133
Household and personal organization and planning	0.09	0.09	100
Household and personal mail and messages (except email)	0.01	0.02	50
Household and personal email	0.06	0.06	100
Caring for and helping household members	**0.87**	**0.45**	**193**
Caring for and helping household children	0.74	0.37	200
Physical care for household children	0.33	0.17	194
Reading to or with household children	0.03	0.01	300
Playing with household children (except sports)	0.14	0.09	156
Talking with, listening to household children	0.04	0.02	200
Looking after household children as a primary activity	0.04	0.03	133
Picking up or dropping off household children	0.04	0.02	200
Activities related to household children's education	0.08	0.04	200
Helping household children with homework	0.07	0.03	233
Helping household adults	0.01	0.01	100
Caring for and helping people in other households	**0.10**	**0.16**	**63**
Caring for and helping children in other households	0.04	0.09	44

	average hours		index, people aged 35 to 44
	people aged 35 to 44	total people	to total people
Helping adults in other households	0.06	0.06	100
Picking up or dropping off adults in other households	0.01	0.01	100
Work and work-related activities	**4.56**	**3.45**	**132**
Work, main job	4.32	3.28	132
Work, other job(s)	0.14	0.09	156
Education	**0.08**	**0.44**	**18**
Taking class	0.03	0.27	11
Taking class for degree, certification, or licensure	0.02	0.26	8
Research, homework	0.05	0.16	31
Consumer purchases (store, telephone, Internet)	**0.43**	**0.38**	**113**
Grocery shopping	0.10	0.10	100
Purchasing gas	0.01	0.01	100
Purchasing food (except groceries)	0.02	0.02	100
Shopping, except groceries, food, and gas	0.30	0.25	120
Professional and personal care services	**0.06**	**0.08**	**75**
Financial services and banking	0.00	0.01	0
Banking	0.00	0.01	0
Medical and care services	0.03	0.05	60
Using health and care services outside the home	0.03	0.04	75
Household services	**0.01**	**0.01**	**100**
Eating and drinking	**1.08**	**1.11**	**97**
Socializing, relaxing, and leisure	**3.68**	**4.62**	**80**
Socializing and communicating	0.56	0.64	88
Attending or hosting social events	0.07	0.07	100
Relaxing and leisure	2.96	3.83	77
Relaxing, thinking	0.15	0.27	56
Television	2.29	2.77	83
Listening to the radio	0.01	0.03	33
Listening to or playing music (not radio)	0.01	0.03	33
Playing games (including computer)	0.12	0.20	60
Computer use for leisure (except games)	0.15	0.14	107
Reading for personal interest	0.19	0.34	56
Arts and entertainment (except sports)	0.09	0.09	100
Sports, exercise, and recreation	**0.30**	**0.33**	**91**
Participating in sports, exercise, or recreation	0.25	0.29	86
Using cardiovascular equipment	0.01	0.02	50
Walking	0.02	0.04	50
Working out, unspecified	0.03	0.03	100
Religious and spiritual activities	**0.12**	**0.14**	**86**
Attending religious services	0.08	0.09	89
Participation in religious practices	0.03	0.04	75

	average hours		index, people aged 35 to 44 to total people
	people aged 35 to 44	total people	
Volunteer activities	**0.14**	**0.15**	**93**
Administrative and support activities	0.04	0.04	100
Telephone calls	**0.07**	**0.13**	**54**
Telephone calls to or from family members	0.03	0.04	75
Telephone calls to or from friends, neighbors, or acquaintances	0.02	0.04	50
Traveling	**1.32**	**1.20**	**110**
Travel related to personal care	0.01	0.01	100
Travel related to household activities	0.03	0.04	75
Travel related to household management	0.02	0.02	100
Travel related to caring for and helping household members	0.16	0.08	200
Travel related to caring for and helping household children	0.14	0.06	233
Travel related to helping household adults	0.01	0.02	50
Travel related to caring for and helping people in other households	0.06	0.06	100
Travel related to caring for and helping children in other households	0.02	0.02	100
Travel related to helping adults in other households	0.05	0.04	125
Travel related to work	0.38	0.28	136
Travel related to education	0.01	0.03	33
Travel related to taking class	0.01	0.03	33
Travel related to consumer purchases	0.26	0.24	108
Travel related to grocery shopping	0.05	0.05	100
Travel related to purchasing gas	0.02	0.02	100
Travel related to purchasing food (except groceries)	0.04	0.04	100
Travel related to shopping (except groceries, food, and gas)	0.15	0.12	125
Travel related to using professional and personal care services	0.03	0.04	75
Travel related to using financial services and banking	0.00	0.01	0
Travel related to using medical services	0.01	0.02	50
Travel related to eating and drinking	0.11	0.12	92
Travel related to socializing, relaxing, and leisure	0.14	0.18	78
Travel related to socializing and communicating	0.08	0.09	89
Travel related to attending or hosting social events	0.01	0.01	100
Travel related to relaxing and leisure	0.03	0.04	75
Travel related to arts and entertainment	0.01	0.02	50
Travel related to sports, exercise, and recreation	0.05	0.04	125
Travel related to participating in sports, exercise, recreation	0.04	0.04	100
Travel related to religious and spiritual activities	0.02	0.02	100
Travel related to volunteer activities	0.02	0.02	100

Note: The index is calculated by dividing average time spent by people in the age group doing primary activity by average time spent by total people doing primary activity and multiplying by 100. Primary activities are those respondents identified as their main activity. Other activities done simultaneously, such as eating while watching TV, are not included. Numbers may not add to total because not all subcategories are shown. If fewer than 2.0 percent of the total population participated in a primary activity, then the primary activity is not shown.
Source: Bureau of Labor Statistics, unpublished tables from the 2008 American Time Use Survey, Internet site http://www.bls .gov/tus/home.htm; calculations by New Strategist

Table 5.5 Indexed Time Use of Men Aged 35 to 44, 2008

(hours spent doing primary activities on an average day by men aged 35 to 44 and by total men aged 15 or older, and index of time spent by men aged 35 to 44 to total men, 2008)

	average hours		index, men aged 35 to 44 to total men
	men aged 35 to 44	total men	
TOTAL, ALL ACTIVITIES	**24.00**	**24.00**	**100**
Personal care	**8.90**	**9.21**	**97**
Sleeping	8.31	8.56	97
Sleeplessness	0.04	0.05	80
Grooming	0.54	0.56	96
Health-related self-care	0.04	0.07	57
Household activities	**1.35**	**1.32**	**102**
Housework	0.26	0.24	108
Interior cleaning	0.17	0.17	100
Laundry	0.07	0.06	117
Storing interior household items, including food	0.01	0.01	100
Food and drink preparation, presentation, and clean-up	0.33	0.30	110
Food and drink preparation	0.28	0.25	112
Kitchen and food clean-up	0.05	0.05	100
Interior maintenance, repair, and decoration	0.12	0.10	120
Interior arrangement, decoration, and repairs	0.09	0.08	113
Exterior maintenance, repair, and decoration	0.10	0.08	125
Lawn, garden, and houseplants	0.23	0.26	88
Animals and pets (not veterinary care)	0.07	0.08	88
Walking, exercising, and playing with pets	0.04	0.04	100
Vehicles	0.09	0.07	129
Household management	0.14	0.16	88
Financial management	0.02	0.03	67
Household and personal organization and planning	0.07	0.07	100
Household and personal mail and messages (except email)	0.01	0.02	50
Household and personal email	0.04	0.05	80
Caring for and helping household members	**0.62**	**0.30**	**207**
Caring for and helping household children	0.52	0.25	208
Physical care for household children	0.21	0.09	233
Reading to or with household children	0.02	0.01	200
Playing with household children (except sports)	0.14	0.08	175
Talking with, listening to household children	0.02	0.01	200
Looking after household children as a primary activity	0.03	0.02	150
Picking up or dropping off household children	0.03	0.01	300
Activities related to household children's education	0.05	0.02	250
Helping household children with homework	0.05	0.02	250
Helping household adults	0.01	0.01	100
Caring for and helping people in other households	**0.11**	**0.13**	**85**
Caring for and helping children in other households	0.03	0.05	60

	average hours		index, men aged 35 to 44 to total men
	men aged 35 to 44	total men	
Helping adults in other households	0.07	0.07	100
Picking up or dropping off adults in other households	0.01	0.01	100
Work and work-related activities	**5.64**	**4.16**	**136**
Work, main job	5.36	3.96	135
Work, other job(s)	0.14	0.10	140
Education	**0.04**	**0.39**	**10**
Taking class	0.01	0.27	4
Taking class for degree, certification, or licensure	0.01	0.27	4
Research, homework	0.03	0.12	25
Consumer purchases (store, telephone, Internet)	**0.32**	**0.28**	**114**
Grocery shopping	0.06	0.06	100
Purchasing gas	0.01	0.01	100
Purchasing food (except groceries)	0.02	0.02	100
Shopping, except groceries, food, and gas	0.23	0.19	121
Professional and personal care services	**0.02**	**0.06**	**33**
Financial services and banking	0.00	0.01	0
Banking	0.00	0.00	–
Medical and care services	0.01	0.04	25
Using health and care services outside the home	0.01	0.03	33
Household services	**0.01**	**0.01**	**100**
Eating and drinking	**1.14**	**1.15**	**99**
Socializing, relaxing, and leisure	**3.73**	**4.83**	**77**
Socializing and communicating	0.52	0.59	88
Attending or hosting social events	0.06	0.06	100
Relaxing and leisure	3.07	4.09	75
Relaxing, thinking	0.15	0.27	56
Television	2.42	3.01	80
Listening to the radio	0.01	0.03	33
Listening to or playing music (not radio)	0.02	0.04	50
Playing games (including computer)	0.13	0.25	52
Computer use for leisure (except games)	0.16	0.15	107
Reading for personal interest	0.14	0.29	48
Arts and entertainment (except sports)	0.08	0.09	89
Sports, exercise, and recreation	**0.37**	**0.44**	**84**
Participating in sports, exercise, or recreation	0.33	0.40	83
Using cardiovascular equipment	0.01	0.01	100
Walking	0.02	0.04	50
Working out, unspecified	0.03	0.04	75
Religious and spiritual activities	**0.10**	**0.12**	**83**
Attending religious services	0.07	0.07	100
Participation in religious practices	0.02	0.03	67

	average hours		index, men aged 35 to 44 to total men
	men aged 35 to 44	total men	
Volunteer activities	**0.10**	**0.14**	**71**
Administrative and support activities	0.02	0.03	67
Telephone calls	**0.05**	**0.07**	**71**
Telephone calls to or from family members	0.02	0.02	100
Telephone calls to or from friends, neighbors, or acquaintances	0.01	0.02	50
Traveling	**1.37**	**1.23**	**111**
Travel related to personal care	0.01	0.01	100
Travel related to household activities	0.04	0.04	100
Travel related to household management	0.02	0.03	67
Travel related to caring for and helping household members	0.10	0.06	167
Travel related to caring for and helping household children	0.09	0.04	225
Travel related to helping household adults	0.01	0.02	50
Travel related to caring for and helping people in other households	0.07	0.06	117
Travel related to caring for and helping children in other households	0.01	0.01	100
Travel related to helping adults in other households	0.06	0.04	150
Travel related to work	0.50	0.36	139
Travel related to education	0.00	0.03	0
Travel related to taking class	0.00	0.02	0
Travel related to consumer purchases	0.20	0.21	95
Travel related to grocery shopping	0.04	0.04	100
Travel related to purchasing gas	0.01	0.02	50
Travel related to purchasing food (except groceries)	0.04	0.04	100
Travel related to shopping (except groceries, food, and gas)	0.11	0.11	100
Travel related to using professional and personal care services	0.02	0.03	67
Travel related to using financial services and banking	0.01	0.01	100
Travel related to using medical services	0.01	0.01	100
Travel related to eating and drinking	0.12	0.13	92
Travel related to socializing, relaxing, and leisure	0.16	0.18	89
Travel related to socializing and communicating	0.09	0.09	100
Travel related to attending or hosting social events	0.01	0.01	100
Travel related to relaxing and leisure	0.03	0.04	75
Travel related to arts and entertainment	0.01	0.02	50
Travel related to sports, exercise, and recreation	0.06	0.06	100
Travel related to participating in sports, exercise, recreation	0.05	0.05	100
Travel related to religious and spiritual activities	0.02	0.02	100
Travel related to volunteer activities	0.02	0.02	100

Note: The index is calculated by dividing average time spent by men in the age group doing primary activity by average time spent by total men doing primary activity and multiplying by 100. Primary activities are those respondents identified as their main activity. Other activities done simultaneously, such as eating while watching TV, are not included. Numbers may not add to total because not all subcategories are shown. If fewer than 2.0 percent of the total population participated in a primary activity, then the primary activity is not shown. "–" means denominator is zero.
Source: Bureau of Labor Statistics, unpublished tables from the 2008 American Time Use Survey, Internet site http://www.bls .gov/tus/home.htm; calculations by New Strategist

Table 5.6 Indexed Time Use of Women Aged 35 to 44, 2008

(hours spent doing primary activities on an average day by women aged 35 to 44 and by total women aged 15 or older, and index of time spent by women aged 35 to 44 to total women, 2008)

	average hours		index, women aged 35 to 44
	women aged 35 to 44	total women	to total women
TOTAL, ALL ACTIVITIES	**24.00**	**24.00**	**100**
Personal care	**9.32**	**9.54**	**98**
Sleeping	8.44	8.64	98
Sleeplessness	0.07	0.07	100
Grooming	0.72	0.78	92
Health-related self-care	0.13	0.11	118
Household activities	**2.42**	**2.19**	**111**
Housework	1.01	0.90	112
Interior cleaning	0.62	0.55	113
Laundry	0.35	0.28	125
Storing interior household items, including food	0.02	0.02	100
Food and drink preparation, presentation, and clean-up	0.88	0.73	121
Food and drink preparation	0.65	0.55	118
Kitchen and food clean-up	0.22	0.18	122
Interior maintenance, repair, and decoration	0.04	0.04	100
Interior arrangement, decoration, and repairs	0.03	0.03	100
Exterior maintenance, repair, and decoration	0.03	0.03	100
Lawn, garden, and houseplants	0.09	0.12	75
Animals and pets (not veterinary care)	0.09	0.10	90
Walking, exercising, and playing with pets	0.05	0.04	125
Vehicles	0.01	0.01	100
Household management	0.26	0.25	104
Financial management	0.06	0.04	150
Household and personal organization and planning	0.12	0.11	109
Household and personal mail and messages (except email)	0.01	0.03	33
Household and personal email	0.07	0.07	100
Caring for and helping household members	**1.12**	**0.59**	**190**
Caring for and helping household children	0.96	0.48	200
Physical care for household children	0.44	0.24	183
Reading to or with household children	0.04	0.02	200
Playing with household children (except sports)	0.14	0.09	156
Talking with, listening to household children	0.07	0.02	350
Looking after household children as a primary activity	0.06	0.03	200
Picking up or dropping off household children	0.06	0.03	200
Activities related to household children's education	0.11	0.05	220
Helping household children with homework	0.09	0.04	234
Helping household adults	0.01	0.01	100
Caring for and helping people in other households	**0.09**	**0.20**	**45**
Caring for and helping children in other households	0.04	0.12	33

	average hours		index, women aged 35 to 44 to total women
	women aged 35 to 44	total women	
Helping adults in other households	0.04	0.05	80
Picking up or dropping off adults in other households	0.01	0.01	100
Work and work-related activities	**3.50**	**2.79**	**125**
Work, main job	3.30	2.63	125
Work, other job(s)	0.15	0.09	167
Education	**0.12**	**0.48**	**25**
Taking class	0.04	0.27	15
Taking class for degree, certification, or licensure	0.02	0.25	9
Research, homework	0.08	0.20	40
Consumer purchases (store, telephone, Internet)	**0.54**	**0.48**	**113**
Grocery shopping	0.14	0.13	108
Purchasing gas	0.01	0.01	100
Purchasing food (except groceries)	0.03	0.02	150
Shopping, except groceries, food, and gas	0.36	0.31	116
Professional and personal care services	**0.09**	**0.11**	**82**
Financial services and banking	0.00	0.01	0
Banking	0.00	0.01	0
Medical and care services	0.05	0.06	85
Using health and care services outside the home	0.05	0.05	100
Household services	**0.02**	**0.01**	**171**
Eating and drinking	**1.02**	**1.07**	**95**
Socializing, relaxing, and leisure	**3.62**	**4.42**	**82**
Socializing and communicating	0.59	0.68	87
Attending or hosting social events	0.08	0.08	100
Relaxing and leisure	2.86	3.58	80
Relaxing, thinking	0.15	0.26	58
Television	2.17	2.54	85
Listening to the radio	0.01	0.02	50
Listening to or playing music (not radio)	0.01	0.02	50
Playing games (including computer)	0.10	0.15	67
Computer use for leisure (except games)	0.14	0.14	100
Reading for personal interest	0.24	0.40	60
Arts and entertainment (except sports)	0.09	0.08	114
Sports, exercise, and recreation	**0.23**	**0.23**	**100**
Participating in sports, exercise, or recreation	0.18	0.20	90
Using cardiovascular equipment	0.02	0.02	100
Walking	0.03	0.04	75
Working out, unspecified	0.02	0.02	107
Religious and spiritual activities	**0.14**	**0.17**	**82**
Attending religious services	0.09	0.10	90
Participation in religious practices	0.04	0.05	80

	average hours		index, women aged 35 to 44 to total women
	women aged 35 to 44	total women	
Volunteer activities	**0.18**	**0.16**	**113**
Administrative and support activities	0.06	0.04	150
Telephone calls	**0.10**	**0.18**	**56**
Telephone calls to or from family members	0.05	0.07	71
Telephone calls to or from friends, neighbors, or acquaintances	0.03	0.06	50
Traveling	**1.28**	**1.17**	**109**
Travel related to personal care	0.02	0.01	175
Travel related to household activities	0.03	0.04	75
Travel related to household management	0.02	0.02	100
Travel related to caring for and helping household members	0.22	0.11	200
Travel related to caring for and helping household children	0.19	0.08	238
Travel related to helping household adults	0.02	0.02	100
Travel related to caring for and helping people in other households	0.06	0.07	86
Travel related to caring for and helping children in other households	0.02	0.02	100
Travel related to helping adults in other households	0.03	0.04	75
Travel related to work	0.26	0.20	130
Travel related to education	0.02	0.04	50
Travel related to taking class	0.01	0.03	33
Travel related to consumer purchases	0.31	0.27	115
Travel related to grocery shopping	0.07	0.06	117
Travel related to purchasing gas	0.02	0.02	100
Travel related to purchasing food (except groceries)	0.04	0.04	100
Travel related to shopping (except groceries, food, and gas)	0.18	0.14	129
Travel related to using professional and personal care services	0.04	0.05	80
Travel related to using financial services and banking	0.00	0.01	0
Travel related to using medical services	0.02	0.02	100
Travel related to eating and drinking	0.10	0.11	91
Travel related to socializing, relaxing, and leisure	0.11	0.17	65
Travel related to socializing and communicating	0.06	0.10	60
Travel related to attending or hosting social events	0.01	0.01	100
Travel related to relaxing and leisure	0.02	0.03	67
Travel related to arts and entertainment	0.01	0.02	50
Travel related to sports, exercise, and recreation	0.04	0.03	133
Travel related to participating in sports, exercise, recreation	0.03	0.03	100
Travel related to religious and spiritual activities	0.02	0.02	100
Travel related to volunteer activities	0.03	0.02	150

Note: The index is calculated by dividing average time spent by women in the age group doing primary activity by average time spent by total women doing primary activity and multiplying by 100. Primary activities are those respondents identified as their main activity. Other activities done simultaneously, such as eating while watching TV, are not included. Numbers may not add to total because not all subcategories are shown. If fewer than 2.0 percent of the total population participated in a primary activity, then the primary activity is not shown.
Source: Bureau of Labor Statistics, unpublished tables from the 2008 American Time Use Survey, Internet site http://www.bls .gov/tus/home.htm; calculations by New Strategist

Table 5.7 Indexed Time Use on of People Aged 35 to 44 by Sex, 2008

(average hours spent by people aged 35 to 44 doing primary activities on an average day by sex, and index of women's time to men's, 2008)

	average hours, aged 35 to 44		index of women to men
	men	women	
TOTAL, ALL ACTIVITIES	**24.00**	**24.00**	**100**
Personal care	**8.90**	**9.32**	**105**
Sleeping	8.31	8.44	102
Sleeplessness	0.04	0.07	175
Grooming	0.54	0.72	133
Health-related self-care	0.04	0.13	325
Household activities	**1.35**	**2.42**	**179**
Housework	0.26	1.01	388
Interior cleaning	0.17	0.62	365
Laundry	0.07	0.35	500
Storing interior household items, including food	0.01	0.02	200
Food and drink preparation, presentation, and clean-up	0.33	0.88	267
Food and drink preparation	0.28	0.65	232
Kitchen and food clean-up	0.05	0.22	440
Interior maintenance, repair, and decoration	0.12	0.04	33
Interior arrangement, decoration, and repairs	0.09	0.03	33
Exterior maintenance, repair, and decoration	0.10	0.03	30
Lawn, garden, and houseplants	0.23	0.09	39
Animals and pets (not veterinary care)	0.07	0.09	129
Walking, exercising, and playing with pets	0.04	0.05	125
Vehicles	0.09	0.01	11
Household management	0.14	0.26	186
Financial management	0.02	0.06	300
Household and personal organization and planning	0.07	0.12	171
Household and personal mail and messages (except email)	0.01	0.01	100
Household and personal email	0.04	0.07	175
Caring for and helping household members	**0.62**	**1.12**	**181**
Caring for and helping household children	0.52	0.96	185
Physical care for household children	0.21	0.44	210
Reading to or with household children	0.02	0.04	200
Playing with household children (except sports)	0.14	0.14	100
Talking with, listening to household children	0.02	0.07	350
Looking after household children as a primary activity	0.03	0.06	200
Picking up or dropping off household children	0.03	0.06	200
Activities related to household children's education	0.05	0.11	220
Helping household children with homework	0.05	0.09	187
Helping household adults	0.01	0.01	100
Caring for and helping people in other households	**0.11**	**0.09**	**82**
Caring for and helping children in other households	0.03	0.04	133

	average hours, aged 35 to 44		index of women to men
	men	women	
Helping adults in other households	0.07	0.04	57
Picking up or dropping off adults in other households	0.01	0.01	100
Work and work-related activities	**5.64**	**3.50**	**62**
Work, main job	5.36	3.30	62
Work, other job(s)	0.14	0.15	107
Education	**0.04**	**0.12**	**300**
Taking class	0.01	0.04	400
Taking class for degree, certification, or licensure	0.01	0.02	224
Research, homework	0.03	0.08	267
Consumer purchases (store, telephone, Internet)	**0.32**	**0.54**	**169**
Grocery shopping	0.06	0.14	233
Purchasing gas	0.01	0.01	100
Purchasing food (except groceries)	0.02	0.03	150
Shopping, except groceries, food, and gas	0.23	0.36	157
Professional and personal care services	**0.02**	**0.09**	**450**
Financial services and banking	0.00	0.00	–
Banking	0.00	0.00	–
Medical and care services	0.01	0.05	510
Using health and care services outside the home	0.01	0.05	500
Household services	**0.01**	**0.02**	**171**
Eating and drinking	**1.14**	**1.02**	**89**
Socializing, relaxing, and leisure	**3.73**	**3.62**	**97**
Socializing and communicating	0.52	0.59	113
Attending or hosting social events	0.06	0.08	133
Relaxing and leisure	3.07	2.86	93
Relaxing, thinking	0.15	0.15	100
Television	2.42	2.17	90
Listening to the radio	0.01	0.01	100
Listening to or playing music (not radio)	0.02	0.01	50
Playing games (including computer)	0.13	0.10	77
Computer use for leisure (except games)	0.16	0.14	88
Reading for personal interest	0.14	0.24	171
Arts and entertainment (except sports)	0.08	0.09	114
Sports, exercise, and recreation	**0.37**	**0.23**	**62**
Participating in sports, exercise, or recreation	0.33	0.18	55
Using cardiovascular equipment	0.01	0.02	200
Walking	0.02	0.03	150
Working out, unspecified	0.03	0.02	71
Religious and spiritual activities	**0.10**	**0.14**	**140**
Attending religious services	0.07	0.09	129
Participation in religious practices	0.02	0.04	200

	average hours, aged 35 to 44		index of women to men
	men	women	
Volunteer activities	**0.10**	**0.18**	**180**
Administrative and support activities	0.02	0.06	300
Telephone calls	**0.05**	**0.10**	**200**
Telephone calls to or from family members	0.02	0.05	250
Telephone calls to or from friends, neighbors, or acquaintances	0.01	0.03	300
Traveling	**1.37**	**1.28**	**93**
Travel related to personal care	0.01	0.02	175
Travel related to household activities	0.04	0.03	75
Travel related to household management	0.02	0.02	100
Travel related to caring for and helping household members	0.10	0.22	220
Travel related to caring for and helping household children	0.09	0.19	211
Travel related to helping household adults	0.01	0.02	200
Travel related to caring for and helping people in other households	0.07	0.06	86
Travel related to caring for and helping children in other households	0.01	0.02	200
Travel related to helping adults in other households	0.06	0.03	50
Travel related to work	0.50	0.26	52
Travel related to education	0.00	0.02	–
Travel related to taking class	0.00	0.01	–
Travel related to consumer purchases	0.20	0.31	155
Travel related to grocery shopping	0.04	0.07	175
Travel related to purchasing gas	0.01	0.02	200
Travel related to purchasing food (except groceries)	0.04	0.04	100
Travel related to shopping (except groceries, food, and gas)	0.11	0.18	164
Travel related to using professional and personal care services	0.02	0.04	200
Travel related to using financial services and banking	0.01	0.00	0
Travel related to using medical services	0.01	0.02	200
Travel related to eating and drinking	0.12	0.10	83
Travel related to socializing, relaxing, and leisure	0.16	0.11	69
Travel related to socializing and communicating	0.09	0.06	67
Travel related to attending or hosting social events	0.01	0.01	100
Travel related to relaxing and leisure	0.03	0.02	67
Travel related to arts and entertainment	0.01	0.01	100
Travel related to sports, exercise, and recreation	0.06	0.04	67
Travel related to participating in sports, exercise, recreation	0.05	0.03	60
Travel related to religious and spiritual activities	0.02	0.02	100
Travel related to volunteer activities	0.02	0.03	150

Note: The index is calculated by dividing women's time by men's time and multiplying by 100. Primary activities are those respondents identified as their main activity. Other activities done simultaneously, such as eating while watching TV, are not included. Numbers may not add to total because not all subcategories are shown. If fewer than 2.0 percent of the total population participated in a primary activity, then the primary activity is not shown. "–" means denominator is zero.
Source: Bureau of Labor Statistics, unpublished tables from the 2008 American Time Use Survey, Internet site http://www.bls .gov/tus/home.htm; calculations by New Strategist

Table 5.8 Indexed Participation in Primary Activities by Total People Aged 35 to 44, 2008

(percent of people aged 35 to 44 and total people aged 15 or older participating in primary activities on an average day, and index of participation by people aged 35 to 44 to total people, 2008)

	percent participating		index, people aged 35 to 44 to total
	people aged 35 to 44	total people	
TOTAL, ALL ACTIVITIES	**100.0%**	**100.0%**	**100**
Personal care	**99.9**	**100.0**	**100**
Sleeping	99.9	99.9	100
Sleeplessness	4.2	5.2	81
Grooming	81.2	79.3	102
Health-related self-care	3.9	6.4	62
Household activities	**79.5**	**75.5**	**105**
Housework	38.3	35.5	108
Interior cleaning	24.9	24.5	102
Laundry	20.6	16.2	127
Storing interior household items, including food	4.7	5.0	94
Food and drink preparation, presentation, and clean-up	59.1	52.3	113
Food and drink preparation	56.3	49.3	114
Kitchen and food clean-up	25.1	20.8	120
Interior maintenance, repair, and decoration	3.1	3.0	102
Interior arrangement, decoration, and repairs	1.7	2.0	89
Exterior maintenance, repair, and decoration	2.8	2.7	103
Lawn, garden, and houseplants	8.1	9.4	86
Animals and pets (not veterinary care)	12.7	14.5	87
Walking, exercising, and playing with pets	5.9	5.8	102
Vehicles	2.8	2.7	104
Household management	30.4	29.0	105
Financial management	4.2	4.0	104
Household and personal organization and planning	16.4	14.1	117
Household and personal mail and messages (except email)	5.3	6.9	77
Household and personal email	10.5	9.4	111
Caring for and helping household members	**48.9**	**26.1**	**187**
Caring for and helping household children	45.9	21.9	210
Physical care for household children	32.9	15.7	210
Reading to or with household children	7.4	2.6	284
Playing with household children (except sports)	10.2	5.4	188
Talking with, listening to household children	7.6	3.0	252
Looking after household children as a primary activity	4.6	2.3	201
Picking up or dropping off household children	20.8	9.2	225
Activities related to household children's education	9.8	3.8	256
Helping household children with homework	9.0	3.4	260
Helping household adults	3.5	3.6	96
Caring for and helping people in other households	**10.6**	**13.3**	**80**
Caring for and helping children in other households	4.0	5.6	72

	percent participating		index, people aged 35 to 44 to total
	people aged 35 to 44	total people	
Helping adults in other households	6.9%	8.0%	86
Picking up or dropping off adults in other households	4.1	5.0	84
Work and work-related activities	**60.4**	**46.6**	**130**
Work, main job	57.3	43.9	131
Work, other job(s)	3.4	2.4	141
Education	**2.4**	**7.9**	**31**
Taking class	1.1	5.2	21
Taking class for degree, certification, or licensure	0.6	4.8	12
Research, homework	1.8	5.8	32
Consumer purchases (store, telephone, Internet)	**44.9**	**40.7**	**110**
Grocery shopping	14.0	12.9	109
Purchasing gas	4.2	4.0	105
Purchasing food (except groceries)	14.5	12.0	121
Shopping, except groceries, food, and gas	25.9	23.5	110
Professional and personal care services	**6.6**	**8.9**	**75**
Financial services and banking	2.2	3.2	70
Banking	2.2	3.0	72
Medical and care services	2.4	3.6	67
Using health and care services outside the home	2.4	3.4	71
Household services	**1.7**	**2.1**	**82**
Eating and drinking	**95.4**	**96.0**	**99**
Socializing, relaxing, and leisure	**93.7**	**95.4**	**98**
Socializing and communicating	36.2	37.6	96
Attending or hosting social events	2.1	2.3	91
Relaxing and leisure	88.8	91.3	97
Relaxing, thinking	16.6	19.9	84
Television	78.6	80.9	97
Listening to the radio	1.3	2.0	64
Listening to or playing music (not radio)	1.3	2.6	50
Playing games (including computer)	6.0	9.0	67
Computer use for leisure (except games)	9.6	9.5	101
Reading for personal interest	17.3	23.9	72
Arts and entertainment (except sports)	3.3	3.2	102
Sports, exercise, and recreation	**16.6**	**18.9**	**88**
Participating in sports, exercise, or recreation	15.1	17.9	84
Using cardiovascular equipment	2.2	2.2	103
Walking	2.7	4.8	56
Working out, unspecified	3.3	3.2	105
Religious and spiritual activities	**8.0**	**9.2**	**86**
Attending religious services	4.2	4.9	86
Participation in religious practices	4.1	4.6	89

| | percent participating | | index, people aged 35 to 44 |
	people aged 35 to 44	total people	to total
Volunteer activities	**6.9%**	**6.7%**	**103**
Administrative and support activities	2.8	2.5	110
Telephone calls	**11.6**	**15.4**	**75**
Telephone calls to or from family members	5.3	7.3	73
Telephone calls to or from friends, neighbors, or acquaintances	4.1	5.6	73
Traveling	**90.6**	**86.9**	**104**
Travel related to personal care	1.8	2.5	71
Travel related to household activities	8.4	9.4	90
Travel related to household management	5.9	6.1	96
Travel related to caring for and helping household members	27.1	13.6	199
Travel related to caring for and helping household children	24.4	11.0	223
Travel related to helping household adults	2.6	2.6	103
Travel related to caring for and helping people in other households	9.3	10.5	89
Travel related to caring for and helping children in other households	3.2	3.5	90
Travel related to helping adults in other households	6.2	7.1	87
Travel related to work	48.9	38.2	128
Travel related to education	1.0	5.0	19
Travel related to taking class	0.9	4.4	20
Travel related to consumer purchases	43.2	39.6	109
Travel related to grocery shopping	14.0	12.9	109
Travel related to purchasing gas	4.2	3.9	106
Travel related to purchasing food (except groceries)	13.5	11.2	120
Travel related to shopping (except groceries, food, and gas)	24.9	22.7	110
Travel related to using professional and personal care services	5.9	8.1	73
Travel related to using financial services and banking	2.0	3.0	65
Travel related to using medical services	2.4	3.3	72
Travel related to eating and drinking	24.9	25.0	100
Travel related to socializing, relaxing, and leisure	24.7	28.6	86
Travel related to socializing and communicating	15.4	18.6	83
Travel related to attending or hosting social events	1.8	2.0	88
Travel related to relaxing and leisure	6.8	8.9	76
Travel related to arts and entertainment	2.5	2.6	98
Travel related to sports, exercise, and recreation	9.1	9.6	96
Travel related to participating in sports, exercise, recreation	7.7	8.6	90
Travel related to religious and spiritual activities	4.2	5.1	82
Travel related to volunteer activities	4.8	4.3	113

Note: The index is calculated by dividing percent of people in the age group doing primary activity by percent of total people doing primary activity and multiplying by 100. Primary activities are those respondents identified as their main activity. Other activities done simultaneously, such as eating while watching TV, are not included. If fewer than 2.0 percent of the total population participated in a primary activity, then the primary activity is not shown.
Source: Bureau of Labor Statistics, unpublished tables from the 2008 American Time Use Survey, Internet site http://www.bls .gov/tus/home.htm; calculations by New Strategist

Table 5.9 Indexed Participation in Primary Activities by Men Aged 35 to 44, 2008

(percent of men aged 35 to 44 and total men aged 15 or older participating in primary activities on an average day, and index of participation by men aged 35 to 44 to total men, 2008)

	percent participating		index, men aged 35 to 44 to total men
	men aged 35 to 44	total men	
TOTAL, ALL ACTIVITIES	**100.0%**	**100.0%**	**100**
Personal care	**99.9**	**100.0**	**100**
Sleeping	99.8	99.9	100
Sleeplessness	3.0	4.5	65
Grooming	79.1	76.6	103
Health-related self-care	2.8	4.8	57
Household activities	**69.2**	**66.6**	**104**
Housework	19.8	19.7	101
Interior cleaning	12.3	13.5	92
Laundry	7.5	6.3	119
Storing interior household items, including food	2.4	2.9	84
Food and drink preparation, presentation, and clean-up	41.4	38.4	108
Food and drink preparation	38.5	36.0	107
Kitchen and food clean-up	10.8	9.5	114
Interior maintenance, repair, and decoration	4.1	3.9	104
Interior arrangement, decoration, and repairs	2.6	2.4	105
Exterior maintenance, repair, and decoration	4.3	3.8	113
Lawn, garden, and houseplants	9.6	11.0	87
Animals and pets (not veterinary care)	10.7	12.1	88
Walking, exercising, and playing with pets	4.3	5.2	82
Vehicles	4.9	4.5	109
Household management	23.9	24.0	100
Financial management	3.1	3.2	98
Household and personal organization and planning	11.9	11.1	107
Household and personal mail and messages (except email)	4.0	5.5	73
Household and personal email	8.0	7.4	108
Caring for and helping household members	**40.0**	**20.7**	**193**
Caring for and helping household children	37.5	16.8	223
Physical care for household children	24.3	10.4	233
Reading to or with household children	5.1	1.7	298
Playing with household children (except sports)	8.9	4.7	189
Talking with, listening to household children	3.8	1.7	218
Looking after household children as a primary activity	3.0	1.5	204
Picking up or dropping off household children	14.4	6.2	232
Activities related to household children's education	5.6	2.2	258
Helping household children with homework	5.4	2.0	264
Helping household adults	2.6	3.5	73
Caring for and helping people in other households	**9.5**	**11.0**	**86**
Caring for and helping children in other households	2.6	3.6	70

	percent participating		index, men aged 35 to 44 to total men
	men aged 35 to 44	total men	
Helping adults in other households	7.1%	7.5%	95
Picking up or dropping off adults in other households	4.1	4.4	92
Work and work-related activities	**70.8**	**53.4**	**133**
Work, main job	67.1	50.1	134
Work, other job(s)	3.2	2.3	140
Education	**1.7**	**6.9**	**25**
Taking class	0.5	5.0	10
Taking class for degree, certification, or licensure	0.3	4.8	5
Research, homework	1.2	4.6	26
Consumer purchases (store, telephone, Internet)	**38.3**	**35.6**	**108**
Grocery shopping	9.3	9.6	97
Purchasing gas	3.6	4.3	83
Purchasing food (except groceries)	14.4	11.8	122
Shopping, except groceries, food, and gas	20.8	19.6	106
Professional and personal care services	**4.3**	**6.7**	**64**
Financial services and banking	2.3	3.1	72
Banking	2.1	2.8	76
Medical and care services	1.0	2.4	41
Using health and care services outside the home	1.0	2.3	43
Household services	**2.0**	**2.1**	**95**
Eating and drinking	**95.8**	**96.5**	**99**
Socializing, relaxing, and leisure	**94.0**	**95.4**	**99**
Socializing and communicating	31.9	34.9	92
Attending or hosting social events	2.1	2.0	108
Relaxing and leisure	89.6	92.1	97
Relaxing, thinking	16.4	20.4	81
Television	80.5	82.3	98
Listening to the radio	1.3	2.5	51
Listening to or playing music (not radio)	1.3	3.3	41
Playing games (including computer)	6.1	9.6	63
Computer use for leisure (except games)	10.4	9.5	109
Reading for personal interest	13.6	21.1	64
Arts and entertainment (except sports)	3.1	3.3	95
Sports, exercise, and recreation	**17.0**	**22.0**	**77**
Participating in sports, exercise, or recreation	15.6	21.0	74
Using cardiovascular equipment	1.2	1.8	67
Walking	1.9	4.9	38
Working out, unspecified	3.1	3.5	89
Religious and spiritual activities	**6.9**	**7.7**	**90**
Attending religious services	3.6	4.0	89
Participation in religious practices	3.3	3.7	88

	percent participating		index, men aged 35 to 44 to total men
	men aged 35 to 44	total men	
Volunteer activities	**5.0%**	**5.7%**	**86**
Administrative and support activities	1.6	1.9	80
Telephone calls	**6.6**	**10.0**	**66**
Telephone calls to or from family members	2.5	3.8	65
Telephone calls to or from friends, neighbors, or acquaintances	2.4	3.7	66
Traveling	**90.9**	**88.5**	**103**
Travel related to personal care	1.7	3.1	56
Travel related to household activities	8.1	8.5	96
Travel related to household management	5.2	5.5	94
Travel related to caring for and helping household members	19.5	9.9	197
Travel related to caring for and helping household children	17.3	7.4	235
Travel related to helping household adults	2.0	2.4	83
Travel related to caring for and helping people in other households	8.5	9.3	92
Travel related to caring for and helping children in other households	2.1	2.5	83
Travel related to helping adults in other households	6.5	6.7	97
Travel related to work	59.3	44.4	134
Travel related to education	0.4	4.6	8
Travel related to taking class	0.3	4.1	8
Travel related to consumer purchases	36.6	34.5	106
Travel related to grocery shopping	9.3	9.5	97
Travel related to purchasing gas	3.5	4.2	84
Travel related to purchasing food (except groceries)	13.5	11.0	123
Travel related to shopping (except groceries, food, and gas)	19.6	18.9	104
Travel related to using professional and personal care services	4.3	6.3	68
Travel related to using financial services and banking	2.2	3.0	73
Travel related to using medical services	1.0	2.3	43
Travel related to eating and drinking	28.1	27.3	103
Travel related to socializing, relaxing, and leisure	23.1	28.0	83
Travel related to socializing and communicating	14.2	17.5	81
Travel related to attending or hosting social events	1.9	1.7	111
Travel related to relaxing and leisure	6.8	9.4	73
Travel related to arts and entertainment	2.8	2.8	101
Travel related to sports, exercise, and recreation	9.5	11.5	82
Travel related to participating in sports, exercise, recreation	8.1	10.4	78
Travel related to religious and spiritual activities	4.2	4.4	95
Travel related to volunteer activities	3.4	3.8	89

Note: The index is calculated by dividing percent of men in the age group doing primary activity by percent of total men doing primary activity and multiplying by 100. Primary activities are those respondents identified as their main activity. Other activities done simultaneously, such as eating while watching TV, are not included. If fewer than 2.0 percent of the total population participated in a primary activity, then the primary activity is not shown.
Source: Bureau of Labor Statistics, unpublished tables from the 2008 American Time Use Survey, Internet site http://www.bls .gov/tus/home.htm; calculations by New Strategist

Table 5.10 Indexed Participation in Primary Activities by Women Aged 35 to 44, 2008

(percent of women aged 35 to 44 and total women aged 15 or older participating in primary activities on an average day, and index of participation by women aged 35 to 44 to total women, 2008)

	percent participating		index, women aged 35 to 44 to total women
	women aged 35 to 44	total women	
TOTAL, ALL ACTIVITIES	**100.0%**	**100.0%**	**100**
Personal care	**100.0**	**100.0**	**100**
Sleeping	100.0	99.9	100
Sleeplessness	5.5	5.8	94
Grooming	83.3	81.8	102
Health-related self-care	5.1	7.8	65
Household activities	**89.6**	**84.0**	**107**
Housework	56.3	50.3	112
Interior cleaning	37.2	34.9	107
Laundry	33.4	25.5	131
Storing interior household items, including food	6.9	7.0	99
Food and drink preparation, presentation, and clean-up	76.3	65.3	117
Food and drink preparation	73.6	61.8	119
Kitchen and food clean-up	39.0	31.5	124
Interior maintenance, repair, and decoration	2.1	2.2	97
Interior arrangement, decoration, and repairs	1.0	1.5	63
Exterior maintenance, repair, and decoration	1.4	1.8	81
Lawn, garden, and houseplants	6.6	7.9	84
Animals and pets (not veterinary care)	14.6	16.7	87
Walking, exercising, and playing with pets	7.4	6.3	119
Vehicles	0.7	1.0	74
Household management	36.8	33.8	109
Financial management	5.3	4.9	109
Household and personal organization and planning	20.9	16.8	124
Household and personal mail and messages (except email)	6.6	8.2	81
Household and personal email	12.9	11.3	114
Caring for and helping household members	**57.6**	**31.2**	**185**
Caring for and helping household children	54.1	26.7	203
Physical care for household children	41.3	20.6	200
Reading to or with household children	9.7	3.5	279
Playing with household children (except sports)	11.4	6.1	187
Talking with, listening to household children	11.4	4.3	267
Looking after household children as a primary activity	6.1	3.0	201
Picking up or dropping off household children	27.0	12.1	224
Activities related to household children's education	13.8	5.4	258
Helping household children with homework	12.5	4.8	262
Helping household adults	4.4	3.7	117
Caring for and helping people in other households	**11.8**	**15.5**	**76**
Caring for and helping children in other households	5.4	7.4	73

	percent participating		index, women aged 35 to 44 to total women
	women aged 35 to 44	total women	
Helping adults in other households	6.7%	8.5%	79
Picking up or dropping off adults in other households	4.2	5.4	77
Work and work-related activities	**50.3**	**40.3**	**125**
Work, main job	47.8	38.0	126
Work, other job(s)	3.5	2.4	143
Education	**3.1**	**8.9**	**35**
Taking class	1.6	5.3	31
Taking class for degree, certification, or licensure	0.9	4.7	18
Research, homework	2.5	7.0	35
Consumer purchases (store, telephone, Internet)	**51.2**	**45.4**	**113**
Grocery shopping	18.7	16.1	116
Purchasing gas	4.8	3.7	129
Purchasing food (except groceries)	14.7	12.3	119
Shopping, except groceries, food, and gas	30.8	27.2	113
Professional and personal care services	**8.9**	**11.0**	**81**
Financial services and banking	2.2	3.3	67
Banking	2.2	3.3	68
Medical and care services	3.9	4.8	81
Using health and care services outside the home	3.9	4.5	86
Household services	**1.4**	**2.1**	**68**
Eating and drinking	**94.9**	**95.6**	**99**
Socializing, relaxing, and leisure	**93.4**	**95.4**	**98**
Socializing and communicating	40.3	40.1	100
Attending or hosting social events	2.1	2.7	79
Relaxing and leisure	88.0	90.6	97
Relaxing, thinking	16.9	19.5	86
Television	76.8	79.5	97
Listening to the radio	1.3	1.5	84
Listening to or playing music (not radio)	1.3	2.0	65
Playing games (including computer)	5.9	8.4	70
Computer use for leisure (except games)	8.8	9.5	93
Reading for personal interest	20.9	26.5	79
Arts and entertainment (except sports)	3.4	3.2	109
Sports, exercise, and recreation	**16.1**	**15.9**	**101**
Participating in sports, exercise, or recreation	14.5	15.0	97
Using cardiovascular equipment	3.2	2.5	129
Walking	3.5	4.7	75
Working out, unspecified	3.5	2.9	123
Religious and spiritual activities	**9.0**	**10.7**	**84**
Attending religious services	4.8	5.7	85
Participation in religious practices	4.9	5.4	90

| | percent participating | | index, women aged 35 to 44 |
	women aged 35 to 44	total women	to total women
Volunteer activities	**8.8%**	**7.6%**	**116**
Administrative and support activities	4.0	3.1	130
Telephone calls	**16.4**	**20.4**	**80**
Telephone calls to or from family members	8.1	10.7	76
Telephone calls to or from friends, neighbors, or acquaintances	5.7	7.4	78
Traveling	**90.2**	**85.5**	**106**
Travel related to personal care	1.9	2.0	94
Travel related to household activities	8.8	10.3	85
Travel related to household management	6.5	6.7	98
Travel related to caring for and helping household members	34.5	17.1	202
Travel related to caring for and helping household children	31.4	14.3	219
Travel related to helping household adults	3.3	2.7	121
Travel related to caring for and helping people in other households	10.1	11.6	87
Travel related to caring for and helping children in other households	4.2	4.5	94
Travel related to helping adults in other households	5.8	7.4	78
Travel related to work	38.7	32.2	120
Travel related to education	1.6	5.4	29
Travel related to taking class	1.4	4.6	30
Travel related to consumer purchases	49.6	44.4	112
Travel related to grocery shopping	18.6	16.0	116
Travel related to purchasing gas	4.8	3.7	129
Travel related to purchasing food (except groceries)	13.6	11.5	118
Travel related to shopping (except groceries, food, and gas)	30.1	26.3	114
Travel related to using professional and personal care services	7.5	9.8	76
Travel related to using financial services and banking	1.7	3.1	56
Travel related to using medical services	3.8	4.3	89
Travel related to eating and drinking	21.9	22.8	96
Travel related to socializing, relaxing, and leisure	26.2	29.2	90
Travel related to socializing and communicating	16.6	19.5	85
Travel related to attending or hosting social events	1.6	2.3	72
Travel related to relaxing and leisure	6.8	8.5	80
Travel related to arts and entertainment	2.2	2.4	93
Travel related to sports, exercise, and recreation	8.8	7.7	114
Travel related to participating in sports, exercise, recreation	7.2	6.8	107
Travel related to religious and spiritual activities	4.2	5.8	72
Travel related to volunteer activities	6.2	4.7	133

Note: The index is calculated by dividing percent of women in the age group doing primary activity by percent of total women doing primary activity and multiplying by 100. Primary activities are those respondents identified as their main activity. Other activities done simultaneously, such as eating while watching TV, are not included. If fewer than 2.0 percent of the total population participated in a primary activity, then the primary activity is not shown.
Source: Bureau of Labor Statistics, unpublished tables from the 2008 American Time Use Survey, Internet site http://www.bls.gov/tus/home.htm; calculations by New Strategist

Table 5.11 Indexed Participation in Primary Activities of People Aged 35 to 44 by Sex, 2008

(percent of people aged 35 to 44 participating in primary activities on an average day by sex, and index of women's participation to men's, 2008)

	aged 35 to 44, percent participating		index of women to men
	men	women	
TOTAL, ALL ACTIVITIES	**100.0%**	**100.0%**	**100**
Personal care	**99.9**	**100.0**	**100**
Sleeping	99.8	100.0	100
Sleeplessness	3.0	5.5	186
Grooming	79.1	83.3	105
Health-related self-care	2.8	5.1	184
Household activities	**69.2**	**89.6**	**130**
Housework	19.8	56.3	284
Interior cleaning	12.3	37.2	301
Laundry	7.5	33.4	445
Storing interior household items, including food	2.4	6.9	287
Food and drink preparation, presentation, and clean-up	41.4	76.3	185
Food and drink preparation	38.5	73.6	191
Kitchen and food clean-up	10.8	39.0	361
Interior maintenance, repair, and decoration	4.1	2.1	52
Interior arrangement, decoration, and repairs	2.6	1.0	37
Exterior maintenance, repair, and decoration	4.3	1.4	33
Lawn, garden, and houseplants	9.6	6.6	69
Animals and pets (not veterinary care)	10.7	14.6	137
Walking, exercising, and playing with pets	4.3	7.4	174
Vehicles	4.9	0.7	15
Household management	23.9	36.8	154
Financial management	3.1	5.3	168
Household and personal organization and planning	11.9	20.9	176
Household and personal mail and messages (except email)	4.0	6.6	166
Household and personal email	8.0	12.9	160
Caring for and helping household members	**40.0**	**57.6**	**144**
Caring for and helping household children	37.5	54.1	144
Physical care for household children	24.3	41.3	170
Reading to or with household children	5.1	9.7	189
Playing with household children (except sports)	8.9	11.4	128
Talking with, listening to household children	3.8	11.4	299
Looking after household children as a primary activity	3.0	6.1	206
Picking up or dropping off household children	14.4	27.0	188
Activities related to household children's education	5.6	13.8	247
Helping household children with homework	5.4	12.5	233
Helping household adults	2.6	4.4	171
Caring for and helping people in other households	**9.5**	**11.8**	**125**
Caring for and helping children in other households	2.6	5.4	212

	aged 35 to 44, percent participating		index of women to men
	men	women	
Helping adults in other households	7.1%	6.7%	94
Picking up or dropping off adults in other households	4.1	4.2	101
Work and work-related activities	**70.8**	**50.3**	**71**
Work, main job	67.1	47.8	71
Work, other job(s)	3.2	3.5	107
Education	**1.7**	**3.1**	**180**
Taking class	0.5	1.6	320
Taking class for degree, certification, or licensure	0.3	0.9	332
Research, homework	1.2	2.5	207
Consumer purchases (store, telephone, Internet)	**38.3**	**51.2**	**134**
Grocery shopping	9.3	18.7	201
Purchasing gas	3.6	4.8	133
Purchasing food (except groceries)	14.4	14.7	102
Shopping, except groceries, food, and gas	20.8	30.8	148
Professional and personal care services	**4.3**	**8.9**	**207**
Financial services and banking	2.3	2.2	99
Banking	2.1	2.2	105
Medical and care services	1.0	3.9	391
Using health and care services outside the home	1.0	3.9	391
Household services	**2.0**	**1.4**	**71**
Eating and drinking	**95.8**	**94.9**	**99**
Socializing, relaxing, and leisure	**94.0**	**93.4**	**99**
Socializing and communicating	31.9	40.3	126
Attending or hosting social events	2.1	2.1	99
Relaxing and leisure	89.6	88.0	98
Relaxing, thinking	16.4	16.9	103
Television	80.5	76.8	95
Listening to the radio	1.3	1.3	100
Listening to or playing music (not radio)	1.3	1.3	95
Playing games (including computer)	6.1	5.9	97
Computer use for leisure (except games)	10.4	8.8	85
Reading for personal interest	13.6	20.9	154
Arts and entertainment (except sports)	3.1	3.4	109
Sports, exercise, and recreation	**17.0**	**16.1**	**95**
Participating in sports, exercise, or recreation	15.6	14.5	93
Using cardiovascular equipment	1.2	3.2	260
Walking	1.9	3.5	189
Working out, unspecified	3.1	3.5	113
Religious and spiritual activities	**6.9**	**9.0**	**129**
Attending religious services	3.6	4.8	134
Participation in religious practices	3.3	4.9	150

	aged 35 to 44, percent participating		index of women to men
	men	women	
Volunteer activities	**5.0%**	**8.8%**	**178**
Administrative and support activities	1.6	4.0	255
Telephone calls	**6.6**	**16.4**	**249**
Telephone calls to or from family members	2.5	8.1	329
Telephone calls to or from friends, neighbors, or acquaintances	2.4	5.7	235
Traveling	**90.9**	**90.2**	**99**
Travel related to personal care	1.7	1.9	110
Travel related to household activities	8.1	8.8	108
Travel related to household management	5.2	6.5	127
Travel related to caring for and helping household members	19.5	34.5	176
Travel related to caring for and helping household children	17.3	31.4	182
Travel related to helping household adults	2.0	3.3	166
Travel related to caring for and helping people in other households	8.5	10.1	119
Travel related to caring for and helping children in other households	2.1	4.2	205
Travel related to helping adults in other households	6.5	5.8	89
Travel related to work	59.3	38.7	65
Travel related to education	0.4	1.6	444
Travel related to taking class	0.3	1.4	441
Travel related to consumer purchases	36.6	49.6	135
Travel related to grocery shopping	9.3	18.6	200
Travel related to purchasing gas	3.5	4.8	135
Travel related to purchasing food (except groceries)	13.5	13.6	100
Travel related to shopping (except groceries, food, and gas)	19.6	30.1	153
Travel related to using professional and personal care services	4.3	7.5	175
Travel related to using financial services and banking	2.2	1.7	77
Travel related to using medical services	1.0	3.8	383
Travel related to eating and drinking	28.1	21.9	78
Travel related to socializing, relaxing, and leisure	23.1	26.2	113
Travel related to socializing and communicating	14.2	16.6	117
Travel related to attending or hosting social events	1.9	1.6	88
Travel related to relaxing and leisure	6.8	6.8	99
Travel related to arts and entertainment	2.8	2.2	80
Travel related to sports, exercise, and recreation	9.5	8.8	93
Travel related to participating in sports, exercise, recreation	8.1	7.2	89
Travel related to religious and spiritual activities	4.2	4.2	100
Travel related to volunteer activities	3.4	6.2	184

Note: The index is calculated by dividing percent of women participating in primary activity by percent of men participating in primary activity and multiplying by 100. Primary activities are those respondents identified as their main activity. Other activities done simultaneously, such as eating while watching TV, are not included. If fewer than 2.0 percent of the total population participated in a primary activity, then the primary activity is not shown.
Source: Bureau of Labor Statistics, unpublished tables from the 2008 American Time Use Survey, Internet site http://www.bls .gov/tus/home.htm; calculations by New Strategist

Table 5.12 Ranking: Average Hours per Day Spent Doing Primary Activities by Total People Aged 35 to 44, 2008

(average hours per day spent by people aged 35 to 44 doing primary activities, ranked by time spent doing activity, 2008)

		average hours per day spent by people aged 35 to 44
	Total, all activities	**24.00**
1.	Sleeping	8.38
2.	Work, main job	4.32
3.	Television	2.29
4.	Eating and drinking	1.08
5.	Caring for and helping household children	0.74
6.	Grooming	0.63
7.	Socializing and communicating	0.56
8.	Food and drink preparation	0.47
9.	Interior cleaning	0.40
10.	Travel related to work	0.38
11.	Shopping, except groceries, food, and gas	0.30
12.	Participating in sports, exercise, or recreation	0.25
13.	Laundry	0.21
14.	Reading for personal interest	0.19
15.	Lawn, garden, and houseplants	0.16
16.	Relaxing, thinking	0.15
17.	Computer use for leisure (except games)	0.15
18.	Travel related to shopping (except groceries, food, and gas)	0.15
19.	Work, other job(s)	0.14
20.	Volunteer activities	0.14
21.	Travel related to caring for and helping household children	0.14
22.	Kitchen and food clean-up	0.13
23.	Playing games (including computer)	0.12
24.	Travel related to eating and drinking	0.11
25.	Grocery shopping	0.10
26.	Household and personal organization and planning	0.09
27.	Arts and entertainment (except sports)	0.09
28.	Health-related self-care	0.08
29.	Interior maintenance, repair, and decoration	0.08
30.	Animals and pets (not veterinary care)	0.08
31.	Activities related to household children's education	0.08
32.	Attending religious services	0.08
33.	Travel related to socializing and communicating	0.08
34.	Exterior maintenance, repair, and decoration	0.07
35.	Attending or hosting social events	0.07
36.	Telephone calls	0.07
37.	Household and personal email	0.06
38.	Helping adults in other households	0.06
39.	Research, homework	0.05

	average hours per day spent by people aged 35 to 44
40. Travel related to helping adults in other households	0.05
41. Travel related to grocery shopping	0.05
42. Travel related to sports, exercise, and recreation	0.05
43. Vehicles	0.04
44. Financial management	0.04
45. Caring for and helping children in other households	0.04
46. Travel related to purchasing food (except groceries)	0.04
47. Taking class	0.03
48. Medical and care services	0.03
49. Participation in religious practices	0.03
50. Travel related to household activities	0.03
51. Travel related to relaxing and leisure	0.03
52. Storing interior household items, including food	0.02
53. Purchasing food (except groceries)	0.02
54. Travel related to caring for and helping children in other households	0.02
55. Travel related to purchasing gas	0.02
56. Travel related to religious and spiritual activities	0.02
57. Travel related to volunteer activities	0.02
58. Household and personal mail and messages (except email)	0.01
59. Helping household adults	0.01
60. Purchasing gas	0.01
61. Household services	0.01
62. Listening to the radio	0.01
63. Listening to or playing music (not radio)	0.01
64. Travel related to personal care	0.01
65. Travel related to helping household adults	0.01
66. Travel related to education	0.01
67. Travel related to using medical services	0.01
68. Travel related to attending or hosting social events	0.01
69. Travel related to arts and entertainment	0.01
70. Financial services and banking	0.00
71. Travel related to using financial services and banking	0.00

Note: Primary activities are those respondents identified as their main activity. Other activities done simultaneously, such as eating while watching TV, are not included. If fewer than 2.0 percent of the total population participated in a primary activity, then the primary activity is not shown.
Source: Bureau of Labor Statistics, unpublished tables from the 2008 American Time Use Survey, Internet site http://www.bls .gov/tus/home.htm; calculations by New Strategist

Table 5.13 Ranking: Average Hours per Day Spent Doing Primary Activities by Men Aged 35 to 44, 2008

(average hours per day spent by men aged 35 to 44 doing primary activities, ranked by time spent doing activity, 2008)

		average hours per day spent by men aged 35 to 44
	Total, all activities	**24.00**
1.	Sleeping	8.31
2.	Work, main job	5.36
3.	Television	2.42
4.	Eating and drinking	1.14
5.	Grooming	0.54
6.	Caring for and helping household children	0.52
7.	Socializing and communicating	0.52
8.	Travel related to work	0.50
9.	Participating in sports, exercise, or recreation	0.33
10.	Food and drink preparation	0.28
11.	Lawn, garden, and houseplants	0.23
12.	Shopping, except groceries, food, and gas	0.23
13.	Interior cleaning	0.17
14.	Computer use for leisure (except games)	0.16
15.	Relaxing, thinking	0.15
16.	Work, other job(s)	0.14
17.	Reading for personal interest	0.14
18.	Playing games (including computer)	0.13
19.	Interior maintenance, repair, and decoration	0.12
20.	Travel related to eating and drinking	0.12
21.	Travel related to shopping (except groceries, food, and gas)	0.11
22.	Exterior maintenance, repair, and decoration	0.10
23.	Volunteer activities	0.10
24.	Vehicles	0.09
25.	Travel related to caring for and helping household children	0.09
26.	Travel related to socializing and communicating	0.09
27.	Arts and entertainment (except sports)	0.08
28.	Laundry	0.07
29.	Animals and pets (not veterinary care)	0.07
30.	Household and personal organization and planning	0.07
31.	Helping adults in other households	0.07
32.	Attending religious services	0.07
33.	Grocery shopping	0.06
34.	Attending or hosting social events	0.06
35.	Travel related to helping adults in other households	0.06
36.	Travel related to sports, exercise, and recreation	0.06
37.	Kitchen and food clean-up	0.05
38.	Activities related to household children's education	0.05
39.	Telephone calls	0.05

		average hours per day spent by men aged 35 to 44
40.	Health-related self-care	0.04
41.	Household and personal email	0.04
42.	Travel related to household activities	0.04
43.	Travel related to grocery shopping	0.04
44.	Travel related to purchasing food (except groceries)	0.04
45.	Caring for and helping children in other households	0.03
46.	Research, homework	0.03
47.	Travel related to relaxing and leisure	0.03
48.	Financial management	0.02
49.	Purchasing food (except groceries)	0.02
50.	Listening to or playing music (not radio)	0.02
51.	Participation in religious practices	0.02
52.	Travel related to religious and spiritual activities	0.02
53.	Travel related to volunteer activities	0.02
54.	Storing interior household items, including food	0.01
55.	Household and personal mail and messages (except email)	0.01
56.	Helping household adults	0.01
57.	Taking class	0.01
58.	Purchasing gas	0.01
59.	Medical and care services	0.01
60.	Household services	0.01
61.	Listening to the radio	0.01
62.	Travel related to personal care	0.01
63.	Travel related to helping household adults	0.01
64.	Travel related to caring for and helping children in other households	0.01
65.	Travel related to purchasing gas	0.01
66.	Travel related to using financial services and banking	0.01
67.	Travel related to using medical services	0.01
68.	Travel related to attending or hosting social events	0.01
69.	Travel related to arts and entertainment	0.01
70.	Financial services and banking	0.00
71.	Travel related to education	0.00

Note: Primary activities are those respondents identified as their main activity. Other activities done simultaneously, such as eating while watching TV, are not included. If fewer than 2.0 percent of the total population participated in a primary activity, then the primary activity is not shown.
Source: Bureau of Labor Statistics, unpublished tables from the 2008 American Time Use Survey, Internet site http://www.bls .gov/tus/home.htm; calculations by New Strategist

Table 5.14 Ranking: Average Hours per Day Spent Doing Primary Activities by Women Aged 35 to 44, 2008

(average hours per day spent by women aged 35 to 44 doing primary activities, ranked by time spent doing activity, 2008)

		average hours per day spent by women aged 35 to 44
	Total, all activities	**24.00**
1.	Sleeping	8.44
2.	Work, main job	3.30
3.	Television	2.17
4.	Eating and drinking	1.02
5.	Caring for and helping household children	0.96
6.	Grooming	0.72
7.	Food and drink preparation	0.65
8.	Interior cleaning	0.62
9.	Socializing and communicating	0.59
10.	Shopping, except groceries, food, and gas	0.36
11.	Laundry	0.35
12.	Travel related to work	0.26
13.	Reading for personal interest	0.24
14.	Kitchen and food clean-up	0.22
15.	Travel related to caring for and helping household children	0.19
16.	Participating in sports, exercise, or recreation	0.18
17.	Volunteer activities	0.18
18.	Travel related to shopping (except groceries, food, and gas)	0.18
19.	Work, other job(s)	0.15
20.	Relaxing, thinking	0.15
21.	Grocery shopping	0.14
22.	Computer use for leisure (except games)	0.14
23.	Health-related self-care	0.13
24.	Household and personal organization and planning	0.12
25.	Activities related to household children's education	0.11
26.	Playing games (including computer)	0.10
27.	Telephone calls	0.10
28.	Travel related to eating and drinking	0.10
29.	Arts and entertainment (except sports)	0.09
30.	Lawn, garden, and houseplants	0.09
31.	Animals and pets (not veterinary care)	0.09
32.	Attending religious services	0.09
33.	Research, homework	0.08
34.	Attending or hosting social events	0.08
35.	Household and personal email	0.07
36.	Travel related to grocery shopping	0.07
37.	Financial management	0.06
38.	Travel related to socializing and communicating	0.06
39.	Medical and care services	0.05

	average hours per day spent by women aged 35 to 44
40. Interior maintenance, repair, and decoration	0.04
41. Caring for and helping children in other households	0.04
42. Helping adults in other households	0.04
43. Taking class	0.04
44. Participation in religious practices	0.04
45. Travel related to purchasing food (except groceries)	0.04
46. Travel related to sports, exercise, and recreation	0.04
47. Exterior maintenance, repair, and decoration	0.03
48. Purchasing food (except groceries)	0.03
49. Travel related to household activities	0.03
50. Travel related to helping adults in other households	0.03
51. Travel related to volunteer activities	0.03
52. Storing interior household items, including food	0.02
53. Travel related to helping household adults	0.02
54. Travel related to caring for and helping children in other households	0.02
55. Travel related to education	0.02
56. Travel related to purchasing gas	0.02
57. Travel related to using medical services	0.02
58. Travel related to relaxing and leisure	0.02
59. Travel related to religious and spiritual activities	0.02
60. Travel related to personal care	0.02
61. Household services	0.02
62. Vehicles	0.01
63. Household and personal mail and messages (except email)	0.01
64. Helping household adults	0.01
65. Purchasing gas	0.01
66. Listening to the radio	0.01
67. Listening to or playing music (not radio)	0.01
68. Travel related to attending or hosting social events	0.01
69. Travel related to arts and entertainment	0.01
70. Financial services and banking	0.00
71. Travel related to using financial services and banking	0.00

Note: Primary activities are those respondents identified as their main activity. Other activities done simultaneously, such as eating while watching TV, are not included. If fewer than 2.0 percent of the total population participated in a primary activity, then the primary activity is not shown.
Source: Bureau of Labor Statistics, unpublished tables from the 2008 American Time Use Survey, Internet site http://www.bls .gov/tus/home.htm; calculations by New Strategist

Table 5.15 Ranking: Percent of Total People Aged 35 to 44 Participating in Primary Activities on an Average Day, 2008

(percent of people aged 35 to 44 participating in primary activities on an average day, ranked by percent participating, 2008)

		percent of people aged 35 to 44 participating in activity
	Total, all activities	**100.0%**
1.	Sleeping	99.9
2.	Eating and drinking	95.4
3.	Grooming	81.2
4.	Television	78.6
5.	Work, main job	57.3
6.	Food and drink preparation	56.3
7.	Travel related to work	48.9
8.	Caring for and helping household children	45.9
9.	Socializing and communicating	36.2
10.	Shopping, except groceries, food, and gas	25.9
11.	Kitchen and food clean-up	25.1
12.	Travel related to shopping (except groceries, food, and gas)	24.9
13.	Interior cleaning	24.9
14.	Travel related to eating and drinking	24.9
15.	Travel related to caring for and helping household children	24.4
16.	Laundry	20.6
17.	Reading for personal interest	17.3
18.	Relaxing, thinking	16.6
19.	Household and personal organization and planning	16.4
20.	Travel related to socializing and communicating	15.4
21.	Participating in sports, exercise, or recreation	15.1
22.	Purchasing food (except groceries)	14.5
23.	Grocery shopping	14.0
24.	Travel related to grocery shopping	14.0
25.	Travel related to purchasing food (except groceries)	13.5
26.	Animals and pets (not veterinary care)	12.7
27.	Telephone calls	11.6
28.	Household and personal email	10.5
29.	Activities related to household children's education	9.8
30.	Computer use for leisure (except games)	9.6
31.	Travel related to sports, exercise, and recreation	9.1
32.	Travel related to household activities	8.4
33.	Lawn, garden, and houseplants	8.1
34.	Volunteer activities	6.9
35.	Helping adults in other households	6.9
36.	Travel related to relaxing and leisure	6.8
37.	Travel related to helping adults in other households	6.2
38.	Playing games (including computer)	6.0
39.	Household and personal mail and messages (except email)	5.3

		percent of people aged 35 to 44 participating in activity
40.	Travel related to volunteer activities	4.8%
41.	Storing interior household items, including food	4.7
42.	Financial management	4.2
43.	Attending religious services	4.2
44.	Travel related to religious and spiritual activities	4.2
45.	Purchasing gas	4.2
46.	Travel related to purchasing gas	4.2
47.	Participation in religious practices	4.1
48.	Caring for and helping children in other households	4.0
49.	Health-related self-care	3.9
50.	Helping household adults	3.5
51.	Work, other job(s)	3.4
52.	Arts and entertainment (except sports)	3.3
53.	Travel related to caring for and helping children in other households	3.2
54.	Interior maintenance, repair, and decoration	3.1
55.	Exterior maintenance, repair, and decoration	2.8
56.	Vehicles	2.8
57.	Travel related to helping household adults	2.6
58.	Travel related to arts and entertainment	2.5
59.	Medical and care services	2.4
60.	Travel related to using medical services	2.4
61.	Financial services and banking	2.2
62.	Attending or hosting social events	2.1
63.	Travel related to using financial services and banking	2.0
64.	Research, homework	1.8
65.	Travel related to personal care	1.8
66.	Travel related to attending or hosting social events	1.8
67.	Household services	1.7
68.	Listening to or playing music (not radio)	1.3
69.	Listening to the radio	1.3
70.	Taking class	1.1
71.	Travel related to education	1.0

Note: Primary activities are those respondents identified as their main activity. Other activities done simultaneously, such as eating while watching TV, are not included. If fewer than 2.0 percent of the total population participated in a primary activity, then the primary activity is not shown.
Source: Bureau of Labor Statistics, unpublished tables from the 2008 American Time Use Survey, Internet site http://www.bls .gov/tus/home.htm; calculations by New Strategist

Table 5.16   Ranking: Percent of Men Aged 35 to 44 Participating in Primary Activities on an Average Day, 2008

(percent of men aged 35 to 44 participating in primary activities on an average day, ranked by percent participating, 2008)

		percent of men aged 35 to 44 participating in activity
	Total, all activities	**100.0%**
1.	Sleeping	99.8
2.	Eating and drinking	95.8
3.	Television	80.5
4.	Grooming	79.1
5.	Work, main job	67.1
6.	Travel related to work	59.3
7.	Food and drink preparation	38.5
8.	Caring for and helping household children	37.5
9.	Socializing and communicating	31.9
10.	Travel related to eating and drinking	28.1
11.	Shopping, except groceries, food, and gas	20.8
12.	Travel related to shopping (except groceries, food, and gas)	19.6
13.	Travel related to caring for and helping household children	17.3
14.	Relaxing, thinking	16.4
15.	Participating in sports, exercise, or recreation	15.6
16.	Purchasing food (except groceries)	14.4
17.	Travel related to socializing and communicating	14.2
18.	Reading for personal interest	13.6
19.	Travel related to purchasing food (except groceries)	13.5
20.	Interior cleaning	12.3
21.	Household and personal organization and planning	11.9
22.	Kitchen and food clean-up	10.8
23.	Animals and pets (not veterinary care)	10.7
24.	Computer use for leisure (except games)	10.4
25.	Lawn, garden, and houseplants	9.6
26.	Travel related to sports, exercise, and recreation	9.5
27.	Grocery shopping	9.3
28.	Travel related to grocery shopping	9.3
29.	Travel related to household activities	8.1
30.	Household and personal email	8.0
31.	Laundry	7.5
32.	Helping adults in other households	7.1
33.	Travel related to relaxing and leisure	6.8
34.	Telephone calls	6.6
35.	Travel related to helping adults in other households	6.5
36.	Playing games (including computer)	6.1
37.	Activities related to household children's education	5.6
38.	Volunteer activities	5.0
39.	Vehicles	4.9

	percent of men aged 35 to 44 participating in activity
40. Exterior maintenance, repair, and decoration	4.3%
41. Travel related to religious and spiritual activities	4.2
42. Interior maintenance, repair, and decoration	4.1
43. Household and personal mail and messages (except email)	4.0
44. Attending religious services	3.6
45. Purchasing gas	3.6
46. Travel related to purchasing gas	3.5
47. Travel related to volunteer activities	3.4
48. Participation in religious practices	3.3
49. Work, other job(s)	3.2
50. Arts and entertainment (except sports)	3.1
51. Financial management	3.1
52. Travel related to arts and entertainment	2.8
53. Health-related self-care	2.8
54. Caring for and helping children in other households	2.6
55. Helping household adults	2.6
56. Storing interior household items, including food	2.4
57. Financial services and banking	2.3
58. Travel related to using financial services and banking	2.2
59. Attending or hosting social events	2.1
60. Travel related to caring for and helping children in other households	2.1
61. Household services	2.0
62. Travel related to helping household adults	2.0
63. Travel related to attending or hosting social events	1.9
64. Travel related to personal care	1.7
65. Listening to or playing music (not radio)	1.3
66. Listening to the radio	1.3
67. Research, homework	1.2
68. Medical and care services	1.0
69. Travel related to using medical services	1.0
70. Taking class	0.5
71. Travel related to education	0.4

Note: Primary activities are those respondents identified as their main activity. Other activities done simultaneously, such as eating while watching TV, are not included. If fewer than 2.0 percent of the total population participated in a primary activity, then the primary activity is not shown.
Source: Bureau of Labor Statistics, unpublished tables from the 2008 American Time Use Survey, Internet site http://www.bls .gov/tus/home.htm; calculations by New Strategist

Table 5.17 **Ranking: Percent of Women Aged 35 to 44 Participating in Primary Activities on an Average Day, 2008**

(percent of women aged 35 to 44 participating in primary activities on an average day, ranked by percent participating, 2008)

		percent of women aged 35 to 44 participating in activity
	Total, all activities	**100.0%**
1.	Sleeping	100.0
2.	Eating and drinking	94.9
3.	Grooming	83.3
4.	Television	76.8
5.	Food and drink preparation	73.6
6.	Caring for and helping household children	54.1
7.	Work, main job	47.8
8.	Socializing and communicating	40.3
9.	Kitchen and food clean-up	39.0
10.	Travel related to work	38.7
11.	Interior cleaning	37.2
12.	Laundry	33.4
13.	Travel related to caring for and helping household children	31.4
14.	Shopping, except groceries, food, and gas	30.8
15.	Travel related to shopping (except groceries, food, and gas)	30.1
16.	Travel related to eating and drinking	21.9
17.	Reading for personal interest	20.9
18.	Household and personal organization and planning	20.9
19.	Grocery shopping	18.7
20.	Travel related to grocery shopping	18.6
21.	Relaxing, thinking	16.9
22.	Travel related to socializing and communicating	16.6
23.	Telephone calls	16.4
24.	Purchasing food (except groceries)	14.7
25.	Animals and pets (not veterinary care)	14.6
26.	Participating in sports, exercise, or recreation	14.5
27.	Activities related to household children's education	13.8
28.	Travel related to purchasing food (except groceries)	13.6
29.	Household and personal email	12.9
30.	Computer use for leisure (except games)	8.8
31.	Volunteer activities	8.8
32.	Travel related to sports, exercise, and recreation	8.8
33.	Travel related to household activities	8.8
34.	Storing interior household items, including food	6.9
35.	Travel related to relaxing and leisure	6.8
36.	Helping adults in other households	6.7
37.	Lawn, garden, and houseplants	6.6
38.	Household and personal mail and messages (except email)	6.6
39.	Travel related to volunteer activities	6.2

	percent of women aged 35 to 44 participating in activity
40. Playing games (including computer)	5.9%
41. Travel related to helping adults in other households	5.8
42. Caring for and helping children in other households	5.4
43. Financial management	5.3
44. Health-related self-care	5.1
45. Participation in religious practices	4.9
46. Attending religious services	4.8
47. Purchasing gas	4.8
48. Travel related to purchasing gas	4.8
49. Helping household adults	4.4
50. Travel related to caring for and helping children in other households	4.2
51. Travel related to religious and spiritual activities	4.2
52. Medical and care services	3.9
53. Travel related to using medical services	3.8
54. Work, other job(s)	3.5
55. Arts and entertainment (except sports)	3.4
56. Travel related to helping household adults	3.3
57. Research, homework	2.5
58. Travel related to arts and entertainment	2.2
59. Financial services and banking	2.2
60. Interior maintenance, repair, and decoration	2.1
61. Attending or hosting social events	2.1
62. Travel related to personal care	1.9
63. Travel related to using financial services and banking	1.7
64. Taking class	1.6
65. Travel related to attending or hosting social events	1.6
66. Travel related to education	1.6
67. Exterior maintenance, repair, and decoration	1.4
68. Household services	1.4
69. Listening to or playing music (not radio)	1.3
70. Listening to the radio	1.3
71. Vehicles	0.7

Note: Primary activities are those respondents identified as their main activity. Other activities done simultaneously, such as eating while watching TV, are not included. If fewer than 2.0 percent of the total population participated in a primary activity, then the primary activity is not shown.
Source: Bureau of Labor Statistics, unpublished tables from the 2008 American Time Use Survey, Internet site http://www.bls .gov/tus/home.htm; calculations by New Strategist

Table 5.18   Ranking: Average Hours per Day Spent Doing Primary Activities by Total Participants Aged 35 to 44, 2008

(hours per day spent by participants aged 35 to 44 doing primary activities, ranked by time spent doing activity, 2008)

		average hours per day spent by participants aged 35 to 44
	Total, all activities	**24.00**
1.	Sleeping	8.39
2.	Work, main job	7.53
3.	Work, other job(s)	4.30
4.	Attending or hosting social events	3.37
5.	Television	2.92
6.	Arts and entertainment (except sports)	2.60
7.	Interior maintenance, repair, and decoration	2.60
8.	Exterior maintenance, repair, and decoration	2.33
9.	Health-related self-care	2.13
10.	Volunteer activities	2.03
11.	Lawn, garden, and houseplants	1.97
12.	Playing games (including computer)	1.94
13.	Attending religious services	1.89
14.	Participating in sports, exercise, or recreation	1.67
15.	Caring for and helping household children	1.62
16.	Vehicles	1.61
17.	Interior cleaning	1.60
18.	Computer use for leisure (except games)	1.54
19.	Socializing and communicating	1.53
20.	Shopping, except groceries, food, and gas	1.14
21.	Eating and drinking	1.13
22.	Reading for personal interest	1.11
23.	Laundry	1.03
24.	Financial management	1.01
25.	Caring for and helping children in other households	0.96
26.	Relaxing, thinking	0.93
27.	Activities related to household children's education	0.85
28.	Helping adults in other households	0.84
29.	Food and drink preparation	0.83
30.	Participation in religious practices	0.79
31.	Grooming	0.78
32.	Travel related to work	0.77
33.	Grocery shopping	0.74
34.	Travel related to helping adults in other households	0.74
35.	Travel related to attending or hosting social events	0.74
36.	Telephone calls	0.64
37.	Animals and pets (not veterinary care)	0.62
38.	Travel related to shopping (except groceries, food, and gas)	0.58
39.	Travel related to caring for and helping household children	0.57

	average hours per day spent by participants aged 35 to 44
40. Household and personal organization and planning	0.57
41. Travel related to sports, exercise, and recreation	0.55
42. Kitchen and food clean-up	0.53
43. Household and personal email	0.53
44. Travel related to socializing and communicating	0.51
45. Travel related to caring for and helping children in other households	0.50
46. Travel related to religious and spiritual activities	0.48
47. Travel related to arts and entertainment	0.47
48. Travel related to eating and drinking	0.44
49. Travel related to volunteer activities	0.44
50. Travel related to grocery shopping	0.39
51. Travel related to household activities	0.39
52. Travel related to relaxing and leisure	0.38
53. Travel related to purchasing gas	0.37
54. Storing interior household items, including food	0.34
55. Travel related to purchasing food (except groceries)	0.31
56. Helping household adults	0.26
57. Financial services and banking	0.22
58. Household and personal mail and messages (except email)	0.20
59. Purchasing food (except groceries)	0.17
60. Purchasing gas	0.16

Note: Primary activities are those respondents identified as their main activity. Other activities done simultaneously, such as eating while watching TV, are not included. The primary activities shown are those for which data by age are available.
Source: Bureau of Labor Statistics, unpublished tables from the 2008 American Time Use Survey, Internet site http://www.bls. gov/tus/home.htm; calculations by New Strategist

Table 5.19 Ranking: Average Hours per Day Spent Doing Primary Activities by Male Participants Aged 35 to 44, 2008

(hours per day spent by male participants aged 35 to 44 doing primary activities, ranked by time spent doing activity, 2008)

		average hours per day spent by male participants aged 35 to 44
	Total, all activities	**24.00**
1.	Sleeping	8.33
2.	Work, main job	7.99
3.	Television	3.01
4.	Lawn, garden, and houseplants	2.38
5.	Playing games (including computer)	2.21
6.	Participating in sports, exercise, or recreation	2.11
7.	Volunteer activities	2.07
8.	Attending religious services	1.97
9.	Socializing and communicating	1.62
10.	Computer use for leisure (except games)	1.52
11.	Interior cleaning	1.41
12.	Caring for and helping household children	1.39
13.	Eating and drinking	1.19
14.	Shopping, except groceries, food, and gas	1.09
15.	Reading for personal interest	1.06
16.	Helping adults in other households	1.05
17.	Laundry	0.98
18.	Relaxing, thinking	0.93
19.	Travel related to helping adults in other households	0.89
20.	Travel related to work	0.84
21.	Food and drink preparation	0.72
22.	Telephone calls	0.69
23.	Grooming	0.68
24.	Grocery shopping	0.68
25.	Travel related to socializing and communicating	0.65
26.	Animals and pets (not veterinary care)	0.63
27.	Travel related to sports, exercise, and recreation	0.58
28.	Household and personal organization and planning	0.56
29.	Household and personal email	0.56
30.	Travel related to shopping (except groceries, food, and gas)	0.53
31.	Travel related to caring for and helping household children	0.50
32.	Kitchen and food clean-up	0.45
33.	Travel related to household activities	0.45
34.	Travel related to grocery shopping	0.44
35.	Travel related to eating and drinking	0.44
36.	Travel related to relaxing and leisure	0.44
37.	Travel related to religious and spiritual activities	0.44
38.	Travel related to purchasing food (except groceries)	0.31
39.	Purchasing food (except groceries)	0.17

Note: Primary activities are those respondents identified as their main activity. Other activities done simultaneously, such as eating while watching TV, are not included. The primary activities shown are those for which data by age are available.
Source: Bureau of Labor Statistics, unpublished tables from the 2008 American Time Use Survey, Internet site http://www.bls .gov/tus/home.htm; calculations by New Strategist

Table 5.20 Ranking: Average Hours per Day Spent Doing Primary Activities by Female Participants Aged 35 to 44, 2008

(hours per day spent by female participants aged 35 to 44 doing primary activities, ranked by time spent doing activity, 2008)

		average hours per day spent by female participants aged 35 to 44
	Total, all activities	**24.00**
1.	Sleeping	8.44
2.	Work, main job	6.90
3.	Television	2.83
4.	Volunteer activities	2.00
5.	Attending religious services	1.84
6.	Caring for and helping household children	1.77
7.	Interior cleaning	1.67
8.	Playing games (including computer)	1.66
9.	Computer use for leisure (except games)	1.57
10.	Socializing and communicating	1.47
11.	Lawn, garden, and houseplants	1.40
12.	Participating in sports, exercise, or recreation	1.22
13.	Shopping, except groceries, food, and gas	1.18
14.	Reading for personal interest	1.14
15.	Eating and drinking	1.07
16.	Laundry	1.05
17.	Relaxing, thinking	0.92
18.	Food and drink preparation	0.89
19.	Grooming	0.87
20.	Caring for and helping children in other households	0.83
21.	Participation in religious practices	0.82
22.	Activities related to household children's education	0.81
23.	Grocery shopping	0.77
24.	Travel related to work	0.67
25.	Helping adults in other households	0.63
26.	Animals and pets (not veterinary care)	0.62
27.	Travel related to shopping (except groceries, food, and gas)	0.61
28.	Travel related to caring for and helping household children	0.61
29.	Telephone calls	0.61
30.	Household and personal organization and planning	0.57
31.	Travel related to helping adults in other households	0.57
32.	Kitchen and food clean-up	0.55
33.	Travel related to religious and spiritual activities	0.52
34.	Household and personal email	0.51
35.	Travel related to sports, exercise, and recreation	0.51
36.	Travel related to eating and drinking	0.44
37.	Travel related to volunteer activities	0.42
38.	Travel related to socializing and communicating	0.39
39.	Travel related to grocery shopping	0.36

	average hours per day spent by female participants aged 35 to 44
40. Storing interior household items, including food	0.35
41. Travel related to purchasing gas	0.35
42. Travel related to household activities	0.34
43. Travel related to relaxing and leisure	0.32
44. Travel related to purchasing food (except groceries)	0.31
45. Household and personal mail and messages (except email)	0.21
46. Purchasing food (except groceries)	0.17
47. Purchasing gas	0.15

Note: Primary activities are those respondents identified as their main activity. Other activities done simultaneously, such as eating while watching TV, are not included. The primary activities shown are those for which data by age are available.
Source: Bureau of Labor Statistics, unpublished tables from the 2008 American Time Use Survey, Internet site http://www.bls .gov/tus/home.htm; calculations by New Strategist

6

Time Use, 2008: People Aged 45 to 54

For people aged 45 to 54, family responsibilities are easing. Some have teenagers at home, but many are empty-nesters. Caring for household children as the primary activity does not even crack the top ten list of time-consuming activities for the average 45-to-54-year-old. People in the age group spend more time grooming and socializing than caring for children. Only 18 percent, in fact, care for household children on an average day. With fewer family responsibilities, people aged 45 to 54 have more time to indulge in personal interests. Reading for personal interest ranks tenth in time use (excluding sleep). Relaxing and thinking—perhaps the ultimate indulgence—ranks ninth.

No other age group spends more time working than 45-to-54-year-olds. The average person in the age group spends 4.38 hours working at his or her main job on an average day (the figure seems low because it includes both weekdays and weekends). Sixty-two percent of men and 52 percent of women in the age group work at their main job on an average day. The 62 percent of men who work spend almost as much time on the job as they do sleeping (8.16 hours). Commuting to work ranks sixth in time use among men aged 45 to 54 (excluding sleep).

Because of their expanded free time, people aged 45 to 54 spend more time than those aged 35 to 44 watching television as the primary activity. With children grown up and gone, many people aged 45 to 54 devote themselves to caring for their pets. The percentage of people who spend time

No other age group spends as much time working as 45-to-54-year-olds

(average hours per day spent by people aged 45 to 54 doing primary activities, for the 10 activities on which the average 45-to-54-year-old spends the most time, excluding sleep, 2008)

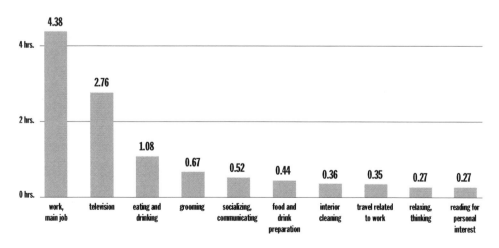

caring for pets rises from 13 percent in the 35-to-44 age group to 18 percent in the 45-to-54 age group. Sleeplessness is becoming more of a problem, with 6 percent reporting sleeplessness in the previous 24 hours.

Housework still requires a great deal of time. Cooking and housecleaning rank sixth and seventh in time use for the average 45-to-54-year-old (excluding sleep). Fifty-five percent prepare a meal on an average day, 25 percent clean the house, 20 percent do the laundry, and 14 percent go grocery shopping.

Women aged 45 to 54 spend much more time than their male counterparts doing stereotypical female chores such as housecleaning, laundry, cooking, kitchen cleanup, and grocery shopping. They also spend more time caring for pets, attending religious services, and talking on the phone. Men spend more time than women working, participating in sports, caring for their lawn and garden, and maintaining the exterior of their home. They are also more likely than women to spend time managing household finances.

Table 6.1 Time Use by Total People Aged 45 to 54, 2008

(number and percent of total people aged 45 to 54 participating in primary activities on an average day, hours spent doing activity by the average person aged 45 to 54 and by those aged 45 to 54 who participated in the activity, 2008; numbers of participants in thousands)

	participants aged 45 to 54		time spent doing activity (hours)	
	number	percent	average person aged 45 to 54	participants aged 45 to 54
TOTAL, ALL ACTIVITIES	**43,959**	**100.0%**	**24.00**	**24.00**
Personal care	**43,936**	**99.9**	**9.09**	**9.10**
Sleeping	43,889	99.8	8.27	8.29
Sleeplessness	2,640	6.0	0.06	1.01
Grooming	35,401	80.5	0.67	0.83
Health-related self-care	3,045	6.9	0.12	1.80
Household activities	**35,511**	**80.8**	**1.94**	**2.40**
Housework	17,231	39.2	0.61	1.55
Interior cleaning	11,000	25.0	0.36	1.45
Laundry	8,947	20.4	0.21	1.01
Storing interior household items, including food	2,491	5.7	0.01	0.26
Food and drink preparation, presentation, and clean-up	25,371	57.7	0.56	0.98
Food and drink preparation	24,148	54.9	0.44	0.79
Kitchen and food clean-up	10,581	24.1	0.12	0.52
Interior maintenance, repair, and decoration	1,787	4.1	0.11	2.73
Interior arrangement, decoration, and repairs	1,356	3.1	0.10	3.28
Exterior maintenance, repair, and decoration	1,286	2.9	0.06	1.91
Lawn, garden, and houseplants	5,243	11.9	0.23	1.92
Animals and pets (not veterinary care)	8,015	18.2	0.09	0.49
Walking, exercising, and playing with pets	2,346	5.3	0.04	0.69
Vehicles	1,523	3.5	0.05	1.49
Household management	12,989	29.5	0.21	0.72
Financial management	1,593	3.6	0.04	0.99
Household and personal organization and planning	6,376	14.5	0.09	0.61
Household and personal mail and messages (except email)	3,617	8.2	0.03	0.34
Household and personal email	3,916	8.9	0.06	0.63
Caring for and helping household members	**10,257**	**23.3**	**0.32**	**1.36**
Caring for and helping household children	8,077	18.4	0.23	1.27
Physical care for household children	4,332	9.9	0.08	0.83
Reading to or with household children	338	0.8	0.00	–
Playing with household children (except sports)	866	2.0	0.04	1.79
Talking with, listening to household children	1,845	4.2	0.03	0.60
Looking after household children as a primary activity	857	1.9	0.02	0.83
Picking up or dropping off household children	3,837	8.7	0.01	0.16
Activities related to household children's education	1,831	4.2	0.05	1.21
Helping household children with homework	1,610	3.7	0.04	1.03
Helping household adults	127	0.3	0.00	0.29
Caring for and helping people in other households	**5,600**	**12.7**	**0.16**	**1.29**
Caring for and helping children in other households	2,260	5.1	0.08	1.59

	participants aged 45 to 54		time spent doing activity (hours)	
	number	percent	average person aged 45 to 54	participants aged 45 to 54
Helping adults in other households	3,434	7.8%	0.06	0.83
Picking up or dropping off adults in other households	1,984	4.5	0.01	0.18
Work and work-related activities	**26,123**	**59.4**	**4.60**	**7.74**
Work, main job	24,916	56.7	4.38	7.73
Work, other job(s)	1,567	3.6	0.13	3.69
Education	**822**	**1.9**	**0.08**	–
Taking class	313	0.7	0.02	–
Taking class for degree, certification, or licensure	139	0.3	0.01	–
Research, homework	568	1.3	0.06	–
Consumer purchases (store, telephone, Internet)	**18,117**	**41.2**	**0.36**	**0.86**
Grocery shopping	6,307	14.3	0.10	0.73
Purchasing gas	2,112	4.8	0.01	0.16
Purchasing food (except groceries)	4,431	10.1	0.02	0.15
Shopping, except groceries, food, and gas	10,412	23.7	0.22	0.94
Professional and personal care services	**4,477**	**10.2**	**0.08**	**0.80**
Financial services and banking	1,834	4.2	0.01	0.18
Banking	1,762	4.0	0.01	0.15
Medical and care services	1,998	4.5	0.05	1.18
Using health and care services outside the home	1,958	4.5	0.04	0.94
Household services	**987**	**2.2**	**0.01**	–
Eating and drinking	**42,144**	**95.9**	**1.08**	**1.13**
Socializing, relaxing, and leisure	**42,040**	**95.6**	**4.20**	**4.39**
Socializing and communicating	15,113	34.4	0.52	1.52
Attending or hosting social events	985	2.2	0.06	2.65
Relaxing and leisure	40,405	91.9	3.56	3.87
Relaxing, thinking	9,596	21.8	0.27	1.23
Television	36,040	82.0	2.76	3.37
Listening to the radio	842	1.9	0.02	–
Listening to or playing music (not radio)	642	1.5	0.02	–
Playing games (including computer)	2,174	4.9	0.09	1.78
Computer use for leisure (except games)	3,467	7.9	0.09	1.16
Reading for personal interest	10,283	23.4	0.27	1.16
Arts and entertainment (except sports)	1,025	2.3	0.06	2.71
Sports, exercise, and recreation	**8,122**	**18.5**	**0.28**	**1.52**
Participating in sports, exercise, or recreation	7,798	17.7	0.25	1.40
Using cardiovascular equipment	1,515	3.4	0.02	–
Walking	2,514	5.7	0.05	0.85
Working out, unspecified	1,316	3.0	0.02	0.83
Religious and spiritual activities	**4,098**	**9.3**	**0.15**	**1.62**
Attending religious services	2,192	5.0	0.10	1.96
Participation in religious practices	2,174	4.9	0.04	0.80

	participants aged 45 to 54		time spent doing activity (hours)	
	number	percent	average person aged 45 to 54	participants aged 45 to 54
Volunteer activities	**3,283**	**7.5%**	**0.17**	**2.30**
Administrative and support activities	1,295	2.9	0.04	1.25
Telephone calls	**6,264**	**14.2**	**0.10**	**0.72**
Telephone calls to or from family members	3,707	8.4	0.06	0.66
Telephone calls to or from friends, neighbors, or acquaintances	1,439	3.3	0.02	0.51
Traveling	**38,347**	**87.2**	**1.21**	**1.39**
Travel related to personal care	1,032	2.3	0.02	–
Travel related to household activities	3,851	8.8	0.04	0.43
Travel related to household management	2,637	6.0	0.03	0.46
Travel related to caring for and helping household members	6,002	13.7	0.08	0.61
Travel related to caring for and helping household children	4,591	10.4	0.06	0.57
Travel related to helping household adults	1,439	3.3	0.02	–
Travel related to caring for and helping people in other households	4,166	9.5	0.06	0.60
Travel related to caring for and helping children in other households	1,271	2.9	0.01	0.45
Travel related to helping adults in other households	2,901	6.6	0.04	0.60
Travel related to work	20,970	47.7	0.35	0.74
Travel related to education	287	0.7	0.01	–
Travel related to taking class	258	0.6	0.01	–
Travel related to consumer purchases	17,896	40.7	0.25	0.60
Travel related to grocery shopping	6,232	14.2	0.06	0.44
Travel related to purchasing gas	2,093	4.8	0.02	0.42
Travel related to purchasing food (except groceries)	4,242	9.6	0.04	0.41
Travel related to shopping (except groceries, food, and gas)	10,211	23.2	0.12	0.53
Travel related to using professional and personal care services	4,171	9.5	0.05	0.55
Travel related to using financial services and banking	1,706	3.9	0.01	0.26
Travel related to using medical services	1,885	4.3	0.03	0.71
Travel related to eating and drinking	10,409	23.7	0.11	0.45
Travel related to socializing, relaxing, and leisure	11,138	25.3	0.15	0.58
Travel related to socializing and communicating	7,367	16.8	0.08	0.48
Travel related to attending or hosting social events	841	1.9	0.01	–
Travel related to relaxing and leisure	2,831	6.4	0.02	0.39
Travel related to arts and entertainment	890	2.0	0.01	0.61
Travel related to sports, exercise, and recreation	3,278	7.5	0.04	0.51
Travel related to participating in sports, exercise, recreation	2,953	6.7	0.03	0.48
Travel related to religious and spiritual activities	2,286	5.2	0.02	0.40
Travel related to volunteer activities	2,043	4.6	0.02	0.43

Note: Primary activities are those respondents identified as their main activity. Other activities done simultaneously, such as eating while watching TV, are not included. Numbers may not add to total because not all subcategories are shown. If fewer than 2.0 percent of the total population participated in a primary activity, then the primary activity is not shown. "–" means sample is too small to make a reliable estimate.
Source: Bureau of Labor Statistics, unpublished tables from the 2008 American Time Use Survey, Internet site http://www.bls .gov/tus/home.htm; calculations by New Strategist

Table 6.2 Time Use by Men Aged 45 to 54, 2008

(number and percent of men aged 45 to 54 participating in primary activities on an average day, hours spent doing activity by the average man aged 45 to 54 and by men aged 45 to 54 who participated in the activity, 2008; numbers of participants in thousands)

	men aged 45 to 54 participating		time spent doing activity (hours)	
	number	percent	average man aged 45 to 54	male participants aged 45 to 54
TOTAL, ALL ACTIVITIES	**21,529**	**100.0%**	**24.00**	**24.00**
Personal care	**21,523**	**100.0**	**8.80**	**8.81**
Sleeping	21,491	99.8	8.16	8.17
Sleeplessness	1,027	4.8	0.04	–
Grooming	16,562	76.9	0.56	0.72
Health-related self-care	1,143	5.3	0.06	–
Household activities	**15,857**	**73.7**	**1.51**	**2.05**
Housework	4,684	21.8	0.25	1.13
Interior cleaning	3,329	15.5	0.16	1.05
Laundry	1,648	7.7	0.08	1.01
Storing interior household items, including food	517	2.4	0.01	–
Food and drink preparation, presentation, and clean-up	9,715	45.1	0.32	0.71
Food and drink preparation	9,132	42.4	0.27	0.64
Kitchen and food clean-up	2,306	10.7	0.05	0.47
Interior maintenance, repair, and decoration	1,141	5.3	0.17	–
Interior arrangement, decoration, and repairs	829	3.9	0.16	–
Exterior maintenance, repair, and decoration	937	4.4	0.08	–
Lawn, garden, and houseplants	3,149	14.6	0.31	2.15
Animals and pets (not veterinary care)	3,242	15.1	0.07	0.49
Walking, exercising, and playing with pets	1,020	4.7	0.04	0.75
Vehicles	1,223	5.7	0.09	–
Household management	5,363	24.9	0.18	0.72
Financial management	506	2.4	0.04	–
Household and personal organization and planning	2,375	11.0	0.06	0.56
Household and personal mail and messages (except email)	1,470	6.8	0.03	–
Household and personal email	1,513	7.0	0.05	0.66
Caring for and helping household members	**4,204**	**19.5**	**0.28**	**1.41**
Caring for and helping household children	3,402	15.8	0.22	1.39
Physical care for household children	1,472	6.8	0.07	0.96
Reading to or with household children	91	0.4	0.00	–
Playing with household children (except sports)	557	2.6	0.05	–
Talking with, listening to household children	700	3.3	0.02	–
Looking after household children as a primary activity	366	1.7	0.01	–
Picking up or dropping off household children	1,552	7.2	0.01	0.18
Activities related to household children's education	754	3.5	0.04	–
Helping household children with homework	676	3.1	0.04	–
Helping household adults	24	0.1	0.00	–
Caring for and helping people in other households	**1,886**	**8.8**	**0.11**	**1.21**
Caring for and helping children in other households	589	2.7	0.02	–

	men aged 45 to 54 participating		time spent doing activity (hours)	
	number	percent	average man aged 45 to 54	male participants aged 45 to 54
Helping adults in other households	1,285	6.0%	0.07	1.22
Picking up or dropping off adults in other households	581	2.7	0.01	–
Work and work-related activities	**14,081**	**65.4**	**5.32**	**8.13**
Work, main job	13,286	61.7	5.03	8.16
Work, other job(s)	851	4.0	0.18	–
Education	**184**	**0.9**	**0.02**	**–**
Taking class	93	0.4	0.01	–
Taking class for degree, certification, or licensure	22	0.1	0.01	–
Research, homework	92	0.4	0.01	–
Consumer purchases (store, telephone, Internet)	**7,980**	**37.1**	**0.25**	**0.67**
Grocery shopping	2,174	10.1	0.06	0.57
Purchasing gas	1,180	5.5	0.01	0.16
Purchasing food (except groceries)	1,994	9.3	0.02	0.16
Shopping, except groceries, food, and gas	4,708	21.9	0.17	0.76
Professional and personal care services	**1,461**	**6.8**	**0.05**	**0.70**
Financial services and banking	723	3.4	0.01	–
Banking	674	3.1	0.00	–
Medical and care services	634	2.9	0.03	–
Using health and care services outside the home	595	2.8	0.02	–
Household services	**359**	**1.7**	**0.01**	**–**
Eating and drinking	**20,866**	**96.9**	**1.14**	**1.18**
Socializing, relaxing, and leisure	**20,424**	**94.9**	**4.41**	**4.65**
Socializing and communicating	6,423	29.8	0.46	1.54
Attending or hosting social events	336	1.6	0.05	–
Relaxing and leisure	20,004	92.9	3.86	4.15
Relaxing, thinking	5,140	23.9	0.29	1.19
Television	18,141	84.3	3.09	3.67
Listening to the radio	588	2.7	0.02	–
Listening to or playing music (not radio)	405	1.9	0.02	–
Playing games (including computer)	720	3.3	0.06	–
Computer use for leisure (except games)	1,468	6.8	0.09	1.30
Reading for personal interest	4,571	21.2	0.24	1.11
Arts and entertainment (except sports)	406	1.9	0.05	–
Sports, exercise, and recreation	**4,401**	**20.4**	**0.37**	**1.79**
Participating in sports, exercise, or recreation	4,191	19.5	0.32	1.63
Using cardiovascular equipment	644	3.0	0.02	–
Walking	1,228	5.7	0.05	–
Working out, unspecified	718	3.3	0.03	–
Religious and spiritual activities	**1,786**	**8.3**	**0.13**	**1.58**
Attending religious services	844	3.9	0.09	2.20
Participation in religious practices	947	4.4	0.03	–

	men aged 45 to 54 participating		time spent doing activity (hours)	
	number	percent	average man aged 45 to 54	male participants aged 45 to 54
Volunteer activities	**1,445**	**6.7%**	**0.19**	**2.82**
Administrative and support activities	499	2.3	0.02	–
Telephone calls	**1,703**	**7.9**	**0.04**	**0.51**
Telephone calls to or from family members	904	4.2	0.02	–
Telephone calls to or from friends, neighbors, or acquaintances	420	2.0	0.01	–
Traveling	**19,007**	**88.3**	**1.25**	**1.41**
Travel related to personal care	746	3.5	0.03	–
Travel related to household activities	1,486	6.9	0.04	0.57
Travel related to household management	993	4.6	0.03	–
Travel related to caring for and helping household members	2,501	11.6	0.07	0.60
Travel related to caring for and helping household children	1,947	9.0	0.05	0.56
Travel related to helping household adults	539	2.5	0.02	–
Travel related to caring for and helping people in other households	1,617	7.5	0.04	0.56
Travel related to caring for and helping children in other households	480	2.2	0.01	–
Travel related to helping adults in other households	1,103	5.1	0.03	–
Travel related to work	11,238	52.2	0.43	0.83
Travel related to education	98	0.5	0.00	–
Travel related to taking class	93	0.4	0.00	–
Travel related to consumer purchases	7,935	36.9	0.22	0.60
Travel related to grocery shopping	2,169	10.1	0.05	0.52
Travel related to purchasing gas	1,162	5.4	0.02	0.36
Travel related to purchasing food (except groceries)	1,885	8.8	0.03	0.34
Travel related to shopping (except groceries, food, and gas)	4,631	21.5	0.12	0.55
Travel related to using professional and personal care services	1,338	6.2	0.03	–
Travel related to using financial services and banking	612	2.8	0.01	–
Travel related to using medical services	597	2.8	0.02	–
Travel related to eating and drinking	5,760	26.8	0.12	0.43
Travel related to socializing, relaxing, and leisure	5,360	24.9	0.15	0.59
Travel related to socializing and communicating	3,513	16.3	0.08	0.49
Travel related to attending or hosting social events	274	1.3	0.01	–
Travel related to relaxing and leisure	1,464	6.8	0.03	0.40
Travel related to arts and entertainment	385	1.8	0.01	–
Travel related to sports, exercise, and recreation	1,912	8.9	0.06	0.64
Travel related to participating in sports, exercise, recreation	1,702	7.9	0.05	0.61
Travel related to religious and spiritual activities	925	4.3	0.02	0.36
Travel related to volunteer activities	969	4.5	0.02	–

Note: Primary activities are those respondents identified as their main activity. Other activities done simultaneously, such as eating while watching TV, are not included. Numbers may not add to total because not all subcategories are shown. If fewer than 2.0 percent of the total population participated in a primary activity, then the primary activity is not shown. "–" means sample is too small to make a reliable estimate.

Source: Bureau of Labor Statistics, unpublished tables from the 2008 American Time Use Survey, Internet site http://www.bls.gov/tus/home.htm; calculations by New Strategist

Table 6.3 Time Use by Women Aged 45 to 54, 2008

(number and percent of women aged 45 to 54 participating in primary activities on an average day, hours spent doing activity by the average woman aged 45 to 54 and by women aged 45 to 54 who participated in the activity, 2008; numbers of participants in thousands)

	women aged 45 to 54 participating		time spent doing activity (hours)	
	number	percent	average woman aged 45 to 54	female participants aged 45 to 54
TOTAL, ALL ACTIVITIES	**22,430**	**100.0%**	**24.00**	**24.00**
Personal care	**22,413**	**99.9**	**9.37**	**9.38**
Sleeping	22,398	99.9	8.39	8.40
Sleeplessness	1,613	7.2	0.08	1.07
Grooming	18,839	84.0	0.78	0.93
Health-related self-care	1,902	8.5	0.18	2.17
Household activities	**19,654**	**87.6**	**2.34**	**2.68**
Housework	12,546	55.9	0.95	1.70
Interior cleaning	7,671	34.2	0.55	1.62
Laundry	7,299	32.5	0.33	1.01
Storing interior household items, including food	1,974	8.8	0.02	0.26
Food and drink preparation, presentation, and clean-up	15,656	69.8	0.80	1.14
Food and drink preparation	15,016	66.9	0.59	0.88
Kitchen and food clean-up	8,275	36.9	0.20	0.53
Interior maintenance, repair, and decoration	646	2.9	0.05	–
Interior arrangement, decoration, and repairs	527	2.3	0.05	–
Exterior maintenance, repair, and decoration	349	1.6	0.03	–
Lawn, garden, and houseplants	2,094	9.3	0.15	1.56
Animals and pets (not veterinary care)	4,773	21.3	0.11	0.50
Walking, exercising, and playing with pets	1,325	5.9	0.04	0.64
Vehicles	300	1.3	0.01	–
Household management	7,626	34.0	0.24	0.72
Financial management	1,086	4.8	0.03	–
Household and personal organization and planning	4,001	17.8	0.11	0.64
Household and personal mail and messages (except email)	2,147	9.6	0.03	0.30
Household and personal email	2,403	10.7	0.07	0.62
Caring for and helping household members	**6,053**	**27.0**	**0.36**	**1.33**
Caring for and helping household children	4,675	20.8	0.25	1.18
Physical care for household children	2,860	12.8	0.10	0.76
Reading to or with household children	297	1.3	0.01	–
Playing with household children (except sports)	309	1.4	0.02	–
Talking with, listening to household children	1,145	5.1	0.03	0.52
Looking after household children as a primary activity	491	2.2	0.02	–
Picking up or dropping off household children	2,285	10.2	0.02	0.15
Activities related to household children's education	1,076	4.8	0.06	1.23
Helping household children with homework	934	4.2	0.04	–
Helping household adults	103	0.5	0.01	–
Caring for and helping people in other households	**3,715**	**16.6**	**0.22**	**1.33**
Caring for and helping children in other households	1,671	7.4	0.14	1.84

	women aged 45 to 54 participating		time spent doing activity (hours)	
	number	percent	average woman aged 45 to 54	female participants aged 45 to 54
Helping adults in other households	2,149	9.6%	0.06	0.59
Picking up or dropping off adults in other households	1,400	6.2	0.01	0.17
Work and work-related activities	**12,041**	**53.7**	**3.91**	**7.28**
Work, main job	11,629	51.8	3.75	7.24
Work, other job(s)	716	3.2	0.09	–
Education	**638**	**2.8**	**0.13**	**–**
Taking class	220	1.0	0.03	–
Taking class for degree, certification, or licensure	117	0.5	0.01	–
Research, homework	477	2.1	0.10	–
Consumer purchases (store, telephone, Internet)	**10,138**	**45.2**	**0.46**	**1.01**
Grocery shopping	4,133	18.4	0.15	0.81
Purchasing gas	931	4.2	0.01	–
Purchasing food (except groceries)	2,437	10.9	0.02	0.15
Shopping, except groceries, food, and gas	5,704	25.4	0.28	1.08
Professional and personal care services	**3,015**	**13.4**	**0.11**	**0.84**
Financial services and banking	1,111	5.0	0.01	–
Banking	1,108	4.9	0.01	–
Medical and care services	1,364	6.1	0.07	–
Using health and care services outside the home	1,364	6.1	0.06	–
Household services	**628**	**2.8**	**0.02**	**–**
Eating and drinking	**21,258**	**94.8**	**1.02**	**1.07**
Socializing, relaxing, and leisure	**21,616**	**96.4**	**4.00**	**4.15**
Socializing and communicating	8,690	38.7	0.58	1.50
Attending or hosting social events	650	2.9	0.07	–
Relaxing and leisure	20,401	91.0	3.27	3.60
Relaxing, thinking	4,456	19.9	0.25	1.27
Television	17,900	79.8	2.44	3.06
Listening to the radio	254	1.1	0.02	–
Listening to or playing music (not radio)	238	1.1	0.01	–
Playing games (including computer)	1,454	6.5	0.11	1.74
Computer use for leisure (except games)	1,999	8.9	0.09	1.06
Reading for personal interest	5,712	25.5	0.31	1.20
Arts and entertainment (except sports)	619	2.8	0.08	–
Sports, exercise, and recreation	**3,721**	**16.6**	**0.20**	**1.21**
Participating in sports, exercise, or recreation	3,608	16.1	0.18	1.12
Using cardiovascular equipment	871	3.9	0.03	–
Walking	1,286	5.7	0.05	0.88
Working out, unspecified	598	2.7	0.02	–
Religious and spiritual activities	**2,312**	**10.3**	**0.17**	**1.66**
Attending religious services	1,348	6.0	0.11	1.82
Participation in religious practices	1,227	5.5	0.05	0.88

	women aged 45 to 54 participating		time spent doing activity (hours)	
	number	percent	average woman aged 45 to 54	female participants aged 45 to 54
Volunteer activities	**1,838**	**8.2%**	**0.15**	**1.88**
Administrative and support activities	796	3.5	0.06	–
Telephone calls	**4,561**	**20.3**	**0.16**	**0.80**
Telephone calls to or from family members	2,802	12.5	0.09	0.75
Telephone calls to or from friends, neighbors, or acquaintances	1,019	4.5	0.02	0.53
Traveling	**19,340**	**86.2**	**1.18**	**1.37**
Travel related to personal care	287	1.3	0.01	–
Travel related to household activities	2,365	10.5	0.04	0.34
Travel related to household management	1,644	7.3	0.03	0.37
Travel related to caring for and helping household members	3,502	15.6	0.10	0.61
Travel related to caring for and helping household children	2,644	11.8%	0.07	0.57
Travel related to helping household adults	900	4.0	0.02	–
Travel related to caring for and helping people in other households	2,549	11.4	0.07	0.63
Travel related to caring for and helping children in other households	791	3.5	0.01	–
Travel related to helping adults in other households	1,798	8.0	0.05	0.62
Travel related to work	9,732	43.4	0.27	0.63
Travel related to education	190	0.8	0.01	–
Travel related to taking class	165	0.7	0.01	–
Travel related to consumer purchases	9,961	44.4	0.27	0.61
Travel related to grocery shopping	4,063	18.1	0.07	0.39
Travel related to purchasing gas	931	4.2	0.02	–
Travel related to purchasing food (except groceries)	2,357	10.5	0.05	0.47
Travel related to shopping (except groceries, food, and gas)	5,581	24.9	0.13	0.52
Travel related to using professional and personal care services	2,833	12.6	0.07	0.59
Travel related to using financial services and banking	1,094	4.9	0.01	–
Travel related to using medical services	1,288	5.7	0.04	–
Travel related to eating and drinking	4,649	20.7	0.10	0.47
Travel related to socializing, relaxing, and leisure	5,778	25.8	0.15	0.57
Travel related to socializing and communicating	3,854	17.2	0.08	0.47
Travel related to attending or hosting social events	567	2.5	0.02	–
Travel related to relaxing and leisure	1,367	6.1	0.02	0.37
Travel related to arts and entertainment	505	2.3	0.01	–
Travel related to sports, exercise, and recreation	1,366	6.1	0.02	0.33
Travel related to participating in sports, exercise, recreation	1,251	5.6	0.02	0.30
Travel related to religious and spiritual activities	1,361	6.1	0.03	0.43
Travel related to volunteer activities	1,074	4.8	0.02	0.44

Note: Primary activities are those respondents identified as their main activity. Other activities done simultaneously, such as eating while watching TV, are not included. Numbers may not add to total because not all subcategories are shown. If fewer than 2.0 percent of the total population participated in a primary activity, then the primary activity is not shown. "–" means sample is too small to make a reliable estimate.
Source: Bureau of Labor Statistics, unpublished tables from the 2008 American Time Use Survey, Internet site http://www.bls.gov/tus/home.htm; calculations by New Strategist

Table 6.4 Indexed Time Use of Total People Aged 45 to 54, 2008

(hours spent doing primary activities on an average day by people aged 45 to 54 and by total people aged 15 or older, and index of time spent by people aged 45 to 54 to total people, 2008)

	average hours		index, people aged 45 to 54 to total people
	people aged 45 to 54	total people	
TOTAL, ALL ACTIVITIES	**24.00**	**24.00**	**100**
Personal care	**9.09**	**9.38**	**97**
Sleeping	8.27	8.60	96
Sleeplessness	0.06	0.06	100
Grooming	0.67	0.67	100
Health-related self-care	0.12	0.09	133
Household activities	**1.94**	**1.77**	**110**
Housework	0.61	0.58	105
Interior cleaning	0.36	0.37	97
Laundry	0.21	0.17	124
Storing interior household items, including food	0.01	0.02	50
Food and drink preparation, presentation, and clean-up	0.56	0.52	108
Food and drink preparation	0.44	0.40	110
Kitchen and food clean-up	0.12	0.12	100
Interior maintenance, repair, and decoration	0.11	0.07	157
Interior arrangement, decoration, and repairs	0.10	0.05	200
Exterior maintenance, repair, and decoration	0.06	0.06	100
Lawn, garden, and houseplants	0.23	0.19	121
Animals and pets (not veterinary care)	0.09	0.09	100
Walking, exercising, and playing with pets	0.04	0.04	100
Vehicles	0.05	0.04	125
Household management	0.21	0.21	100
Financial management	0.04	0.03	133
Household and personal organization and planning	0.09	0.09	100
Household and personal mail and messages (except email)	0.03	0.02	150
Household and personal email	0.06	0.06	100
Caring for and helping household members	**0.32**	**0.45**	**71**
Caring for and helping household children	0.23	0.37	62
Physical care for household children	0.08	0.17	47
Reading to or with household children	0.00	0.01	0
Playing with household children (except sports)	0.04	0.09	44
Talking with, listening to household children	0.03	0.02	150
Looking after household children as a primary activity	0.02	0.03	67
Picking up or dropping off household children	0.01	0.02	50
Activities related to household children's education	0.05	0.04	125
Helping household children with homework	0.04	0.03	133
Helping household adults	0.00	0.01	0
Caring for and helping people in other households	**0.16**	**0.16**	**100**
Caring for and helping children in other households	0.08	0.09	89

	average hours		index, people aged 45 to 54 to total people
	people aged 45 to 54	total people	
Helping adults in other households	0.06	0.06	100
Picking up or dropping off adults in other households	0.01	0.01	100
Work and work-related activities	**4.60**	**3.45**	**133**
Work, main job	4.38	3.28	134
Work, other job(s)	0.13	0.09	144
Education	**0.08**	**0.44**	**18**
Taking class	0.02	0.27	7
Taking class for degree, certification, or licensure	0.01	0.26	4
Research, homework	0.06	0.16	38
Consumer purchases (store, telephone, Internet)	**0.36**	**0.38**	**95**
Grocery shopping	0.10	0.10	100
Purchasing gas	0.01	0.01	100
Purchasing food (except groceries)	0.02	0.02	100
Shopping, except groceries, food, and gas	0.22	0.25	88
Professional and personal care services	**0.08**	**0.08**	**100**
Financial services and banking	0.01	0.01	100
Banking	0.01	0.01	100
Medical and care services	0.05	0.05	100
Using health and care services outside the home	0.04	0.04	100
Household services	**0.01**	**0.01**	**100**
Eating and drinking	**1.08**	**1.11**	**97**
Socializing, relaxing, and leisure	**4.20**	**4.62**	**91**
Socializing and communicating	0.52	0.64	81
Attending or hosting social events	0.06	0.07	86
Relaxing and leisure	3.56	3.83	93
Relaxing, thinking	0.27	0.27	100
Television	2.76	2.77	100
Listening to the radio	0.02	0.03	67
Listening to or playing music (not radio)	0.02	0.03	67
Playing games (including computer)	0.09	0.20	45
Computer use for leisure (except games)	0.09	0.14	64
Reading for personal interest	0.27	0.34	79
Arts and entertainment (except sports)	0.06	0.09	67
Sports, exercise, and recreation	**0.28**	**0.33**	**85**
Participating in sports, exercise, or recreation	0.25	0.29	86
Using cardiovascular equipment	0.02	0.02	100
Walking	0.05	0.04	125
Working out, unspecified	0.02	0.03	67
Religious and spiritual activities	**0.15**	**0.14**	**107**
Attending religious services	0.10	0.09	111
Participation in religious practices	0.04	0.04	100

	average hours		index, people aged 45 to 54
	people aged 45 to 54	total people	to total people
Volunteer activities	**0.17**	**0.15**	**113**
Administrative and support activities	0.04	0.04	100
Telephone calls	**0.10**	**0.13**	**77**
Telephone calls to or from family members	0.06	0.04	150
Telephone calls to or from friends, neighbors, or acquaintances	0.02	0.04	50
Traveling	**1.21**	**1.20**	**101**
Travel related to personal care	0.02	0.01	200
Travel related to household activities	0.04	0.04	100
Travel related to household management	0.03	0.02	150
Travel related to caring for and helping household members	0.08	0.08	100
Travel related to caring for and helping household children	0.06	0.06	100
Travel related to helping household adults	0.02	0.02	100
Travel related to caring for and helping people in other households	0.06	0.06	100
Travel related to caring for and helping children in other households	0.01	0.02	50
Travel related to helping adults in other households	0.04	0.04	100
Travel related to work	0.35	0.28	125
Travel related to education	0.01	0.03	33
Travel related to taking class	0.01	0.03	33
Travel related to consumer purchases	0.25	0.24	104
Travel related to grocery shopping	0.06	0.05	120
Travel related to purchasing gas	0.02	0.02	100
Travel related to purchasing food (except groceries)	0.04	0.04	100
Travel related to shopping (except groceries, food, and gas)	0.12	0.12	100
Travel related to using professional and personal care services	0.05	0.04	125
Travel related to using financial services and banking	0.01	0.01	100
Travel related to using medical services	0.03	0.02	150
Travel related to eating and drinking	0.11	0.12	92
Travel related to socializing, relaxing, and leisure	0.15	0.18	83
Travel related to socializing and communicating	0.08	0.09	89
Travel related to attending or hosting social events	0.01	0.01	100
Travel related to relaxing and leisure	0.02	0.04	50
Travel related to arts and entertainment	0.01	0.02	50
Travel related to sports, exercise, and recreation	0.04	0.04	100
Travel related to participating in sports, exercise, recreation	0.03	0.04	75
Travel related to religious and spiritual activities	0.02	0.02	100
Travel related to volunteer activities	0.02	0.02	100

Note: The index is calculated by dividing average time spent by people in the age group doing primary activity by average time spent by total people doing primary activity and multiplying by 100. Primary activities are those respondents identified as their main activity. Other activities done simultaneously, such as eating while watching TV, are not included. Numbers may not add to total because not all subcategories are shown. If fewer than 2.0 percent of the total population participated in a primary activity, then the primary activity is not shown.
Source: Bureau of Labor Statistics, unpublished tables from the 2008 American Time Use Survey, Internet site http://www.bls .gov/tus/home.htm; calculations by New Strategist

Table 6.5 Indexed Time Use of Men Aged 45 to 54, 2008

(hours spent doing primary activities on an average day by men aged 45 to 54 and by total men aged 15 or older, and index of time spent by men aged 45 to 54 to total men, 2008)

	average hours		index, men aged 45 to 54 to total men
	men aged 45 to 54	total men	
TOTAL, ALL ACTIVITIES	**24.00**	**24.00**	**100**
Personal care	**8.80**	**9.21**	**96**
Sleeping	8.16	8.56	95
Sleeplessness	0.04	0.05	80
Grooming	0.56	0.56	100
Health-related self-care	0.06	0.07	86
Household activities	**1.51**	**1.32**	**114**
Housework	0.25	0.24	104
Interior cleaning	0.16	0.17	94
Laundry	0.08	0.06	133
Storing interior household items, including food	0.01	0.01	100
Food and drink preparation, presentation, and clean-up	0.32	0.30	107
Food and drink preparation	0.27	0.25	108
Kitchen and food clean-up	0.05	0.05	100
Interior maintenance, repair, and decoration	0.17	0.10	170
Interior arrangement, decoration, and repairs	0.16	0.08	200
Exterior maintenance, repair, and decoration	0.08	0.08	100
Lawn, garden, and houseplants	0.31	0.26	119
Animals and pets (not veterinary care)	0.07	0.08	88
Walking, exercising, and playing with pets	0.04	0.04	100
Vehicles	0.09	0.07	129
Household management	0.18	0.16	113
Financial management	0.04	0.03	133
Household and personal organization and planning	0.06	0.07	86
Household and personal mail and messages (except email)	0.03	0.02	150
Household and personal email	0.05	0.05	100
Caring for and helping household members	**0.28**	**0.30**	**93**
Caring for and helping household children	0.22	0.25	88
Physical care for household children	0.07	0.09	78
Reading to or with household children	0.00	0.01	0
Playing with household children (except sports)	0.05	0.08	63
Talking with, listening to household children	0.02	0.01	200
Looking after household children as a primary activity	0.01	0.02	50
Picking up or dropping off household children	0.01	0.01	100
Activities related to household children's education	0.04	0.02	200
Helping household children with homework	0.04	0.02	200
Helping household adults	0.00	0.01	0
Caring for and helping people in other households	**0.11**	**0.13**	**85**
Caring for and helping children in other households	0.02	0.05	40

	average hours		index, men aged 45 to 54 to total men
	men aged 45 to 54	total men	
Helping adults in other households	0.07	0.07	100
Picking up or dropping off adults in other households	0.01	0.01	100
Work and work-related activities	**5.32**	**4.16**	**128**
Work, main job	5.03	3.96	127
Work, other job(s)	0.18	0.10	180
Education	**0.02**	**0.39**	**5**
Taking class	0.01	0.27	4
Taking class for degree, certification, or licensure	0.01	0.27	4
Research, homework	0.01	0.12	8
Consumer purchases (store, telephone, Internet)	**0.25**	**0.28**	**89**
Grocery shopping	0.06	0.06	100
Purchasing gas	0.01	0.01	100
Purchasing food (except groceries)	0.02	0.02	100
Shopping, except groceries, food, and gas	0.17	0.19	89
Professional and personal care services	**0.05**	**0.06**	**83**
Financial services and banking	0.01	0.01	100
Banking	0.00	0.00	–
Medical and care services	0.03	0.04	75
Using health and care services outside the home	0.02	0.03	67
Household services	**0.01**	**0.01**	**100**
Eating and drinking	**1.14**	**1.15**	**99**
Socializing, relaxing, and leisure	**4.41**	**4.83**	**91**
Socializing and communicating	0.46	0.59	78
Attending or hosting social events	0.05	0.06	83
Relaxing and leisure	3.86	4.09	94
Relaxing, thinking	0.29	0.27	107
Television	3.09	3.01	103
Listening to the radio	0.02	0.03	67
Listening to or playing music (not radio)	0.02	0.04	50
Playing games (including computer)	0.06	0.25	24
Computer use for leisure (except games)	0.09	0.15	60
Reading for personal interest	0.24	0.29	83
Arts and entertainment (except sports)	0.05	0.09	56
Sports, exercise, and recreation	**0.37**	**0.44**	**84**
Participating in sports, exercise, or recreation	0.32	0.40	80
Using cardiovascular equipment	0.02	0.01	200
Walking	0.05	0.04	125
Working out, unspecified	0.03	0.04	75
Religious and spiritual activities	**0.13**	**0.12**	**108**
Attending religious services	0.09	0.07	129
Participation in religious practices	0.03	0.03	100

	average hours		index, men aged 45 to 54 to total men
	men aged 45 to 54	total men	
Volunteer activities	**0.19**	**0.14**	**136**
Administrative and support activities	0.02	0.03	67
Telephone calls	**0.04**	**0.07**	**57**
Telephone calls to or from family members	0.02	0.02	100
Telephone calls to or from friends, neighbors, or acquaintances	0.01	0.02	50
Traveling	**1.25**	**1.23**	**102**
Travel related to personal care	0.03	0.01	300
Travel related to household activities	0.04	0.04	100
Travel related to household management	0.03	0.03	100
Travel related to caring for and helping household members	0.07	0.06	117
Travel related to caring for and helping household children	0.05	0.04	125
Travel related to helping household adults	0.02	0.02	100
Travel related to caring for and helping people in other households	0.04	0.06	67
Travel related to caring for and helping children in other households	0.01	0.01	100
Travel related to helping adults in other households	0.03	0.04	75
Travel related to work	0.43	0.36	119
Travel related to education	0.00	0.03	0
Travel related to taking class	0.00	0.02	0
Travel related to consumer purchases	0.22	0.21	105
Travel related to grocery shopping	0.05	0.04	125
Travel related to purchasing gas	0.02	0.02	100
Travel related to purchasing food (except groceries)	0.03	0.04	75
Travel related to shopping (except groceries, food, and gas)	0.12	0.11	109
Travel related to using professional and personal care services	0.03	0.03	100
Travel related to using financial services and banking	0.01	0.01	100
Travel related to using medical services	0.02	0.01	200
Travel related to eating and drinking	0.12	0.13	92
Travel related to socializing, relaxing, and leisure	0.15	0.18	83
Travel related to socializing and communicating	0.08	0.09	89
Travel related to attending or hosting social events	0.01	0.01	100
Travel related to relaxing and leisure	0.03	0.04	75
Travel related to arts and entertainment	0.01	0.02	50
Travel related to sports, exercise, and recreation	0.06	0.06	100
Travel related to participating in sports, exercise, recreation	0.05	0.05	100
Travel related to religious and spiritual activities	0.02	0.02	100
Travel related to volunteer activities	0.02	0.02	100

Note: The index is calculated by dividing average time spent by men in the age group doing primary activity by average time spent by total men doing primary activity and multiplying by 100. Primary activities are those respondents identified as their main activity. Other activities done simultaneously, such as eating while watching TV, are not included. Numbers may not add to total because not all subcategories are shown. If fewer than 2.0 percent of the total population participated in a primary activity, then the primary activity is not shown. "–" means denominator is zero.
Source: Bureau of Labor Statistics, unpublished tables from the 2008 American Time Use Survey, Internet site http://www.bls .gov/tus/home.htm; calculations by New Strategist

Table 6.6 Indexed Time Use of Women Aged 45 to 54, 2008

(hours spent doing primary activities on an average day by women aged 45 to 54 and by total women aged 15 or older, and index of time spent by women aged 45 to 54 to total women, 2008)

	average hours		index, women aged 45 to 54 to total women
	women aged 45 to 54	total women	
TOTAL, ALL ACTIVITIES	**24.00**	**24.00**	**100**
Personal care	**9.37**	**9.54**	**98**
Sleeping	8.39	8.64	97
Sleeplessness	0.08	0.07	114
Grooming	0.78	0.78	100
Health-related self-care	0.18	0.11	164
Household activities	**2.34**	**2.19**	**107**
Housework	0.95	0.90	106
Interior cleaning	0.55	0.55	100
Laundry	0.33	0.28	118
Storing interior household items, including food	0.02	0.02	100
Food and drink preparation, presentation, and clean-up	0.80	0.73	110
Food and drink preparation	0.59	0.55	107
Kitchen and food clean-up	0.20	0.18	111
Interior maintenance, repair, and decoration	0.05	0.04	125
Interior arrangement, decoration, and repairs	0.05	0.03	167
Exterior maintenance, repair, and decoration	0.03	0.03	100
Lawn, garden, and houseplants	0.15	0.12	125
Animals and pets (not veterinary care)	0.11	0.10	110
Walking, exercising, and playing with pets	0.04	0.04	100
Vehicles	0.01	0.01	100
Household management	0.24	0.25	96
Financial management	0.03	0.04	75
Household and personal organization and planning	0.11	0.11	100
Household and personal mail and messages (except email)	0.03	0.03	100
Household and personal email	0.07	0.07	100
Caring for and helping household members	**0.36**	**0.59**	**61**
Caring for and helping household children	0.25	0.48	52
Physical care for household children	0.10	0.24	42
Reading to or with household children	0.01	0.02	50
Playing with household children (except sports)	0.02	0.09	22
Talking with, listening to household children	0.03	0.02	150
Looking after household children as a primary activity	0.02	0.03	67
Picking up or dropping off household children	0.02	0.03	67
Activities related to household children's education	0.06	0.05	120
Helping household children with homework	0.04	0.04	100
Helping household adults	0.01	0.01	100
Caring for and helping people in other households	**0.22**	**0.20**	**110**
Caring for and helping children in other households	0.14	0.12	117

	average hours		index, women aged 45 to 54 to total women
	women aged 45 to 54	total women	
Helping adults in other households	0.06	0.05	120
Picking up or dropping off adults in other households	0.01	0.01	100
Work and work-related activities	**3.91**	**2.79**	**140**
Work, main job	3.75	2.63	143
Work, other job(s)	0.09	0.09	100
Education	**0.13**	**0.48**	**27**
Taking class	0.03	0.27	11
Taking class for degree, certification, or licensure	0.01	0.25	4
Research, homework	0.10	0.20	50
Consumer purchases (store, telephone, Internet)	**0.46**	**0.48**	**96**
Grocery shopping	0.15	0.13	115
Purchasing gas	0.01	0.01	100
Purchasing food (except groceries)	0.02	0.02	100
Shopping, except groceries, food, and gas	0.28	0.31	90
Professional and personal care services	**0.11**	**0.11**	**100**
Financial services and banking	0.01	0.01	100
Banking	0.01	0.01	100
Medical and care services	0.07	0.06	117
Using health and care services outside the home	0.06	0.05	120
Household services	**0.02**	**0.01**	**200**
Eating and drinking	**1.02**	**1.07**	**95**
Socializing, relaxing, and leisure	**4.00**	**4.42**	**90**
Socializing and communicating	0.58	0.68	85
Attending or hosting social events	0.07	0.08	88
Relaxing and leisure	3.27	3.58	91
Relaxing, thinking	0.25	0.26	96
Television	2.44	2.54	96
Listening to the radio	0.02	0.02	100
Listening to or playing music (not radio)	0.01	0.02	50
Playing games (including computer)	0.11	0.15	73
Computer use for leisure (except games)	0.09	0.14	64
Reading for personal interest	0.31	0.40	78
Arts and entertainment (except sports)	0.08	0.08	100
Sports, exercise, and recreation	**0.20**	**0.23**	**87**
Participating in sports, exercise, or recreation	0.18	0.20	90
Using cardiovascular equipment	0.03	0.02	150
Walking	0.05	0.04	125
Working out, unspecified	0.02	0.02	100
Religious and spiritual activities	**0.17**	**0.17**	**100**
Attending religious services	0.11	0.10	110
Participation in religious practices	0.05	0.05	100

	average hours		index, women aged 45 to 54 to total women
	women aged 45 to 54	total women	
Volunteer activities	**0.15**	**0.16**	**94**
Administrative and support activities	0.06	0.04	150
Telephone calls	**0.16**	**0.18**	**89**
Telephone calls to or from family members	0.09	0.07	129
Telephone calls to or from friends, neighbors, or acquaintances	0.02	0.06	33
Traveling	**1.18**	**1.17**	**101**
Travel related to personal care	0.01	0.01	100
Travel related to household activities	0.04	0.04	100
Travel related to household management	0.03	0.02	150
Travel related to caring for and helping household members	0.10	0.11	91
Travel related to caring for and helping household children	0.07	0.08	88
Travel related to helping household adults	0.02	0.02	100
Travel related to caring for and helping people in other households	0.07	0.07	100
Travel related to caring for and helping children in other households	0.01	0.02	50
Travel related to helping adults in other households	0.05	0.04	125
Travel related to work	0.27	0.20	135
Travel related to education	0.01	0.04	25
Travel related to taking class	0.01	0.03	33
Travel related to consumer purchases	0.27	0.27	100
Travel related to grocery shopping	0.07	0.06	117
Travel related to purchasing gas	0.02	0.02	100
Travel related to purchasing food (except groceries)	0.05	0.04	125
Travel related to shopping (except groceries, food, and gas)	0.13	0.14	93
Travel related to using professional and personal care services	0.07	0.05	140
Travel related to using financial services and banking	0.01	0.01	100
Travel related to using medical services	0.04	0.02	200
Travel related to eating and drinking	0.10	0.11	91
Travel related to socializing, relaxing, and leisure	0.15	0.17	88
Travel related to socializing and communicating	0.08	0.10	80
Travel related to attending or hosting social events	0.02	0.01	200
Travel related to relaxing and leisure	0.02	0.03	67
Travel related to arts and entertainment	0.01	0.02	50
Travel related to sports, exercise, and recreation	0.02	0.03	67
Travel related to participating in sports, exercise, recreation	0.02	0.03	67
Travel related to religious and spiritual activities	0.03	0.02	150
Travel related to volunteer activities	0.02	0.02	100

Note: The index is calculated by dividing average time spent by women in the age group doing primary activity by average time spent by total women doing primary activity and multiplying by 100. Primary activities are those respondents identified as their main activity. Other activities done simultaneously, such as eating while watching TV, are not included. Numbers may not add to total because not all subcategories are shown. If fewer than 2.0 percent of the total population participated in a primary activity, then the primary activity is not shown.

Source: Bureau of Labor Statistics, unpublished tables from the 2008 American Time Use Survey, Internet site http://www.bls .gov/tus/home.htm; calculations by New Strategist

Table 6.7 Indexed Time Use on of People Aged 45 to 54 by Sex, 2008

(average hours spent by people aged 45 to 54 doing primary activities on an average day by sex, and index of women's time to men's, 2008)

	average hours, aged 45 to 54		index of women to men
	men	women	
TOTAL, ALL ACTIVITIES	**24.00**	**24.00**	**100**
Personal care	**8.80**	**9.37**	**106**
Sleeping	8.16	8.39	103
Sleeplessness	0.04	0.08	200
Grooming	0.56	0.78	139
Health-related self-care	0.06	0.18	300
Household activities	**1.51**	**2.34**	**155**
Housework	0.25	0.95	380
Interior cleaning	0.16	0.55	344
Laundry	0.08	0.33	413
Storing interior household items, including food	0.01	0.02	200
Food and drink preparation, presentation, and clean-up	0.32	0.80	250
Food and drink preparation	0.27	0.59	219
Kitchen and food clean-up	0.05	0.20	400
Interior maintenance, repair, and decoration	0.17	0.05	29
Interior arrangement, decoration, and repairs	0.16	0.05	31
Exterior maintenance, repair, and decoration	0.08	0.03	38
Lawn, garden, and houseplants	0.31	0.15	48
Animals and pets (not veterinary care)	0.07	0.11	157
Walking, exercising, and playing with pets	0.04	0.04	100
Vehicles	0.09	0.01	11
Household management	0.18	0.24	133
Financial management	0.04	0.03	75
Household and personal organization and planning	0.06	0.11	183
Household and personal mail and messages (except email)	0.03	0.03	100
Household and personal email	0.05	0.07	140
Caring for and helping household members	**0.28**	**0.36**	**129**
Caring for and helping household children	0.22	0.25	114
Physical care for household children	0.07	0.10	143
Reading to or with household children	0.00	0.01	–
Playing with household children (except sports)	0.05	0.02	40
Talking with, listening to household children	0.02	0.03	150
Looking after household children as a primary activity	0.01	0.02	200
Picking up or dropping off household children	0.01	0.02	200
Activities related to household children's education	0.04	0.06	150
Helping household children with homework	0.04	0.04	100
Helping household adults	0.00	0.01	–
Caring for and helping people in other households	**0.11**	**0.22**	**200**
Caring for and helping children in other households	0.02	0.14	700

	average hours, aged 45 to 54		index of women to men
	men	women	
Helping adults in other households	0.07	0.06	86
Picking up or dropping off adults in other households	0.01	0.01	100
Work and work-related activities	**5.32**	**3.91**	**73**
Work, main job	5.03	3.75	75
Work, other job(s)	0.18	0.09	50
Education	**0.02**	**0.13**	**650**
Taking class	0.01	0.03	300
Taking class for degree, certification, or licensure	0.01	0.01	100
Research, homework	0.01	0.10	1000
Consumer purchases (store, telephone, Internet)	**0.25**	**0.46**	**184**
Grocery shopping	0.06	0.15	250
Purchasing gas	0.01	0.01	100
Purchasing food (except groceries)	0.02	0.02	100
Shopping, except groceries, food, and gas	0.17	0.28	165
Professional and personal care services	**0.05**	**0.11**	**220**
Financial services and banking	0.01	0.01	100
Banking	0.00	0.01	—
Medical and care services	0.03	0.07	233
Using health and care services outside the home	0.02	0.06	300
Household services	**0.01**	**0.02**	**200**
Eating and drinking	**1.14**	**1.02**	**89**
Socializing, relaxing, and leisure	**4.41**	**4.00**	**91**
Socializing and communicating	0.46	0.58	126
Attending or hosting social events	0.05	0.07	140
Relaxing and leisure	3.86	3.27	85
Relaxing, thinking	0.29	0.25	86
Television	3.09	2.44	79
Listening to the radio	0.02	0.02	100
Listening to or playing music (not radio)	0.02	0.01	50
Playing games (including computer)	0.06	0.11	183
Computer use for leisure (except games)	0.09	0.09	100
Reading for personal interest	0.24	0.31	129
Arts and entertainment (except sports)	0.05	0.08	160
Sports, exercise, and recreation	**0.37**	**0.20**	**54**
Participating in sports, exercise, or recreation	0.32	0.18	56
Using cardiovascular equipment	0.02	0.03	150
Walking	0.05	0.05	100
Working out, unspecified	0.03	0.02	67
Religious and spiritual activities	**0.13**	**0.17**	**131**
Attending religious services	0.09	0.11	122
Participation in religious practices	0.03	0.05	167

	average hours, aged 45 to 54		index of women to men
	men	women	
Volunteer activities	**0.19**	**0.15**	**79**
Administrative and support activities	0.02	0.06	300
Telephone calls	**0.04**	**0.16**	**400**
Telephone calls to or from family members	0.02	0.09	450
Telephone calls to or from friends, neighbors, or acquaintances	0.01	0.02	200
Traveling	**1.25**	**1.18**	**94**
Travel related to personal care	0.03	0.01	33
Travel related to household activities	0.04	0.04	100
Travel related to household management	0.03	0.03	100
Travel related to caring for and helping household members	0.07	0.10	143
Travel related to caring for and helping household children	0.05	0.07	140
Travel related to helping household adults	0.02	0.02	100
Travel related to caring for and helping people in other households	0.04	0.07	175
Travel related to caring for and helping children in other households	0.01	0.01	100
Travel related to helping adults in other households	0.03	0.05	167
Travel related to work	0.43	0.27	63
Travel related to education	0.00	0.01	–
Travel related to taking class	0.00	0.01	–
Travel related to consumer purchases	0.22	0.27	123
Travel related to grocery shopping	0.05	0.07	140
Travel related to purchasing gas	0.02	0.02	100
Travel related to purchasing food (except groceries)	0.03	0.05	167
Travel related to shopping (except groceries, food, and gas)	0.12	0.13	108
Travel related to using professional and personal care services	0.03	0.07	233
Travel related to using financial services and banking	0.01	0.01	100
Travel related to using medical services	0.02	0.04	200
Travel related to eating and drinking	0.12	0.10	83
Travel related to socializing, relaxing, and leisure	0.15	0.15	100
Travel related to socializing and communicating	0.08	0.08	100
Travel related to attending or hosting social events	0.01	0.02	200
Travel related to relaxing and leisure	0.03	0.02	67
Travel related to arts and entertainment	0.01	0.01	100
Travel related to sports, exercise, and recreation	0.06	0.02	33
Travel related to participating in sports, exercise, recreation	0.05	0.02	40
Travel related to religious and spiritual activities	0.02	0.03	150
Travel related to volunteer activities	0.02	0.02	100

Note: The index is calculated by dividing women's time by men's time and multiplying by 100. Primary activities are those respondents identified as their main activity. Other activities done simultaneously, such as eating while watching TV, are not included. Numbers may not add to total because not all subcategories are shown. If fewer than 2.0 percent of the total population participated in a primary activity, then the primary activity is not shown. "–" means denominator is zero.
Source: Bureau of Labor Statistics, unpublished tables from the 2008 American Time Use Survey, Internet site http://www.bls.gov/tus/home.htm; calculations by New Strategist

Table 6.8 Indexed Participation in Primary Activities by Total People Aged 45 to 54, 2008

(percent of people aged 45 to 54 and total people aged 15 or older participating in primary activities on an average day, and index of participation by people aged 45 to 54 to total people, 2008)

	percent participating		index, people aged 45 to 54 to total
	people aged 45 to 54	total people	
TOTAL, ALL ACTIVITIES	**100.0%**	**100.0%**	**100**
Personal care	**99.9**	**100.0**	**100**
Sleeping	99.8	99.9	100
Sleeplessness	6.0	5.2	115
Grooming	80.5	79.3	101
Health-related self-care	6.9	6.4	109
Household activities	**80.8**	**75.5**	**107**
Housework	39.2	35.5	111
Interior cleaning	25.0	24.5	102
Laundry	20.4	16.2	126
Storing interior household items, including food	5.7	5.0	114
Food and drink preparation, presentation, and clean-up	57.7	52.3	110
Food and drink preparation	54.9	49.3	111
Kitchen and food clean-up	24.1	20.8	115
Interior maintenance, repair, and decoration	4.1	3.0	134
Interior arrangement, decoration, and repairs	3.1	2.0	157
Exterior maintenance, repair, and decoration	2.9	2.7	107
Lawn, garden, and houseplants	11.9	9.4	127
Animals and pets (not veterinary care)	18.2	14.5	126
Walking, exercising, and playing with pets	5.3	5.8	93
Vehicles	3.5	2.7	129
Household management	29.5	29.0	102
Financial management	3.6	4.0	89
Household and personal organization and planning	14.5	14.1	103
Household and personal mail and messages (except email)	8.2	6.9	120
Household and personal email	8.9	9.4	94
Caring for and helping household members	**23.3**	**26.1**	**89**
Caring for and helping household children	18.4	21.9	84
Physical care for household children	9.9	15.7	63
Reading to or with household children	0.8	2.6	29
Playing with household children (except sports)	2.0	5.4	36
Talking with, listening to household children	4.2	3.0	138
Looking after household children as a primary activity	1.9	2.3	86
Picking up or dropping off household children	8.7	9.2	95
Activities related to household children's education	4.2	3.8	109
Helping household children with homework	3.7	3.4	106
Helping household adults	0.3	3.6	8
Caring for and helping people in other households	**12.7**	**13.3**	**96**
Caring for and helping children in other households	5.1	5.6	92

	percent participating		index, people aged 45 to 54 to total
	people aged 45 to 54	total people	
Helping adults in other households	7.8%	8.0%	97
Picking up or dropping off adults in other households	4.5	5.0	91
Work and work-related activities	**59.4**	**46.6**	**127**
Work, main job	56.7	43.9	129
Work, other job(s)	3.6	2.4	150
Education	**1.9**	**7.9**	**24**
Taking class	0.7	5.2	14
Taking class for degree, certification, or licensure	0.3	4.8	7
Research, homework	1.3	5.8	22
Consumer purchases (store, telephone, Internet)	**41.2**	**40.7**	**101**
Grocery shopping	14.3	12.9	111
Purchasing gas	4.8	4.0	121
Purchasing food (except groceries)	10.1	12.0	84
Shopping, except groceries, food, and gas	23.7	23.5	101
Professional and personal care services	**10.2**	**8.9**	**115**
Financial services and banking	4.2	3.2	129
Banking	4.0	3.0	132
Medical and care services	4.5	3.6	125
Using health and care services outside the home	4.5	3.4	130
Household services	**2.2**	**2.1**	**108**
Eating and drinking	**95.9**	**96.0**	**100**
Socializing, relaxing, and leisure	**95.6**	**95.4**	**100**
Socializing and communicating	34.4	37.6	91
Attending or hosting social events	2.2	2.3	96
Relaxing and leisure	91.9	91.3	101
Relaxing, thinking	21.8	19.9	110
Television	82.0	80.9	101
Listening to the radio	1.9	2.0	95
Listening to or playing music (not radio)	1.5	2.6	56
Playing games (including computer)	4.9	9.0	55
Computer use for leisure (except games)	7.9	9.5	83
Reading for personal interest	23.4	23.9	98
Arts and entertainment (except sports)	2.3	3.2	72
Sports, exercise, and recreation	**18.5**	**18.9**	**98**
Participating in sports, exercise, or recreation	17.7	17.9	99
Using cardiovascular equipment	3.4	2.2	158
Walking	5.7	4.8	119
Working out, unspecified	3.0	3.2	94
Religious and spiritual activities	**9.3**	**9.2**	**101**
Attending religious services	5.0	4.9	102
Participation in religious practices	4.9	4.6	108

	percent participating		index, people aged 45 to 54
	people aged 45 to 54	total people	to total
Volunteer activities	**7.5%**	**6.7%**	**111**
Administrative and support activities	2.9	2.5	116
Telephone calls	**14.2**	**15.4**	**93**
Telephone calls to or from family members	8.4	7.3	115
Telephone calls to or from friends, neighbors, or acquaintances	3.3	5.6	59
Traveling	**87.2**	**86.9**	**100**
Travel related to personal care	2.3	2.5	93
Travel related to household activities	8.8	9.4	93
Travel related to household management	6.0	6.1	98
Travel related to caring for and helping household members	13.7	13.6	100
Travel related to caring for and helping household children	10.4	11.0	95
Travel related to helping household adults	3.3	2.6	128
Travel related to caring for and helping people in other households	9.5	10.5	90
Travel related to caring for and helping children in other households	2.9	3.5	82
Travel related to helping adults in other households	6.6	7.1	93
Travel related to work	47.7	38.2	125
Travel related to education	0.7	5.0	13
Travel related to taking class	0.6	4.4	13
Travel related to consumer purchases	40.7	39.6	103
Travel related to grocery shopping	14.2	12.9	110
Travel related to purchasing gas	4.8	3.9	121
Travel related to purchasing food (except groceries)	9.6	11.2	86
Travel related to shopping (except groceries, food, and gas)	23.2	22.7	102
Travel related to using professional and personal care services	9.5	8.1	117
Travel related to using financial services and banking	3.9	3.0	128
Travel related to using medical services	4.3	3.3	129
Travel related to eating and drinking	23.7	25.0	95
Travel related to socializing, relaxing, and leisure	25.3	28.6	89
Travel related to socializing and communicating	16.8	18.6	90
Travel related to attending or hosting social events	1.9	2.0	96
Travel related to relaxing and leisure	6.4	8.9	72
Travel related to arts and entertainment	2.0	2.6	78
Travel related to sports, exercise, and recreation	7.5	9.6	78
Travel related to participating in sports, exercise, recreation	6.7	8.6	78
Travel related to religious and spiritual activities	5.2	5.1	101
Travel related to volunteer activities	4.6	4.3	109

Note: The index is calculated by dividing percent of people in the age group doing primary activity by percent of total people doing primary activity and multiplying by 100. Primary activities are those respondents identified as their main activity. Other activities done simultaneously, such as eating while watching TV, are not included. If fewer than 2.0 percent of the total population participated in a primary activity, then the primary activity is not shown.
Source: Bureau of Labor Statistics, unpublished tables from the 2008 American Time Use Survey, Internet site http://www.bls.gov/tus/home.htm; calculations by New Strategist

Table 6.9 Indexed Participation in Primary Activities by Men Aged 45 to 54, 2008

(percent of men aged 45 to 54 and total men aged 15 or older participating in primary activities on an average day, and index of participation by men aged 45 to 54 to total men, 2008)

	percent participating		index, men aged 45 to 54 to total men
	men aged 45 to 54	total men	
TOTAL, ALL ACTIVITIES	**100.0%**	**100.0%**	**100**
Personal care	**100.0**	**100.0**	**100**
Sleeping	99.8	99.9	100
Sleeplessness	4.8	4.5	106
Grooming	76.9	76.6	100
Health-related self-care	5.3	4.8	110
Household activities	**73.7**	**66.6**	**111**
Housework	21.8	19.7	111
Interior cleaning	15.5	13.5	115
Laundry	7.7	6.3	122
Storing interior household items, including food	2.4	2.9	84
Food and drink preparation, presentation, and clean-up	45.1	38.4	117
Food and drink preparation	42.4	36.0	118
Kitchen and food clean-up	10.7	9.5	113
Interior maintenance, repair, and decoration	5.3	3.9	136
Interior arrangement, decoration, and repairs	3.9	2.4	157
Exterior maintenance, repair, and decoration	4.4	3.8	115
Lawn, garden, and houseplants	14.6	11.0	133
Animals and pets (not veterinary care)	15.1	12.1	124
Walking, exercising, and playing with pets	4.7	5.2	91
Vehicles	5.7	4.5	126
Household management	24.9	24.0	104
Financial management	2.4	3.2	74
Household and personal organization and planning	11.0	11.1	99
Household and personal mail and messages (except email)	6.8	5.5	125
Household and personal email	7.0	7.4	95
Caring for and helping household members	**19.5**	**20.7**	**94**
Caring for and helping household children	15.8	16.8	94
Physical care for household children	6.8	10.4	66
Reading to or with household children	0.4	1.7	25
Playing with household children (except sports)	2.6	4.7	55
Talking with, listening to household children	3.3	1.7	186
Looking after household children as a primary activity	1.7	1.5	117
Picking up or dropping off household children	7.2	6.2	116
Activities related to household children's education	3.5	2.2	161
Helping household children with homework	3.1	2.0	155
Helping household adults	0.1	3.5	3
Caring for and helping people in other households	**8.8**	**11.0**	**80**
Caring for and helping children in other households	2.7	3.6	75

	percent participating		index, men aged 45 to 54
	men aged 45 to 54	total men	to total men
Helping adults in other households	6.0%	7.5%	80
Picking up or dropping off adults in other households	2.7	4.4	61
Work and work-related activities	**65.4**	**53.4**	**123**
Work, main job	61.7	50.1	123
Work, other job(s)	4.0	2.3	170
Education	**0.9**	**6.9**	**12**
Taking class	0.4	5.0	9
Taking class for degree, certification, or licensure	0.1	4.8	2
Research, homework	0.4	4.6	9
Consumer purchases (store, telephone, Internet)	**37.1**	**35.6**	**104**
Grocery shopping	10.1	9.6	106
Purchasing gas	5.5	4.3	128
Purchasing food (except groceries)	9.3	11.8	78
Shopping, except groceries, food, and gas	21.9	19.6	112
Professional and personal care services	**6.8**	**6.7**	**102**
Financial services and banking	3.4	3.1	107
Banking	3.1	2.8	113
Medical and care services	2.9	2.4	121
Using health and care services outside the home	2.8	2.3	120
Household services	**1.7**	**2.1**	**80**
Eating and drinking	**96.9**	**96.5**	**100**
Socializing, relaxing, and leisure	**94.9**	**95.4**	**99**
Socializing and communicating	29.8	34.9	85
Attending or hosting social events	1.6	2.0	79
Relaxing and leisure	92.9	92.1	101
Relaxing, thinking	23.9	20.4	117
Television	84.3	82.3	102
Listening to the radio	2.7	2.5	108
Listening to or playing music (not radio)	1.9	3.3	58
Playing games (including computer)	3.3	9.6	35
Computer use for leisure (except games)	6.8	9.5	72
Reading for personal interest	21.2	21.1	101
Arts and entertainment (except sports)	1.9	3.3	57
Sports, exercise, and recreation	**20.4**	**22.0**	**93**
Participating in sports, exercise, or recreation	19.5	21.0	93
Using cardiovascular equipment	3.0	1.8	162
Walking	5.7	4.9	116
Working out, unspecified	3.3	3.5	95
Religious and spiritual activities	**8.3**	**7.7**	**108**
Attending religious services	3.9	4.0	98
Participation in religious practices	4.4	3.7	119

	percent participating		index, men aged 45 to 54 to total men
	men aged 45 to 54	total men	
Volunteer activities	**6.7%**	**5.7%**	**117**
Administrative and support activities	2.3	1.9	119
Telephone calls	**7.9**	**10.0**	**79**
Telephone calls to or from family members	4.2	3.8	110
Telephone calls to or from friends, neighbors, or acquaintances	2.0	3.7	53
Traveling	**88.3**	**88.5**	**100**
Travel related to personal care	3.5	3.1	113
Travel related to household activities	6.9	8.5	82
Travel related to household management	4.6	5.5	84
Travel related to caring for and helping household members	11.6	9.9	117
Travel related to caring for and helping household children	9.0	7.4	123
Travel related to helping household adults	2.5	2.4	105
Travel related to caring for and helping people in other households	7.5	9.3	81
Travel related to caring for and helping children in other households	2.2	2.5	90
Travel related to helping adults in other households	5.1	6.7	76
Travel related to work	52.2	44.4	117
Travel related to education	0.5	4.6	10
Travel related to taking class	0.4	4.1	10
Travel related to consumer purchases	36.9	34.5	107
Travel related to grocery shopping	10.1	9.5	106
Travel related to purchasing gas	5.4	4.2	129
Travel related to purchasing food (except groceries)	8.8	11.0	80
Travel related to shopping (except groceries, food, and gas)	21.5	18.9	114
Travel related to using professional and personal care services	6.2	6.3	98
Travel related to using financial services and banking	2.8	3.0	94
Travel related to using medical services	2.8	2.3	120
Travel related to eating and drinking	26.8	27.3	98
Travel related to socializing, relaxing, and leisure	24.9	28.0	89
Travel related to socializing and communicating	16.3	17.5	93
Travel related to attending or hosting social events	1.3	1.7	75
Travel related to relaxing and leisure	6.8	9.4	72
Travel related to arts and entertainment	1.8	2.8	64
Travel related to sports, exercise, and recreation	8.9	11.5	77
Travel related to participating in sports, exercise, recreation	7.9	10.4	76
Travel related to religious and spiritual activities	4.3	4.4	98
Travel related to volunteer activities	4.5	3.8	118

Note: The index is calculated by dividing percent of men in the age group doing primary activity by percent of total men doing primary activity and multiplying by 100. Primary activities are those respondents identified as their main activity. Other activities done simultaneously, such as eating while watching TV, are not included. If fewer than 2.0 percent of the total population participated in a primary activity, then the primary activity is not shown.
Source: Bureau of Labor Statistics, unpublished tables from the 2008 American Time Use Survey, Internet site http://www.bls .gov/tus/home.htm; calculations by New Strategist

Table 6.10 Indexed Participation in Primary Activities by Women Aged 45 to 54, 2008

(percent of women aged 45 to 54 and total women aged 15 or older participating in primary activities on an average day, and index of participation by women aged 45 to 54 to total women, 2008)

	percent participating		index, women aged 45 to 54 to total women
	women aged 45 to 54	total women	
TOTAL, ALL ACTIVITIES	**100.0%**	**100.0%**	**100**
Personal care	**99.9**	**100.0**	**100**
Sleeping	99.9	99.9	100
Sleeplessness	7.2	5.8	123
Grooming	84.0	81.8	103
Health-related self-care	8.5	7.8	109
Household activities	**87.6**	**84.0**	**104**
Housework	55.9	50.3	111
Interior cleaning	34.2	34.9	98
Laundry	32.5	25.5	128
Storing interior household items, including food	8.8	7.0	126
Food and drink preparation, presentation, and clean-up	69.8	65.3	107
Food and drink preparation	66.9	61.8	108
Kitchen and food clean-up	36.9	31.5	117
Interior maintenance, repair, and decoration	2.9	2.2	131
Interior arrangement, decoration, and repairs	2.3	1.5	155
Exterior maintenance, repair, and decoration	1.6	1.8	88
Lawn, garden, and houseplants	9.3	7.9	118
Animals and pets (not veterinary care)	21.3	16.7	127
Walking, exercising, and playing with pets	5.9	6.3	94
Vehicles	1.3	1.0	136
Household management	34.0	33.8	101
Financial management	4.8	4.9	100
Household and personal organization and planning	17.8	16.8	106
Household and personal mail and messages (except email)	9.6	8.2	117
Household and personal email	10.7	11.3	95
Caring for and helping household members	**27.0**	**31.2**	**87**
Caring for and helping household children	20.8	26.7	78
Physical care for household children	12.8	20.6	62
Reading to or with household children	1.3	3.5	38
Playing with household children (except sports)	1.4	6.1	23
Talking with, listening to household children	5.1	4.3	120
Looking after household children as a primary activity	2.2	3.0	72
Picking up or dropping off household children	10.2	12.1	84
Activities related to household children's education	4.8	5.4	89
Helping household children with homework	4.2	4.8	87
Helping household adults	0.5	3.7	12
Caring for and helping people in other households	**16.6**	**15.5**	**107**
Caring for and helping children in other households	7.4	7.4	101

	percent participating		index, women aged 45 to 54
	women aged 45 to 54	total women	to total women
Helping adults in other households	9.6%	8.5%	112
Picking up or dropping off adults in other households	6.2	5.4	115
Work and work-related activities	**53.7**	**40.3**	**133**
Work, main job	51.8	38.0	136
Work, other job(s)	3.2	2.4	131
Education	**2.8**	**8.9**	**32**
Taking class	1.0	5.3	18
Taking class for degree, certification, or licensure	0.5	4.7	11
Research, homework	2.1	7.0	30
Consumer purchases (store, telephone, Internet)	**45.2**	**45.4**	**99**
Grocery shopping	18.4	16.1	115
Purchasing gas	4.2	3.7	113
Purchasing food (except groceries)	10.9	12.3	88
Shopping, except groceries, food, and gas	25.4	27.2	94
Professional and personal care services	**13.4**	**11.0**	**122**
Financial services and banking	5.0	3.3	149
Banking	4.9	3.3	152
Medical and care services	6.1	4.8	128
Using health and care services outside the home	6.1	4.5	135
Household services	**2.8**	**2.1**	**135**
Eating and drinking	**94.8**	**95.6**	**99**
Socializing, relaxing, and leisure	**96.4**	**95.4**	**101**
Socializing and communicating	38.7	40.1	97
Attending or hosting social events	2.9	2.7	109
Relaxing and leisure	91.0	90.6	100
Relaxing, thinking	19.9	19.5	102
Television	79.8	79.5	100
Listening to the radio	1.1	1.5	74
Listening to or playing music (not radio)	1.1	2.0	54
Playing games (including computer)	6.5	8.4	77
Computer use for leisure (except games)	8.9	9.5	94
Reading for personal interest	25.5	26.5	96
Arts and entertainment (except sports)	2.8	3.2	88
Sports, exercise, and recreation	**16.6**	**15.9**	**104**
Participating in sports, exercise, or recreation	16.1	15.0	107
Using cardiovascular equipment	3.9	2.5	155
Walking	5.7	4.7	122
Working out, unspecified	2.7	2.9	93
Religious and spiritual activities	**10.3**	**10.7**	**97**
Attending religious services	6.0	5.7	106
Participation in religious practices	5.5	5.4	101

| | percent participating | | index, women aged 45 to 54 |
	women aged 45 to 54	total women	to total women
Volunteer activities	**8.2%**	**7.6%**	**107**
Administrative and support activities	3.5	3.1	115
Telephone calls	**20.3**	**20.4**	**100**
Telephone calls to or from family members	12.5	10.7	117
Telephone calls to or from friends, neighbors, or acquaintances	4.5	7.4	62
Traveling	**86.2**	**85.5**	**101**
Travel related to personal care	1.3	2.0	64
Travel related to household activities	10.5	10.3	103
Travel related to household management	7.3	6.7	109
Travel related to caring for and helping household members	15.6	17.1	91
Travel related to caring for and helping household children	11.8	14.3	82
Travel related to helping household adults	4.0	2.7	148
Travel related to caring for and helping people in other households	11.4	11.6	98
Travel related to caring for and helping children in other households	3.5	4.5	78
Travel related to helping adults in other households	8.0	7.4	108
Travel related to work	43.4	32.2	135
Travel related to education	0.8	5.4	16
Travel related to taking class	0.7	4.6	16
Travel related to consumer purchases	44.4	44.4	100
Travel related to grocery shopping	18.1	16.0	113
Travel related to purchasing gas	4.2	3.7	113
Travel related to purchasing food (except groceries)	10.5	11.5	92
Travel related to shopping (except groceries, food, and gas)	24.9	26.3	94
Travel related to using professional and personal care services	12.6	9.8	129
Travel related to using financial services and banking	4.9	3.1	160
Travel related to using medical services	5.7	4.3	135
Travel related to eating and drinking	20.7	22.8	91
Travel related to socializing, relaxing, and leisure	25.8	29.2	88
Travel related to socializing and communicating	17.2	19.5	88
Travel related to attending or hosting social events	2.5	2.3	111
Travel related to relaxing and leisure	6.1	8.5	72
Travel related to arts and entertainment	2.3	2.4	93
Travel related to sports, exercise, and recreation	6.1	7.7	79
Travel related to participating in sports, exercise, recreation	5.6	6.8	82
Travel related to religious and spiritual activities	6.1	5.8	104
Travel related to volunteer activities	4.8	4.7	102

Note: The index is calculated by dividing percent of women in the age group doing primary activity by percent of total women doing primary activity and multiplying by 100. Primary activities are those respondents identified as their main activity. Other activities done simultaneously, such as eating while watching TV, are not included. If fewer than 2.0 percent of the total population participated in a primary activity, then the primary activity is not shown.
Source: Bureau of Labor Statistics, unpublished tables from the 2008 American Time Use Survey, Internet site http://www.bls .gov/tus/home.htm; calculations by New Strategist

Table 6.11 Indexed Participation in Primary Activities of People Aged 45 to 54 by Sex, 2008

(percent of people aged 45 to 54 participating in primary activities on an average day by sex, and index of women's participation to men's, 2008)

	aged 45 to 54, percent participating		index of women to men
	men	women	
TOTAL, ALL ACTIVITIES	**100.0%**	**100.0%**	**100**
Personal care	**100.0**	**99.9**	**100**
Sleeping	99.8	99.9	100
Sleeplessness	4.8	7.2	151
Grooming	76.9	84.0	109
Health-related self-care	5.3	8.5	160
Household activities	**73.7**	**87.6**	**119**
Housework	21.8	55.9	257
Interior cleaning	15.5	34.2	221
Laundry	7.7	32.5	425
Storing interior household items, including food	2.4	8.8	366
Food and drink preparation, presentation, and clean-up	45.1	69.8	155
Food and drink preparation	42.4	66.9	158
Kitchen and food clean-up	10.7	36.9	344
Interior maintenance, repair, and decoration	5.3	2.9	54
Interior arrangement, decoration, and repairs	3.9	2.3	61
Exterior maintenance, repair, and decoration	4.4	1.6	36
Lawn, garden, and houseplants	14.6	9.3	64
Animals and pets (not veterinary care)	15.1	21.3	141
Walking, exercising, and playing with pets	4.7	5.9	125
Vehicles	5.7	1.3	24
Household management	24.9	34.0	136
Financial management	2.4	4.8	206
Household and personal organization and planning	11.0	17.8	162
Household and personal mail and messages (except email)	6.8	9.6	140
Household and personal email	7.0	10.7	152
Caring for and helping household members	**19.5**	**27.0**	**138**
Caring for and helping household children	15.8	20.8	132
Physical care for household children	6.8	12.8	186
Reading to or with household children	0.4	1.3	313
Playing with household children (except sports)	2.6	1.4	53
Talking with, listening to household children	3.3	5.1	157
Looking after household children as a primary activity	1.7	2.2	129
Picking up or dropping off household children	7.2	10.2	141
Activities related to household children's education	3.5	4.8	137
Helping household children with homework	3.1	4.2	133
Helping household adults	0.1	0.5	412
Caring for and helping people in other households	**8.8**	**16.6**	**189**
Caring for and helping children in other households	2.7	7.4	272

	aged 45 to 54, percent participating		index of women to men
	men	women	
Helping adults in other households	6.0%	9.6%	161
Picking up or dropping off adults in other households	2.7	6.2	231
Work and work-related activities	**65.4**	**53.7**	**82**
Work, main job	61.7	51.8	84
Work, other job(s)	4.0	3.2	81
Education	**0.9**	**2.8**	**333**
Taking class	0.4	1.0	227
Taking class for degree, certification, or licensure	0.1	0.5	510
Research, homework	0.4	2.1	498
Consumer purchases (store, telephone, Internet)	**37.1**	**45.2**	**122**
Grocery shopping	10.1	18.4	182
Purchasing gas	5.5	4.2	76
Purchasing food (except groceries)	9.3	10.9	117
Shopping, except groceries, food, and gas	21.9	25.4	116
Professional and personal care services	**6.8**	**13.4**	**198**
Financial services and banking	3.4	5.0	147
Banking	3.1	4.9	158
Medical and care services	2.9	6.1	206
Using health and care services outside the home	2.8	6.1	220
Household services	**1.7**	**2.8**	**168**
Eating and drinking	**96.9**	**94.8**	**98**
Socializing, relaxing, and leisure	**94.9**	**96.4**	**102**
Socializing and communicating	29.8	38.7	130
Attending or hosting social events	1.6	2.9	186
Relaxing and leisure	92.9	91.0	98
Relaxing, thinking	23.9	19.9	83
Television	84.3	79.8	95
Listening to the radio	2.7	1.1	41
Listening to or playing music (not radio)	1.9	1.1	56
Playing games (including computer)	3.3	6.5	194
Computer use for leisure (except games)	6.8	8.9	131
Reading for personal interest	21.2	25.5	120
Arts and entertainment (except sports)	1.9	2.8	146
Sports, exercise, and recreation	**20.4**	**16.6**	**81**
Participating in sports, exercise, or recreation	19.5	16.1	83
Using cardiovascular equipment	3.0	3.9	130
Walking	5.7	5.7	101
Working out, unspecified	3.3	2.7	80
Religious and spiritual activities	**8.3**	**10.3**	**124**
Attending religious services	3.9	6.0	153
Participation in religious practices	4.4	5.5	124

	aged 45 to 54, percent participating		index of women to men
	men	women	
Volunteer activities	**6.7%**	**8.2%**	**122**
Administrative and support activities	2.3	3.5	153
Telephone calls	**7.9**	**20.3**	**257**
Telephone calls to or from family members	4.2	12.5	298
Telephone calls to or from friends, neighbors, or acquaintances	2.0	4.5	233
Traveling	**88.3**	**86.2**	**98**
Travel related to personal care	3.5	1.3	37
Travel related to household activities	6.9	10.5	153
Travel related to household management	4.6	7.3	159
Travel related to caring for and helping household members	11.6	15.6	134
Travel related to caring for and helping household children	9.0	11.8	130
Travel related to helping household adults	2.5	4.0	160
Travel related to caring for and helping people in other households	7.5	11.4	151
Travel related to caring for and helping children in other households	2.2	3.5	158
Travel related to helping adults in other households	5.1	8.0	156
Travel related to work	52.2	43.4	83
Travel related to education	0.5	0.8	186
Travel related to taking class	0.4	0.7	170
Travel related to consumer purchases	36.9	44.4	120
Travel related to grocery shopping	10.1	18.1	180
Travel related to purchasing gas	5.4	4.2	77
Travel related to purchasing food (except groceries)	8.8	10.5	120
Travel related to shopping (except groceries, food, and gas)	21.5	24.9	116
Travel related to using professional and personal care services	6.2	12.6	203
Travel related to using financial services and banking	2.8	4.9	172
Travel related to using medical services	2.8	5.7	207
Travel related to eating and drinking	26.8	20.7	77
Travel related to socializing, relaxing, and leisure	24.9	25.8	103
Travel related to socializing and communicating	16.3	17.2	105
Travel related to attending or hosting social events	1.3	2.5	199
Travel related to relaxing and leisure	6.8	6.1	90
Travel related to arts and entertainment	1.8	2.3	126
Travel related to sports, exercise, and recreation	8.9	6.1	69
Travel related to participating in sports, exercise, recreation	7.9	5.6	71
Travel related to religious and spiritual activities	4.3	6.1	141
Travel related to volunteer activities	4.5	4.8	106

Note: The index is calculated by dividing percent of women participating in primary activity by percent of men participating in primary activity and multiplying by 100. Primary activities are those respondents identified as their main activity. Other activities done simultaneously, such as eating while watching TV, are not included. If fewer than 2.0 percent of the total population participated in a primary activity, then the primary activity is not shown.
Source: Bureau of Labor Statistics, unpublished tables from the 2008 American Time Use Survey, Internet site http://www.bls .gov/tus/home.htm; calculations by New Strategist

Table 6.12   Ranking: Average Hours per Day Spent Doing Primary Activities by Total People Aged 45 to 54, 2008

(average hours per day spent by people aged 45 to 54 doing primary activities, ranked by time spent doing activity, 2008)

		average hours per day spent by people aged 45 to 54
	Total, all activities	**24.00**
1.	Sleeping	8.27
2.	Work, main job	4.38
3.	Television	2.76
4.	Eating and drinking	1.08
5.	Grooming	0.67
6.	Socializing and communicating	0.52
7.	Food and drink preparation	0.44
8.	Interior cleaning	0.36
9.	Travel related to work	0.35
10.	Relaxing, thinking	0.27
11.	Reading for personal interest	0.27
12.	Participating in sports, exercise, or recreation	0.25
13.	Lawn, garden, and houseplants	0.23
14.	Caring for and helping household children	0.23
15.	Shopping, except groceries, food, and gas	0.22
16.	Laundry	0.21
17.	Volunteer activities	0.17
18.	Work, other job(s)	0.13
19.	Health-related self-care	0.12
20.	Kitchen and food clean-up	0.12
21.	Travel related to shopping (except groceries, food, and gas)	0.12
22.	Interior maintenance, repair, and decoration	0.11
23.	Travel related to eating and drinking	0.11
24.	Grocery shopping	0.10
25.	Attending religious services	0.10
26.	Telephone calls	0.10
27.	Animals and pets (not veterinary care)	0.09
28.	Household and personal organization and planning	0.09
29.	Playing games (including computer)	0.09
30.	Computer use for leisure (except games)	0.09
31.	Caring for and helping children in other households	0.08
32.	Travel related to socializing and communicating	0.08
33.	Exterior maintenance, repair, and decoration	0.06
34.	Household and personal email	0.06
35.	Helping adults in other households	0.06
36.	Research, homework	0.06
37.	Attending or hosting social events	0.06
38.	Arts and entertainment (except sports)	0.06
39.	Travel related to caring for and helping household children	0.06

	average hours per day spent by people aged 45 to 54
40. Travel related to grocery shopping	0.06
41. Vehicles	0.05
42. Activities related to household children's education	0.05
43. Medical and care services	0.05
44. Financial management	0.04
45. Participation in religious practices	0.04
46. Travel related to household activities	0.04
47. Travel related to helping adults in other households	0.04
48. Travel related to purchasing food (except groceries)	0.04
49. Travel related to sports, exercise, and recreation	0.04
50. Household and personal mail and messages (except email)	0.03
51. Travel related to using medical services	0.03
52. Taking class	0.02
53. Purchasing food (except groceries)	0.02
54. Listening to the radio	0.02
55. Listening to or playing music (not radio)	0.02
56. Travel related to personal care	0.02
57. Travel related to helping household adults	0.02
58. Travel related to purchasing gas	0.02
59. Travel related to relaxing and leisure	0.02
60. Travel related to religious and spiritual activities	0.02
61. Travel related to volunteer activities	0.02
62. Storing interior household items, including food	0.01
63. Purchasing gas	0.01
64. Financial services and banking	0.01
65. Household services	0.01
66. Travel related to caring for and helping children in other households	0.01
67. Travel related to education	0.01
68. Travel related to using financial services and banking	0.01
69. Travel related to attending or hosting social events	0.01
70. Travel related to arts and entertainment	0.01
71. Helping household adults	0.00

Note: Primary activities are those respondents identified as their main activity. Other activities done simultaneously, such as eating while watching TV, are not included. If fewer than 2.0 percent of the total population participated in a primary activity, then the primary activity is not shown.
Source: Bureau of Labor Statistics, unpublished tables from the 2008 American Time Use Survey, Internet site http://www.bls .gov/tus/home.htm; calculations by New Strategist

Table 6.13 Ranking: Average Hours per Day Spent Doing Primary Activities by Men Aged 45 to 54, 2008

(average hours per day spent by men aged 45 to 54 doing primary activities, ranked by time spent doing activity, 2008)

		average hours per day spent by men aged 45 to 54
	Total, all activities	**24.00**
1.	Sleeping	8.16
2.	Work, main job	5.03
3.	Television	3.09
4.	Eating and drinking	1.14
5.	Grooming	0.56
6.	Socializing and communicating	0.46
7.	Travel related to work	0.43
8.	Participating in sports, exercise, or recreation	0.32
9.	Lawn, garden, and houseplants	0.31
10.	Relaxing, thinking	0.29
11.	Food and drink preparation	0.27
12.	Reading for personal interest	0.24
13.	Caring for and helping household children	0.22
14.	Volunteer activities	0.19
15.	Work, other job(s)	0.18
16.	Interior maintenance, repair, and decoration	0.17
17.	Shopping, except groceries, food, and gas	0.17
18.	Interior cleaning	0.16
19.	Travel related to shopping (except groceries, food, and gas)	0.12
20.	Travel related to eating and drinking	0.12
21.	Vehicles	0.09
22.	Computer use for leisure (except games)	0.09
23.	Attending religious services	0.09
24.	Laundry	0.08
25.	Exterior maintenance, repair, and decoration	0.08
26.	Travel related to socializing and communicating	0.08
27.	Animals and pets (not veterinary care)	0.07
28.	Helping adults in other households	0.07
29.	Health-related self-care	0.06
30.	Household and personal organization and planning	0.06
31.	Grocery shopping	0.06
32.	Playing games (including computer)	0.06
33.	Travel related to sports, exercise, and recreation	0.06
34.	Kitchen and food clean-up	0.05
35.	Household and personal email	0.05
36.	Attending or hosting social events	0.05
37.	Arts and entertainment (except sports)	0.05
38.	Travel related to caring for and helping household children	0.05
39.	Travel related to grocery shopping	0.05

	average hours per day spent by men aged 45 to 54
40. Financial management	0.04
41. Activities related to household children's education	0.04
42. Telephone calls	0.04
43. Travel related to household activities	0.04
44. Household and personal mail and messages (except email)	0.03
45. Medical and care services	0.03
46. Participation in religious practices	0.03
47. Travel related to personal care	0.03
48. Travel related to helping adults in other households	0.03
49. Travel related to purchasing food (except groceries)	0.03
50. Travel related to relaxing and leisure	0.03
51. Caring for and helping children in other households	0.02
52. Purchasing food (except groceries)	0.02
53. Listening to the radio	0.02
54. Listening to or playing music (not radio)	0.02
55. Travel related to helping household adults	0.02
56. Travel related to purchasing gas	0.02
57. Travel related to using medical services	0.02
58. Travel related to religious and spiritual activities	0.02
59. Travel related to volunteer activities	0.02
60. Storing interior household items, including food	0.01
61. Taking class	0.01
62. Research, homework	0.01
63. Purchasing gas	0.01
64. Financial services and banking	0.01
65. Household services	0.01
66. Travel related to caring for and helping children in other households	0.01
67. Travel related to using financial services and banking	0.01
68. Travel related to attending or hosting social events	0.01
69. Travel related to arts and entertainment	0.01
70. Helping household adults	0.00
71. Travel related to education	0.00

Note: Primary activities are those respondents identified as their main activity. Other activities done simultaneously, such as eating while watching TV, are not included. If fewer than 2.0 percent of the total population participated in a primary activity, then the primary activity is not shown.
Source: Bureau of Labor Statistics, unpublished tables from the 2008 American Time Use Survey, Internet site http://www.bls .gov/tus/home.htm; calculations by New Strategist

Table 6.14 Ranking: Average Hours per Day Spent Doing Primary Activities by Women Aged 45 to 54, 2008

(average hours per day spent by women aged 45 to 54 doing primary activities, ranked by time spent doing activity, 2008)

		average hours per day spent by women aged 45 to 54
	Total, all activities	**24.00**
1.	Sleeping	8.39
2.	Work, main job	3.75
3.	Television	2.44
4.	Eating and drinking	1.02
5.	Grooming	0.78
6.	Food and drink preparation	0.59
7.	Socializing and communicating	0.58
8.	Interior cleaning	0.55
9.	Laundry	0.33
10.	Reading for personal interest	0.31
11.	Shopping, except groceries, food, and gas	0.28
12.	Travel related to work	0.27
13.	Caring for and helping household children	0.25
14.	Relaxing, thinking	0.25
15.	Kitchen and food clean-up	0.20
16.	Health-related self-care	0.18
17.	Participating in sports, exercise, or recreation	0.18
18.	Telephone calls	0.16
19.	Lawn, garden, and houseplants	0.15
20.	Grocery shopping	0.15
21.	Volunteer activities	0.15
22.	Caring for and helping children in other households	0.14
23.	Travel related to shopping (except groceries, food, and gas)	0.13
24.	Animals and pets (not veterinary care)	0.11
25.	Household and personal organization and planning	0.11
26.	Playing games (including computer)	0.11
27.	Attending religious services	0.11
28.	Research, homework	0.10
29.	Travel related to eating and drinking	0.10
30.	Work, other job(s)	0.09
31.	Computer use for leisure (except games)	0.09
32.	Arts and entertainment (except sports)	0.08
33.	Travel related to socializing and communicating	0.08
34.	Household and personal email	0.07
35.	Medical and care services	0.07
36.	Attending or hosting social events	0.07
37.	Travel related to caring for and helping household children	0.07
38.	Travel related to grocery shopping	0.07
39.	Activities related to household children's education	0.06

	average hours per day spent by women aged 45 to 54
40. Helping adults in other households	0.06
41. Interior maintenance, repair, and decoration	0.05
42. Participation in religious practices	0.05
43. Travel related to helping adults in other households	0.05
44. Travel related to purchasing food (except groceries)	0.05
45. Travel related to household activities	0.04
46. Travel related to using medical services	0.04
47. Exterior maintenance, repair, and decoration	0.03
48. Financial management	0.03
49. Household and personal mail and messages (except email)	0.03
50. Taking class	0.03
51. Travel related to religious and spiritual activities	0.03
52. Storing interior household items, including food	0.02
53. Purchasing food (except groceries)	0.02
54. Household services	0.02
55. Listening to the radio	0.02
56. Travel related to helping household adults	0.02
57. Travel related to purchasing gas	0.02
58. Travel related to attending or hosting social events	0.02
59. Travel related to relaxing and leisure	0.02
60. Travel related to sports, exercise, and recreation	0.02
61. Travel related to volunteer activities	0.02
62. Vehicles	0.01
63. Helping household adults	0.01
64. Purchasing gas	0.01
65. Financial services and banking	0.01
66. Listening to or playing music (not radio)	0.01
67. Travel related to personal care	0.01
68. Travel related to caring for and helping children in other households	0.01
69. Travel related to education	0.01
70. Travel related to using financial services and banking	0.01
71. Travel related to arts and entertainment	0.01

Note: Primary activities are those respondents identified as their main activity. Other activities done simultaneously, such as eating while watching TV, are not included. If fewer than 2.0 percent of the total population participated in a primary activity, then the primary activity is not shown.
Source: Bureau of Labor Statistics, unpublished tables from the 2008 American Time Use Survey, Internet site http://www.bls .gov/tus/home.htm; calculations by New Strategist

Table 6.15 Ranking: Percent of Total People Aged 45 to 54 Participating in Primary Activities on an Average Day, 2008

(percent of people aged 45 to 54 participating in primary activities on an average day, ranked by percent participating, 2008)

		percent of people aged 45 to 54 participating in activity
	Total, all activities	**100.0%**
1.	Sleeping	99.8
2.	Eating and drinking	95.9
3.	Television	82.0
4.	Grooming	80.5
5.	Work, main job	56.7
6.	Food and drink preparation	54.9
7.	Travel related to work	47.7
8.	Socializing and communicating	34.4
9.	Interior cleaning	25.0
10.	Kitchen and food clean-up	24.1
11.	Shopping, except groceries, food, and gas	23.7
12.	Travel related to eating and drinking	23.7
13.	Reading for personal interest	23.4
14.	Travel related to shopping (except groceries, food, and gas)	23.2
15.	Relaxing, thinking	21.8
16.	Laundry	20.4
17.	Caring for and helping household children	18.4
18.	Animals and pets (not veterinary care)	18.2
19.	Participating in sports, exercise, or recreation	17.7
20.	Travel related to socializing and communicating	16.8
21.	Household and personal organization and planning	14.5
22.	Grocery shopping	14.3
23.	Telephone calls	14.2
24.	Travel related to grocery shopping	14.2
25.	Lawn, garden, and houseplants	11.9
26.	Travel related to caring for and helping household children	10.4
27.	Purchasing food (except groceries)	10.1
28.	Travel related to purchasing food (except groceries)	9.6
29.	Household and personal email	8.9
30.	Travel related to household activities	8.8
31.	Household and personal mail and messages (except email)	8.2
32.	Computer use for leisure (except games)	7.9
33.	Helping adults in other households	7.8
34.	Volunteer activities	7.5
35.	Travel related to sports, exercise, and recreation	7.5
36.	Health-related self-care	6.9
37.	Travel related to helping adults in other households	6.6
38.	Travel related to relaxing and leisure	6.4
39.	Storing interior household items, including food	5.7

		percent of people aged 45 to 54 participating in activity
40.	Travel related to religious and spiritual activities	5.2%
41.	Caring for and helping children in other households	5.1
42.	Attending religious services	5.0
43.	Playing games (including computer)	4.9
44.	Participation in religious practices	4.9
45.	Purchasing gas	4.8
46.	Travel related to purchasing gas	4.8
47.	Travel related to volunteer activities	4.6
48.	Medical and care services	4.5
49.	Travel related to using medical services	4.3
50.	Financial services and banking	4.2
51.	Activities related to household children's education	4.2
52.	Interior maintenance, repair, and decoration	4.1
53.	Travel related to using financial services and banking	3.9
54.	Financial management	3.6
55.	Work, other job(s)	3.6
56.	Vehicles	3.5
57.	Travel related to helping household adults	3.3
58.	Exterior maintenance, repair, and decoration	2.9
59.	Travel related to caring for and helping children in other households	2.9
60.	Travel related to personal care	2.3
61.	Arts and entertainment (except sports)	2.3
62.	Household services	2.2
63.	Attending or hosting social events	2.2
64.	Travel related to arts and entertainment	2.0
65.	Listening to the radio	1.9
66.	Travel related to attending or hosting social events	1.9
67.	Listening to or playing music (not radio)	1.5
68.	Research, homework	1.3
69.	Taking class	0.7
70.	Travel related to education	0.7
71.	Helping household adults	0.3

Note: Primary activities are those respondents identified as their main activity. Other activities done simultaneously, such as eating while watching TV, are not included. If fewer than 2.0 percent of the total population participated in a primary activity, then the primary activity is not shown.
Source: Bureau of Labor Statistics, unpublished tables from the 2008 American Time Use Survey, Internet site http://www.bls .gov/tus/home.htm; calculations by New Strategist

Table 6.16 **Ranking: Percent of Men Aged 45 to 54 Participating in Primary Activities on an Average Day, 2008**

(percent of men aged 45 to 54 participating in primary activities on an average day, ranked by percent participating, 2008)

		percent of men aged 45 to 54 participating in activity
	Total, all activities	100.0%
1.	Sleeping	99.8
2.	Eating and drinking	96.9
3.	Television	84.3
4.	Grooming	76.9
5.	Work, main job	61.7
6.	Travel related to work	52.2
7.	Food and drink preparation	42.4
8.	Socializing and communicating	29.8
9.	Travel related to eating and drinking	26.8
10.	Relaxing, thinking	23.9
11.	Shopping, except groceries, food, and gas	21.9
12.	Travel related to shopping (except groceries, food, and gas)	21.5
13.	Reading for personal interest	21.2
14.	Participating in sports, exercise, or recreation	19.5
15.	Travel related to socializing and communicating	16.3
16.	Caring for and helping household children	15.8
17.	Interior cleaning	15.5
18.	Animals and pets (not veterinary care)	15.1
19.	Lawn, garden, and houseplants	14.6
20.	Household and personal organization and planning	11.0
21.	Kitchen and food clean-up	10.7
22.	Grocery shopping	10.1
23.	Travel related to grocery shopping	10.1
24.	Purchasing food (except groceries)	9.3
25.	Travel related to caring for and helping household children	9.0
26.	Travel related to sports, exercise, and recreation	8.9
27.	Travel related to purchasing food (except groceries)	8.8
28.	Telephone calls	7.9
29.	Laundry	7.7
30.	Household and personal email	7.0
31.	Travel related to household activities	6.9
32.	Household and personal mail and messages (except email)	6.8
33.	Computer use for leisure (except games)	6.8
34.	Travel related to relaxing and leisure	6.8
35.	Volunteer activities	6.7
36.	Helping adults in other households	6.0
37.	Vehicles	5.7
38.	Purchasing gas	5.5
39.	Travel related to purchasing gas	5.4

	percent of men aged 45 to 54 participating in activity
40. Health-related self-care	5.3%
41. Interior maintenance, repair, and decoration	5.3
42. Travel related to helping adults in other households	5.1
43. Travel related to volunteer activities	4.5
44. Participation in religious practices	4.4
45. Exterior maintenance, repair, and decoration	4.4
46. Travel related to religious and spiritual activities	4.3
47. Work, other job(s)	4.0
48. Attending religious services	3.9
49. Activities related to household children's education	3.5
50. Travel related to personal care	3.5
51. Financial services and banking	3.4
52. Playing games (including computer)	3.3
53. Medical and care services	2.9
54. Travel related to using financial services and banking	2.8
55. Travel related to using medical services	2.8
56. Caring for and helping children in other households	2.7
57. Listening to the radio	2.7
58. Travel related to helping household adults	2.5
59. Storing interior household items, including food	2.4
60. Financial management	2.4
61. Travel related to caring for and helping children in other households	2.2
62. Arts and entertainment (except sports)	1.9
63. Listening to or playing music (not radio)	1.9
64. Travel related to arts and entertainment	1.8
65. Household services	1.7
66. Attending or hosting social events	1.6
67. Travel related to attending or hosting social events	1.3
68. Travel related to education	0.5
69. Taking class	0.4
70. Research, homework	0.4
71. Helping household adults	0.1

Note: Primary activities are those respondents identified as their main activity. Other activities done simultaneously, such as eating while watching TV, are not included. If fewer than 2.0 percent of the total population participated in a primary activity, then the primary activity is not shown.
Source: Bureau of Labor Statistics, unpublished tables from the 2008 American Time Use Survey, Internet site http://www.bls .gov/tus/home.htm; calculations by New Strategist

Table 6.17 **Ranking: Percent of Women Aged 45 to 54 Participating in Primary Activities on an Average Day, 2008**

(percent of women aged 45 to 54 participating in primary activities on an average day, ranked by percent participating, 2008)

		percent of women aged 45 to 54 participating in activity
	Total, all activities	**100.0%**
1.	Sleeping	99.9
2.	Eating and drinking	94.8
3.	Grooming	84.0
4.	Television	79.8
5.	Food and drink preparation	66.9
6.	Work, main job	51.8
7.	Travel related to work	43.4
8.	Socializing and communicating	38.7
9.	Kitchen and food clean-up	36.9
10.	Interior cleaning	34.2
11.	Laundry	32.5
12.	Reading for personal interest	25.5
13.	Shopping, except groceries, food, and gas	25.4
14.	Travel related to shopping (except groceries, food, and gas)	24.9
15.	Animals and pets (not veterinary care)	21.3
16.	Caring for and helping household children	20.8
17.	Travel related to eating and drinking	20.7
18.	Telephone calls	20.3
19.	Relaxing, thinking	19.9
20.	Grocery shopping	18.4
21.	Travel related to grocery shopping	18.1
22.	Household and personal organization and planning	17.8
23.	Travel related to socializing and communicating	17.2
24.	Participating in sports, exercise, or recreation	16.1
25.	Travel related to caring for and helping household children	11.8
26.	Purchasing food (except groceries)	10.9
27.	Household and personal email	10.7
28.	Travel related to household activities	10.5
29.	Travel related to purchasing food (except groceries)	10.5
30.	Helping adults in other households	9.6
31.	Household and personal mail and messages (except email)	9.6
32.	Lawn, garden, and houseplants	9.3
33.	Computer use for leisure (except games)	8.9
34.	Storing interior household items, including food	8.8
35.	Health-related self-care	8.5
36.	Volunteer activities	8.2
37.	Travel related to helping adults in other households	8.0
38.	Caring for and helping children in other households	7.4
39.	Playing games (including computer)	6.5

	percent of women aged 45 to 54 participating in activity
40. Travel related to relaxing and leisure	6.1%
41. Travel related to sports, exercise, and recreation	6.1
42. Medical and care services	6.1
43. Travel related to religious and spiritual activities	6.1
44. Attending religious services	6.0
45. Travel related to using medical services	5.7
46. Participation in religious practices	5.5
47. Financial services and banking	5.0
48. Travel related to using financial services and banking	4.9
49. Financial management	4.8
50. Activities related to household children's education	4.8
51. Travel related to volunteer activities	4.8
52. Travel related to purchasing gas	4.2
53. Purchasing gas	4.2
54. Travel related to helping household adults	4.0
55. Travel related to caring for and helping children in other households	3.5
56. Work, other job(s)	3.2
57. Attending or hosting social events	2.9
58. Interior maintenance, repair, and decoration	2.9
59. Household services	2.8
60. Arts and entertainment (except sports)	2.8
61. Travel related to attending or hosting social events	2.5
62. Travel related to arts and entertainment	2.3
63. Research, homework	2.1
64. Exterior maintenance, repair, and decoration	1.6
65. Vehicles	1.3
66. Travel related to personal care	1.3
67. Listening to the radio	1.1
68. Listening to or playing music (not radio)	1.1
69. Taking class	1.0
70. Travel related to education	0.8
71. Helping household adults	0.5

Note: Primary activities are those respondents identified as their main activity. Other activities done simultaneously, such as eating while watching TV, are not included. If fewer than 2.0 percent of the total population participated in a primary activity, then the primary activity is not shown.
Source: Bureau of Labor Statistics, unpublished tables from the 2008 American Time Use Survey, Internet site http://www.bls .gov/tus/home.htm; calculations by New Strategist

Table 6.18 **Ranking: Average Hours per Day Spent Doing Primary Activities by Total Participants Aged 45 to 54, 2008**

(hours per day spent by participants aged 45 to 54 doing primary activities, ranked by time spent doing activity, 2008)

		average hours per day spent by participants aged 45 to 54
	Total, all activities	**24.00**
1.	Sleeping	8.29
2.	Work, main job	7.73
3.	Work, other job(s)	3.69
4.	Television	3.37
5.	Interior maintenance, repair, and decoration	2.73
6.	Arts and entertainment (except sports)	2.71
7.	Attending or hosting social events	2.65
8.	Volunteer activities	2.30
9.	Attending religious services	1.96
10.	Lawn, garden, and houseplants	1.92
11.	Exterior maintenance, repair, and decoration	1.91
12.	Health-related self-care	1.80
13.	Playing games (including computer)	1.78
14.	Caring for and helping children in other households	1.59
15.	Socializing and communicating	1.52
16.	Vehicles	1.49
17.	Interior cleaning	1.45
18.	Participating in sports, exercise, or recreation	1.40
19.	Caring for and helping household children	1.27
20.	Relaxing, thinking	1.23
21.	Activities related to household children's education	1.21
22.	Medical and care services	1.18
23.	Reading for personal interest	1.16
24.	Computer use for leisure (except games)	1.16
25.	Eating and drinking	1.13
26.	Laundry	1.01
27.	Financial management	0.99
28.	Shopping, except groceries, food, and gas	0.94
29.	Grooming	0.83
30.	Helping adults in other households	0.83
31.	Participation in religious practices	0.80
32.	Food and drink preparation	0.79
33.	Travel related to work	0.74
34.	Grocery shopping	0.73
35.	Telephone calls	0.72
36.	Travel related to using medical services	0.71
37.	Household and personal email	0.63
38.	Household and personal organization and planning	0.61
39.	Travel related to arts and entertainment	0.61

		average hours per day spent by participants aged 45 to 54
40.	Travel related to helping adults in other households	0.60
41.	Travel related to caring for and helping household children	0.57
42.	Travel related to shopping (except groceries, food, and gas)	0.53
43.	Kitchen and food clean-up	0.52
44.	Travel related to sports, exercise, and recreation	0.51
45.	Animals and pets (not veterinary care)	0.49
46.	Travel related to socializing and communicating	0.48
47.	Travel related to eating and drinking	0.45
48.	Travel related to caring for and helping children in other households	0.45
49.	Travel related to grocery shopping	0.44
50.	Travel related to household activities	0.43
51.	Travel related to volunteer activities	0.43
52.	Travel related to purchasing gas	0.42
53.	Travel related to purchasing food (except groceries)	0.41
54.	Travel related to religious and spiritual activities	0.40
55.	Travel related to relaxing and leisure	0.39
56.	Household and personal mail and messages (except email)	0.34
57.	Helping household adults	0.29
58.	Storing interior household items, including food	0.26
59.	Travel related to using financial services and banking	0.26
60.	Financial services and banking	0.18
61.	Purchasing gas	0.16
62.	Purchasing food (except groceries)	0.15

Note: Primary activities are those respondents identified as their main activity. Other activities done simultaneously, such as eating while watching TV, are not included. The primary activities shown are those for which data by age are available.
Source: Bureau of Labor Statistics, unpublished tables from the 2008 American Time Use Survey, Internet site http://www.bls.gov/tus/home.htm; calculations by New Strategist

Table 6.19 Ranking: Average Hours per Day Spent Doing Primary Activities by Male Participants Aged 45 to 54, 2008

(hours per day spent by male participants aged 45 to 54 doing primary activities, ranked by time spent doing activity, 2008)

		average hours per day spent by male participants aged 45 to 54
	Total, all activities	**24.00**
1.	Sleeping	8.17
2.	Work, main job	8.16
3.	Television	3.67
4.	Volunteer activities	2.82
5.	Attending religious services	2.20
6.	Lawn, garden, and houseplants	2.15
7.	Participating in sports, exercise, or recreation	1.63
8.	Socializing and communicating	1.54
9.	Caring for and helping household children	1.39
10.	Computer use for leisure (except games)	1.30
11.	Helping adults in other households	1.22
12.	Relaxing, thinking	1.19
13.	Eating and drinking	1.18
14.	Reading for personal interest	1.11
15.	Interior cleaning	1.05
16.	Laundry	1.01
17.	Travel related to work	0.83
18.	Shopping, except groceries, food, and gas	0.76
19.	Grooming	0.72
20.	Household and personal email	0.66
21.	Food and drink preparation	0.64
22.	Travel related to sports, exercise, and recreation	0.64
23.	Grocery shopping	0.57
24.	Travel related to household activities	0.57
25.	Household and personal organization and planning	0.56
26.	Travel related to caring for and helping household children	0.56
27.	Travel related to shopping (except groceries, food, and gas)	0.55
28.	Travel related to grocery shopping	0.52
29.	Telephone calls	0.51
30.	Travel related to socializing and communicating	0.49
31.	Animals and pets (not veterinary care)	0.49
32.	Kitchen and food clean-up	0.47
33.	Travel related to eating and drinking	0.43
34.	Travel related to relaxing and leisure	0.40
35.	Travel related to purchasing gas	0.36
36.	Travel related to religious and spiritual activities	0.36
37.	Travel related to purchasing food (except groceries)	0.34
38.	Purchasing food (except groceries)	0.16
39.	Purchasing gas	0.16

Note: Primary activities are those respondents identified as their main activity. Other activities done simultaneously, such as eating while watching TV, are not included. The primary activities shown are those for which data by age are available.
Source: Bureau of Labor Statistics, unpublished tables from the 2008 American Time Use Survey, Internet site http://www.bls .gov/tus/home.htm; calculations by New Strategist

Table 6.20 Ranking: Average Hours per Day Spent Doing Primary Activities by Female Participants Aged 45 to 54, 2008

(hours per day spent by female participants aged 45 to 54 doing primary activities, ranked by time spent doing activity, 2008)

		average hours per day spent by female participants aged 45 to 54
	Total, all activities	**24.00**
1.	Sleeping	8.40
2.	Work, main job	7.24
3.	Television	3.06
4.	Health-related self-care	2.17
5.	Volunteer activities	1.88
6.	Caring for and helping children in other households	1.84
7.	Attending religious services	1.82
8.	Playing games (including computer)	1.74
9.	Interior cleaning	1.62
10.	Lawn, garden, and houseplants	1.56
11.	Socializing and communicating	1.50
12.	Relaxing, thinking	1.27
13.	Activities related to household children's education	1.23
14.	Reading for personal interest	1.20
15.	Caring for and helping household children	1.18
16.	Participating in sports, exercise, or recreation	1.12
17.	Shopping, except groceries, food, and gas	1.08
18.	Eating and drinking	1.07
19.	Computer use for leisure (except games)	1.06
20.	Laundry	1.01
21.	Grooming	0.93
22.	Food and drink preparation	0.88
23.	Participation in religious practices	0.88
24.	Grocery shopping	0.81
25.	Telephone calls	0.80
26.	Household and personal organization and planning	0.64
27.	Travel related to work	0.63
28.	Household and personal email	0.62
29.	Travel related to helping adults in other households	0.62
30.	Helping adults in other households	0.59
31.	Travel related to caring for and helping household children	0.57
32.	Kitchen and food clean-up	0.53
33.	Travel related to shopping (except groceries, food, and gas)	0.52
34.	Animals and pets (not veterinary care)	0.50
35.	Travel related to eating and drinking	0.47
36.	Travel related to socializing and communicating	0.47
37.	Travel related to purchasing food (except groceries)	0.47
38.	Travel related to volunteer activities	0.44
39.	Travel related to religious and spiritual activities	0.43

	average hours per day spent by female participants aged 45 to 54
40. Travel related to grocery shopping	0.39
41. Travel related to relaxing and leisure	0.37
42. Travel related to household activities	0.34
43. Travel related to sports, exercise, and recreation	0.33
44. Household and personal mail and messages (except email)	0.30
45. Storing interior household items, including food	0.26
46. Purchasing food (except groceries)	0.15

Note: Primary activities are those respondents identified as their main activity. Other activities done simultaneously, such as eating while watching TV, are not included. The primary activities shown are those for which data by age are available.
Source: Bureau of Labor Statistics, unpublished tables from the 2008 American Time Use Survey, Internet site http://www.bls .gov/tus/home.htm; calculations by New Strategist

7

Time Use, 2008: People Aged 55 to 64

People aged 55-to-64 are a diverse group. Some are already retired and enjoying more leisure time. Others are still in the workforce. Because many 55-to-64-year-olds do not work, television is the single most time-consuming activity for the average person in the age group (after sleep), with 3.27 hours a day devoted to watching television as the primary activity. Working at a main job as the primary activity consumes only 3.13 hours on an average day. The age group devotes less time to work than any of the younger age groups except teenagers. Only 44 percent of men aged 55 to 64 work at a main job on an average day. Among women the figure is 38 percent.

The increased amount of leisure time available to many people aged 55 to 64 can be seen in the time use statistics. The age group spends significantly more time than younger adults watching television. Reading for personal interest is the sixth most time-consuming activity for 55-to-64-year-olds (excluding sleep). Taking care of the lawn is in ninth place.

Caring for children in other households becomes an important activity in this age group as people become grandparents. On an average day, a substantial 8 percent of 55-to-64-year-olds care for children in other households. Pet care is even more important than helping out with grandchildren. Twenty percent of people aged 55 to 64 take care of pets as a primary activity on an average day, a larger proportion than in any other age group.

Leisure activities are increasingly important to 55-to-64-year-olds

(average hours per day spent by people aged 55 to 64 doing primary activities, for the 10 activities on which the average 55-to-64-year-old spends the most time, excluding sleep, 2008)

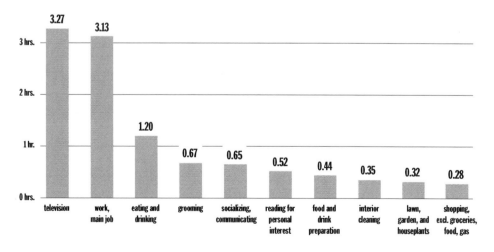

Having more free time, many 55-to-64-year-olds spend it doing housework. Although most are childfree, this age group is just as likely to clean the house on an average day as younger adults with children at home. In fact, cleaning the house ranks eighth among activities on which this age group devotes the most time (excluding sleep). Cooking ranks seventh. Talking to family members on the phone becomes an increasingly important activity as people age. Among 55-to-64-year-olds, a substantial 11 percent talk to family members on the phone during an average day as a primary activity. Among women, the proportion is 16 percent.

In the empty-nest households of most 55-to-64-year-olds, sex roles remain as sharply divided as they are in younger age groups with children in the home. Women overwhelmingly do the cooking, cleaning, and laundry. They are also much more likely than men to care for children in other households (their grandchildren) on an average day (11 versus 5 percent). Men are more likely than women to take care of the lawn (16 versus 12 percent).

Table 7.1 Time Use by Total People Aged 55 to 64, 2008

(number and percent of total people aged 55 to 64 participating in primary activities on an average day, hours spent doing activity by the average person aged 55 to 64 and by those aged 55 to 64 who participated in the activity, 2008; numbers of participants in thousands)

	participants aged 55 to 64		time spent doing activity (hours)	
	number	percent	average person aged 55 to 64	participants aged 55 to 64
TOTAL, ALL ACTIVITIES	**33,492**	**100.0%**	**24.00**	**24.00**
Personal care	**33,458**	**99.9**	**9.03**	**9.04**
Sleeping	33,400	99.7	8.26	8.28
Sleeplessness	1,940	5.8	0.08	1.31
Grooming	25,757	76.9	0.67	0.87
Health-related self-care	2,669	8.0	0.09	1.13
Household activities	**26,915**	**80.4**	**2.14**	**2.66**
Housework	13,068	39.0	0.61	1.55
Interior cleaning	8,683	25.9	0.35	1.36
Laundry	6,127	18.3	0.19	1.04
Storing interior household items, including food	2,362	7.1	0.03	0.46
Food and drink preparation, presentation, and clean-up	19,520	58.3	0.59	1.01
Food and drink preparation	18,379	54.9	0.44	0.81
Kitchen and food clean-up	8,140	24.3	0.14	0.58
Interior maintenance, repair, and decoration	1,205	3.6	0.09	2.50
Interior arrangement, decoration, and repairs	913	2.7	0.08	–
Exterior maintenance, repair, and decoration	1,265	3.8	0.08	2.14
Lawn, garden, and houseplants	4,656	13.9	0.32	2.29
Animals and pets (not veterinary care)	6,631	19.8	0.13	0.66
Walking, exercising, and playing with pets	2,705	8.1	0.06	0.68
Vehicles	831	2.5	0.04	–
Household management	10,326	30.8	0.26	0.85
Financial management	1,908	5.7	0.05	0.81
Household and personal organization and planning	4,425	13.2	0.12	0.91
Household and personal mail and messages (except email)	2,994	8.9	0.03	0.31
Household and personal email	3,371	10.1	0.06	0.61
Caring for and helping household members	**3,814**	**11.4**	**0.16**	**1.41**
Caring for and helping household children	1,694	5.1	0.06	1.20
Physical care for household children	1,048	3.1	0.02	0.80
Reading to or with household children	49	0.1	0.00	–
Playing with household children (except sports)	201	0.6	0.01	–
Talking with, listening to household children	360	1.1	0.01	–
Looking after household children as a primary activity	307	0.9	0.01	–
Picking up or dropping off household children	804	2.4	0.00	–
Activities related to household children's education	287	0.9	0.01	–
Helping household children with homework	256	0.8	0.01	–
Helping household adults	1,292	3.9	0.02	–
Caring for and helping people in other households	**5,257**	**15.7**	**0.32**	**2.02**
Caring for and helping children in other households	2,666	8.0	0.20	2.51

	participants aged 55 to 64		time spent doing activity (hours)	
	number	percent	average person aged 55 to 64	participants aged 55 to 64
Helping adults in other households	2,637	7.9%	0.09	1.10
Picking up or dropping off adults in other households	1,514	4.5	0.01	0.15
Work and work-related activities	**14,868**	**44.4**	**3.28**	**7.38**
Work, main job	14,165	42.3	3.13	7.39
Work, other job(s)	962	2.9	0.10	–
Education	**320**	**1.0**	**0.02**	–
Taking class	182	0.5	0.02	–
Taking class for degree, certification, or licensure	82	0.2	0.01	–
Research, homework	150	0.4	0.01	
Consumer purchases (store, telephone, Internet)	**13,917**	**41.6**	**0.42**	**1.00**
Grocery shopping	4,825	14.4	0.11	0.76
Purchasing gas	1,538	4.6	0.01	0.18
Purchasing food (except groceries)	3,708	11.1	0.02	0.18
Shopping, except groceries, food, and gas	8,154	24.3	0.28	1.14
Professional and personal care services	**3,632**	**10.8**	**0.12**	**1.09**
Financial services and banking	1,398	4.2	0.01	–
Banking	1,343	4.0	0.01	–
Medical and care services	1,577	4.7	0.08	1.64
Using health and care services outside the home	1,477	4.4	0.06	–
Household services	**604**	**1.8**	**0.01**	–
Eating and drinking	**32,183**	**96.1**	**1.20**	**1.25**
Socializing, relaxing, and leisure	**32,167**	**96.0**	**5.22**	**5.43**
Socializing and communicating	13,170	39.3	0.65	1.66
Attending or hosting social events	604	1.8	0.05	–
Relaxing and leisure	31,254	93.3	4.45	4.76
Relaxing, thinking	7,465	22.3	0.28	1.27
Television	28,111	83.9	3.27	3.89
Listening to the radio	596	1.8	0.03	–
Listening to or playing music (not radio)	598	1.8	0.02	–
Playing games (including computer)	2,504	7.5	0.13	1.73
Computer use for leisure (except games)	2,533	7.6	0.10	1.35
Reading for personal interest	11,622	34.7	0.52	1.51
Arts and entertainment (except sports)	901	2.7	0.06	–
Sports, exercise, and recreation	**5,653**	**16.9**	**0.25**	**1.46**
Participating in sports, exercise, or recreation	5,528	16.5	0.23	1.42
Using cardiovascular equipment	665	2.0	0.02	–
Walking	2,067	6.2	0.05	0.85
Working out, unspecified	1,081	3.2	0.03	–
Religious and spiritual activities	**3,727**	**11.1**	**0.17**	**1.52**
Attending religious services	1,977	5.9	0.10	1.62
Participation in religious practices	1,946	5.8	0.06	1.02

	participants aged 55 to 64		time spent doing activity (hours)	
	number	percent	average person aged 55 to 64	participants aged 55 to 64
Volunteer activities	**2,761**	**8.2%**	**0.19**	**2.28**
Administrative and support activities	986	2.9	0.05	–
Telephone calls	**5,787**	**17.3**	**0.12**	**0.68**
Telephone calls to or from family members	3,690	11.0	0.06	0.59
Telephone calls to or from friends, neighbors, or acquaintances	1,552	4.6	0.03	0.55
Traveling	**28,136**	**84.0**	**1.17**	**1.39**
Travel related to personal care	891	2.7	0.02	–
Travel related to household activities	3,478	10.4	0.04	0.38
Travel related to household management	2,081	6.2	0.02	–
Travel related to caring for and helping household members	1,777	5.3	0.03	0.66
Travel related to caring for and helping household children	942	2.8	0.01	–
Travel related to helping household adults	750	2.2	0.02	–
Travel related to caring for and helping people in other households	3,989	11.9	0.08	0.67
Travel related to caring for and helping children in other households	1,507	4.5	0.02	0.49
Travel related to helping adults in other households	2,399	7.2	0.05	0.72
Travel related to work	11,796	35.2	0.26	0.74
Travel related to education	182	0.5	0.01	–
Travel related to taking class	88	0.3	0.00	–
Travel related to consumer purchases	13,554	40.5	0.27	0.66
Travel related to grocery shopping	4,766	14.2	0.05	0.38
Travel related to purchasing gas	1,538	4.6	0.03	0.58
Travel related to purchasing food (except groceries)	3,494	10.4	0.04	0.36
Travel related to shopping (except groceries, food, and gas)	7,908	23.6	0.15	0.63
Travel related to using professional and personal care services	3,319	9.9	0.05	0.46
Travel related to using financial services and banking	1,283	3.8	0.01	–
Travel related to using medical services	1,452	4.3	0.02	–
Travel related to eating and drinking	8,757	26.1	0.14	0.53
Travel related to socializing, relaxing, and leisure	8,737	26.1	0.17	0.67
Travel related to socializing and communicating	5,951	17.8	0.09	0.53
Travel related to attending or hosting social events	475	1.4	0.01	–
Travel related to relaxing and leisure	2,415	7.2	0.03	0.42
Travel related to arts and entertainment	660	2.0	0.01	–
Travel related to sports, exercise, and recreation	2,171	6.5	0.02	0.38
Travel related to participating in sports, exercise, recreation	2,054	6.1	0.02	0.36
Travel related to religious and spiritual activities	2,060	6.2	0.03	0.42
Travel related to volunteer activities	1,621	4.8	0.03	0.53

Note: Primary activities are those respondents identified as their main activity. Other activities done simultaneously, such as eating while watching TV, are not included. Numbers may not add to total because not all subcategories are shown. If fewer than 2.0 percent of the total population participated in a primary activity, then the primary activity is not shown. "–" means sample is too small to make a reliable estimate.

Source: Bureau of Labor Statistics, unpublished tables from the 2008 American Time Use Survey, Internet site http://www.bls .gov/tus/home.htm; calculations by New Strategist

Table 7.2 Time Use by Men Aged 55 to 64, 2008

(number and percent of men aged 55 to 64 participating in primary activities on an average day, hours spent doing activity by the average man aged 55 to 64 and by men aged 55 to 64 who participated in the activity, 2008; numbers of participants in thousands)

	men aged 55 to 64 participating		time spent doing activity (hours)	
	number	percent	average man aged 55 to 64	male participants aged 55 to 64
TOTAL, ALL ACTIVITIES	**16,132**	**100.0%**	**24.00**	**24.00**
Personal care	**16,124**	**100.0**	**8.91**	**8.92**
Sleeping	16,124	100.0	8.24	8.24
Sleeplessness	845	5.2	0.06	–
Grooming	11,681	72.4	0.57	0.79
Health-related self-care	1,170	7.3	0.10	1.38
Household activities	**11,281**	**69.9**	**1.67**	**2.39**
Housework	3,625	22.5	0.26	1.17
Interior cleaning	2,415	15.0	0.17	1.16
Laundry	933	5.8	0.06	0.97
Storing interior household items, including food	871	5.4	0.03	–
Food and drink preparation, presentation, and clean-up	6,895	42.7	0.34	0.80
Food and drink preparation	6,476	40.1	0.28	0.70
Kitchen and food clean-up	1,697	10.5	0.06	0.60
Interior maintenance, repair, and decoration	703	4.4	0.11	–
Interior arrangement, decoration, and repairs	468	2.9	0.08	–
Exterior maintenance, repair, and decoration	809	5.0	0.12	–
Lawn, garden, and houseplants	2,515	15.6	0.42	2.66
Animals and pets (not veterinary care)	2,288	14.2	0.10	0.73
Walking, exercising, and playing with pets	1,131	7.0	0.06	–
Vehicles	677	4.2	0.08	–
Household management	4,046	25.1	0.21	0.82
Financial management	703	4.4	0.03	–
Household and personal organization and planning	1,576	9.8	0.10	0.98
Household and personal mail and messages (except email)	1,220	7.6	0.02	0.29
Household and personal email	1,291	8.0	0.05	0.68
Caring for and helping household members	**1,552**	**9.6**	**0.11**	**1.13**
Caring for and helping household children	630	3.9	0.06	–
Physical care for household children	367	2.3	0.02	–
Reading to or with household children	15	0.1	0.00	–
Playing with household children (except sports)	98	0.6	0.01	–
Talking with, listening to household children	75	0.5	0.00	–
Looking after household children as a primary activity	116	0.7	0.02	–
Picking up or dropping off household children	287	1.8	0.00	–
Activities related to household children's education	95	0.6	0.01	–
Helping household children with homework	95	0.6	0.01	–
Helping household adults	709	4.4	0.02	–
Caring for and helping people in other households	**1,996**	**12.4**	**0.23**	**1.84**
Caring for and helping children in other households	757	4.7	0.09	–

	men aged 55 to 64 participating		time spent doing activity (hours)	
	number	percent	average man aged 55 to 64	male participants aged 55 to 64
Helping adults in other households	1,264	7.8%	0.13	1.61
Picking up or dropping off adults in other households	596	3.7	0.01	–
Work and work-related activities	**7,839**	**48.6**	**3.81**	**7.85**
Work, main job	7,495	46.5	3.64	7.84
Work, other job(s)	376	2.3	0.09	–
Education	**51**	**0.3**	**0.01**	–
Taking class	7	0.0	0.00	–
Taking class for degree, certification, or licensure	7	0.0	0.00	–
Research, homework	44	0.3	0.01	–
Consumer purchases (store, telephone, Internet)	**5,677**	**35.2**	**0.29**	**0.83**
Grocery shopping	1,698	10.5	0.07	0.68
Purchasing gas	788	4.9	0.01	–
Purchasing food (except groceries)	1,767	11.0	0.02	0.17
Shopping, except groceries, food, and gas	3,108	19.3	0.19	0.99
Professional and personal care services	**1,429**	**8.9**	**0.10**	–
Financial services and banking	585	3.6	0.01	–
Banking	529	3.3	0.01	–
Medical and care services	652	4.0	0.08	–
Using health and care services outside the home	602	3.7	0.07	–
Household services	**316**	**2.0**	**0.01**	–
Eating and drinking	**15,584**	**96.6**	**1.24**	**1.29**
Socializing, relaxing, and leisure	**15,606**	**96.7**	**5.63**	**5.82**
Socializing and communicating	5,608	34.8	0.56	1.61
Attending or hosting social events	299	1.9	0.04	–
Relaxing and leisure	15,233	94.4	4.96	5.25
Relaxing, thinking	3,655	22.7	0.31	1.38
Television	13,951	86.5	3.81	4.40
Listening to the radio	348	2.2	0.04	–
Listening to or playing music (not radio)	262	1.6	0.03	–
Playing games (including computer)	796	4.9	0.08	–
Computer use for leisure (except games)	1,361	8.4	0.13	1.49
Reading for personal interest	5,194	32.2	0.48	1.48
Arts and entertainment (except sports)	460	2.9	0.07	–
Sports, exercise, and recreation	**3,239**	**20.1**	**0.33**	**1.65**
Participating in sports, exercise, or recreation	3,138	19.5	0.31	1.57
Using cardiovascular equipment	448	2.8	0.02	–
Walking	1,126	7.0	0.06	–
Working out, unspecified	673	4.2	0.04	–
Religious and spiritual activities	**1,342**	**8.3**	**0.11**	**1.36**
Attending religious services	722	4.5	0.07	–
Participation in religious practices	728	4.5	0.04	–

	men aged 55 to 64 participating		time spent doing activity (hours)	
	number	percent	average man aged 55 to 64	male participants aged 55 to 64
Volunteer activities	**985**	**6.1%**	**0.16**	–
Administrative and support activities	408	2.5	0.04	–
Telephone calls	**1,626**	**10.1**	**0.05**	**0.47**
Telephone calls to or from family members	883	5.5	0.02	–
Telephone calls to or from friends, neighbors, or acquaintances	332	2.1	0.01	–
Traveling	**13,461**	**83.4**	**1.16**	**1.39**
Travel related to personal care	571	3.5	0.03	–
Travel related to household activities	1,423	8.8	0.03	0.39
Travel related to household management	887	5.5	0.02	–
Travel related to caring for and helping household members	816	5.1	0.04	–
Travel related to caring for and helping household children	351	2.2	0.01	–
Travel related to helping household adults	425	2.6	0.03	–
Travel related to caring for and helping people in other households	1,551	9.6	0.07	0.71
Travel related to caring for and helping children in other households	303	1.9	0.01	–
Travel related to helping adults in other households	1,188	7.4	0.06	–
Travel related to work	6,506	40.3	0.33	0.83
Travel related to education	7	0.0	0.00	–
Travel related to taking class	7	0.0	0.00	–
Travel related to consumer purchases	5,566	34.5	0.22	0.63
Travel related to grocery shopping	1,677	10.4	0.04	0.42
Travel related to purchasing gas	788	4.9	0.03	–
Travel related to purchasing food (except groceries)	1,702	10.6	0.04	0.38
Travel related to shopping (except groceries, food, and gas)	3,008	18.6	0.10	0.55
Travel related to using professional and personal care services	1,253	7.8	0.04	–
Travel related to using financial services and banking	585	3.6	0.01	–
Travel related to using medical services	568	3.5	0.02	–
Travel related to eating and drinking	4,403	27.3	0.13	0.47
Travel related to socializing, relaxing, and leisure	3,912	24.2	0.17	0.69
Travel related to socializing and communicating	2,375	14.7	0.08	0.52
Travel related to attending or hosting social events	210	1.3	0.01	–
Travel related to relaxing and leisure	1,184	7.3	0.04	0.52
Travel related to arts and entertainment	388	2.4	0.02	–
Travel related to sports, exercise, and recreation	1,204	7.5	0.03	0.34
Travel related to participating in sports, exercise, recreation	1,117	6.9	0.02	–
Travel related to religious and spiritual activities	715	4.4	0.02	–
Travel related to volunteer activities	688	4.3	0.03	–

Note: Primary activities are those respondents identified as their main activity. Other activities done simultaneously, such as eating while watching TV, are not included. Numbers may not add to total because not all subcategories are shown. If fewer than 2.0 percent of the total population participated in a primary activity, then the primary activity is not shown. "–" means sample is too small to make a reliable estimate.
Source: Bureau of Labor Statistics, unpublished tables from the 2008 American Time Use Survey, Internet site http://www.bls .gov/tus/home.htm; calculations by New Strategist

Table 7.3 Time Use by Women Aged 55 to 64, 2008

(number and percent of women aged 55 to 64 participating in primary activities on an average day, hours spent doing activity by the average woman aged 55 to 64 and by women aged 55 to 64 who participated in the activity, 2008; numbers of participants in thousands)

	women aged 55 to 64 participating		time spent doing activity (hours)	
	number	percent	average woman aged 55 to 64	female participants aged 55 to 64
TOTAL, ALL ACTIVITIES	**17,360**	**100.0%**	**24.00**	**24.00**
Personal care	**17,334**	**99.9**	**9.14**	**9.15**
Sleeping	17,316	99.7	8.29	8.31
Sleeplessness	1,095	6.3	0.09	1.41
Grooming	14,077	81.1	0.76	0.93
Health-related self-care	1,499	8.6	0.08	0.94
Household activities	**15,634**	**90.1**	**2.58**	**2.86**
Housework	9,443	54.4	0.93	1.70
Interior cleaning	6,268	36.1	0.52	1.44
Laundry	5,194	29.9	0.31	1.05
Storing interior household items, including food	1,491	8.6	0.03	0.39
Food and drink preparation, presentation, and clean-up	12,626	72.7	0.82	1.13
Food and drink preparation	11,904	68.6	0.60	0.87
Kitchen and food clean-up	6,444	37.1	0.21	0.58
Interior maintenance, repair, and decoration	502	2.9	0.07	–
Interior arrangement, decoration, and repairs	444	2.6	0.07	–
Exterior maintenance, repair, and decoration	456	2.6	0.05	–
Lawn, garden, and houseplants	2,140	12.3	0.23	1.86
Animals and pets (not veterinary care)	4,343	25.0	0.15	0.62
Walking, exercising, and playing with pets	1,574	9.1	0.06	0.61
Vehicles	154	0.9	0.01	–
Household management	6,279	36.2	0.31	0.86
Financial management	1,204	6.9	0.06	–
Household and personal organization and planning	2,848	16.4	0.14	0.87
Household and personal mail and messages (except email)	1,774	10.2	0.03	0.33
Household and personal email	2,080	12.0	0.07	0.57
Caring for and helping household members	**2,262**	**13.0**	**0.21**	**1.60**
Caring for and helping household children	1,064	6.1	0.06	1.06
Physical care for household children	681	3.9	0.03	–
Reading to or with household children	34	0.2	0.00	–
Playing with household children (except sports)	103	0.6	0.01	–
Talking with, listening to household children	286	1.6	0.01	–
Looking after household children as a primary activity	191	1.1	0.01	–
Picking up or dropping off household children	517	3.0	0.00	–
Activities related to household children's education	192	1.1	0.02	–
Helping household children with homework	160	0.9	0.01	–
Helping household adults	583	3.4	0.01	–
Caring for and helping people in other households	**3,261**	**18.8**	**0.40**	**2.13**
Caring for and helping children in other households	1,909	11.0	0.30	2.77

	women aged 55 to 64 participating		time spent doing activity (hours)	
	number	percent	average woman aged 55 to 64	female participants aged 55 to 64
Helping adults in other households	1,373	7.9%	0.05	0.63
Picking up or dropping off adults in other households	918	5.3	0.01	–
Work and work-related activities	**7,029**	**40.5**	**2.78**	**6.86**
Work, main job	6,670	38.4	2.65	6.89
Work, other job(s)	586	3.4	0.10	–
Education	**269**	**1.5**	**0.04**	**–**
Taking class	175	1.0	0.03	–
Taking class for degree, certification, or licensure	75	0.4	0.01	–
Research, homework	106	0.6	0.01	–
Consumer purchases (store, telephone, Internet)	**8,241**	**47.5**	**0.53**	**1.13**
Grocery shopping	3,126	18.0	0.15	0.81
Purchasing gas	750	4.3	0.01	–
Purchasing food (except groceries)	1,940	11.2	0.02	0.19
Shopping, except groceries, food, and gas	5,047	29.1	0.36	1.23
Professional and personal care services	**2,204**	**12.7**	**0.13**	**1.03**
Financial services and banking	813	4.7	0.01	–
Banking	813	4.7	0.01	–
Medical and care services	924	5.3	0.07	–
Using health and care services outside the home	875	5.0	0.06	–
Household services	**288**	**1.7**	**0.01**	**–**
Eating and drinking	**16,600**	**95.6**	**1.16**	**1.21**
Socializing, relaxing, and leisure	**16,561**	**95.4**	**4.83**	**5.07**
Socializing and communicating	7,562	43.6	0.74	1.70
Attending or hosting social events	305	1.8	0.06	–
Relaxing and leisure	16,021	92.3	3.97	4.30
Relaxing, thinking	3,811	22.0	0.25	1.16
Television	14,160	81.6	2.76	3.39
Listening to the radio	248	1.4	0.02	–
Listening to or playing music (not radio)	337	1.9	0.02	–
Playing games (including computer)	1,708	9.8	0.17	1.77
Computer use for leisure (except games)	1,172	6.8	0.08	1.19
Reading for personal interest	6,429	37.0	0.57	1.53
Arts and entertainment (except sports)	441	2.5	0.06	–
Sports, exercise, and recreation	**2,414**	**13.9**	**0.17**	**1.21**
Participating in sports, exercise, or recreation	2,390	13.8	0.17	1.21
Using cardiovascular equipment	216	1.2	0.01	–
Walking	940	5.4	0.05	–
Working out, unspecified	407	2.3	0.02	–
Religious and spiritual activities	**2,385**	**13.7**	**0.22**	**1.61**
Attending religious services	1,255	7.2	0.12	1.71
Participation in religious practices	1,218	7.0	0.08	1.10

	women aged 55 to 64 participating		time spent doing activity (hours)	
	number	percent	average woman aged 55 to 64	female participants aged 55 to 64
Volunteer activities	**1,776**	**10.2%**	**0.21**	**2.08**
Administrative and support activities	578	3.3	0.05	–
Telephone calls	**4,160**	**24.0**	**0.18**	**0.76**
Telephone calls to or from family members	2,806	16.2	0.10	0.63
Telephone calls to or from friends, neighbors, or acquaintances	1,220	7.0	0.04	0.60
Traveling	**14,676**	**84.5**	**1.18**	**1.39**
Travel related to personal care	320	1.8	0.01	–
Travel related to household activities	2,055	11.8	0.04	0.37
Travel related to household management	1,195	6.9	0.02	–
Travel related to caring for and helping household members	961	5.5	0.03	–
Travel related to caring for and helping household children	591	3.4	0.02	–
Travel related to helping household adults	325	1.9	0.01	–
Travel related to caring for and helping people in other households	2,438	14.0	0.09	0.64
Travel related to caring for and helping children in other households	1,204	6.9	0.03	–
Travel related to helping adults in other households	1,211	7.0	0.05	0.70
Travel related to work	5,290	30.5	0.19	0.63
Travel related to education	175	1.0	0.01	–
Travel related to taking class	81	0.5	0.00	–
Travel related to consumer purchases	7,989	46.0	0.31	0.68
Travel related to grocery shopping	3,089	17.8	0.06	0.35
Travel related to purchasing gas	750	4.3	0.02	–
Travel related to purchasing food (except groceries)	1,792	10.3	0.03	0.34
Travel related to shopping (except groceries, food, and gas)	4,900	28.2	0.19	0.67
Travel related to using professional and personal care services	2,066	11.9	0.05	0.42
Travel related to using financial services and banking	698	4.0	0.01	–
Travel related to using medical services	885	5.1	0.02	–
Travel related to eating and drinking	4,654	26.8	0.15	0.58
Travel related to socializing, relaxing, and leisure	4,824	27.8	0.18	0.65
Travel related to socializing and communicating	3,576	20.6	0.11	0.53
Travel related to attending or hosting social events	266	1.5	0.01	–
Travel related to relaxing and leisure	1,231	7.1	0.02	0.32
Travel related to arts and entertainment	271	1.6	0.01	–
Travel related to sports, exercise, and recreation	967	5.6	0.02	–
Travel related to participating in sports, exercise, recreation	937	5.4	0.02	–
Travel related to religious and spiritual activities	1,345	7.7	0.03	0.39
Travel related to volunteer activities	933	5.4	0.02	–

Note: Primary activities are those respondents identified as their main activity. Other activities done simultaneously, such as eating while watching TV, are not included. Numbers may not add to total because not all subcategories are shown. If fewer than 2.0 percent of the total population participated in a primary activity, then the primary activity is not shown. "–" means sample is too small to make a reliable estimate.
Source: Bureau of Labor Statistics, unpublished tables from the 2008 American Time Use Survey, Internet site http://www.bls .gov/tus/home.htm; calculations by New Strategist

Table 7.4 Indexed Time Use of Total People Aged 55 to 64, 2008

(hours spent doing primary activities on an average day by people aged 55 to 64 and by total people aged 15 or older, and index of time spent by people aged 55 to 64 to total people, 2008)

	average hours		index, people aged 55 to 64 to total people
	people aged 55 to 64	total people	
TOTAL, ALL ACTIVITIES	**24.00**	**24.00**	**100**
Personal care	**9.03**	**9.38**	**96**
Sleeping	8.26	8.60	96
Sleeplessness	0.08	0.06	133
Grooming	0.67	0.67	100
Health-related self-care	0.09	0.09	100
Household activities	**2.14**	**1.77**	**121**
Housework	0.61	0.58	105
Interior cleaning	0.35	0.37	95
Laundry	0.19	0.17	112
Storing interior household items, including food	0.03	0.02	150
Food and drink preparation, presentation, and clean-up	0.59	0.52	113
Food and drink preparation	0.44	0.40	110
Kitchen and food clean-up	0.14	0.12	117
Interior maintenance, repair, and decoration	0.09	0.07	129
Interior arrangement, decoration, and repairs	0.08	0.05	160
Exterior maintenance, repair, and decoration	0.08	0.06	133
Lawn, garden, and houseplants	0.32	0.19	168
Animals and pets (not veterinary care)	0.13	0.09	144
Walking, exercising, and playing with pets	0.06	0.04	150
Vehicles	0.04	0.04	100
Household management	0.26	0.21	124
Financial management	0.05	0.03	167
Household and personal organization and planning	0.12	0.09	133
Household and personal mail and messages (except email)	0.03	0.02	150
Household and personal email	0.06	0.06	100
Caring for and helping household members	**0.16**	**0.45**	**36**
Caring for and helping household children	0.06	0.37	16
Physical care for household children	0.02	0.17	12
Reading to or with household children	0.00	0.01	0
Playing with household children (except sports)	0.01	0.09	11
Talking with, listening to household children	0.01	0.02	50
Looking after household children as a primary activity	0.01	0.03	33
Picking up or dropping off household children	0.00	0.02	0
Activities related to household children's education	0.01	0.04	25
Helping household children with homework	0.01	0.03	33
Helping household adults	0.02	0.01	200
Caring for and helping people in other households	**0.32**	**0.16**	**200**
Caring for and helping children in other households	0.20	0.09	222

	average hours		index, people aged 55 to 64 to total people
	people aged 55 to 64	total people	
Helping adults in other households	0.09	0.06	150
Picking up or dropping off adults in other households	0.01	0.01	100
Work and work-related activities	**3.28**	**3.45**	**95**
Work, main job	3.13	3.28	95
Work, other job(s)	0.10	0.09	111
Education	**0.02**	**0.44**	**5**
Taking class	0.02	0.27	7
Taking class for degree, certification, or licensure	0.01	0.26	4
Research, homework	0.01	0.16	6
Consumer purchases (store, telephone, Internet)	**0.42**	**0.38**	**111**
Grocery shopping	0.11	0.10	110
Purchasing gas	0.01	0.01	100
Purchasing food (except groceries)	0.02	0.02	100
Shopping, except groceries, food, and gas	0.28	0.25	112
Professional and personal care services	**0.12**	**0.08**	**150**
Financial services and banking	0.01	0.01	100
Banking	0.01	0.01	100
Medical and care services	0.08	0.05	160
Using health and care services outside the home	0.06	0.04	150
Household services	**0.01**	**0.01**	**100**
Eating and drinking	**1.20**	**1.11**	**108**
Socializing, relaxing, and leisure	**5.22**	**4.62**	**113**
Socializing and communicating	0.65	0.64	102
Attending or hosting social events	0.05	0.07	71
Relaxing and leisure	4.45	3.83	116
Relaxing, thinking	0.28	0.27	104
Television	3.27	2.77	118
Listening to the radio	0.03	0.03	100
Listening to or playing music (not radio)	0.02	0.03	67
Playing games (including computer)	0.13	0.20	65
Computer use for leisure (except games)	0.10	0.14	71
Reading for personal interest	0.52	0.34	153
Arts and entertainment (except sports)	0.06	0.09	67
Sports, exercise, and recreation	**0.25**	**0.33**	**76**
Participating in sports, exercise, or recreation	0.23	0.29	79
Using cardiovascular equipment	0.02	0.02	100
Walking	0.05	0.04	125
Working out, unspecified	0.03	0.03	100
Religious and spiritual activities	**0.17**	**0.14**	**121**
Attending religious services	0.10	0.09	111
Participation in religious practices	0.06	0.04	150

	average hours		index, people aged 55 to 64
	people aged 55 to 64	total people	to total people
Volunteer activities	**0.19**	**0.15**	**127**
Administrative and support activities	0.05	0.04	125
Telephone calls	**0.12**	**0.13**	**92**
Telephone calls to or from family members	0.06	0.04	150
Telephone calls to or from friends, neighbors, or acquaintances	0.03	0.04	75
Traveling	**1.17**	**1.20**	**98**
Travel related to personal care	0.02	0.01	200
Travel related to household activities	0.04	0.04	100
Travel related to household management	0.02	0.02	100
Travel related to caring for and helping household members	0.03	0.08	38
Travel related to caring for and helping household children	0.01	0.06	17
Travel related to helping household adults	0.02	0.02	100
Travel related to caring for and helping people in other households	0.08	0.06	133
Travel related to caring for and helping children in other households	0.02	0.02	100
Travel related to helping adults in other households	0.05	0.04	125
Travel related to work	0.26	0.28	93
Travel related to education	0.01	0.03	33
Travel related to taking class	0.00	0.03	0
Travel related to consumer purchases	0.27	0.24	113
Travel related to grocery shopping	0.05	0.05	100
Travel related to purchasing gas	0.03	0.02	150
Travel related to purchasing food (except groceries)	0.04	0.04	100
Travel related to shopping (except groceries, food, and gas)	0.15	0.12	125
Travel related to using professional and personal care services	0.05	0.04	125
Travel related to using financial services and banking	0.01	0.01	100
Travel related to using medical services	0.02	0.02	100
Travel related to eating and drinking	0.14	0.12	117
Travel related to socializing, relaxing, and leisure	0.17	0.18	94
Travel related to socializing and communicating	0.09	0.09	100
Travel related to attending or hosting social events	0.01	0.01	100
Travel related to relaxing and leisure	0.03	0.04	75
Travel related to arts and entertainment	0.01	0.02	50
Travel related to sports, exercise, and recreation	0.02	0.04	50
Travel related to participating in sports, exercise, recreation	0.02	0.04	50
Travel related to religious and spiritual activities	0.03	0.02	150
Travel related to volunteer activities	0.03	0.02	150

Note: The index is calculated by dividing average time spent by people in the age group doing primary activity by average time spent by total people doing primary activity and multiplying by 100. Primary activities are those respondents identified as their main activity. Other activities done simultaneously, such as eating while watching TV, are not included. Numbers may not add to total because not all subcategories are shown. If fewer than 2.0 percent of the total population participated in a primary activity, then the primary activity is not shown.
Source: Bureau of Labor Statistics, unpublished tables from the 2008 American Time Use Survey, Internet site http://www.bls .gov/tus/home.htm; calculations by New Strategist

Table 7.5 Indexed Time Use of Men Aged 55 to 64, 2008

(hours spent doing primary activities on an average day by men aged 55 to 64 and by total men aged 15 or older, and index of time spent by men aged 55 to 64 to total men, 2008)

	average hours		index, men aged 55 to 64
	men aged 55 to 64	total men	to total men
TOTAL, ALL ACTIVITIES	**24.00**	**24.00**	**100**
Personal care	**8.91**	**9.21**	**97**
Sleeping	8.24	8.56	96
Sleeplessness	0.06	0.05	120
Grooming	0.57	0.56	102
Health-related self-care	0.10	0.07	143
Household activities	**1.67**	**1.32**	**127**
Housework	0.26	0.24	108
Interior cleaning	0.17	0.17	100
Laundry	0.06	0.06	100
Storing interior household items, including food	0.03	0.01	300
Food and drink preparation, presentation, and clean-up	0.34	0.30	113
Food and drink preparation	0.28	0.25	112
Kitchen and food clean-up	0.06	0.05	120
Interior maintenance, repair, and decoration	0.11	0.10	110
Interior arrangement, decoration, and repairs	0.08	0.08	100
Exterior maintenance, repair, and decoration	0.12	0.08	150
Lawn, garden, and houseplants	0.42	0.26	162
Animals and pets (not veterinary care)	0.10	0.08	125
Walking, exercising, and playing with pets	0.06	0.04	150
Vehicles	0.08	0.07	114
Household management	0.21	0.16	131
Financial management	0.03	0.03	100
Household and personal organization and planning	0.10	0.07	143
Household and personal mail and messages (except email)	0.02	0.02	100
Household and personal email	0.05	0.05	100
Caring for and helping household members	**0.11**	**0.30**	**37**
Caring for and helping household children	0.06	0.25	24
Physical care for household children	0.02	0.09	22
Reading to or with household children	0.00	0.01	0
Playing with household children (except sports)	0.01	0.08	13
Talking with, listening to household children	0.00	0.01	0
Looking after household children as a primary activity	0.02	0.02	100
Picking up or dropping off household children	0.00	0.01	0
Activities related to household children's education	0.01	0.02	50
Helping household children with homework	0.01	0.02	50
Helping household adults	0.02	0.01	200
Caring for and helping people in other households	**0.23**	**0.13**	**177**
Caring for and helping children in other households	0.09	0.05	180

	average hours		index, men aged 55 to 64 to total men
	men aged 55 to 64	total men	
Helping adults in other households	0.13	0.07	186
Picking up or dropping off adults in other households	0.01	0.01	100
Work and work-related activities	**3.81**	**4.16**	**92**
Work, main job	3.64	3.96	92
Work, other job(s)	0.09	0.10	90
Education	**0.01**	**0.39**	**3**
Taking class	0.00	0.27	0
Taking class for degree, certification, or licensure	0.00	0.27	0
Research, homework	0.01	0.12	8
Consumer purchases (store, telephone, Internet)	**0.29**	**0.28**	**104**
Grocery shopping	0.07	0.06	117
Purchasing gas	0.01	0.01	100
Purchasing food (except groceries)	0.02	0.02	100
Shopping, except groceries, food, and gas	0.19	0.19	100
Professional and personal care services	**0.10**	**0.06**	**167**
Financial services and banking	0.01	0.01	100
Banking	0.01	0.00	–
Medical and care services	0.08	0.04	200
Using health and care services outside the home	0.07	0.03	233
Household services	**0.01**	**0.01**	**100**
Eating and drinking	**1.24**	**1.15**	**108**
Socializing, relaxing, and leisure	**5.63**	**4.83**	**117**
Socializing and communicating	0.56	0.59	95
Attending or hosting social events	0.04	0.06	67
Relaxing and leisure	4.96	4.09	121
Relaxing, thinking	0.31	0.27	115
Television	3.81	3.01	127
Listening to the radio	0.04	0.03	133
Listening to or playing music (not radio)	0.03	0.04	75
Playing games (including computer)	0.08	0.25	32
Computer use for leisure (except games)	0.13	0.15	87
Reading for personal interest	0.48	0.29	166
Arts and entertainment (except sports)	0.07	0.09	78
Sports, exercise, and recreation	**0.33**	**0.44**	**75**
Participating in sports, exercise, or recreation	0.31	0.40	78
Using cardiovascular equipment	0.02	0.01	200
Walking	0.06	0.04	150
Working out, unspecified	0.04	0.04	100
Religious and spiritual activities	**0.11**	**0.12**	**92**
Attending religious services	0.07	0.07	100
Participation in religious practices	0.04	0.03	133

	average hours		index, men aged 55 to 64 to total men
	men aged 55 to 64	total men	
Volunteer activities	**0.16**	**0.14**	**114**
Administrative and support activities	0.04	0.03	133
Telephone calls	**0.05**	**0.07**	**71**
Telephone calls to or from family members	0.02	0.02	100
Telephone calls to or from friends, neighbors, or acquaintances	0.01	0.02	50
Traveling	**1.16**	**1.23**	**94**
Travel related to personal care	0.03	0.01	300
Travel related to household activities	0.03	0.04	75
Travel related to household management	0.02	0.03	67
Travel related to caring for and helping household members	0.04	0.06	67
Travel related to caring for and helping household children	0.01	0.04	25
Travel related to helping household adults	0.03	0.02	150
Travel related to caring for and helping people in other households	0.07	0.06	117
Travel related to caring for and helping children in other households	0.01	0.01	100
Travel related to helping adults in other households	0.06	0.04	150
Travel related to work	0.33	0.36	92
Travel related to education	0.00	0.03	0
Travel related to taking class	0.00	0.02	0
Travel related to consumer purchases	0.22	0.21	105
Travel related to grocery shopping	0.04	0.04	100
Travel related to purchasing gas	0.03	0.02	150
Travel related to purchasing food (except groceries)	0.04	0.04	100
Travel related to shopping (except groceries, food, and gas)	0.10	0.11	91
Travel related to using professional and personal care services	0.04	0.03	133
Travel related to using financial services and banking	0.01	0.01	100
Travel related to using medical services	0.02	0.01	200
Travel related to eating and drinking	0.13	0.13	100
Travel related to socializing, relaxing, and leisure	0.17	0.18	94
Travel related to socializing and communicating	0.08	0.09	89
Travel related to attending or hosting social events	0.01	0.01	100
Travel related to relaxing and leisure	0.04	0.04	100
Travel related to arts and entertainment	0.02	0.02	100
Travel related to sports, exercise, and recreation	0.03	0.06	50
Travel related to participating in sports, exercise, recreation	0.02	0.05	40
Travel related to religious and spiritual activities	0.02	0.02	100
Travel related to volunteer activities	0.03	0.02	150

Note: The index is calculated by dividing average time spent by men in the age group doing primary activity by average time spent by total men doing primary activity and multiplying by 100. Primary activities are those respondents identified as their main activity. Other activities done simultaneously, such as eating while watching TV, are not included. Numbers may not add to total because not all subcategories are shown. If fewer than 2.0 percent of the total population participated in a primary activity, then the primary activity is not shown. "–" means denominator is zero.
Source: Bureau of Labor Statistics, unpublished tables from the 2008 American Time Use Survey, Internet site http://www.bls .gov/tus/home.htm; calculations by New Strategist

Table 7.6 Indexed Time Use of Women Aged 55 to 64, 2008

(hours spent doing primary activities on an average day by women aged 55 to 64 and by total women aged 15 or older, and index of time spent by women aged 55 to 64 to total women, 2008)

	average hours		index, women aged 55 to 64 to total women
	women aged 55 to 64	total women	
TOTAL, ALL ACTIVITIES	**24.00**	**24.00**	**100**
Personal care	**9.14**	**9.54**	**96**
Sleeping	8.29	8.64	96
Sleeplessness	0.09	0.07	129
Grooming	0.76	0.78	97
Health-related self-care	0.08	0.11	73
Household activities	**2.58**	**2.19**	**118**
Housework	0.93	0.90	103
Interior cleaning	0.52	0.55	95
Laundry	0.31	0.28	111
Storing interior household items, including food	0.03	0.02	150
Food and drink preparation, presentation, and clean-up	0.82	0.73	112
Food and drink preparation	0.60	0.55	109
Kitchen and food clean-up	0.21	0.18	117
Interior maintenance, repair, and decoration	0.07	0.04	175
Interior arrangement, decoration, and repairs	0.07	0.03	233
Exterior maintenance, repair, and decoration	0.05	0.03	167
Lawn, garden, and houseplants	0.23	0.12	192
Animals and pets (not veterinary care)	0.15	0.10	150
Walking, exercising, and playing with pets	0.06	0.04	150
Vehicles	0.01	0.01	100
Household management	0.31	0.25	124
Financial management	0.06	0.04	150
Household and personal organization and planning	0.14	0.11	127
Household and personal mail and messages (except email)	0.03	0.03	100
Household and personal email	0.07	0.07	100
Caring for and helping household members	**0.21**	**0.59**	**36**
Caring for and helping household children	0.06	0.48	13
Physical care for household children	0.03	0.24	13
Reading to or with household children	0.00	0.02	0
Playing with household children (except sports)	0.01	0.09	11
Talking with, listening to household children	0.01	0.02	50
Looking after household children as a primary activity	0.01	0.03	33
Picking up or dropping off household children	0.00	0.03	0
Activities related to household children's education	0.02	0.05	40
Helping household children with homework	0.01	0.04	25
Helping household adults	0.01	0.01	100
Caring for and helping people in other households	**0.40**	**0.20**	**200**
Caring for and helping children in other households	0.30	0.12	250

	average hours		index, women aged 55 to 64 to total women
	women aged 55 to 64	total women	
Helping adults in other households	0.05	0.05	100
Picking up or dropping off adults in other households	0.01	0.01	100
Work and work-related activities	**2.78**	**2.79**	**100**
Work, main job	2.65	2.63	101
Work, other job(s)	0.10	0.09	111
Education	**0.04**	**0.48**	**8**
Taking class	0.03	0.27	11
Taking class for degree, certification, or licensure	0.01	0.25	4
Research, homework	0.01	0.20	5
Consumer purchases (store, telephone, Internet)	**0.53**	**0.48**	**110**
Grocery shopping	0.15	0.13	115
Purchasing gas	0.01	0.01	100
Purchasing food (except groceries)	0.02	0.02	100
Shopping, except groceries, food, and gas	0.36	0.31	116
Professional and personal care services	**0.13**	**0.11**	**118**
Financial services and banking	0.01	0.01	100
Banking	0.01	0.01	100
Medical and care services	0.07	0.06	117
Using health and care services outside the home	0.06	0.05	120
Household services	**0.01**	**0.01**	**100**
Eating and drinking	**1.16**	**1.07**	**108**
Socializing, relaxing, and leisure	**4.83**	**4.42**	**109**
Socializing and communicating	0.74	0.68	109
Attending or hosting social events	0.06	0.08	75
Relaxing and leisure	3.97	3.58	111
Relaxing, thinking	0.25	0.26	96
Television	2.76	2.54	109
Listening to the radio	0.02	0.02	100
Listening to or playing music (not radio)	0.02	0.02	100
Playing games (including computer)	0.17	0.15	113
Computer use for leisure (except games)	0.08	0.14	57
Reading for personal interest	0.57	0.40	143
Arts and entertainment (except sports)	0.06	0.08	75
Sports, exercise, and recreation	**0.17**	**0.23**	**74**
Participating in sports, exercise, or recreation	0.17	0.20	85
Using cardiovascular equipment	0.01	0.02	50
Walking	0.05	0.04	125
Working out, unspecified	0.02	0.02	100
Religious and spiritual activities	**0.22**	**0.17**	**129**
Attending religious services	0.12	0.10	120
Participation in religious practices	0.08	0.05	160

	average hours		index, women aged 55 to 64 to total women
	women aged 55 to 64	total women	
Volunteer activities	**0.21**	**0.16**	**131**
Administrative and support activities	0.05	0.04	125
Telephone calls	**0.18**	**0.18**	**100**
Telephone calls to or from family members	0.10	0.07	143
Telephone calls to or from friends, neighbors, or acquaintances	0.04	0.06	67
Traveling	**1.18**	**1.17**	**101**
Travel related to personal care	0.01	0.01	100
Travel related to household activities	0.04	0.04	100
Travel related to household management	0.02	0.02	100
Travel related to caring for and helping household members	0.03	0.11	27
Travel related to caring for and helping household children	0.02	0.08	25
Travel related to helping household adults	0.01	0.02	50
Travel related to caring for and helping people in other households	0.09	0.07	129
Travel related to caring for and helping children in other households	0.03	0.02	150
Travel related to helping adults in other households	0.05	0.04	125
Travel related to work	0.19	0.20	95
Travel related to education	0.01	0.04	25
Travel related to taking class	0.00	0.03	0
Travel related to consumer purchases	0.31	0.27	115
Travel related to grocery shopping	0.06	0.06	100
Travel related to purchasing gas	0.02	0.02	100
Travel related to purchasing food (except groceries)	0.03	0.04	75
Travel related to shopping (except groceries, food, and gas)	0.19	0.14	136
Travel related to using professional and personal care services	0.05	0.05	100
Travel related to using financial services and banking	0.01	0.01	100
Travel related to using medical services	0.02	0.02	100
Travel related to eating and drinking	0.15	0.11	136
Travel related to socializing, relaxing, and leisure	0.18	0.17	106
Travel related to socializing and communicating	0.11	0.10	110
Travel related to attending or hosting social events	0.01	0.01	100
Travel related to relaxing and leisure	0.02	0.03	67
Travel related to arts and entertainment	0.01	0.02	50
Travel related to sports, exercise, and recreation	0.02	0.03	67
Travel related to participating in sports, exercise, recreation	0.02	0.03	67
Travel related to religious and spiritual activities	0.03	0.02	150
Travel related to volunteer activities	0.02	0.02	100

Note: The index is calculated by dividing average time spent by women in the age group doing primary activity by average time spent by total women doing primary activity and multiplying by 100. Primary activities are those respondents identified as their main activity. Other activities done simultaneously, such as eating while watching TV, are not included. Numbers may not add to total because not all subcategories are shown. If fewer than 2.0 percent of the total population participated in a primary activity, then the primary activity is not shown.

Source: Bureau of Labor Statistics, unpublished tables from the 2008 American Time Use Survey, Internet site http://www.bls.gov/tus/home.htm; calculations by New Strategist

Table 7.7 Indexed Time Use on of People Aged 55 to 64 by Sex, 2008

(average hours spent by people aged 55 to 64 doing primary activities on an average day by sex, and index of women's time to men's, 2008)

	average hours, aged 55 to 64		index of women to men
	men	women	
TOTAL, ALL ACTIVITIES	**24.00**	**24.00**	**100**
Personal care	**8.91**	**9.14**	**103**
Sleeping	8.24	8.29	101
Sleeplessness	0.06	0.09	150
Grooming	0.57	0.76	133
Health-related self-care	0.10	0.08	80
Household activities	**1.67**	**2.58**	**154**
Housework	0.26	0.93	358
Interior cleaning	0.17	0.52	306
Laundry	0.06	0.31	517
Storing interior household items, including food	0.03	0.03	100
Food and drink preparation, presentation, and clean-up	0.34	0.82	241
Food and drink preparation	0.28	0.60	214
Kitchen and food clean-up	0.06	0.21	350
Interior maintenance, repair, and decoration	0.11	0.07	64
Interior arrangement, decoration, and repairs	0.08	0.07	88
Exterior maintenance, repair, and decoration	0.12	0.05	42
Lawn, garden, and houseplants	0.42	0.23	55
Animals and pets (not veterinary care)	0.10	0.15	150
Walking, exercising, and playing with pets	0.06	0.06	100
Vehicles	0.08	0.01	13
Household management	0.21	0.31	148
Financial management	0.03	0.06	200
Household and personal organization and planning	0.10	0.14	140
Household and personal mail and messages (except email)	0.02	0.03	150
Household and personal email	0.05	0.07	140
Caring for and helping household members	**0.11**	**0.21**	**191**
Caring for and helping household children	0.06	0.06	100
Physical care for household children	0.02	0.03	150
Reading to or with household children	0.00	0.00	–
Playing with household children (except sports)	0.01	0.01	100
Talking with, listening to household children	0.00	0.01	–
Looking after household children as a primary activity	0.02	0.01	50
Picking up or dropping off household children	0.00	0.00	–
Activities related to household children's education	0.01	0.02	200
Helping household children with homework	0.01	0.01	100
Helping household adults	0.02	0.01	50
Caring for and helping people in other households	**0.23**	**0.40**	**174**
Caring for and helping children in other households	0.09	0.30	333

	average hours, aged 55 to 64		index of women to men
	men	women	
Helping adults in other households	0.13	0.05	38
Picking up or dropping off adults in other households	0.01	0.01	100
Work and work-related activities	**3.81**	**2.78**	**73**
Work, main job	3.64	2.65	73
Work, other job(s)	0.09	0.10	111
Education	**0.01**	**0.04**	**400**
Taking class	0.00	0.03	–
Taking class for degree, certification, or licensure	0.00	0.01	–
Research, homework	0.01	0.01	100
Consumer purchases (store, telephone, Internet)	**0.29**	**0.53**	**183**
Grocery shopping	0.07	0.15	214
Purchasing gas	0.01	0.01	100
Purchasing food (except groceries)	0.02	0.02	100
Shopping, except groceries, food, and gas	0.19	0.36	189
Professional and personal care services	**0.10**	**0.13**	**130**
Financial services and banking	0.01	0.01	100
Banking	0.01	0.01	100
Medical and care services	0.08	0.07	88
Using health and care services outside the home	0.07	0.06	86
Household services	**0.01**	**0.01**	**100**
Eating and drinking	**1.24**	**1.16**	**94**
Socializing, relaxing, and leisure	**5.63**	**4.83**	**86**
Socializing and communicating	0.56	0.74	132
Attending or hosting social events	0.04	0.06	150
Relaxing and leisure	4.96	3.97	80
Relaxing, thinking	0.31	0.25	81
Television	3.81	2.76	72
Listening to the radio	0.04	0.02	50
Listening to or playing music (not radio)	0.03	0.02	67
Playing games (including computer)	0.08	0.17	213
Computer use for leisure (except games)	0.13	0.08	62
Reading for personal interest	0.48	0.57	119
Arts and entertainment (except sports)	0.07	0.06	86
Sports, exercise, and recreation	**0.33**	**0.17**	**52**
Participating in sports, exercise, or recreation	0.31	0.17	55
Using cardiovascular equipment	0.02	0.01	50
Walking	0.06	0.05	83
Working out, unspecified	0.04	0.02	50
Religious and spiritual activities	**0.11**	**0.22**	**200**
Attending religious services	0.07	0.12	171
Participation in religious practices	0.04	0.08	200

	average hours, aged 55 to 64		index of women to men
	men	women	
Volunteer activities	0.16	0.21	131
Administrative and support activities	0.04	0.05	125
Telephone calls	0.05	0.18	360
Telephone calls to or from family members	0.02	0.10	500
Telephone calls to or from friends, neighbors, or acquaintances	0.01	0.04	400
Traveling	1.16	1.18	102
Travel related to personal care	0.03	0.01	33
Travel related to household activities	0.03	0.04	133
Travel related to household management	0.02	0.02	100
Travel related to caring for and helping household members	0.04	0.03	75
Travel related to caring for and helping household children	0.01	0.02	200
Travel related to helping household adults	0.03	0.01	33
Travel related to caring for and helping people in other households	0.07	0.09	129
Travel related to caring for and helping children in other households	0.01	0.03	300
Travel related to helping adults in other households	0.06	0.05	83
Travel related to work	0.33	0.19	58
Travel related to education	0.00	0.01	–
Travel related to taking class	0.00	0.00	–
Travel related to consumer purchases	0.22	0.31	141
Travel related to grocery shopping	0.04	0.06	150
Travel related to purchasing gas	0.03	0.02	67
Travel related to purchasing food (except groceries)	0.04	0.03	75
Travel related to shopping (except groceries, food, and gas)	0.10	0.19	190
Travel related to using professional and personal care services	0.04	0.05	125
Travel related to using financial services and banking	0.01	0.01	100
Travel related to using medical services	0.02	0.02	100
Travel related to eating and drinking	0.13	0.15	115
Travel related to socializing, relaxing, and leisure	0.17	0.18	106
Travel related to socializing and communicating	0.08	0.11	138
Travel related to attending or hosting social events	0.01	0.01	100
Travel related to relaxing and leisure	0.04	0.02	50
Travel related to arts and entertainment	0.02	0.01	50
Travel related to sports, exercise, and recreation	0.03	0.02	67
Travel related to participating in sports, exercise, recreation	0.02	0.02	100
Travel related to religious and spiritual activities	0.02	0.03	150
Travel related to volunteer activities	0.03	0.02	67

Note: The index is calculated by dividing women's time by men's time and multiplying by 100. Primary activities are those respondents identified as their main activity. Other activities done simultaneously, such as eating while watching TV, are not included. Numbers may not add to total because not all subcategories are shown. If fewer than 2.0 percent of the total population participated in a primary activity, then the primary activity is not shown. "–" means denominator is zero.
Source: Bureau of Labor Statistics, unpublished tables from the 2008 American Time Use Survey, Internet site http://www.bls.gov/tus/home.htm; calculations by New Strategist

Table 7.8 Indexed Participation in Primary Activities by Total People Aged 55 to 64, 2008

(percent of people aged 55 to 64 and total people aged 15 or older participating in primary activities on an average day, and index of participation by people aged 55 to 64 to total people, 2008)

	percent participating		index, people aged 55 to 64 to total
	people aged 55 to 64	total people	
TOTAL, ALL ACTIVITIES	**100.0%**	**100.0%**	**100**
Personal care	**99.9**	**100.0**	**100**
Sleeping	99.7	99.9	100
Sleeplessness	5.8	5.2	111
Grooming	76.9	79.3	97
Health-related self-care	8.0	6.4	125
Household activities	**80.4**	**75.5**	**106**
Housework	39.0	35.5	110
Interior cleaning	25.9	24.5	106
Laundry	18.3	16.2	113
Storing interior household items, including food	7.1	5.0	141
Food and drink preparation, presentation, and clean-up	58.3	52.3	111
Food and drink preparation	54.9	49.3	111
Kitchen and food clean-up	24.3	20.8	117
Interior maintenance, repair, and decoration	3.6	3.0	119
Interior arrangement, decoration, and repairs	2.7	2.0	138
Exterior maintenance, repair, and decoration	3.8	2.7	138
Lawn, garden, and houseplants	13.9	9.4	148
Animals and pets (not veterinary care)	19.8	14.5	136
Walking, exercising, and playing with pets	8.1	5.8	140
Vehicles	2.5	2.7	92
Household management	30.8	29.0	106
Financial management	5.7	4.0	141
Household and personal organization and planning	13.2	14.1	94
Household and personal mail and messages (except email)	8.9	6.9	130
Household and personal email	10.1	9.4	107
Caring for and helping household members	**11.4**	**26.1**	**44**
Caring for and helping household children	5.1	21.9	23
Physical care for household children	3.1	15.7	20
Reading to or with household children	0.1	2.6	6
Playing with household children (except sports)	0.6	5.4	11
Talking with, listening to household children	1.1	3.0	35
Looking after household children as a primary activity	0.9	2.3	40
Picking up or dropping off household children	2.4	9.2	26
Activities related to household children's education	0.9	3.8	22
Helping household children with homework	0.8	3.4	22
Helping household adults	3.9	3.6	106
Caring for and helping people in other households	**15.7**	**13.3**	**118**
Caring for and helping children in other households	8.0	5.6	143

	percent participating		index, people aged 55 to 64 to total
	people aged 55 to 64	total people	
Helping adults in other households	7.9%	8.0%	98
Picking up or dropping off adults in other households	4.5	5.0	91
Work and work-related activities	**44.4**	**46.6**	**95**
Work, main job	42.3	43.9	96
Work, other job(s)	2.9	2.4	121
Education	**1.0**	**7.9**	**12**
Taking class	0.5	5.2	10
Taking class for degree, certification, or licensure	0.2	4.8	5
Research, homework	0.4	5.8	8
Consumer purchases (store, telephone, Internet)	**41.6**	**40.7**	**102**
Grocery shopping	14.4	12.9	112
Purchasing gas	4.6	4.0	116
Purchasing food (except groceries)	11.1	12.0	92
Shopping, except groceries, food, and gas	24.3	23.5	104
Professional and personal care services	**10.8**	**8.9**	**122**
Financial services and banking	4.2	3.2	129
Banking	4.0	3.0	133
Medical and care services	4.7	3.6	130
Using health and care services outside the home	4.4	3.4	128
Household services	**1.8**	**2.1**	**86**
Eating and drinking	**96.1**	**96.0**	**100**
Socializing, relaxing, and leisure	**96.0**	**95.4**	**101**
Socializing and communicating	39.3	37.6	105
Attending or hosting social events	1.8	2.3	78
Relaxing and leisure	93.3	91.3	102
Relaxing, thinking	22.3	19.9	112
Television	83.9	80.9	104
Listening to the radio	1.8	2.0	88
Listening to or playing music (not radio)	1.8	2.6	68
Playing games (including computer)	7.5	9.0	83
Computer use for leisure (except games)	7.6	9.5	80
Reading for personal interest	34.7	23.9	145
Arts and entertainment (except sports)	2.7	3.2	83
Sports, exercise, and recreation	**16.9**	**18.9**	**89**
Participating in sports, exercise, or recreation	16.5	17.9	92
Using cardiovascular equipment	2.0	2.2	91
Walking	6.2	4.8	128
Working out, unspecified	3.2	3.2	101
Religious and spiritual activities	**11.1**	**9.2**	**121**
Attending religious services	5.9	4.9	121
Participation in religious practices	5.8	4.6	127

	percent participating		index, people aged 55 to 64
	people aged 55 to 64	total people	to total
Volunteer activities	**8.2%**	**6.7%**	**123**
Administrative and support activities	2.9	2.5	116
Telephone calls	**17.3**	**15.4**	**112**
Telephone calls to or from family members	11.0	7.3	150
Telephone calls to or from friends, neighbors, or acquaintances	4.6	5.6	83
Traveling	**84.0**	**86.9**	**97**
Travel related to personal care	2.7	2.5	105
Travel related to household activities	10.4	9.4	111
Travel related to household management	6.2	6.1	102
Travel related to caring for and helping household members	5.3	13.6	39
Travel related to caring for and helping household children	2.8	11.0	26
Travel related to helping household adults	2.2	2.6	88
Travel related to caring for and helping people in other households	11.9	10.5	114
Travel related to caring for and helping children in other households	4.5	3.5	128
Travel related to helping adults in other households	7.2	7.1	101
Travel related to work	35.2	38.2	92
Travel related to education	0.5	5.0	11
Travel related to taking class	0.3	4.4	6
Travel related to consumer purchases	40.5	39.6	102
Travel related to grocery shopping	14.2	12.9	110
Travel related to purchasing gas	4.6	3.9	117
Travel related to purchasing food (except groceries)	10.4	11.2	93
Travel related to shopping (except groceries, food, and gas)	23.6	22.7	104
Travel related to using professional and personal care services	9.9	8.1	122
Travel related to using financial services and banking	3.8	3.0	126
Travel related to using medical services	4.3	3.3	131
Travel related to eating and drinking	26.1	25.0	105
Travel related to socializing, relaxing, and leisure	26.1	28.6	91
Travel related to socializing and communicating	17.8	18.6	96
Travel related to attending or hosting social events	1.4	2.0	71
Travel related to relaxing and leisure	7.2	8.9	81
Travel related to arts and entertainment	2.0	2.6	76
Travel related to sports, exercise, and recreation	6.5	9.6	68
Travel related to participating in sports, exercise, recreation	6.1	8.6	72
Travel related to religious and spiritual activities	6.2	5.1	120
Travel related to volunteer activities	4.8	4.3	113

Note: The index is calculated by dividing percent of people in the age group doing primary activity by percent of total people doing primary activity and multiplying by 100. Primary activities are those respondents identified as their main activity. Other activities done simultaneously, such as eating while watching TV, are not included. If fewer than 2.0 percent of the total population participated in a primary activity, then the primary activity is not shown.
Source: Bureau of Labor Statistics, unpublished tables from the 2008 American Time Use Survey, Internet site http://www.bls .gov/tus/home.htm; calculations by New Strategist

Table 7.9 Indexed Participation in Primary Activities by Men Aged 55 to 64, 2008

(percent of men aged 55 to 64 and total men aged 15 or older participating in primary activities on an average day, and index of participation by men aged 55 to 64 to total men, 2008)

	percent participating		index, men aged 55 to 64 to total men
	men aged 55 to 64	total men	
TOTAL, ALL ACTIVITIES	**100.0%**	**100.0%**	**100**
Personal care	**100.0**	**100.0**	**100**
Sleeping	100.0	99.9	100
Sleeplessness	5.2	4.5	116
Grooming	72.4	76.6	94
Health-related self-care	7.3	4.8	151
Household activities	**69.9**	**66.6**	**105**
Housework	22.5	19.7	114
Interior cleaning	15.0	13.5	111
Laundry	5.8	6.3	92
Storing interior household items, including food	5.4	2.9	188
Food and drink preparation, presentation, and clean-up	42.7	38.4	111
Food and drink preparation	40.1	36.0	111
Kitchen and food clean-up	10.5	9.5	111
Interior maintenance, repair, and decoration	4.4	3.9	111
Interior arrangement, decoration, and repairs	2.9	2.4	119
Exterior maintenance, repair, and decoration	5.0	3.8	132
Lawn, garden, and houseplants	15.6	11.0	142
Animals and pets (not veterinary care)	14.2	12.1	117
Walking, exercising, and playing with pets	7.0	5.2	134
Vehicles	4.2	4.5	93
Household management	25.1	24.0	105
Financial management	4.4	3.2	137
Household and personal organization and planning	9.8	11.1	88
Household and personal mail and messages (except email)	7.6	5.5	138
Household and personal email	8.0	7.4	108
Caring for and helping household members	**9.6**	**20.7**	**46**
Caring for and helping household children	3.9	16.8	23
Physical care for household children	2.3	10.4	22
Reading to or with household children	0.1	1.7	5
Playing with household children (except sports)	0.6	4.7	13
Talking with, listening to household children	0.5	1.7	27
Looking after household children as a primary activity	0.7	1.5	49
Picking up or dropping off household children	1.8	6.2	29
Activities related to household children's education	0.6	2.2	27
Helping household children with homework	0.6	2.0	29
Helping household adults	4.4	3.5	126
Caring for and helping people in other households	**12.4**	**11.0**	**113**
Caring for and helping children in other households	4.7	3.6	129

	percent participating		index, men aged 55 to 64 to total men
	men aged 55 to 64	total men	
Helping adults in other households	7.8%	7.5%	105
Picking up or dropping off adults in other households	3.7	4.4	83
Work and work-related activities	**48.6**	**53.4**	**91**
Work, main job	46.5	50.1	93
Work, other job(s)	2.3	2.3	101
Education	**0.3**	**6.9**	**5**
Taking class	0.0	5.0	1
Taking class for degree, certification, or licensure	0.0	4.8	1
Research, homework	0.3	4.6	6
Consumer purchases (store, telephone, Internet)	**35.2**	**35.6**	**99**
Grocery shopping	10.5	9.6	110
Purchasing gas	4.9	4.3	114
Purchasing food (except groceries)	11.0	11.8	93
Shopping, except groceries, food, and gas	19.3	19.6	98
Professional and personal care services	**8.9**	**6.7**	**133**
Financial services and banking	3.6	3.1	116
Banking	3.3	2.8	118
Medical and care services	4.0	2.4	166
Using health and care services outside the home	3.7	2.3	163
Household services	**2.0**	**2.1**	**93**
Eating and drinking	**96.6**	**96.5**	**100**
Socializing, relaxing, and leisure	**96.7**	**95.4**	**101**
Socializing and communicating	34.8	34.9	100
Attending or hosting social events	1.9	2.0	94
Relaxing and leisure	94.4	92.1	103
Relaxing, thinking	22.7	20.4	111
Television	86.5	82.3	105
Listening to the radio	2.2	2.5	85
Listening to or playing music (not radio)	1.6	3.3	50
Playing games (including computer)	4.9	9.6	52
Computer use for leisure (except games)	8.4	9.5	89
Reading for personal interest	32.2	21.1	153
Arts and entertainment (except sports)	2.9	3.3	86
Sports, exercise, and recreation	**20.1**	**22.0**	**91**
Participating in sports, exercise, or recreation	19.5	21.0	92
Using cardiovascular equipment	2.8	1.8	150
Walking	7.0	4.9	142
Working out, unspecified	4.2	3.5	118
Religious and spiritual activities	**8.3**	**7.7**	**108**
Attending religious services	4.5	4.0	112
Participation in religious practices	4.5	3.7	122

	percent participating		index, men aged 55 to 64 to total men
	men aged 55 to 64	total men	
Volunteer activities	**6.1%**	**5.7%**	**106**
Administrative and support activities	2.5	1.9	130
Telephone calls	**10.1**	**10.0**	**101**
Telephone calls to or from family members	5.5	3.8	144
Telephone calls to or from friends, neighbors, or acquaintances	2.1	3.7	56
Traveling	**83.4**	**88.5**	**94**
Travel related to personal care	3.5	3.1	115
Travel related to household activities	8.8	8.5	104
Travel related to household management	5.5	5.5	100
Travel related to caring for and helping household members	5.1	9.9	51
Travel related to caring for and helping household children	2.2	7.4	30
Travel related to helping household adults	2.6	2.4	110
Travel related to caring for and helping people in other households	9.6	9.3	104
Travel related to caring for and helping children in other households	1.9	2.5	76
Travel related to helping adults in other households	7.4	6.7	109
Travel related to work	40.3	44.4	91
Travel related to education	0.0	4.6	1
Travel related to taking class	0.0	4.1	1
Travel related to consumer purchases	34.5	34.5	100
Travel related to grocery shopping	10.4	9.5	109
Travel related to purchasing gas	4.9	4.2	116
Travel related to purchasing food (except groceries)	10.6	11.0	96
Travel related to shopping (except groceries, food, and gas)	18.6	18.9	99
Travel related to using professional and personal care services	7.8	6.3	122
Travel related to using financial services and banking	3.6	3.0	120
Travel related to using medical services	3.5	2.3	153
Travel related to eating and drinking	27.3	27.3	100
Travel related to socializing, relaxing, and leisure	24.2	28.0	87
Travel related to socializing and communicating	14.7	17.5	84
Travel related to attending or hosting social events	1.3	1.7	77
Travel related to relaxing and leisure	7.3	9.4	78
Travel related to arts and entertainment	2.4	2.8	87
Travel related to sports, exercise, and recreation	7.5	11.5	65
Travel related to participating in sports, exercise, recreation	6.9	10.4	66
Travel related to religious and spiritual activities	4.4	4.4	101
Travel related to volunteer activities	4.3	3.8	112

Note: The index is calculated by dividing percent of men in the age group doing primary activity by percent of total men doing primary activity and multiplying by 100. Primary activities are those respondents identified as their main activity. Other activities done simultaneously, such as eating while watching TV, are not included. If fewer than 2.0 percent of the total population participated in a primary activity, then the primary activity is not shown.
Source: Bureau of Labor Statistics, unpublished tables from the 2008 American Time Use Survey, Internet site http://www.bls .gov/tus/home.htm; calculations by New Strategist

Table 7.10 Indexed Participation in Primary Activities by Women Aged 55 to 64, 2008

(percent of women aged 55 to 64 and total women aged 15 or older participating in primary activities on an average day, and index of participation by women aged 55 to 64 to total women, 2008)

	percent participating		index, women aged 55 to 64 to total women
	women aged 55 to 64	total women	
TOTAL, ALL ACTIVITIES	**100.0%**	**100.0%**	**100**
Personal care	**99.9**	**100.0**	**100**
Sleeping	99.7	99.9	100
Sleeplessness	6.3	5.8	108
Grooming	81.1	81.8	99
Health-related self-care	8.6	7.8	111
Household activities	**90.1**	**84.0**	**107**
Housework	54.4	50.3	108
Interior cleaning	36.1	34.9	104
Laundry	29.9	25.5	118
Storing interior household items, including food	8.6	7.0	123
Food and drink preparation, presentation, and clean-up	72.7	65.3	111
Food and drink preparation	68.6	61.8	111
Kitchen and food clean-up	37.1	31.5	118
Interior maintenance, repair, and decoration	2.9	2.2	132
Interior arrangement, decoration, and repairs	2.6	1.5	168
Exterior maintenance, repair, and decoration	2.6	1.8	149
Lawn, garden, and houseplants	12.3	7.9	156
Animals and pets (not veterinary care)	25.0	16.7	150
Walking, exercising, and playing with pets	9.1	6.3	144
Vehicles	0.9	1.0	90
Household management	36.2	33.8	107
Financial management	6.9	4.9	143
Household and personal organization and planning	16.4	16.8	97
Household and personal mail and messages (except email)	10.2	8.2	125
Household and personal email	12.0	11.3	106
Caring for and helping household members	**13.0**	**31.2**	**42**
Caring for and helping household children	6.1	26.7	23
Physical care for household children	3.9	20.6	19
Reading to or with household children	0.2	3.5	6
Playing with household children (except sports)	0.6	6.1	10
Talking with, listening to household children	1.6	4.3	39
Looking after household children as a primary activity	1.1	3.0	36
Picking up or dropping off household children	3.0	12.1	25
Activities related to household children's education	1.1	5.4	21
Helping household children with homework	0.9	4.8	19
Helping household adults	3.4	3.7	90
Caring for and helping people in other households	**18.8**	**15.5**	**122**
Caring for and helping children in other households	11.0	7.4	149

	percent participating		index, women aged 55 to 64 to total women
	women aged 55 to 64	total women	
Helping adults in other households	7.9%	8.5%	93
Picking up or dropping off adults in other households	5.3	5.4	97
Work and work-related activities	**40.5**	**40.3**	**101**
Work, main job	38.4	38.0	101
Work, other job(s)	3.4	2.4	139
Education	**1.5**	**8.9**	**17**
Taking class	1.0	5.3	19
Taking class for degree, certification, or licensure	0.4	4.7	9
Research, homework	0.6	7.0	9
Consumer purchases (store, telephone, Internet)	**47.5**	**45.4**	**105**
Grocery shopping	18.0	16.1	112
Purchasing gas	4.3	3.7	117
Purchasing food (except groceries)	11.2	12.3	91
Shopping, except groceries, food, and gas	29.1	27.2	107
Professional and personal care services	**12.7**	**11.0**	**116**
Financial services and banking	4.7	3.3	141
Banking	4.7	3.3	144
Medical and care services	5.3	4.8	112
Using health and care services outside the home	5.0	4.5	112
Household services	**1.7**	**2.1**	**80**
Eating and drinking	**95.6**	**95.6**	**100**
Socializing, relaxing, and leisure	**95.4**	**95.4**	**100**
Socializing and communicating	43.6	40.1	109
Attending or hosting social events	1.8	2.7	66
Relaxing and leisure	92.3	90.6	102
Relaxing, thinking	22.0	19.5	112
Television	81.6	79.5	103
Listening to the radio	1.4	1.5	94
Listening to or playing music (not radio)	1.9	2.0	98
Playing games (including computer)	9.8	8.4	116
Computer use for leisure (except games)	6.8	9.5	71
Reading for personal interest	37.0	26.5	140
Arts and entertainment (except sports)	2.5	3.2	81
Sports, exercise, and recreation	**13.9**	**15.9**	**87**
Participating in sports, exercise, or recreation	13.8	15.0	92
Using cardiovascular equipment	1.2	2.5	50
Walking	5.4	4.7	115
Working out, unspecified	2.3	2.9	81
Religious and spiritual activities	**13.7**	**10.7**	**129**
Attending religious services	7.2	5.7	127
Participation in religious practices	7.0	5.4	130

| | percent participating | | index, women aged 55 to 64 |
	women aged 55 to 64	total women	to total women
Volunteer activities	**10.2%**	**7.6%**	**134**
Administrative and support activities	3.3	3.1	108
Telephone calls	**24.0**	**20.4**	**117**
Telephone calls to or from family members	16.2	10.7	151
Telephone calls to or from friends, neighbors, or acquaintances	7.0	7.4	95
Traveling	**84.5**	**85.5**	**99**
Travel related to personal care	1.8	2.0	92
Travel related to household activities	11.8	10.3	115
Travel related to household management	6.9	6.7	103
Travel related to caring for and helping household members	5.5	17.1	32
Travel related to caring for and helping household children	3.4	14.3	24
Travel related to helping household adults	1.9	2.7	69
Travel related to caring for and helping people in other households	14.0	11.6	121
Travel related to caring for and helping children in other households	6.9	4.5	154
Travel related to helping adults in other households	7.0	7.4	94
Travel related to work	30.5	32.2	95
Travel related to education	1.0	5.4	19
Travel related to taking class	0.5	4.6	10
Travel related to consumer purchases	46.0	44.4	104
Travel related to grocery shopping	17.8	16.0	111
Travel related to purchasing gas	4.3	3.7	118
Travel related to purchasing food (except groceries)	10.3	11.5	90
Travel related to shopping (except groceries, food, and gas)	28.2	26.3	107
Travel related to using professional and personal care services	11.9	9.8	122
Travel related to using financial services and banking	4.0	3.1	132
Travel related to using medical services	5.1	4.3	120
Travel related to eating and drinking	26.8	22.8	117
Travel related to socializing, relaxing, and leisure	27.8	29.2	95
Travel related to socializing and communicating	20.6	19.5	106
Travel related to attending or hosting social events	1.5	2.3	67
Travel related to relaxing and leisure	7.1	8.5	84
Travel related to arts and entertainment	1.6	2.4	65
Travel related to sports, exercise, and recreation	5.6	7.7	72
Travel related to participating in sports, exercise, recreation	5.4	6.8	80
Travel related to religious and spiritual activities	7.7	5.8	133
Travel related to volunteer activities	5.4	4.7	114

Note: The index is calculated by dividing percent of women in the age group doing primary activity by percent of total women doing primary activity and multiplying by 100. Primary activities are those respondents identified as their main activity. Other activities done simultaneously, such as eating while watching TV, are not included. If fewer than 2.0 percent of the total population participated in a primary activity, then the primary activity is not shown.
Source: Bureau of Labor Statistics, unpublished tables from the 2008 American Time Use Survey, Internet site http://www.bls .gov/tus/home.htm; calculations by New Strategist

Table 7.11 Indexed Participation in Primary Activities of People Aged 55 to 64 by Sex, 2008

(percent of people aged 55 to 64 participating in primary activities on an average day by sex, and index of women's participation to men's, 2008)

	aged 55 to 64, percent participating		index of women to men
	men	women	
TOTAL, ALL ACTIVITIES	**100.0%**	**100.0%**	**100**
Personal care	**100.0**	**99.9**	**100**
Sleeping	100.0	99.7	100
Sleeplessness	5.2	6.3	120
Grooming	72.4	81.1	112
Health-related self-care	7.3	8.6	119
Household activities	**69.9**	**90.1**	**129**
Housework	22.5	54.4	242
Interior cleaning	15.0	36.1	241
Laundry	5.8	29.9	517
Storing interior household items, including food	5.4	8.6	159
Food and drink preparation, presentation, and clean-up	42.7	72.7	170
Food and drink preparation	40.1	68.6	171
Kitchen and food clean-up	10.5	37.1	353
Interior maintenance, repair, and decoration	4.4	2.9	66
Interior arrangement, decoration, and repairs	2.9	2.6	88
Exterior maintenance, repair, and decoration	5.0	2.6	52
Lawn, garden, and houseplants	15.6	12.3	79
Animals and pets (not veterinary care)	14.2	25.0	176
Walking, exercising, and playing with pets	7.0	9.1	129
Vehicles	4.2	0.9	21
Household management	25.1	36.2	144
Financial management	4.4	6.9	159
Household and personal organization and planning	9.8	16.4	168
Household and personal mail and messages (except email)	7.6	10.2	135
Household and personal email	8.0	12.0	150
Caring for and helping household members	**9.6**	**13.0**	**135**
Caring for and helping household children	3.9	6.1	157
Physical care for household children	2.3	3.9	172
Reading to or with household children	0.1	0.2	211
Playing with household children (except sports)	0.6	0.6	98
Talking with, listening to household children	0.5	1.6	354
Looking after household children as a primary activity	0.7	1.1	153
Picking up or dropping off household children	1.8	3.0	167
Activities related to household children's education	0.6	1.1	188
Helping household children with homework	0.6	0.9	157
Helping household adults	4.4	3.4	76
Caring for and helping people in other households	**12.4**	**18.8**	**152**
Caring for and helping children in other households	4.7	11.0	234

	aged 55 to 64, percent participating		index of women to men
	men	women	
Helping adults in other households	7.8%	7.9%	101
Picking up or dropping off adults in other households	3.7	5.3	143
Work and work-related activities	**48.6**	**40.5**	**83**
Work, main job	46.5	38.4	83
Work, other job(s)	2.3	3.4	145
Education	**0.3**	**1.5**	**490**
Taking class	0.0	1.0	2323
Taking class for degree, certification, or licensure	0.0	0.4	996
Research, homework	0.3	0.6	224
Consumer purchases (store, telephone, Internet)	**35.2**	**47.5**	**135**
Grocery shopping	10.5	18.0	171
Purchasing gas	4.9	4.3	88
Purchasing food (except groceries)	11.0	11.2	102
Shopping, except groceries, food, and gas	19.3	29.1	151
Professional and personal care services	**8.9**	**12.7**	**143**
Financial services and banking	3.6	4.7	129
Banking	3.3	4.7	143
Medical and care services	4.0	5.3	132
Using health and care services outside the home	3.7	5.0	135
Household services	**2.0**	**1.7**	**85**
Eating and drinking	**96.6**	**95.6**	**99**
Socializing, relaxing, and leisure	**96.7**	**95.4**	**99**
Socializing and communicating	34.8	43.6	125
Attending or hosting social events	1.9	1.8	95
Relaxing and leisure	94.4	92.3	98
Relaxing, thinking	22.7	22.0	97
Television	86.5	81.6	94
Listening to the radio	2.2	1.4	66
Listening to or playing music (not radio)	1.6	1.9	120
Playing games (including computer)	4.9	9.8	199
Computer use for leisure (except games)	8.4	6.8	80
Reading for personal interest	32.2	37.0	115
Arts and entertainment (except sports)	2.9	2.5	89
Sports, exercise, and recreation	**20.1**	**13.9**	**69**
Participating in sports, exercise, or recreation	19.5	13.8	71
Using cardiovascular equipment	2.8	1.2	45
Walking	7.0	5.4	78
Working out, unspecified	4.2	2.3	56
Religious and spiritual activities	**8.3**	**13.7**	**165**
Attending religious services	4.5	7.2	162
Participation in religious practices	4.5	7.0	155

	aged 55 to 64, percent participating		index of women to men
	men	women	
Volunteer activities	**6.1%**	**10.2%**	**168**
Administrative and support activities	2.5	3.3	132
Telephone calls	**10.1**	**24.0**	**238**
Telephone calls to or from family members	5.5	16.2	295
Telephone calls to or from friends, neighbors, or acquaintances	2.1	7.0	341
Traveling	**83.4**	**84.5**	**101**
Travel related to personal care	3.5	1.8	52
Travel related to household activities	8.8	11.8	134
Travel related to household management	5.5	6.9	125
Travel related to caring for and helping household members	5.1	5.5	109
Travel related to caring for and helping household children	2.2	3.4	156
Travel related to helping household adults	2.6	1.9	71
Travel related to caring for and helping people in other households	9.6	14.0	146
Travel related to caring for and helping children in other households	1.9	6.9	369
Travel related to helping adults in other households	7.4	7.0	95
Travel related to work	40.3	30.5	76
Travel related to education	0.0	1.0	2323
Travel related to taking class	0.0	0.5	1075
Travel related to consumer purchases	34.5	46.0	133
Travel related to grocery shopping	10.4	17.8	171
Travel related to purchasing gas	4.9	4.3	88
Travel related to purchasing food (except groceries)	10.6	10.3	98
Travel related to shopping (except groceries, food, and gas)	18.6	28.2	151
Travel related to using professional and personal care services	7.8	11.9	153
Travel related to using financial services and banking	3.6	4.0	111
Travel related to using medical services	3.5	5.1	145
Travel related to eating and drinking	27.3	26.8	98
Travel related to socializing, relaxing, and leisure	24.2	27.8	115
Travel related to socializing and communicating	14.7	20.6	140
Travel related to attending or hosting social events	1.3	1.5	118
Travel related to relaxing and leisure	7.3	7.1	97
Travel related to arts and entertainment	2.4	1.6	65
Travel related to sports, exercise, and recreation	7.5	5.6	75
Travel related to participating in sports, exercise, recreation	6.9	5.4	78
Travel related to religious and spiritual activities	4.4	7.7	175
Travel related to volunteer activities	4.3	5.4	126

Note: The index is calculated by dividing percent of women participating in primary activity by percent of men participating in primary activity and multiplying by 100. Primary activities are those respondents identified as their main activity. Other activities done simultaneously, such as eating while watching TV, are not included. If fewer than 2.0 percent of the total population participated in a primary activity, then the primary activity is not shown.
Source: Bureau of Labor Statistics, unpublished tables from the 2008 American Time Use Survey, Internet site http://www.bls .gov/tus/home.htm; calculations by New Strategist

Table 7.12 **Ranking: Average Hours per Day Spent Doing Primary Activities by Total People Aged 55 to 64, 2008**

(average hours per day spent by people aged 55 to 64 doing primary activities, ranked by time spent doing activity, 2008)

		average hours per day spent by people aged 55 to 64
	Total, all activities	**24.00**
1.	Sleeping	8.26
2.	Television	3.27
3.	Work, main job	3.13
4.	Eating and drinking	1.20
5.	Grooming	0.67
6.	Socializing and communicating	0.65
7.	Reading for personal interest	0.52
8.	Food and drink preparation	0.44
9.	Interior cleaning	0.35
10.	Lawn, garden, and houseplants	0.32
11.	Shopping, except groceries, food, and gas	0.28
12.	Relaxing, thinking	0.28
13.	Travel related to work	0.26
14.	Participating in sports, exercise, or recreation	0.23
15.	Caring for and helping children in other households	0.20
16.	Laundry	0.19
17.	Volunteer activities	0.19
18.	Travel related to shopping (except groceries, food, and gas)	0.15
19.	Kitchen and food clean-up	0.14
20.	Travel related to eating and drinking	0.14
21.	Animals and pets (not veterinary care)	0.13
22.	Playing games (including computer)	0.13
23.	Household and personal organization and planning	0.12
24.	Telephone calls	0.12
25.	Grocery shopping	0.11
26.	Work, other job(s)	0.10
27.	Computer use for leisure (except games)	0.10
28.	Attending religious services	0.10
29.	Health-related self-care	0.09
30.	Interior maintenance, repair, and decoration	0.09
31.	Helping adults in other households	0.09
32.	Travel related to socializing and communicating	0.09
33.	Exterior maintenance, repair, and decoration	0.08
34.	Medical and care services	0.08
35.	Household and personal email	0.06
36.	Caring for and helping household children	0.06
37.	Arts and entertainment (except sports)	0.06
38.	Participation in religious practices	0.06
39.	Financial management	0.05

	average hours per day spent by people aged 55 to 64
40. Attending or hosting social events	0.05
41. Travel related to helping adults in other households	0.05
42. Travel related to grocery shopping	0.05
43. Vehicles	0.04
44. Travel related to household activities	0.04
45. Travel related to purchasing food (except groceries)	0.04
46. Storing interior household items, including food	0.03
47. Household and personal mail and messages (except email)	0.03
48. Listening to the radio	0.03
49. Travel related to purchasing gas	0.03
50. Travel related to relaxing and leisure	0.03
51. Travel related to religious and spiritual activities	0.03
52. Travel related to volunteer activities	0.03
53. Helping household adults	0.02
54. Taking class	0.02
55. Purchasing food (except groceries)	0.02
56. Listening to or playing music (not radio)	0.02
57. Travel related to personal care	0.02
58. Travel related to helping household adults	0.02
59. Travel related to caring for and helping children in other households	0.02
60. Travel related to using medical services	0.02
61. Travel related to sports, exercise, and recreation	0.02
62. Activities related to household children's education	0.01
63. Research, homework	0.01
64. Purchasing gas	0.01
65. Financial services and banking	0.01
66. Household services	0.01
67. Travel related to caring for and helping household children	0.01
68. Travel related to education	0.01
69. Travel related to using financial services and banking	0.01
70. Travel related to attending or hosting social events	0.01
71. Travel related to arts and entertainment	0.01

Note: Primary activities are those respondents identified as their main activity. Other activities done simultaneously, such as eating while watching TV, are not included. If fewer than 2.0 percent of the total population participated in a primary activity, then the primary activity is not shown.
Source: Bureau of Labor Statistics, unpublished tables from the 2008 American Time Use Survey, Internet site http://www.bls .gov/tus/home.htm; calculations by New Strategist

Table 7.13   Ranking: Average Hours per Day Spent Doing Primary Activities by Men Aged 55 to 64, 2008

(average hours per day spent by men aged 55 to 64 doing primary activities, ranked by time spent doing activity, 2008)

		average hours per day spent by men aged 55 to 64
	Total, all activities	**24.00**
1.	Sleeping	8.24
2.	Television	3.81
3.	Work, main job	3.64
4.	Eating and drinking	1.24
5.	Grooming	0.57
6.	Socializing and communicating	0.56
7.	Reading for personal interest	0.48
8.	Lawn, garden, and houseplants	0.42
9.	Travel related to work	0.33
10.	Relaxing, thinking	0.31
11.	Participating in sports, exercise, or recreation	0.31
12.	Food and drink preparation	0.28
13.	Shopping, except groceries, food, and gas	0.19
14.	Interior cleaning	0.17
15.	Volunteer activities	0.16
16.	Helping adults in other households	0.13
17.	Computer use for leisure (except games)	0.13
18.	Travel related to eating and drinking	0.13
19.	Exterior maintenance, repair, and decoration	0.12
20.	Interior maintenance, repair, and decoration	0.11
21.	Health-related self-care	0.10
22.	Animals and pets (not veterinary care)	0.10
23.	Household and personal organization and planning	0.10
24.	Travel related to shopping (except groceries, food, and gas)	0.10
25.	Caring for and helping children in other households	0.09
26.	Work, other job(s)	0.09
27.	Vehicles	0.08
28.	Medical and care services	0.08
29.	Playing games (including computer)	0.08
30.	Travel related to socializing and communicating	0.08
31.	Grocery shopping	0.07
32.	Arts and entertainment (except sports)	0.07
33.	Attending religious services	0.07
34.	Laundry	0.06
35.	Kitchen and food clean-up	0.06
36.	Caring for and helping household children	0.06
37.	Travel related to helping adults in other households	0.06
38.	Household and personal email	0.05
39.	Telephone calls	0.05

	average hours per day spent by men aged 55 to 64
40. Attending or hosting social events	0.04
41. Listening to the radio	0.04
42. Participation in religious practices	0.04
43. Travel related to grocery shopping	0.04
44. Travel related to purchasing food (except groceries)	0.04
45. Travel related to relaxing and leisure	0.04
46. Storing interior household items, including food	0.03
47. Financial management	0.03
48. Listening to or playing music (not radio)	0.03
49. Travel related to personal care	0.03
50. Travel related to household activities	0.03
51. Travel related to helping household adults	0.03
52. Travel related to purchasing gas	0.03
53. Travel related to sports, exercise, and recreation	0.03
54. Travel related to volunteer activities	0.03
55. Household and personal mail and messages (except email)	0.02
56. Helping household adults	0.02
57. Purchasing food (except groceries)	0.02
58. Travel related to using medical services	0.02
59. Travel related to arts and entertainment	0.02
60. Travel related to religious and spiritual activities	0.02
61. Activities related to household children's education	0.01
62. Research, homework	0.01
63. Purchasing gas	0.01
64. Financial services and banking	0.01
65. Household services	0.01
66. Travel related to caring for and helping household children	0.01
67. Travel related to caring for and helping children in other households	0.01
68. Travel related to using financial services and banking	0.01
69. Travel related to attending or hosting social events	0.01
70. Taking class	0.00
71. Travel related to education	0.00

Note: Primary activities are those respondents identified as their main activity. Other activities done simultaneously, such as eating while watching TV, are not included. If fewer than 2.0 percent of the total population participated in a primary activity, then the primary activity is not shown.
Source: Bureau of Labor Statistics, unpublished tables from the 2008 American Time Use Survey, Internet site http://www.bls .gov/tus/home.htm; calculations by New Strategist

Table 7.14 Ranking: Average Hours per Day Spent Doing Primary Activities by Women Aged 55 to 64, 2008

(average hours per day spent by women aged 55 to 64 doing primary activities, ranked by time spent doing activity, 2008)

		average hours per day spent by women aged 55 to 64
	Total, all activities	**24.00**
1.	Sleeping	8.29
2.	Television	2.76
3.	Work, main job	2.65
4.	Eating and drinking	1.16
5.	Grooming	0.76
6.	Socializing and communicating	0.74
7.	Food and drink preparation	0.60
8.	Reading for personal interest	0.57
9.	Interior cleaning	0.52
10.	Shopping, except groceries, food, and gas	0.36
11.	Laundry	0.31
12.	Caring for and helping children in other households	0.30
13.	Relaxing, thinking	0.25
14.	Lawn, garden, and houseplants	0.23
15.	Kitchen and food clean-up	0.21
16.	Volunteer activities	0.21
17.	Travel related to work	0.19
18.	Travel related to shopping (except groceries, food, and gas)	0.19
19.	Telephone calls	0.18
20.	Playing games (including computer)	0.17
21.	Participating in sports, exercise, or recreation	0.17
22.	Animals and pets (not veterinary care)	0.15
23.	Grocery shopping	0.15
24.	Travel related to eating and drinking	0.15
25.	Household and personal organization and planning	0.14
26.	Attending religious services	0.12
27.	Travel related to socializing and communicating	0.11
28.	Work, other job(s)	0.10
29.	Health-related self-care	0.08
30.	Computer use for leisure (except games)	0.08
31.	Participation in religious practices	0.08
32.	Interior maintenance, repair, and decoration	0.07
33.	Household and personal email	0.07
34.	Medical and care services	0.07
35.	Financial management	0.06
36.	Caring for and helping household children	0.06
37.	Attending or hosting social events	0.06
38.	Arts and entertainment (except sports)	0.06
39.	Travel related to grocery shopping	0.06

	average hours per day spent by women aged 55 to 64
40. Exterior maintenance, repair, and decoration	0.05
41. Helping adults in other households	0.05
42. Travel related to helping adults in other households	0.05
43. Travel related to household activities	0.04
44. Storing interior household items, including food	0.03
45. Household and personal mail and messages (except email)	0.03
46. Taking class	0.03
47. Travel related to caring for and helping children in other households	0.03
48. Travel related to purchasing food (except groceries)	0.03
49. Travel related to religious and spiritual activities	0.03
50. Activities related to household children's education	0.02
51. Purchasing food (except groceries)	0.02
52. Listening to the radio	0.02
53. Listening to or playing music (not radio)	0.02
54. Travel related to caring for and helping household children	0.02
55. Travel related to purchasing gas	0.02
56. Travel related to using medical services	0.02
57. Travel related to relaxing and leisure	0.02
58. Travel related to sports, exercise, and recreation	0.02
59. Travel related to volunteer activities	0.02
60. Vehicles	0.01
61. Helping household adults	0.01
62. Research, homework	0.01
63. Purchasing gas	0.01
64. Financial services and banking	0.01
65. Household services	0.01
66. Travel related to personal care	0.01
67. Travel related to helping household adults	0.01
68. Travel related to education	0.01
69. Travel related to using financial services and banking	0.01
70. Travel related to attending or hosting social events	0.01
71. Travel related to arts and entertainment	0.01

Note: Primary activities are those respondents identified as their main activity. Other activities done simultaneously, such as eating while watching TV, are not included. If fewer than 2.0 percent of the total population participated in a primary activity, then the primary activity is not shown.
Source: Bureau of Labor Statistics, unpublished tables from the 2008 American Time Use Survey, Internet site http://www.bls .gov/tus/home.htm; calculations by New Strategist

Table 7.15 Ranking: Percent of Total People Aged 55 to 64 Participating in Primary Activities on an Average Day, 2008

(percent of people aged 55 to 64 participating in primary activities on an average day, ranked by percent participating, 2008)

		percent of people aged 55 to 64 participating in activity
	Total, all activities	**100.0%**
1.	Sleeping	99.7
2.	Eating and drinking	96.1
3.	Television	83.9
4.	Grooming	76.9
5.	Food and drink preparation	54.9
6.	Work, main job	42.3
7.	Socializing and communicating	39.3
8.	Travel related to work	35.2
9.	Reading for personal interest	34.7
10.	Travel related to eating and drinking	26.1
11.	Interior cleaning	25.9
12.	Shopping, except groceries, food, and gas	24.3
13.	Kitchen and food clean-up	24.3
14.	Travel related to shopping (except groceries, food, and gas)	23.6
15.	Relaxing, thinking	22.3
16.	Animals and pets (not veterinary care)	19.8
17.	Laundry	18.3
18.	Travel related to socializing and communicating	17.8
19.	Telephone calls	17.3
20.	Participating in sports, exercise, or recreation	16.5
21.	Grocery shopping	14.4
22.	Travel related to grocery shopping	14.2
23.	Lawn, garden, and houseplants	13.9
24.	Household and personal organization and planning	13.2
25.	Purchasing food (except groceries)	11.1
26.	Travel related to purchasing food (except groceries)	10.4
27.	Travel related to household activities	10.4
28.	Household and personal email	10.1
29.	Household and personal mail and messages (except email)	8.9
30.	Volunteer activities	8.2
31.	Health-related self-care	8.0
32.	Caring for and helping children in other households	8.0
33.	Helping adults in other households	7.9
34.	Computer use for leisure (except games)	7.6
35.	Playing games (including computer)	7.5
36.	Travel related to relaxing and leisure	7.2
37.	Travel related to helping adults in other households	7.2
38.	Storing interior household items, including food	7.1
39.	Travel related to sports, exercise, and recreation	6.5

	percent of people aged 55 to 64 participating in activity
40. Travel related to religious and spiritual activities	6.2%
41. Attending religious services	5.9
42. Participation in religious practices	5.8
43. Financial management	5.7
44. Caring for and helping household children	5.1
45. Travel related to volunteer activities	4.8
46. Medical and care services	4.7
47. Travel related to purchasing gas	4.6
48. Purchasing gas	4.6
49. Travel related to caring for and helping children in other households	4.5
50. Travel related to using medical services	4.3
51. Financial services and banking	4.2
52. Helping household adults	3.9
53. Travel related to using financial services and banking	3.8
54. Exterior maintenance, repair, and decoration	3.8
55. Interior maintenance, repair, and decoration	3.6
56. Work, other job(s)	2.9
57. Travel related to caring for and helping household children	2.8
58. Arts and entertainment (except sports)	2.7
59. Travel related to personal care	2.7
60. Vehicles	2.5
61. Travel related to helping household adults	2.2
62. Travel related to arts and entertainment	2.0
63. Attending or hosting social events	1.8
64. Household services	1.8
65. Listening to or playing music (not radio)	1.8
66. Listening to the radio	1.8
67. Travel related to attending or hosting social events	1.4
68. Activities related to household children's education	0.9
69. Taking class	0.5
70. Travel related to education	0.5
71. Research, homework	0.4

Note: Primary activities are those respondents identified as their main activity. Other activities done simultaneously, such as eating while watching TV, are not included. If fewer than 2.0 percent of the total population participated in a primary activity, then the primary activity is not shown.
Source: Bureau of Labor Statistics, unpublished tables from the 2008 American Time Use Survey, Internet site http://www.bls .gov/tus/home.htm; calculations by New Strategist

Table 7.16 Ranking: Percent of Men Aged 55 to 64 Participating in Primary Activities on an Average Day, 2008

(percent of men aged 55 to 64 participating in primary activities on an average day, ranked by percent participating, 2008)

		percent of men aged 55 to 64 participating in activity
	Total, all activities	**100.0%**
1.	Sleeping	100.0
2.	Eating and drinking	96.6
3.	Television	86.5
4.	Grooming	72.4
5.	Work, main job	46.5
6.	Travel related to work	40.3
7.	Food and drink preparation	40.1
8.	Socializing and communicating	34.8
9.	Reading for personal interest	32.2
10.	Travel related to eating and drinking	27.3
11.	Relaxing, thinking	22.7
12.	Participating in sports, exercise, or recreation	19.5
13.	Shopping, except groceries, food, and gas	19.3
14.	Travel related to shopping (except groceries, food, and gas)	18.6
15.	Lawn, garden, and houseplants	15.6
16.	Interior cleaning	15.0
17.	Travel related to socializing and communicating	14.7
18.	Animals and pets (not veterinary care)	14.2
19.	Purchasing food (except groceries)	11.0
20.	Travel related to purchasing food (except groceries)	10.6
21.	Grocery shopping	10.5
22.	Kitchen and food clean-up	10.5
23.	Travel related to grocery shopping	10.4
24.	Telephone calls	10.1
25.	Household and personal organization and planning	9.8
26.	Travel related to household activities	8.8
27.	Computer use for leisure (except games)	8.4
28.	Household and personal email	8.0
29.	Helping adults in other households	7.8
30.	Household and personal mail and messages (except email)	7.6
31.	Travel related to sports, exercise, and recreation	7.5
32.	Travel related to helping adults in other households	7.4
33.	Travel related to relaxing and leisure	7.3
34.	Health-related self-care	7.3
35.	Volunteer activities	6.1
36.	Laundry	5.8
37.	Storing interior household items, including food	5.4
38.	Exterior maintenance, repair, and decoration	5.0
39.	Playing games (including computer)	4.9

	percent of men aged 55 to 64 participating in activity
40. Travel related to purchasing gas	4.9%
41. Purchasing gas	4.9
42. Caring for and helping children in other households	4.7
43. Participation in religious practices	4.5
44. Attending religious services	4.5
45. Travel related to religious and spiritual activities	4.4
46. Helping household adults	4.4
47. Interior maintenance, repair, and decoration	4.4
48. Financial management	4.4
49. Travel related to volunteer activities	4.3
50. Vehicles	4.2
51. Medical and care services	4.0
52. Caring for and helping household children	3.9
53. Financial services and banking	3.6
54. Travel related to using financial services and banking	3.6
55. Travel related to personal care	3.5
56. Travel related to using medical services	3.5
57. Arts and entertainment (except sports)	2.9
58. Travel related to helping household adults	2.6
59. Travel related to arts and entertainment	2.4
60. Work, other job(s)	2.3
61. Travel related to caring for and helping household children	2.2
62. Listening to the radio	2.2
63. Household services	2.0
64. Travel related to caring for and helping children in other households	1.9
65. Attending or hosting social events	1.9
66. Listening to or playing music (not radio)	1.6
67. Travel related to attending or hosting social events	1.3
68. Activities related to household children's education	0.6
69. Research, homework	0.3
70. Taking class	0.0
71. Travel related to education	0.0

Note: Primary activities are those respondents identified as their main activity. Other activities done simultaneously, such as eating while watching TV, are not included. If fewer than 2.0 percent of the total population participated in a primary activity, then the primary activity is not shown.

Source: Bureau of Labor Statistics, unpublished tables from the 2008 American Time Use Survey, Internet site http://www.bls .gov/tus/home.htm; calculations by New Strategist"

Table 7.17 Ranking: Percent of Women Aged 55 to 64 Participating in Primary Activities on an Average Day, 2008

(percent of women aged 55 to 64 participating in primary activities on an average day, ranked by percent participating, 2008)

		percent of women aged 55 to 64 participating in activity
	Total, all activities	**100.0%**
1.	Sleeping	99.7
2.	Eating and drinking	95.6
3.	Television	81.6
4.	Grooming	81.1
5.	Food and drink preparation	68.6
6.	Socializing and communicating	43.6
7.	Work, main job	38.4
8.	Kitchen and food clean-up	37.1
9.	Reading for personal interest	37.0
10.	Interior cleaning	36.1
11.	Travel related to work	30.5
12.	Laundry	29.9
13.	Shopping, except groceries, food, and gas	29.1
14.	Travel related to shopping (except groceries, food, and gas)	28.2
15.	Travel related to eating and drinking	26.8
16.	Animals and pets (not veterinary care)	25.0
17.	Telephone calls	24.0
18.	Relaxing, thinking	22.0
19.	Travel related to socializing and communicating	20.6
20.	Grocery shopping	18.0
21.	Travel related to grocery shopping	17.8
22.	Household and personal organization and planning	16.4
23.	Participating in sports, exercise, or recreation	13.8
24.	Lawn, garden, and houseplants	12.3
25.	Household and personal email	12.0
26.	Travel related to household activities	11.8
27.	Purchasing food (except groceries)	11.2
28.	Caring for and helping children in other households	11.0
29.	Travel related to purchasing food (except groceries)	10.3
30.	Volunteer activities	10.2
31.	Household and personal mail and messages (except email)	10.2
32.	Playing games (including computer)	9.8
33.	Health-related self-care	8.6
34.	Storing interior household items, including food	8.6
35.	Helping adults in other households	7.9
36.	Travel related to religious and spiritual activities	7.7
37.	Attending religious services	7.2
38.	Travel related to relaxing and leisure	7.1
39.	Participation in religious practices	7.0

	percent of women aged 55 to 64 participating in activity
40. Travel related to helping adults in other households	7.0%
41. Financial management	6.9
42. Travel related to caring for and helping children in other households	6.9
43. Computer use for leisure (except games)	6.8
44. Caring for and helping household children	6.1
45. Travel related to sports, exercise, and recreation	5.6
46. Travel related to volunteer activities	5.4
47. Medical and care services	5.3
48. Travel related to using medical services	5.1
49. Financial services and banking	4.7
50. Travel related to purchasing gas	4.3
51. Purchasing gas	4.3
52. Travel related to using financial services and banking	4.0
53. Travel related to caring for and helping household children	3.4
54. Work, other job(s)	3.4
55. Helping household adults	3.4
56. Interior maintenance, repair, and decoration	2.9
57. Exterior maintenance, repair, and decoration	2.6
58. Arts and entertainment (except sports)	2.5
59. Listening to or playing music (not radio)	1.9
60. Travel related to helping household adults	1.9
61. Travel related to personal care	1.8
62. Attending or hosting social events	1.8
63. Household services	1.7
64. Travel related to arts and entertainment	1.6
65. Travel related to attending or hosting social events	1.5
66. Listening to the radio	1.4
67. Activities related to household children's education	1.1
68. Taking class	1.0
69. Travel related to education	1.0
70. Vehicles	0.9
71. Research, homework	0.6

Note: Primary activities are those respondents identified as their main activity. Other activities done simultaneously, such as eating while watching TV, are not included. If fewer than 2.0 percent of the total population participated in a primary activity, then the primary activity is not shown.
Source: Bureau of Labor Statistics, unpublished tables from the 2008 American Time Use Survey, Internet site http://www.bls .gov/tus/home.htm; calculations by New Strategist

Table 7.18 Ranking: Average Hours per Day Spent Doing Primary Activities by Total Participants Aged 55 to 64, 2008

(hours per day spent by participants aged 55 to 64 doing primary activities, ranked by time spent doing activity, 2008)

		average hours per day spent by participants aged 55 to 64
	Total, all activities	**24.00**
1.	Sleeping	8.28
2.	Work, main job	7.39
3.	Television	3.89
4.	Caring for and helping children in other households	2.51
5.	Interior maintenance, repair, and decoration	2.50
6.	Lawn, garden, and houseplants	2.29
7.	Volunteer activities	2.28
8.	Exterior maintenance, repair, and decoration	2.14
9.	Playing games (including computer)	1.73
10.	Socializing and communicating	1.66
11.	Medical and care services	1.64
12.	Attending religious services	1.62
13.	Reading for personal interest	1.51
14.	Participating in sports, exercise, or recreation	1.42
15.	Interior cleaning	1.36
16.	Computer use for leisure (except games)	1.35
17.	Relaxing, thinking	1.27
18.	Eating and drinking	1.25
19.	Caring for and helping household children	1.20
20.	Shopping, except groceries, food, and gas	1.14
21.	Health-related self-care	1.13
22.	Helping adults in other households	1.10
23.	Laundry	1.04
24.	Participation in religious practices	1.02
25.	Household and personal organization and planning	0.91
26.	Grooming	0.87
27.	Food and drink preparation	0.81
28.	Financial management	0.81
29.	Grocery shopping	0.76
30.	Travel related to work	0.74
31.	Travel related to helping adults in other households	0.72
32.	Telephone calls	0.68
33.	Animals and pets (not veterinary care)	0.66
34.	Travel related to shopping (except groceries, food, and gas)	0.63
35.	Household and personal email	0.61
36.	Kitchen and food clean-up	0.58
37.	Travel related to purchasing gas	0.58
38.	Travel related to eating and drinking	0.53
39.	Travel related to socializing and communicating	0.53

	average hours per day spent by participants aged 55 to 64
40. Travel related to volunteer activities	0.53
41. Travel related to caring for and helping children in other households	0.49
42. Storing interior household items, including food	0.46
43. Travel related to relaxing and leisure	0.42
44. Travel related to religious and spiritual activities	0.42
45. Travel related to grocery shopping	0.38
46. Travel related to household activities	0.38
47. Travel related to sports, exercise, and recreation	0.38
48. Travel related to purchasing food (except groceries)	0.36
49. Household and personal mail and messages (except email)	0.31
50. Purchasing food (except groceries)	0.18
51. Purchasing gas	0.18

Note: Primary activities are those respondents identified as their main activity. Other activities done simultaneously, such as eating while watching TV, are not included. The primary activities shown are those for which data by age are available.
Source: Bureau of Labor Statistics, unpublished tables from the 2008 American Time Use Survey, Internet site http://www.bls .gov/tus/home.htm; calculations by New Strategist

Table 7.19 Ranking: Average Hours per Day Spent Doing Primary Activities by Male Participants Aged 55 to 64, 2008

(hours per day spent by male participants aged 55 to 64 doing primary activities, ranked by time spent doing activity, 2008)

		average hours per day spent by male participants aged 55 to 64
	Total, all activities	**24.00**
1.	Sleeping	8.24
2.	Work, main job	7.84
3.	Television	4.40
4.	Lawn, garden, and houseplants	2.66
5.	Socializing and communicating	1.61
6.	Helping adults in other households	1.61
7.	Participating in sports, exercise, or recreation	1.57
8.	Computer use for leisure (except games)	1.49
9.	Reading for personal interest	1.48
10.	Relaxing, thinking	1.38
11.	Health-related self-care	1.38
12.	Eating and drinking	1.29
13.	Interior cleaning	1.16
14.	Shopping, except groceries, food, and gas	0.99
15.	Household and personal organization and planning	0.98
16.	Laundry	0.97
17.	Travel related to work	0.83
18.	Grooming	0.79
19.	Animals and pets (not veterinary care)	0.73
20.	Food and drink preparation	0.70
21.	Grocery shopping	0.68
22.	Household and personal email	0.68
23.	Kitchen and food clean-up	0.60
24.	Travel related to shopping (except groceries, food, and gas)	0.55
25.	Travel related to socializing and communicating	0.52
26.	Travel related to relaxing and leisure	0.52
27.	Travel related to eating and drinking	0.47
28.	Telephone calls	0.47
29.	Travel related to grocery shopping	0.42
30.	Travel related to household activities	0.39
31.	Travel related to purchasing food (except groceries)	0.38
32.	Travel related to sports, exercise, and recreation	0.34
33.	Household and personal mail and messages (except email)	0.29
34.	Purchasing food (except groceries)	0.17

Note: Primary activities are those respondents identified as their main activity. Other activities done simultaneously, such as eating while watching TV, are not included. The primary activities shown are those for which data by age are available.
Source: Bureau of Labor Statistics, unpublished tables from the 2008 American Time Use Survey, Internet site http://www.bls .gov/tus/home.htm; calculations by New Strategist

Table 7.20 Ranking: Average Hours per Day Spent Doing Primary Activities by Female Participants Aged 55 to 64, 2008

(hours per day spent by female participants aged 55 to 64 doing primary activities, ranked by time spent doing activity, 2008)

		average hours per day spent by female participants aged 55 to 64
	Total, all activities	**24.00**
1.	Sleeping	8.31
2.	Work, main job	6.89
3.	Television	3.39
4.	Caring for and helping children in other households	2.77
5.	Volunteer activities	2.08
6.	Lawn, garden, and houseplants	1.86
7.	Playing games (including computer)	1.77
8.	Attending religious services	1.71
9.	Socializing and communicating	1.70
10.	Reading for personal interest	1.53
11.	Interior cleaning	1.44
12.	Shopping, except groceries, food, and gas	1.23
13.	Eating and drinking	1.21
14.	Participating in sports, exercise, or recreation	1.21
15.	Computer use for leisure (except games)	1.19
16.	Relaxing, thinking	1.16
17.	Participation in religious practices	1.10
18.	Caring for and helping household children	1.06
19.	Laundry	1.05
20.	Health-related self-care	0.94
21.	Grooming	0.93
22.	Food and drink preparation	0.87
23.	Household and personal organization and planning	0.87
24.	Grocery shopping	0.81
25.	Telephone calls	0.76
26.	Travel related to helping adults in other households	0.70
27.	Travel related to shopping (except groceries, food, and gas)	0.67
28.	Travel related to work	0.63
29.	Helping adults in other households	0.63
30.	Animals and pets (not veterinary care)	0.62
31.	Kitchen and food clean-up	0.58
32.	Travel related to eating and drinking	0.58
33.	Household and personal email	0.57
34.	Travel related to socializing and communicating	0.53
35.	Storing interior household items, including food	0.39
36.	Travel related to religious and spiritual activities	0.39
37.	Travel related to household activities	0.37
38.	Travel related to grocery shopping	0.35
39.	Travel related to purchasing food (except groceries)	0.34

	average hours per day spent by female participants aged 55 to 64
40. Household and personal mail and messages (except email)	0.33
41. Travel related to relaxing and leisure	0.32
42. Purchasing food (except groceries)	0.19

Note: Primary activities are those respondents identified as their main activity. Other activities done simultaneously, such as eating while watching TV, are not included. The primary activities shown are those for which data by age are available.
Source: Bureau of Labor Statistics, unpublished tables from the 2008 American Time Use Survey, Internet site http://www.bls .gov/tus/home.htm; calculations by New Strategist

8

Time Use, 2008: People Aged 65 to 74

Most people aged 65-to-74 have put work behind them, making leisure pursuits their top priorities. Working at a main job is in third place on the time-use list of 65-to-74-year-olds (excluding sleep)—behind watching television and eating and drinking. Only 21 percent of men and 14 percent of women aged 65 to 74 spend time working at a main job on an average day.

Watching television is the most important activity of 65-to-74-year-olds, ranking number-one in time use (excluding sleep). Eighty-seven percent of people aged 65 to 74 watch television as a primary activity on an average day, spending a substantial 4.00 hours in front of the TV—or more than one-fourth of their waking hours. Reading for personal interest ranks fourth in time use, with 45 percent of 65-to-74-year-olds reading on an average day. Relaxing and thinking ranks ninth.

Caring for children in other households (i.e., grandchildren) is more important to 65-to-74-year-olds than it is for 55-to-64-year-olds. The percentage who care for children in other households on an average day rises to 9 percent in this age group. A substantial 16 percent of people aged 65 to 74 care for pets on an average day.

The maxim that work expands to fill the time available is evident in the time use statistics for this age group. Having so much free time available, 65-to-74-year-olds fill it with household

Leisure activities dominate the schedules of 65-to-74-year-olds

(average hours per day spent by people aged 65 to 74 doing primary activities, for the 10 activities on which the average 65-to-74-year-old spends the most time, excluding sleep, 2008)

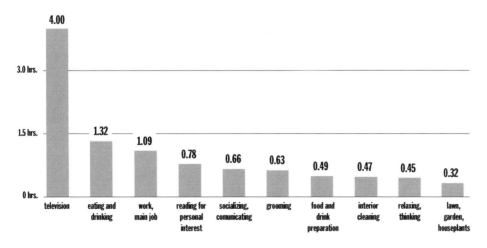

chores. People aged 65 to 74 are more likely to clean the house on an average day than people in the crowded-nest lifestage. Twenty-nine percent spend time cleaning the house, placing this activity eighth in importance on their time-use list (excluding sleep).

People aged 65 to 74 are more likely than any other age group to go grocery shopping on an average day, with 17 percent doing so. Lawn and garden care ranks 10th on their time-use list, with 19 percent of men and 13 percent of women in the age group caring for lawn and garden on an average day. Sixteen percent of 65-to-74-year-olds take part in religious activities on an average day.

Men aged 65 to 74 spend more time than their female counterparts on interior and exterior home maintenance. Women spend more time than men doing the laundry, housecleaning, and cooking. They also spend more time engaged in religious practices (such as reading the Bible or praying). Twelve percent of women and 5 percent of men participate in religious practices on an average day. Women are more likely than men to talk to family members on the phone on an average day—14 percent of women versus 6 percent of men.

Table 8.1 Time Use by Total People Aged 65 to 74, 2008

(number and percent of total people aged 65 to 74 participating in primary activities on an average day, hours spent doing activity by the average person aged 65 to 74 and by those aged 65 to 74 who participated in the activity, 2008; numbers of participants in thousands)

	participants aged 65 to 74		time spent doing activity (hours)	
	number	percent	average person aged 65 to 74	participants aged 65 to 74
TOTAL, ALL ACTIVITIES	**19,885**	**100.0%**	**24.00**	**24.00**
Personal care	**19,885**	**100.0**	**9.51**	**9.51**
Sleeping	19,885	100.0	8.77	8.77
Sleeplessness	1,174	5.9	0.10	1.61
Grooming	14,694	73.9	0.63	0.85
Health-related self-care	2,793	14.0	0.11	0.75
Household activities	**16,722**	**84.1**	**2.34**	**2.78**
Housework	7,832	39.4	0.77	1.95
Interior cleaning	5,806	29.2	0.47	1.60
Laundry	3,159	15.9	0.19	1.19
Storing interior household items, including food	1,510	7.6	0.03	0.41
Food and drink preparation, presentation, and clean-up	11,739	59.0	0.63	1.07
Food and drink preparation	10,917	54.9	0.49	0.89
Kitchen and food clean-up	4,645	23.4	0.14	0.59
Interior maintenance, repair, and decoration	897	4.5	0.06	–
Interior arrangement, decoration, and repairs	417	2.1	0.04	–
Exterior maintenance, repair, and decoration	1,181	5.9	0.15	–
Lawn, garden, and houseplants	3,184	16.0	0.32	1.99
Animals and pets (not veterinary care)	3,096	15.6	0.10	0.66
Walking, exercising, and playing with pets	1,165	5.9	0.04	0.64
Vehicles	608	3.1	0.03	–
Household management	6,645	33.4	0.26	0.78
Financial management	1,079	5.4	0.05	–
Household and personal organization and planning	2,853	14.3	0.09	0.64
Household and personal mail and messages (except email)	2,530	12.7	0.05	0.40
Household and personal email	1,839	9.2	0.07	0.74
Caring for and helping household members	**1,405**	**7.1**	**0.07**	–
Caring for and helping household children	321	1.6	0.02	–
Physical care for household children	177	0.9	0.00	–
Reading to or with household children	–	–	–	–
Playing with household children (except sports)	79	0.4	0.01	–
Talking with, listening to household children	11	0.1	0.00	–
Looking after household children as a primary activity	50	0.3	0.00	–
Picking up or dropping off household children	132	0.7	0.00	–
Activities related to household children's education	58	0.3	0.00	–
Helping household children with homework	58	0.3	0.00	–
Helping household adults	699	3.5	0.02	–
Caring for and helping people in other households	**3,310**	**16.6**	**0.24**	**1.43**
Caring for and helping children in other households	1,788	9.0	0.17	1.92

	participants aged 65 to 74		time spent doing activity (hours)	
	number	percent	average person aged 65 to 74	participants aged 65 to 74
Helping adults in other households	1,760	8.9%	0.05	0.61
Picking up or dropping off adults in other households	947	4.8	0.01	0.20
Work and work-related activities	**3,599**	**18.1**	**1.14**	**6.30**
Work, main job	3,441	17.3	1.09	6.32
Work, other job(s)	54	0.3	0.01	–
Education	**143**	**0.7**	**0.01**	–
Taking class	62	0.3	0.01	–
Taking class for degree, certification, or licensure	62	0.3	0.01	–
Research, homework	81	0.4	0.00	–
Consumer purchases (store, telephone, Internet)	**7,888**	**39.7**	**0.42**	**1.06**
Grocery shopping	3,327	16.7	0.14	0.86
Purchasing gas	605	3.0	0.01	–
Purchasing food (except groceries)	1,461	7.3	0.01	0.20
Shopping, except groceries, food, and gas	4,901	24.6	0.26	1.04
Professional and personal care services	**2,210**	**11.1**	**0.13**	**1.16**
Financial services and banking	700	3.5	0.01	–
Banking	624	3.1	0.01	–
Medical and care services	1,032	5.2	0.08	–
Using health and care services outside the home	859	4.3	0.06	–
Household services	**741**	**3.7**	**0.03**	–
Eating and drinking	**19,587**	**98.5**	**1.32**	**1.34**
Socializing, relaxing, and leisure	**19,552**	**98.3**	**6.56**	**6.67**
Socializing and communicating	7,806	39.3	0.66	1.69
Attending or hosting social events	494	2.5	0.06	–
Relaxing and leisure	19,224	96.7	5.75	5.95
Relaxing, thinking	4,328	21.8	0.45	2.06
Television	17,348	87.2	4.00	4.59
Listening to the radio	542	2.7	0.06	–
Listening to or playing music (not radio)	351	1.8	0.02	–
Playing games (including computer)	2,253	11.3	0.23	2.05
Computer use for leisure (except games)	1,295	6.5	0.13	2.03
Reading for personal interest	8,860	44.6	0.78	1.76
Arts and entertainment (except sports)	587	3.0	0.07	–
Sports, exercise, and recreation	**3,553**	**17.9**	**0.33**	**1.83**
Participating in sports, exercise, or recreation	3,473	17.5	0.30	1.73
Using cardiovascular equipment	246	1.2	0.01	–
Walking	1,597	8.0	0.07	0.81
Working out, unspecified	710	3.6	0.04	–
Religious and spiritual activities	**3,253**	**16.4**	**0.25**	**1.51**
Attending religious services	1,516	7.6	0.14	1.80
Participation in religious practices	1,747	8.8	0.08	0.95

	participants aged 65 to 74		time spent doing activity (hours)	
	number	percent	average person aged 65 to 74	participants aged 65 to 74
Volunteer activities	**1,701**	**8.6%**	**0.23**	**2.74**
Administrative and support activities	867	4.4	0.10	–
Telephone calls	**3,527**	**17.7**	**0.13**	**0.71**
Telephone calls to or from family members	2,075	10.4	0.06	0.57
Telephone calls to or from friends, neighbors, or acquaintances	1,019	5.1	0.04	0.74
Traveling	**15,192**	**76.4**	**1.05**	**1.38**
Travel related to personal care	213	1.1	0.00	–
Travel related to household activities	2,211	11.1	0.05	0.48
Travel related to household management	1,490	7.5	0.03	0.45
Travel related to caring for and helping household members	752	3.8	0.02	–
Travel related to caring for and helping household children	172	0.9	0.00	–
Travel related to helping household adults	523	2.6	0.02	–
Travel related to caring for and helping people in other households	2,102	10.6	0.07	0.71
Travel related to caring for and helping children in other households	771	3.9	0.03	–
Travel related to helping adults in other households	1,451	7.3	0.04	0.53
Travel related to work	2,584	13.0	0.09	0.66
Travel related to education	52	0.3	0.00	–
Travel related to taking class	45	0.2	0.00	–
Travel related to consumer purchases	7,805	39.3	0.28	0.71
Travel related to grocery shopping	3,322	16.7	0.07	0.39
Travel related to purchasing gas	590	3.0	0.01	–
Travel related to purchasing food (except groceries)	1,420	7.1	0.04	0.57
Travel related to shopping (except groceries, food, and gas)	4,832	24.3	0.16	0.65
Travel related to using professional and personal care services	1,931	9.7	0.05	0.49
Travel related to using financial services and banking	649	3.3	0.01	–
Travel related to using medical services	791	4.0	0.03	–
Travel related to eating and drinking	5,265	26.5	0.15	0.55
Travel related to socializing, relaxing, and leisure	5,831	29.3	0.20	0.68
Travel related to socializing and communicating	3,971	20.0	0.11	0.56
Travel related to attending or hosting social events	414	2.1	0.02	–
Travel related to relaxing and leisure	1,296	6.5	0.03	0.49
Travel related to arts and entertainment	545	2.7	0.02	–
Travel related to sports, exercise, and recreation	1,653	8.3	0.04	0.43
Travel related to participating in sports, exercise, recreation	1,558	7.8	0.03	0.40
Travel related to religious and spiritual activities	1,597	8.0	0.03	0.34
Travel related to volunteer activities	1,082	5.4	0.02	–

Note: Primary activities are those respondents identified as their main activity. Other activities done simultaneously, such as eating while watching TV, are not included. Numbers may not add to total because not all subcategories are shown. If fewer than 2.0 percent of the total population participated in a primary activity, then the primary activity is not shown. "–" means sample is too small to make a reliable estimate.
Source: Bureau of Labor Statistics, unpublished tables from the 2008 American Time Use Survey, Internet site http://www.bls .gov/tus/home.htm; calculations by New Strategist

Table 8.2 Time Use by Men Aged 65 to 74, 2008

(number and percent of men aged 65 to 74 participating in primary activities on an average day, hours spent doing activity by the average man aged 65 to 74 and by men aged 65 to 74 who participated in the activity, 2008; numbers of participants in thousands)

	men aged 65 to 74 participating		time spent doing activity (hours)	
	number	percent	average man aged 65 to 74	male participants aged 65 to 74
TOTAL, ALL ACTIVITIES	**9,163**	**100.0%**	**24.00**	**24.00**
Personal care	**9,163**	**100.0**	**9.40**	**9.40**
Sleeping	9,163	100.0	8.88	8.88
Sleeplessness	339	3.7	0.08	–
Grooming	6,081	66.4	0.48	0.72
Health-related self-care	1,051	11.5	0.04	–
Household activities	**7,106**	**77.6**	**1.82**	**2.35**
Housework	1,529	16.7	0.22	1.34
Interior cleaning	1,092	11.9	0.16	1.31
Laundry	375	4.1	0.05	–
Storing interior household items, including food	265	2.9	0.02	–
Food and drink preparation, presentation, and clean-up	3,835	41.9	0.34	0.80
Food and drink preparation	3,654	39.9	0.29	0.73
Kitchen and food clean-up	829	9.0	0.05	–
Interior maintenance, repair, and decoration	659	7.2	0.10	–
Interior arrangement, decoration, and repairs	258	2.8	0.06	–
Exterior maintenance, repair, and decoration	878	9.6	0.28	–
Lawn, garden, and houseplants	1,784	19.5	0.47	2.41
Animals and pets (not veterinary care)	1,397	15.2	0.12	0.77
Walking, exercising, and playing with pets	571	6.2	0.04	–
Vehicles	417	4.6	0.06	–
Household management	2,736	29.9	0.22	0.74
Financial management	472	5.2	0.05	–
Household and personal organization and planning	1,119	12.2	0.07	–
Household and personal mail and messages (except email)	926	10.1	0.03	–
Household and personal email	764	8.3	0.06	–
Caring for and helping household members	**771**	**8.4**	**0.05**	**–**
Caring for and helping household children	146	1.6	0.02	–
Physical care for household children	57	0.6	0.00	–
Reading to or with household children		0.0		
Playing with household children (except sports)	32	0.3	0.01	–
Talking with, listening to household children	11	0.1	0.00	–
Looking after household children as a primary activity	45	0.5	0.01	–
Picking up or dropping off household children	51	0.6	0.00	–
Activities related to household children's education	12	0.1	0.00	–
Helping household children with homework	12	0.1	0.00	–
Helping household adults	505	5.5	0.03	–
Caring for and helping people in other households	**1,405**	**15.3**	**0.20**	**1.33**
Caring for and helping children in other households	682	7.4	0.12	–

	men aged 65 to 74 participating		time spent doing activity (hours)	
	number	percent	average man aged 65 to 74	male participants aged 65 to 74
Helping adults in other households	843	9.2%	0.08	–
Picking up or dropping off adults in other households	446	4.9	0.01	–
Work and work-related activities	**1,979**	**21.6**	**1.32**	**6.09**
Work, main job	1,922	21.0	1.30	6.19
Work, other job(s)	11	0.1	0.00	–
Education	**33**	**0.4**	**0.00**	**–**
Taking class	4	0.0	0.00	–
Taking class for degree, certification, or licensure	4	0.0	0.00	–
Research, homework	29	0.3	0.00	–
Consumer purchases (store, telephone, Internet)	**3,499**	**38.2**	**0.38**	**1.01**
Grocery shopping	1,278	13.9	0.11	0.76
Purchasing gas	384	4.2	0.01	–
Purchasing food (except groceries)	606	6.6	0.01	–
Shopping, except groceries, food, and gas	2,229	24.3	0.26	1.06
Professional and personal care services	**877**	**9.6**	**0.11**	**–**
Financial services and banking	348	3.8	0.01	–
Banking	280	3.1	0.00	–
Medical and care services	387	4.2	0.08	–
Using health and care services outside the home	387	4.2	0.07	–
Household services	**461**	**5.0**	**0.04**	**–**
Eating and drinking	**9,019**	**98.4**	**1.42**	**1.45**
Socializing, relaxing, and leisure	**9,059**	**98.9**	**6.94**	**7.02**
Socializing and communicating	3,451	37.7	0.56	1.49
Attending or hosting social events	216	2.4	0.06	–
Relaxing and leisure	8,948	97.7	6.24	6.39
Relaxing, thinking	1,629	17.8	0.43	2.42
Television	8,182	89.3	4.60	5.16
Listening to the radio	226	2.5	0.06	–
Listening to or playing music (not radio)	261	2.8	0.03	–
Playing games (including computer)	744	8.1	0.19	–
Computer use for leisure (except games)	587	6.4	0.14	–
Reading for personal interest	3,748	40.9	0.69	1.68
Arts and entertainment (except sports)	295	3.2	0.07	–
Sports, exercise, and recreation	**2,130**	**23.2**	**0.53**	**2.30**
Participating in sports, exercise, or recreation	2,080	22.7	0.50	2.21
Using cardiovascular equipment	117	1.3	0.01	–
Walking	851	9.3	0.08	–
Working out, unspecified	375	4.1	0.06	–
Religious and spiritual activities	**1,107**	**12.1**	**0.21**	**1.76**
Attending religious services	623	6.8	0.12	–
Participation in religious practices	433	4.7	0.07	–

	men aged 65 to 74 participating		time spent doing activity (hours)	
	number	percent	average man aged 65 to 74	male participants aged 65 to 74
Volunteer activities	**718**	**7.8%**	**0.26**	–
Administrative and support activities	356	3.9	0.11	–
Telephone calls	**905**	**9.9**	**0.08**	–
Telephone calls to or from family members	539	5.9	0.03	–
Telephone calls to or from friends, neighbors, or acquaintances	236	2.6	0.02	–
Traveling	**7,494**	**81.8**	**0.98**	**1.20**
Travel related to personal care	99	1.1	0.00	–
Travel related to household activities	907	9.9	0.04	–
Travel related to household management	557	6.1	0.03	–
Travel related to caring for and helping household members	495	5.4	0.03	–
Travel related to caring for and helping household children	81	0.9	0.00	–
Travel related to helping household adults	392	4.3	0.03	–
Travel related to caring for and helping people in other households	906	9.9	0.07	–
Travel related to caring for and helping children in other households	309	3.4	0.02	–
Travel related to helping adults in other households	649	7.1	0.04	–
Travel related to work	1,382	15.1	0.11	0.72
Travel related to education	7	0.1	0.00	–
Travel related to taking class	0	0.0	0.00	–
Travel related to consumer purchases	3,429	37.4	0.26	0.70
Travel related to grocery shopping	1,278	13.9	0.05	0.39
Travel related to purchasing gas	384	4.2	0.03	–
Travel related to purchasing food (except groceries)	571	6.2	0.02	–
Travel related to shopping (except groceries, food, and gas)	2,178	23.8	0.16	0.67
Travel related to using professional and personal care services	863	9.4	0.05	–
Travel related to using financial services and banking	334	3.6	0.01	–
Travel related to using medical services	371	4.0	0.03	–
Travel related to eating and drinking	2,509	27.4	0.12	0.43
Travel related to socializing, relaxing, and leisure	2,653	29.0	0.16	0.55
Travel related to socializing and communicating	1,772	19.3	0.09	0.47
Travel related to attending or hosting social events	171	1.9	0.01	–
Travel related to relaxing and leisure	558	6.1	0.02	–
Travel related to arts and entertainment	288	3.1	0.02	–
Travel related to sports, exercise, and recreation	1,042	11.4	0.05	–
Travel related to participating in sports, exercise, recreation	963	10.5	0.05	–
Travel related to religious and spiritual activities	670	7.3	0.02	–
Travel related to volunteer activities	491	5.4	0.03	–

Note: Primary activities are those respondents identified as their main activity. Other activities done simultaneously, such as eating while watching TV, are not included. Numbers may not add to total because not all subcategories are shown. If fewer than 2.0 percent of the total population participated in a primary activity, then the primary activity is not shown. "–" means sample is too small to make a reliable estimate.
Source: Bureau of Labor Statistics, unpublished tables from the 2008 American Time Use Survey, Internet site http://www.bls .gov/tus/home.htm; calculations by New Strategist

Table 8.3 Time Use by Women Aged 65 to 74, 2008

(number and percent of women aged 65 to 74 participating in primary activities on an average day, hours spent doing activity by the average woman aged 65 to 74 and by women aged 65 to 74 who participated in the activity, 2008; numbers of participants in thousands)

	women aged 65 to 74 participating		time spent doing activity (hours)	
	number	percent	average woman aged 65 to 74	female participants aged 65 to 74
TOTAL, ALL ACTIVITIES	10,723	100.0%	24.00	24.00
Personal care	**10,723**	**100.0**	**9.60**	**9.60**
Sleeping	10,723	100.0	8.67	8.67
Sleeplessness	835	7.8	0.11	–
Grooming	8,613	80.3	0.76	0.95
Health-related self-care	1,741	16.2	0.16	1.00
Household activities	**9,617**	**89.7**	**2.77**	**3.09**
Housework	6,303	58.8	1.23	2.10
Interior cleaning	4,714	44.0	0.74	1.67
Laundry	2,784	26.0	0.31	1.19
Storing interior household items, including food	1,245	11.6	0.04	0.35
Food and drink preparation, presentation, and clean-up	7,905	73.7	0.89	1.20
Food and drink preparation	7,263	67.7	0.66	0.98
Kitchen and food clean-up	3,815	35.6	0.22	0.61
Interior maintenance, repair, and decoration	238	2.2	0.03	–
Interior arrangement, decoration, and repairs	159	1.5	0.02	–
Exterior maintenance, repair, and decoration	303	2.8	0.04	–
Lawn, garden, and houseplants	1,400	13.1	0.19	1.45
Animals and pets (not veterinary care)	1,699	15.8	0.09	0.56
Walking, exercising, and playing with pets	594	5.5	0.04	–
Vehicles	191	1.8	0.01	–
Household management	3,908	36.4	0.29	0.80
Financial management	607	5.7	0.04	–
Household and personal organization and planning	1,734	16.2	0.11	0.67
Household and personal mail and messages (except email)	1,604	15.0	0.06	0.43
Household and personal email	1,075	10.0	0.08	–
Caring for and helping household members	**634**	**5.9**	**0.08**	**–**
Caring for and helping household children	175	1.6	0.03	–
Physical care for household children	119	1.1	0.01	–
Reading to or with household children		0.0		
Playing with household children (except sports)	48	0.4	0.02	–
Talking with, listening to household children	0	0.0	0.00	–
Looking after household children as a primary activity	5	0.0	0.00	–
Picking up or dropping off household children	81	0.8	0.00	–
Activities related to household children's education	46	0.4	0.00	–
Helping household children with homework	46	0.4	0.00	–
Helping household adults	194	1.8	0.02	–
Caring for and helping people in other households	**1,904**	**17.8**	**0.27**	**1.50**
Caring for and helping children in other households	1,106	10.3	0.21	

	women aged 65 to 74 participating		time spent doing activity (hours)	
	number	percent	average woman aged 65 to 74	female participants aged 65 to 74
Helping adults in other households	917	8.6%	0.04	–
Picking up or dropping off adults in other households	501	4.7	0.01	–
Work and work-related activities	**1,619**	**15.1**	**0.99**	**6.55**
Work, main job	1,519	14.2	0.92	6.48
Work, other job(s)	43	0.4	0.02	–
Education	**110**	**1.0**	**0.02**	**–**
Taking class	58	0.5	0.02	–
Taking class for degree, certification, or licensure	58	0.5	0.02	–
Research, homework	52	0.5	0.00	–
Consumer purchases (store, telephone, Internet)	**4,388**	**40.9**	**0.45**	**1.10**
Grocery shopping	2,049	19.1	0.18	0.92
Purchasing gas	222	2.1	0.00	–
Purchasing food (except groceries)	855	8.0	0.02	–
Shopping, except groceries, food, and gas	2,673	24.9	0.26	1.02
Professional and personal care services	**1,333**	**12.4**	**0.14**	**1.14**
Financial services and banking	352	3.3	0.01	–
Banking	344	3.2	0.01	–
Medical and care services	645	6.0	0.08	–
Using health and care services outside the home	471	4.4	0.05	–
Household services	**281**	**2.6**	**0.02**	**–**
Eating and drinking	**10,568**	**98.6**	**1.23**	**1.24**
Socializing, relaxing, and leisure	**10,493**	**97.9**	**6.22**	**6.36**
Socializing and communicating	4,355	40.6	0.75	1.85
Attending or hosting social events	278	2.6	0.06	–
Relaxing and leisure	10,276	95.8	5.34	5.57
Relaxing, thinking	2,699	25.2	0.46	1.84
Television	9,166	85.5	3.49	4.08
Listening to the radio	316	2.9	0.06	–
Listening to or playing music (not radio)	90	0.8	0.01	–
Playing games (including computer)	1,509	14.1	0.27	1.91
Computer use for leisure (except games)	708	6.6	0.12	–
Reading for personal interest	5,112	47.7	0.87	1.81
Arts and entertainment (except sports)	293	2.7	0.07	–
Sports, exercise, and recreation	**1,423**	**13.3**	**0.15**	**1.14**
Participating in sports, exercise, or recreation	1,393	13.0	0.13	1.02
Using cardiovascular equipment	129	1.2	0.01	–
Walking	746	7.0	0.05	–
Working out, unspecified	335	3.1	0.03	–
Religious and spiritual activities	**2,146**	**20.0**	**0.28**	**1.38**
Attending religious services	892	8.3	0.15	1.83
Participation in religious practices	1,314	12.3	0.09	0.75

	women aged 65 to 74 participating		time spent doing activity (hours)	
	number	percent	average woman aged 65 to 74	female participants aged 65 to 74
Volunteer activities	**983**	**9.2%**	**0.21**	–
Administrative and support activities	512	4.8	0.08	–
Telephone calls	**2,622**	**24.5**	**0.16**	**0.67**
Telephone calls to or from family members	1,536	14.3	0.08	0.56
Telephone calls to or from friends, neighbors, or acquaintances	783	7.3	0.05	0.73
Traveling	**7,699**	**71.8**	**1.12**	**1.56**
Travel related to personal care	114	1.1	0.00	–
Travel related to household activities	1,304	12.2	0.06	0.51
Travel related to household management	933	8.7	0.04	–
Travel related to caring for and helping household members	257	2.4	0.02	–
Travel related to caring for and helping household children	90	0.8	0.00	–
Travel related to helping household adults	131	1.2	0.01	–
Travel related to caring for and helping people in other households	1,196	11.2	0.08	0.74
Travel related to caring for and helping children in other households	462	4.3	0.04	–
Travel related to helping adults in other households	802	7.5	0.03	–
Travel related to work	1,202	11.2	0.07	0.60
Travel related to education	45	0.4	0.00	–
Travel related to taking class	45	0.4	0.00	–
Travel related to consumer purchases	4,376	40.8	0.29	0.71
Travel related to grocery shopping	2,044	19.1	0.08	0.40
Travel related to purchasing gas	207	1.9	0.00	–
Travel related to purchasing food (except groceries)	849	7.9	0.05	–
Travel related to shopping (except groceries, food, and gas)	2,654	24.8	0.16	0.63
Travel related to using professional and personal care services	1,068	10.0	0.05	–
Travel related to using financial services and banking	315	2.9	0.01	–
Travel related to using medical services	420	3.9	0.03	–
Travel related to eating and drinking	2,755	25.7	0.17	0.67
Travel related to socializing, relaxing, and leisure	3,178	29.6	0.23	0.78
Travel related to socializing and communicating	2,199	20.5	0.13	0.64
Travel related to attending or hosting social events	243	2.3	0.02	–
Travel related to relaxing and leisure	738	6.9	0.04	–
Travel related to arts and entertainment	256	2.4	0.02	–
Travel related to sports, exercise, and recreation	611	5.7	0.02	–
Travel related to participating in sports, exercise, recreation	595	5.5	0.02	–
Travel related to religious and spiritual activities	927	8.6	0.03	0.35
Travel related to volunteer activities	591	5.5	0.02	–

Note: Primary activities are those respondents identified as their main activity. Other activities done simultaneously, such as eating while watching TV, are not included. Numbers may not add to total because not all subcategories are shown. If fewer than 2.0 percent of the total population participated in a primary activity, then the primary activity is not shown. "–" means sample is too small to make a reliable estimate.
Source: Bureau of Labor Statistics, unpublished tables from the 2008 American Time Use Survey, Internet site http://www.bls .gov/tus/home.htm; calculations by New Strategist

Table 8.4 Indexed Time Use of Total People Aged 65 to 74, 2008

(hours spent doing primary activities on an average day by people aged 65 to 74 and by total people aged 15 or older, and index of time spent by people aged 65 to 74 to total people, 2008)

	average hours		index, people aged 65 to 74
	people aged 65 to 74	total people	to total people
TOTAL, ALL ACTIVITIES	**24.00**	**24.00**	**100**
Personal care	**9.51**	**9.38**	**101**
Sleeping	8.77	8.60	102
Sleeplessness	0.10	0.06	167
Grooming	0.63	0.67	94
Health-related self-care	0.11	0.09	122
Household activities	**2.34**	**1.77**	**132**
Housework	0.77	0.58	133
Interior cleaning	0.47	0.37	127
Laundry	0.19	0.17	112
Storing interior household items, including food	0.03	0.02	150
Food and drink preparation, presentation, and clean-up	0.63	0.52	121
Food and drink preparation	0.49	0.40	123
Kitchen and food clean-up	0.14	0.12	117
Interior maintenance, repair, and decoration	0.06	0.07	86
Interior arrangement, decoration, and repairs	0.04	0.05	80
Exterior maintenance, repair, and decoration	0.15	0.06	250
Lawn, garden, and houseplants	0.32	0.19	168
Animals and pets (not veterinary care)	0.10	0.09	111
Walking, exercising, and playing with pets	0.04	0.04	100
Vehicles	0.03	0.04	75
Household management	0.26	0.21	124
Financial management	0.05	0.03	167
Household and personal organization and planning	0.09	0.09	100
Household and personal mail and messages (except email)	0.05	0.02	250
Household and personal email	0.07	0.06	117
Caring for and helping household members	**0.07**	**0.45**	**16**
Caring for and helping household children	0.02	0.37	5
Physical care for household children	0.00	0.17	0
Reading to or with household children	–	0.01	–
Playing with household children (except sports)	0.01	0.09	11
Talking with, listening to household children	0.00	0.02	0
Looking after household children as a primary activity	0.00	0.03	0
Picking up or dropping off household children	0.00	0.02	0
Activities related to household children's education	0.00	0.04	0
Helping household children with homework	0.00	0.03	0
Helping household adults	0.02	0.01	200
Caring for and helping people in other households	**0.24**	**0.16**	**150**
Caring for and helping children in other households	0.17	0.09	189

	average hours		index, people aged 65 to 74 to total people
	people aged 65 to 74	total people	
Helping adults in other households	0.05	0.06	83
Picking up or dropping off adults in other households	0.01	0.01	100
Work and work-related activities	**1.14**	**3.45**	**33**
Work, main job	1.09	3.28	33
Work, other job(s)	0.01	0.09	11
Education	**0.01**	**0.44**	**2**
Taking class	0.01	0.27	4
Taking class for degree, certification, or licensure	0.01	0.26	4
Research, homework	0.00	0.16	0
Consumer purchases (store, telephone, Internet)	**0.42**	**0.38**	**111**
Grocery shopping	0.14	0.10	140
Purchasing gas	0.01	0.01	100
Purchasing food (except groceries)	0.01	0.02	50
Shopping, except groceries, food, and gas	0.26	0.25	104
Professional and personal care services	**0.13**	**0.08**	**163**
Financial services and banking	0.01	0.01	100
Banking	0.01	0.01	100
Medical and care services	0.08	0.05	160
Using health and care services outside the home	0.06	0.04	150
Household services	**0.03**	**0.01**	**300**
Eating and drinking	**1.32**	**1.11**	**119**
Socializing, relaxing, and leisure	**6.56**	**4.62**	**142**
Socializing and communicating	0.66	0.64	103
Attending or hosting social events	0.06	0.07	86
Relaxing and leisure	5.75	3.83	150
Relaxing, thinking	0.45	0.27	167
Television	4.00	2.77	144
Listening to the radio	0.06	0.03	200
Listening to or playing music (not radio)	0.02	0.03	67
Playing games (including computer)	0.23	0.20	115
Computer use for leisure (except games)	0.13	0.14	93
Reading for personal interest	0.78	0.34	229
Arts and entertainment (except sports)	0.07	0.09	78
Sports, exercise, and recreation	**0.33**	**0.33**	**100**
Participating in sports, exercise, or recreation	0.30	0.29	103
Using cardiovascular equipment	0.01	0.02	50
Walking	0.07	0.04	175
Working out, unspecified	0.04	0.03	133
Religious and spiritual activities	**0.25**	**0.14**	**179**
Attending religious services	0.14	0.09	156
Participation in religious practices	0.08	0.04	200

	average hours		index, people aged 65 to 74 to total people
	people aged 65 to 74	total people	
Volunteer activities	**0.23**	**0.15**	**153**
Administrative and support activities	0.10	0.04	250
Telephone calls	**0.13**	**0.13**	**100**
Telephone calls to or from family members	0.06	0.04	150
Telephone calls to or from friends, neighbors, or acquaintances	0.04	0.04	100
Traveling	**1.05**	**1.20**	**88**
Travel related to personal care	0.00	0.01	0
Travel related to household activities	0.05	0.04	125
Travel related to household management	0.03	0.02	150
Travel related to caring for and helping household members	0.02	0.08	25
Travel related to caring for and helping household children	0.00	0.06	0
Travel related to helping household adults	0.02	0.02	100
Travel related to caring for and helping people in other households	0.07	0.06	117
Travel related to caring for and helping children in other households	0.03	0.02	150
Travel related to helping adults in other households	0.04	0.04	100
Travel related to work	0.09	0.28	32
Travel related to education	0.00	0.03	0
Travel related to taking class	0.00	0.03	0
Travel related to consumer purchases	0.28	0.24	117
Travel related to grocery shopping	0.07	0.05	140
Travel related to purchasing gas	0.01	0.02	50
Travel related to purchasing food (except groceries)	0.04	0.04	100
Travel related to shopping (except groceries, food, and gas)	0.16	0.12	133
Travel related to using professional and personal care services	0.05	0.04	125
Travel related to using financial services and banking	0.01	0.01	100
Travel related to using medical services	0.03	0.02	150
Travel related to eating and drinking	0.15	0.12	125
Travel related to socializing, relaxing, and leisure	0.20	0.18	111
Travel related to socializing and communicating	0.11	0.09	122
Travel related to attending or hosting social events	0.02	0.01	200
Travel related to relaxing and leisure	0.03	0.04	75
Travel related to arts and entertainment	0.02	0.02	100
Travel related to sports, exercise, and recreation	0.04	0.04	100
Travel related to participating in sports, exercise, recreation	0.03	0.04	75
Travel related to religious and spiritual activities	0.03	0.02	150
Travel related to volunteer activities	0.02	0.02	100

Note: The index is calculated by dividing average time spent by people in the age group doing primary activity by average time spent by total people doing primary activity and multiplying by 100. Primary activities are those respondents identified as their main activity. Other activities done simultaneously, such as eating while watching TV, are not included. Numbers may not add to total because not all subcategories are shown. If fewer than 2.0 percent of the total population participated in a primary activity, then the primary activity is not shown. "–" means sample is too small to make a reliable estimate.
Source: Bureau of Labor Statistics, unpublished tables from the 2008 American Time Use Survey, Internet site http://www.bls .gov/tus/home.htm; calculations by New Strategist

Table 8.5 Indexed Time Use of Men Aged 65 to 74, 2008

(hours spent doing primary activities on an average day by men aged 65 to 74 and by total men aged 15 or older, and index of time spent by men aged 65 to 74 to total men, 2008)

	average hours		index, men aged 65 to 74 to total men
	men aged 65 to 74	total men	
TOTAL, ALL ACTIVITIES	**24.00**	**24.00**	**100**
Personal care	**9.40**	**9.21**	**102**
Sleeping	8.88	8.56	104
Sleeplessness	0.08	0.05	160
Grooming	0.48	0.56	86
Health-related self-care	0.04	0.07	57
Household activities	**1.82**	**1.32**	**138**
Housework	0.22	0.24	92
Interior cleaning	0.16	0.17	94
Laundry	0.05	0.06	83
Storing interior household items, including food	0.02	0.01	200
Food and drink preparation, presentation, and clean-up	0.34	0.30	113
Food and drink preparation	0.29	0.25	116
Kitchen and food clean-up	0.05	0.05	100
Interior maintenance, repair, and decoration	0.10	0.10	100
Interior arrangement, decoration, and repairs	0.06	0.08	75
Exterior maintenance, repair, and decoration	0.28	0.08	350
Lawn, garden, and houseplants	0.47	0.26	181
Animals and pets (not veterinary care)	0.12	0.08	150
Walking, exercising, and playing with pets	0.04	0.04	100
Vehicles	0.06	0.07	86
Household management	0.22	0.16	138
Financial management	0.05	0.03	167
Household and personal organization and planning	0.07	0.07	100
Household and personal mail and messages (except email)	0.03	0.02	150
Household and personal email	0.06	0.05	120
Caring for and helping household members	**0.05**	**0.30**	**17**
Caring for and helping household children	0.02	0.25	8
Physical care for household children	0.00	0.09	0
Reading to or with household children	–	0.01	–
Playing with household children (except sports)	0.01	0.08	13
Talking with, listening to household children	0.00	0.01	0
Looking after household children as a primary activity	0.01	0.02	50
Picking up or dropping off household children	0.00	0.01	0
Activities related to household children's education	0.00	0.02	0
Helping household children with homework	0.00	0.02	0
Helping household adults	0.03	0.01	300
Caring for and helping people in other households	**0.20**	**0.13**	**154**
Caring for and helping children in other households	0.12	0.05	240

	average hours		index, men aged 65 to 74 to total men
	men aged 65 to 74	total men	
Helping adults in other households	0.08	0.07	114
Picking up or dropping off adults in other households	0.01	0.01	100
Work and work-related activities	**1.32**	**4.16**	**32**
Work, main job	1.30	3.96	33
Work, other job(s)	0.00	0.10	0
Education	**0.00**	**0.39**	**0**
Taking class	0.00	0.27	0
Taking class for degree, certification, or licensure	0.00	0.27	0
Research, homework	0.00	0.12	0
Consumer purchases (store, telephone, Internet)	**0.38**	**0.28**	**136**
Grocery shopping	0.11	0.06	183
Purchasing gas	0.01	0.01	100
Purchasing food (except groceries)	0.01	0.02	50
Shopping, except groceries, food, and gas	0.26	0.19	137
Professional and personal care services	**0.11**	**0.06**	**183**
Financial services and banking	0.01	0.01	100
Banking	0.00	0.00	–
Medical and care services	0.08	0.04	200
Using health and care services outside the home	0.07	0.03	233
Household services	**0.04**	**0.01**	**400**
Eating and drinking	**1.42**	**1.15**	**123**
Socializing, relaxing, and leisure	**6.94**	**4.83**	**144**
Socializing and communicating	0.56	0.59	95
Attending or hosting social events	0.06	0.06	100
Relaxing and leisure	6.24	4.09	153
Relaxing, thinking	0.43	0.27	159
Television	4.60	3.01	153
Listening to the radio	0.06	0.03	200
Listening to or playing music (not radio)	0.03	0.04	75
Playing games (including computer)	0.19	0.25	76
Computer use for leisure (except games)	0.14	0.15	93
Reading for personal interest	0.69	0.29	238
Arts and entertainment (except sports)	0.07	0.09	78
Sports, exercise, and recreation	**0.53**	**0.44**	**120**
Participating in sports, exercise, or recreation	0.50	0.40	125
Using cardiovascular equipment	0.01	0.01	100
Walking	0.08	0.04	200
Working out, unspecified	0.06	0.04	150
Religious and spiritual activities	**0.21**	**0.12**	**175**
Attending religious services	0.12	0.07	171
Participation in religious practices	0.07	0.03	233

	average hours		index, men aged 65 to 74 to total men
	men aged 65 to 74	total men	
Volunteer activities	**0.26**	**0.14**	**186**
Administrative and support activities	0.11	0.03	367
Telephone calls	**0.08**	**0.07**	**114**
Telephone calls to or from family members	0.03	0.02	150
Telephone calls to or from friends, neighbors, or acquaintances	0.02	0.02	100
Traveling	**0.98**	**1.23**	**80**
Travel related to personal care	0.00	0.01	0
Travel related to household activities	0.04	0.04	100
Travel related to household management	0.03	0.03	100
Travel related to caring for and helping household members	0.03	0.06	50
Travel related to caring for and helping household children	0.00	0.04	0
Travel related to helping household adults	0.03	0.02	150
Travel related to caring for and helping people in other households	0.07	0.06	117
Travel related to caring for and helping children in other households	0.02	0.01	200
Travel related to helping adults in other households	0.04	0.04	100
Travel related to work	0.11	0.36	31
Travel related to education	0.00	0.03	0
Travel related to taking class	0.00	0.02	0
Travel related to consumer purchases	0.26	0.21	124
Travel related to grocery shopping	0.05	0.04	125
Travel related to purchasing gas	0.03	0.02	150
Travel related to purchasing food (except groceries)	0.02	0.04	50
Travel related to shopping (except groceries, food, and gas)	0.16	0.11	145
Travel related to using professional and personal care services	0.05	0.03	167
Travel related to using financial services and banking	0.01	0.01	100
Travel related to using medical services	0.03	0.01	300
Travel related to eating and drinking	0.12	0.13	92
Travel related to socializing, relaxing, and leisure	0.16	0.18	89
Travel related to socializing and communicating	0.09	0.09	100
Travel related to attending or hosting social events	0.01	0.01	100
Travel related to relaxing and leisure	0.02	0.04	50
Travel related to arts and entertainment	0.02	0.02	100
Travel related to sports, exercise, and recreation	0.05	0.06	83
Travel related to participating in sports, exercise, recreation	0.05	0.05	100
Travel related to religious and spiritual activities	0.02	0.02	100
Travel related to volunteer activities	0.03	0.02	150

Note: The index is calculated by dividing average time spent by men in the age group doing primary activity by average time spent by total men doing primary activity and multiplying by 100. Primary activities are those respondents identified as their main activity. Other activities done simultaneously, such as eating while watching TV, are not included. Numbers may not add to total because not all subcategories are shown. If fewer than 2.0 percent of the total population participated in a primary activity, then the primary activity is not shown. "—" means denominator is zero or sample is too small to make a reliable estimate. Source: Bureau of Labor Statistics, unpublished tables from the 2008 American Time Use Survey, Internet site http://www.bls .gov/tus/home.htm; calculations by New Strategist

Table 8.6 Indexed Time Use of Women Aged 65 to 74, 2008

(hours spent doing primary activities on an average day by women aged 65 to 74 and by total women aged 15 or older, and index of time spent by women aged 65 to 74 to total women, 2008)

	average hours		index, women aged 65 to 74 to total women
	women aged 65 to 74	total women	
TOTAL, ALL ACTIVITIES	**24.00**	**24.00**	**100**
Personal care	**9.60**	**9.54**	**101**
Sleeping	8.67	8.64	100
Sleeplessness	0.11	0.07	157
Grooming	0.76	0.78	97
Health-related self-care	0.16	0.11	145
Household activities	**2.77**	**2.19**	**126**
Housework	1.23	0.90	137
Interior cleaning	0.74	0.55	135
Laundry	0.31	0.28	111
Storing interior household items, including food	0.04	0.02	200
Food and drink preparation, presentation, and clean-up	0.89	0.73	122
Food and drink preparation	0.66	0.55	120
Kitchen and food clean-up	0.22	0.18	122
Interior maintenance, repair, and decoration	0.03	0.04	75
Interior arrangement, decoration, and repairs	0.02	0.03	67
Exterior maintenance, repair, and decoration	0.04	0.03	133
Lawn, garden, and houseplants	0.19	0.12	158
Animals and pets (not veterinary care)	0.09	0.10	90
Walking, exercising, and playing with pets	0.04	0.04	100
Vehicles	0.01	0.01	100
Household management	0.29	0.25	116
Financial management	0.04	0.04	100
Household and personal organization and planning	0.11	0.11	100
Household and personal mail and messages (except email)	0.06	0.03	200
Household and personal email	0.08	0.07	114
Caring for and helping household members	**0.08**	**0.59**	**14**
Caring for and helping household children	0.03	0.48	6
Physical care for household children	0.01	0.24	4
Reading to or with household children	–	0.02	–
Playing with household children (except sports)	0.02	0.09	22
Talking with, listening to household children	0.00	0.02	0
Looking after household children as a primary activity	0.00	0.03	0
Picking up or dropping off household children	0.00	0.03	0
Activities related to household children's education	0.00	0.05	0
Helping household children with homework	0.00	0.04	0
Helping household adults	0.02	0.01	200
Caring for and helping people in other households	**0.27**	**0.20**	**135**
Caring for and helping children in other households	0.21	0.12	175

	average hours		index, women aged 65 to 74 to total women
	women aged 65 to 74	total women	
Helping adults in other households	0.04	0.05	80
Picking up or dropping off adults in other households	0.01	0.01	100
Work and work-related activities	**0.99**	**2.79**	**35**
Work, main job	0.92	2.63	35
Work, other job(s)	0.02	0.09	22
Education	**0.02**	**0.48**	**4**
Taking class	0.02	0.27	7
Taking class for degree, certification, or licensure	0.02	0.25	8
Research, homework	0.00	0.20	0
Consumer purchases (store, telephone, Internet)	**0.45**	**0.48**	**94**
Grocery shopping	0.18	0.13	138
Purchasing gas	0.00	0.01	0
Purchasing food (except groceries)	0.02	0.02	100
Shopping, except groceries, food, and gas	0.26	0.31	84
Professional and personal care services	**0.14**	**0.11**	**127**
Financial services and banking	0.01	0.01	100
Banking	0.01	0.01	100
Medical and care services	0.08	0.06	133
Using health and care services outside the home	0.05	0.05	100
Household services	**0.02**	**0.01**	**200**
Eating and drinking	**1.23**	**1.07**	**115**
Socializing, relaxing, and leisure	**6.22**	**4.42**	**141**
Socializing and communicating	0.75	0.68	110
Attending or hosting social events	0.06	0.08	75
Relaxing and leisure	5.34	3.58	149
Relaxing, thinking	0.46	0.26	177
Television	3.49	2.54	137
Listening to the radio	0.06	0.02	300
Listening to or playing music (not radio)	0.01	0.02	50
Playing games (including computer)	0.27	0.15	180
Computer use for leisure (except games)	0.12	0.14	86
Reading for personal interest	0.87	0.40	218
Arts and entertainment (except sports)	0.07	0.08	88
Sports, exercise, and recreation	**0.15**	**0.23**	**65**
Participating in sports, exercise, or recreation	0.13	0.20	65
Using cardiovascular equipment	0.01	0.02	50
Walking	0.05	0.04	125
Working out, unspecified	0.03	0.02	150
Religious and spiritual activities	**0.28**	**0.17**	**165**
Attending religious services	0.15	0.10	150
Participation in religious practices	0.09	0.05	180

	average hours		index, women aged 65 to 74 to total women
	women aged 65 to 74	total women	
Volunteer activities	**0.21**	**0.16**	**131**
Administrative and support activities	0.08	0.04	200
Telephone calls	**0.16**	**0.18**	**89**
Telephone calls to or from family members	0.08	0.07	114
Telephone calls to or from friends, neighbors, or acquaintances	0.05	0.06	83
Traveling	**1.12**	**1.17**	**96**
Travel related to personal care	0.00	0.01	0
Travel related to household activities	0.06	0.04	150
Travel related to household management	0.04	0.02	200
Travel related to caring for and helping household members	0.02	0.11	18
Travel related to caring for and helping household children	0.00	0.08	0
Travel related to helping household adults	0.01	0.02	50
Travel related to caring for and helping people in other households	0.08	0.07	114
Travel related to caring for and helping children in other households	0.04	0.02	200
Travel related to helping adults in other households	0.03	0.04	75
Travel related to work	0.07	0.20	35
Travel related to education	0.00	0.04	0
Travel related to taking class	0.00	0.03	0
Travel related to consumer purchases	0.29	0.27	107
Travel related to grocery shopping	0.08	0.06	133
Travel related to purchasing gas	0.00	0.02	0
Travel related to purchasing food (except groceries)	0.05	0.04	125
Travel related to shopping (except groceries, food, and gas)	0.16	0.14	114
Travel related to using professional and personal care services	0.05	0.05	100
Travel related to using financial services and banking	0.01	0.01	100
Travel related to using medical services	0.03	0.02	150
Travel related to eating and drinking	0.17	0.11	155
Travel related to socializing, relaxing, and leisure	0.23	0.17	135
Travel related to socializing and communicating	0.13	0.10	130
Travel related to attending or hosting social events	0.02	0.01	200
Travel related to relaxing and leisure	0.04	0.03	133
Travel related to arts and entertainment	0.02	0.02	100
Travel related to sports, exercise, and recreation	0.02	0.03	67
Travel related to participating in sports, exercise, recreation	0.02	0.03	67
Travel related to religious and spiritual activities	0.03	0.02	150
Travel related to volunteer activities	0.02	0.02	100

Note: The index is calculated by dividing average time spent by women in the age group doing primary activity by average time spent by total women doing primary activity and multiplying by 100. Primary activities are those respondents identified as their main activity. Other activities done simultaneously, such as eating while watching TV, are not included. Numbers may not add to total because not all subcategories are shown. If fewer than 2.0 percent of the total population participated in a primary activity, then the primary activity is not shown. "–" means sample is too small to make a reliable estimate.
Source: Bureau of Labor Statistics, unpublished tables from the 2008 American Time Use Survey, Internet site http://www.bls .gov/tus/home.htm; calculations by New Strategist

Table 8.7 Indexed Time Use on of People Aged 65 to 74 by Sex, 2008

(average hours spent by people aged 65 to 74 doing primary activities on an average day by sex, and index of women's time to men's, 2008)

	average hours, aged 65 to 74		index of women to men
	men	women	
TOTAL, ALL ACTIVITIES	**24.00**	**24.00**	**100**
Personal care	**9.40**	**9.60**	**102**
Sleeping	8.88	8.67	98
Sleeplessness	0.08	0.11	138
Grooming	0.48	0.76	158
Health-related self-care	0.04	0.16	400
Household activities	**1.82**	**2.77**	**152**
Housework	0.22	1.23	559
Interior cleaning	0.16	0.74	463
Laundry	0.05	0.31	620
Storing interior household items, including food	0.02	0.04	200
Food and drink preparation, presentation, and clean-up	0.34	0.89	262
Food and drink preparation	0.29	0.66	228
Kitchen and food clean-up	0.05	0.22	440
Interior maintenance, repair, and decoration	0.10	0.03	30
Interior arrangement, decoration, and repairs	0.06	0.02	33
Exterior maintenance, repair, and decoration	0.28	0.04	14
Lawn, garden, and houseplants	0.47	0.19	40
Animals and pets (not veterinary care)	0.12	0.09	75
Walking, exercising, and playing with pets	0.04	0.04	100
Vehicles	0.06	0.01	17
Household management	0.22	0.29	132
Financial management	0.05	0.04	80
Household and personal organization and planning	0.07	0.11	157
Household and personal mail and messages (except email)	0.03	0.06	200
Household and personal email	0.06	0.08	133
Caring for and helping household members	**0.05**	**0.08**	**160**
Caring for and helping household children	0.02	0.03	150
Physical care for household children	0.00	0.01	–
Reading to or with household children	–	–	–
Playing with household children (except sports)	0.01	0.02	200
Talking with, listening to household children	0.00	0.00	–
Looking after household children as a primary activity	0.01	0.00	0
Picking up or dropping off household children	0.00	0.00	–
Activities related to household children's education	0.00	0.00	–
Helping household children with homework	0.00	0.00	–
Helping household adults	0.03	0.02	67
Caring for and helping people in other households	**0.20**	**0.27**	**135**
Caring for and helping children in other households	0.12	0.21	175

	average hours, aged 65 to 74		index of women to men
	men	women	
Helping adults in other households	0.08	0.04	50
Picking up or dropping off adults in other households	0.01	0.01	100
Work and work-related activities	**1.32**	**0.99**	**75**
Work, main job	1.30	0.92	71
Work, other job(s)	0.00	0.02	–
Education	**0.00**	**0.02**	**–**
Taking class	0.00	0.02	–
Taking class for degree, certification, or licensure	0.00	0.02	–
Research, homework	0.00	0.00	–
Consumer purchases (store, telephone, Internet)	**0.38**	**0.45**	**118**
Grocery shopping	0.11	0.18	164
Purchasing gas	0.01	0.00	0
Purchasing food (except groceries)	0.01	0.02	200
Shopping, except groceries, food, and gas	0.26	0.26	100
Professional and personal care services	**0.11**	**0.14**	**127**
Financial services and banking	0.01	0.01	100
Banking	0.00	0.01	–
Medical and care services	0.08	0.08	100
Using health and care services outside the home	0.07	0.05	71
Household services	**0.04**	**0.02**	**50**
Eating and drinking	**1.42**	**1.23**	**87**
Socializing, relaxing, and leisure	**6.94**	**6.22**	**90**
Socializing and communicating	0.56	0.75	134
Attending or hosting social events	0.06	0.06	100
Relaxing and leisure	6.24	5.34	86
Relaxing, thinking	0.43	0.46	107
Television	4.60	3.49	76
Listening to the radio	0.06	0.06	100
Listening to or playing music (not radio)	0.03	0.01	33
Playing games (including computer)	0.19	0.27	142
Computer use for leisure (except games)	0.14	0.12	86
Reading for personal interest	0.69	0.87	126
Arts and entertainment (except sports)	0.07	0.07	100
Sports, exercise, and recreation	**0.53**	**0.15**	**28**
Participating in sports, exercise, or recreation	0.50	0.13	26
Using cardiovascular equipment	0.01	0.01	100
Walking	0.08	0.05	63
Working out, unspecified	0.06	0.03	50
Religious and spiritual activities	**0.21**	**0.28**	**133**
Attending religious services	0.12	0.15	125
Participation in religious practices	0.07	0.09	129

	average hours, aged 65 to 74		index of women to men
	men	women	
Volunteer activities	**0.26**	**0.21**	**81**
Administrative and support activities	0.11	0.08	73
Telephone calls	**0.08**	**0.16**	**200**
Telephone calls to or from family members	0.03	0.08	267
Telephone calls to or from friends, neighbors, or acquaintances	0.02	0.05	250
Traveling	**0.98**	**1.12**	**114**
Travel related to personal care	0.00	0.00	–
Travel related to household activities	0.04	0.06	150
Travel related to household management	0.03	0.04	133
Travel related to caring for and helping household members	0.03	0.02	67
Travel related to caring for and helping household children	0.00	0.00	–
Travel related to helping household adults	0.03	0.01	33
Travel related to caring for and helping people in other households	0.07	0.08	114
Travel related to caring for and helping children in other households	0.02	0.04	200
Travel related to helping adults in other households	0.04	0.03	75
Travel related to work	0.11	0.07	64
Travel related to education	0.00	0.00	–
Travel related to taking class	0.00	0.00	–
Travel related to consumer purchases	0.26	0.29	112
Travel related to grocery shopping	0.05	0.08	160
Travel related to purchasing gas	0.03	0.00	0
Travel related to purchasing food (except groceries)	0.02	0.05	250
Travel related to shopping (except groceries, food, and gas)	0.16	0.16	100
Travel related to using professional and personal care services	0.05	0.05	100
Travel related to using financial services and banking	0.01	0.01	100
Travel related to using medical services	0.03	0.03	100
Travel related to eating and drinking	0.12	0.17	142
Travel related to socializing, relaxing, and leisure	0.16	0.23	144
Travel related to socializing and communicating	0.09	0.13	144
Travel related to attending or hosting social events	0.01	0.02	200
Travel related to relaxing and leisure	0.02	0.04	200
Travel related to arts and entertainment	0.02	0.02	100
Travel related to sports, exercise, and recreation	0.05	0.02	40
Travel related to participating in sports, exercise, recreation	0.05	0.02	40
Travel related to religious and spiritual activities	0.02	0.03	150
Travel related to volunteer activities	0.03	0.02	67

Note: The index is calculated by dividing women's time by men's time and multiplying by 100. Primary activities are those respondents identified as their main activity. Other activities done simultaneously, such as eating while watching TV, are not included. Numbers may not add to total because not all subcategories are shown. If fewer than 2.0 percent of the total population participated in a primary activity, then the primary activity is not shown. "–" means denominator is zero or sample is too small to make a reliable estimate.
Source: Bureau of Labor Statistics, unpublished tables from the 2008 American Time Use Survey, Internet site http://www.bls.gov/tus/home.htm; calculations by New Strategist

Table 8.8 Indexed Participation in Primary Activities by Total People Aged 65 to 74, 2008

(percent of people aged 65 to 74 and total people aged 15 or older participating in primary activities on an average day, and index of participation by people aged 65 to 74 to total people, 2008)

	percent participating		index, people aged 65 to 74 to total
	people aged 65 to 74	total people	
TOTAL, ALL ACTIVITIES	**100.0%**	**100.0%**	**100**
Personal care	**100.0**	**100.0**	**100**
Sleeping	100.0	99.9	100
Sleeplessness	5.9	5.2	113
Grooming	73.9	79.3	93
Health-related self-care	14.0	6.4	221
Household activities	**84.1**	**75.5**	**111**
Housework	39.4	35.5	111
Interior cleaning	29.2	24.5	119
Laundry	15.9	16.2	98
Storing interior household items, including food	7.6	5.0	152
Food and drink preparation, presentation, and clean-up	59.0	52.3	113
Food and drink preparation	54.9	49.3	111
Kitchen and food clean-up	23.4	20.8	112
Interior maintenance, repair, and decoration	4.5	3.0	149
Interior arrangement, decoration, and repairs	2.1	2.0	107
Exterior maintenance, repair, and decoration	5.9	2.7	216
Lawn, garden, and houseplants	16.0	9.4	171
Animals and pets (not veterinary care)	15.6	14.5	107
Walking, exercising, and playing with pets	5.9	5.8	102
Vehicles	3.1	2.7	114
Household management	33.4	29.0	115
Financial management	5.4	4.0	134
Household and personal organization and planning	14.3	14.1	102
Household and personal mail and messages (except email)	12.7	6.9	186
Household and personal email	9.2	9.4	98
Caring for and helping household members	**7.1**	**26.1**	**27**
Caring for and helping household children	1.6	21.9	7
Physical care for household children	0.9	15.7	6
Reading to or with household children	–	2.6	–
Playing with household children (except sports)	0.4	5.4	7
Talking with, listening to household children	0.1	3.0	2
Looking after household children as a primary activity	0.3	2.3	11
Picking up or dropping off household children	0.7	9.2	7
Activities related to household children's education	0.3	3.8	8
Helping household children with homework	0.3	3.4	8
Helping household adults	3.5	3.6	97
Caring for and helping people in other households	**16.6**	**13.3**	**125**
Caring for and helping children in other households	9.0	5.6	162

	percent participating		index, people aged 65 to 74 to total
	people aged 65 to 74	total people	
Helping adults in other households	8.9%	8.0%	110
Picking up or dropping off adults in other households	4.8	5.0	96
Work and work-related activities	**18.1**	**46.6**	**39**
Work, main job	17.3	43.9	39
Work, other job(s)	0.3	2.4	11
Education	**0.7**	**7.9**	**9**
Taking class	0.3	5.2	6
Taking class for degree, certification, or licensure	0.3	4.8	7
Research, homework	0.4	5.8	7
Consumer purchases (store, telephone, Internet)	**39.7**	**40.7**	**98**
Grocery shopping	16.7	12.9	130
Purchasing gas	3.0	4.0	77
Purchasing food (except groceries)	7.3	12.0	61
Shopping, except groceries, food, and gas	24.6	23.5	105
Professional and personal care services	**11.1**	**8.9**	**125**
Financial services and banking	3.5	3.2	109
Banking	3.1	3.0	104
Medical and care services	5.2	3.6	143
Using health and care services outside the home	4.3	3.4	126
Household services	**3.7**	**2.1**	**178**
Eating and drinking	**98.5**	**96.0**	**103**
Socializing, relaxing, and leisure	**98.3**	**95.4**	**103**
Socializing and communicating	39.3	37.6	104
Attending or hosting social events	2.5	2.3	107
Relaxing and leisure	96.7	91.3	106
Relaxing, thinking	21.8	19.9	109
Television	87.2	80.9	108
Listening to the radio	2.7	2.0	136
Listening to or playing music (not radio)	1.8	2.6	68
Playing games (including computer)	11.3	9.0	126
Computer use for leisure (except games)	6.5	9.5	69
Reading for personal interest	44.6	23.9	187
Arts and entertainment (except sports)	3.0	3.2	91
Sports, exercise, and recreation	**17.9**	**18.9**	**95**
Participating in sports, exercise, or recreation	17.5	17.9	97
Using cardiovascular equipment	1.2	2.2	57
Walking	8.0	4.8	167
Working out, unspecified	3.6	3.2	112
Religious and spiritual activities	**16.4**	**9.2**	**177**
Attending religious services	7.6	4.9	156
Participation in religious practices	8.8	4.6	192

	percent participating		index, people aged 65 to 74 to total
	people aged 65 to 74	total people	
Volunteer activities	**8.6%**	**6.7%**	**128**
Administrative and support activities	4.4	2.5	172
Telephone calls	**17.7**	**15.4**	**115**
Telephone calls to or from family members	10.4	7.3	142
Telephone calls to or from friends, neighbors, or acquaintances	5.1	5.6	92
Traveling	**76.4**	**86.9**	**88**
Travel related to personal care	1.1	2.5	42
Travel related to household activities	11.1	9.4	118
Travel related to household management	7.5	6.1	123
Travel related to caring for and helping household members	3.8	13.6	28
Travel related to caring for and helping household children	0.9	11.0	8
Travel related to helping household adults	2.6	2.6	103
Travel related to caring for and helping people in other households	10.6	10.5	101
Travel related to caring for and helping children in other households	3.9	3.5	110
Travel related to helping adults in other households	7.3	7.1	103
Travel related to work	13.0	38.2	34
Travel related to education	0.3	5.0	5
Travel related to taking class	0.2	4.4	5
Travel related to consumer purchases	39.3	39.6	99
Travel related to grocery shopping	16.7	12.9	130
Travel related to purchasing gas	3.0	3.9	76
Travel related to purchasing food (except groceries)	7.1	11.2	64
Travel related to shopping (except groceries, food, and gas)	24.3	22.7	107
Travel related to using professional and personal care services	9.7	8.1	120
Travel related to using financial services and banking	3.3	3.0	108
Travel related to using medical services	4.0	3.3	120
Travel related to eating and drinking	26.5	25.0	106
Travel related to socializing, relaxing, and leisure	29.3	28.6	102
Travel related to socializing and communicating	20.0	18.6	108
Travel related to attending or hosting social events	2.1	2.0	104
Travel related to relaxing and leisure	6.5	8.9	73
Travel related to arts and entertainment	2.7	2.6	106
Travel related to sports, exercise, and recreation	8.3	9.6	87
Travel related to participating in sports, exercise, recreation	7.8	8.6	92
Travel related to religious and spiritual activities	8.0	5.1	157
Travel related to volunteer activities	5.4	4.3	127

Note: The index is calculated by dividing percent of people in the age group doing primary activity by percent of total people doing primary activity and multiplying by 100. Primary activities are those respondents identified as their main activity. Other activities done simultaneously, such as eating while watching TV, are not included. If fewer than 2.0 percent of the total population participated in a primary activity, then the primary activity is not shown. "–" means sample is too small to make a reliable estimate.
Source: Bureau of Labor Statistics, unpublished tables from the 2008 American Time Use Survey, Internet site http://www.bls.gov/tus/home.htm; calculations by New Strategist

Table 8.9 Indexed Participation in Primary Activities by Men Aged 65 to 74, 2008

(percent of men aged 65 to 74 and total men aged 15 or older participating in primary activities on an average day, and index of participation by men aged 65 to 74 to total men, 2008)

	percent participating		index, men aged 65 to 74 to total men
	men aged 65 to 74	total men	
TOTAL, ALL ACTIVITIES	**100.0%**	**100.0**	**100**
Personal care	**100.0**	**100.0**	**100**
Sleeping	100.0	99.9	100
Sleeplessness	3.7	4.5	82
Grooming	66.4	76.6	87
Health-related self-care	11.5	4.8	238
Household activities	**77.6**	**66.6**	**117**
Housework	16.7	19.7	85
Interior cleaning	11.9	13.5	89
Laundry	4.1	6.3	65
Storing interior household items, including food	2.9	2.9	101
Food and drink preparation, presentation, and clean-up	41.9	38.4	109
Food and drink preparation	39.9	36.0	111
Kitchen and food clean-up	9.0	9.5	95
Interior maintenance, repair, and decoration	7.2	3.9	184
Interior arrangement, decoration, and repairs	2.8	2.4	115
Exterior maintenance, repair, and decoration	9.6	3.8	253
Lawn, garden, and houseplants	19.5	11.0	177
Animals and pets (not veterinary care)	15.2	12.1	126
Walking, exercising, and playing with pets	6.2	5.2	119
Vehicles	4.6	4.5	101
Household management	29.9	24.0	125
Financial management	5.2	3.2	162
Household and personal organization and planning	12.2	11.1	110
Household and personal mail and messages (except email)	10.1	5.5	185
Household and personal email	8.3	7.4	112
Caring for and helping household members	**8.4**	**20.7**	**41**
Caring for and helping household children	1.6	16.8	9
Physical care for household children	0.6	10.4	6
Reading to or with household children	–	1.7	–
Playing with household children (except sports)	0.3	4.7	7
Talking with, listening to household children	0.1	1.7	7
Looking after household children as a primary activity	0.5	1.5	34
Picking up or dropping off household children	0.6	6.2	9
Activities related to household children's education	0.1	2.2	6
Helping household children with homework	0.1	2.0	6
Helping household adults	5.5	3.5	158
Caring for and helping people in other households	**15.3**	**11.0**	**140**
Caring for and helping children in other households	7.4	3.6	205

	percent participating		index, men aged 65 to 74 to total men
	men aged 65 to 74	total men	
Helping adults in other households	9.2%	7.5%	123
Picking up or dropping off adults in other households	4.9	4.4	109
Work and work-related activities	**21.6**	**53.4**	**40**
Work, main job	21.0	50.1	42
Work, other job(s)	0.1	2.3	5
Education	**0.4**	**6.9**	**5**
Taking class	0.0	5.0	1
Taking class for degree, certification, or licensure	0.0	4.8	1
Research, homework	0.3	4.6	7
Consumer purchases (store, telephone, Internet)	**38.2**	**35.6**	**107**
Grocery shopping	13.9	9.6	146
Purchasing gas	4.2	4.3	98
Purchasing food (except groceries)	6.6	11.8	56
Shopping, except groceries, food, and gas	24.3	19.6	124
Professional and personal care services	**9.6**	**6.7**	**144**
Financial services and banking	3.8	3.1	121
Banking	3.1	2.8	110
Medical and care services	4.2	2.4	173
Using health and care services outside the home	4.2	2.3	184
Household services	**5.0**	**2.1**	**240**
Eating and drinking	**98.4**	**96.5**	**102**
Socializing, relaxing, and leisure	**98.9**	**95.4**	**104**
Socializing and communicating	37.7	34.9	108
Attending or hosting social events	2.4	2.0	120
Relaxing and leisure	97.7	92.1	106
Relaxing, thinking	17.8	20.4	87
Television	89.3	82.3	108
Listening to the radio	2.5	2.5	97
Listening to or playing music (not radio)	2.8	3.3	87
Playing games (including computer)	8.1	9.6	85
Computer use for leisure (except games)	6.4	9.5	67
Reading for personal interest	40.9	21.1	194
Arts and entertainment (except sports)	3.2	3.3	97
Sports, exercise, and recreation	**23.2**	**22.0**	**105**
Participating in sports, exercise, or recreation	22.7	21.0	108
Using cardiovascular equipment	1.3	1.8	69
Walking	9.3	4.9	188
Working out, unspecified	4.1	3.5	116
Religious and spiritual activities	**12.1**	**7.7**	**157**
Attending religious services	6.8	4.0	169
Participation in religious practices	4.7	3.7	128

	percent participating		index, men aged 65 to 74 to total men
	men aged 65 to 74	total men	
Volunteer activities	**7.8%**	**5.7%**	**137**
Administrative and support activities	3.9	1.9	199
Telephone calls	**9.9**	**10.0**	**99**
Telephone calls to or from family members	5.9	3.8	154
Telephone calls to or from friends, neighbors, or acquaintances	2.6	3.7	70
Traveling	**81.8**	**88.5**	**92**
Travel related to personal care	1.1	3.1	35
Travel related to household activities	9.9	8.5	117
Travel related to household management	6.1	5.5	111
Travel related to caring for and helping household members	5.4	9.9	55
Travel related to caring for and helping household children	0.9	7.4	12
Travel related to helping household adults	4.3	2.4	179
Travel related to caring for and helping people in other households	9.9	9.3	107
Travel related to caring for and helping children in other households	3.4	2.5	136
Travel related to helping adults in other households	7.1	6.7	105
Travel related to work	15.1	44.4	34
Travel related to education	0.1	4.6	2
Travel related to taking class	–	4.1	–
Travel related to consumer purchases	37.4	34.5	108
Travel related to grocery shopping	13.9	9.5	146
Travel related to purchasing gas	4.2	4.2	100
Travel related to purchasing food (except groceries)	6.2	11.0	57
Travel related to shopping (except groceries, food, and gas)	23.8	18.9	126
Travel related to using professional and personal care services	9.4	6.3	149
Travel related to using financial services and banking	3.6	3.0	121
Travel related to using medical services	4.0	2.3	175
Travel related to eating and drinking	27.4	27.3	100
Travel related to socializing, relaxing, and leisure	29.0	28.0	103
Travel related to socializing and communicating	19.3	17.5	110
Travel related to attending or hosting social events	1.9	1.7	110
Travel related to relaxing and leisure	6.1	9.4	65
Travel related to arts and entertainment	3.1	2.8	113
Travel related to sports, exercise, and recreation	11.4	11.5	99
Travel related to participating in sports, exercise, recreation	10.5	10.4	101
Travel related to religious and spiritual activities	7.3	4.4	167
Travel related to volunteer activities	5.4	3.8	140

Note: The index is calculated by dividing percent of men in the age group doing primary activity by percent of total men doing primary activity and multiplying by 100. Primary activities are those respondents identified as their main activity. Other activities done simultaneously, such as eating while watching TV, are not included. If fewer than 2.0 percent of the total population participated in a primary activity, then the primary activity is not shown. "–" means sample is too small to make a reliable estimate.
Source: Bureau of Labor Statistics, unpublished tables from the 2008 American Time Use Survey, Internet site http://www.bls .gov/tus/home.htm; calculations by New Strategist

Table 8.10 Indexed Participation in Primary Activities by Women Aged 65 to 74, 2008

(percent of women aged 65 to 74 and total women aged 15 or older participating in primary activities on an average day, and index of participation by women aged 65 to 74 to total women, 2008)

	percent participating		index, women aged 65 to 74 to total women
	women aged 65 to 74	total women	
TOTAL, ALL ACTIVITIES	**100.0%**	**100.0%**	**100**
Personal care	**100.0**	**100.0**	**100**
Sleeping	100.0	99.9	100
Sleeplessness	7.8	5.8	133
Grooming	80.3	81.8	98
Health-related self-care	16.2	7.8	208
Household activities	**89.7**	**84.0**	**107**
Housework	58.8	50.3	117
Interior cleaning	44.0	34.9	126
Laundry	26.0	25.5	102
Storing interior household items, including food	11.6	7.0	166
Food and drink preparation, presentation, and clean-up	73.7	65.3	113
Food and drink preparation	67.7	61.8	110
Kitchen and food clean-up	35.6	31.5	113
Interior maintenance, repair, and decoration	2.2	2.2	101
Interior arrangement, decoration, and repairs	1.5	1.5	98
Exterior maintenance, repair, and decoration	2.8	1.8	160
Lawn, garden, and houseplants	13.1	7.9	165
Animals and pets (not veterinary care)	15.8	16.7	95
Walking, exercising, and playing with pets	5.5	6.3	88
Vehicles	1.8	1.0	181
Household management	36.4	33.8	108
Financial management	5.7	4.9	116
Household and personal organization and planning	16.2	16.8	96
Household and personal mail and messages (except email)	15.0	8.2	183
Household and personal email	10.0	11.3	89
Caring for and helping household members	**5.9**	**31.2**	**19**
Caring for and helping household children	1.6	26.7	6
Physical care for household children	1.1	20.6	5
Reading to or with household children	–	3.5	–
Playing with household children (except sports)	0.4	6.1	7
Talking with, listening to household children	–	4.3	–
Looking after household children as a primary activity	0.0	3.0	2
Picking up or dropping off household children	0.8	12.1	6
Activities related to household children's education	0.4	5.4	8
Helping household children with homework	0.4	4.8	9
Helping household adults	1.8	3.7	48
Caring for and helping people in other households	**17.8**	**15.5**	**115**
Caring for and helping children in other households	10.3	7.4	140

	percent participating		index, women aged 65 to 74 to total women
	women aged 65 to 74	total women	
Helping adults in other households	8.6%	8.5%	100
Picking up or dropping off adults in other households	4.7	5.4	86
Work and work-related activities	**15.1**	**40.3**	**37**
Work, main job	14.2	38.0	37
Work, other job(s)	0.4	2.4	17
Education	**1.0**	**8.9**	**12**
Taking class	0.5	5.3	10
Taking class for degree, certification, or licensure	0.5	4.7	11
Research, homework	0.5	7.0	7
Consumer purchases (store, telephone, Internet)	**40.9**	**45.4**	**90**
Grocery shopping	19.1	16.1	119
Purchasing gas	2.1	3.7	56
Purchasing food (except groceries)	8.0	12.3	65
Shopping, except groceries, food, and gas	24.9	27.2	92
Professional and personal care services	**12.4**	**11.0**	**113**
Financial services and banking	3.3	3.3	99
Banking	3.2	3.3	99
Medical and care services	6.0	4.8	127
Using health and care services outside the home	4.4	4.5	98
Household services	**2.6**	**2.1**	**126**
Eating and drinking	**98.6**	**95.6**	**103**
Socializing, relaxing, and leisure	**97.9**	**95.4**	**103**
Socializing and communicating	40.6	40.1	101
Attending or hosting social events	2.6	2.7	97
Relaxing and leisure	95.8	90.6	106
Relaxing, thinking	25.2	19.5	129
Television	85.5	79.5	107
Listening to the radio	2.9	1.5	194
Listening to or playing music (not radio)	0.8	2.0	42
Playing games (including computer)	14.1	8.4	167
Computer use for leisure (except games)	6.6	9.5	70
Reading for personal interest	47.7	26.5	180
Arts and entertainment (except sports)	2.7	3.2	87
Sports, exercise, and recreation	**13.3**	**15.9**	**83**
Participating in sports, exercise, or recreation	13.0	15.0	87
Using cardiovascular equipment	1.2	2.5	48
Walking	7.0	4.7	148
Working out, unspecified	3.1	2.9	108
Religious and spiritual activities	**20.0**	**10.7**	**188**
Attending religious services	8.3	5.7	146
Participation in religious practices	12.3	5.4	227

| | percent participating | | index, women aged 65 to 74 |
	women aged 65 to 74	total women	to total women
Volunteer activities	**9.2%**	**7.6%**	**120**
Administrative and support activities	4.8	3.1	155
Telephone calls	**24.5**	**20.4**	**120**
Telephone calls to or from family members	14.3	10.7	134
Telephone calls to or from friends, neighbors, or acquaintances	7.3	7.4	99
Traveling	**71.8**	**85.5**	**84**
Travel related to personal care	1.1	2.0	53
Travel related to household activities	12.2	10.3	119
Travel related to household management	8.7	6.7	130
Travel related to caring for and helping household members	2.4	17.1	14
Travel related to caring for and helping household children	0.8	14.3	6
Travel related to helping household adults	1.2	2.7	45
Travel related to caring for and helping people in other households	11.2	11.6	96
Travel related to caring for and helping children in other households	4.3	4.5	96
Travel related to helping adults in other households	7.5	7.4	101
Travel related to work	11.2	32.2	35
Travel related to education	0.4	5.4	8
Travel related to taking class	0.4	4.6	9
Travel related to consumer purchases	40.8	44.4	92
Travel related to grocery shopping	19.1	16.0	119
Travel related to purchasing gas	1.9	3.7	53
Travel related to purchasing food (except groceries)	7.9	11.5	69
Travel related to shopping (except groceries, food, and gas)	24.8	26.3	94
Travel related to using professional and personal care services	10.0	9.8	102
Travel related to using financial services and banking	2.9	3.1	96
Travel related to using medical services	3.9	4.3	92
Travel related to eating and drinking	25.7	22.8	113
Travel related to socializing, relaxing, and leisure	29.6	29.2	101
Travel related to socializing and communicating	20.5	19.5	105
Travel related to attending or hosting social events	2.3	2.3	99
Travel related to relaxing and leisure	6.9	8.5	81
Travel related to arts and entertainment	2.4	2.4	99
Travel related to sports, exercise, and recreation	5.7	7.7	74
Travel related to participating in sports, exercise, recreation	5.5	6.8	82
Travel related to religious and spiritual activities	8.6	5.8	148
Travel related to volunteer activities	5.5	4.7	117

Note: The index is calculated by dividing percent of women in the age group doing primary activity by percent of total women doing primary activity and multiplying by 100. Primary activities are those respondents identified as their main activity. Other activities done simultaneously, such as eating while watching TV, are not included. If fewer than 2.0 percent of the total population participated in a primary activity, then the primary activity is not shown. "–" means sample is too small to make a reliable estimate.

Source: Bureau of Labor Statistics, unpublished tables from the 2008 American Time Use Survey, Internet site http://www.bls .gov/tus/home.htm; calculations by New Strategist

Table 8.11 Indexed Participation in Primary Activities of People Aged 65 to 74 by Sex, 2008

(percent of people aged 65 to 74 participating in primary activities on an average day by sex, and index of women's participation to men's, 2008)

	aged 65 to 74, percent participating		index of women to men
	men	women	
TOTAL, ALL ACTIVITIES	**100.0%**	**100.0%**	**100**
Personal care	**100.0**	**100.0**	**100**
Sleeping	100.0	100.0	100
Sleeplessness	3.7	7.8	210
Grooming	66.4	80.3	121
Health-related self-care	11.5	16.2	142
Household activities	**77.6**	**89.7**	**116**
Housework	16.7	58.8	352
Interior cleaning	11.9	44.0	369
Laundry	4.1	26.0	634
Storing interior household items, including food	2.9	11.6	401
Food and drink preparation, presentation, and clean-up	41.9	73.7	176
Food and drink preparation	39.9	67.7	170
Kitchen and food clean-up	9.0	35.6	393
Interior maintenance, repair, and decoration	7.2	2.2	31
Interior arrangement, decoration, and repairs	2.8	1.5	53
Exterior maintenance, repair, and decoration	9.6	2.8	29
Lawn, garden, and houseplants	19.5	13.1	67
Animals and pets (not veterinary care)	15.2	15.8	104
Walking, exercising, and playing with pets	6.2	5.5	89
Vehicles	4.6	1.8	39
Household management	29.9	36.4	122
Financial management	5.2	5.7	110
Household and personal organization and planning	12.2	16.2	132
Household and personal mail and messages (except email)	10.1	15.0	148
Household and personal email	8.3	10.0	120
Caring for and helping household members	**8.4**	**5.9**	**70**
Caring for and helping household children	1.6	1.6	102
Physical care for household children	0.6	1.1	178
Reading to or with household children	–	–	–
Playing with household children (except sports)	0.3	0.4	128
Talking with, listening to household children	0.1	–	–
Looking after household children as a primary activity	0.5	0.0	9
Picking up or dropping off household children	0.6	0.8	136
Activities related to household children's education	0.1	0.4	328
Helping household children with homework	0.1	0.4	328
Helping household adults	5.5	1.8	33
Caring for and helping people in other households	**15.3**	**17.8**	**116**
Caring for and helping children in other households	7.4	10.3	139

	aged 65 to 74, percent participating		index of women to men
	men	women	
Helping adults in other households	9.2%	8.6%	93
Picking up or dropping off adults in other households	4.9	4.7	96
Work and work-related activities	**21.6**	**15.1**	**70**
Work, main job	21.0	14.2	68
Work, other job(s)	0.1	0.4	334
Education	**0.4**	**1.0**	**285**
Taking class	0.0	0.5	1239
Taking class for degree, certification, or licensure	0.0	0.5	1239
Research, homework	0.3	0.5	153
Consumer purchases (store, telephone, Internet)	**38.2**	**40.9**	**107**
Grocery shopping	13.9	19.1	137
Purchasing gas	4.2	2.1	49
Purchasing food (except groceries)	6.6	8.0	121
Shopping, except groceries, food, and gas	24.3	24.9	102
Professional and personal care services	**9.6**	**12.4**	**130**
Financial services and banking	3.8	3.3	86
Banking	3.1	3.2	105
Medical and care services	4.2	6.0	142
Using health and care services outside the home	4.2	4.4	104
Household services	**5.0**	**2.6**	**52**
Eating and drinking	**98.4**	**98.6**	**100**
Socializing, relaxing, and leisure	**98.9**	**97.9**	**99**
Socializing and communicating	37.7	40.6	108
Attending or hosting social events	2.4	2.6	110
Relaxing and leisure	97.7	95.8	98
Relaxing, thinking	17.8	25.2	142
Television	89.3	85.5	96
Listening to the radio	2.5	2.9	119
Listening to or playing music (not radio)	2.8	0.8	29
Playing games (including computer)	8.1	14.1	173
Computer use for leisure (except games)	6.4	6.6	103
Reading for personal interest	40.9	47.7	117
Arts and entertainment (except sports)	3.2	2.7	85
Sports, exercise, and recreation	**23.2**	**13.3**	**57**
Participating in sports, exercise, or recreation	22.7	13.0	57
Using cardiovascular equipment	1.3	1.2	94
Walking	9.3	7.0	75
Working out, unspecified	4.1	3.1	76
Religious and spiritual activities	**12.1**	**20.0**	**166**
Attending religious services	6.8	8.3	122
Participation in religious practices	4.7	12.3	259

	aged 65 to 74, percent participating		index of women to men
	men	women	
Volunteer activities	**7.8%**	**9.2%**	**117**
Administrative and support activities	3.9	4.8	123
Telephone calls	**9.9**	**24.5**	**248**
Telephone calls to or from family members	5.9	14.3	244
Telephone calls to or from friends, neighbors, or acquaintances	2.6	7.3	284
Traveling	**81.8**	**71.8**	**88**
Travel related to personal care	1.1	1.1	98
Travel related to household activities	9.9	12.2	123
Travel related to household management	6.1	8.7	143
Travel related to caring for and helping household members	5.4	2.4	44
Travel related to caring for and helping household children	0.9	0.8	95
Travel related to helping household adults	4.3	1.2	29
Travel related to caring for and helping people in other households	9.9	11.2	113
Travel related to caring for and helping children in other households	3.4	4.3	128
Travel related to helping adults in other households	7.1	7.5	106
Travel related to work	15.1	11.2	74
Travel related to education	0.1	0.4	549
Travel related to taking class	–	0.4	–
Travel related to consumer purchases	37.4	40.8	109
Travel related to grocery shopping	13.9	19.1	137
Travel related to purchasing gas	4.2	1.9	46
Travel related to purchasing food (except groceries)	6.2	7.9	127
Travel related to shopping (except groceries, food, and gas)	23.8	24.8	104
Travel related to using professional and personal care services	9.4	10.0	106
Travel related to using financial services and banking	3.6	2.9	81
Travel related to using medical services	4.0	3.9	97
Travel related to eating and drinking	27.4	25.7	94
Travel related to socializing, relaxing, and leisure	29.0	29.6	102
Travel related to socializing and communicating	19.3	20.5	106
Travel related to attending or hosting social events	1.9	2.3	121
Travel related to relaxing and leisure	6.1	6.9	113
Travel related to arts and entertainment	3.1	2.4	76
Travel related to sports, exercise, and recreation	11.4	5.7	50
Travel related to participating in sports, exercise, recreation	10.5	5.5	53
Travel related to religious and spiritual activities	7.3	8.6	118
Travel related to volunteer activities	5.4	5.5	103

Note: The index is calculated by dividing percent of women participating in primary activity by percent of men participating in primary activity and multiplying by 100. Primary activities are those respondents identified as their main activity. Other activities done simultaneously, such as eating while watching TV, are not included. If fewer than 2.0 percent of the total population participated in a primary activity, then the primary activity is not shown. "–" means sample is too small to make a reliable estimate.
Source: Bureau of Labor Statistics, unpublished tables from the 2008 American Time Use Survey, Internet site http://www.bls.gov/tus/home.htm; calculations by New Strategist

Table 8.12 Ranking: Average Hours per Day Spent Doing Primary Activities by Total People Aged 65 to 74, 2008

(average hours per day spent by people aged 65 to 74 doing primary activities, ranked by time spent doing activity, 2008)

		average hours per day spent by people aged 65 to 74
	Total, all activities	**24.00**
1.	Sleeping	8.77
2.	Television	4.00
3.	Eating and drinking	1.32
4.	Work, main job	1.09
5.	Reading for personal interest	0.78
6.	Socializing and communicating	0.66
7.	Grooming	0.63
8.	Food and drink preparation	0.49
9.	Interior cleaning	0.47
10.	Relaxing, thinking	0.45
11.	Lawn, garden, and houseplants	0.32
12.	Participating in sports, exercise, or recreation	0.30
13.	Shopping, except groceries, food, and gas	0.26
14.	Playing games (including computer)	0.23
15.	Volunteer activities	0.23
16.	Laundry	0.19
17.	Caring for and helping children in other households	0.17
18.	Travel related to shopping (except groceries, food, and gas)	0.16
19.	Exterior maintenance, repair, and decoration	0.15
20.	Travel related to eating and drinking	0.15
21.	Kitchen and food clean-up	0.14
22.	Grocery shopping	0.14
23.	Attending religious services	0.14
24.	Computer use for leisure (except games)	0.13
25.	Telephone calls	0.13
26.	Health-related self-care	0.11
27.	Travel related to socializing and communicating	0.11
28.	Animals and pets (not veterinary care)	0.10
29.	Household and personal organization and planning	0.09
30.	Travel related to work	0.09
31.	Medical and care services	0.08
32.	Participation in religious practices	0.08
33.	Household and personal email	0.07
34.	Arts and entertainment (except sports)	0.07
35.	Travel related to grocery shopping	0.07
36.	Interior maintenance, repair, and decoration	0.06
37.	Attending or hosting social events	0.06
38.	Listening to the radio	0.06
39.	Financial management	0.05

	average hours per day spent by people aged 65 to 74
40. Household and personal mail and messages (except email)	0.05
41. Helping adults in other households	0.05
42. Travel related to household activities	0.05
43. Travel related to helping adults in other households	0.04
44. Travel related to purchasing food (except groceries)	0.04
45. Travel related to sports, exercise, and recreation	0.04
46. Storing interior household items, including food	0.03
47. Vehicles	0.03
48. Household services	0.03
49. Travel related to caring for and helping children in other households	0.03
50. Travel related to using medical services	0.03
51. Travel related to relaxing and leisure	0.03
52. Travel related to religious and spiritual activities	0.03
53. Caring for and helping household children	0.02
54. Helping household adults	0.02
55. Listening to or playing music (not radio)	0.02
56. Travel related to helping household adults	0.02
57. Travel related to attending or hosting social events	0.02
58. Travel related to arts and entertainment	0.02
59. Travel related to volunteer activities	0.02
60. Work, other job(s)	0.01
61. Taking class	0.01
62. Purchasing gas	0.01
63. Purchasing food (except groceries)	0.01
64. Financial services and banking	0.01
65. Travel related to purchasing gas	0.01
66. Travel related to using financial services and banking	0.01
67. Activities related to household children's education	0.00
68. Research, homework	0.00
69. Travel related to personal care	0.00
70. Travel related to caring for and helping household children	0.00
71. Travel related to education	0.00

Note: Primary activities are those respondents identified as their main activity. Other activities done simultaneously, such as eating while watching TV, are not included. If fewer than 2.0 percent of the total population participated in a primary activity, then the primary activity is not shown.
Source: Bureau of Labor Statistics, unpublished tables from the 2008 American Time Use Survey, Internet site http://www.bls.gov/tus/home.htm; calculations by New Strategist

Table 8.13   Ranking: Average Hours per Day Spent Doing Primary Activities by Men Aged 65 to 74, 2008

(average hours per day spent by men aged 65 to 74 doing primary activities, ranked by time spent doing activity, 2008)

		average hours per day spent by men aged 65 to 74
	Total, all activities	**24.00**
1.	Sleeping	8.88
2.	Television	4.60
3.	Eating and drinking	1.42
4.	Work, main job	1.30
5.	Reading for personal interest	0.69
6.	Socializing and communicating	0.56
7.	Participating in sports, exercise, or recreation	0.50
8.	Grooming	0.48
9.	Lawn, garden, and houseplants	0.47
10.	Relaxing, thinking	0.43
11.	Food and drink preparation	0.29
12.	Exterior maintenance, repair, and decoration	0.28
13.	Shopping, except groceries, food, and gas	0.26
14.	Volunteer activities	0.26
15.	Playing games (including computer)	0.19
16.	Interior cleaning	0.16
17.	Travel related to shopping (except groceries, food, and gas)	0.16
18.	Computer use for leisure (except games)	0.14
19.	Animals and pets (not veterinary care)	0.12
20.	Caring for and helping children in other households	0.12
21.	Attending religious services	0.12
22.	Travel related to eating and drinking	0.12
23.	Grocery shopping	0.11
24.	Travel related to work	0.11
25.	Interior maintenance, repair, and decoration	0.10
26.	Travel related to socializing and communicating	0.09
27.	Helping adults in other households	0.08
28.	Medical and care services	0.08
29.	Telephone calls	0.08
30.	Household and personal organization and planning	0.07
31.	Arts and entertainment (except sports)	0.07
32.	Participation in religious practices	0.07
33.	Vehicles	0.06
34.	Household and personal email	0.06
35.	Attending or hosting social events	0.06
36.	Listening to the radio	0.06
37.	Laundry	0.05
38.	Kitchen and food clean-up	0.05
39.	Financial management	0.05

	average hours per day spent by men aged 65 to 74
40. Travel related to grocery shopping	0.05
41. Travel related to sports, exercise, and recreation	0.05
42. Health-related self-care	0.04
43. Household services	0.04
44. Travel related to household activities	0.04
45. Travel related to helping adults in other households	0.04
46. Household and personal mail and messages (except email)	0.03
47. Helping household adults	0.03
48. Listening to or playing music (not radio)	0.03
49. Travel related to helping household adults	0.03
50. Travel related to purchasing gas	0.03
51. Travel related to using medical services	0.03
52. Travel related to volunteer activities	0.03
53. Storing interior household items, including food	0.02
54. Caring for and helping household children	0.02
55. Travel related to caring for and helping children in other households	0.02
56. Travel related to purchasing food (except groceries)	0.02
57. Travel related to relaxing and leisure	0.02
58. Travel related to arts and entertainment	0.02
59. Travel related to religious and spiritual activities	0.02
60. Purchasing gas	0.01
61. Purchasing food (except groceries)	0.01
62. Financial services and banking	0.01
63. Travel related to using financial services and banking	0.01
64. Travel related to attending or hosting social events	0.01
65. Activities related to household children's education	0.00
66. Work, other job(s)	0.00
67. Taking class	0.00
68. Research, homework	0.00
69. Travel related to personal care	0.00
70. Travel related to caring for and helping household children	0.00
71. Travel related to education	0.00

Note: Primary activities are those respondents identified as their main activity. Other activities done simultaneously, such as eating while watching TV, are not included. If fewer than 2.0 percent of the total population participated in a primary activity, then the primary activity is not shown.
Source: Bureau of Labor Statistics, unpublished tables from the 2008 American Time Use Survey, Internet site http://www.bls .gov/tus/home.htm; calculations by New Strategist

Table 8.14 Ranking: Average Hours per Day Spent Doing Primary Activities by Women Aged 65 to 74, 2008

(average hours per day spent by women aged 65 to 74 doing primary activities, ranked by time spent doing activity, 2008)

		average hours per day spent by women aged 65 to 74
	Total, all activities	**24.00**
1.	Sleeping	8.67
2.	Television	3.49
3.	Eating and drinking	1.23
4.	Work, main job	0.92
5.	Reading for personal interest	0.87
6.	Grooming	0.76
7.	Socializing and communicating	0.75
8.	Interior cleaning	0.74
9.	Food and drink preparation	0.66
10.	Relaxing, thinking	0.46
11.	Laundry	0.31
12.	Playing games (including computer)	0.27
13.	Shopping, except groceries, food, and gas	0.26
14.	Kitchen and food clean-up	0.22
15.	Caring for and helping children in other households	0.21
16.	Volunteer activities	0.21
17.	Lawn, garden, and houseplants	0.19
18.	Grocery shopping	0.18
19.	Travel related to eating and drinking	0.17
20.	Health-related self-care	0.16
21.	Telephone calls	0.16
22.	Travel related to shopping (except groceries, food, and gas)	0.16
23.	Attending religious services	0.15
24.	Participating in sports, exercise, or recreation	0.13
25.	Travel related to socializing and communicating	0.13
26.	Computer use for leisure (except games)	0.12
27.	Household and personal organization and planning	0.11
28.	Animals and pets (not veterinary care)	0.09
29.	Participation in religious practices	0.09
30.	Household and personal email	0.08
31.	Medical and care services	0.08
32.	Travel related to grocery shopping	0.08
33.	Arts and entertainment (except sports)	0.07
34.	Travel related to work	0.07
35.	Household and personal mail and messages (except email)	0.06
36.	Attending or hosting social events	0.06
37.	Listening to the radio	0.06
38.	Travel related to household activities	0.06
39.	Travel related to purchasing food (except groceries)	0.05

	average hours per day spent by women aged 65 to 74
40. Storing interior household items, including food	0.04
41. Exterior maintenance, repair, and decoration	0.04
42. Financial management	0.04
43. Helping adults in other households	0.04
44. Travel related to caring for and helping children in other households	0.04
45. Travel related to relaxing and leisure	0.04
46. Interior maintenance, repair, and decoration	0.03
47. Caring for and helping household children	0.03
48. Travel related to helping adults in other households	0.03
49. Travel related to using medical services	0.03
50. Travel related to religious and spiritual activities	0.03
51. Helping household adults	0.02
52. Work, other job(s)	0.02
53. Taking class	0.02
54. Purchasing food (except groceries)	0.02
55. Household services	0.02
56. Travel related to attending or hosting social events	0.02
57. Travel related to arts and entertainment	0.02
58. Travel related to sports, exercise, and recreation	0.02
59. Travel related to volunteer activities	0.02
60. Vehicles	0.01
61. Financial services and banking	0.01
62. Listening to or playing music (not radio)	0.01
63. Travel related to helping household adults	0.01
64. Travel related to using financial services and banking	0.01
65. Activities related to household children's education	0.00
66. Research, homework	0.00
67. Purchasing gas	0.00
68. Travel related to personal care	0.00
69. Travel related to caring for and helping household children	0.00
70. Travel related to education	0.00
71. Travel related to purchasing gas	0.00

Note: Primary activities are those respondents identified as their main activity. Other activities done simultaneously, such as eating while watching TV, are not included. If fewer than 2.0 percent of the total population participated in a primary activity, then the primary activity is not shown.
Source: Bureau of Labor Statistics, unpublished tables from the 2008 American Time Use Survey, Internet site http://www.bls .gov/tus/home.htm; calculations by New Strategist

Table 8.15 Ranking: Percent of Total People Aged 65 to 74 Participating in Primary Activities on an Average Day, 2008

(percent of people aged 65 to 74 participating in primary activities on an average day, ranked by percent participating, 2008)

		percent of people aged 65 to 74 participating in activity
	Total, all activities	**100.0%**
1.	Sleeping	100.0
2.	Eating and drinking	98.5
3.	Television	87.2
4.	Grooming	73.9
5.	Food and drink preparation	54.9
6.	Reading for personal interest	44.6
7.	Socializing and communicating	39.3
8.	Interior cleaning	29.2
9.	Travel related to eating and drinking	26.5
10.	Shopping, except groceries, food, and gas	24.6
11.	Travel related to shopping (except groceries, food, and gas)	24.3
12.	Kitchen and food clean-up	23.4
13.	Relaxing, thinking	21.8
14.	Travel related to socializing and communicating	20.0
15.	Telephone calls	17.7
16.	Participating in sports, exercise, or recreation	17.5
17.	Work, main job	17.3
18.	Grocery shopping	16.7
19.	Travel related to grocery shopping	16.7
20.	Lawn, garden, and houseplants	16.0
21.	Laundry	15.9
22.	Animals and pets (not veterinary care)	15.6
23.	Household and personal organization and planning	14.3
24.	Health-related self-care	14.0
25.	Travel related to work	13.0
26.	Household and personal mail and messages (except email)	12.7
27.	Playing games (including computer)	11.3
28.	Travel related to household activities	11.1
29.	Household and personal email	9.2
30.	Caring for and helping children in other households	9.0
31.	Helping adults in other households	8.9
32.	Participation in religious practices	8.8
33.	Volunteer activities	8.6
34.	Travel related to sports, exercise, and recreation	8.3
35.	Travel related to religious and spiritual activities	8.0
36.	Attending religious services	7.6
37.	Storing interior household items, including food	7.6
38.	Purchasing food (except groceries)	7.3
39.	Travel related to helping adults in other households	7.3

	percent of people aged 65 to 74 participating in activity
40. Travel related to purchasing food (except groceries)	7.1%
41. Travel related to relaxing and leisure	6.5
42. Computer use for leisure (except games)	6.5
43. Exterior maintenance, repair, and decoration	5.9
44. Travel related to volunteer activities	5.4
45. Financial management	5.4
46. Medical and care services	5.2
47. Interior maintenance, repair, and decoration	4.5
48. Travel related to using medical services	4.0
49. Travel related to caring for and helping children in other households	3.9
50. Household services	3.7
51. Financial services and banking	3.5
52. Helping household adults	3.5
53. Travel related to using financial services and banking	3.3
54. Vehicles	3.1
55. Purchasing gas	3.0
56. Travel related to purchasing gas	3.0
57. Arts and entertainment (except sports)	3.0
58. Travel related to arts and entertainment	2.7
59. Listening to the radio	2.7
60. Travel related to helping household adults	2.6
61. Attending or hosting social events	2.5
62. Travel related to attending or hosting social events	2.1
63. Listening to or playing music (not radio)	1.8
64. Caring for and helping household children	1.6
65. Travel related to personal care	1.1
66. Travel related to caring for and helping household children	0.9
67. Research, homework	0.4
68. Taking class	0.3
69. Activities related to household children's education	0.3
70. Work, other job(s)	0.3
71. Travel related to education	0.3

Note: Primary activities are those respondents identified as their main activity. Other activities done simultaneously, such as eating while watching TV, are not included. If fewer than 2.0 percent of the total population participated in a primary activity, then the primary activity is not shown.
Source: Bureau of Labor Statistics, unpublished tables from the 2008 American Time Use Survey, Internet site http://www.bls .gov/tus/home.htm; calculations by New Strategist

Table 8.16 Ranking: Percent of Men Aged 65 to 74 Participating in Primary Activities on an Average Day, 2008

(percent of men aged 65 to 74 participating in primary activities on an average day, ranked by percent participating, 2008)

		percent of men aged 65 to 74 participating in activity
	Total, all activities	**100.0%**
1.	Sleeping	100.0
2.	Eating and drinking	98.4
3.	Television	89.3
4.	Grooming	66.4
5.	Reading for personal interest	40.9
6.	Food and drink preparation	39.9
7.	Socializing and communicating	37.7
8.	Travel related to eating and drinking	27.4
9.	Shopping, except groceries, food, and gas	24.3
10.	Travel related to shopping (except groceries, food, and gas)	23.8
11.	Participating in sports, exercise, or recreation	22.7
12.	Work, main job	21.0
13.	Lawn, garden, and houseplants	19.5
14.	Travel related to socializing and communicating	19.3
15.	Relaxing, thinking	17.8
16.	Animals and pets (not veterinary care)	15.2
17.	Travel related to work	15.1
18.	Grocery shopping	13.9
19.	Travel related to grocery shopping	13.9
20.	Household and personal organization and planning	12.2
21.	Interior cleaning	11.9
22.	Health-related self-care	11.5
23.	Travel related to sports, exercise, and recreation	11.4
24.	Household and personal mail and messages (except email)	10.1
25.	Travel related to household activities	9.9
26.	Telephone calls	9.9
27.	Exterior maintenance, repair, and decoration	9.6
28.	Helping adults in other households	9.2
29.	Kitchen and food clean-up	9.0
30.	Household and personal email	8.3
31.	Playing games (including computer)	8.1
32.	Volunteer activities	7.8
33.	Caring for and helping children in other households	7.4
34.	Travel related to religious and spiritual activities	7.3
35.	Interior maintenance, repair, and decoration	7.2
36.	Travel related to helping adults in other households	7.1
37.	Attending religious services	6.8
38.	Purchasing food (except groceries)	6.6
39.	Computer use for leisure (except games)	6.4

	percent of men aged 65 to 74 participating in activity
40. Travel related to purchasing food (except groceries)	6.2%
41. Travel related to relaxing and leisure	6.1
42. Helping household adults	5.5
43. Travel related to volunteer activities	5.4
44. Financial management	5.2
45. Household services	5.0
46. Participation in religious practices	4.7
47. Vehicles	4.6
48. Travel related to helping household adults	4.3
49. Medical and care services	4.2
50. Travel related to purchasing gas	4.2
51. Purchasing gas	4.2
52. Laundry	4.1
53. Travel related to using medical services	4.0
54. Financial services and banking	3.8
55. Travel related to using financial services and banking	3.6
56. Travel related to caring for and helping children in other households	3.4
57. Arts and entertainment (except sports)	3.2
58. Travel related to arts and entertainment	3.1
59. Storing interior household items, including food	2.9
60. Listening to or playing music (not radio)	2.8
61. Listening to the radio	2.5
62. Attending or hosting social events	2.4
63. Travel related to attending or hosting social events	1.9
64. Caring for and helping household children	1.6
65. Travel related to personal care	1.1
66. Travel related to caring for and helping household children	0.9
67. Research, homework	0.3
68. Activities related to household children's education	0.1
69. Work, other job(s)	0.1
70. Travel related to education	0.1
71. Taking class	0.0

Note: Primary activities are those respondents identified as their main activity. Other activities done simultaneously, such as eating while watching TV, are not included. If fewer than 2.0 percent of the total population participated in a primary activity, then the primary activity is not shown.
Source: Bureau of Labor Statistics, unpublished tables from the 2008 American Time Use Survey, Internet site http://www.bls .gov/tus/home.htm; calculations by New Strategist

Table 8.17 Ranking: Percent of Women Aged 65 to 74 Participating in Primary Activities on an Average Day, 2008

(percent of women aged 65 to 74 participating in primary activities on an average day, ranked by percent participating, 2008)

		percent of women aged 65 to 74 participating in activity
	Total, all activities	**100.0%**
1.	Sleeping	100.0
2.	Eating and drinking	98.6
3.	Television	85.5
4.	Grooming	80.3
5.	Food and drink preparation	67.7
6.	Reading for personal interest	47.7
7.	Interior cleaning	44.0
8.	Socializing and communicating	40.6
9.	Kitchen and food clean-up	35.6
10.	Laundry	26.0
11.	Travel related to eating and drinking	25.7
12.	Relaxing, thinking	25.2
13.	Shopping, except groceries, food, and gas	24.9
14.	Travel related to shopping (except groceries, food, and gas)	24.8
15.	Telephone calls	24.5
16.	Travel related to socializing and communicating	20.5
17.	Grocery shopping	19.1
18.	Travel related to grocery shopping	19.1
19.	Health-related self-care	16.2
20.	Household and personal organization and planning	16.2
21.	Animals and pets (not veterinary care)	15.8
22.	Household and personal mail and messages (except email)	15.0
23.	Work, main job	14.2
24.	Playing games (including computer)	14.1
25.	Lawn, garden, and houseplants	13.1
26.	Participating in sports, exercise, or recreation	13.0
27.	Participation in religious practices	12.3
28.	Travel related to household activities	12.2
29.	Storing interior household items, including food	11.6
30.	Travel related to work	11.2
31.	Caring for and helping children in other households	10.3
32.	Household and personal email	10.0
33.	Volunteer activities	9.2
34.	Travel related to religious and spiritual activities	8.6
35.	Helping adults in other households	8.6
36.	Attending religious services	8.3
37.	Purchasing food (except groceries)	8.0
38.	Travel related to purchasing food (except groceries)	7.9
39.	Travel related to helping adults in other households	7.5

		percent of women aged 65 to 74 participating in activity
40.	Travel related to relaxing and leisure	6.9%
41.	Computer use for leisure (except games)	6.6
42.	Medical and care services	6.0
43.	Travel related to sports, exercise, and recreation	5.7
44.	Financial management	5.7
45.	Travel related to volunteer activities	5.5
46.	Travel related to caring for and helping children in other households	4.3
47.	Travel related to using medical services	3.9
48.	Financial services and banking	3.3
49.	Listening to the radio	2.9
50.	Travel related to using financial services and banking	2.9
51.	Exterior maintenance, repair, and decoration	2.8
52.	Arts and entertainment (except sports)	2.7
53.	Household services	2.6
54.	Attending or hosting social events	2.6
55.	Travel related to arts and entertainment	2.4
56.	Travel related to attending or hosting social events	2.3
57.	Interior maintenance, repair, and decoration	2.2
58.	Purchasing gas	2.1
59.	Travel related to purchasing gas	1.9
60.	Helping household adults	1.8
61.	Vehicles	1.8
62.	Caring for and helping household children	1.6
63.	Travel related to helping household adults	1.2
64.	Travel related to personal care	1.1
65.	Listening to or playing music (not radio)	0.8
66.	Travel related to caring for and helping household children	0.8
67.	Taking class	0.5
68.	Research, homework	0.5
69.	Activities related to household children's education	0.4
70.	Travel related to education	0.4
71.	Work, other job(s)	0.4

Note: Primary activities are those respondents identified as their main activity. Other activities done simultaneously, such as eating while watching TV, are not included. If fewer than 2.0 percent of the total population participated in a primary activity, then the primary activity is not shown.

Source: Bureau of Labor Statistics, unpublished tables from the 2008 American Time Use Survey, Internet site http://www.bls .gov/tus/home.htm; calculations by New Strategist

(hours per day spent by participants aged 65 to 74 doing primary activities, ranked by time spent doing activity, 2008)

		average hours per day spent by participants aged 65 to 74
	Total, all activities	**24.00**
1.	Sleeping	8.77
2.	Work, main job	6.32
3.	Television	4.59
4.	Volunteer activities	2.74
5.	Relaxing, thinking	2.06
6.	Playing games (including computer)	2.05
7.	Computer use for leisure (except games)	2.03
8.	Lawn, garden, and houseplants	1.99
9.	Caring for and helping children in other households	1.92
10.	Attending religious services	1.80
11.	Reading for personal interest	1.76
12.	Participating in sports, exercise, or recreation	1.73
13.	Socializing and communicating	1.69
14.	Interior cleaning	1.60
15.	Eating and drinking	1.34
16.	Laundry	1.19
17.	Shopping, except groceries, food, and gas	1.04
18.	Participation in religious practices	0.95
19.	Food and drink preparation	0.89
20.	Grocery shopping	0.86
21.	Grooming	0.85
22.	Health-related self-care	0.75
23.	Household and personal email	0.74
24.	Telephone calls	0.71
25.	Animals and pets (not veterinary care)	0.66
26.	Travel related to work	0.66
27.	Travel related to shopping (except groceries, food, and gas)	0.65
28.	Household and personal organization and planning	0.64
29.	Helping adults in other households	0.61
30.	Kitchen and food clean-up	0.59
31.	Travel related to purchasing food (except groceries)	0.57
32.	Travel related to socializing and communicating	0.56
33.	Travel related to eating and drinking	0.55
34.	Travel related to helping adults in other households	0.53
35.	Travel related to relaxing and leisure	0.49
36.	Travel related to household activities	0.48
37.	Travel related to sports, exercise, and recreation	0.43
38.	Storing interior household items, including food	0.41
39.	Household and personal mail and messages (except email)	0.40

		average hours per day spent by participants aged 65 to 74
40.	Travel related to grocery shopping	0.39
41.	Travel related to religious and spiritual activities	0.34
42.	Purchasing food (except groceries)	0.20

Note: Primary activities are those respondents identified as their main activity. Other activities done simultaneously, such as eating while watching TV, are not included. The primary activities shown are those for which data by age are available.
Source: Bureau of Labor Statistics, unpublished tables from the 2008 American Time Use Survey, Internet site http://www .bl.gov/tus/home.htm; calculations by New Strategist

Table 8.19 Ranking: Average Hours per Day Spent Doing Primary Activities by Male Participants Aged 65 to 74, 2008

(hours per day spent by male participants aged 65 to 74 doing primary activities, ranked by time spent doing activity, 2008)

		average hours per day spent by male participants aged 65 to 74
	Total, all activities	**24.00**
1.	Sleeping	8.88
2.	Work, main job	6.19
3.	Television	5.16
4.	Relaxing, thinking	2.42
5.	Lawn, garden, and houseplants	2.41
6.	Participating in sports, exercise, or recreation	2.21
7.	Reading for personal interest	1.68
8.	Socializing and communicating	1.49
9.	Eating and drinking	1.45
10.	Interior cleaning	1.31
11.	Shopping, except groceries, food, and gas	1.06
12.	Animals and pets (not veterinary care)	0.77
13.	Grocery shopping	0.76
14.	Food and drink preparation	0.73
15.	Grooming	0.72
16.	Travel related to work	0.72
17.	Travel related to shopping (except groceries, food, and gas)	0.67
18.	Travel related to socializing and communicating	0.47
19.	Travel related to eating and drinking	0.43
20.	Travel related to grocery shopping	0.39

Note: Primary activities are those respondents identified as their main activity. Other activities done simultaneously, such as eating while watching TV, are not included. The primary activities shown are those for which data by age are available.
Source: Bureau of Labor Statistics, unpublished tables from the 2008 American Time Use Survey, Internet site http://www.bls.gov/tus/home.htm; calculations by New Strategist

Table 8.20 Ranking: Average Hours per Day Spent Doing Primary Activities by Female Participants Aged 65 to 74, 2008

(hours per day spent by female participants aged 65 to 74 doing primary activities, ranked by time spent doing activity, 2008)

		average hours per day spent by female participants aged 65 to 74
	Total, all activities	**24.00**
1.	Sleeping	8.67
2.	Work, main job	6.48
3.	Television	4.08
4.	Playing games (including computer)	1.91
5.	Socializing and communicating	1.85
6.	Relaxing, thinking	1.84
7.	Attending religious services	1.83
8.	Reading for personal interest	1.81
9.	Interior cleaning	1.67
10.	Lawn, garden, and houseplants	1.45
11.	Eating and drinking	1.24
12.	Laundry	1.19
13.	Shopping, except groceries, food, and gas	1.02
14.	Participating in sports, exercise, or recreation	1.02
15.	Health-related self-care	1.00
16.	Food and drink preparation	0.98
17.	Grooming	0.95
18.	Grocery shopping	0.92
19.	Participation in religious practices	0.75
20.	Travel related to eating and drinking	0.67
21.	Telephone calls	0.67
22.	Household and personal organization and planning	0.67
23.	Travel related to socializing and communicating	0.64
24.	Travel related to shopping (except groceries, food, and gas)	0.63
25.	Kitchen and food clean-up	0.61
26.	Travel related to work	0.60
27.	Animals and pets (not veterinary care)	0.56
28.	Travel related to household activities	0.51
29.	Household and personal mail and messages (except email)	0.43
30.	Travel related to grocery shopping	0.40
31.	Storing interior household items, including food	0.35
32.	Travel related to religious and spiritual activities	0.35

Note: Primary activities are those respondents identified as their main activity. Other activities done simultaneously, such as eating while watching TV, are not included. The primary activities shown are those for which data by age are available.
Source: Bureau of Labor Statistics, unpublished tables from the 2008 American Time Use Survey, Internet site http://www.bls .gov/tus/home.htm; calculations by New Strategist

Time Use, 2008: People Aged 75 or Older

The oldest Americans are the ones with the greatest amount of leisure time. Unfortunately, health problems mount at this age, limiting activities. Perhaps that is why no age group spends as much time watching television as people aged 75 or older. Ninety-one percent watch television as a primary activity on an average day, spending 4.19 hours doing so—more than one-fourth of their waking hours. Few people aged 75 or older are still in the labor force, which is why work ranks 10th in time use (excluding sleep) for the age group. Only 8 percent of men and 4 percent of women aged 75 or older work on an average day.

People aged 75 or older are the most avid readers. Reading for personal interest ranks third in time use for the age group (excluding sleep), with the average person reading for more than one hour a day on average. Relaxing and thinking is the fourth most time-consuming activity among people aged 75 or older.

Few people aged 75 or older care for children in other households (i.e., grandchildren) on an average day. Only 3 percent do so, well below the 15 percent who take care of pets on an average day.

Sleeplessness is more of a problem in the 75-or-older age group than in any other. In an average 24-hour period, 8 percent of people aged 75 or older have trouble sleeping.

People aged 75 or older spend more than four hours a day watching television

(average hours per day spent by people aged 75 or older doing primary activities, for the 10 activities on which the average person aged 75 or older spends the most time, excluding sleep, 2008)

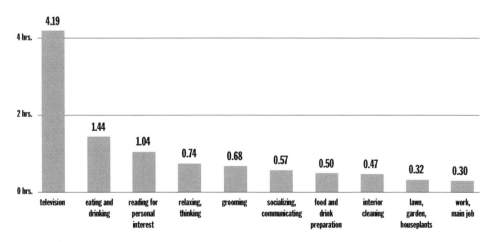

As is true for 65-to-74-year-olds, the average person aged 75 or older fills much of his or her free time with household chores. No other age group is as likely to clean the house on an average day, with 34 percent doing so. No other age group spends more time cooking or cleaning up in the kitchen. Not surprisingly, this age group spends the most time getting medical care, 8 percent seeing a health care provider on an average day. Time spent in religious activities peaks in the 75-or-older age group, with 18 percent participating on an average day.

Among people aged 75 or older, men's and women's time use differs in the stereotypical ways. Older men spend more time than women on household financial management, lawn care, and exterior home maintenance. Older women spend more time than older men doing the laundry, housecleaning, and cooking. Interestingly, the time people spend playing games peaks among 15-to-19-year-olds and among people aged 75 or older. But the two age groups are playing very different types of games. Most teens are playing computer games. Most older Americans are likely playing board or card games.

Table 9.1 Time Use by Total People Aged 75 or Older, 2008

(number and percent of total people aged 75 or older participating in primary activities on an average day, hours spent doing activity by the average person aged 75 or older and by those aged 75 or older who participated in the activity, 2008; numbers of participants in thousands)

	participants aged 75 or older		time spent doing activity (hours)	
	number	percent	average person aged 75 or older	participants aged 75 or older
TOTAL, ALL ACTIVITIES	**17,278**	**100.0%**	**24.00**	**24.00**
Personal care	**17,278**	**100.0**	**10.02**	**10.02**
Sleeping	17,246	99.8	9.14	9.16
Sleeplessness	1,393	8.1	0.13	1.58
Grooming	12,490	72.3	0.68	0.94
Health-related self-care	3,122	18.1	0.20	1.09
Household activities	**14,067**	**81.4**	**2.42**	**2.98**
Housework	7,376	42.7	0.78	1.83
Interior cleaning	5,791	33.5	0.47	1.40
Laundry	2,510	14.5	0.19	1.30
Storing interior household items, including food	1,455	8.4	0.03	0.37
Food and drink preparation, presentation, and clean-up	10,358	59.9	0.70	1.16
Food and drink preparation	9,558	55.3	0.50	0.91
Kitchen and food clean-up	5,184	30.0	0.18	0.61
Interior maintenance, repair, and decoration	649	3.8	0.06	–
Interior arrangement, decoration, and repairs	267	1.5	0.04	–
Exterior maintenance, repair, and decoration	637	3.7	0.07	–
Lawn, garden, and houseplants	2,886	16.7	0.32	1.92
Animals and pets (not veterinary care)	2,597	15.0	0.13	0.86
Walking, exercising, and playing with pets	991	5.7	0.06	–
Vehicles	203	1.2	0.01	–
Household management	5,948	34.4	0.33	0.97
Financial management	1,247	7.2	0.07	1.00
Household and personal organization and planning	2,355	13.6	0.14	1.03
Household and personal mail and messages (except email)	3,012	17.4	0.08	0.45
Household and personal email	919	5.3	0.04	–
Caring for and helping household members	**1,091**	**6.3**	**0.06**	**–**
Caring for and helping household children	124	0.7	0.01	–
Physical care for household children	51	0.3	0.00	–
Reading to or with household children	–	–	–	–
Playing with household children (except sports)	32	0.2	0.00	–
Talking with, listening to household children	36	0.2	0.00	–
Looking after household children as a primary activity	115	0.7	0.00	–
Picking up or dropping off household children	52	0.3	0.00	–
Activities related to household children's education	–	–	–	–
Helping household children with homework	–	–	–	–
Helping household adults	301	1.7	0.00	–
Caring for and helping people in other households	**1,465**	**8.5**	**0.11**	**1.24**
Caring for and helping children in other households	472	2.7	0.06	–

	participants aged 75 or older		time spent doing activity (hours)	
	number	percent	average person aged 75 or older	participants aged 75 or older
Helping adults in other households	880	5.1%	0.04	–
Picking up or dropping off adults in other households	564	3.3	0.00	–
Work and work-related activities	**1,104**	**6.4**	**0.34**	–
Work, main job	953	5.5	0.30	–
Work, other job(s)	–	–	–	–
Education	**147**	**0.9**	**0.03**	–
Taking class	83	0.5	0.01	–
Taking class for degree, certification, or licensure	4	0.0	0.00	–
Research, homework	67	0.4	0.02	–
Consumer purchases (store, telephone, Internet)	**5,741**	**33.2**	**0.33**	**0.98**
Grocery shopping	2,187	12.7	0.11	0.83
Purchasing gas	317	1.8	0.01	–
Purchasing food (except groceries)	648	3.8	0.01	–
Shopping, except groceries, food, and gas	3,358	19.4	0.21	1.06
Professional and personal care services	**2,490**	**14.4**	**0.16**	**1.11**
Financial services and banking	603	3.5	0.01	–
Banking	574	3.3	0.01	–
Medical and care services	1,436	8.3	0.11	–
Using health and care services outside the home	1,344	7.8	0.08	–
Household services	**416**	**2.4**	**0.02**	–
Eating and drinking	**17,050**	**98.7**	**1.44**	**1.46**
Socializing, relaxing, and leisure	**17,201**	**99.6**	**7.27**	**7.30**
Socializing and communicating	6,039	35.0	0.57	1.63
Attending or hosting social events	468	2.7	0.07	–
Relaxing and leisure	17,126	99.1	6.56	6.62
Relaxing, thinking	5,329	30.8	0.74	2.39
Television	15,700	90.9	4.19	4.62
Listening to the radio	787	4.6	0.09	–
Listening to or playing music (not radio)	186	1.1	0.02	–
Playing games (including computer)	2,230	12.9	0.29	2.23
Computer use for leisure (except games)	951	5.5	0.10	–
Reading for personal interest	8,902	51.5	1.04	2.02
Arts and entertainment (except sports)	344	2.0	0.07	–
Sports, exercise, and recreation	**3,036**	**17.6**	**0.18**	**1.03**
Participating in sports, exercise, or recreation	3,018	17.5	0.18	1.01
Using cardiovascular equipment	405	2.3	0.02	–
Walking	1,991	11.5	0.08	0.69
Working out, unspecified	542	3.1	0.03	–
Religious and spiritual activities	**3,079**	**17.8**	**0.26**	**1.46**
Attending religious services	1,612	9.3	0.15	1.61
Participation in religious practices	1,595	9.2	0.08	0.86

	participants aged 75 or older		time spent doing activity (hours)	
	number	percent	average person aged 75 or older	participants aged 75 or older
Volunteer activities	**1,590**	**9.2%**	**0.22**	**2.34**
Administrative and support activities	633	3.7	0.06	–
Telephone calls	**3,774**	**21.8**	**0.20**	**0.90**
Telephone calls to or from family members	2,297	13.3	0.09	0.70
Telephone calls to or from friends, neighbors, or acquaintances	1,448	8.4	0.05	0.57
Traveling	**11,632**	**67.3**	**0.70**	**1.04**
Travel related to personal care	143	0.8	0.00	–
Travel related to household activities	1,494	8.6	0.03	0.36
Travel related to household management	1,067	6.2	0.02	–
Travel related to caring for and helping household members	453	2.6	0.02	–
Travel related to caring for and helping household children	52	0.3	0.00	–
Travel related to helping household adults	209	1.2	0.01	–
Travel related to caring for and helping people in other households	1,082	6.3	0.04	0.58
Travel related to caring for and helping children in other households	198	1.1	0.01	–
Travel related to helping adults in other households	64	0.4	0.00	–
Travel related to work	860	5.0	0.03	–
Travel related to education	79	0.5	0.00	–
Travel related to taking class	79	0.5	0.00	–
Travel related to consumer purchases	5,676	32.9	0.17	0.51
Travel related to grocery shopping	2,252	13.0	0.04	0.34
Travel related to purchasing gas	317	1.8	0.01	–
Travel related to purchasing food (except groceries)	643	3.7	0.01	–
Travel related to shopping (except groceries, food, and gas)	3,250	18.8	0.10	0.55
Travel related to using professional and personal care services	2,291	13.3	0.06	0.47
Travel related to using financial services and banking	603	3.5	0.02	–
Travel related to using medical services	1,289	7.5	0.04	–
Travel related to eating and drinking	3,066	17.7	0.09	0.49
Travel related to socializing, relaxing, and leisure	4,327	25.0	0.15	0.61
Travel related to socializing and communicating	2,610	15.1	0.07	0.47
Travel related to attending or hosting social events	364	2.1	0.01	–
Travel related to relaxing and leisure	1,322	7.7	0.03	0.42
Travel related to arts and entertainment	285	1.6	0.02	–
Travel related to sports, exercise, and recreation	747	4.3	0.02	–
Travel related to participating in sports, exercise, recreation	730	4.2	0.02	–
Travel related to religious and spiritual activities	1,547	9.0	0.04	0.44
Travel related to volunteer activities	909	5.3	0.02	–

Note: Primary activities are those respondents identified as their main activity. Other activities done simultaneously, such as eating while watching TV, are not included. Numbers may not add to total because not all subcategories are shown. If fewer than 2.0 percent of the total population participated in a primary activity, then the primary activity is not shown. "–" means sample is too small to make a reliable estimate.
Source: Bureau of Labor Statistics, unpublished tables from the 2008 American Time Use Survey, Internet site http://www.bls .gov/tus/home.htm; calculations by New Strategist

Table 9.2 Time Use by Men Aged 75 or Older, 2008

(number and percent of men aged 75 or older participating in primary activities on an average day, hours spent doing activity by the average man aged 75 or older and by men aged 75 or older who participated in the activity, 2008; numbers of participants in thousands)

	men aged 75 or older participating		time spent doing activity (hours)	
	number	percent	average man aged 75 or older	male participants aged 75 or older
TOTAL, ALL ACTIVITIES	**6,843**	**100.0%**	**24.00**	**24.00**
Personal care	**6,843**	**100.0**	**9.83**	**9.83**
Sleeping	6,828	99.8	9.03	9.05
Sleeplessness	409	6.0	0.09	–
Grooming	4,664	68.2	0.60	0.87
Health-related self-care	755	11.0	0.21	–
Household activities	**5,014**	**73.3**	**1.76**	**2.41**
Housework	1,301	19.0	0.22	1.15
Interior cleaning	1,016	14.8	0.16	–
Laundry	214	3.1	0.04	–
Storing interior household items, including food	398	5.8	0.02	–
Food and drink preparation, presentation, and clean-up	2,882	42.1	0.39	0.93
Food and drink preparation	2,614	38.2	0.29	0.75
Kitchen and food clean-up	1,038	15.2	0.10	–
Interior maintenance, repair, and decoration	333	4.9	0.11	–
Interior arrangement, decoration, and repairs	152	2.2	0.07	–
Exterior maintenance, repair, and decoration	326	4.8	0.10	–
Lawn, garden, and houseplants	1,348	19.7	0.45	2.26
Animals and pets (not veterinary care)	1,043	15.2	0.14	–
Walking, exercising, and playing with pets	448	6.5	0.07	–
Vehicles	175	2.6	0.03	–
Household management	2,012	29.4	0.30	1.02
Financial management	437	6.4	0.09	–
Household and personal organization and planning	723	10.6	0.12	–
Household and personal mail and messages (except email)	926	13.5	0.04	–
Household and personal email	355	5.2	0.04	–
Caring for and helping household members	**468**	**6.8**	**0.04**	**–**
Caring for and helping household children	52	0.8	0.00	–
Physical care for household children	11	0.2	0.00	–
Reading to or with household children	–	–	–	–
Playing with household children (except sports)	–	–	–	–
Talking with, listening to household children	–	–	–	–
Looking after household children as a primary activity	–	–	–	
Picking up or dropping off household children	52	0.8	0.00	–
Activities related to household children's education	–	–	–	–
Helping household children with homework	–	–	–	–
Helping household adults	283	4.1	0.01	–
Caring for and helping people in other households	**513**	**7.5**	**0.12**	**–**
Caring for and helping children in other households	186	2.7	0.05	–

414 AMERICAN TIME USE

	men aged 75 or older participating		time spent doing activity (hours)	
	number	percent	average man aged 75 or older	male participants aged 75 or older
Helping adults in other households	327	4.8%	0.06	–
Picking up or dropping off adults in other households	175	2.6	0.00	–
Work and work-related activities	**703**	**10.3**	**0.51**	–
Work, main job	565	8.3	0.41	–
Work, other job(s)		0.0		
Education	**16**	**0.2**	**0.01**	–
Taking class	–	–	–	–
Taking class for degree, certification, or licensure	–	–	–	–
Research, homework	16	0.2	0.01	–
Consumer purchases (store, telephone, Internet)	**2,249**	**32.9**	**0.29**	**0.89**
Grocery shopping	651	9.5	0.17	–
Purchasing gas	198	2.9	0.01	–
Purchasing food (except groceries)	302	4.4	0.01	–
Shopping, except groceries, food, and gas	1,364	19.9	0.21	–
Professional and personal care services	**980**	**14.3**	**0.14**	–
Financial services and banking	343	5.0	0.01	–
Banking	335	4.9	0.01	–
Medical and care services	608	8.9	0.13	–
Using health and care services outside the home	583	8.5	0.09	–
Household services	**239**	**3.5**	**0.02**	–
Eating and drinking	**6,753**	**98.7**	**1.51**	**1.53**
Socializing, relaxing, and leisure	**6,799**	**99.4**	**7.89**	**7.94**
Socializing and communicating	2,084	30.5	0.55	1.81
Attending or hosting social events	108	1.6	0.05	–
Relaxing and leisure	6,799	99.4	7.20	7.24
Relaxing, thinking	2,171	31.7	0.87	2.75
Television	6,263	91.5	4.66	5.09
Listening to the radio	459	6.7	0.12	–
Listening to or playing music (not radio)	95	1.4	0.03	–
Playing games (including computer)	675	9.9	0.25	–
Computer use for leisure (except games)	480	7.0	0.13	–
Reading for personal interest	3,440	50.3	1.02	2.04
Arts and entertainment (except sports)	158	2.3	0.09	–
Sports, exercise, and recreation	**1,385**	**20.2**	**0.20**	**1.00**
Participating in sports, exercise, or recreation	1,385	20.2	0.20	1.00
Using cardiovascular equipment	299	4.4	0.03	–
Walking	906	13.2	0.07	–
Working out, unspecified	224	3.3	0.03	–
Religious and spiritual activities	**1,139**	**16.6**	**0.28**	**1.67**
Attending religious services	761	11.1	0.19	–
Participation in religious practices	433	6.3	0.06	–

	men aged 75 or older participating		time spent doing activity (hours)	
	number	percent	average man aged 75 or older	male participants aged 75 or older
Volunteer activities	**652**	**9.5%**	**0.24**	–
Administrative and support activities	229	3.3	0.08	–
Telephone calls	**678**	**9.9**	**0.08**	–
Telephone calls to or from family members	329	4.8	0.03	–
Telephone calls to or from friends, neighbors, or acquaintances	121	1.8	0.01	–
Traveling	**5,093**	**74.4**	**0.85**	**1.15**
Travel related to personal care	43	0.6	0.00	–
Travel related to household activities	535	7.8	0.02	–
Travel related to household management	348	5.1	0.02	–
Travel related to caring for and helping household members	310	4.5	0.04	–
Travel related to caring for and helping household children	52	0.8	0.01	–
Travel related to helping household adults	191	2.8	0.03	–
Travel related to caring for and helping people in other households	404	5.9	0.04	–
Travel related to caring for and helping children in other households	109	1.6	0.02	–
Travel related to helping adults in other households	–	–	–	–
Travel related to work	562	8.2	0.04	–
Travel related to education	–	–	–	–
Travel related to taking class	–	–	–	–
Travel related to consumer purchases	2,189	32.0	0.19	0.61
Travel related to grocery shopping	651	9.5	0.03	–
Travel related to purchasing gas	198	2.9	0.01	–
Travel related to purchasing food (except groceries)	297	4.3	0.01	–
Travel related to shopping (except groceries, food, and gas)	1,330	19.4	0.14	–
Travel related to using professional and personal care services	980	14.3	0.07	–
Travel related to using financial services and banking	343	5.0	0.02	–
Travel related to using medical services	608	8.9	0.05	–
Travel related to eating and drinking	1,445	21.1	0.11	0.53
Travel related to socializing, relaxing, and leisure	1,880	27.5	0.18	0.65
Travel related to socializing and communicating	989	14.5	0.08	–
Travel related to attending or hosting social events	88	1.3	0.02	–
Travel related to relaxing and leisure	659	9.6	0.04	–
Travel related to arts and entertainment	158	2.3	0.02	–
Travel related to sports, exercise, and recreation	330	4.8	0.02	–
Travel related to participating in sports, exercise, recreation	330	4.8	0.02	–
Travel related to religious and spiritual activities	682	10.0	0.06	–
Travel related to volunteer activities	359	5.2	0.02	–

Note: Primary activities are those respondents identified as their main activity. Other activities done simultaneously, such as eating while watching TV, are not included. Numbers may not add to total because not all subcategories are shown. If fewer than 2.0 percent of the total population participated in a primary activity, then the primary activity is not shown. "–" means sample is too small to make a reliable estimate.
Source: Bureau of Labor Statistics, unpublished tables from the 2008 American Time Use Survey, Internet site http://www.bls .gov/tus/home.htm; calculations by New Strategist

Table 9.3 Time Use by Women Aged 75 or Older, 2008

(number and percent of women aged 75 or older participating in primary activities on an average day, hours spent doing activity by the average woman aged 75 or older and by women aged 75 or older who participated in the activity, 2008; numbers of participants in thousands)

	women aged 75 or older participating		time spent doing activity (hours)	
	number	percent	average woman aged 75 or older	female participants aged 75 or older
TOTAL, ALL ACTIVITIES	**10,434**	**100.0%**	**24.00**	**24.00**
Personal care	**10,434**	**100.0**	**10.14**	**10.14**
Sleeping	10,418	99.8	9.22	9.23
Sleeplessness	984	9.4	0.15	–
Grooming	7,826	75.0	0.73	0.97
Health-related self-care	2,367	22.7	0.19	0.84
Household activities	**9,053**	**86.8**	**2.86**	**3.29**
Housework	6,075	58.2	1.15	1.98
Interior cleaning	4,775	45.8	0.67	1.47
Laundry	2,295	22.0	0.29	1.30
Storing interior household items, including food	1,057	10.1	0.04	0.38
Food and drink preparation, presentation, and clean-up	7,476	71.7	0.90	1.25
Food and drink preparation	6,944	66.6	0.65	0.97
Kitchen and food clean-up	4,146	39.7	0.24	0.60
Interior maintenance, repair, and decoration	316	3.0	0.03	–
Interior arrangement, decoration, and repairs	115	1.1	0.02	–
Exterior maintenance, repair, and decoration	311	3.0	0.05	–
Lawn, garden, and houseplants	1,539	14.7	0.24	1.62
Animals and pets (not veterinary care)	1,554	14.9	0.12	0.84
Walking, exercising, and playing with pets	543	5.2	0.05	–
Vehicles	27	0.3	0.00	–
Household management	3,935	37.7	0.36	0.95
Financial management	809	7.8	0.06	–
Household and personal organization and planning	1,632	15.6	0.15	0.96
Household and personal mail and messages (except email)	2,086	20.0	0.10	0.51
Household and personal email	564	5.4	0.04	–
Caring for and helping household members	**624**	**6.0**	**0.07**	**–**
Caring for and helping household children	72	0.7	0.01	–
Physical care for household children	40	0.4	0.00	–
Reading to or with household children	–	–	–	–
Playing with household children (except sports)	32	0.3	0.00	–
Talking with, listening to household children	36	0.3	0.00	–
Looking after household children as a primary activity	115	1.1	0.00	–
Picking up or dropping off household children	–	–	–	–
Activities related to household children's education	–	–	–	–
Helping household children with homework	–	–	–	–
Helping household adults	18	0.2	0.00	–
Caring for and helping people in other households	**952**	**9.1**	**0.10**	**–**
Caring for and helping children in other households	286	2.7	0.06	–

	women aged 75 or older participating		time spent doing activity (hours)	
	number	percent	average woman aged 75 or older	female participants aged 75 or older
Helping adults in other households	553	5.3%	0.03	–
Picking up or dropping off adults in other households	389	3.7	0.01	–
Work and work-related activities	**401**	**3.8**	**0.23**	**–**
Work, main job	388	3.7	0.23	–
Work, other job(s)	–	–	–	–
Education	**130**	**1.2**	**0.04**	**–**
Taking class	83	0.8	0.02	–
Taking class for degree, certification, or licensure	4	0.0	0.00	–
Research, homework	51	0.5	0.02	–
Consumer purchases (store, telephone, Internet)	**3,493**	**33.5**	**0.35**	**1.04**
Grocery shopping	1,536	14.7	0.13	0.88
Purchasing gas	119	1.1	0.00	–
Purchasing food (except groceries)	347	3.3	0.01	–
Shopping, except groceries, food, and gas	1,994	19.1	0.21	1.08
Professional and personal care services	**1,511**	**14.5**	**0.17**	**1.18**
Financial services and banking	260	2.5	0.01	–
Banking	239	2.3	0.00	–
Medical and care services	828	7.9	0.10	–
Using health and care services outside the home	761	7.3	0.08	–
Household services	**177**	**1.7**	**0.03**	**–**
Eating and drinking	**10,297**	**98.7**	**1.39**	**1.40**
Socializing, relaxing, and leisure	**10,402**	**99.7**	**6.86**	**6.88**
Socializing and communicating	3,955	37.9	0.58	1.54
Attending or hosting social events	360	3.5	0.08	–
Relaxing and leisure	10,327	99.0	6.15	6.21
Relaxing, thinking	3,158	30.3	0.65	2.13
Television	9,437	90.4	3.89	4.30
Listening to the radio	328	3.1	0.08	–
Listening to or playing music (not radio)	91	0.9	0.01	–
Playing games (including computer)	1,555	14.9	0.31	2.09
Computer use for leisure (except games)	471	4.5	0.08	–
Reading for personal interest	5,462	52.3	1.05	2.01
Arts and entertainment (except sports)	185	1.8	0.06	–
Sports, exercise, and recreation	**1,651**	**15.8**	**0.17**	**1.06**
Participating in sports, exercise, or recreation	1,634	15.7	0.16	1.01
Using cardiovascular equipment	106	1.0	0.01	–
Walking	1,085	10.4	0.08	0.80
Working out, unspecified	319	3.1	0.02	–
Religious and spiritual activities	**1,940**	**18.6**	**0.25**	**1.33**
Attending religious services	851	8.2	0.12	1.50
Participation in religious practices	1,163	11.1	0.09	0.81

	women aged 75 or older participating		time spent doing activity (hours)	
	number	percent	average woman aged 75 or older	female participants aged 75 or older
Volunteer activities	**938**	**9.0%**	**0.20**	**2.20**
Administrative and support activities	404	3.9	0.05	–
Telephone calls	**3,096**	**29.7**	**0.27**	**0.92**
Telephone calls to or from family members	1,968	18.9	0.14	0.73
Telephone calls to or from friends, neighbors, or acquaintances	1,327	12.7	0.07	0.59
Traveling	**6,539**	**62.7**	**0.60**	**0.95**
Travel related to personal care	101	1.0	0.00	–
Travel related to household activities	960	9.2	0.04	–
Travel related to household management	719	6.9	0.02	–
Travel related to caring for and helping household members	142	1.4	0.00	–
Travel related to caring for and helping household children	–	–	–	–
Travel related to helping household adults	18	0.2	0.00	–
Travel related to caring for and helping people in other households	678	6.5	0.03	–
Travel related to caring for and helping children in other households	88	0.8	0.00	–
Travel related to helping adults in other households	64	0.6	0.00	–
Travel related to work	298	2.9	0.02	–
Travel related to education	79	0.8	0.00	–
Travel related to taking class	79	0.8	0.00	–
Travel related to consumer purchases	3,487	33.4	0.15	0.45
Travel related to grocery shopping	1,601	15.3	0.05	0.34
Travel related to purchasing gas	119	1.1	0.00	–
Travel related to purchasing food (except groceries)	347	3.3	0.01	–
Travel related to shopping (except groceries, food, and gas)	1,920	18.4	0.08	0.44
Travel related to using professional and personal care services	1,312	12.6	0.06	–
Travel related to using financial services and banking	260	2.5	0.01	–
Travel related to using medical services	681	6.5	0.03	–
Travel related to eating and drinking	1,621	15.5	0.07	0.45
Travel related to socializing, relaxing, and leisure	2,447	23.5	0.14	0.58
Travel related to socializing and communicating	1,621	15.5	0.07	0.43
Travel related to attending or hosting social events	276	2.6	0.01	–
Travel related to relaxing and leisure	663	6.4	0.02	–
Travel related to arts and entertainment	126	1.2	0.02	–
Travel related to sports, exercise, and recreation	417	4.0	0.01	–
Travel related to participating in sports, exercise, recreation	400	3.8	0.01	–
Travel related to religious and spiritual activities	865	8.3	0.03	0.34
Travel related to volunteer activities	549	5.3	0.02	–

Note: Primary activities are those respondents identified as their main activity. Other activities done simultaneously, such as eating while watching TV, are not included. Numbers may not add to total because not all subcategories are shown. If fewer than 2.0 percent of the total population participated in a primary activity, then the primary activity is not shown. "–" means sample is too small to make a reliable estimate.
Source: Bureau of Labor Statistics, unpublished tables from the 2008 American Time Use Survey, Internet site http://www.bls .gov/tus/home.htm; calculations by New Strategist

Table 9.4 Indexed Time Use of Total People Aged 75 or Older, 2008

(hours spent doing primary activities on an average day by people aged 75 or older and by total people aged 15 or older, and index of time spent by people aged 75 or older to total people, 2008)

	average hours		index, people aged 75 or older to total people
	people aged 75 or older	total people	
TOTAL, ALL ACTIVITIES	**24.00**	**24.00**	**100**
Personal care	**10.02**	**9.38**	**107**
Sleeping	9.14	8.60	106
Sleeplessness	0.13	0.06	217
Grooming	0.68	0.67	101
Health-related self-care	0.20	0.09	222
Household activities	**2.42**	**1.77**	**137**
Housework	0.78	0.58	134
Interior cleaning	0.47	0.37	127
Laundry	0.19	0.17	112
Storing interior household items, including food	0.03	0.02	150
Food and drink preparation, presentation, and clean-up	0.70	0.52	135
Food and drink preparation	0.50	0.40	125
Kitchen and food clean-up	0.18	0.12	150
Interior maintenance, repair, and decoration	0.06	0.07	86
Interior arrangement, decoration, and repairs	0.04	0.05	80
Exterior maintenance, repair, and decoration	0.07	0.06	117
Lawn, garden, and houseplants	0.32	0.19	168
Animals and pets (not veterinary care)	0.13	0.09	144
Walking, exercising, and playing with pets	0.06	0.04	150
Vehicles	0.01	0.04	25
Household management	0.33	0.21	157
Financial management	0.07	0.03	233
Household and personal organization and planning	0.14	0.09	156
Household and personal mail and messages (except email)	0.08	0.02	400
Household and personal email	0.04	0.06	67
Caring for and helping household members	**0.06**	**0.45**	**13**
Caring for and helping household children	0.01	0.37	3
Physical care for household children	0.00	0.17	0
Reading to or with household children	–	0.01	–
Playing with household children (except sports)	0.00	0.09	0
Talking with, listening to household children	0.00	0.02	0
Looking after household children as a primary activity	0.00	0.03	0
Picking up or dropping off household children	0.00	0.02	0
Activities related to household children's education	–	0.04	–
Helping household children with homework	–	0.03	–
Helping household adults	0.00	0.01	0
Caring for and helping people in other households	**0.11**	**0.16**	**69**
Caring for and helping children in other households	0.06	0.09	67

	average hours		index, people aged 75 or older to total people
	people aged 75 or older	total people	
Helping adults in other households	0.04	0.06	67
Picking up or dropping off adults in other households	0.00	0.01	0
Work and work-related activities	**0.34**	**3.45**	**10**
Work, main job	0.30	3.28	9
Work, other job(s)	–	0.09	–
Education	**0.03**	**0.44**	**7**
Taking class	0.01	0.27	4
Taking class for degree, certification, or licensure	0.00	0.26	0
Research, homework	0.02	0.16	13
Consumer purchases (store, telephone, Internet)	**0.33**	**0.38**	**87**
Grocery shopping	0.11	0.10	110
Purchasing gas	0.01	0.01	100
Purchasing food (except groceries)	0.01	0.02	50
Shopping, except groceries, food, and gas	0.21	0.25	84
Professional and personal care services	**0.16**	**0.08**	**200**
Financial services and banking	0.01	0.01	100
Banking	0.01	0.01	100
Medical and care services	0.11	0.05	220
Using health and care services outside the home	0.08	0.04	200
Household services	**0.02**	**0.01**	**200**
Eating and drinking	**1.44**	**1.11**	**130**
Socializing, relaxing, and leisure	**7.27**	**4.62**	**157**
Socializing and communicating	0.57	0.64	89
Attending or hosting social events	0.07	0.07	100
Relaxing and leisure	6.56	3.83	171
Relaxing, thinking	0.74	0.27	274
Television	4.19	2.77	151
Listening to the radio	0.09	0.03	300
Listening to or playing music (not radio)	0.02	0.03	67
Playing games (including computer)	0.29	0.20	145
Computer use for leisure (except games)	0.10	0.14	71
Reading for personal interest	1.04	0.34	306
Arts and entertainment (except sports)	0.07	0.09	78
Sports, exercise, and recreation	**0.18**	**0.33**	**55**
Participating in sports, exercise, or recreation	0.18	0.29	62
Using cardiovascular equipment	0.02	0.02	100
Walking	0.08	0.04	200
Working out, unspecified	0.03	0.03	100
Religious and spiritual activities	**0.26**	**0.14**	**186**
Attending religious services	0.15	0.09	167
Participation in religious practices	0.08	0.04	200

	average hours		index, people aged 75 or older to total people
	people aged 75 or older	total people	
Volunteer activities	**0.22**	**0.15**	**147**
Administrative and support activities	0.06	0.04	150
Telephone calls	**0.20**	**0.13**	**154**
Telephone calls to or from family members	0.09	0.04	225
Telephone calls to or from friends, neighbors, or acquaintances	0.05	0.04	125
Traveling	**0.70**	**1.20**	**58**
Travel related to personal care	0.00	0.01	0
Travel related to household activities	0.03	0.04	75
Travel related to household management	0.02	0.02	100
Travel related to caring for and helping household members	0.02	0.08	25
Travel related to caring for and helping household children	0.00	0.06	0
Travel related to helping household adults	0.01	0.02	50
Travel related to caring for and helping people in other households	0.04	0.06	67
Travel related to caring for and helping children in other households	0.01	0.02	50
Travel related to helping adults in other households	0.00	0.04	0
Travel related to work	0.03	0.28	11
Travel related to education	0.00	0.03	0
Travel related to taking class	0.00	0.03	0
Travel related to consumer purchases	0.17	0.24	71
Travel related to grocery shopping	0.04	0.05	80
Travel related to purchasing gas	0.01	0.02	50
Travel related to purchasing food (except groceries)	0.01	0.04	25
Travel related to shopping (except groceries, food, and gas)	0.10	0.12	83
Travel related to using professional and personal care services	0.06	0.04	150
Travel related to using financial services and banking	0.02	0.01	200
Travel related to using medical services	0.04	0.02	200
Travel related to eating and drinking	0.09	0.12	75
Travel related to socializing, relaxing, and leisure	0.15	0.18	83
Travel related to socializing and communicating	0.07	0.09	78
Travel related to attending or hosting social events	0.01	0.01	100
Travel related to relaxing and leisure	0.03	0.04	75
Travel related to arts and entertainment	0.02	0.02	100
Travel related to sports, exercise, and recreation	0.02	0.04	50
Travel related to participating in sports, exercise, recreation	0.02	0.04	50
Travel related to religious and spiritual activities	0.04	0.02	200
Travel related to volunteer activities	0.02	0.02	100

Note: The index is calculated by dividing average time spent by people in the age group doing primary activity by average time spent by total people doing primary activity and multiplying by 100. Primary activities are those respondents identified as their main activity. Other activities done simultaneously, such as eating while watching TV, are not included. Numbers may not add to total because not all subcategories are shown. If fewer than 2.0 percent of the total population participated in a primary activity, then the primary activity is not shown. "–" means sample is too small to make a reliable estimate.
Source: Bureau of Labor Statistics, unpublished tables from the 2008 American Time Use Survey, Internet site http://www.bls .gov/tus/home.htm; calculations by New Strategist

Table 9.5 Indexed Time Use of Men Aged 75 or Older, 2008

(hours spent doing primary activities on an average day by men aged 75 or older and by total men aged 15 or older, and index of time spent by men aged 75 or older to total men, 2008)

	average hours		index, men aged 75 or older to total men
	men aged 75 or older	total men	
TOTAL, ALL ACTIVITIES	**24.00**	**24.00**	**100**
Personal care	**9.83**	**9.21**	**107**
Sleeping	9.03	8.56	105
Sleeplessness	0.09	0.05	180
Grooming	0.60	0.56	107
Health-related self-care	0.21	0.07	300
Household activities	**1.76**	**1.32**	**133**
Housework	0.22	0.24	92
Interior cleaning	0.16	0.17	94
Laundry	0.04	0.06	67
Storing interior household items, including food	0.02	0.01	200
Food and drink preparation, presentation, and clean-up	0.39	0.30	130
Food and drink preparation	0.29	0.25	116
Kitchen and food clean-up	0.10	0.05	200
Interior maintenance, repair, and decoration	0.11	0.10	110
Interior arrangement, decoration, and repairs	0.07	0.08	88
Exterior maintenance, repair, and decoration	0.10	0.08	125
Lawn, garden, and houseplants	0.45	0.26	173
Animals and pets (not veterinary care)	0.14	0.08	175
Walking, exercising, and playing with pets	0.07	0.04	175
Vehicles	0.03	0.07	43
Household management	0.30	0.16	188
Financial management	0.09	0.03	300
Household and personal organization and planning	0.12	0.07	171
Household and personal mail and messages (except email)	0.04	0.02	200
Household and personal email	0.04	0.05	80
Caring for and helping household members	**0.04**	**0.30**	**13**
Caring for and helping household children	0.00	0.25	0
Physical care for household children	0.00	0.09	0
Reading to or with household children	–	0.01	–
Playing with household children (except sports)	–	0.08	–
Talking with, listening to household children	–	0.01	–
Looking after household children as a primary activity	–	0.02	–
Picking up or dropping off household children	0.00	0.01	0
Activities related to household children's education	–	0.02	–
Helping household children with homework	–	0.02	–
Helping household adults	0.01	0.01	100
Caring for and helping people in other households	**0.12**	**0.13**	**92**
Caring for and helping children in other households	0.05	0.05	100

	average hours		index, men aged 75 or older to total men
	men aged 75 or older	total men	
Helping adults in other households	0.06	0.07	86
Picking up or dropping off adults in other households	0.00	0.01	0
Work and work-related activities	**0.51**	**4.16**	**12**
Work, main job	0.41	3.96	10
Work, other job(s)	–	0.10	–
Education	**0.01**	**0.39**	**3**
Taking class	–	0.27	–
Taking class for degree, certification, or licensure	–	0.27	–
Research, homework	0.01	0.12	8
Consumer purchases (store, telephone, Internet)	**0.29**	**0.28**	**104**
Grocery shopping	0.17	0.06	283
Purchasing gas	0.01	0.01	100
Purchasing food (except groceries)	0.01	0.02	50
Shopping, except groceries, food, and gas	0.21	0.19	111
Professional and personal care services	**0.14**	**0.06**	**233**
Financial services and banking	0.01	0.01	100
Banking	0.01	0.00	–
Medical and care services	0.13	0.04	325
Using health and care services outside the home	0.09	0.03	300
Household services	**0.02**	**0.01**	**200**
Eating and drinking	**1.51**	**1.15**	**131**
Socializing, relaxing, and leisure	**7.89**	**4.83**	**163**
Socializing and communicating	0.55	0.59	93
Attending or hosting social events	0.05	0.06	83
Relaxing and leisure	7.20	4.09	176
Relaxing, thinking	0.87	0.27	322
Television	4.66	3.01	155
Listening to the radio	0.12	0.03	400
Listening to or playing music (not radio)	0.03	0.04	75
Playing games (including computer)	0.25	0.25	100
Computer use for leisure (except games)	0.13	0.15	87
Reading for personal interest	1.02	0.29	352
Arts and entertainment (except sports)	0.09	0.09	100
Sports, exercise, and recreation	**0.20**	**0.44**	**45**
Participating in sports, exercise, or recreation	0.20	0.40	50
Using cardiovascular equipment	0.03	0.01	300
Walking	0.07	0.04	175
Working out, unspecified	0.03	0.04	75
Religious and spiritual activities	**0.28**	**0.12**	**233**
Attending religious services	0.19	0.07	271
Participation in religious practices	0.06	0.03	200

	average hours		index, men aged 75 or older to total men
	men aged 75 or older	total men	
Volunteer activities	**0.24**	**0.14**	**171**
Administrative and support activities	0.08	0.03	267
Telephone calls	**0.08**	**0.07**	**114**
Telephone calls to or from family members	0.03	0.02	150
Telephone calls to or from friends, neighbors, or acquaintances	0.01	0.02	50
Traveling	**0.85**	**1.23**	**69**
Travel related to personal care	0.00	0.01	0
Travel related to household activities	0.02	0.04	50
Travel related to household management	0.02	0.03	67
Travel related to caring for and helping household members	0.04	0.06	67
Travel related to caring for and helping household children	0.01	0.04	25
Travel related to helping household adults	0.03	0.02	150
Travel related to caring for and helping people in other households	0.04	0.06	67
Travel related to caring for and helping children in other households	0.02	0.01	200
Travel related to helping adults in other households	–	0.04	–
Travel related to work	0.04	0.36	11
Travel related to education	–	0.03	–
Travel related to taking class	–	0.02	–
Travel related to consumer purchases	0.19	0.21	90
Travel related to grocery shopping	0.03	0.04	75
Travel related to purchasing gas	0.01	0.02	50
Travel related to purchasing food (except groceries)	0.01	0.04	25
Travel related to shopping (except groceries, food, and gas)	0.14	0.11	127
Travel related to using professional and personal care services	0.07	0.03	233
Travel related to using financial services and banking	0.02	0.01	200
Travel related to using medical services	0.05	0.01	500
Travel related to eating and drinking	0.11	0.13	85
Travel related to socializing, relaxing, and leisure	0.18	0.18	100
Travel related to socializing and communicating	0.08	0.09	89
Travel related to attending or hosting social events	0.02	0.01	200
Travel related to relaxing and leisure	0.04	0.04	100
Travel related to arts and entertainment	0.02	0.02	100
Travel related to sports, exercise, and recreation	0.02	0.06	33
Travel related to participating in sports, exercise, recreation	0.02	0.05	40
Travel related to religious and spiritual activities	0.06	0.02	300
Travel related to volunteer activities	0.02	0.02	100

Note: The index is calculated by dividing average time spent by men in the age group doing primary activity by average time spent by total men doing primary activity and multiplying by 100. Primary activities are those respondents identified as their main activity. Other activities done simultaneously, such as eating while watching TV, are not included. Numbers may not add to total because not all subcategories are shown. If fewer than 2.0 percent of the total population participated in a primary activity, then the primary activity is not shown. "–" means denominator is zero or sample is too small to make a reliable estimate. Source: Bureau of Labor Statistics, unpublished tables from the 2008 American Time Use Survey, Internet site http://www.bls .gov/tus/home.htm; calculations by New Strategist

Table 9.6 Indexed Time Use of Women Aged 75 or Older, 2008

(hours spent doing primary activities on an average day by women aged 75 or older and by total women aged 15 or older, and index of time spent by women aged 75 or older to total women, 2008)

	average hours		index, women aged 75 or older to total women
	women aged 75 or older	total women	
TOTAL, ALL ACTIVITIES	**24.00**	**24.00**	**100**
Personal care	**10.14**	**9.54**	**106**
Sleeping	9.22	8.64	107
Sleeplessness	0.15	0.07	214
Grooming	0.73	0.78	94
Health-related self-care	0.19	0.11	173
Household activities	**2.86**	**2.19**	**131**
Housework	1.15	0.90	128
Interior cleaning	0.67	0.55	122
Laundry	0.29	0.28	104
Storing interior household items, including food	0.04	0.02	200
Food and drink preparation, presentation, and clean-up	0.90	0.73	123
Food and drink preparation	0.65	0.55	118
Kitchen and food clean-up	0.24	0.18	133
Interior maintenance, repair, and decoration	0.03	0.04	75
Interior arrangement, decoration, and repairs	0.02	0.03	67
Exterior maintenance, repair, and decoration	0.05	0.03	167
Lawn, garden, and houseplants	0.24	0.12	200
Animals and pets (not veterinary care)	0.12	0.10	120
Walking, exercising, and playing with pets	0.05	0.04	125
Vehicles	0.00	0.01	0
Household management	0.36	0.25	144
Financial management	0.06	0.04	150
Household and personal organization and planning	0.15	0.11	136
Household and personal mail and messages (except email)	0.10	0.03	333
Household and personal email	0.04	0.07	57
Caring for and helping household members	**0.07**	**0.59**	**12**
Caring for and helping household children	0.01	0.48	2
Physical care for household children	0.00	0.24	0
Reading to or with household children	–	0.02	–
Playing with household children (except sports)	0.00	0.09	0
Talking with, listening to household children	0.00	0.02	0
Looking after household children as a primary activity	0.00	0.03	0
Picking up or dropping off household children	–	0.03	–
Activities related to household children's education	–	0.05	–
Helping household children with homework	–	0.04	–
Helping household adults	–	0.01	–
Caring for and helping people in other households	**0.10**	**0.20**	**50**
Caring for and helping children in other households	0.06	0.12	50

	average hours		index, women aged 75 or older to total women
	women aged 75 or older	total women	
Helping adults in other households	0.03	0.05	60
Picking up or dropping off adults in other households	0.01	0.01	100
Work and work-related activities	**0.23**	**2.79**	**8**
Work, main job	0.23	2.63	9
Work, other job(s)	–	0.09	–
Education	**0.04**	**0.48**	**8**
Taking class	0.02	0.27	7
Taking class for degree, certification, or licensure	0.00	0.25	0
Research, homework	0.02	0.20	10
Consumer purchases (store, telephone, Internet)	**0.35**	**0.48**	**73**
Grocery shopping	0.13	0.13	100
Purchasing gas	0.00	0.01	0
Purchasing food (except groceries)	0.01	0.02	50
Shopping, except groceries, food, and gas	0.21	0.31	68
Professional and personal care services	**0.17**	**0.11**	**155**
Financial services and banking	0.01	0.01	100
Banking	0.00	0.01	0
Medical and care services	0.10	0.06	167
Using health and care services outside the home	0.08	0.05	160
Household services	**0.03**	**0.01**	**300**
Eating and drinking	**1.39**	**1.07**	**130**
Socializing, relaxing, and leisure	**6.86**	**4.42**	**155**
Socializing and communicating	0.58	0.68	85
Attending or hosting social events	0.08	0.08	100
Relaxing and leisure	6.15	3.58	172
Relaxing, thinking	0.65	0.26	250
Television	3.89	2.54	153
Listening to the radio	0.08	0.02	400
Listening to or playing music (not radio)	0.01	0.02	50
Playing games (including computer)	0.31	0.15	207
Computer use for leisure (except games)	0.08	0.14	57
Reading for personal interest	1.05	0.40	263
Arts and entertainment (except sports)	0.06	0.08	75
Sports, exercise, and recreation	**0.17**	**0.23**	**74**
Participating in sports, exercise, or recreation	0.16	0.20	80
Using cardiovascular equipment	0.01	0.02	50
Walking	0.08	0.04	200
Working out, unspecified	0.02	0.02	100
Religious and spiritual activities	**0.25**	**0.17**	**147**
Attending religious services	0.12	0.10	120
Participation in religious practices	0.09	0.05	180

	average hours		index, women aged 75 or older
	women aged 75 or older	total women	to total women
Volunteer activities	**0.20**	**0.16**	**125**
Administrative and support activities	0.05	0.04	125
Telephone calls	**0.27**	**0.18**	**150**
Telephone calls to or from family members	0.14	0.07	200
Telephone calls to or from friends, neighbors, or acquaintances	0.07	0.06	117
Traveling	**0.60**	**1.17**	**51**
Travel related to personal care	0.00	0.01	0
Travel related to household activities	0.04	0.04	100
Travel related to household management	0.02	0.02	100
Travel related to caring for and helping household members	0.00	0.11	0
Travel related to caring for and helping household children	–	0.08	–
Travel related to helping household adults	0.00	0.02	0
Travel related to caring for and helping people in other households	0.03	0.07	43
Travel related to caring for and helping children in other households	0.00	0.02	0
Travel related to helping adults in other households	0.00	0.04	0
Travel related to work	0.02	0.20	10
Travel related to education	0.00	0.04	0
Travel related to taking class	0.00	0.03	0
Travel related to consumer purchases	0.15	0.27	56
Travel related to grocery shopping	0.05	0.06	83
Travel related to purchasing gas	0.00	0.02	0
Travel related to purchasing food (except groceries)	0.01	0.04	25
Travel related to shopping (except groceries, food, and gas)	0.08	0.14	57
Travel related to using professional and personal care services	0.06	0.05	120
Travel related to using financial services and banking	0.01	0.01	100
Travel related to using medical services	0.03	0.02	150
Travel related to eating and drinking	0.07	0.11	64
Travel related to socializing, relaxing, and leisure	0.14	0.17	82
Travel related to socializing and communicating	0.07	0.10	70
Travel related to attending or hosting social events	0.01	0.01	100
Travel related to relaxing and leisure	0.02	0.03	67
Travel related to arts and entertainment	0.02	0.02	100
Travel related to sports, exercise, and recreation	0.01	0.03	33
Travel related to participating in sports, exercise, recreation	0.01	0.03	33
Travel related to religious and spiritual activities	0.03	0.02	150
Travel related to volunteer activities	0.02	0.02	100

Note: The index is calculated by dividing average time spent by women in the age group doing primary activity by average time spent by total women doing primary activity and multiplying by 100. Primary activities are those respondents identified as their main activity. Other activities done simultaneously, such as eating while watching TV, are not included. Numbers may not add to total because not all subcategories are shown. If fewer than 2.0 percent of the total population participated in a primary activity, then the primary activity is not shown. "–" means sample is too small to make a reliable estimate.
Source: Bureau of Labor Statistics, unpublished tables from the 2008 American Time Use Survey, Internet site http://www.bls .gov/tus/home.htm; calculations by New Strategist

Table 9.7 Indexed Time Use of People Aged 75 or Older by Sex, 2008

(average hours spent by people aged 75 or older doing primary activities on an average day by sex, and index of women's time to men's, 2008)

	average hours, aged 75 or older		index of women to men
	men	women	
TOTAL, ALL ACTIVITIES	**24.00**	**24.00**	**100**
Personal care	**9.83**	**10.14**	**103**
Sleeping	9.03	9.22	102
Sleeplessness	0.09	0.15	167
Grooming	0.60	0.73	122
Health-related self-care	0.21	0.19	90
Household activities	**1.76**	**2.86**	**163**
Housework	0.22	1.15	523
Interior cleaning	0.16	0.67	419
Laundry	0.04	0.29	725
Storing interior household items, including food	0.02	0.04	200
Food and drink preparation, presentation, and clean-up	0.39	0.90	231
Food and drink preparation	0.29	0.65	224
Kitchen and food clean-up	0.10	0.24	240
Interior maintenance, repair, and decoration	0.11	0.03	27
Interior arrangement, decoration, and repairs	0.07	0.02	29
Exterior maintenance, repair, and decoration	0.10	0.05	50
Lawn, garden, and houseplants	0.45	0.24	53
Animals and pets (not veterinary care)	0.14	0.12	86
Walking, exercising, and playing with pets	0.07	0.05	71
Vehicles	0.03	0.00	0
Household management	0.30	0.36	120
Financial management	0.09	0.06	67
Household and personal organization and planning	0.12	0.15	125
Household and personal mail and messages (except email)	0.04	0.10	250
Household and personal email	0.04	0.04	100
Caring for and helping household members	**0.04**	**0.07**	**175**
Caring for and helping household children	0.00	0.01	–
Physical care for household children	0.00	0.00	–
Reading to or with household children	–	–	–
Playing with household children (except sports)	–	0.00	–
Talking with, listening to household children	–	0.00	–
Looking after household children as a primary activity	–	0.00	–
Picking up or dropping off household children	0.00	–	–
Activities related to household children's education	–	–	–
Helping household children with homework	–	–	–
Helping household adults	0.01	–	–
Caring for and helping people in other households	**0.12**	**0.10**	**83**
Caring for and helping children in other households	0.05	0.06	120

	average hours, aged 75 or older		index of women to men
	men	women	
Helping adults in other households	0.06	0.03	50
Picking up or dropping off adults in other households	0.00	0.01	–
Work and work-related activities	**0.51**	**0.23**	**45**
Work, main job	0.41	0.23	56
Work, other job(s)	–	–	–
Education	**0.01**	**0.04**	**400**
Taking class	–	0.02	–
Taking class for degree, certification, or licensure	–	0.00	–
Research, homework	0.01	0.02	200
Consumer purchases (store, telephone, Internet)	**0.29**	**0.35**	**121**
Grocery shopping	0.17	0.13	76
Purchasing gas	0.01	0.00	0
Purchasing food (except groceries)	0.01	0.01	100
Shopping, except groceries, food, and gas	0.21	0.21	100
Professional and personal care services	**0.14**	**0.17**	**121**
Financial services and banking	0.01	0.01	100
Banking	0.01	0.00	0
Medical and care services	0.13	0.10	77
Using health and care services outside the home	0.09	0.08	89
Household services	**0.02**	**0.03**	**150**
Eating and drinking	**1.51**	**1.39**	**92**
Socializing, relaxing, and leisure	**7.89**	**6.86**	**87**
Socializing and communicating	0.55	0.58	105
Attending or hosting social events	0.05	0.08	160
Relaxing and leisure	7.20	6.15	85
Relaxing, thinking	0.87	0.65	75
Television	4.66	3.89	83
Listening to the radio	0.12	0.08	67
Listening to or playing music (not radio)	0.03	0.01	33
Playing games (including computer)	0.25	0.31	124
Computer use for leisure (except games)	0.13	0.08	62
Reading for personal interest	1.02	1.05	103
Arts and entertainment (except sports)	0.09	0.06	67
Sports, exercise, and recreation	**0.20**	**0.17**	**85**
Participating in sports, exercise, or recreation	0.20	0.16	80
Using cardiovascular equipment	0.03	0.01	33
Walking	0.07	0.08	114
Working out, unspecified	0.03	0.02	67
Religious and spiritual activities	**0.28**	**0.25**	**89**
Attending religious services	0.19	0.12	63
Participation in religious practices	0.06	0.09	150

	average hours, aged 75 or older		index of women to men
	men	women	
Volunteer activities	**0.24**	**0.20**	**83**
Administrative and support activities	0.08	0.05	63
Telephone calls	**0.08**	**0.27**	**338**
Telephone calls to or from family members	0.03	0.14	467
Telephone calls to or from friends, neighbors, or acquaintances	0.01	0.07	700
Traveling	**0.85**	**0.60**	**71**
Travel related to personal care	0.00	0.00	–
Travel related to household activities	0.02	0.04	200
Travel related to household management	0.02	0.02	100
Travel related to caring for and helping household members	0.04	0.00	0
Travel related to caring for and helping household children	0.01	–	–
Travel related to helping household adults	0.03	0.00	0
Travel related to caring for and helping people in other households	0.04	0.03	75
Travel related to caring for and helping children in other households	0.02	0.00	0
Travel related to helping adults in other households	–	0.00	–
Travel related to work	0.04	0.02	50
Travel related to education	–	0.00	–
Travel related to taking class	–	0.00	–
Travel related to consumer purchases	0.19	0.15	79
Travel related to grocery shopping	0.03	0.05	167
Travel related to purchasing gas	0.01	0.00	0
Travel related to purchasing food (except groceries)	0.01	0.01	100
Travel related to shopping (except groceries, food, and gas)	0.14	0.08	57
Travel related to using professional and personal care services	0.07	0.06	86
Travel related to using financial services and banking	0.02	0.01	50
Travel related to using medical services	0.05	0.03	60
Travel related to eating and drinking	0.11	0.07	64
Travel related to socializing, relaxing, and leisure	0.18	0.14	78
Travel related to socializing and communicating	0.08	0.07	88
Travel related to attending or hosting social events	0.02	0.01	50
Travel related to relaxing and leisure	0.04	0.02	50
Travel related to arts and entertainment	0.02	0.02	100
Travel related to sports, exercise, and recreation	0.02	0.01	50
Travel related to participating in sports, exercise, recreation	0.02	0.01	50
Travel related to religious and spiritual activities	0.06	0.03	50
Travel related to volunteer activities	0.02	0.02	100

Note: The index is calculated by dividing women's time by men's time and multiplying by 100. Primary activities are those respondents identified as their main activity. Other activities done simultaneously, such as eating while watching TV, are not included. Numbers may not add to total because not all subcategories are shown. If fewer than 2.0 percent of the total population participated in a primary activity, then the primary activity is not shown. "–" means denominator is zero or sample is too small to make a reliable estimate.

Source: Bureau of Labor Statistics, unpublished tables from the 2008 American Time Use Survey, Internet site http://www.bls.gov/tus/home.htm; calculations by New Strategist

Table 9.8 Indexed Participation in Primary Activities by Total People Aged 75 or Older, 2008

(percent of people aged 75 or older and total people aged 15 or older participating in primary activities on an average day, and index of participation by people aged 75 or older to total people, 2008)

	percent participating		index, people aged 75 or older to total
	people aged 75 or older	total people	
TOTAL, ALL ACTIVITIES	**100.0%**	**100.0%**	**100**
Personal care	**100.0**	**100.0**	**100**
Sleeping	99.8	99.9	100
Sleeplessness	8.1	5.2	155
Grooming	72.3	79.3	91
Health-related self-care	18.1	6.4	284
Household activities	**81.4**	**75.5**	**108**
Housework	42.7	35.5	120
Interior cleaning	33.5	24.5	137
Laundry	14.5	16.2	90
Storing interior household items, including food	8.4	5.0	169
Food and drink preparation, presentation, and clean-up	59.9	52.3	115
Food and drink preparation	55.3	49.3	112
Kitchen and food clean-up	30.0	20.8	144
Interior maintenance, repair, and decoration	3.8	3.0	124
Interior arrangement, decoration, and repairs	1.5	2.0	79
Exterior maintenance, repair, and decoration	3.7	2.7	134
Lawn, garden, and houseplants	16.7	9.4	178
Animals and pets (not veterinary care)	15.0	14.5	104
Walking, exercising, and playing with pets	5.7	5.8	99
Vehicles	1.2	2.7	44
Household management	34.4	29.0	119
Financial management	7.2	4.0	178
Household and personal organization and planning	13.6	14.1	97
Household and personal mail and messages (except email)	17.4	6.9	254
Household and personal email	5.3	9.4	56
Caring for and helping household members	**6.3**	**26.1**	**24**
Caring for and helping household children	0.7	21.9	3
Physical care for household children	0.3	15.7	2
Reading to or with household children	–	2.6	–
Playing with household children (except sports)	0.2	5.4	3
Talking with, listening to household children	0.2	3.0	7
Looking after household children as a primary activity	0.7	2.3	29
Picking up or dropping off household children	0.3	9.2	3
Activities related to household children's education	–	3.8	–
Helping household children with homework	–	3.4	–
Helping household adults	1.7	3.6	48
Caring for and helping people in other households	**8.5**	**13.3**	**64**
Caring for and helping children in other households	2.7	5.6	49

	percent participating		index, people aged 75 or older to total
	people aged 75 or older	total people	
Helping adults in other households	5.1%	8.0%	64
Picking up or dropping off adults in other households	3.3	5.0	66
Work and work-related activities	**6.4**	**46.6**	**14**
Work, main job	5.5	43.9	13
Work, other job(s)	–	2.4	–
Education	**0.9**	**7.9**	**11**
Taking class	0.5	5.2	9
Taking class for degree, certification, or licensure	–	4.8	–
Research, homework	0.4	5.8	7
Consumer purchases (store, telephone, Internet)	**33.2**	**40.7**	**82**
Grocery shopping	12.7	12.9	98
Purchasing gas	1.8	4.0	46
Purchasing food (except groceries)	3.8	12.0	31
Shopping, except groceries, food, and gas	19.4	23.5	83
Professional and personal care services	**14.4**	**8.9**	**162**
Financial services and banking	3.5	3.2	108
Banking	3.3	3.0	110
Medical and care services	8.3	3.6	229
Using health and care services outside the home	7.8	3.4	227
Household services	**2.4**	**2.1**	**115**
Eating and drinking	**98.7**	**96.0**	**103**
Socializing, relaxing, and leisure	**99.6**	**95.4**	**104**
Socializing and communicating	35.0	37.6	93
Attending or hosting social events	2.7	2.3	116
Relaxing and leisure	99.1	91.3	109
Relaxing, thinking	30.8	19.9	155
Television	90.9	80.9	112
Listening to the radio	4.6	2.0	226
Listening to or playing music (not radio)	1.1	2.6	41
Playing games (including computer)	12.9	9.0	144
Computer use for leisure (except games)	5.5	9.5	58
Reading for personal interest	51.5	23.9	216
Arts and entertainment (except sports)	2.0	3.2	62
Sports, exercise, and recreation	**17.6**	**18.9**	**93**
Participating in sports, exercise, or recreation	17.5	17.9	97
Using cardiovascular equipment	2.3	2.2	107
Walking	11.5	4.8	240
Working out, unspecified	3.1	3.2	98
Religious and spiritual activities	**17.8**	**9.2**	**193**
Attending religious services	9.3	4.9	191
Participation in religious practices	9.2	4.6	202

	percent participating		index, people aged 75 or older
	people aged 75 or older	total people	to total
Volunteer activities	**9.2%**	**6.7%**	**137**
Administrative and support activities	3.7	2.5	145
Telephone calls	**21.8**	**15.4**	**142**
Telephone calls to or from family members	13.3	7.3	181
Telephone calls to or from friends, neighbors, or acquaintances	8.4	5.6	150
Traveling	**67.3**	**86.9**	**77**
Travel related to personal care	0.8	2.5	33
Travel related to household activities	8.6	9.4	92
Travel related to household management	6.2	6.1	101
Travel related to caring for and helping household members	2.6	13.6	19
Travel related to caring for and helping household children	0.3	11.0	3
Travel related to helping household adults	1.2	2.6	47
Travel related to caring for and helping people in other households	6.3	10.5	60
Travel related to caring for and helping children in other households	1.1	3.5	33
Travel related to helping adults in other households	0.4	7.1	5
Travel related to work	5.0	38.2	13
Travel related to education	0.5	5.0	9
Travel related to taking class	0.5	4.4	10
Travel related to consumer purchases	32.9	39.6	83
Travel related to grocery shopping	13.0	12.9	101
Travel related to purchasing gas	1.8	3.9	47
Travel related to purchasing food (except groceries)	3.7	11.2	33
Travel related to shopping (except groceries, food, and gas)	18.8	22.7	83
Travel related to using professional and personal care services	13.3	8.1	163
Travel related to using financial services and banking	3.5	3.0	115
Travel related to using medical services	7.5	3.3	225
Travel related to eating and drinking	17.7	25.0	71
Travel related to socializing, relaxing, and leisure	25.0	28.6	87
Travel related to socializing and communicating	15.1	18.6	81
Travel related to attending or hosting social events	2.1	2.0	105
Travel related to relaxing and leisure	7.7	8.9	86
Travel related to arts and entertainment	1.6	2.6	64
Travel related to sports, exercise, and recreation	4.3	9.6	45
Travel related to participating in sports, exercise, recreation	4.2	8.6	49
Travel related to religious and spiritual activities	9.0	5.1	175
Travel related to volunteer activities	5.3	4.3	123

Note: The index is calculated by dividing percent of people in the age group doing primary activity by percent of total people doing primary activity and multiplying by 100. Primary activities are those respondents identified as their main activity. Other activities done simultaneously, such as eating while watching TV, are not included. If fewer than 2.0 percent of the total population participated in a primary activity, then the primary activity is not shown. "–" means sample is too small to make a reliable estimate.
Source: Bureau of Labor Statistics, unpublished tables from the 2008 American Time Use Survey, Internet site http://www.bls .gov/tus/home.htm; calculations by New Strategist

Table 9.9 Indexed Participation in Primary Activities by Men Aged 75 or Older, 2008

(percent of men aged 75 or older and total men aged 15 or older participating in primary activities on an average day, and index of participation by men aged 75 or older to total men, 2008)

	percent participating		index, men aged 75 or older to total men
	men aged 75 or older	total men	
TOTAL, ALL ACTIVITIES	**100.0%**	**100.0%**	**100**
Personal care	**100.0**	**100.0**	**100**
Sleeping	99.8	99.9	100
Sleeplessness	6.0	4.5	132
Grooming	68.2	76.6	89
Health-related self-care	11.0	4.8	229
Household activities	**73.3**	**66.6**	**110**
Housework	19.0	19.7	97
Interior cleaning	14.8	13.5	110
Laundry	3.1	6.3	50
Storing interior household items, including food	5.8	2.9	202
Food and drink preparation, presentation, and clean-up	42.1	38.4	110
Food and drink preparation	38.2	36.0	106
Kitchen and food clean-up	15.2	9.5	160
Interior maintenance, repair, and decoration	4.9	3.9	125
Interior arrangement, decoration, and repairs	2.2	2.4	91
Exterior maintenance, repair, and decoration	4.8	3.8	126
Lawn, garden, and houseplants	19.7	11.0	179
Animals and pets (not veterinary care)	15.2	12.1	126
Walking, exercising, and playing with pets	6.5	5.2	125
Vehicles	2.6	4.5	57
Household management	29.4	24.0	123
Financial management	6.4	3.2	200
Household and personal organization and planning	10.6	11.1	95
Household and personal mail and messages (except email)	13.5	5.5	247
Household and personal email	5.2	7.4	70
Caring for and helping household members	**6.8**	**20.7**	**33**
Caring for and helping household children	0.8	16.8	5
Physical care for household children	0.2	10.4	2
Reading to or with household children	–	1.7	–
Playing with household children (except sports)	–	4.7	–
Talking with, listening to household children	–	1.7	–
Looking after household children as a primary activity	–	1.5	–
Picking up or dropping off household children	0.8	6.2	12
Activities related to household children's education	–	2.2	–
Helping household children with homework	–	2.0	–
Helping household adults	4.1	3.5	118
Caring for and helping people in other households	**7.5**	**11.0**	**68**
Caring for and helping children in other households	2.7	3.6	75

	percent participating		index, men aged 75 or older
	men aged 75 or older	total men	to total men
Helping adults in other households	4.8%	7.5%	64
Picking up or dropping off adults in other households	2.6	4.4	58
Work and work-related activities	**10.3**	**53.4**	**19**
Work, main job	8.3	50.1	16
Work, other job(s)	–	2.3	–
Education	**0.2**	**6.9**	**3**
Taking class	–	5.0	–
Taking class for degree, certification, or licensure	–	4.8	–
Research, homework	0.2	4.6	5
Consumer purchases (store, telephone, Internet)	**32.9**	**35.6**	**92**
Grocery shopping	9.5	9.6	99
Purchasing gas	2.9	4.3	68
Purchasing food (except groceries)	4.4	11.8	37
Shopping, except groceries, food, and gas	19.9	19.6	102
Professional and personal care services	**14.3**	**6.7**	**215**
Financial services and banking	5.0	3.1	160
Banking	4.9	2.8	176
Medical and care services	8.9	2.4	365
Using health and care services outside the home	8.5	2.3	371
Household services	**3.5**	**2.1**	**167**
Eating and drinking	**98.7**	**96.5**	**102**
Socializing, relaxing, and leisure	**99.4**	**95.4**	**104**
Socializing and communicating	30.5	34.9	87
Attending or hosting social events	1.6	2.0	80
Relaxing and leisure	99.4	92.1	108
Relaxing, thinking	31.7	20.4	156
Television	91.5	82.3	111
Listening to the radio	6.7	2.5	265
Listening to or playing music (not radio)	1.4	3.3	42
Playing games (including computer)	9.9	9.6	103
Computer use for leisure (except games)	7.0	9.5	74
Reading for personal interest	50.3	21.1	239
Arts and entertainment (except sports)	2.3	3.3	70
Sports, exercise, and recreation	**20.2**	**22.0**	**92**
Participating in sports, exercise, or recreation	20.2	21.0	96
Using cardiovascular equipment	4.4	1.8	237
Walking	13.2	4.9	269
Working out, unspecified	3.3	3.5	93
Religious and spiritual activities	**16.6**	**7.7**	**216**
Attending religious services	11.1	4.0	277
Participation in religious practices	6.3	3.7	171

	percent participating		index, men aged 75 or older to total men
	men aged 75 or older	total men	
Volunteer activities	**9.5%**	**5.7%**	**166**
Administrative and support activities	3.3	1.9	172
Telephone calls	**9.9**	**10.0**	**99**
Telephone calls to or from family members	4.8	3.8	126
Telephone calls to or from friends, neighbors, or acquaintances	1.8	3.7	48
Traveling	**74.4**	**88.5**	**84**
Travel related to personal care	0.6	3.1	20
Travel related to household activities	7.8	8.5	92
Travel related to household management	5.1	5.5	93
Travel related to caring for and helping household members	4.5	9.9	46
Travel related to caring for and helping household children	0.8	7.4	10
Travel related to helping household adults	2.8	2.4	117
Travel related to caring for and helping people in other households	5.9	9.3	64
Travel related to caring for and helping children in other households	1.6	2.5	64
Travel related to helping adults in other households	–	6.7	–
Travel related to work	8.2	44.4	18
Travel related to education	–	4.6	–
Travel related to taking class	–	4.1	–
Travel related to consumer purchases	32.0	34.5	93
Travel related to grocery shopping	9.5	9.5	100
Travel related to purchasing gas	2.9	4.2	69
Travel related to purchasing food (except groceries)	4.3	11.0	39
Travel related to shopping (except groceries, food, and gas)	19.4	18.9	103
Travel related to using professional and personal care services	14.3	6.3	226
Travel related to using financial services and banking	5.0	3.0	166
Travel related to using medical services	8.9	2.3	385
Travel related to eating and drinking	21.1	27.3	77
Travel related to socializing, relaxing, and leisure	27.5	28.0	98
Travel related to socializing and communicating	14.5	17.5	82
Travel related to attending or hosting social events	1.3	1.7	76
Travel related to relaxing and leisure	9.6	9.4	103
Travel related to arts and entertainment	2.3	2.8	83
Travel related to sports, exercise, and recreation	4.8	11.5	42
Travel related to participating in sports, exercise, recreation	4.8	10.4	46
Travel related to religious and spiritual activities	10.0	4.4	227
Travel related to volunteer activities	5.2	3.8	137

Note: The index is calculated by dividing percent of men in the age group doing primary activity by percent of total men doing primary activity and multiplying by 100. Primary activities are those respondents identified as their main activity. Other activities done simultaneously, such as eating while watching TV, are not included. If fewer than 2.0 percent of the total population participated in a primary activity, then the primary activity is not shown. "–" means sample is too small to make a reliable estimate.

Source: Bureau of Labor Statistics, unpublished tables from the 2008 American Time Use Survey, Internet site http://www.bls.gov/tus/home.htm; calculations by New Strategist

Table 9.10 Indexed Participation in Primary Activities by Women Aged 75 or Older, 2008

(percent of women aged 75 or older and total women aged 15 or older participating in primary activities on an average day, and index of participation by women aged 75 or older to total women, 2008)

	percent participating		index, women aged 75 or older to total women
	women aged 75 or older	total women	
TOTAL, ALL ACTIVITIES	**100.0%**	**100.0%**	**100**
Personal care	**100.0**	**100.0**	**100**
Sleeping	99.8	99.9	100
Sleeplessness	9.4	5.8	161
Grooming	75.0	81.8	92
Health-related self-care	22.7	7.8	291
Household activities	**86.8**	**84.0**	**103**
Housework	58.2	50.3	116
Interior cleaning	45.8	34.9	131
Laundry	22.0	25.5	86
Storing interior household items, including food	10.1	7.0	145
Food and drink preparation, presentation, and clean-up	71.7	65.3	110
Food and drink preparation	66.6	61.8	108
Kitchen and food clean-up	39.7	31.5	126
Interior maintenance, repair, and decoration	3.0	2.2	138
Interior arrangement, decoration, and repairs	1.1	1.5	73
Exterior maintenance, repair, and decoration	3.0	1.8	169
Lawn, garden, and houseplants	14.7	7.9	187
Animals and pets (not veterinary care)	14.9	16.7	89
Walking, exercising, and playing with pets	5.2	6.3	83
Vehicles	0.3	1.0	26
Household management	37.7	33.8	112
Financial management	7.8	4.9	160
Household and personal organization and planning	15.6	16.8	93
Household and personal mail and messages (except email)	20.0	8.2	245
Household and personal email	5.4	11.3	48
Caring for and helping household members	**6.0**	**31.2**	**19**
Caring for and helping household children	0.7	26.7	3
Physical care for household children	0.4	20.6	2
Reading to or with household children	–	3.5	–
Playing with household children (except sports)	0.3	6.1	5
Talking with, listening to household children	0.3	4.3	7
Looking after household children as a primary activity	1.1	3.0	36
Picking up or dropping off household children	–	12.1	–
Activities related to household children's education	–	5.4	–
Helping household children with homework	–	4.8	–
Helping household adults	0.2	3.7	5
Caring for and helping people in other households	**9.1**	**15.5**	**59**
Caring for and helping children in other households	2.7	7.4	37

	percent participating		index, women aged 75 or older to total women
	women aged 75 or older	total women	
Helping adults in other households	5.3%	8.5%	62
Picking up or dropping off adults in other households	3.7	5.4	69
Work and work-related activities	**3.8**	**40.3**	**10**
Work, main job	3.7	38.0	10
Work, other job(s)	–	2.4	–
Education	**1.2**	**8.9**	**14**
Taking class	0.8	5.3	15
Taking class for degree, certification, or licensure	0.0	4.7	1
Research, homework	0.5	7.0	7
Consumer purchases (store, telephone, Internet)	**33.5**	**45.4**	**74**
Grocery shopping	14.7	16.1	92
Purchasing gas	1.1	3.7	31
Purchasing food (except groceries)	3.3	12.3	27
Shopping, except groceries, food, and gas	19.1	27.2	70
Professional and personal care services	**14.5**	**11.0**	**132**
Financial services and banking	2.5	3.3	75
Banking	2.3	3.3	70
Medical and care services	7.9	4.8	167
Using health and care services outside the home	7.3	4.5	162
Household services	**1.7**	**2.1**	**82**
Eating and drinking	**98.7**	**95.6**	**103**
Socializing, relaxing, and leisure	**99.7**	**95.4**	**104**
Socializing and communicating	37.9	40.1	94
Attending or hosting social events	3.5	2.7	130
Relaxing and leisure	99.0	90.6	109
Relaxing, thinking	30.3	19.5	155
Television	90.4	79.5	114
Listening to the radio	3.1	1.5	206
Listening to or playing music (not radio)	0.9	2.0	44
Playing games (including computer)	14.9	8.4	176
Computer use for leisure (except games)	4.5	9.5	48
Reading for personal interest	52.3	26.5	197
Arts and entertainment (except sports)	1.8	3.2	56
Sports, exercise, and recreation	**15.8**	**15.9**	**99**
Participating in sports, exercise, or recreation	15.7	15.0	104
Using cardiovascular equipment	1.0	2.5	41
Walking	10.4	4.7	221
Working out, unspecified	3.1	2.9	106
Religious and spiritual activities	**18.6**	**10.7**	**175**
Attending religious services	8.2	5.7	144
Participation in religious practices	11.1	5.4	206

	percent participating		index, women aged 75 or older to total women
	women aged 75 or older	total women	
Volunteer activities	**9.0%**	**7.6%**	**118**
Administrative and support activities	3.9	3.1	126
Telephone calls	**29.7**	**20.4**	**145**
Telephone calls to or from family members	18.9	10.7	177
Telephone calls to or from friends, neighbors, or acquaintances	12.7	7.4	173
Traveling	**62.7**	**85.5**	**73**
Travel related to personal care	1.0	2.0	48
Travel related to household activities	9.2	10.3	90
Travel related to household management	6.9	6.7	103
Travel related to caring for and helping household members	1.4	17.1	8
Travel related to caring for and helping household children	–	14.3	–
Travel related to helping household adults	0.2	2.7	6
Travel related to caring for and helping people in other households	6.5	11.6	56
Travel related to caring for and helping children in other households	0.8	4.5	19
Travel related to helping adults in other households	0.6	7.4	8
Travel related to work	2.9	32.2	9
Travel related to education	0.8	5.4	14
Travel related to taking class	0.8	4.6	16
Travel related to consumer purchases	33.4	44.4	75
Travel related to grocery shopping	15.3	16.0	96
Travel related to purchasing gas	1.1	3.7	31
Travel related to purchasing food (except groceries)	3.3	11.5	29
Travel related to shopping (except groceries, food, and gas)	18.4	26.3	70
Travel related to using professional and personal care services	12.6	9.8	128
Travel related to using financial services and banking	2.5	3.1	82
Travel related to using medical services	6.5	4.3	153
Travel related to eating and drinking	15.5	22.8	68
Travel related to socializing, relaxing, and leisure	23.5	29.2	80
Travel related to socializing and communicating	15.5	19.5	80
Travel related to attending or hosting social events	2.6	2.3	116
Travel related to relaxing and leisure	6.4	8.5	75
Travel related to arts and entertainment	1.2	2.4	50
Travel related to sports, exercise, and recreation	4.0	7.7	52
Travel related to participating in sports, exercise, recreation	3.8	6.8	56
Travel related to religious and spiritual activities	8.3	5.8	142
Travel related to volunteer activities	5.3	4.7	112

Note: The index is calculated by dividing percent of women in the age group doing primary activity by percent of total women doing primary activity and multiplying by 100. Primary activities are those respondents identified as their main activity. Other activities done simultaneously, such as eating while watching TV, are not included. If fewer than 2.0 percent of the total population participated in a primary activity, then the primary activity is not shown. "–" means sample is too small to make a reliable estimate.
Source: Bureau of Labor Statistics, unpublished tables from the 2008 American Time Use Survey, Internet site http://www.bls.gov/tus/home.htm; calculations by New Strategist

Table 9.11 Indexed Participation in Primary Activities of People Aged 75 or Older by Sex, 2008

(percent of people aged 75 or older participating in primary activities on an average day by sex, and index of women's participation to men's, 2008)

	aged 75 or older, percent participating		index of women to men
	men	women	
TOTAL, ALL ACTIVITIES	**100.0%**	**100.0%**	**100**
Personal care	**100.0**	**100.0**	**100**
Sleeping	99.8	99.8	100
Sleeplessness	6.0	9.4	158
Grooming	68.2	75.0	110
Health-related self-care	11.0	22.7	206
Household activities	**73.3**	**86.8**	**118**
Housework	19.0	58.2	306
Interior cleaning	14.8	45.8	308
Laundry	3.1	22.0	703
Storing interior household items, including food	5.8	10.1	174
Food and drink preparation, presentation, and clean-up	42.1	71.7	170
Food and drink preparation	38.2	66.6	174
Kitchen and food clean-up	15.2	39.7	262
Interior maintenance, repair, and decoration	4.9	3.0	62
Interior arrangement, decoration, and repairs	2.2	1.1	50
Exterior maintenance, repair, and decoration	4.8	3.0	63
Lawn, garden, and houseplants	19.7	14.7	75
Animals and pets (not veterinary care)	15.2	14.9	98
Walking, exercising, and playing with pets	6.5	5.2	79
Vehicles	2.6	0.3	10
Household management	29.4	37.7	128
Financial management	6.4	7.8	121
Household and personal organization and planning	10.6	15.6	148
Household and personal mail and messages (except email)	13.5	20.0	148
Household and personal email	5.2	5.4	104
Caring for and helping household members	**6.8**	**6.0**	**87**
Caring for and helping household children	0.8	0.7	91
Physical care for household children	0.2	0.4	238
Reading to or with household children	–	–	–
Playing with household children (except sports)	–	0.3	–
Talking with, listening to household children	–	0.3	–
Looking after household children as a primary activity	–	1.1	–
Picking up or dropping off household children	0.8	–	–
Activities related to household children's education	–	–	–
Helping household children with homework	–	–	–
Helping household adults	4.1	0.2	4
Caring for and helping people in other households	**7.5**	**9.1**	**122**
Caring for and helping children in other households	2.7	2.7	101

	aged 75 or older, percent participating		index of women to men
	men	women	
Helping adults in other households	4.8%	5.3%	111
Picking up or dropping off adults in other households	2.6	3.7	146
Work and work-related activities	**10.3**	**3.8**	**37**
Work, main job	8.3	3.7	45
Work, other job(s)	–	–	–
Education	**0.2**	**1.2**	**533**
Taking class	–	0.8	–
Taking class for degree, certification, or licensure	–	0.0	–
Research, homework	0.2	0.5	209
Consumer purchases (store, telephone, Internet)	**32.9**	**33.5**	**102**
Grocery shopping	9.5	14.7	155
Purchasing gas	2.9	1.1	39
Purchasing food (except groceries)	4.4	3.3	75
Shopping, except groceries, food, and gas	19.9	19.1	96
Professional and personal care services	**14.3**	**14.5**	**101**
Financial services and banking	5.0	2.5	50
Banking	4.9	2.3	47
Medical and care services	8.9	7.9	89
Using health and care services outside the home	8.5	7.3	86
Household services	**3.5**	**1.7**	**49**
Eating and drinking	**98.7**	**98.7**	**100**
Socializing, relaxing, and leisure	**99.4**	**99.7**	**100**
Socializing and communicating	30.5	37.9	124
Attending or hosting social events	1.6	3.5	219
Relaxing and leisure	99.4	99.0	100
Relaxing, thinking	31.7	30.3	95
Television	91.5	90.4	99
Listening to the radio	6.7	3.1	47
Listening to or playing music (not radio)	1.4	0.9	63
Playing games (including computer)	9.9	14.9	151
Computer use for leisure (except games)	7.0	4.5	64
Reading for personal interest	50.3	52.3	104
Arts and entertainment (except sports)	2.3	1.8	77
Sports, exercise, and recreation	**20.2**	**15.8**	**78**
Participating in sports, exercise, or recreation	20.2	15.7	77
Using cardiovascular equipment	4.4	1.0	23
Walking	13.2	10.4	79
Working out, unspecified	3.3	3.1	93
Religious and spiritual activities	**16.6**	**18.6**	**112**
Attending religious services	11.1	8.2	73
Participation in religious practices	6.3	11.1	176

	aged 75 or older, percent participating		index of women to men
	men	women	
Volunteer activities	**9.5%**	**9.0%**	**94**
Administrative and support activities	3.3	3.9	116
Telephone calls	**9.9**	**29.7**	**299**
Telephone calls to or from family members	4.8	18.9	392
Telephone calls to or from friends, neighbors, or acquaintances	1.8	12.7	719
Traveling	**74.4**	**62.7**	**84**
Travel related to personal care	0.6	1.0	154
Travel related to household activities	7.8	9.2	118
Travel related to household management	5.1	6.9	136
Travel related to caring for and helping household members	4.5	1.4	30
Travel related to caring for and helping household children	0.8	–	–
Travel related to helping household adults	2.8	0.2	6
Travel related to caring for and helping people in other households	5.9	6.5	110
Travel related to caring for and helping children in other households	1.6	0.8	53
Travel related to helping adults in other households	–	0.6	–
Travel related to work	8.2	2.9	35
Travel related to education	–	0.8	–
Travel related to taking class	–	0.8	–
Travel related to consumer purchases	32.0	33.4	104
Travel related to grocery shopping	9.5	15.3	161
Travel related to purchasing gas	2.9	1.1	39
Travel related to purchasing food (except groceries)	4.3	3.3	77
Travel related to shopping (except groceries, food, and gas)	19.4	18.4	95
Travel related to using professional and personal care services	14.3	12.6	88
Travel related to using financial services and banking	5.0	2.5	50
Travel related to using medical services	8.9	6.5	73
Travel related to eating and drinking	21.1	15.5	74
Travel related to socializing, relaxing, and leisure	27.5	23.5	85
Travel related to socializing and communicating	14.5	15.5	107
Travel related to attending or hosting social events	1.3	2.6	206
Travel related to relaxing and leisure	9.6	6.4	66
Travel related to arts and entertainment	2.3	1.2	52
Travel related to sports, exercise, and recreation	4.8	4.0	83
Travel related to participating in sports, exercise, recreation	4.8	3.8	79
Travel related to religious and spiritual activities	10.0	8.3	83
Travel related to volunteer activities	5.2	5.3	100

Note: The index is calculated by dividing percent of women participating in primary activity by percent of men participating in primary activity and multiplying by 100. Primary activities are those respondents identified as their main activity. Other activities done simultaneously, such as eating while watching TV, are not included. If fewer than 2.0 percent of the total population participated in a primary activity, then the primary activity is not shown. "–" means sample is too small to make a reliable estimate.

Source: Bureau of Labor Statistics, unpublished tables from the 2008 American Time Use Survey, Internet site http://www.bls .gov/tus/home.htm; calculations by New Strategist

Table 9.12 Ranking: Average Hours per Day Spent Doing Primary Activities by Total People Aged 75 or Older, 2008

(average hours per day spent by people aged 75 or older doing primary activities, ranked by time spent doing activity, 2008)

		average hours per day spent by people aged 75 or older
	Total, all activities	**24.00**
1.	Sleeping	9.14
2.	Television	4.19
3.	Eating and drinking	1.44
4.	Reading for personal interest	1.04
5.	Relaxing, thinking	0.74
6.	Grooming	0.68
7.	Socializing and communicating	0.57
8.	Food and drink preparation	0.50
9.	Interior cleaning	0.47
10.	Lawn, garden, and houseplants	0.32
11.	Work, main job	0.30
12.	Playing games (including computer)	0.29
13.	Volunteer activities	0.22
14.	Shopping, except groceries, food, and gas	0.21
15.	Health-related self-care	0.20
16.	Telephone calls	0.20
17.	Laundry	0.19
18.	Kitchen and food clean-up	0.18
19.	Participating in sports, exercise, or recreation	0.18
20.	Attending religious services	0.15
21.	Household and personal organization and planning	0.14
22.	Animals and pets (not veterinary care)	0.13
23.	Grocery shopping	0.11
24.	Medical and care services	0.11
25.	Computer use for leisure (except games)	0.10
26.	Travel related to shopping (except groceries, food, and gas)	0.10
27.	Listening to the radio	0.09
28.	Travel related to eating and drinking	0.09
29.	Household and personal mail and messages (except email)	0.08
30.	Participation in religious practices	0.08
31.	Exterior maintenance, repair, and decoration	0.07
32.	Financial management	0.07
33.	Attending or hosting social events	0.07
34.	Arts and entertainment (except sports)	0.07
35.	Travel related to socializing and communicating	0.07
36.	Interior maintenance, repair, and decoration	0.06
37.	Caring for and helping children in other households	0.06
38.	Household and personal email	0.04
39.	Helping adults in other households	0.04

	average hours per day spent by people aged 75 or older
40. Travel related to grocery shopping	0.04
41. Travel related to using medical services	0.04
42. Travel related to religious and spiritual activities	0.04
43. Storing interior household items, including food	0.03
44. Travel related to household activities	0.03
45. Travel related to work	0.03
46. Travel related to relaxing and leisure	0.03
47. Research, homework	0.02
48. Household services	0.02
49. Listening to or playing music (not radio)	0.02
50. Travel related to using financial services and banking	0.02
51. Travel related to arts and entertainment	0.02
52. Travel related to sports, exercise, and recreation	0.02
53. Travel related to volunteer activities	0.02
54. Vehicles	0.01
55. Caring for and helping household children	0.01
56. Taking class	0.01
57. Purchasing gas	0.01
58. Purchasing food (except groceries)	0.01
59. Financial services and banking	0.01
60. Travel related to helping household adults	0.01
61. Travel related to caring for and helping children in other households	0.01
62. Travel related to purchasing gas	0.01
63. Travel related to purchasing food (except groceries)	0.01
64. Travel related to attending or hosting social events	0.01
65. Helping household adults	0.00
66. Travel related to personal care	0.00
67. Travel related to caring for and helping household children	0.00
68. Travel related to helping adults in other households	0.00
69. Travel related to education	0.00
70. Activities related to household children's education	–
71. Work, other job(s)	–

Note: Primary activities are those respondents identified as their main activity. Other activities done simultaneously, such as eating while watching TV, are not included. If fewer than 2.0 percent of the total population participated in a primary activity, then the primary activity is not shown. "–" means sample is too small to make a reliable estimate.
Source: Bureau of Labor Statistics, unpublished tables from the 2008 American Time Use Survey, Internet site http://www.bls .gov/tus/home.htm; calculations by New Strategist

Table 9.13 **Ranking: Average Hours per Day Spent Doing Primary Activities by Men Aged 75 or Older, 2008**

(average hours per day spent by men aged 75 or older doing primary activities, ranked by time spent doing activity, 2008)

		average hours per day spent by men aged 75 or older
	Total, all activities	**24.00**
1.	Sleeping	9.03
2.	Television	4.66
3.	Eating and drinking	1.51
4.	Reading for personal interest	1.02
5.	Relaxing, thinking	0.87
6.	Grooming	0.60
7.	Socializing and communicating	0.55
8.	Lawn, garden, and houseplants	0.45
9.	Work, main job	0.41
10.	Food and drink preparation	0.29
11.	Playing games (including computer)	0.25
12.	Volunteer activities	0.24
13.	Health-related self-care	0.21
14.	Shopping, except groceries, food, and gas	0.21
15.	Participating in sports, exercise, or recreation	0.20
16.	Attending religious services	0.19
17.	Grocery shopping	0.17
18.	Interior cleaning	0.16
19.	Animals and pets (not veterinary care)	0.14
20.	Travel related to shopping (except groceries, food, and gas)	0.14
21.	Medical and care services	0.13
22.	Computer use for leisure (except games)	0.13
23.	Household and personal organization and planning	0.12
24.	Listening to the radio	0.12
25.	Interior maintenance, repair, and decoration	0.11
26.	Travel related to eating and drinking	0.11
27.	Kitchen and food clean-up	0.10
28.	Exterior maintenance, repair, and decoration	0.10
29.	Financial management	0.09
30.	Arts and entertainment (except sports)	0.09
31.	Telephone calls	0.08
32.	Travel related to socializing and communicating	0.08
33.	Helping adults in other households	0.06
34.	Participation in religious practices	0.06
35.	Travel related to religious and spiritual activities	0.06
36.	Caring for and helping children in other households	0.05
37.	Attending or hosting social events	0.05
38.	Travel related to using medical services	0.05
39.	Laundry	0.04

	average hours per day spent by men aged 75 or older
40. Household and personal mail and messages (except email)	0.04
41. Household and personal email	0.04
42. Travel related to work	0.04
43. Travel related to relaxing and leisure	0.04
44. Vehicles	0.03
45. Listening to or playing music (not radio)	0.03
46. Travel related to helping household adults	0.03
47. Travel related to grocery shopping	0.03
48. Storing interior household items, including food	0.02
49. Household services	0.02
50. Travel related to household activities	0.02
51. Travel related to caring for and helping children in other households	0.02
52. Travel related to using financial services and banking	0.02
53. Travel related to attending or hosting social events	0.02
54. Travel related to arts and entertainment	0.02
55. Travel related to sports, exercise, and recreation	0.02
56. Travel related to volunteer activities	0.02
57. Helping household adults	0.01
58. Research, homework	0.01
59. Purchasing gas	0.01
60. Purchasing food (except groceries)	0.01
61. Financial services and banking	0.01
62. Travel related to caring for and helping household children	0.01
63. Travel related to purchasing gas	0.01
64. Travel related to purchasing food (except groceries)	0.01
65. Caring for and helping household children	0.00
66. Travel related to personal care	0.00
67. Work, other job(s)	–
68. Activities related to household children's education	–
69. Taking class	–
70. Travel related to helping adults in other households	–
71. Travel related to education	–

Note: Primary activities are those respondents identified as their main activity. Other activities done simultaneously, such as eating while watching TV, are not included. If fewer than 2.0 percent of the total population participated in a primary activity, then the primary activity is not shown. "–" means sample is too small to make a reliable estimate.
Source: Bureau of Labor Statistics, unpublished tables from the 2008 American Time Use Survey, Internet site http://www.bls.gov/tus/home.htm; calculations by New Strategist

Table 9.14 Ranking: Average Hours per Day Spent Doing Primary Activities by Women Aged 75 or Older, 2008

(average hours per day spent by women aged 75 or older doing primary activities, ranked by time spent doing activity, 2008)

		average hours per day spent by women aged 75 or older
	Total, all activities	**24.00**
1.	Sleeping	9.22
2.	Television	3.89
3.	Eating and drinking	1.39
4.	Reading for personal interest	1.05
5.	Grooming	0.73
6.	Interior cleaning	0.67
7.	Food and drink preparation	0.65
8.	Relaxing, thinking	0.65
9.	Socializing and communicating	0.58
10.	Playing games (including computer)	0.31
11.	Laundry	0.29
12.	Telephone calls	0.27
13.	Kitchen and food clean-up	0.24
14.	Lawn, garden, and houseplants	0.24
15.	Work, main job	0.23
16.	Shopping, except groceries, food, and gas	0.21
17.	Volunteer activities	0.20
18.	Health-related self-care	0.19
19.	Participating in sports, exercise, or recreation	0.16
20.	Household and personal organization and planning	0.15
21.	Grocery shopping	0.13
22.	Animals and pets (not veterinary care)	0.12
23.	Attending religious services	0.12
24.	Household and personal mail and messages (except email)	0.10
25.	Medical and care services	0.10
26.	Participation in religious practices	0.09
27.	Attending or hosting social events	0.08
28.	Listening to the radio	0.08
29.	Computer use for leisure (except games)	0.08
30.	Travel related to shopping (except groceries, food, and gas)	0.08
31.	Travel related to eating and drinking	0.07
32.	Travel related to socializing and communicating	0.07
33.	Financial management	0.06
34.	Caring for and helping children in other households	0.06
35.	Arts and entertainment (except sports)	0.06
36.	Exterior maintenance, repair, and decoration	0.05
37.	Travel related to grocery shopping	0.05
38.	Storing interior household items, including food	0.04
39.	Household and personal email	0.04

	average hours per day spent by women aged 75 or older
40. Travel related to household activities	0.04
41. Interior maintenance, repair, and decoration	0.03
42. Helping adults in other households	0.03
43. Household services	0.03
44. Travel related to using medical services	0.03
45. Travel related to religious and spiritual activities	0.03
46. Taking class	0.02
47. Research, homework	0.02
48. Travel related to work	0.02
49. Travel related to relaxing and leisure	0.02
50. Travel related to arts and entertainment	0.02
51. Travel related to volunteer activities	0.02
52. Caring for and helping household children	0.01
53. Purchasing food (except groceries)	0.01
54. Financial services and banking	0.01
55. Listening to or playing music (not radio)	0.01
56. Travel related to purchasing food (except groceries)	0.01
57. Travel related to using financial services and banking	0.01
58. Travel related to attending or hosting social events	0.01
59. Travel related to sports, exercise, and recreation	0.01
60. Vehicles	0.00
61. Helping household adults	0.00
62. Purchasing gas	0.00
63. Travel related to personal care	0.00
64. Travel related to helping household adults	0.00
65. Travel related to caring for and helping children in other households	0.00
66. Travel related to helping adults in other households	0.00
67. Travel related to education	0.00
68. Travel related to purchasing gas	0.00
69. Work, other job(s)	–
70. Activities related to household children's education	–
71. Travel related to caring for and helping household children	–

Note: Primary activities are those respondents identified as their main activity. Other activities done simultaneously, such as eating while watching TV, are not included. If fewer than 2.0 percent of the total population participated in a primary activity, then the primary activity is not shown. "–" means sample is too small to make a reliable estimate.
Source: Bureau of Labor Statistics, unpublished tables from the 2008 American Time Use Survey, Internet site http://www.bls.gov/tus/home.htm; calculations by New Strategist

Table 9.15 Ranking: Percent of Total People Aged 75 or Older Participating in Primary Activities on an Average Day, 2008

(percent of people aged 75 or older participating in primary activities on an average day, ranked by percent participating, 2008)

		percent of people aged 75 or older participating in activity
	Total, all activities	**100.0%**
1.	Sleeping	99.8
2.	Eating and drinking	98.7
3.	Television	90.9
4.	Grooming	72.3
5.	Food and drink preparation	55.3
6.	Reading for personal interest	51.5
7.	Socializing and communicating	35.0
8.	Interior cleaning	33.5
9.	Relaxing, thinking	30.8
10.	Kitchen and food clean-up	30.0
11.	Telephone calls	21.8
12.	Shopping, except groceries, food, and gas	19.4
13.	Travel related to shopping (except groceries, food, and gas)	18.8
14.	Health-related self-care	18.1
15.	Travel related to eating and drinking	17.7
16.	Participating in sports, exercise, or recreation	17.5
17.	Household and personal mail and messages (except email)	17.4
18.	Lawn, garden, and houseplants	16.7
19.	Travel related to socializing and communicating	15.1
20.	Animals and pets (not veterinary care)	15.0
21.	Laundry	14.5
22.	Household and personal organization and planning	13.6
23.	Travel related to grocery shopping	13.0
24.	Playing games (including computer)	12.9
25.	Grocery shopping	12.7
26.	Attending religious services	9.3
27.	Participation in religious practices	9.2
28.	Volunteer activities	9.2
29.	Travel related to religious and spiritual activities	9.0
30.	Travel related to household activities	8.6
31.	Storing interior household items, including food	8.4
32.	Medical and care services	8.3
33.	Travel related to relaxing and leisure	7.7
34.	Travel related to using medical services	7.5
35.	Financial management	7.2
36.	Work, main job	5.5
37.	Computer use for leisure (except games)	5.5
38.	Household and personal email	5.3
39.	Travel related to volunteer activities	5.3

	percent of people aged 75 or older participating in activity
40. Helping adults in other households	5.1%
41. Travel related to work	5.0
42. Listening to the radio	4.6
43. Travel related to sports, exercise, and recreation	4.3
44. Interior maintenance, repair, and decoration	3.8
45. Purchasing food (except groceries)	3.8
46. Travel related to purchasing food (except groceries)	3.7
47. Exterior maintenance, repair, and decoration	3.7
48. Travel related to using financial services and banking	3.5
49. Financial services and banking	3.5
50. Caring for and helping children in other households	2.7
51. Attending or hosting social events	2.7
52. Household services	2.4
53. Travel related to attending or hosting social events	2.1
54. Arts and entertainment (except sports)	2.0
55. Purchasing gas	1.8
56. Travel related to purchasing gas	1.8
57. Helping household adults	1.7
58. Travel related to arts and entertainment	1.6
59. Travel related to helping household adults	1.2
60. Vehicles	1.2
61. Travel related to caring for and helping children in other households	1.1
62. Listening to or playing music (not radio)	1.1
63. Travel related to personal care	0.8
64. Caring for and helping household children	0.7
65. Taking class	0.5
66. Travel related to education	0.5
67. Research, homework	0.4
68. Travel related to helping adults in other households	0.4
69. Travel related to caring for and helping household children	0.3
70. Activities related to household children's education	–
71. Work, other job(s)	–

Note: Primary activities are those respondents identified as their main activity. Other activities done simultaneously, such as eating while watching TV, are not included. If fewer than 2.0 percent of the total population participated in a primary activity, then the primary activity is not shown. "–" means sample is too small to make a reliable estimate.
Source: Bureau of Labor Statistics, unpublished tables from the 2008 American Time Use Survey, Internet site http://www.bls.gov/tus/home.htm; calculations by New Strategist

Table 9.16 **Ranking: Percent of Men Aged 75 or Older Participating in Primary Activities on an Average Day, 2008**

(percent of men aged 75 or older participating in primary activities on an average day, ranked by percent participating, 2008)

		percent of men aged 75 or older participating in activity
	Total, all activities	**100.0%**
1.	Sleeping	99.8
2.	Eating and drinking	98.7
3.	Television	91.5
4.	Grooming	68.2
5.	Reading for personal interest	50.3
6.	Food and drink preparation	38.2
7.	Relaxing, thinking	31.7
8.	Socializing and communicating	30.5
9.	Travel related to eating and drinking	21.1
10.	Participating in sports, exercise, or recreation	20.2
11.	Shopping, except groceries, food, and gas	19.9
12.	Lawn, garden, and houseplants	19.7
13.	Travel related to shopping (except groceries, food, and gas)	19.4
14.	Animals and pets (not veterinary care)	15.2
15.	Kitchen and food clean-up	15.2
16.	Interior cleaning	14.8
17.	Travel related to socializing and communicating	14.5
18.	Household and personal mail and messages (except email)	13.5
19.	Attending religious services	11.1
20.	Health-related self-care	11.0
21.	Household and personal organization and planning	10.6
22.	Travel related to religious and spiritual activities	10.0
23.	Telephone calls	9.9
24.	Playing games (including computer)	9.9
25.	Travel related to relaxing and leisure	9.6
26.	Volunteer activities	9.5
27.	Grocery shopping	9.5
28.	Travel related to grocery shopping	9.5
29.	Medical and care services	8.9
30.	Travel related to using medical services	8.9
31.	Work, main job	8.3
32.	Travel related to work	8.2
33.	Travel related to household activities	7.8
34.	Computer use for leisure (except games)	7.0
35.	Listening to the radio	6.7
36.	Financial management	6.4
37.	Participation in religious practices	6.3
38.	Storing interior household items, including food	5.8
39.	Travel related to volunteer activities	5.2

	percent of men aged 75 or older participating in activity
40. Household and personal email	5.2%
41. Travel related to using financial services and banking	5.0
42. Financial services and banking	5.0
43. Interior maintenance, repair, and decoration	4.9
44. Travel related to sports, exercise, and recreation	4.8
45. Helping adults in other households	4.8
46. Exterior maintenance, repair, and decoration	4.8
47. Purchasing food (except groceries)	4.4
48. Travel related to purchasing food (except groceries)	4.3
49. Helping household adults	4.1
50. Household services	3.5
51. Laundry	3.1
52. Purchasing gas	2.9
53. Travel related to purchasing gas	2.9
54. Travel related to helping household adults	2.8
55. Caring for and helping children in other households	2.7
56. Vehicles	2.6
57. Arts and entertainment (except sports)	2.3
58. Travel related to arts and entertainment	2.3
59. Travel related to caring for and helping children in other households	1.6
60. Attending or hosting social events	1.6
61. Listening to or playing music (not radio)	1.4
62. Travel related to attending or hosting social events	1.3
63. Travel related to caring for and helping household children	0.8
64. Caring for and helping household children	0.8
65. Travel related to personal care	0.6
66. Research, homework	0.2
67. Work, other job(s)	0.0
68. Activities related to household children's education	–
69. Taking class	–
70. Travel related to helping adults in other households	–
71. Travel related to education	–

Note: Primary activities are those respondents identified as their main activity. Other activities done simultaneously, such as eating while watching TV, are not included. If fewer than 2.0 percent of the total population participated in a primary activity, then the primary activity is not shown. "–" means sample is too small to make a reliable estimate.
Source: Bureau of Labor Statistics, unpublished tables from the 2008 American Time Use Survey, Internet site http://www.bls .gov/tus/home.htm; calculations by New Strategist

Table 9.17 Ranking: Percent of Women Aged 75 or Older Participating in Primary Activities on an Average Day, 2008

(percent of women aged 75 or older participating in primary activities on an average day, ranked by percent participating, 2008)

		percent of women aged 75 or older participating in activity
	Total, all activities	**100.0%**
1.	Sleeping	99.8
2.	Eating and drinking	98.7
3.	Television	90.4
4.	Grooming	75.0
5.	Food and drink preparation	66.6
6.	Reading for personal interest	52.3
7.	Interior cleaning	45.8
8.	Kitchen and food clean-up	39.7
9.	Socializing and communicating	37.9
10.	Relaxing, thinking	30.3
11.	Telephone calls	29.7
12.	Health-related self-care	22.7
13.	Laundry	22.0
14.	Household and personal mail and messages (except email)	20.0
15.	Shopping, except groceries, food, and gas	19.1
16.	Travel related to shopping (except groceries, food, and gas)	18.4
17.	Participating in sports, exercise, or recreation	15.7
18.	Household and personal organization and planning	15.6
19.	Travel related to eating and drinking	15.5
20.	Travel related to socializing and communicating	15.5
21.	Travel related to grocery shopping	15.3
22.	Playing games (including computer)	14.9
23.	Animals and pets (not veterinary care)	14.9
24.	Lawn, garden, and houseplants	14.7
25.	Grocery shopping	14.7
26.	Participation in religious practices	11.1
27.	Storing interior household items, including food	10.1
28.	Travel related to household activities	9.2
29.	Volunteer activities	9.0
30.	Travel related to religious and spiritual activities	8.3
31.	Attending religious services	8.2
32.	Medical and care services	7.9
33.	Financial management	7.8
34.	Travel related to using medical services	6.5
35.	Travel related to relaxing and leisure	6.4
36.	Household and personal email	5.4
37.	Helping adults in other households	5.3
38.	Travel related to volunteer activities	5.3
39.	Computer use for leisure (except games)	4.5

	percent of women aged 75 or older participating in activity
40. Travel related to sports, exercise, and recreation	4.0%
41. Work, main job	3.7
42. Attending or hosting social events	3.5
43. Purchasing food (except groceries)	3.3
44. Travel related to purchasing food (except groceries)	3.3
45. Listening to the radio	3.1
46. Interior maintenance, repair, and decoration	3.0
47. Exterior maintenance, repair, and decoration	3.0
48. Travel related to work	2.9
49. Caring for and helping children in other households	2.7
50. Travel related to attending or hosting social events	2.6
51. Financial services and banking	2.5
52. Travel related to using financial services and banking	2.5
53. Arts and entertainment (except sports)	1.8
54. Household services	1.7
55. Travel related to arts and entertainment	1.2
56. Purchasing gas	1.1
57. Travel related to purchasing gas	1.1
58. Travel related to personal care	1.0
59. Listening to or playing music (not radio)	0.9
60. Travel related to caring for and helping children in other households	0.8
61. Taking class	0.8
62. Travel related to education	0.8
63. Caring for and helping household children	0.7
64. Travel related to helping adults in other households	0.6
65. Research, homework	0.5
66. Vehicles	0.3
67. Helping household adults	0.2
68. Travel related to helping household adults	0.2
69. Work, other job(s)	0.0
70. Activities related to household children's education	–
71. Travel related to caring for and helping household children	–

Note: Primary activities are those respondents identified as their main activity. Other activities done simultaneously, such as eating while watching TV, are not included. If fewer than 2.0 percent of the total population participated in a primary activity, then the primary activity is not shown. "–" means sample is too small to make a reliable estimate.
Source: Bureau of Labor Statistics, unpublished tables from the 2008 American Time Use Survey, Internet site http://www.bls.gov/tus/home.htm; calculations by New Strategist

Table 9.18 Ranking: Average Hours per Day Spent Doing Primary Activities by Total Participants Aged 75 or Older, 2008

(hours per day spent by participants aged 75 or older doing primary activities, ranked by time spent doing activity, 2008)

		average hours per day spent by participants aged 75 or older
	Total, all activities	**24.00**
1.	Sleeping	9.16
2.	Television	4.62
3.	Relaxing, thinking	2.39
4.	Volunteer activities	2.34
5.	Playing games (including computer)	2.23
6.	Reading for personal interest	2.02
7.	Lawn, garden, and houseplants	1.92
8.	Socializing and communicating	1.63
9.	Attending religious services	1.61
10.	Eating and drinking	1.46
11.	Interior cleaning	1.40
12.	Laundry	1.30
13.	Health-related self-care	1.09
14.	Shopping, except groceries, food, and gas	1.06
15.	Household and personal organization and planning	1.03
16.	Participating in sports, exercise, or recreation	1.01
17.	Financial management	1.00
18.	Grooming	0.94
19.	Food and drink preparation	0.91
20.	Telephone calls	0.90
21.	Animals and pets (not veterinary care)	0.86
22.	Participation in religious practices	0.86
23.	Grocery shopping	0.83
24.	Kitchen and food clean-up	0.61
25.	Travel related to shopping (except groceries, food, and gas)	0.55
26.	Travel related to eating and drinking	0.49
27.	Travel related to socializing and communicating	0.47
28.	Household and personal mail and messages (except email)	0.45
29.	Travel related to religious and spiritual activities	0.44
30.	Travel related to relaxing and leisure	0.42
31.	Storing interior household items, including food	0.37
32.	Travel related to household activities	0.36
33.	Travel related to grocery shopping	0.34

Note: Primary activities are those respondents identified as their main activity. Other activities done simultaneously, such as eating while watching TV, are not included. The primary activities shown are those for which data by age are available.
Source: Bureau of Labor Statistics, unpublished tables from the 2008 American Time Use Survey, Internet site http://www.bls.gov/tus/home.htm; calculations by New Strategist

Table 9.19 Ranking: Average Hours per Day Spent Doing Primary Activities by Male Participants Aged 75 or Older, 2008

(hours per day spent by male participants aged 75 or older doing primary activities, ranked by time spent doing activity, 2008)

		average hours per day spent by male participants aged 75 or older
	Total, all activities	**24.00**
1.	Sleeping	9.05
2.	Television	5.09
3.	Relaxing, thinking	2.75
4.	Lawn, garden, and houseplants	2.26
5.	Reading for personal interest	2.04
6.	Socializing and communicating	1.81
7.	Eating and drinking	1.53
8.	Participating in sports, exercise, or recreation	1.00
9.	Grooming	0.87
10.	Food and drink preparation	0.75
11.	Travel related to eating and drinking	0.53

Note: Primary activities are those respondents identified as their main activity. Other activities done simultaneously, such as eating while watching TV, are not included. The primary activities shown are those for which data by age are available.
Source: Bureau of Labor Statistics, unpublished tables from the 2008 American Time Use Survey, Internet site http://www.bls .gov/tus/home.htm; calculations by New Strategist

Table 9.20 Ranking: Average Hours per Day Spent Doing Primary Activities by Female Participants Aged 75 or Older, 2008

(hours per day spent by female participants aged 75 or older doing primary activities, ranked by time spent doing activity, 2008)

		average hours per day spent by female participants aged 75 or older
	Total, all activities	**24.00**
1.	Sleeping	9.23
2.	Television	4.30
3.	Volunteer activities	2.20
4.	Relaxing, thinking	2.13
5.	Playing games (including computer)	2.09
6.	Reading for personal interest	2.01
7.	Lawn, garden, and houseplants	1.62
8.	Socializing and communicating	1.54
9.	Attending religious services	1.50
10.	Interior cleaning	1.47
11.	Eating and drinking	1.40
12.	Laundry	1.30
13.	Shopping, except groceries, food, and gas	1.08
14.	Participating in sports, exercise, or recreation	1.01
15.	Grooming	0.97
16.	Food and drink preparation	0.97
17.	Household and personal organization and planning	0.96
18.	Telephone calls	0.92
19.	Grocery shopping	0.88
20.	Health-related self-care	0.84
21.	Animals and pets (not veterinary care)	0.84
22.	Participation in religious practices	0.81
23.	Kitchen and food clean-up	0.60
24.	Household and personal mail and messages (except email)	0.51
25.	Travel related to eating and drinking	0.45
26.	Travel related to shopping (except groceries, food, and gas)	0.44
27.	Travel related to socializing and communicating	0.43
28.	Storing interior household items, including food	0.38
29.	Travel related to grocery shopping	0.34
30.	Travel related to religious and spiritual activities	0.34

Note: Primary activities are those respondents identified as their main activity. Other activities done simultaneously, such as eating while watching TV, are not included. The primary activities shown are those for which data by age are available.
Source: Bureau of Labor Statistics, unpublished tables from the 2008 American Time Use Survey, Internet site http://www.bls .gov/tus/home.htm; calculations by New Strategist

Appendix A: About the American Time Use Survey

What does the American Time Use Survey measure?

The American Time Use Survey (ATUS) is the Nation's first federally administered, continuous survey on time use in the United States. The goal of the survey is to measure how people divide their time among life's activities. After years of planning and development, the first ATUS results were collected in 2003. ATUS results are now available annually approximately one to two years after the survey year, and can be obtained from the ATUS web site, http://www.bls.gov/tus/home.htm.

In ATUS, individuals are randomly selected from a subset of households that have completed their eighth and final month of interviews for the Current Population Survey (CPS). ATUS respondents are interviewed only one time about how they spent their time on the previous day, where they were, and whom they were with. The survey is sponsored by the Bureau of Labor Statistics and is conducted by the U.S. Census Bureau.

The major purpose of ATUS is to develop nationally representative estimates of how people spend their time. Many ATUS users are interested in the amount of time Americans spend doing unpaid, nonmarket work. These include unpaid childcare and adult care, housework, and volunteering. The survey also provides information on the amount of time people spend in many other activities, such as religious activities, socializing, exercising, and relaxing. In addition to collecting data about what people did on the day before the interview, ATUS collects information about where and with whom each activity occurred, and whether the activities were done for one's job or business. Demographic information—including sex, race, age, educational attainment, occupation, income, marital status, and the presence of children in the household—also is available for each respondent. Although some of these variables are updated during the ATUS interview, most of this information comes from earlier CPS interviews.

How can the survey results be used?

ATUS significantly furthers understanding about how Americans spend their time. Because ATUS data are collected on an ongoing, monthly basis, time-series data eventually will be available, enabling analysts to identify any changes in how people spend their time. ATUS data can provide a wide range of applications for different users.

For example, many economists are interested in estimating the monetary value of nonmarket work. Lawyers can use this type of information when calculating the value of lost time (or life) in personal injury or wrongful death cases, thus allowing judges and juries to more accurately determine reasonable compensation in such cases. Policymakers can use ATUS data to better understand the economic and noneconomic effects of their policy decisions. Likewise, businesses can use ATUS data on how people spend their time to determine what kinds of goods and services to develop or market to a particular group.

ATUS data also include information on with whom and where respondents spend their time. From this, sociologists can determine, for example, the average amount of time fathers or mothers spend with their children or how much time people spend with colleagues and friends. It also is possible to determine how much time people spend working outside of the office. All of this information can help researchers understand how people in the United States are dividing their time among the duties of childcare; the demands of their jobs; their need to relax or exercise; and their religious, volunteer, and other commitments.

Many other countries have done time-use surveys, and more are planning to conduct them in the future. Time-use data are currently collected in North America, South America, Europe, Australia, and New Zealand. ATUS was designed to ensure that time- use information in the United States can be compared, at broad levels, with information from other countries.

ATUS methodology

ATUS covers all residents living in households in the United States who are at least 15 years of age, with the exception of active military personnel and people residing in institutions such as nursing homes and prisons.

Data collection for the ATUS began in January 2003. Sample cases for the survey are selected monthly and interviews are conducted continuously throughout the year. In 2008, approximately 12,700 individuals were interviewed. Estimates are released annually.

ATUS sample households are chosen from the households that completed their eighth (final) interview for the Current Population Survey (CPS), the nation's monthly household labor force survey. ATUS sample households are selected to ensure that estimates will be nationally representative. One individual age 15 or over is randomly chosen from each sampled household. This "designated person" is interviewed by telephone once about his or her activities on the day before the interview—the "diary day."

All ATUS interviews are conducted using Computer Assisted Telephone Interviewing. Procedures are in place to collect information from the small number of households that did not provide a telephone number during the CPS interview.

ATUS designated persons are pre-assigned a day of the week about which to report. Pre-assignment is designed to reduce variability in response rates across the week and to allow oversampling of weekend days so that accurate weekend day measures can be developed. Interviews occur on the day following the assigned day. For example, a person assigned to report about a Monday would be contacted on the following Tuesday. Ten percent of designated persons are assigned to report about each of the five weekdays. Twenty-five percent are assigned to report about each weekend day. Households are called for up to 8 consecutive weeks (for example, 8 Tuesdays) in order to secure an interview.

In the time diary portion of the ATUS interview, survey respondents sequentially report activities they did between 4 a.m. on the day before the interview ("yesterday") until 4 a.m.

on the day of the interview. For each activity, respondents are asked how long the activity lasted. For activities other than personal care activities (such as sleeping and grooming), interviewers also ask respondents where they were. And for activities other than personal care and work, they are asked who was in the room with them (if at home) or who accompanied them (if away from home). If respondents report doing more than one activity at a time, they are asked to identify which one was the "main" (primary) activity. If none can be identified, then the interviewer records the first activity mentioned. After completing the time diary, interviewers ask respondents additional questions to clearly identify work, volunteering, and secondary childcare activities. Secondary childcare is defined as having a child under age 13 in one's care while doing other activities.

The ATUS coding lexicon, or activity classification system, was originally based on the one used for the Australian Bureau of Statistics 1997 time-use survey. Codes are periodically evaluated and updated prior to the start of each year's data collection. The 2008 ATUS Coding Lexicon can be accessed online at http://www.bls.gove/tus/lexicons.htm.

• **Limitations of the data**

While attempts have been made to collect the most accurate data possible, the ATUS data do have limitations. With the exception of childcare, information on secondary activities (activities that are done at the same time as the primary activity) is not collected. This could lead to underestimates of the amount of time people spend doing activities that are frequently done in combination with other activities. For example, ATUS estimates likely underestimate the amount of time people spend listening to music since so many people listen to music while doing other things.

Survey estimates are subject to nonsampling errors that may arise from many different sources, such as an inability to obtain information from all households in the sample, data entry errors, coding errors, and misinterpretation of definitions. Errors also could occur if nonresponse is correlated with time use. Nonsampling errors were not measured. However, the Census Bureau uses quality-assurance procedures to minimize nonsampling data entry and coding errors in the survey estimates.

Obtaining ATUS data

• **BLS publications** Each year the BLS publishes press releases of time-use estimates. These press releases are available on the ATUS web site, **www.bls.gov/tus/**. The releases include descriptive highlights and selected tables showing estimates of time-use data for the previous year. The ATUS web site also contains a list of titles of, and links to, ATUS-related papers published in BLS publications, as well as BLS working papers. The ATUS staff plans to release topical issues papers on the ATUS web site periodically.

• **Unpublished tables from BLS** In addition to the selected tables published with the annual press release, ATUS data are compiled in numerous tables showing time use by various groups of respondents. These include tables of time use by various combinations of respondents' demographic characteristics, marital status, employment status, educational attainment, geographic location, and the presence and age of household children. These unpublished tables are available in PDF format on request.

• **Public use data files** Public use files containing ATUS microdata are released at least once each year. These files contain records of respondents' answers to the survey questions as well as other information about the respondent and his or her household. These data are intended for users who wish to do their own tabulations and analyses. These files are available for downloading on the ATUS web site.

• **For more information** The ATUS Web site is a resource for up-to-date information about the American Time Use Survey. It includes background information about the survey, as well as links to time-use news releases, publications, and the public use files. The ATUS homepage is available at www.bls.gov/tus/. Information about ATUS also is available by e-mail (ATUSinfo@bls.gov) or by telephone (202-691-6339).

Appendix B: Time Use Category Examples

For the complete list of activity examples, see http://www.bls.gov/tus/lexicons.htm.

Animals and pets Includes activities such as taking pets for a walk, petting animals, feeding and watering pets, adopting a pet, cleaning the litter box, playing with animals, feeding ducks, and caring for orphaned animals.

Appliances, tools, and toys Includes activities such as setting up or fixing a computer, setting clocks, changing batteries, hooking up a VCR, installing a printer, connecting a washing machine, loading software onto a computer, repairing sports equipment, repairing appliances, and cleaning tools and equipment.

Arts and crafts as a hobby Includes activities such as woodworking, photography, and making holiday decorations.

Arts and entertainment (other than sports) Includes activities such as attending concerts and plays, visiting an art gallery or museum, attending movies, gambling, and taking a guided nature walk.

Attending or hosting social events Includes activities such as attending birthday parties, graduation ceremonies, boy scouts, book clubs, and AA meetings.

Attending religious services Includes activities such as attending weddings, funerals, confirmation services, and wakes.

Caring for adults (in household or in other households) Includes activities such as feeding, bathing, dressing, supervising, or providing medical care.

Caring for and helping household children Includes the subcategories physical care, reading, playing (not sports), arts and crafts, playing sports, talking with household children, organization and planning for household children, looking after household children as a primary activity, attending household children's events, waiting for/with household children, and picking up and dropping off household children.

Computer use for leisure (excluding games) Includes activities such as surfing the Internet, downloading files for personal interest, and designing or updating a web site for personal use.

Exterior cleaning A subcategory of Exterior Maintenance, Repair, and Decoration, this includes activities such as sweeping steps, cleaning the garage, shoveling snow, and putting away bicycles.

Exterior maintenance, repair and decoration Includes activities such as exterior cleaning (see separate listing) and home maintenance activities such as fixing the roof, replacing screens, building a deck, putting up outdoor holiday decorations, fixing a mailbox, setting up garden furniture, and hanging flags.

Financial management Includes activities such as balancing the checkbook, buying or selling stocks, paying bills, filling out tax forms, using a computer to pay bills, and giving money to household children.

Financial services and banking Includes activities such as using an ATM, applying for a loan or mortgage, talking to a bank teller, meeting with a broker or accountant, completing a credit card application, meeting with an insurance agent, and meeting with a claims adjuster.

Food and drink preparation Includes activities such as cooking meals, packing lunches, mixing drinks, making coffee, canning food, getting a drink, and breast pumping.

Food presentation Includes activities such as serving a meal, setting the table, polishing silver, garnishing food, and putting out condiments.

Grooming Includes activities such as bathing, blow-drying hair, putting on makeup, shaving, laying clothes out, cleaning ears, and using the bathroom.

Health-related self care Includes activities such as doing childbirth exercises, taking vitamins, resting because of illness, meditating, taking insulin, and exercising for medical reasons.

Heating and cooling A subcategory of the category Interior Maintenance, Repair and Decoration, this includes activities such as chopping wood, lighting a fireplace, changing furnace filters, and opening and closing windows.

Helping adults in other households Includes activities such as helping with housework, laundry, shopping, cooking, lawn care, trash disposal, pet care, vehicle care, computers, taxes, bills, running errands, dropping off, and picking up.

Helping household adults Includes activities such as helping with computers, taxes, bills, or shopping, and picking up and dropping off at events.

Home security Includes activities such as installing smoke detectors, checking or changing locks, breaking into home if locked out, setting security alarm, turning out lights, and closing curtains.

Household and personal email Includes instant messaging.

Household and personal mail and messages (except email) Includes activities such as mailing letters and payments, checking phone messages, bringing in the newspaper, writing letters, and writing Christmas cards.

Household and personal organization and planning Includes activities such as making shopping lists, planning household trips, planning household meals, packing suitcases, putting pictures in albums, filling Christmas stockings, loading and unloading the car, and wrapping presents.

Household services Includes activities such as hiring a maid, hiring a caterer, dropping off clothes at a drycleaners, hiring an electrician, hiring someone to remodel, hiring movers, paying a decorator, paying a pet groomer, hiring someone to mow the lawn or shovel snow, paying for an oil change, paying for a car wash,

Interior arrangement, decoration, and repairs Includes activities such as decorating, rearranging furniture, hanging pictures, painting walls, remodeling the interior of the house, fixing leaks, changing light bulbs, putting up Christmas lights, setting mousetraps, decorating the Christmas tree, and carving pumpkins.

Interior cleaning A subcategory of Interior Maintenance, Repair, and Decoration, this includes activities such as vacuuming, dusting, making the bed, changing sheets, taking out the trash, recycling, and picking up the house.

Kitchen and food clean-up Includes activities such as clearing the table, loading or emptying the dishwasher, putting leftovers away, and cleaning the refrigerator or freezer.

Laundry Includes activities such as putting laundry in the washer or dryer, folding laundry, ironing, putting towels in the bathroom, and hanging clothes.

Lawn, garden, and houseplant care Includes activities such as raking leaves, planting vegetables or flowers, watering houseplants, gathering eggs, gathering honey, planting a garden, picking fruits and vegetables, and mowing the lawn.

Listening to or playing music (not radio) Includes activities such as listening to CDs, playing a musical instrument, singing, singing karaoke, listening to someone play the piano.

Looking after household children as a primary activity A subcategory of Caring for and Helping Household Children, this includes activities such as supervising children swimming, accompanying children while trick-or-treating, accompanying children while visiting Santa Claus, checking on children, and watching but not interacting with children.

Medical and care services Includes activities such as having dental work done, having an eye exam, paying for health care services, attending group therapy, paying for long-term care, and talking with a pharmacist.

Organization and planning for household children Includes activities such as packing children's school bag, planning play dates, planning and helping with children's parties, signing children up for activities, and making children's costumes.

Other income-generating activities Includes activities such as making artwork, furniture, baskets, quilts, or dinners for sale; playing in a band for pay, babysitting for pay, mowing lawns for pay, doing household chores for pay, maintaining rental property, selling items at a garage sale, and redeeming a winning lottery ticket.

Participating in religious practices Includes activities such as singing in a church choir, praying, visiting graves, and opening Advent calendars.

Personal care services Includes activities such as getting a haircut, having nails done, and getting a massage.

Physical care for household children Includes activities such as feeding and dressing children, breastfeeding, changing diapers, cuddling children, tucking children into bed, waking children up, cutting children's hair, helping children use the bathroom, and getting children ready for school.

Playing games Includes activities such as playing computer games, playing board games, playing cards, working a crossword puzzle, and hiding Easter eggs.

Purchasing food (not groceries) Includes activities such as paying a pizza delivery person, paying for a meal at a restaurant, and picking up take-out food.

Reading for personal interest Includes activities such as reading the newspaper, listening to books on tape, and borrowing books from a library.

Relaxing and thinking Includes activities such as hanging around alone, sunbathing, sitting in a hot tub, grieving, crying, watching husband assemble lawnmower, and watching wife garden.

Sewing, repairing, and maintaining textiles Includes activities such as sewing on buttons, hemming garments, knitting, and polishing shoes,

Shopping (except groceries, food, and gas) Includes activities such as buying movie tickets, test-driving a vehicle, window shopping, buying or ordering clothes, shopping on e-Bay, renting a movie, and looking through catalogs.

Sleeping Includes dozing off, napping, falling asleep, getting up, and dreaming.

Sleeplessness Includes activities such as insomnia, tossing and turning, lying awake, and counting sheep.

Socializing and communicating Includes activities such as hanging out with friends, hanging out with family, talking to neighbors, accompanying friends or family while they run errands, giving gifts, and visiting people in hospitals or nursing homes.

Storing interior household items including food Includes activities such as putting groceries away, putting stuff in the attic or basement, and putting decorations away.

Talking with and listening to household children Includes activities such as lecturing children, scolding children, listening to children sing or recite, telling children to brush their teeth or get ready for bed, and singing to or with household children.

Vehicles Includes activities such as changing oil, scraping ice and snow from a vehicle, checking to make sure a car is locked, checking tire pressure, cleaning boats, fixing bikes, cleaning or vacuuming a vehicle, and covering boats.

Volunteering, administrative and support activities Includes activities such as stuffing envelopes, making phone calls, and raising money for charitable causes.

Volunteering, social service and care activities Includes activities such as volunteering in a soup kitchen, preparing food for a fundraiser, baking cookies for the PTA, collecting or donating clothes or books, tutoring, working for a hotline, and teaching Sunday school.

Watching television Includes activities such as watching movies on DVD.

Work, main job Includes all activities done at or for main job including job training. Commuting to work is excluded because it is in the category Travel Related to Work.

Work, other job Includes all activities done at or for jobs other than main job, except commuting to work. which is included in Travel Related to Work.

Glossary

Average hours per day The average number of hours spent in a 24-hour day (between 4 a.m. on the diary day and 4 a.m. on the interview day) doing a specified activity. Estimates are adjusted for variability in response rates across days of the week. Average hours per day are shown in decimals. To convert decimal portions of an hour into minutes, multiply 60 by the decimal. For example, if the average is 1.2 hours, multiply 60 by 0.2 to get 12 minutes, so the average is 1 hour and 12 minutes. If the average is 0.05 hours, multiply 60 by .05 to get 3 minutes. If the average is 5.36 hours, multiply 60 by 0.36 to get 21.6, so the average is 5 hours and about 22 minutes.

Caring for and helping household members Time spent doing activities to care for or help any child or adult in the respondent's household, regardless of relationship to the respondent or the physical or mental health status of the person being helped, is classified here. Caring and helping activities for household children and adults are coded separately in subcategories. Household members are considered children if they are under age 18.

Primary childcare activities include physical care; playing with children; reading with children; assistance with homework; attending children's events; taking care of children's health care needs; and dropping off, picking up, and waiting for children. Passive childcare done as a primary activity (such as "keeping an eye on my son while he swam in the pool") also is included. A child's presence during the respondent's activity is not enough in itself to classify the activity as childcare. For example, "watching television with my child" is coded as a leisure activity, not childcare.

Caring for and helping household members also includes a range of activities done to benefit adult members of households, such as providing physical and medical care or obtaining medical services. Doing something as a favor for or helping another household adult does not automatically result in classification as a helping activity. For example, a report of "helping my spouse cook dinner" is considered a household activity (food preparation), not a helping activity, because cooking dinner benefits the household as a whole. By contrast, doing paperwork for another person usually benefits the individual, so a report of "filling out an insurance application for my spouse" is considered a helping activity.

Caring for and helping people in other households Activities done to care for or help any child or adult who is not part of the respondent's household, regardless of relationship to the respondent or the physical or mental health status of the person being helped, are classified here. Caring for and helping activities for children and adults in other households are coded separately in subcategories. Nonhousehold members are considered children if they are under age 18. When done for or through an organization, time spent helping people in other households is classified as volunteering. Caring for or helping children in other households, even when done as a favor or helping activity for another adult, is always classified as nonhousehold childcare, not as helping another adult.

Consumer purchases Most purchases and rentals of consumer goods, regardless of mode or place of purchase or rental (in person, via telephone, over the Internet, at home, or in a store) are classified in this category. Gasoline, groceries, other food purchases, and all other shopping are subcategories

Day of the week Time use estimates include data collected on both weekdays and weekends. Therefore, the percentage of people reporting an activity (such as working at a main job) and the amount of time spent doing certain activities (such as participating in recreation) may appear lower than they would if data were collected only on weekdays or weekends.

Diary day The day about which the survey respondent (designated person) reports. For example, the diary day of a survey respondent interviewed on Tuesday is Monday. Diary days are assigned, and survey respondents may not substitute another day of the week on which to report.

Eating and drinking All time spent eating and drinking (except when identified by the respondent as part of a work or volunteer activity), whether alone, with others, at home, at a place of purchase, in transit, or somewhere else, is classified here. Time spent purchasing or talking related to purchasing meals, snacks, and beverages is not counted as part of this category; time spent doing these activities are counted in Consumer Purchases.

Education Includes taking classes (including Internet or other distance learning courses); doing research and homework; and taking care of administrative tasks, such as registering for classes or obtaining a school ID. For high school students, before- and after-school extracurricular activities (except sports) also are classified as educational activities. Activities are classified separately by whether the educational activity was for a class for a degree or for personal interest. Educational activities do not include time spent for classes or training that respondents identified as part of their job. Time spent helping others with their education-related activities is classified in the caring for and helping categories.

Government services and civic obligations This category captures time spent obtaining and using government services, such as applying for food stamps, and purchasing government-required licenses or paying fines or fees. Civic obligations include government-required duties—such as serving jury duty or appearing in court—and activities that assist or influence government processes, such as voting or attending town hall meetings. The percentage of people participating in these activities on an average day was too small to allow the data to be included in this book.

Household All persons, both related family members and all unrelated persons, who occupy a housing unit and have no other usual address. A house, an apartment, a group of rooms, or a single room is regarded as a housing unit when occupied or intended for occupancy as separate living quarters. A householder is the person (or one of the persons) in whose name the housing unit is owned or rented. The term householder is never applied to either husbands or wives in married-couple families but relates only to persons in families maintained by either men or women without a spouse.

Household activities Activities done by respondents to maintain their households. These include housework; cooking; yard care; pet care; vehicle maintenance and repair; and home maintenance, repair, decoration, and renovation. Food preparation, whether or not reported as done specifically for another household member, is always classified as a household activity, unless the respondent identified it as a volunteer, work, or income-generating activity. For example, "making breakfast for my son" is coded as a household activity, not as childcare. Household management and organizational activities—such as filling out paperwork, balancing a checkbook, or planning a party—also are included in this category.

Household children Children under age 18 residing in the household of the survey respondent. The children may be related to the respondent (such as their own children, grandchildren, nieces or nephews, or brothers or sisters) or not related (such as foster children or children of roommates or boarders).

Household services Time spent arranging for and purchasing household services provided by someone else for pay is classified here. Household services include housecleaning; cooking; lawn care and landscaping; pet care; tailoring, laundering, and dry cleaning; vehicle maintenance and repairs; and home repairs, maintenance, and construction.

Personal care Includes sleeping, bathing, dressing, health-related self-care, and personal or private activities.

Receiving unpaid personal care from others (for example, "my sister put polish on my nails") also is captured in this category.

Population versus participant measures Some ATUS data refer to time use by the population as a whole (such as all 25-to-34-year-olds), while others restrict analysis to those who reported participating in a particular activity. Data referring to the population as a whole include every respondent, even those who did not engage in a specified activity on the diary day. This could result in low averages for the population for activities that are done infrequently (such as volunteering) or are of short duration. Data showing "participants" include only the time durations for specific activities if the respondent reported doing the activity on the diary day.

Primary activity The main activity a respondent was doing at a specified time.

Professional and personal care services Time spent obtaining, receiving, and purchasing professional and personal care services provided by someone else for pay is classified in this category. Professional services include childcare, financial services and banking, legal services, medical and adult care services, real estate services, and veterinary services. Personal care services include day spas, hair salons and barbershops, nail salons, and tanning salons. Activities classified here include time respondents spent paying, meeting with, or talking to service providers, as well as time spent receiving the service or waiting to receive the service.

Religious and spiritual activities Includes those activities normally associated with membership in or identification with specific religions or denominations, such as attending religious services; participating in choirs, youth groups, orchestras, or unpaid teaching (unless identified as volunteer activities); and engaging in personal religious practices, such as praying.

Secondary/simultaneous activities An activity done at the same time as a primary activity. With the exception of the care of children under age 13, information on secondary activities is not systematically collected by ATUS.

Socializing, relaxing, and leisure Includes face-to-face social communication and hosting or attending social functions. Time spent communicating with others using the telephone, mail, or e-mail is not part of this category. Leisure activities include watching television; reading; relaxing or thinking; playing computer, board, or card games; using a computer or the Internet for personal interest; playing or listening to music; and other activities, such as attending arts, cultural, and entertainment events.

Sports, exercise, and recreation Participating in—as well as attending or watching—sports, exercise, and recreational activities, whether team or individual and competitive or noncompetitive, falls into this category. Recreational activities are leisure activities that are active in nature, such as yard games like croquet or horseshoes.

Telephone calls This category captures telephone communication, with the following exceptions. Telephone and Internet purchases of consumer goods are classified in Consumer Purchases. Telephone calls identified as related to work or volunteering are classified as Work or Volunteering.

Traveling All traveling is coded here, regardless of mode or purpose. Walking is considered traveling when used to get from one destination (address or building) to another, but not when the primary purpose is exercise.

Volunteer activities Time spent volunteering for or through an organization.

Working and work-related activities Time spent working, doing activities as part of one's job, engaging in income-generating activities (not as part of one's job), and job search activities. "Working" includes hours spent doing the specific tasks required of one's main or other job, regardless of location or time of day. Activities done outside of regular work hours are classified as work if identified by respondents as part of their job. "Work-related activities" include activities that are not obviously work but are identified by the respondent as being done as part of one's job, such as having a business lunch or playing golf with clients.

"Other income-generating activities" are those done "on the side" or under informal arrangement and are not part of the respondent's regular job. Such activities might include selling homemade crafts, babysitting, maintaining a rental property, or having a yard sale. Respondents identify these activities as ones they "are paid for or will be paid for."

Index

Financial services and banking
    20 to 24 age group, 99–148
    25 to 34 age group, 149–199
    35 to 44 age group, 201–252
    45 to 54 age group, 253–304
    55 to 64 age group, 305–356
    65 to 74 age group, 357–407
    75 or older age group, 409–458
    total population, 13–47
Food and drink preparation
    15 to 19 age group, 49–98
    20 to 24 age group, 99–148
    25 to 34 age group, 149–199
    35 to 44 age group, 201–252
    45 to 54 age group, 253–304
    55 to 64 age group, 305–356
    65 to 74 age group, 357–407
    75 or older age group, 409–458
    total population, 13–47
Grocery shopping
    15 to 19 age group, 49–98
    20 to 24 age group, 99–148
    25 to 34 age group, 149–199
    35 to 44 age group, 201–252
    45 to 54 age group, 253–304
    55 to 64 age group, 305–356
    65 to 74 age group, 357–407
    75 or older age group, 409–458
    total population, 13–47
Grooming
    15 to 19 age group, 49–98
    20 to 24 age group, 99–148
    25 to 34 age group, 149–199
    35 to 44 age group, 201–252
    45 to 54 age group, 253–304
    55 to 64 age group, 305–356
    65 to 74 age group, 357–407
    75 or older age group, 409–458
    total population, 13–47
Health-related self care
    25 to 34 age group, 149–199
    35 to 44 age group, 201–252
    45 to 54 age group, 253–304
    55 to 64 age group, 305–356
    65 to 74 age group, 357–407
    75 or older age group, 409–458
    total population, 13–47
Helping adults in other households
    15 to 19 age group, 49–98
    20 to 24 age group, 99–148
    25 to 34 age group, 149–199
    35 to 44 age group, 201–252
    45 to 54 age group, 253–304
    55 to 64 age group, 305–356
    65 to 74 age group, 357–407
    75 or older age group, 409–458
    total population, 13–47

Helping household adults
    15 to 19 age group, 49–98
    20 to 24 age group, 99–148
    25 to 34 age group, 149–199
    35 to 44 age group, 201–252
    45 to 54 age group, 253–304
    55 to 64 age group, 305–356
    65 to 74 age group, 357–407
    75 or older age group, 409–458
    total population, 13–47
Helping household children with homework
    25 to 34 age group, 149–199
    35 to 44 age group, 201–252
    45 to 54 age group, 253–304
    total population, 13–47
Household and personal email
    15 to 19 age group, 49–98
    20 to 24 age group, 99–148
    25 to 34 age group, 149–199
    35 to 44 age group, 201–252
    45 to 54 age group, 253–304
    55 to 64 age group, 305–356
    65 to 74 age group, 357–407
    75 or older age group, 409–458
    total population, 13–47
Household and personal mail and messages
(except email)
    20 to 24 age group, 99–148
    25 to 34 age group, 149–199
    35 to 44 age group, 201–252
    45 to 54 age group, 253–304
    55 to 64 age group, 305–356
    65 to 74 age group, 357–407
    75 or older age group, 409–458
    total population, 13–47
Household and personal organization and planning
    15 to 19 age group, 49–98
    20 to 24 age group, 99–148
    25 to 34 age group, 149–199
    35 to 44 age group, 201–252
    45 to 54 age group, 253–304
    55 to 64 age group, 305–356
    65 to 74 age group, 357–407
    75 or older age group, 409–458
    total population, 13–47
Household services
    35 to 44 age group, 201–252
    45 to 54 age group, 253–304
    55 to 64 age group, 305–356
    65 to 74 age group, 357–407
    75 or older age group, 409–458
    total population, 13–47
Housework
    15 to 19 age group, 49–98
    20 to 24 age group, 99–148
    25 to 34 age group, 149–199
    35 to 44 age group, 201–252
    45 to 54 age group, 253–304
    55 to 64 age group, 305–356
    65 to 74 age group, 357–407
    75 or older age group, 409–458
    total population, 13–47

Telephone calls to or from family members
    15 to 19 age group, 49–98
    20 to 24 age group, 99–148
    25 to 34 age group, 149–199
    35 to 44 age group, 201–252
    45 to 54 age group, 253–304
    55 to 64 age group, 305–356
    65 to 74 age group, 357–407
    75 or older age group, 409–458
    total population, 13–47
Telephone calls to or from friends, neighbors,
or acquaintances
    15 to 19 age group, 49–98
    20 to 24 age group, 99–148
    25 to 34 age group, 149–199
    35 to 44 age group, 201–252
    45 to 54 age group, 253–304
    55 to 64 age group, 305–356
    65 to 74 age group, 357–407
    75 or older age group, 409–458
    total population, 13–47
Television
    15 to 19 age group, 49–98
    20 to 24 age group, 99–148
    25 to 34 age group, 149–199
    35 to 44 age group, 201–252
    45 to 54 age group, 253–304
    55 to 64 age group, 305–356
    65 to 74 age group, 357–407
    75 or older age group, 409–458
    total population, 13–47
Travel related to arts and entertainment
    25 to 34 age group, 149–199
    35 to 44 age group, 201–252
    45 to 54 age group, 253–304
    55 to 64 age group, 305–356
    65 to 74 age group, 357–407
    75 or older age group, 409–458
    total population, 13–47
Travel related to attending or hosting social events
    25 to 34 age group, 149–199
    35 to 44 age group, 201–252
    55 to 64 age group, 305–356
    total population, 13–47
Travel related to caring for and helping
household children
    25 to 34 age group, 149–199
    35 to 44 age group, 201–252
    45 to 54 age group, 253–304
    total population, 13–47
Travel related to caring for, helping children
in other households
    25 to 34 age group, 149–199
    35 to 44 age group, 201–252
    45 to 54 age group, 253–304
    55 to 64 age group, 305–356
    65 to 74 age group, 357–407
    total population, 13–47

Travel related to consumer purchases
    15 to 19 age group, 49–98
    20 to 24 age group, 99–148
    25 to 34 age group, 149–199
    35 to 44 age group, 201–252
    45 to 54 age group, 253–304
    55 to 64 age group, 305–356
    65 to 74 age group, 357–407
    75 or older age group, 409–458
    total population, 13–47
Travel related to eating and drinking
    15 to 19 age group, 49–98
    20 to 24 age group, 99–148
    25 to 34 age group, 149–199
    35 to 44 age group, 201–252
    45 to 54 age group, 253–304
    55 to 64 age group, 305–356
    65 to 74 age group, 357–407
    75 or older age group, 409–458
    total population, 13–47
Travel related to education
    15 to 19 age group, 49–98
    20 to 24 age group, 99–148
    25 to 34 age group, 149–199
    total population, 13–47
Travel related to grocery shopping
    25 to 34 age group, 149–199
    35 to 44 age group, 201–252
    45 to 54 age group, 253–304
    55 to 64 age group, 305–356
    65 to 74 age group, 357–407
    75 or older age group, 409–458
    total population, 13–47
Travel related to helping adults in other households
    25 to 34 age group, 149–199
    35 to 44 age group, 201–252
    45 to 54 age group, 253–304
    55 to 64 age group, 305–356
    65 to 74 age group, 357–407
    75 or older age group, 409–458
    total population, 13–47
Travel related to helping household adults
    25 to 34 age group, 149–199
    35 to 44 age group, 201–252
    45 to 54 age group, 253–304
    55 to 64 age group, 305–356
    65 to 74 age group, 357–407
    total population, 13–47
Travel related to household management
    35 to 44 age group, 201–252
    45 to 54 age group, 253–304
    55 to 64 age group, 305–356
    65 to 74 age group, 357–407
    75 or older age group, 409–458
    total population, 13–47